THE MIGHT OF NATIONS
World Politics in Our Time

The Might of Nations
World Politics in Our Time

John G. Stoessinger
Trinity University, San Antonio, Texas

EIGHTH EDITION

RANDOM HOUSE   New York

Eighth Edition

987654321

Copyright © 1961, 1965, 1969, 1973, 1975, 1979, 1982, 1986, by John G. Stoessinger

Library of Congress Cataloging in Publication Data

Stoessinger, John George.
 The might of nations.

 Includes bibliographies and index.
 1. World politics—1945–   . I. Title.
D843.S826 1986   327   85-10762
ISBN 0-394-34493-6

Cover design: Jeanette Jacobs

Manufactured in the United States of America

*To My Mother
and the Memory
of My Father*

Preface to the Eighth Edition

A quarter century has passed since the first edition of this book appeared. Since then the international system has changed before our very eyes. It seems almost as if a kaleidoscope had been shaken vigorously and the pieces had formed new patterns. A new generation is in the process of redefining its international relationships. The postwar era has definitely ended.

I first wrote this book in order to make some sense out of the chaos of international relations and to transmit this understanding to my students. I have continued to try, over the years, to present my ideas in clear and simple language, yet without doing violence to the complexity of the subject matter.

The book deals essentially with international relations since the Second World War. While events are described in chronological order, they are also organized conceptually around two basic themes: the struggles for power and for order in world politics.

The revision of a book is always a process of soul-searching. An author is forced to submit his work to the test of time, which is a writer's way of saying that he must face himself. To work on this edition was a joy as well as labor, since my conviction that the basic conception of the book is sound has deepened with the passing years.

In a very basic sense, this book represents a common quest. Over the years, I have had a multitude of letters about it from teachers and students all over the world. Many of these contained suggestions for improvement that have found their way into the present edition. For all these, I am most sincerely grateful. No teacher could be more fortunate.

Of all the revisions this book has undergone, the present one is probably the most extensive. The world has changed quite dramatically during the past three years. In order to bring the book completely up to date, I have incorporated the following major topics into the eighth edition:

United States–Soviet relations during the Reagan administration
The increasing rapprochement between China and the United States
The widening war between Iran and Iraq and its impact on the Persian Gulf
A new case study of the situation in Lebanon
United States missile deployment in Europe and its impact on NATO
The war over the Falkland Islands, and the Grenada Invasion
OPEC and the world energy picture
Developments in Central America
The Latin American debt crisis
Recent developments in the United Nations and regional organizations
The impact of terrorism on diplomacy

Recent developments in the European Common Market
Updating of the bibliographical suggestions following each chapter.

It gives me great happiness to know that this book continues to live. The response of a generation of students gives me the courage to go on searching and growing as a teacher despite the harshness of the times. A dear friend of mine, a poet, has expressed this feeling very poignantly in a fable of our times, which I should like to share with my readers:

> One day a teacher came to Sodom. Night and day he walked the streets speaking out against evil and indifference. In the beginning, people listened and smiled ironically. Then they stopped listening; he no longer even amused them. The killers went on killing just the same.
>
> One day a young student, moved to compassion for the unfortunate teacher, approached him with these words: "Poor stranger, you shout, you expend yourself body and soul; don't you see that it is hopeless?"
>
> "Yes, I see," answered the teacher.
>
> "Then why do you go on?"
>
> "I will tell you why. In the beginning, I thought I could change man. Today, I know that I cannot. If I still shout today, if I still scream, it is to prevent man from ultimately changing me."[*]

J. G. S.
San Antonio
SUMMER 1985

ACKNOWLEDGMENTS

I am indebted for valuable research assistance to Marsene Smith and Anthony Roger, both graduates of Trinity University.

[*] Adapted from Elie Wiesel, *One Generation After* (New York: Random House, 1965), p. 72.

Contents

Part One

THE NATURE
OF INTERNATIONAL
RELATIONS

Part One

THE NATURE
OF INTERNATIONAL
RELATIONS

Chapter 1

Introduction

The struggle itself toward the heights is enough to fill a man's heart. One must imagine Sisyphus happy.

ALBERT CAMUS *The Myth of Sisyphus*

Sisyphus, according to Homeric legend, had been condemned by the gods forever to exert his entire being toward accomplishing nothing. He was to roll a rock to the top of a mountain only to see it fall back each time into the depths. The crime that had won him this dreadful penalty was hubris—presumptuous ambition. His crime was greater even than that of Prometheus, who had attempted to steal the eternal fires. Sisyphus had a passion for life and refused to heed the call from the underworld when his time had come. By decree of the gods, Mercury had to come and snatch him from his joys. Upon arrival in the infernal darkness, Sisyphus managed to trick Death and put her in chains. For a time Hades was deserted and silent. Then Pluto, god of the underworld, dispatched the god of war to liberate Death. The wrath of the gods now descended on the man whose love of life and hatred of death had made him challenge the eternal laws. His rock was waiting for him.

Countless generations have breathed life into this myth. Its underscoring of our impotence in an indifferent and often hostile universe has seemed relevant to people everywhere. In ancient and medieval times, the ever-present threat to humanity's existence lay chiefly in the vast and inscrutable forces of nature. Today, these physical conditions of our survival are for the most part understood and, in the Western world at least, controlled. Yet the menace to the species has, if anything, become more ominous than ever before. And, tragically, it is no longer anything preordained or mysterious that now confronts us with the possibility of our doom. It is the instruments of destruction that we have fashioned ourselves.

Nowhere would we have better reason for abandoning ourselves to a sense of hopelessness about the fate of modern man than when we contemplate the state of relations among today's nations, the great collective actors in whose hands the decisions as to whether we survive or perish ultimately rest. Who of us, in witnessing the frantic preparations for yet another world war, has not at times despaired and concluded that the entire spectacle was a manifestation of organized insanity? Who of us has not had moments in which he

3

has been tempted to dismiss the efforts of those working for peace as a futile Sisyphean labor?

Yet it is from this very myth of Sisyphus, as the great French writer Albert Camus has told us, that humanity can take heart. For, according to Camus, the important part of the story is not really Sisyphus' ascent up the mountain. It is during his return to the plain that the hero is most inspiring. "That hour," as Camus sees it, "like a breathing-space which returns as surely as his suffering, that is the hour of consciousness. At each of those moments when he leaves the heights and gradually sinks toward the lairs of the gods, he is superior to his fate. He is stronger than his rock." [1]

In Camus' view, therefore, Sisyphus' fate does not teach us a lesson of acceptance and resignation. Rather, it serves as a symbol of that higher courage that revolts against our fate and raises rocks even with the knowledge that this revolt may be in vain. It shows us that so long as the rock is still rolling, the struggle is not futile. Man says Yes and his effort must be unceasing.

The relevance of this interpretation of the Sisyphean myth to modern world politics is clear. In many respects, modern man has descended to unprecedented depths, yet in others he has soared to greater heights than ever before. He has not only built concentration camps and perfected weapons of mass destruction; he has also learned to control hunger and disease and has created the United Nations. Never before have nations made such intensive preparations to destroy each other. But at no previous time has mankind striven more desperately to avert such destruction. Our generation is involved in the fiercest struggles for power in history. Yet it also has the privilege of participating in the most determined struggle for order ever waged. If, therefore, we have cause for shame and despair, we also have grounds for pride and hope. We may never solve the problems of our human condition—in international relations or in anything else—completely and permanently. But what remains crucial for us, as it was for Sisyphus, is that we do not permit our rock to crush us.

It is the purpose of this book to contribute in whatever small measure it can to this effort. While it hopes to offer more than a mere description of our crisis-ridden international situation, it does not pretend to advance any full-scale theory of international relations. It is my judgment that until the discipline of international relations becomes more developed, a much more useful task is to review and analyze its vast and complex subject matter in terms of certain major organizing concepts.

The treatment of international relations here presented is focused in terms of three such broad conceptual principles. The first of these is the ever-present *tension between the struggle for power and the struggle for order.* Throughout the book, care is taken to emphasize that these two processes of international intercourse are always closely interrelated, that every form of relationship, even war itself, includes elements of cooperation, while every form of order, even the most tranquil condition of peace, bears within it seeds of conflict. The second and related organizing concept here employed is that of the *divergence between the images that nations entertain of world affairs and of each other and the international realities as they actually are.* This divergence between what is and what is taken to be often exacerbates the international struggle for power and slows the international struggle for order. Finally, the book is focused upon what the author believes are the two truly dominant events of our time: *the struggle of East versus West,* and *the struggle of North versus South—the rich and the poor.* It is chiefly with reference to the latter two struggles—and the linkages between them—that the data and analyses offered are topically organized.

The book is divided into four sections. Part I examines the nation-state system and the nature of power. Part II deals with the international struggle for power—including both the East-West conflict and the North-South struggle, as well as the many linkages between them. Part III undertakes a similar analysis of the political, military, and economic dimensions of the international struggle for order. And Part IV attempts a fuller development of the three key concepts, in terms of which the empirical materials presented in the body of the book are analyzed and interpreted.

The general approach to the subject is an interdisciplinary one. Nothing less will do in a field that requires both breadth and depth. I am painfully aware of serious shortcomings in my command of both these dimensions. Yet, taking my inspiration from Camus' version of the myth of Sisyphus, I feel that the struggle to make international relations into a coherent discipline must continue. The pages which follow constitute an effort in that direction.

REFERENCE

1. Albert Camus, *The Myth of Sisyphus and Other Essays,* New York: Knopf, 1955, p. 121.

Chapter 2

The Nation-State System and the Nature of Power

Some are born great; some achieve greatness; And some have greatness thrust upon 'em.

SHAKESPEARE *Twelfth Night*, II, 5

THE ANATOMY OF THE NATION-STATE

Our world is made up of over one hundred sixty political units called nation-states. There is hardly a place on this planet that is not claimed by a nation-state. Only a century ago the world still abounded with frontiers and lands that remained unpreempted. But in our time, one can no longer escape from the nation-state system—unless he or she migrates to the frozen polar zones or to the stars. The nation-state has become ubiquitous. And everywhere it is the highest secular authority. It may decree that a person dies; and, with no less effort, it may offer the protection that enables a person to live. When no state wants him—when man is naked in his humanity and nothing but a man—he thereby loses the very first precondition for his fellows even to be able to acknowledge his existence. Whether it be to be born, to live, or to die, no one can do without official recognition—the recognition of a nation-state.

This modern-day fact of life is astounding when one considers that the nations that possess this inescapable power of life and death are in many ways only abstractions, figments of the human imagination. For though the power that is brought to bear to implement a nation's will is ultimately physical, the will itself is chiefly the result of human images, images of what a nation is and about why and how its will should be expressed and obeyed.

There are two principal aspects of this universal political image. In the first place, humans have endowed the nation-state with a quality that it shares with no other human association—the attribute of *sovereignty*. It is indeed no coincidence that the theory of sovereignty was first formulated in the sixteenth century, at a time when the nation-state system was in the process of emerging from the universalism of the medieval world. Its first systematic presentation was contained in the writings of the French political thinker Jean Bodin. Bodin's definition of sovereignty as "the state's supreme authority over citizens and subjects," set forth in his *De La République* in 1576, is still largely valid today. The nation remains the final arbiter over the lives of its citizens, leaving them recourse to no higher law. And while this is true in peacetime, it is even more totally and dramatically the case in times of war. For in the latter eventuality, the sovereign state has the right to send its citizens to their death and, through its sanction, to transform even the most brutal forms of killing into acts of patriotic heroism.

It is frequently asserted that the concept of sovereignty is about to become obsolete. We are undergoing a "systemic revolution." Just as the Greek and Roman city-states and the medieval church-state were destined to pass, so the nation-state system is in turn bound to yield to a different form of political organization. As one thinker has pointed out, the very core of sovereignty, the "impermeability and impenetrability" of nation-states, has been brought to an abrupt end by the advent of the atomic age:

> In a symbolic way (in addition to their possible practical use for hostile purposes) satellites circling the globe and penetrating the space above any territory of the globe, regardless of "sovereign" rights over air spaces and duties of "nonintervention," serve to emphasize the new openness and penetrability of everything to everybody.[1]

There is much to be said for the argument that the first atomic weapon "blew the roof off the sovereign nation-state." It is probably true that in case of nuclear war, little sovereign impermeability would remain. But it is equally true that in the absence of violent conflict, and especially in what the state continues to be able to demand of its citizens, sovereignty remains very much intact.

The truth is that in our time sovereignty is being both strengthened and weakened. This apparent contradiction is resolved if we survey the different parts of the globe. The Atlantic Community, especially Western Europe, seems to be slowly relaxing the grip of sovereignty. In that part of the world, sovereign states are moving toward larger units of political integration such as the European Common Market. But if sovereignty is "obsolete" in Western Europe, it is just coming into its own in Asia, the Middle East, and Africa. While the Atlantic Community is moving toward cohesion, these other areas are veering toward fragmentation. In fact, more sovereign states have been born in our generation than in the preceding three-hundred-year history of the nation-state system. As a result of the triumph of sovereignty among the nonwhite peoples of the earth, the membership of the United Nations has, since 1945, more than tripled. Hence, we would seem to be living in one of those rare and fascinating transitional periods in history in which the human race is at the same time looking both forward and backward. When we consider the Western world and see sovereignty beginning to be replaced by various new forms of regionalism, we see signs of the future. When we turn to the new nationalism in Asia, the Middle East, and Africa, we witness what is in effect a rekindling of the past. Until, therefore, the world has internationally evolved somewhat further, sovereignty is bound to remain an integral part of our lives.

Despite the fact that sovereignty is omnipresent in the nation-state system, it is very difficult, if not impossible, to discover where and in whom this sovereignty is actually vested. The reason for this is that the concept is essentially an abstraction that defies precise and concrete location. The problem was much simpler as long as states in international relations were identified with their absolute rulers. Louis XIV's alleged claim "L'Etat, c'est moi," left little doubt about the locus of sovereignty. But the advent of modern forms of government, both democratic and totalitarian, complicated the task enormously. Who, precisely, is the "sovereign" United States in international relations? Is it the President, the Congress, or the Supreme Court? The American separation of powers and the principle of "checks and balances" prevent the concentration of sovereignty in any one center. Yet the very essence of sovereignty, according to Bodin, is its absoluteness and indivisibility. The Soviet Union, too, claims absolute sovereignty in international relations. But does it reside in the person of the premier? Or in the Presidium of the Communist party? Or, as Soviet dialecticians maintain, in the multinational Soviet people? No easy or precise answer is possible.

Despite all its contradictions, however, sovereignty remains an essential characteristic of the nation-state system. Even if the term itself should disappear, the substance of sovereignty—the absolute authority of states in international relations—will probably survive as long as the nation-state system itself. It is sovereignty, more than any other single factor, that is responsible for the anarchic condition of international relations. Bodin conceived of sovereignty as essentially an *internal* phenomenon, "the state's supreme authority over citizens and subjects." While the advent of democratic government has rendered this power far less than absolute, no government, democratic or totalitarian, has been willing to yield major portions of its sovereignty in its relations with *other* nation-states. Hence, it would seem that sovereignty in our time is fundamentally a phenomenon of *international* relations, a fact of life in political intercourse among nations. Over three hundred years ago the image of Leviathan was created. In some parts of the world Leviathan is humanity's servant; in others, he remains the master. But no Leviathan yields to another except by its own consent. Sovereignty, originally no more than a political construct defining man's relationship to the state, has taken on a life of its own on the international scene. In the internal affairs of states, sovereignty has often created political order and stability. In international relations it has led to anarchy.

The second key component that has come into the making of nations has been the phenomenon of *nationalism*. In the broadest terms nationalism may be defined as a people's sense of collective destiny through a common past and the vision of a common future. (For an analysis of the anatomy of the new nationalism of Asia, the Middle East, and Africa, see Chapter 4.) In a very real sense, a nation's "personality" is its common past, or history. Empirically, a nation is merely a group of people occupying geographic space. But nations exist much more in time than in space. The history of common triumphs and suffering evokes powerful bonds of solidarity for nations large and small. Common suffering seems to be more important in this respect than are victories. The Civil War was probably the most tragic—and continues to be the most written-about—experience of the American nation. Yet both North and South have come to regard this grim American tragedy as a period of glory. The case of Israel affords an even clearer illustration. Ethnically and culturally, the Jews of Israel are certainly anything but homogeneous. Even in their religion they range from strict orthodoxy to frank agnosticism. Yet what gives Israel its national identity in spite of these differences is the common history of suffering experienced by its people in the Diaspora. Since a similar logic characterizes nationalism everywhere, it is clear that this image of a common past exercises a most crucial function. It enables the citizens of the state to share vicariously in collective greatness and to merge their own identity, often colorless and insecure, into the larger identity of the nation. It is significant that Ernest Renan's definition of a nation, advanced in 1882 at the Sorbonne, has become a classic: "What constitutes a nation," he said, "is not speaking the same tongue or belonging to the same ethnic group, but having accomplished great things in common in the past and the wish to accomplish them in the future."

The vision of a common future constitutes the second ingredient of nationalism. Here, too, an individual's aspirations are often projected onto the larger stage of politics and international relations. The unconscious realization that one's personal future may be bleak and devoid of larger meaning is often unbearable. Hence, as Erich Fromm has brilliantly demonstrated in his *Escape from Freedom,* people may seek compensation for their lack of a personal future in the reflected glory of the nation's collective future.[2] This form of identification may manifest itself in socially constructive ways; it may also lend itself to nationalism of a more destructive kind, as it did, for example, in Nazi Germany. The process whereby the identification is generated takes place largely in the "illogical, irrational, and fantastic world of the unconscious."[3] Hence, the insights of social psychology and psychoanalysis may have a profound bearing on the study of international relations. A case study of the development of one such image of the future, that of Nazi Germany, will serve to illustrate the point.

Many scholars now believe that the Nazi image of the ultimate enthronement of the "Aryan" superman had its roots in the authoritarian structure of the German family.[4] Erik Erikson paints a convincing portrait of the German father whose frequent remoteness and tyranny over his children made the maturation process excessively difficult:

> When the father comes home from work, even the walls seem to pull themselves together. The children hold their breath, for the father does not approve of "nonsense"—that is, neither of the mother's feminine moods nor of the children's playfulness. . . . Later when the boy comes to observe the father in company, when he notices his father's subservience to superiors, and when he observes his excessive sentimentality when he drinks and sings with his equals, the boy acquires the first ingredient of *Weltschmerz:* a deep doubt of the dignity of man—or at any rate of the "old man." . . . The average German father's dominance and harshness was not blended with the tenderness and dignity which comes from

participation in an integrating cause. Rather, the average father, either habitually or in decisive moments, came to represent the habits and ethics of the German top sergeant and petty official who—"dress'd in a little brief authority"—would never be more but was in constant danger of becoming less; and who had sold the birthright of a free man for an official title or a life pension.[5]

This kind of father, of course, creates for the son an unusually difficult adolescence, a period of "storm and stress," in Goethe's words, which becomes a strange mixture of open rebellion and submissive obedience, of romanticism and despondency. For each act of rebellion the boy suffers profound pangs of guilt, but for each act of submission he is punished by self-disgust. Hence the search for identify frequently ends in stunned exhaustion, with the boy's "reverting to type" and, despite everything, identifying with his father. The excessively severe *superego* implanted by the father in his son during childhood has entrenched itself like a garrison in a conquered city. The boy now becomes a "bourgeois" after all, but with an eternal sense of shame for having succumbed.

The catalytic agent that during the 1930s offered the possibility of escape from this vicious circle was Adolf Hitler. In the Fuehrer's world the adolescent could feel emancipated. "Youth shapes its own destiny"—the motto of the Hitler Youth—was profoundly appealing to a youth whose psychological quest for identity was often thwarted. Erikson points out that Hitler did not fill the role of the father image. Had he done so, he would have elicited great ambivalence in the German youth. Rather, he became the symbol of a glorified older brother, a rebel whose will could never be crushed, an unbroken adolescent who could lead others into self-sufficiency—in short, a leader. Since he had become their conscience, he made it possible for the young to rebel against authority without incurring guilt. Hermann Goering echoes the sentiments of the Hitler Youth when he stated categorically that his conscience was Adolf Hitler. Parents were to be silenced if their views conflicted with the official doctrines of the Third Reich: "All those who from the perspective of their experience and from that alone combat our method of letting youth lead youth, must be silenced."[6] The young Nazi was taught that he was destined by Providence to bring a new order to the world, *das tausendjahrige Reich*, the Aryan millennium of the superman. Young Nazi women, too, felt a surge of pride when they were told that childbirth, legitimate or illegitimate, was a meaningful act because "German women must give children to the Fuehrer." This writer recalls how, on numerous occasions, large groups of young women would march the streets chanting in chorus: "We want to beget children for our Fuehrer." National Socialism made it possible for the young to rid themselves of their profound personal insecurities by merging their identity into the image of a superior and glorious German nation. This image of a common future was well expressed in the famous Nazi marching song: "Let everything go to pieces, we shall march on. For today Germany is ours; tomorrow the whole world."

The dynamics and forms of expression that characterized the imagery of Nazi nationalism are not, of course, typical. Indeed, the precise nature of the relationship between family structure and national and international imagery varies with each nation and is in all cases difficult to ascertain empirically. Yet subtle and complex or not, its role in the genesis of nationalism is always crucial.

It would, of course, be a mistake to claim that the psychological phenomenon of nationalism and the legal institution of sovereignty are the sole foundations of a nation. There are also a number of more "objective" ingredients that play an essential part. Most prominent among these are territorial and economic ties and the presence of common language, culture, and religion.

Clearly, the very first requirement of a nation would seem that it possess a *geographical base*, a territory of its own. Yet, as the struggle of the Palestinians for a homeland indicates, a people may consider itself a nation even though it still has no sovereign territory to call its own. However, it is not necessarily true that attachment to the soil of a homeland primarily explains the fact of national unity. The insights of social psychology would seem to indicate that individuals may remain attached to a much more specific and limited location, such as their place of birth or the countryside where they were raised. In fact, people may feel more "at home" in a spot in a foreign land that reminds them of their youth than in an unfamiliar locale in their own country. Moreover, powerful emotional ties to specific locales may even divide a nation. When this is the case, the nation in question tends to be vulnerable to serious disunity and, frequently, internecine strife. Yet even when strong local attachments are not present, a really active attachment to the national territory as a whole usually results only from powerful nationalistic propaganda.

Another major contributing factor to the existence and unity of a nation lies in its common and interdependent *economic patterns*. Especially has this come to be the case since the advent of modern technology and mass production, with their need for vast national markets. Yet this same economic logic has also tended to undermine the nation-state system. For why limit production and distribution to nationally protected markets? And significantly, the only genuinely "supranational" organizations in existence in our time are of a primarily economic character. (For a full analysis of these organizations, see Chapter 13.) It is therefore incorrect to assert that economic ties reinforce the nation exclusively. Modern technology and the enlargement of markets work equally for the development of economic patterns that reach far beyond national boundaries.

It is similarly difficult to generalize about the part that is played in the making of a nation by the presence of a *common language*. In many countries, as for example the United States, a common tongue is an important integrative factor. In other nations, the fact that the same common language may be spoken in many different versions definitely constitutes a divisive influence. This is very notably the case with the Chinese language, for instance, which consists of hundreds of dialects. Thus, if a native of Shanghai wants to communicate with a Cantonese, he or she can do so only by falling back on written Chinese or by resorting to some third language that both may know. Switzerland, on the other hand, with its three different major languages, has achieved a very high degree of national unity. Still other nations have hoped to increase national cohesion by resurrecting a dead language. The revitalization of the Hebrew language in Israel is a case in point. (But it is safe to assume that language is a relatively minor factor in Israeli unity.) At times the quest for a national language has caused endless internal friction. The attempt to make Urdu the national language of Pakistan met with bitter resistance from that part of the Pakistani population which spoke Bengali. And India, after independence, had to accept English, a "foreign" language, as its temporary *lingua franca*. Hence the role of language in the life of nations is clearly a rather ambiguous one.

Surely one of the most perplexing concepts is that of *"national character."* Few social scientists would deny that certain cultural patterns occur more frequently and are more highly valued in one nation than in another. But it is almost impossible to find agreement among scholars on precisely what these common patterns are. In other words, we are faced with the paradox that national character seems to be an indisputable factor but that no one knows exactly what it is. This confusion probably stems from the fact that cultural patterns continue to live as stereotypes. For example, the stereotypes of the "volatile Frenchman" and of the "materialistic American" are strictly time-bound. Only a century ago almost opposite images were current. Moreover, patterns may differ from region to region in the same country. And it is never difficult to find exceptions to the prevailing images. On the whole, it would therefore appear that though national character patterns are a fact, their uniqueness and their significance in supporting national unity vary from nation to nation. Perhaps the concept "national character" is itself obsolete and it would be more accurate to speak of a "political culture."

The role of *religion,* finally, is equally two-edged. In the United States, religion has neither substantially contributed to nor detracted from national unity. In other countries, Israel for example, religion has proved a very significant factor in making for unity in national terms. Yet in certain other cases religion has played a key part in preventing national unity. Thus it was chiefly the religious friction between Moslems and Hindus that in 1947 made necessary the partition of the Indian subcontinent into two separate nations—India and Pakistan. Religions have probably tended as much to keep nations divided as to aid their unity.

In summary, then, what constitutes a nation-state in our time may be characterized as follows. First and foremost, it is a sovereign political unit. Second, it is a population that in being committed to a particular collective identity through a common image of past and future shares a greater or lesser degree of nationalism. And finally, it is a population inhabiting a definite territory, acknowledging a common government, and usually—though not always—exhibiting common linguistic and cultural patterns.

Having examined the structure of the nation-state, we can now focus our attention on the heart of our subject matter—the behavior *among* nations. As a first step in this larger analysis, we must devote some attention to that most crucial of all the concepts in the study of international relations, the concept of *power.*

THE NATURE OF POWER

The nature of a nation's power vis-à-vis other nations is one of the most elusive aspects of international relations. It is frequently suggested that a nation's *power* is simply the sum total of its *capabilities.* Yet such a definition fails to do the concept of power full justice. For though power always involves capabilities, it concerns other dimensions as well. Most importantly, while capabilities are objectively measurable, power must in every case be evaluated in more subtle psychological and relational terms.

The psychological aspect of power is crucial, since a nation's power may depend in considerable measure on what other nations think it is or even on what it thinks other nations think it is. The relational aspect of power can be illustrated as follows. Let us assume that two nations, for example the United States and the Soviet Union, are approximately balanced in their capabilities. To the extent that this condition prevails, the power of either nation vis-à-vis the other is almost nil, even though their capabilities might suffice to wipe each other from the face of the earth. Hence, because power is a relational thing, whereas capabilities are not, there may upon occasion be no correlation whatsoever between the two. Indeed, when capabilities are equal, as in a stalemate, power tends to disappear altogether. To put it crassly, when everybody is somebody, nobody may be anybody.[7] By the same token, of course, even a small increase in the capabilities of one of the two nations might mean a really major advantage in terms of its power.

Under certain circumstances there may even turn out to be an inverse correlation between power and capabilities. Just as an experienced driver would probably give a car marked "Auto School" a wide berth, a leading nation might be doubly careful not to provoke the volatile leader of some smaller nation. The United States, for example, might be more inclined to appease a small state armed with atomic missiles than it would a major nuclear power like the Soviet Union. Paradoxically, a weakness in capabilities—instability of leadership—might actually enhance such a small state's relative power. Indeed, as a scholar of the role of small states in international relations has pointed out, the East-West struggle has resulted in giving greater power and freedom of maneuver to small nations at the very time that their inferiority in military capabilities has vastly increased.[8]

In the above illustration of the experienced driver, of course, there is little doubt that the person in question would make it a general rule also to accord the right of way to a large truck. Similarly, a small nation is likely to do its utmost not to provoke one of the superpowers. Yet, as the Iranian hostage crisis has made clear, there may be striking exceptions to this rule. Fanaticism and the willingness to die for a cause may contribute greatly to a nation's power.

The psychological and relational aspects of power must, therefore, be recognized as hardly less significant than the objectively measurable capabilities themselves.

Coming now to the analysis of the anatomy of power as a whole, including its tangible capability aspects, we find it frequently asserted that "the most stable factor upon which the power of a nation depends is geography." [9] In the words of Hans J. Morgenthau:

> The fact that the continental territory of the United States is separated from other continents by bodies of water three thousand miles wide to the east and more than six thousand miles wide to the west is a permanent factor that determines the position of the United States in the world.[10]

In the opinion of other scholars, however, the advent of the atomic age and the development of intercontinental ballistic missiles have brought about the obsolescence of "territoriality." As John H. Herz has put it, "now that power can destroy power from center to center, everything is different." [11]

It would be difficult to agree with Morgenthau that *geography* is always and necessarily a crucial factor in the power of nations. No doubt the enormous land mass of the Soviet Union prevented that country from being conquered by three different invaders in three succeeding centuries. Yet there may also be circumstances in which geographical considerations are much less relevant. Thus, the same Russia whose vast expanses proved the undoing of Charles XII of Sweden, Napoleon, and Hitler, was in 1904 brought low in a naval battle by tiny Japan. It would be misleading, however, to go all the way with Professor Herz and suggest that the role of geography has drastically declined. Even the coming of nuclear weapons and intercontinental missiles may be less significant in this regard than is often claimed. As many military strategists have pointed out, mutual nuclear deterrence on the part of the superpowers may result in the wars of the future being "limited" to weapons and strategies not much different from those that have been used in the past. And to the extent that this might be the case, facts of national geography, location, and topography would continue to retain very considerable importance in the balancing of international power.

Nevertheless, it would seem that, all in all, the significance of geography as a factor in the power of nations has been decreasing. Only a generation ago it was still possible for scholars to regard the influence of geography on international relations as decisive and to elevate its study into an entirely separate discipline, the "science of geopolitics." The Scottish geographer and strategist Sir Halford Mackinder, for example, in 1904 advanced the geopolitical formula that "he who rules Eastern Europe commands the Heartland of Eurasia; who rules the Heartland, commands the World Island of Europe, Asia and Africa; and who rules the World Island commands the World." [12] The determinism of Mackinder's heartland theory was matched by that of Alfred T. Mahan, an American geopolitician of the late nineteenth century who believed in the decisive importance of sea power.[13] Even during World War II, power calculations of nations were still influenced by geopolitical thinking. A

German geographer, Dr. Karl Haushofer, deeply impressed by Mackinder's heartland theory, argued for a German-Russian-Japanese axis. He predicted a German defeat if Hitler were to attempt an invasion of the Soviet Union. Hitler not only ignored his advice but sent Haushofer to a concentration camp. Today such geographical determinism would not find the wide audience it did in the 1920s and 1930s. With the coming of the atomic age, the "science" of geopolitics has largely disappeared from the scene.

A second major element in a nation's international power is usually considered to be its possession of *natural resources*. Yet though this factor is always significant it, too, is in itself by no means decisive. For it is not primarily the possession of raw materials that makes a nation powerful; it is above all the *use* that nation is able to make of the resources it has available. So long as the Arab states of the Middle East were unable to coordinate their oil policies toward the Western world, even their huge oil deposits did not make them into powerful nations. But when in 1973 they managed to agree on a common oil embargo policy vis-à-vis the West, and to establish an oil price cartel, they suddenly acquired formidable power on the world stage. The result was a serious "energy crisis" that threatened the economic bases of some of the richest and most powerful nations on earth.

What use a nation is able to make of the raw materials it possesses depends primarily on the extent of its economic and industrial development. To develop a powerful military establishment, nations today must first command an advanced technological base. How vital this requirement may be can be seen from the examples of Germany, Italy, and Japan in World War II. In the possession of strategic raw materials, all three of these countries are relatively poor. Yet because of their highly developed industry and technology, they proved able to build military machines that almost succeeded in bringing about an Axis victory. That the power of the Allies triumphed in the end is largely attributable to the fact that the latter possessed *both* an abundance of essential raw materials *and* the advanced industrial apparatus.

Since World War II a strong industrial economy has become even more important as a factor in the power of nations. This may be seen in the degree to which both the United States and the Soviet Union are admired and envied by the smaller and economically less developed countries. The two superpowers have been fully aware of this and have capitalized on it by using foreign aid and technical assistance to influence the nations in question. Though the "lesser developed" states concerned have often felt ambivalent about the superpowers themselves, they have done their best to conduct themselves so as to induce the superpowers to give them the greatest possible amount of such aid and assistance. To the extent that this pattern has occurred, the superpowers' relative power position versus the rest of the world has, of course, grown. (For a detailed analysis of this subject, see Chapter 7.)

It is possible that the gradual dispersion of atomic energy among most of the world's nations will diminish the importance of industrialization as a power factor. The two superpowers have used atomic energy as an object of competition in the East-West struggle and have made it easier for some of their respective allies to produce nuclear weapons on their own. As a result, some nations are in the incongruous position of controlling the most sophisticated product of an advanced technology without having the supporting base of an industrial economy. A small nation equipped with atomic weapons might, through atomic blackmail, prove as powerful as one of the superpowers. Yet its advantage would be military only, and would be operative only in terms of a one-shot nuclear war. It is probable that as conventional sources of energy are increasingly replaced by the harnessed energy of the atom, the economic and hence general power of nations with large uranium deposits will somewhat increase. But unless such nations also possess the advanced technology necessary to turn uranium into actual atomic energy, their initiative in the power struggle is likely to remain limited.

The same point that has been noted in regard to geography and natural resources is also true of a third major element of national power, *population.* Once again, though a nation's population is certain always to be important as a factor in its power, the actual extent of its significance depends on many other considerations as well. Though both very populous, neither China nor India was in the past considered very powerful. Indeed, as the case of China illustrates, population is primarily *potential* power. As a result, it has been possible for nations with large populations to be weak, but impossible for nations without large populations to be powerful. Though the advent of atomic weapons may diminish the importance of manpower in warfare, the Vietnamese war would seem to have shown that the foot soldier has by no means been superseded. In the future as in the past, large populations are likely to remain an important military advantage. Hitler found it necessary to import slave labor from Eastern Europe to make up for labor shortages in Germany. An armed conflict with a nation as populous as China would prove a struggle of the most overwhelming proportions. Even though it at the time had little else but its vast population, China was at the end of World War II accorded great-power status in the United Nations.

Population becomes most important of all as a power factor when it is combined with industrialization. It is common knowledge that those countries now going through the process of industrialization are also the ones that are growing most rapidly in population. This fact, known as the "demographic transition," significantly affects a nation's power. Industrialization leads to an increase in population, which in turn may make possible further industrialization. As the case of China demonstrates once again, the potential power of population is actualized only when it is *used,* most profitably in the development of a modern industrial base which in turn makes possible a first-rate military establishment. In the view of many observers, once China succeeds in harnessing its immense population, it may in time become the most powerful nation on earth.

On the other hand, it is well to remember that population is not in itself any guarantee of power. The *will* to commit the population in battle must be present. Hence, once again the impact of a national image may be decisive. India has great population resources; yet, judging by the image of itself that it projects upon the world, India has been fairly reluctant, until recently, to mobilize its population for military combat. Fascist Italy, on the other hand, with a relatively small population, was whipped into a fighting frenzy by Mussolini. On balance, even in the atomic age there is still a partial truth in the nineteenth-century dictum that "God is on the side of the biggest battalions"— provided a nation has the will and resources to mobilize them.

A fourth element of national power whose effects it is difficult to assess concerns the nature of a country's *government.* It is tempting to assume that a democratic form of government provides greater national strength than a dictatorship. Yet though the historical record does not invalidate this assumption, it certainly places it in question. The victory of Sparta over Athens is only one of many instances in which a dictatorship emerged triumphant. But any analysis of this issue must remain inconclusive. There are simply too many imponderables involved to permit any easy conclusion.

It is generally assumed that a dictatorial government has its greatest advantages for national power in time of war, when centralized control, secrecy, and swiftness of execution are most important. Actually, the record does not support this conclusion. In wartime, most democracies have managed to fashion temporary "constitutional dictatorships," which quickly balanced the initial advantages of the aggressive dictator. Britain's wartime cabinet and America's reaction to Pearl Harbor are cases in point. Centralized control and self-discipline have usually been an effective counterpoise to secrecy and regimentation.

Many observers point out that democracy has a great advantage because it rests on the consent and voluntary support of the governed, where dictatorship requires coercion. While there is much truth in this oft-repeated assertion, it has been overdone. Modern totalitarianism has developed highly effective means of psychological indoctrination. Nazi Germany, Fascist Italy, the Soviet Union, and China each developed a highly organized youth movement for this express purpose. In addition, "brainwashing"—a kind of psychoanalysis in reverse—was widely applied to "reactionary elements" in China during the Cultural Revolution. These techniques, when coupled with the fact that modern totalitarianism deprives a population of standards of comparison in both time and space, have made possible the emergence of a new type of government: "totalitarianism with the consent of the governed." At times, totalitarian governments do not have to create popular support through these methods. The Nazi dictatorship, for example, enjoyed the fanatical support of most of the German population before 1941. Hence, a broad base of popular support as a source of power is not a monopoly of the democracies.

A dictatorship seems to have an advantage in the development of its industrial resources. Forced collectivization and industrialization of the Soviet and Chinese varieties would be unthinkable in a democratic framework. In both countries there resulted a great increase in power status, albeit at the cost of millions of human lives. But the democracies have been more generously endowed with prosperous economies and this has been a balancing factor. It is probably not an accident that most modern dictatorships have tended to be "have-not" nations. A totalitarian nation with a wealthy economy might indeed have a decisive advantage.

The total record is inconclusive. Perhaps the only democratic source of power which is denied to dictatorship is the fact that most people *think* that a democracy is inherently more powerful. Even the Soviet Union and China have found it necessary to camouflage totalitarian reality behind the democratic facade of a "people's democracy." The Soviet Constitution of 1936 was hailed by Stalin as "the most democratic in the world." In a world in which most of the nations of Africa, the Middle East, and Southeast Asia are uncommitted in the struggle between democracy and dictatorship, the image of democracy's greater power might be decisive. In short, democracy exerts a magnetism and possesses a kind of mystique which dictatorship cannot muster. Yet we must remember that very few of these uncommitted nations have any tradition in democratic government. If, despite this handicap, the new nations should embrace democracy, such an act might in large measure depend upon their conviction that democracy is compatible with the dictates of power.

It appears from the above that the objective or "capability" attributes of a nation's power depend, above all, on the *use* which its government makes of such physical factors as geography, population, and natural wealth. In the hands of a resourceful government, democratic or totalitarian, geography is turned to strategic advantage, and population and natural resources become twin pillars of power—military preparedness and industrialization. But as we have stated at the outset, despite their great importance these objective bases of national power are by no means the whole story. Of no less importance for a nation's power arsenal are its image of itself and, perhaps most crucial of all, the way it is viewed by other nations. To understand the latter dimension of power we must consider chiefly the factors of national character and morale, ideology, and national leadership.

We have seen earlier that the concept of *national character*, or "political culture," is highly elusive, and that it refers to something that is constantly changing. Its relevance to power does not lie so much in its objective existence, which is still disputed by many scholars, but in the persistence of stereotypes that are imputed by one nation to another. The instability of these stereotypes themselves denies the permanence of national character. Yet that they vitally affect a nation's power nevertheless can be seen from the following situation. Before the United States had established any physical contact with Japan, the American image of the Japanese was that of a quaint, romantic, and picturesque society, almost rococo in its fragility. Hence when the Americans decided to "open" Japan to the West in the mid-nineteenth century, they simply sent Commodore Perry and a few warships to force the door. Actually, the Japan of 1850 was a rigidly stratified society that had been ruled for over two hundred years by an authoritarian military clan, the Tokugawa. Under the Western impact, Japan modernized with astounding rapidity.

For centuries, the Japanese image of China had been that of a great master. Japan's written language, its art and literature—even its political institutions—had been copied from China, though they often had to be foisted onto the Japanese scene artificially. But between 1850 and 1900 the Japanese image of China swung to the other extreme, with the West now assuming the role of teacher and master. By 1915 Japan had only contempt for China and presented its former idol with the "Twenty-One Demands," which would have turned China into a Japanese colony had the West not interceded. When in 1931 Japan invaded China, most Japanese militarists were convinced that China would crumble in a matter of weeks. By this time many Japanese regarded the Chinese as less than human.

Americans' image of Japan had also changed rapidly. The "sweet and doll-like" Japanese of Perry's day had become "leering, bespectacled sadists" who raped and murdered innocent women and children. By the late 1930s, the Japanese image of the West, especially of the United States, became that of a decadent, corrupt, and spineless society which would disintegrate in the wake of a determined military attack. This distorted perception of America was matched by a Japanese self-image of absolute superiority and invincibility. In other words, a high *national morale* now became a major power factor. If the Japanese in 1941 had perceived themselves and the United States as they really were, there would have been no Pearl Harbor. It would have been obvious that Japan could not possibly win a war against the United States, that, in short, the objective fact of vastly superior capabilities was bound to overwhelm her. It was the power of an image that precipitated the Japanese attack. The incredible feats of little Japan during World War II cannot be explained in terms of its meager objective resources, but must be attributed above all to the existence of a self-image that was translated into superior national morale. This national morale became an immense storehouse of power. A well-known student of Japan, Ruth Benedict, provides a fascinating illustration of this morale factor in her report of a Japanese radio broadcast describing the behavior of a Japanese pilot during the war:

> After the air battles were over, the Japanese planes returned to their base in small formations of three or four. A Captain was in one of the first planes to return. After alighting from his plane, he stood on the ground and gazed into the sky through binoculars. As his men returned, he counted. He looked rather pale, but he was quite steady. After the last plane returned he made out a report and proceeded to Headquarters. At Headquarters he made his report to the Commanding Officer. As soon as he had finished his report, however, he suddenly dropped to the ground. The officers on the spot rushed to give assistance but alas! he was dead. On examining his body it was found that it was already cold, and he had a bullet wound in his chest, which had proved fatal. It is impossible for the body of a newly-dead person to be cold. Nevertheless the body of the dead Captain was as cold as ice. The Captain must have been dead long before, and it was his spirit that made the report. Such a miraculous feat must have been achieved by the strict sense of responsibility that the dead Captain possessed.[14]

To a non-Japanese, this story might seem like an outrageous yarn. But this writer himself heard the particular broadcast and was able to observe the reaction of Japanese military personnel in occupied Shanghai. The story was believed almost without exception. It was common knowledge that a disciplined spirit was master of the body, that indeed "a composed spirit could last a thousand years." [15] Why should it not be possible that the spirit of a man could outlive his body by a few hours if that man had made duty and responsibility to the Emperor the central tenets of his life?

Iran, under the leadership of the Ayatollah Khomeini, may be another case in point. Shi'ite Moslems believe that if they die in a holy war, they go directly to paradise. Perhaps American reluctance to take forceful military action against Iran during the hostage crisis was motivated not only by fear for the lives of the captives, but also by the despairing realization that the Iranian people might virtually welcome death as martyrdom in a sacred revolutionary cause. In other words, the intensity of Iran's religious fanaticism significantly enhanced its national morale and power. This was true not only during Iran's lengthy showdown with the United States, but also in its war with neighboring Iraq. There, too, Iran held out surprisingly well. "They fought like fanatics," a surprised Iraqi general exclaimed after a particularly bloody battle in which the Iranians had held out to the last man.

The roots of national character and national morale as sources of power are probably to be found in the culture, historical experience, and social and religious structure of nations. Once again, the insights of the social psychologist and sociologist have relevance to the study of international relations. Empirical research has not advanced sufficiently to permit definite conclusions in this vital area of study, but it has provided some important clues. And certainly the phenomena to be explained are remarkable indeed. The German social scene, for example, changed significantly between the two world wars. Is there any connection between these changes and the fact that Germany capitulated with relative ease in 1918 but fought on fanatically in 1945? If so, what is that connection? What explains the Germans' conviction in 1941 that they would dictate peace terms to Stalin in a matter of weeks? And what, on the other hand, accounted for the tremendous staying power of the Red Army? What made British morale during World War II the object of almost universal admiration, whereas France collapsed within a few weeks? What made the United States gather its resources after Pearl Harbor in an iron determination to force the enemy into unconditional surrender? The answers to these questions must await further insights into the nature of political culture. What is clear is that political culture and morale provide tremendous reservoirs of power.

We have seen earlier that the very essence of nationalism is a nation's image of a common past and a common future. Hence, it goes without saying that nationalism vitally affects a nation's power. Under certain conditions, moreover, the vision of a common future may become an *ideology*. This occurs when a nation's image of the future includes *the notion of a dynamic evolution toward some universal utopia.* Ideology has largely become the monopoly of totalitarian nations. Napoleon's vision of universal empire was rationalized by the ideology of the French *"mission civilisatrice."* The ultimate vision of Nazi Germany was the enthronement of the "Aryan race." To accomplish this end, it became necessary for Germany to expand into ever wider areas of *Lebensraum,* or "living space." The Japanese "Co-Prosperity Sphere" was based on similar assumptions. The Communists, in turn, have their own blueprint for the world, which predicts the growing influence of the Soviet Union and China. In all these cases, the nation is seen as the dynamic instrument for world-wide dominion.

It would be too simple to assert, as does Morgenthau, that ideology is simply "a flattering unction" for the concealment of imperialist expansion:

> It is a characteristic aspect of all politics, domestic as well as international, that frequently its basic manifestations do not appear as what they actually are— manifestations of a struggle for power. Rather, the element of power as the immediate goal of the policy pursued is explained and justified in ethical, legal, or biological terms. That is to say: the true nature of the policy is concealed by ideological justifications and rationalizations. . . .
>
> Politicians have an ineradicable tendency to deceive themselves about what they are doing by referring to their policies not in terms of power but in terms of either ethical and legal principles or biological necessities. In other words, while all politics is necessarily pursuit of power, ideologies render involvement in that contest for power psychologically and morally acceptable to the actors and their audience.[16]

Not only is it an exaggeration to claim that *all* politics is a pursuit of power, but the relationship between power and ideology is a much more complex and multifaceted one. In the first place, a widespread belief in the "truth" of an ideology may hasten its realization and thus become a power factor. For example, the ideological conviction of many Communists that the victory of communism is ordained by history has added immensely to the power of the Soviet Union. This faith in a metaphysical determinism has tended to inspire communism with a self-image of invincibility. Second, ideology may assume an authority all its own, precisely because its adherents are convinced of its metaphysical validity. Power, in the last analysis, must rest on the capacity of physical force. Authority, on the other hand, may attain similar compliance because it is accepted as legitimate or "true." Ideology serves the peculiar function of "justifying power and transforming it into authority, thus diminishing the amount of power which must be applied to achieve compliance or to produce the desired effect." [17] Moreover, the image of an ideology's ultimate universal ideal takes on a life of its own, which even all-powerful dictators ignore only at their own peril. This inner dynamic has been well stated by one student of ideology:

> Since an important ingredient of the movement's power is the element of explicit and proclaimed purpose which furthers its seizure of political power, the fulfillment of major portions of the ideologically stated objectives becomes a necessity dictated by power, by the inner dynamic of the movement itself. It is therefore doubtful that Hitler could have survived without gradually increasing the scope of the National-Socialist revolution in Germany, or that Stalin and his regime could have maintained the New Economic Policy without ultimately losing power. . . .
>
> A skeptical leader would run a serious risk of undermining his power if he were to allow himself to question the ideology. It is very doubtful that even Stalin could have done it.[18]

The relationship between power and ideology seems, up to a point, to be one of mutual reinforcement. Commitment to an ideology creates an image of the future which is based on the confident expectation of victory. This confidence is a source of tremendous long-range power. The enhancement of power in turn necessitates the further development and refinement of ideology along ever more ambitious lines. Theoretically, this mutual enhancement of ideology and power would end only in world domination. But if the reality lags too far behind the longed-for utopia, if the dichotomy between image and reality is too sharp, ideology begins to erode and lose its authority. It is for this reason that each Soviet Five-Year Plan has been "the final great effort" which would make entrance into the promised utopia a reality. As long as confrontation with reality does not uncover too great discrepancies, as long as image and reality tend to converge, ideology remains a vast fountainhead of power. But the point of diminishing returns is usually reached when no further victories can be won and expansion is brought to a standstill.

In former times, the peculiar character of ideology with its claims of expansion toward universal power was limited to religious movements. Modern ideology has become the psychological counterpart of messianic religion. Although its ultimate goals are secular rather than supernatural, it has been able to command as much power as the most fanatical of religious movements. The implications for international relations of the presence of competing ideologies have been well stated by Hans Morgenthau:

> The claim to universality which inspires the moral code of one particular group is incompatible with the identical claim of another group; the world has room for only one, and the other must yield or be destroyed. Thus, carrying their idols before them, the nationalistic masses of our time meet in the international arena, each group convinced that it executes the mandate of history, that it does for humanity what is seems to do for itself, and that it fulfills a sacred mission ordained by Providence, however defined.[19]

Ideology as a source of power is largely a monopoly of totalitarianism. A democracy may have goals or ideals but not an ideology. Since the very essence of a democracy is the principle of the right of disagreement on substantive goals, such a nation lacks the fanaticism and uniformity that lend an ideology its coherence and drive. The citizens of the United States may disagree on America's "national purpose." A totalitarian society, on the other hand, has only one official ideology. This does not mean, of course, that democracy has no resources to marshal against the aspirations of a universal ideology. As we have seen, it has other great sources of power. Besides, ideology is not *only* a source of power. It is the great overreacher of international relations. By definition, its goals are boundless and its horizons of conquest unlimited. The time must come, as it always has, when the image of a universal ideology is thwarted by an unyielding reality—when power encounters concerted counterpower. Hence each ideology carries within itself the seed of its own destruction, the hubristic assumption that power can expand without limit.

Finally, the quality of a nation's *leadership* and the image which it projects upon the world are important sources of power. If leadership is defective, all other resources may be to no avail. No amount of manpower or industrial and military potential will make a nation powerful unless its leadership *uses* the resources with maximum effect on the international scene. If the tangible resources are the body of power, and the national character its soul, leadership is its brains. It alone can decide how to apply its nation's resources. For example, the United States before World War II possessed virtually every single attribute of a powerful nation. But it played a relatively minor role in international relations because its leadership was committed to a policy of isolation. Hence, as far as American power was concerned, the advantages of geography, natural resources, industrial and military potential, and size and quality of population might as well not have existed at all, for though they did in fact exist, American leadership proceeded as if they did not.[20]

Leadership may build and save nations; it may also destroy them. The former capacity is symbolized in Winston Churchill's immortal challenge to the Nazis: "We shall fight on the beaches, we shall fight on the landing grounds, we shall fight in the fields and in the streets, we shall fight in the hills; we shall never surrender." It would be difficult to understand the power of the young American republic without reference to the outstanding leadership of its early statesmen. What would Britain have been without Castlereagh, Disraeli, and Canning? France without Talleyrand? Czechoslovakia without Masaryk? On the other hand, leadership may provide the power for national extinction. The early triumphs of Nazi Germany were the product of Hitler's mind. But the utter nihilism of the Third Reich and its final act of national suicide also grew out of Hitler's leadership. As historians have demonstrated, Hitler cast an almost hypnotic spell over Germany long after the war was considered lost by most of his entourage. His will alone resulted in the prolongation of the war at the cost of millions of lives. The German image of the Fuehrer invested him with the power of life and death.

In concluding our analysis of power, we must take note of two striking paradoxes: While the power gap between big and small states has never been greater, never have big states been less able to impose their will upon lesser countries. The conflicts between the United States and North Vietnam, France and Algeria, the Soviet Union and Afghanistan, and the United States and Iran and Lebanon are cases in point. Part of the reason for this is, of course, the fact that whenever one superpower is engaged against a lesser state, the other superpower tends to be arrayed on the other side. Yet the French experience in Algeria, the French and American experiences in Indochina as well as the American confrontation with Iran demonstrate that power also has a great deal to do with a nation's will and readiness to accept punishment. American policy in Southeast Asia failed because the threshold of suffering for North Vietnam and the Vietcong was much higher than Washington had assumed, while the American threshold was considerably lower. The United States dropped more bombs on North Vietnam than it dropped on the Axis powers during the entire period of World War II. Yet that little nation virtually fought the United States to a standstill and finally won the war. It seems that, with the coming of the atomic age, the power of big states has diminished while the power of small states has increased. At any rate, power can no longer be calculated simply by adding up a nation's physical capabilities. Psychology and will must be given as much weight as resources and hardware.

Finally, it must be noted that any up-to-date analysis of power must include nonstate entities as well. The rise in recent years of various national liberation groups in different parts of the world suggests that power may no longer be limited to national states alone. It is now also beginning to reside in the cracks of the state system. The Palestine Liberation Organization (PLO) is a case in point. The fact that some of these liberation groups resort to terror and blackmail to enforce their territorial demands only underlines this point. Even though some states have begun to take measures against international terrorism, it is the very randomness and irrationality of the terrorists that give them a measure of power. The helplessness of the American government during the Iranian hostage crisis in 1980 and again in 1985, when forty Americans were hijacked and abducted to Beirut, demonstrated the destructive power of a small but disciplined group of terrorists. And we must also not forget that, in our anarchic world, one person's terrorist may be another's patriot or hero.

Now that we have analyzed the anatomy of power, we may propose the following definition: *Power in international relations is the capacity of a nation to use its tangible and intangible resources in such a way as to affect the behavior of other nations.*

THE BALANCE OF POWER

Perhaps the most enduring "law" of international relations has been the principle of the balance of power. It is generally agreed to have been operative for over three hundred years, since the emergence of the multistate system. In its simplest form, the principle operated as follows: In the anarchic world of nation-states, each protagonist sought to maximize its safety through the enhancement of its power. In this competition, the quest for safety expressed itself chiefly in a search for allies. The safety of all was assured only if no one nation or group of nations was permitted to achieve a preponderance of power—if, in other words, a rough balance was achieved. Whenever the system threatened to break down, a "balancer" would ally itself with the weaker group of nations and thus restore the unstable equilibrium known as the "balance of power." This role was traditionally played by Great Britain. The Pax Britannica, when seen in terms of the balance of power principle, was therefore in essence guaranteed by Britain's capacity to tip the scales by allying itself with the weaker nations against whatever state or combination of states threatened to become predominant.

In order to analyze the concept of its applicability meaningfully and unambiguously, it is necessary to make our definitions as precise as possible. In his *Power and International Relations*, Inis L. Claude, Jr., has pointed out that students of international relations have used the balance of power concept in four different ways.[21] First, and most commonly, it has been used to connote a *system* for the operation of international politics in a world of multiple states. This system can be seen as working automatically, like a physical law; semiautomatically, since Britain seemed exempt from this law in its traditional role as balancer; or manually, with every actor manipulating the system through its own contrivance. Second, writers have referred to the balance of power concept as a *situation,* either of equilibrium or preponderance, between two states. Third, it has been used to describe a *policy* of equilibrium or preponderance. And finally, it has often served as a *symbol* of concern with the problem of power without substantive content. Throughout this book, the term *balance of power* will be used to describe a system of either the semiautomatic or manually operated type. The term *bipolarity,* or *balance of terror,* will connote the rough equilibrium of mutual atomic deterrence between East and West; and *multipolarity* will be used to describe a system of international relations in which a large number of protagonists engage in the balancing process without any one single nation playing the role of balancer.

Essentially, the balance of power system was a process of checking power with counterpower. The favorite technique used to accomplish this end was the formation of alliances and counteralliances. These unions were not permanent; those partner to them frequently switched sides whenever the maintenance of equilibrium seemed to require it. One classic example of the rapidity of such realignments was the Austro-British alliance against France and Prussia in 1740, which only a few years later changed to an Anglo-Prussian alliance against France and Austria. One of the chief alleged benefits of the balance of power system, when it operated successfully, was to guarantee the independence of small nations who were protected by the "balancer" from being devoured by the large ones. And perhaps most important, of course, the system was supposed to ensure peace in an anarchic world.

A careful scrutiny of this theory of the balance of power as almost a kind of "natural law" of classic international relations leaves one with many doubts about its actual validity. First, while the theory assumed that every nation would strive to enhance its power, it curiously viewed at least one nation—the balancer—as somehow exempt from this apparently universal rule. This balancer was seen as motivated not by national egotism but by international altruism. Since it was the British who traditionally played this balancing role, Great Britain was perceived as a sort of Olympian arbiter, allegedly above and exempt from the rules of international intercourse that governed the actions of other nations. As A. F. K. Organski has pointed out,

> The English modestly and the rest of the world credulously assigned this role to England. England has been the balancer because Englishmen believed that she was, said that she was, and the rest of the world believed them. The specifications for the role of balancer have been written with England in mind: the balancer must be a big power slightly removed from the center of controversy, preferably an island and mistress of the seas. Later, the fact that England met these specifications was used as added proof that England was the balancer.

Just why England's motives should differ so from those of other nations is never explained. Why a preponderance of power in England's hands should be a balancing factor is not explained, either, nor can it be, for it is not true.[22]

Actually, of course, Great Britain's balance strategy was as motivated by national interest as were the strategies of all the other European nations. It was grounded, above all, in two circumstances. One was the fact that as an island and the predominant naval power, Britain was likely to prove invulnerable to conquest save possibly by a state that had gained control over the whole European continent. The other was that in view of its size, population, and resources, Britain could not—as France did under Napoleon and Germany did under Hitler—reasonably aspire to win and maintain hegemony over Europe on its own. Hence Britain's optimum strategy was to settle for the compromise policy of playing the European balancer—preventing anyone else from developing control over all of Europe by always siding against whichever happened to be the ascendant power, in alliance with the state or states that potentially, along with Great Britain, seemed at the moment most seriously threatened.

The further assumption that nations participating in the balance of power were free to switch parners at will, like the dancers in a quadrille, also seems open to question. Could international combinations really be formed that mechanically? To be sure, alliances changed their membership in an almost kaleidoscopic fashion, but just as often the bonds of tradition and friendship made rapid shifts difficult and well nigh impossible. This has not, admittedly, been the case in countries whose governments have been authoritarian or totalitarian. Though Hitler and Stalin, for example, had denounced each other for a decade as mortal enemies, in 1939 they proved able to make a complete turnabout and, acknowledging what appeared to them to be the dictates of their respective national interests, overnight became close, if temporary, allies. However, in countries where government, including foreign policy, is directly responsible and responsive to the electorate, such a rapid shift of sides would be impossible. Any major realignment would require a lengthy period of popular rethinking and reconditioning—as the United States' difficulty in facing up to the sudden post–World War II challenges of its former ally, the Soviet Union, amply illustrates. And for the United States to go so far as to throw its weight against such long-standing friends, partners, and allies as Britain and France—even if the maintenance of the balance of power would seem to demand it—is rare indeed.

The most fundamental criticism of the theory concerns the assumption that a rough equilibrium among nations generally ushered in periods of peace. It is well known that the Pax Romana was one of the longest periods of relatively undisturbed peace in the history of Western civilization. This peace was guaranteed not by a balance, but by the absolute predominance of Rome. This example may be dismissed as invalid because it preceded the emergence of the nation-state system; however, it would be difficult to disregard the century of relative stability and peace that was ushered in by the Congress of Vienna in 1815. This peace was guaranteed by the preponderant power of the combined forces of the Concert of Powers: Britain, Austria, Prussia, and Russia. Indeed, the peace was broken only when, once again, a condition of relative balance emerged at the beginning of the twentieth century. Organski goes so far as to state that "the relationship between peace and the balance of power appears to be exactly the opposite of what has been claimed. The periods of balance, real or imagined, are periods of warfare, while the periods of known preponderance are periods of peace."[23] This view, however, falls into the opposite error. Rather, the evidence seems to point to the fact that the long-alleged causal relationship between equilibrium and the attainment of peace simply does not exist.

Whatever success in maintaining peace the balance of power may or may not once have had, its effectiveness definitely ended with the emergence of bipolarity. It might be objected, of course, that bipolarity was merely another form of balance, simple rather than multiple. And it is undoubtedly true that each side has attempted to enhance its position vis-à-vis the other. But who has been the balancer? Britain, allegedly the traditional holder of the balance, has long since lost the independence that the role would require today—as the Suez crisis of 1956 dramatically showed. Moreover, the development of a rough equilibrium between the two superpowers may actually have increased the danger of war. Indeed, so long as the West possessed an atomic monopoly and thus a preponderance of power, there was little danger of a major war.

As we have seen earlier, bipolarity as a type of international power configuration has ample precedent. In such cases, as Organski has pointed out, wars have been most likely to occur when there was an approaching balance between the dominant nation and a major challenger.[24] Peace, on the other hand, has been most likely when one bloc has enjoyed a decided preponderance over the others. Thus, the "bipolar" wars between Sparta and Athens and between Rome and Carthage occurred at a time when the antagonists were in a condition of approaching equilibrium. The balance of terror of our time differed from traditional bipolarity in the fact that it was at the same time a nuclear bipolarity. While the equilibrium between the two military blocs of East and West increased the chances of war, the condition of mutual deterrence acted as a counterweight.

Recent developments indicate, however, that the bipolar international system has been superseded by a multipolar one. A war between the two major superpowers, though possible, is not probable. The ascendancy of China, Japan, and Western Europe has irrevocably changed the power equation. In addition, the widening gulf between rich and poor nations in the "Third World" has decentralized the world's power balance even further. There is, moreover, the constant danger of further nuclear dispersion and even of nuclear theft. The rise of international terrorism conjures up horrendous scenarios if nuclear weapons should ever fall into irresponsible hands in the international community. A "nuclear Sarajevo" triggered by a state such as Libya, for example, has become an almost universal nightmare. Thus, nuclear war, though "unthinkable," still remains a possibility. In view of this fact, the foreign policies of nations are absolutely crucial. Domestic policy can hurt, but foreign policy can kill.

THE NATURE OF FOREIGN POLICY

We have now examined the nation as the unit of action in international relations. We have seen that it consists of both imagery and objective attributes. We have also seen that power—the nation's ability to affect the behavior of others—is more than the sum total of its attributes. It, too, consists of both image and reality. We have yet to see toward what *goals* this power is applied—in brief, the ends toward which a nation's foreign policy is conducted.

A *nation's foreign policy is the expression of its national interest vis-à-vis other nations.* To define foreign policy in this manner is, in a sense, to beg the question: What *is* the national interest? And merely to state that each nation provides its own definition is to underline the obvious. Yet might it nevertheless be possible to discover some universal guiding principle that governs the foreign policies of *all* nations? In brief, is there any one goal that is shared universally in the nation-state system?

One of the most challenging theories of international relations is that advanced by Morgenthau, who considers the central and universal goal of foreign policy to be power. Accordingly, it is always in terms of power that he views the national interest:

> The main signpost that helps political realism to find its way through the landscape of international politics is the concept of interest defined in terms of power. . . . We assume that statesmen think and act in terms of interest defined as power, and the evidence of history bears that assumption out. . . .[25]

In short, Morgenthau postulates that nations will tend to use their power in the quest for further power. Moreover, he rejects as unrealistic the proposition that the national interest may be defined in terms of abstract moral principle. Rather, in his view, the national interest becomes virtually identical with national security. Excessive preoccupation with questions of morality and law is condemned as "moralism" and "legalism." These are out of place in the making of foreign policy:

> Intellectually, the political realist maintains the autonomy of the political sphere, as the economist, the lawyer, the moralist maintain theirs. He thinks in terms of interest defined as power, as the economist thinks in terms of interest defined as wealth; the lawyer, of the conformity of action with legal rules; the moralist, of the conformity of action with moral principles.[26]

Morgenthau's is a brilliant exposition of a single-factor analysis. But like all such efforts, it is a tour de force which simply does not stand up under critical scrutiny. In the first place, we have seen that the essence of power is relational, that it depends upon comparison to be meaningful. To define the national interest in terms of the maximization of power is to assume that the goals of *all* nations are *competitive.* This is incorrect on two counts. First, many nations are interested in enhancing the power and welfare of others, rather than in competing with them. And, more important, the goals of some nations are not competitive but are *absolute,* not being defined in relation to other states at all. It is true that most of the powerful nations are competitive and seek even greater power. But can this be said with equal validity of small nations like Switzerland or Sri Lanka? Neither of these can be said to define its national interest primarily in terms of power. Moreover, competitive goals may change into absolute ones in the same nation. Sweden, for example, was once a powerful nation with fiercely competitive goals. But in our time Sweden's goals are absolute and in essence unrelated to those of other nations. Hence, the maximization of power is a major ingredient of the national interest, but not the only one. Nations have and always have had both competitive and absolute goals.

The statement that power is a vital goal of most of the world's powerful nations does not solve our problem. We have seen that the anatomy of power is highly complex. It also is an oversimplification to assert, as Morgenthau does, that a nation's foreign policy must be based either on national interest or on moral principle and should be based on the former. The two considerations are seldom if ever mutually exclusive. As W. T. R. Fox has aptly pointed out:

> Moral principle necessarily enters into any valid formulation of national interest which must itself reconcile the desirable and the possible. Against the view that there can be no compromise, I assert that there can be no escape from compromise. This is what makes politics a vocation only for the mature, for the responsible, for the man who does not despair when he discovers incommensurate values placed in such a juxtaposition that one or another has to be sacrificed.[27]

Indeed, power and moral principle might be considered as two concentric circles. At times power is the larger and includes morality. This is true when a nation is powerful and can "afford" to act morally. But at other times, and this is equally important, morality may include power; that is, greater power may accrue to a nation from moral behavior. Or, conversely, a nation may lose a measure of its power through immoral behavior. For example, suppose the United States should break a promise to one of its allies in NATO, hence acting "immorally." The ally might leave NATO and become neutralist. The United States would thereby lose a measure of power by ignoring moral principle. (The relationship between power and morality is discussed more fully in Chapter 8.)

We see, therefore, that it is misleading to define the national interest in terms of any one concept. In fact, our definition of foreign policy as the formulation of the national interest is purely *formal.* To say, "Always follow the national interest!" is to devise a kind of categorical imperative. But, like Kant's famous dictum "Always treat man as an end, never as a means," the formula of the national interest is ambiguous and frequently not at all helpful when applied to a concrete situation. Simply to assert that it is identical with power is equally imprecise. Perhaps we can bring the concept of national interest into clearer focus by ascertaining the *types* of goals as well as the goals themselves which nations tend to pursue in international relations.

We have seen above a useful distinction between *competitive* and *absolute* goals. The pursuit of power, by definition, is a competitive goal. The pursuit of peace or order, on the other hand, may be defined as an absolute goal. Another useful distinction may be made between goals that are *clearly defined* and those that are *diffuse.* A clearly defined goal is shared by an entire nation or, at least, an overwhelming majority in that nation. Nazi Germany's aim to annex Austria was such a case. But most of the time it is exceedingly difficult to abstract a national goal which is common to most members of a nation. For example, does the United States have a national interest which can be objectively determined? Is the guideline of its foreign policy the maximization of power, the consolidation of economic prosperity, or the pursuit of peace? Or is it a combination of the three? Moreover, as one scholar has demonstrated, the foreign policy views of most Americans tend to fluctuate greatly and depend primarily on mood.[28] Sometimes diffuse goals may change in the direction of a more clearly defined policy. The foreign policy of France under the Fourth Republic was an example of extreme diffusion, but with the ascendancy of General de Gaulle to the presidency, national goals were set forth with far greater clarity. A third distinction may be drawn between a nation's *declaratory* policy and its *action* policy. Often a nation's stated goals are very different from its real intentions. The Soviet slogan of "peaceful coexistence" during the Khrushchev era was a good example of declaratory policy. But it was quite possible that the Soviet leader conceived of peaceful coexistence as merely a phase in the struggle for world domination. Finally, a foreign policy may be either *static* or *dynamic.* Some nations are interested in the preservation of the status quo in international relations, while others are equally eager for change.

We may now attempt to make some general observations about the national interest. The goals of nations are subject to constant change. There is no single concept that explains the national interest. It is true that many nations use their power for the pursuit of greater power. This is especially true in the case of nations which are already powerful. But it is equally true that nations may employ their power in the pursuit of cooperation and international order. National goals may be competitive or absolute, clear or diffuse, overt or covert, static or dynamic. Beyond this it would be hazardous to generalize.

THE STUDY OF WORLD POLITICS

In a sense, the study of world politics is a study of the interplay of the foreign policies or of the national interests of nations. But while architects of foreign policy tend to regard the world from the vantage point of their own nations, students of world politics must look at the world in the round. It is appropriate, therefore, before concluding this chapter, to describe briefly the various schools of thought in the field of international relations and to locate the place of this book in the mainstream of recent thought about the subject.

World politics—or international relations—as a separate discipline was developed primarily by European scholars in American universities after World War II. Before that time, it was the province of historians, international lawyers, and philosophers. War and conflict were then still regarded as departures from "normal" peaceful relations. World War I, after all, had been "the war to end all wars." Scholars during the interwar period, therefore, tended to be idealists advancing theories of federation, collective security, and even world government. The rise of Nazi and fascist totalitarianism, however, and the death of forty million people during World War II challenged the basic assumptions of the idealists. Their hopes and aspirations lay shattered in the wake of Auschwitz and Hiroshima.

The founder of the new "realist" school of international relations was, not surprisingly, a European refugee from the Nazi holocaust: Hans J. Morgenthau. His belief that power was the most reliable signpost on the landscape of world politics was first advanced in his *Politics Among Nations.* This book, deeply pessimistic about human nature and strongly influenced by Machiavelli's *Prince,* was rejected by several American publishers before it appeared in its first edition in 1948. Thereafter, it went through five editions and gradually attained the status of a classic. Students and practitioners of foreign policy openly acknowledged their intellectual debt. When Morgenthau died in 1980 at the age of seventy-six, the main eulogy was delivered by Henry Kissinger. The former secretary of state opened his remarks by declaring simply: "Hans Morgenthau was my teacher."

During the 1950s and 1960s, a new school of thought emerged that was critical of both the "idealist" and "realist" approaches. These scholars, aiming to give international relations greater scientific content, tended to think in terms of "models," "systems," and "behavioral" approaches, relegating "idealists" and "realists" alike to an outdated traditionalism. In their aim to inject greater precision into the study of world politics, they tended to borrow concepts from the more exact sciences. To name only a few examples from the vast body of "scientific" or "behavioral" literature: Morton Kaplan's *System and Process in International Politics,* which is indebted to physics and talks about "fields of force"; J. David Singer's *Quantitative International Politics,* which explores the possibilities of injecting greater mathematical precision into the field: Karl Deutsch's *The Nerves of Government,* heavily influenced by communications theory; Richard Snyder's *Foreign Policy Decision Making,* which attempts to analyze individual policy decisions under a microscope; Ole Holsti's *The Belief System and National Images: A Case Study,* which seeks to reconstruct a statesman's political beliefs through a content analysis of his books and speeches; Herbert Kelman's *International Behavior,* heavily influenced by behavorial psychology; Thomas Schelling's *Strategy of Conflict,* indebted to games theory; and Richard Sterling's *Macropolitics,* which benefits from the field of economics.

In essence, international relations as a field of study has been dominated ever since the 1960s by a dialogue between the "scientific" and "traditional" approaches. The "scientific" scholars have tended to accuse "traditionalists" of fuzziness and imprecision. They assert, for example, that the "balance of power," a favorite concept of the "realists," is little more than a vague metaphor since no balance in world politics is ever exact or subject to quantitative measurement. The "traditionalists," in turn, challenge the behavioral scholars by asking, for example, how genius in leadership or self-destructive leadership, for that matter, could be quantified, or even subject to scientific analysis. The study of world politics or of foreign policy, they contend, can never be free of values or subjective judgments. In short, it can never be a science, but is destined to remain an art.

This book, while in essence traditionalist, is not limited to Morgenthau's assumptions about the primacy of power. Half of the book analyzes the struggles for power in the world, but the other half examines the struggles for a better world order. If I have borrowed from other disciplines, it has primarily been history. World politics, without history, in my judgment, has no roots, just as history without application to the present may bear no fruits. I was also shocked to read that 60 percent of the freshman class in a leading American university in 1980 did not know the difference between World War I and World War II.[29] The price of such ignorance comes high in blood and treasure.

Most important, however, this book focuses on the human element in world politics. In our time, we have been led to think of states almost as living actors on the world scene. How often do we hear a phrase such as "The United States decided" or "The United States agreed"? To speak of "actors," "powers," or of "systems" merely beclouds the basic truth that human beings, made of flesh and blood, make these decisions on behalf of collectivities called states. States have no existences apart from the lives of men and women. They are creatures of the human will. Hence, I tend to give considerable weight to the personalities of leading figures and their impact on the world—for better or for worse. It makes a difference, in my judgment, *who* is there at a given moment. In summary, I do not believe in the division of human knowledge into neat and separate compartments. World politics, perhaps more than any other field of study, requires a unified renaissance approach. Nothing less will do if we are to begin to understand the tragedy of our human condition.

REFERENCES

1. John H. Herz, *International Politics in the Atomic Age.* New York: Columbia University Press, 1959, p. 22.
2. Erich Fromm, *Escape from Freedom.* New York: Rinehart, 1941, *passim.*
3. Louis L. Snyder, *The Meaning of Nationalism.* New Brunswick, N.J.: Rutgers University Press, 1954, p. 89.
4. See the provocative analysis by Erik Erikson in *Childhood and Society.* New York: Norton, 1950, pp. 284–315.
5. *Ibid.,* p. 289.
6. *Ibid.,* p. 300.
7. Charles P. Kindleberger, "International Political Theory from Outside," in William T. R. Fox, ed., *Theoretical Aspects of International Relations.* South Bend, Ind.: University of Notre Dame Press, 1959.
8. Annette Baker Fox, *The Power of Small States.* Chicago: University of Chicago Press, 1959, p. 186.
9. Hans J. Morgenthau, *Politics Among Nations,* 4th ed. New York: Knopf, 1967, p. 106.
10. *Ibid.*
11. Herz, *op. cit.,* p. 108.

12. Sir Halford Mackinder, *Democratic Ideals and Reality.* New York: Holt, 1919, p. 150.
13. Alfred T. Mahan, *The Influence of Sea Power upon History.* Boston: Little, Brown, 1890, *passim.*
14. Ruth Benedict, *The Chrysanthemum and the Sword.* Boston: Houghton Mifflin, 1946, p. 25.
15. *Ibid.,* p. 26.
16. Morgenthau, *op. cit.,* pp. 83–84.
17. Zbigniew K. Brzezinski, *The Soviet Bloc: Unity and Conflict.* Cambridge, Mass.: Harvard University Press, 1960, pp. 386–387.
18. *Ibid.,* pp. 387–389.
19. Morgenthau, *op. cit.,* p. 249.
20. *Ibid.,* p. 136.
21. Inis L. Claude, Jr., *Power and International Relations.* New York: Random House, 1962, pp. 11–39.
22. A. F. K. Organski, *World Politics.* New York: Knopf, 1958, p. 286.
23. *Ibid.,* p. 292.
24. *Ibid.,* p. 338.
25. Morgenthau, *op. cit.,* p. 5.
26. *Ibid.,* p. 11.
27. William T. R. Fox, "The Reconciliation of the Desirable and the Possible," *The American Scholar,* Spring 1949.
28. Gabriel A. Almond, *The American People and Foreign Policy.* New York: Praeger, 1960, *passim.*
29. Cindy Ris, "Why Johnny Doesn't Know His History," *The Wall Street Journal,* October 29, 1980.

BIBLIOGRAPHY

Almond, Gabriel A. *The American People and Foreign Policy.* New York: Praeger, 1960.
———— and Coleman, James S., eds. *The Politics of the Developing Areas.* Princeton, N.J.: Princeton University Press, 1960.
Arendt, Hannah. *On Revolution.* New York: Viking, 1963.
———— *The Origins of Totalitarianism.* New York: Harcourt, Brace, 1951.
Aron, Raymond. *Peace and War.* New York: Doubleday, 1966.
Ball, George W. *The Past Has Another Pattern: Memoirs.* New York: Norton, 1982.
Beard, Charles A. *The Idea of National Interest, An Analytical Study in American Foreign Policy.* New York: Macmillan, 1934.
Benedict, Ruth. *Patterns of Culture.* Boston: Houghton Mifflin, 1934.
Bruchan, Silviu. *The Dissolution of Power: A Sociology of International Relations and Politics.* New York: Knopf, 1971.
Brzezinski, Zbigniew K. *Between Two Ages: America's Role in the Technetronic Era.* New York: Viking, 1970.
————. *The Soviet Bloc: Unity and Conflict.* Rev. ed. Cambridge, Mass.: Harvard University Press, 1967.
Buchan, Alastair. *Change Without War: The Shifting Structures of World Power.* New York: St. Martin's Press, 1975.
Carr, Edward H. *The Twenty Years' Crisis, 1919–1939: An Introduction to the Study of International Relations.* London: Macmillan and Company, Ltd., 1946.
Chatterjee, Partha. *Arms, Alliances, and Stability: The Development of the Structure of International Politics.* New York: Halsted Press, 1975.

Choucri, Nazli, and North, Robert C. *Nations in Conflict: National Growth and International Violence.* San Francisco: Freeman, 1975.

Claude, Inis. L., Jr. *National Minorities, an International Problem.* Cambridge, Mass.: Harvard University Press, 1955.

————. *Power and International Relations.* New York: Random House, 1962.

Crozier, Brian. *De Gaulle.* New York: Scribner, 1974.

Dallek, Robert. *Ronald Reagan: The Politics of Symbolism.* Cambridge, Mass.: Harvard University Press, 1984.

De Gaulle, Charles. *Memoirs of Hope: Renewal and Endeavor.* New York: Simon and Schuster, 1972.

————. *The War Memoirs of Charles De Gaulle.* Volumes I, II, and III. New York: Simon and Schuster, 1966.

De Rivera, Joseph H. *The Psychological Dimension of Foreign Policy.* Columbus, Ohio: Charles E. Merrill, 1968.

Deutsch, Karl W. *Nationalism and Social Communication.* New York: Massachusetts Institute of Technology Press and Wiley, 1953.

Draper, Theodore. *Present History: On Nuclear War, Détente, and Other Controversies.* New York: Random House, 1983.

Eisenstadt, S. N. *Revolution and the Transformation of Societies.* New York: Free Press, 1978.

Emerson, Rupert. *From Empire to Nation.* Cambridge, Mass.: Harvard University Press, 1960.

Fairbank, John K. *The United States and China.* Fourth ed. Cambridge, Mass.: Harvard University Press, 1978.

Fest, Joachim. *Hitler.* New York: Harcourt Brace Jovanovich, 1974.

Fox, Annette B. *The Power of Small States.* Chicago: University of Chicago Press, 1959.

Gottmann, Jean. *The Significance of Territory.* Charlottesville: University of Virginia Press, 1973.

Graubard, Stephen R., ed. *The State.* New York: Norton, 1981.

Griffith, William E., ed. *The World and the Great-Power Triangles.* Cambridge: Massachusetts Institute of Technology Press, 1975.

Haig, Alexander M., Jr. *Caveat: Realism, Reagan, and Foreign Policy.* New York: Macmillan, 1984.

Henderson, Gregory; Lebow, Richard Ned; and Stoessinger, John G., eds. *Divided Nations in a Divided World.* New York: McKay, 1974.

Herz, John H. *International Politics in the Atomic Age.* New York: Columbia University Press, 1959.

————. *The Nation-State and the Crisis of World Politics.* New York: McKay, 1976.

Hinsley, F. H. *Power and the Pursuit of Peace.* Cambridge: Cambridge University Press, 1963.

Holborn, Hajo. *The Political Collapse of Europe.* New York: Knopf, 1951.

Holbraad, Carsten. *Middle Powers in International Politics.* New York: St. Martin's, 1984.

Kissinger, Henry A. *A World Restored: Metternich, Castlereagh and the Problems of Peace, 1812–1822.* Boston: Houghton Mifflin, 1957.

————. *White House Years.* Boston: Little, Brown, 1979.

Knapp, Wilfred F. *A History of War and Peace: 1939–1965.* New York: Oxford University Press, 1967.

Knorr, Klaus. *The Power of Nations: The Political Economy of International Relations.* New York: Basic Books, 1975.

Lasswell, Harold D. *Power and Personality.* New York: Norton, 1948.

————. *World Politics and Personal Insecurity.* New York: McGraw-Hill, 1935.

————, and Kaplan, Abraham. *Power and Society.* New Haven, Conn.: Yale University Press, 1950.

Lippmann, Walter. *Public Opinion.* New York: Macmillan, 1947.

Liska, George. *Imperial America.* Baltimore: Johns Hopkins Press, 1967.

Mackinder, Halford J. *Democratic Ideals and Reality.* London: Penguin, 1944.

Masters, Roger D. *The Nation Is Burdened.* New York: Knopf, 1967.

Mattingly, Garrett. *Renaissance Diplomacy.* London: Jonathan Cape, 1955.

Meadows, Donella H., et al. *The Limits to Growth.* New York: Universe Books, 1972.

Modelski, George. *A Theory of Foreign Policy.* New York: Praeger, 1962.

Morgenthau, Hans J. *In Defense of the National Interest: A Critical Examination of American Foreign Policy.* New York: Knopf, 1951.

———. *Politics among Nations: The Struggle for Power and Peace.* 5th ed. revised. New York: Knopf, 1978.

Morse, Edward L. *Modernization and the Transformation of International Relations.* New York: Free Press, 1976.

Nicolson, Harold G. *Diplomacy.* New York: Oxford University Press, 1950.

Niebuhr, Reinhold. *The Structure of Nations and Empires.* New York: Scribner, 1959.

Nixon, Richard. *RN: The Memoirs of Richard Nixon.* New York: Grosset & Dunlap, 1978.

Osgood, Robert E. *Ideals and Self-Interest in America's Foreign Relations.* Chicago: University of Chicago Press, 1953.

———, and Tucker, Robert W. *Force, Order, and Justice.* Baltimore: Johns Hopkins Press, 1967.

Plischke, Elmer. *Microstates in World Affairs: Policy Problems and Options.* Washington, D.C.: American Enterprise Institute, 1977.

Rostow, W. W. *Politics and the Stages of Growth.* New York: Cambridge University Press, 1971.

Rothstein, Robert L. *The Weak in the World of the Strong: The Developing Countries in the International System.* New York: Columbia University Press, 1977.

Russell, Bertrand. *Power, a New Social Analysis.* New York: Norton, 1938.

Rustow, Dankwart A. *A World of Nations: Problems of Political Modernization.* Washington, D.C.: Brookings Institution, 1967.

Schell, Jonathan. *The Fate of the Earth.* New York: Knopf, 1982.

Schlesinger, Arthur, Jr., *A Thousand Days.* Boston: Houghton Mifflin, 1965.

Schurmann, Franz. *The Logic of World Power.* New York: Pantheon. 1974.

Schwab, George, ed. *United States Foreign Policy at the Crossroads.* Westport, Conn.: Greenwood Press, 1982.

Spykman, Nicholas J. *America's Strategy in World Politics.* New York: Harcourt, Brace, 1942.

Stoessinger, John G. *Nations in Darkness: China, Russia and America.* 4th ed. New York: Random House, 1985.

———, and Westin, Alan F., eds. *Power and Order: Six Cases in World Politics.* New York: Harcourt, Brace and World, 1964.

Szulc, Tad. *The Illusion of Peace: Foreign Policy in the Nixon Years.* New York: Viking, 1978.

Taylor, Alan J. P. *The Struggle for Mastery in Europe, 1848–1918.* Oxford: Clarendon Press, 1957.

Thompson, Kenneth W. *Morality and Foreign Policy.* Baton Rouge: Louisiana State University Press, 1980.

Tickell, Crispin. *Climatic Change and World Affairs.* Cambridge, Mass.: Harvard Center for International Affairs, 1977.

Tucker, Robert W. *The Inequality of Nations.* New York: Basic Books, 1977.

Ulam, Adam B. *The Unfinished Revolution.* New York: Random House, 1960.

Vital, David. *The Survival of Small States: Studies in Small Power/Great Power Conflict.* New York: Oxford University Press, 1971.

Vogelgesang, Sandy. *American Dream, Global Nightmare: The Dilemma of U.S. Human Rights Policy.* New York: Norton, 1980.

Yost, Charles. *The Insecurity of Nations: International Relations in the Twentieth Century.* New York: Praeger, 1968.

Part Two

THE INTERNATIONAL STRUGGLE FOR POWER

Chapter 3

The United States-
Soviet-China Struggle

*There are at the present time two great nations in the world, which started
from different points, but seem to tend toward the same end. I allude to
the Russians and the Americans.... Their starting point is different and
their courses are not the same; yet each of them seems marked out by the
will of Heaven to sway the destinies of half the globe.*

ALEXIS DE TOCQUEVILLE *Democracy in America,* 1835

THE ROOTS OF THE COLD WAR

"No, I am not a Marxist," Karl Marx was supposed to have said shortly before
his death in 1883. Today, a century later, it is even more important to separate
the man from the myth. Who was the founder of communism and how did his
doctrine get to Russia?

Marx was a German philosopher who was deeply disturbed by the conditions of the workers in mid-nineteenth-century Europe. There were reasons for
his outrage. Sweatshops, child labor, and starvation wages were the order of
the day. Unions did not exist nor did profit-sharing plans. Together with his
collaborator, Friedrich Engels, Marx published the *Communist Manifesto* in
1848. Its clarion call, "workers of the world unite, you have nothing to lose but
your chains," has echoed down to our time. Marx believed that workers had no
homeland since nations were simply the representatives of capitalists whose
only goal was to accumulate ever more wealth. Workers, therefore, would engage in a global "class struggle," and the time would come when, in a spontaneous revolution, they would throw off the capitalist yoke and establish a
socialist state. In such a state, the workers would own the means of production.
In his famous book, *Capital,* published in 1867, Marx asserted that these developments would have to happen, that they were indeed inevitable. History
moved forward through a process of challenge and response, and its great
turning points came about through economic forces. This "dialectical materialism" would ultimately usher in the victory of communism in which struggle
would cease and men and women would live harmoniously in a "classless
society."

Marx believed that the revolution would strike first in the most highly industrialized countries where the misery of the working classes was the greatest: Germany and England. This was not to be, however. In Russia, at the turn of the century, a young seminarian named V. I. Lenin was scarred for life when his brother was executed by the secret police for plotting to assassinate the Tsar. Lenin embraced the ideas of Karl Marx, but with a crucial difference. He did not believe that a workers' revolution would ever happen spontaneously. It would have to be organized by a "dictatorship of the proletariat" made up of professional revolutionaries who dedicated their lives to the cause. There would have to be iron discipline and strict obedience to authority. Lenin soon became the spokesman for these men and women and had to go into exile with a price upon his head. During World War I, he found himself in Germany working for the revolution. The German High Command, however, fighting the British and French in the West and the Russians in the East, proposed a deal to Lenin instead. It would smuggle him into Finland in a sealed train and help him finance the Russian revolution if Lenin would promise to take Russia out of the war with Germany. Lenin agreed and was dropped into Russia like a time bomb in the spring of 1917. By that time, the Tsar had abdicated and a provisional government under Alexander Kerensky had assumed control. Lenin agitated against Kerensky, promising "land to the peasants, factories to the workers, and an end to the war." Not surprisingly, he was successful and in October, in a determined coup, his men toppled the Kerensky government and took over the reins of power. Thus, it came about that a German philosopher inspired a Russian student for the priesthood to spark the Bolshevik Revolution. The world has not been the same since that event.

Today the East-West struggle hovers over us all like a "brooding omnipresence in the sky." It has become so much a part of our daily lives that we have virtually come to accept it as an axiom of international relations. While its presence and fearful implications are obvious to all, its causes are far from simple. It is to these that we must first address ourselves.

It is tempting to explain the genesis of the East-West struggle purely in terms of the expansionary zeal of Communist ideology. Indeed, a fairly good case can be made for such a position. Marxism, with its prediction that the "expropriated" would expropriate the "expropriators" on an international scale, envisaged world revolution as its ultimate goal. Leninism fashioned a network of Communist parties—the Comintern—to "give history a push" and hasten the day of Communist victory. This inherent aggressiveness of the Communist ideology, emanating from the Soviet Union as its citadel and directing center, elicited protective countermeasures in the West. These, in turn, generated suspicions of "capitalist encirclement" in the Soviet Union. Suspicion begot countersuspicion, gradually drawing East and West into a vicious circle. And thus the East-West struggle was launched.

A moment's reflection shows that this description of the "cold war," though tempting, is all too simple. It does not explain the fact that the Soviet Union on many occasions pushed forward its frontiers for reasons other than ideology. For example, it could hardly be said that the absorption of part of Poland and of the Baltic states in the wake of the Nazi-Soviet Pact of 1939 was the result of Communist ideology. Nor could it be assumed without question that the extension of American influence in Europe and Asia during World War II was purely a countermove to Communist expansion. Even a cursory inspection suggests that the East-West struggle may have some of its roots in geographic, historical, or cultural factors. This is not to say that ideology is not important. But the first and crucial question which we must ask is *how much* of the East-West struggle is rooted in the expansionary zeal of Communist ideology?

As one careful scholar of Soviet foreign policy has pointed out, it is a striking fact that Russian expansion can often be explained without reference to Marxist-Leninist ideological factors. For example,

> In the Second World War the Soviets could scarcely have permitted their Anglo-American partners to extend Western influence into all sections of the power vacuum created by the Axis defeat. American expansion in both Europe and Asia has often been hesitant and reluctant. Nevertheless, the war ended with an American general in Berlin and another in Tokyo. This the Soviets could hardly afford to neglect.[1]

It is, of course, impossible to determine the exact contribution of Communist ideology to Soviet expansion. But a perusal of Soviet foreign policy suggests that ideology alone did not prompt the Soviet Union to join or to break any alliance that it would not have joined or broken on the grounds of national interest. There are indications, however, that ideology in some cases retarded the shift or speeded up the change. Certainly, Marxism compounded the difficulties besetting the Grand Alliance during World War II and contributed to its disintegration. Lenin's strategy of Communist party infiltration, put to work so effectively in Eastern Europe following World War II, no doubt hastened the coming of the cold war. This "residual" quality of ideology has had one very important result:

> ... the Marxist-Leninist tradition has made it very difficult to reach a *modus vivendi* with the Soviets, which the Americans have been genuinely anxious to do. A belief in the inherently aggressive tendencies of modern capitalism obviously excludes any agreement except an armed truce of undetermined duration. Likewise, the acceptance of the Leninist theory makes it almost impossible to believe in the friendly intentions of American leaders.[2]

Hence, the Soviet perception of the West is to some degree, at least, colored by the lenses of ideology. And to the extent that this has been the case, the Soviet Union has, in effect, been struggling not so much with the West itself as with its ideologically conditioned image of the West.

More broadly, ideology has lent a Jekyll-and-Hyde quality to Soviet behavior vis-à-vis the West. In one sense, the Soviet Union has de-emphasized ideology and has acted as a nation among nations: it has made and broken alliances with Western nations; it has used diplomacy as an instrument of its national policy; and it has participated in the League of Nations and the United Nations. But on another level, the Soviet Union has always considered itself as the citadel of a revolutionary ideology destined ultimately to dominate the world. Thus, while ideology cannot be considered *the* cause of Soviet expansion and, hence, of the East-West struggle, it is clearly one very important cause.

There are other possible explanations for Soviet expansion that deserve analysis. First, it is often asserted that authoritarian states, by the very nature of their being, have need of an external enemy in order to deflect the frustrations of the population from the government to an external scapegoat. While there is some psychological truth in this claim, it cannot be carried too far. Authoritarian Sparta, for example, had no more expansionary zeal than its "democratic" counterpart, Athens. Nor did authoritarian Japan attack the United States in the nineteenth century; it was democratic America that forced open the door of Japan. We cannot demonstrate empirically that authoritarian regimes are by necessity more aggressive than democracies. Nor can the oft-asserted claim be validated that a good part of Soviet expansion is due to a power drive in the personalities of the Soviet leadership. Another explanation is sometimes sought in historical and geographic factors. Thus, some scholars maintain that Soviet expansion is merely a continuation of Tsarist aggrandizement and that certain Soviet territorial claims have their roots in the historical Russian strategic interest in warm-water ports. While it may well be that Soviet leadership derives some of its inspiration from the expansionist dreams of Tsarism, it is important to bear in mind that though history can teach by analogy, it never repeats itself exactly. The roots of Soviet expansionism must therefore equally be sought in what the men in the Kremlin believe to be the needs and opportunities of their country's contemporary situation. There is no doubt, for example, that economic factors enter into the picture. The Soviet absorption of most of Eastern Europe in the wake of World War II is generally agreed to have been dictated in some measure at least by very conscious economic considerations.

In sum, then, Soviet expansion cannot be explained in terms of any single-factor analysis. Its roots must be seen in a syndrome of forces among which are ideological and economic considerations, as well as factors of historical and geographic continuity. It is quite possible, although this cannot be demonstrated, that ideology constitutes the most important single element in this syndrome.

The temptation to explain American world strategy during and after World War II purely in terms of countermoves to Soviet expansionism is almost as great as the temptation to explain the latter exclusively in terms of Marxist-Leninist ideology. Yet here again we must beware of the pitfall of the single-factor analysis. No doubt there is much truth in such an interpretation of American policies, but it explains only part of the picture. Over a century before the cold war developed, the great De Tocqueville predicted its coming. Indeed, as one scholar has pointed out:

Well before 1945 the map of the world suggested the primacy of America and of Russia. Already by 1850 the United States formed one of the greatest land empires of the globe, stretching from the Atlantic to the Pacific and from the Canadian frontier to the Gulf of Mexico and the Caribbean Sea; already by 1800 the Russian Empire, stretching from Manchuria to Warsaw, covered over one-sixth of the entire land of our globe. Already by 1850 there were as many Russians as there were Frenchmen and Englishmen and Germans; already by 1890 there were more Americans than Frenchmen and Englishmen together; already by 1900 the United States produced more steel than any other country in the world; already during the First World War the financial wealth of the world shifted to America. Well before 1945 the United States and Russia were becoming the two largest Empires in the history of mankind.[3]

It is true that the United States had liquidated many of its possessions by the end of World War II. By 1946 the Philippines were given their independence and the remaining American possessions were being steadily prepared for self-government or statehood. On the other hand, it is quite clear that World War II had broadened the United States' perception of its strategic interests. Soon after hostilities had ended in Europe, the entire North Atlantic, from the Azores to Iceland and Greenland, had come within the sphere of American influence. And as a result of the occupation of Japan, the Pacific was transformed into what was virtually an American strategic lake. Indeed, World War II had created several power vacuums which the United States had decided to fill long before the cold war actually crystallized.

A number of "revisionist" scholars have gone even further and have actually blamed the United States for the outbreak of the cold war. Gar Alperowitz, in his *Atomic Diplomacy*, for example, argued that the United States, using its atomic monopoly, tried to push the Soviet Union out of Europe, and Gabriel Kolko, in his *Politics of War*, advanced the thesis that American capitalist society was, by its very nature, expansionistic. One does not have to be a Marxist, however, to appreciate the fact that the United States was not entirely blameless. The Soviet Union lost more than twenty million men during World War II. Yet Franklin D. Roosevelt twice postponed the creation of a second front against the Nazis in Europe, thus forcing the Russians to take the brunt of the German assault. Little wonder that Stalin was highly suspicious of American postwar intentions and tried to place as much territory as possible between Germany and Russia by the creation of Communist governments in Eastern Europe. It is thus not unreasonable to claim that *both* the United States and the Soviet Union share the responsibility for the origins of the cold war. But now that the two superpowers are caught in their circular predicament, "it is futile to argue which contestant has aggressive intentions and which has peaceable aims, since each move in the struggle calls out its countermove from the opponent."[4] A more useful function is served by analyzing the actual dynamics of the East-West struggle in our time.

THE DYNAMICS OF THE UNITED STATES–SOVIET–CHINA STRUGGLE

Phase One: The Comintern and the West, 1917–1949

When the Soviet Union emerged from the Bolshevik Revolution of 1917 it was largely guided in its relations with the West by the tenets of Marxism-Leninism. Indeed, Lenin proclaimed a complete divorce from the past. The new Soviet Union was to be a revolutionary society that would spread the Communist idea to other lands, beginning with the highly industrialized nations of the West. The first three years of the new state's existence, known as the period of War Communism, were a time of great ferment. Though engaged in a murderous civil war, the Soviet Union embarked on a program of ambitious experimentation in virtually every field of human endeavor. The Communist party assumed complete control of all political activity; the Komsomol (Soviet Youth Movement) was organized; industry was nationalized; atheism became official dogma; marriage was regarded as unnecessary; and education was completely reoriented. In its relations with the Western powers, the new Soviet government repudiated most of the debts contracted by its predecessor. It announced that within a short time the revolutionary tidal wave of communism would engulf the West as well. According to the Soviet leaders, there were omens and portents to justify this prediction: some of the Western nations, especially England and Germany, had reached the point of "capitalist concentration," a reliable signal of impending doom. Moreover, Lenin was confident that the struggle of these nations for colonies in World War I was a final and desperate maneuver to prevent their imminent collapse. To hasten this process, Lenin instructed the Comintern, which over a period of fifteen years had been built into a formidable revolutionary instrument, to concentrate its activity on Germany and England. This network of Communist parties was controlled unequivocally though clandestinely by the Communist party of the Soviet Union. Lenin's tenet of unquestioning obedience to the leadership of the Soviet Union was its governing organizational principle.

The West's reaction was a mixture of awe and terror. Many Western intellectuals were sincerely attracted by the bold new Soviet experiment. But the vast majority among the peoples of Western Europe and the United States recoiled from the "Red Terror." In the United States stringent security measures were taken; under Attorney General A. Mitchell Palmer thousands of arrests and deportations for alleged Communist subversion were made. The Western nations broke off all diplomatic relations with the new Soviet government and intervened in the civil war on the side of the Tsarist generals. In 1918, the Soviet Union stood alone, fighting a battle for survival at home and treated as a pariah abroad.

By 1920 the Soviet government faced imminent catastrophe. Not only had the Comintern failed in its international revolutionary efforts—save for brief Communist interludes in Bavaria and Hungary—but the Soviet Union itself was in desperate straits. Nationalization did not prove to be a magic formula for a country whose resources had been sapped by a destructive civil war, nor was a thorough knowledge of Marxism a substitute for technical competence in the factory and on the farm. The withdrawal of foreign investments and credits left the Soviet Union economically ostracized and on the verge of bankruptcy. Lenin was faced with a difficult dilemma: To continue the pursuit of world revolution would almost certainly lead to the destruction of the Soviet Union itself; on the other hand, to save the Soviet Union from the specter of bankruptcy would mean the betrayal of the revolutionary ideal.

Lenin, shrewd pragmatist that he was, took a middle course. He announced the formula of "One step backward in order to take two steps forward." The answer was to be found in the postponement of world revolution, not its abandonment. The struggle against the West would simply be pursued by other means. Lenin announced the New Economic Policy. Under this directive the Soviet government made an about-face in both domestic and foreign affairs. Almost all industry was denationalized, *Pravda* celebrated Soviet millionaires, social mores were tightened once again, and foreign investors were reinvited to the Soviet Union. Lenin instructed the Comintern to camouflage its tactics and adopt a policy of United Front with other leftist political parties in national parliaments. The Soviet Union concluded its first treaty in 1922—with Germany at Rapallo—and expressed interest in entering nonaggression pacts with France and Czechoslovakia. It seemed as if the Soviet Union had taken its place among the nations of the world community.

The Western world greeted the New Economic Policy with tremendous relief. Most Western observers concluded that the storm and stress period was over and that the Soviet Union had come of age. It now seemed that the "Red Terror" had been but a passing phase and that the Soviet Union had abandoned its struggle against the West. This impression was strengthened when Lenin died in 1924 and a bitter struggle for the succession left the Politburo little time or energy for the business of world revolution. Besides, both the Soviet Union and the West became increasingly apprehensive about the new threat of a remilitarized and aggressive Germany that loomed ever larger as the 1920s passed. The German Communist party, one of the most powerful in the Comintern network, found itself without effective leadership at a time when it was embattled with the National Socialist party for the control of Germany. The German population, harassed by the aftermath of a lost war and tormented by a galloping inflation, was ready to vote for political extremism of either Left or Right. The Nazi party attacked the Communists as agents of a foreign power and pointed to itself as the party of true patriots. The Communist tactic of the United Front proved unavailing and in 1933 the Nazi party assumed complete control of Germany.

The United Front technique proved equally unsuccessful in England— the second Western nation on the revolutionary timetable—when the British Communist party attempted to use a depression in the coal industry to bring England into the Communist orbit. Instead, a Liberal-Labour coalition took power. Thus, ten years after the foundation of the Soviet Union, neither the direct subversion of the early years nor the United Front of the 1920s was able to demonstrate any territorial gains for the cause of world revolution.

Stalin's accession to power in 1928 ushered in a period of complete transformation in Soviet domestic affairs. The New Economic Policy was abruptly terminated. In its place, a rigorous Five-Year Plan was announced, mobilizing the industrial and agricultural resources of the nation in order to build "socialism in one country." Stalin saw no inconsistency between this present emphasis on national power and the future goal of world revolution. The more powerful the Soviet Union was as a national state, he maintained, the better equipped it would be to export its revolutionary ideology later. But to accomplish "socialism in one country" during the 1930s, the complexion of the Soviet state underwent profound changes. Industry was nationalized once again and agriculture was forcibly collectivized in a ruthless campaign. The Communist party changed from a group of ideologues to a group of production experts; ability to overfulfill the Plan rather than a knowledge of Marxism-Leninism became the criterion of party membership. The party itself became an elite. Equality of pay was denounced as a "bourgeois superstition"; "Stakhanovites," or shock workers, were given higher wages and bonuses. In short, Stalin used Western capitalist methods to overcome the West. The goal was clear:

> To slacken the tempo of industrial growth in the Soviet Union would mean to fall behind. And those who fall behind get beaten. But we refuse to be beaten! One feature of the history of old Russia was the continual beatings she suffered for falling behind, for her backwardness. She was beaten by the Mongol khans. She was beaten by the Turkish beys. She was beaten by the Polish gentry. She was beaten by the British and French capitalists. All beat her—for her backwardness. Lenin said during the October Revolution: "Either perish—or overtake and outstrip the capitalist countries; either we do it—or they crush us."[5]

In foreign affairs, Stalin continued the policy of the United Front. A growing fear of Nazi Germany prompted him to de-emphasize Communist subversion of the Western countries. In 1936 he promulgated the so-called Stalin Constitution, which he proclaimed as the world's most democratic. The Soviet Union joined the League of Nations and its representative, Maxim Litvinov, proclaimed the USSR's adherence to the principles of collective security. The early 1930s was a fairly inactive period for the Comintern. One attempt at revolutionary coup—in France—was foiled by the French government. The growing fear of Nazism coupled with the opportunity of at last delivering one country into the orbit of the Soviet Union prompted Soviet intervention in the Spanish Civil War during the late 1930s. When Nazi intervention on the side of General Franco seemed to assure the latter's victory, Stalin decided to aid the Loyalists to redress the balance. But, in the midst of the Spanish war, the Great Purges took place in the Soviet Union. These cost the lives of many of the country's top military leaders. The Comintern, like every other Soviet power structure, was deeply affected by this gigantic bloodletting. It took its toll also in Spain and, coupled with the neutrality of the Western powers in the Spanish Civil War, gave victory to Franco by default. The Comintern had failed once again.

By 1938 Stalin felt increasingly insecure in his temporary alliance with the West. He may even have suspected that the West aimed at encouraging Hitler to strike to the East to promote a death struggle between the Soviet Union and Germany. At any rate, the Western fiasco at Munich confirmed the Soviet leader in his suspicion that an alliance with Hitler, who had just absorbed Austria and was rapidly gaining strength, would yield greater advantages. Stalin calculated that a pact with Hitler would safeguard the Nazi dictator's Eastern flank and thus give him the green light to launch an offensive against the West. Since, in Stalin's view, Nazi Germany and the West were approximately equal in strength, a mutually exhausting war would ensue that would give the Soviet Union an opportunity to grow stronger in peace and ultimately to absorb both adversaries. Besides, Stalin reasoned, a pact with Hitler would buy time and since the Great Purges had seriously weakened the Soviet military machine, time was most necessary. Moreover, the Soviet Union would at last be able to make some territorial gains: part of Poland and the three Baltic states of Latvia, Lithuania, and Estonia. Thus, in 1939, a strange alliance took shape between two incompatible dictators, and Marxism-Leninism was sacrificed on the altar of Machiavelli. As it turned out, Stalin's hopes were premised on a great miscalculation: It took Hitler not years but weeks to conquer most of Western Europe. By 1940, therefore, Stalin was dismayed to see himself confronted with a Nazi colossus preparing to break an alliance that had outlived its usefulness. Moreover, the ill-fated pact with Hitler had cost the Comintern many loyal followers who had been unable to accept the new dictum that the Nazis were to be the allies of the Soviet Union.

On June 22, 1941, Nazi troops crossed the Soviet border. Hitler vowed to dictate peace terms from the Kremlin within six weeks. As the Nazi forces advanced deep into Soviet territory, Soviet foreign policy became one desperate cry to the Western powers for help. The Allies responded with lend-lease supplies in late 1941, but refused to open an immediate second front in Europe. As a condition for further help, they insisted on the dissolution of the Comintern, since they thought it illogical to buoy up a government whose policy it was to subvert them. Accordingly, in 1943, the Comintern was dissolved.

Perhaps the greatest paradox of this phase of the East-West struggle is the fact that the Comintern was most successful at a time when the Soviet Union had reached its lowest ebb. The Communists, who had been suspect in the United Fronts of the 1920s and 1930s, were now welcomed. Their ruthless methods, which were formerly so feared, now proved a valuable asset in the common resistance against the Nazis. Communist party membership swelled again all over Western Europe. As the Red Army pursued the retreating *Wehrmacht* after the victory at Stalingrad, plans were laid for the absorption of liberated territories into the Soviet orbit. During the last two years of the war, preparations were worked out for the absorption of eight Eastern European countries. In carrying out this objective, the Soviet Union generally operated in three stages: first, a genuine anti-Nazi resistance coalition was to be formed with existing socialist and peasant parties; second, the Communist party would attempt to split the opposition parties by exploiting regional and ethnic jealousies, thereby transforming the coalition into a bogus alliance controlled by the Communist party; and finally, a coup d'état would establish complete Soviet control.

While the Soviet Union was thus preparing to take over most of Eastern Europe, American and Russian armies met in the heart of Europe, near the German town of Torgau, in April 1945. This event was the prelude to the division of Germany and most of Europe into American and Russian spheres of influence. Soon after, the first open misunderstanding arose and the "cold war" began to take shape. While the West had lowered its guard, the Soviet Union established control over seven Eastern European countries whose absorption had been prepared during the last years of the war: Albania, Bulgaria, Hungary, Poland, East Germany, Yugoslavia, and Rumania. In March 1946 Winston Churchill visited the United States and delivered his famous "Iron Curtain" speech in which he warned the West of Soviet intentions. During the following year, the United States took two specific steps to counter the Soviet challenge. In March 1947, through the Truman Doctrine, the United States took over from Britain the responsibility of protecting Greece and Turkey from communism. In June 1947 General George Marshall proposed the outline of a vast European Recovery Program at a commencement address at Harvard University. The aim of the Marshall Plan was the ultimate restoration of the economies of Europe through American aid. This aid was also offered to Eastern Europe and the Soviet Union, but Stalin refused to accept it. Relations between the Soviet Union and the United States now deteriorated rapidly. The four-power negotiations over a German peace settlement bogged down and a tougher American policy was adumbrated by George Kennan writing under the pseudonym "Mr. X" in the journal *Foreign Affairs.* Indeed, this policy of "containment" was soon to become the official American posture. In February 1948 the Soviet Union electrified the West by absorbing the eighth Eastern European country, Czechoslovakia, into the Communist orbit. In this case, all three Soviet techniques of subversion described above were employed successfully.

In the United States and Western Europe, the Communist coup in Czechoslovakia came as a most painful shock. Under its two great leaders Thomas G. Masaryk and Eduard Beneš, Czechoslovakia had during the 1920s and 1930s become the only really well-established and sophisticated democracy in Eastern Europe. Moreover, the country had been woven into the Western political community through defense alliances with Britain and France and had received a guarantee from the Soviet Union for help against the Nazi threat provided that Britain and France would fulfill their obligations. From the Czechoslovak point of view, however, the Munich Conference of 1938, resulting in the subsequent absorption of the country by Nazi Germany, signified a complete betrayal by the Western powers of their treaty obligations. This "Munich hangover" played an important role in the Soviet success. The eastward orientation of Czechoslovakia was given further impetus by the fact that the Red Army liberated most of Czechoslovakia, including the capital, Prague, in 1945. Communist party membership at the conclusion of World War II was substantial. The party was instructed to exploit the regional jealousies between the Bohemians and the Slovaks. Capitalizing on its anti-Nazi record, the Communist party now claimed control of the Ministry of the Interior. By 1947 the vote for the Communist party exceeded 40 percent of the population and the Red Army surrounded four-fifths of the Republic. At this juncture, the United States offered economic aid to Czechoslovakia under the Marshall Plan, which President Beneš was eager to accept. Stalin informed the Czechoslovak government that he would take a grave view of Czech acceptance of American aid. When, after an agonizing debate, the Czechoslovak government decided to decline the American offer, the Soviet Union knew that the Czech ship of state was foundering and was no longer an independent entity. In February 1948 Soviet Deputy Foreign Minister Valerian Zorin arrived in Prague, ostensibly to supervise the delivery of Soviet wheat. During the next few days the Communists completed the take-over through a coup d'état.

The success of the Communist coup in Czechoslovakia galvanized the West into action. Twelve nations, under the leadership of the United States, formed the North Atlantic Treaty Organization (NATO), a regional defense alliance for the purpose of containing Soviet expansion. For the United States, membership in a peacetime alliance was a drastic reversal of foreign policy. The fear of the Soviet Union and its newly acquired allies now dominated political thinking in all of the Western nations. The fact that the Comintern was reconstituted by 1947 in Warsaw—although under the innocuous-sounding title of Communist Information Bureau, or Cominform—was widely interpreted in the West as a sign pointing to renewed Soviet emphasis on the goal of world revolution. The West now determined to stand fast.

The showdown came in Germany. In Berlin, the former capital, the cold war reached a point of rigidification. It will be remembered that, in 1945, Germany had been occupied by the four major victorious powers, the United States, Britain, France, and the Soviet Union. The Yalta and Potsdam Agreements of 1945 had divided Germany into four zones, three Western and one Soviet. Berlin, the former capital, was situated in the Soviet zone but was itself divided into four sectors. Under the agreements, none of the Occupation powers was to have the right to change the status quo without the consent of the others. In 1948, however, shortly after the absorption of Czechoslovakia, Stalin began to put pressure on the Western garrisons in Berlin. The Soviet administration suspended all communications between West Berlin and the Western zones of Germany. The object of this blockade was to turn West Berlin into an island and to starve it into submission. The American response was the famous Berlin Air Lift, which effectively countered the Soviet move by supplying the population of West Berlin from the air. In May 1949 the blockade was lifted.

By this time, the division of Germany as a whole had begun to be accepted as a long-time condition. Both superpowers attempted to absorb their zones of occupation into their respective orbits. The three Western zones emerged as the Federal Republic of Germany, with its capital at Bonn, and the Eastern zone was turned into a Soviet dependency. The vast majority of the German people, however, desired the reunification of their country.

The Western condition of German reunification was, in essence, a free election to be held in all of Germany. This was unacceptable to the Soviet Union because both East Berlin and West Berlin would probably opt for the West and thus remove the city from Soviet influence. Moreover, the population of all of Germany would probably prefer the West. Such a development would bring Germany within the Western orbit and extend Western influence to the Czech and Polish borders, thereby threatening Soviet control in Eastern

Europe. The Soviet demand in return for granting German reunification was the neutralization of Germany and Western withdrawal from Berlin. These conditions seemed unacceptable to most Western statesmen. It was felt that the East German Communist government would then be in a position to absorb West Berlin through a process of strangulation. Moreover, the United States alleged that German neutrality would play into the hands of the Soviet Union, since American troops would withdraw across the Atlantic while the Red Army could be based in Eastern Europe and thus return at any moment to fill the power vacuum. Perhaps most important, the West feared that meeting the Soviet conditions would convince the Eastern European nations that they had been abandoned by the West and, hence, cause them to settle in the Soviet orbit for good.

The deadlock over Germany ended the first phase of the East-West struggle, which till then had still been characterized by large areas of maneuverability. It ushered in a period of increasing rigidity, in which each superpower stipulated conditions that were unacceptable to the other. This sort of relationship—mutually exclusive positions short of actual physical conflict—was to characterize the East-West struggle from then on.

At the very time that the Soviet Union encountered stiffened Western resistance in Berlin, the Soviet orbit also began to undergo internal changes with great significance for the East-West struggle. Indeed, the Czech coup was the last major Communist action in which Moscow was the absolute master of communism. For thirty years Moscow's orders had been executed without question by Communist parties everywhere. This relationship was now subjected to profound changes. In 1948, for the first time in Communist history, another Communist party defied Moscow's authority: the Yugoslav party under the leadership of Tito. Tito had always been a loyal Communist; he and his fellow partisans had distinguished themselves in guerrilla warfare against the Nazis, whom they had fought bravely and relentlessly. Stalin, however, let it be known that the Soviet Army had driven the Germans from Yugoslavia while the partisans had just engaged in mopping-up operations. Though Tito took a dim view of this version of events in Yugoslavia, the episode no doubt would have passed without major repercussions if Stalin had permitted the fulfillment of Tito's fond dream of organizing a Balkan Federation. It was Tito's desire to form an empire within an empire, with Yugoslavia exercising its rule over Albania and Bulgaria. Stalin not only scotched this ambition but proceeded to rebuke Tito for the slow advance toward collectivization in Yugoslavia. When Tito defended himself by pointing out the difficult conditions he had to face in coping with the local peasantry, Stalin threatened to send to Yugoslavia Soviet Communist inspectors who were to be paid out of Yugoslav funds. Tito interpreted this as an attack upon his control of the Yugoslav Communist party and refused to follow orders. Stalin thereupon expelled Tito from the Cominform.[6] By this act of excommunication Stalin fully expected to end Tito's political revolt—and probably his life as well. But there was to be no walk to Canossa. Instead, the West immediately offered assistance to Tito's government and Stalin decided not to crush the defector by force. Tito, though continuing to identify himself as a Communist, thenceforth refused to submit to Cominform authority. He remained suspended precariously between East and West.

Later during the same year, the Chinese Communist party came to power on the mainland of China. As we shall see in Chapter 5, this party had been ruggedly independent of Moscow's control from its very beginnings. With its formula for the organization of communism on a peasant, rather than an urban, industrial basis, it had come to power to the surprise of both the West and the Soviet Union. Though describing himself as a Communist, Mao Tse-tung, the political leader of the new China, had, in effect, developed an ideology sharply at variance with the orthodox, Moscow-directed Communist creed. What this of course meant for Stalin was that shortly after the Yugoslav fiasco, he found himself confronted with a second and similar dilemma: should he insist on the ideological conformity of Mao Tse-tung and thereby risk the defection of China from the Communist orbit? Or should he recognize the ideological deviation of the Chinese leader and thereby encourage the development of Peking as an independent Communist power center? Stalin chose the latter course and in late 1949 the Soviet Union extended recognition to the new Communist government in China.

The Yugoslav defection and the developments in China ended Moscow's unquestioned authority within the Communist orbit. By 1949 there were three centers of communism: Moscow, Belgrade, and Peking. In communism's struggle against the West, this internal transformation signified both a strength and a weakness. It portended a greater threat to the West because increased ideological flexibility could be expected to inject new life into a credo threatened by petrification. On the other hand, after 1949 the Cominform was no longer able to count on the blind obedience of its membership, which had guaranteed it such swiftness of political action in the past.

In evaluating this first phase of the East-West struggle, we can come up with at least two interesting observations. The first concerns the striking number of blunders committed by the Comintern during the 1920s and 1930s. Indeed, it did not achieve its first successes until during and immediately after World War II. Nevertheless, the Western view of the Comintern during the interwar decades for the most part remained that of an implacable foe, a kind of consummate chess master impervious to the mistakes of ordinary people. Many acts of the Comintern were seen in the West as carefully worked out and long-planned stratagems and many of its errors were interpreted as strategic retreats according to plan.

What were the reasons for this collective "inferiority complex" on the part of the West? In part, it no doubt stemmed from fear of the "built-in" expansionism of Communist ideology. But the Nazis were equally imperialistic and, moreover, were locked with the West in an all-out military conflict, which communism never was. Yet the West was more afraid of Communist than of Nazi ideology. This may be attributable to the facts that communism attacked private property and was a highly sophisticated ideology that offered something to almost everyone: an ultimate vision of humanitarianism and equality to the democrat; revolution to the revolutionary; a better life for the worker; and a sophisticated dialectic to the intellectual. Most important, it offered a coherent secular religion:

> The dictator becomes God, the only God for that matter; and the Party becomes the church. As a variant, collective leadership becomes a sort of Trinity. The central committee and the local leaders take care of polytheistic needs. The parallels could be pressed further. The point is that all the essential mundane elements of religion except the Virgin Mother are represented.[7]

One group of students even went so far as to state that communism by 1946 had become a "father image the like of which the world had never seen—harsh, revengeful, jealous, and unpredictable."[8] Something like this was implied by John Foster Dulles when he made the following statement in 1946:

> Few men in political life anywhere act without first thinking whether they will please or displease the leaders of the Soviet Union. Never in history have a few men in a single country achieved world-wide influence.[9]

Yet as we have seen, this "superman" image by no means squares with the record. The history of the Comintern until 1949 presents a mixture of failures and successes, of rational and irrational acts, and of much gross distortion of the facts of international life.

The second observation that deserves to be noted about this early phase of the East-West struggle concerns the difficulty of sorting out its "causes." The great importance of Communist ideology is clearly apparent; but it is equally clear that the cold war also grew out of the meeting between Russians and Americans in the heart of Europe at the close of World War II. Indeed, the entire pattern suggests the validity of Barrington Moore's point that it is futile to argue about the primal causes of the struggle since each move by one superpower elicited a countermove from the other. What is important is that the East-West struggle had rigidified in Europe by 1949. There was virtually no maneuverability left as power confronted concerted counterpower. Thus, it was no accident that the major arena of the East-West struggle during the next decade shifted away from Europe. And the rise of China as an independent power center in the Communist orbit helped move this arena to East Asia.

Phase Two: The Rise of China

The most striking development in the context of the East-West struggle during the 1950s and early 1960s was the ascendancy of China, both within the Communist orbit itself and in the power configuration vis-à-vis the West. While Western fears of Communist expansionism continued during the 1950s to concentrate mainly on the Soviet Union, the expansion that actually occurred took place not in Europe but in East Asia. Indeed, the Soviet Union was unable to absorb any territory during the 1950s while, during the same decade, the Chinese Communists fought in Korea, shared in the dismemberment of Indochina, and made expansionary moves into Tibet and India. Not only did the Soviet Union fail to score further advances in Europe during the 1950s, but it had to fight to retain control in Poland and Hungary, which had been absorbed in the 1940s. In August 1961 the erection of the Berlin Wall served notice of yet another Soviet failure: Moscow was forced to fence in its East German ally lest it emigrate out of existence. The sole Soviet territorial advance was the acquisition of a Communist foothold in the Caribbean—Cuba. But this gain was offset by the loss of face Moscow suffered when it was forced to withdraw its missile bases and offensive weapons from Cuba in 1962 and by simultaneous Chinese territorial gains in the Himalayas. Indeed, it seemed that, by the mid-1960s, the center of gravity of Communist expansion had shifted from Moscow to Peking. This transition in the East-West struggle deserves analysis.

China's first participation in the East-West conflict took place in Korea. That peninsula had been partitioned at the thirty-eighth parallel shortly before the end of World War II as a result of the military disposition of Soviet and American forces. The Japanese were to surrender to American troops south of that parallel, to Soviet troops north of it. Since neither half of the country was economically viable and the partition was accepted very reluctantly by the Korean people, Korea's truncated state was seen as only a temporary modus vivendi. During the next two years the United States occupied South Korea, while North Korea was absorbed into the Soviet orbit. All attempts to agree on a formula for unification failed. In the fall of 1947 the United Nations took over the Korean problem and recommended free elections. But since United Nations observers were not permitted to visit North Korea, an election could be held in the southern half only. From this election there emerged the Republic of Korea as a sovereign state; the northern half retaliated by pronouncing itself a sovereign "Democratic People's Republic." During the next two years there occurred a great deal of military posturing on both sides of the parallel. Finally, on June 25, 1950, the North Korean Army attacked. The United Nations Security Council responded immediately by authorizing a "police action." During the summer of 1950 United Nations troops were in retreat, but in October they recrossed the thirty-eighth parallel, shortly thereafter capturing the Communist capital of Pyongyang and advancing toward the Manchurian border. At that point China entered the conflict.

The United Nations action in Korea will be evaluated in another context in Chapter 12. What is important in the present connection is the impact of China on the Korean War. It is not entirely clear why the Chinese Communists decided to intervene. Perhaps they were persuaded to do so by the Soviet Union. On the other hand, the decision may have been made quite independently and for reasons wholly their own. In the opinion of one scholar, there were two overriding reasons for the Chinese Communists' actions. One was their concern that an American-controlled Korea, along with the United States itself and a revived Japan, might develop into an alignment that could dominate all of Northeast Asia. The other was their fear that if they passively accepted an American victory in Korea, their enemies both within and outside China might be so strengthened as to imperil the Chinese Communist regime itself.[10] Moreover, the Chinese may have believed that General Douglas Mac-

Arthur, the commander of the UN forces, intended to cross the Yalu River and invade China. In any case, the entry of China turned the hostilities in Korea into an entirely new war. The lines of battle seesawed for two more years, to come to a standstill approximately where they had been when the war began, with the indefinite partition of the country by the armistice agreement of 1953. Since then, China has competed with the Soviet Union over influence in North Korea.

When, in 1954, the battle of Dienbienphu brought to an end the French Empire in Asia, four new entities emerged from the colony of Indochina: South Vietnam, Laos, Cambodia, and North Vietnam. As a result of the Geneva Conference of 1954, North Vietnam fell under the shadow of communism while South Vietnam established a pro-American regime. The West, alerted to the new threat emanating from China, formed the Southeast Asian Treaty Organization (SEATO), which bound together the United States, Britain, Australia, France, New Zealand, the Philippines, Thailand, and Pakistan in a military defense alliance. Yet the "Pekintern" continued its expansionary drive. In 1959 it suppressed a rebellion in Tibet, which it had "liberated" in 1950, and began moving into areas that it claimed along the Chinese-Indian border. Armed clashes between Chinese and Indian border forces occurred intermittently until the Chinese launched a major offensive in October 1962. The result of this invasion was a cease-fire giving China control over a large section of the disputed border area in Ladakh. Moreover, under SEATO's very nose, China continued its pressures on Laos and its infiltration into Cambodia.

Not only did China fare better than its Soviet partner in the struggle against the West; she also made rapid strides during the 1950s on the internal home front. Most notably, Mao Tse-tung announced the "Great Leap Forward," a vast program of agricultural reform through which he planned to turn China's arable land into a series of gigantic communes far closer to the ideal of pure collectivization than their counterparts in the Soviet Union had ever been. While the Russian peasant on the typical Soviet collective farm continued to enjoy a small private plot of land—a residue of capitalism which neither Stalin nor Khrushchev had been able to eliminate—the Chinese commune aimed at the abolition of all private property. In the more advanced communes, even the bringing up of children was not left a private family matter but was put into the hands of party functionaries. Although the Great Leap Forward was thwarted by poor planning and repeated crop failures, these lapses did not seriously affect China's rising international power status.

As China consolidated its independent position within the Communist orbit, China also began to develop an increasingly independent approach to the East-West struggle. During the late 1950s it became increasingly evident that China's attitude toward the West was more hostile than that of the Soviet Union and that the Chinese leadership showed fewer inhibitions about the use of violence than did their Soviet partners in the struggle. Indeed, Mao Tse-tung was reported to have pointed out that neither the Soviet Union nor the United States could afford an atomic war, whereas if China lost three hundred million people, there would still be over four hundred million left. By 1960 a major doctrinal divergence on the question of how best to bring the West to its knees had arisen between the two major Communist powers. Peking's apparent conviction that "capitalism" could only be defeated through war was at variance with Premier Khrushchev's doctrine of "peaceful coexistence," which postulated a Communist victory without the necessity of armed conflict. However, since both Moscow and Peking were aware of the fact that their continued unity was a crucial factor of strength in the East-West struggle, the Chinese nominally accepted Soviet ideological leadership. While the dialogue continued under the surface, the common dictates of the East-West struggle still kept it well within limits. As one scholar of Sino-Soviet relations astutely observed in 1960:

> In the bargaining process between them [Russia and China], *unity* plays a role analogous to that of a hostage restraining both parties. In a situation involving the exchange of hostages, one may threaten the life of a hostage, but such threat can be effective only as long as the hostage is alive; once he is dead, the threat is meaningless. The same applies to unity. Since loss of unity is the worst eventuality for both, the weaker partner must limit his efforts at self-assertion, the stronger must limit or make oblique his countermoves.[11]

In the early 1960s the Sino-Soviet conflict entered a new and more violent phase. The doctrinal differences grew more intense as the two Communist colossi exchanged veiled insults, with the Chinese attacking "Yugoslav revisionism" and the Soviets retaliating with assaults on "Albanian adventurism." Chinese disenchantment with the Soviet leadership reached a new high when the latter withdrew its technicians from China, thus postponing temporarily China's entrance into the nuclear club. In 1962 two dramatic events brought the conflict into the open: the Cuban missile crisis and the Chinese attack on India. In the former China attacked the Soviets for backing down before a paper tiger while Premier Khrushchev pointed out that the American tiger happened to be equipped with nuclear teeth. In the latter the Soviet Union gave neither aid nor encouragement to the Chinese, but used its influence to bring about a rapid and peaceful settlement. The outcome of these two simultaneous crises again favored the Chinese: While Russia had to back down from one of the most serious East-West confrontations in a decade, China was achieving a major diplomatic and military victory.

By 1963 the doctrinal and "methodological" differences between the two major Communist nations began more and more to take on the coloration of a major power conflict between two great national states. Ideology began to decrease in importance as competitive nationalism began to increase. Serious border disputes broke out along the Sino-Soviet frontier over contested territory in Sinkiang and Mongolia. Communist parties throughout the world were deeply split over the issues raised by the dispute. China no longer recognized the ideological leadership of the Soviet Union and accused Khrushchev of plotting with Washington for Russo-American world domination. In 1964 two dramatic events occurred in quick succession. Premier Khrushchev was ousted by the Soviet Presidium as a "hare-brained schemer" and the Chinese exploded their first atomic device. Thus, while yet another succession crisis shook the Soviet government, China had crashed the gates of the exclusive nuclear club.

By the mid-1960s, moreover, it was clear that some of the expansionary drive of communism had definitely shifted from Moscow to Peking. During the 1950s and early 1960s all the territorial gains for communism, with the exception of Cuba, were made by China. This is not to say, of course, that the Soviet Union's intention to expand had disappeared or even diminished. But it met far more effective Western resistance from NATO than China did from SEATO. Certainly this was true until the United States became deeply involved in the Vietnamese war. Indeed, while China made its gains against the West, the Soviet leadership had to expend its energies in maintaining control over what it had gained earlier. Moreover, Stalin's death in March 1953, marking the end of a heavy-handed personal dictatorship that had lasted since the late 1920s, had triggered a rumble of discontent among the Eastern European nations. The promulgation by the United States government in 1953 of a "policy of liberation" toward Eastern Europe had already caused some ferment in those nations. When Khrushchev publicly denounced Stalin in February 1956, he opened a Pandora's box of revolts. Within the year, Poland, under the leadership of Wladislaw Gomulka, attempted to emulate the Yugoslav move for independence. The Poles demanded the removal of the Soviet secret police and military rule, tolerance for the Catholic Church, and the freedom to "travel their own road to socialism." Almost at the same time, Hungary revolted against Soviet control. The first stage of the Hungarian Revolution was patterned after the Polish precedent. But then the revolutionaries were no longer content with ideological deviation within the Cominform, and wanted to escape from communism altogether. At this point, the Soviet Union moved in with military force and crushed the revolt. The West found itself unable to intervene because of fear of a general war. "Liberation" proved unworkable and the West had to be content with the "containment" of the Soviet Union. Nevertheless, in most Western countries the spectacle of the Hungarian freedom fighters shattered whatever still remained of the old "chessmaster concept" of the Soviet Union.

The instability of the East German regime was indicated in another manner. East Germans were voting against Soviet domination with their feet, emigrating at the rate of about two hundred thousand a year to West Germany via that gaping hole in the Iron Curtain, Berlin. By early 1961 the number of refugees amounted to one quarter of the total population of East Germany at that time. The danger which this loss of skilled workers and professionals represented to the East German economy was matched only by the grave political implications of the exodus. In order to retain East Germany as a dependency, Moscow was forced to turn it into a walled jail. The Berlin Wall, closing off the last gap in the Iron Curtain, was erected in August 1961.

The greatest crisis within the Soviet bloc during the 1960s, however, took place in Czechoslovakia in 1968. These events were of sufficient importance to merit detailed consideration.

For almost two decades Czechoslovakia had been an apparently tranquil nation in the Soviet orbit. Toward the end of 1967, however, many intellectuals in Czechoslovakia began to criticize the lack of literary freedom, and President Antonín Novotný, a Stalinist, found it increasingly difficult to maintain his leadership. In January 1968 Alexander Dubček, a reform-minded liberal, was appointed as First Secretary of the Communist party of Czechoslovakia. Two months later, Novotný was forced to resign and a highly respected elderly military leader, General Ludvík Svoboda, was named to succeed him to the presidency. During the spring of 1968 the Dubček regime decided on a dramatic move: it lifted censorship of the press. As a result, on April 16, 1968, *Rudé Právo,* the Czechoslovak Communist party organ, suggested for the first time that Soviet agents might have been responsible for the death of Jan Masaryk, Czechoslovak foreign minister, who either jumped or was pushed through a window in March 1948. This initiative triggered the first Soviet suspicions about developments in Czechoslovakia. In April 1968, the Dubček leadership issued a manifesto promising fuller civil rights to the Czech people, but, in order to reassure the Soviet Union, reiterated on numerous occasions that Czechoslovakia would remain Communist and a faithful member of the Warsaw Pact.

In May 1968 the Communist party leaders of the Soviet Union, East Germany, Poland, Bulgaria, and Hungary—stung by ever more critical articles in the Czechoslovak press—began talks in Moscow about the Dubček liberalization program. Rumania stayed aloof from this conference. On May 17 Soviet Premier Aleksei Kosygin arrived in Prague for a "continuing exchange of views" as a result of which the Prague regime agreed to Warsaw Pact military maneuvers on Czechoslovak soil. Later that month, a manifesto called "Two Thousand Words" was issued by seventy Czechoslovak intellectuals. This manifesto called for, *inter alia,* the establishment of multiple political parties and proposed that Stalinists be purged from the Czechoslovak Communist party. Although the Dubček leadership strongly objected to this manifesto, it was seen in the Soviet Union as a confirmation of Soviet fears that Dubček would not be able to control events and that anti-Communists were gaining ground in Czechoslovakia.

In June, Warsaw Pact maneuvers took place in Czechoslovakia and on July 9 the Dubček regime rejected a demand from the Soviet Union and its four Warsaw Pact allies for a summit meeting in Warsaw. On July 14 this summit meeting took place without the Czechoslovaks, and the result was a stinging letter demanding an end to the liberalization program. On July 18 the Dubček regime rejected this rebuke and declared its intention to continue the reforms. At the end of July, on Soviet initiative, a dramatic meeting took place between virtually the entire ruling bodies of the Soviet Union and Czechoslovakia in the small Czechoslovak border town of Cierna. The Soviet leaders appeared to yield after three days of talks and on August 3, at Bratislava, Czechoslovakia, the five Warsaw Pact members and Czechoslovakia signed a "unity document" that seemed to ratify the accord reached at Cierna. Shortly thereafter, Soviet troops that had lingered in Czechoslovakia after the June maneuvers left the country. It seemed that Czechoslovakia was the victor in its confrontation with the Soviet Union and its four allies.

Following the conclusion of the Bratislava conference, Czechoslovakia

was host to three Communist leaders. On August 9 President Tito, who had
supported the Dubček leadership all along, visited Prague. Two days later,
however, East German party leader Walter Ulbricht, a mainstay of Communist orthodoxy, arrived in the Czechoslovak capital and received a very cool
reception. On August 15 Rumanian President Nicolai Ceausescu arrived in
Prague to dramatize his regime's support for Dubček. On the following day,
the Soviet press resumed its attacks on Czechoslovakia, charging that "antiso-
cialist forces" were stirring dangerously in the country.

During the night of August 20 the blow fell. Troops from the Soviet
Union, East Germany, Bulgaria, Hungary, and Poland crossed the Czechoslovak border in a surprise move and proceeded to occupy the country. The decision, which seemed to have been the result of many months of disagreement
within the Soviet leadership, came as a profound shock to most of the world
and virtually split the Communist movement down the middle. Rumania and
Yugoslavia as well as China opposed the Soviet move, as did most of the Communist parties in Western Europe. The Czechoslovak population offered resistance through strikes, noncooperation, and, in places, violence. The leading
members of the Dubček regime, including the First Secretary himself, were
arrested, but the Soviets were not able to assemble a regime of Czechoslovaks
that was more to their liking. Instead, while the Czechoslovak foreign minister
placed the case of his nation before the United Nations Security Council, representatives of the liberal Czechoslovak regime continued to meet clandestinely in Prague, virtually under the guns of the occupying powers. Three days
after the invasion, the Soviet Union realized that it had to negotiate with the
Czechoslovak leaders after all. Yet another confrontation now took place, this
time in Moscow. The Soviet leadership and its four Warsaw Pact allies again
faced the Czechoslovaks, including the aged President Svoboda and First
Party Secretary Dubček himself. This time, the agreement that emerged was a
compromise heavily weighted in favor of the Soviet Union. The five occupying
powers insisted that their troops would remain in Czechoslovakia until the situation was "normalized," that is until, in their eyes, the threat of "counterrevolution" had disappeared. In the view of most Western observers, the Moscow
agreement bordered on capitulation. Thus, the Soviet Union managed to
reimpose a degree of orthodoxy on Czechoslovakia, but the price that it paid
was a further fragmentation within the international Communist movement.

In the light of these events, the East-West struggle could by now no
longer be considered exclusively, or perhaps even primarily, in terms of the
Soviet Union and the United States. Competition *within* the two camps had
become almost as important as competition *between* them. The homogeneity
of the Western alliance was seriously challenged by the nationalist policies of
President de Gaulle in Western Europe. In the East, China's bid for ideological leadership of the Communist camp had begun to assume the proportions of
a major national power rivalry with the Soviet Union. In fact, Moscow's control was now threatened from both Left and Right. China and its Eastern European ally Albania took every opportunity to attack Soviet "revisionism" for
its alleged collusion with American "capitalism." On the other side of the

Communist spectrum, Yugoslavia had been free of Moscow's control since Tito's expulsion from the Cominform in 1949 and Rumania, by the late 1960s, had carved out for itself a relatively independent role in the Communist bloc including an independent foreign policy.

Thus, by the late 1960s the bipolar system had begun to loosen even though spheres of influence continued to exist. Some observers noted a similarity in the behavior of the superpowers in their respective spheres of influence. Thus, each superpower still risked intervention by force of arms when faced with the possible loss of a nation that it considered vital to its national interests. The United States took this course in the Dominican Republic and in Vietnam, and the Soviet Union resorted to it in Hungary and Czechoslovakia. There were, however, significant differences in degree between American and Soviet patterns of intervention. While some of the policies of the Dubček regime no doubt seemed provocative to the Soviet Union, Czechoslovakia never threatened to leave the Warsaw Pact. President de Gaulle of France, on the other hand, not only frequently provoked the United States, but came close to pulling France out of the Atlantic Alliance. Yet, no American statesman seriously contemplated an invasion of France. Be that as it may, the world of the late 1960s still seemed divided into fairly well-defined superpower spheres of influence with some gray areas in between which, while remaining objects of competition, were not considered crucial.

Even after the Czechoslovak crisis, United States–Soviet relations continued to exhibit elements of both conflict and cooperation. As the 1960s drew to a close, the Soviet Union and the United States had concluded an agreement to ban the use of outer space for military purposes and had jointly proposed a treaty to halt the further spread of nuclear weapons. In addition, despite conflicting policies in Vietnam and in the Middle East, the two superpowers managed to open talks on limiting their respective missile systems, ratified a long-delayed consular agreement, and arranged for direct New York–Moscow air connections.

There were thus some hopeful signs that the United States–Soviet relationship had moved beyond the cold war into a phase of uneasy coexistence. At least it was possible to gain some perspective on those bleak two decades following World War II. In retrospect, it was impossible to see the cold war simply as a case of Soviet aggression and American response or of American aggression and Soviet response. Only the tragic elements in the developing cold war spiral were clear. But the question remains, as Arthur Schlesinger, Jr., has put it, whether the cold war was an example of Greek tragedy, "the tragedy of necessity," where the feeling aroused in the spectator is "what a pity it had to be this way"—or of Christian tragedy, "the tragedy of possibility," where the feeling aroused is "what a pity it was this way when it might have been otherwise."[12] Perhaps the cold war could have been avoided if Stalin had not been so convinced of the imminent decline of the West and of the inevitability of a Communist victory, and if the United States had not in turn succumbed to its own forms of dogmatism and self-righteousness. In that sense, perhaps, a tragedy of possibility was transformed into one of necessity.

Chinese Communist fortunes began to suffer some significant reversals during this period. In October 1965 the Chinese-controlled Communist party of Indonesia was purged in a bloody coup. And when President Nkrumah of Ghana was ousted a year later, the Chinese were virtually expelled from that African country.

In 1966 the beginnings of a furious internal struggle further weakened China's rule on the world scene. Under the leadership of Mao Tse-tung, a "Great Cultural Revolution" was launched which shook China's political structure to its very foundations. Mao, anxious that China might follow the "revisionist" example of the Soviet Union, made a concerted effort to reinfuse China's masses with the revolutionary fervor of the old Yenan days. Toward this end, hundreds of thousands of young Red Guards, who were to spread Mao's slogans across the land, were mobilized. But these efforts encountered stiff opposition by more pragmatic elements in both the party and the army who were more interested in consolidating the gains China had made since the ascendancy of the Communist regime than in risking these in a war with the West. The ensuing struggle for power between Mao and his opponents was somewhat reminiscent of the struggle between "Reds" and "experts" that had characterized the Soviet Union in the 1920s.

Thus, by the late 1960s, both internal and international developments had brought setbacks to China. In addition, China's relations with the Soviet Union had deteriorated to such an extent that China found itself embattled in a two-front cold war with both superpowers at the same time. The stage was now set for a fundamental change in the nature of the East-West struggle.

Phase Three: American Détente with Russia and China

The Cuban missile crisis of 1962 represented a great turning point in Soviet-American relations. Both superpowers had gone to the edge of the nuclear abyss and turned back just in time. The narrow escape from atomic holocaust left its mark on the Soviet and American leadership alike. Slowly, the frozen hostility of cold war thawed and gave way to a less abrasive relationship characterized by greater realism and a more businesslike approach. Shopworn slogans and polemics were replaced by more objective assessments of each other's character, intent, and power. An atmosphere of confrontation slowly yielded to an attitude conducive to productive negotiations.

The first concrete result was the partial nuclear test-ban treaty, concluded in Moscow in 1963. President John F. Kennedy had called for such a ban in a major address at American University in June 1963. During the remainder of the decade, despite the rapid escalation of the Vietnamese war, Soviet-American relations gradually improved. Agreements were hammered out to prevent the spread of nuclear weapons and to insulate outer space and the ocean floors from the atomic arms race. But it was not until 1969 that the new policy was openly articulated. President Richard Nixon, newly elected, declared that an "era of negotiation" would begin and the Soviet leadership, with a wary eye on China, decided to cooperate with its great capitalist adversary. The process of gradual détente that followed marked the end of the cold war and the beginning of a new pattern of "adversary-partnership." This fundamental change in superpower relations deserves careful and systematic scrutiny.

At first, the new policy was applied selectively, primarily in two fields in which an interest in reaching agreement had been previously defined and where viable options could be identified: Berlin and arms control. The United States and the Soviet Union began talks on the status of Berlin in March 1970. While little visible progress was made during that year, the talks signaled a shift in policy toward the recognition of the status quo in Europe, a necessary prerequisite to further negotiations in this crucial arena of contention. During 1970 two rounds of Strategic Arms Limitation Talks (SALT) were convened in Vienna and in Helsinki, firmly emphasizing the interest of the two superpowers in negotiating bilateral agreements on weapons control. In November 1970 the United States also received private assurances from the Soviet Union that it would not introduce offensive weapons into the Western Hemisphere or establish bases there, a conciliatory gesture on a point of special American concern. The United States, together with other NATO members, also invited "all interested states" to hold exploratory talks on a mutual and balanced reduction of NATO and Warsaw Pact forces. The Warsaw Pact countries suggested a limited discussion on the reduction of foreign armed forces on the territory of European states, but indicated that such talks should follow a conference on general European security. The NATO countries agreed that such a conference was desirable, but suggested that it be held after the successful conclusion of the negotiations over Berlin.

During 1971 the negotiations on both Berlin and SALT continued. The first phase of the quadripartite negotiations on Berlin was completed, leading to subsequent negotiations between the German authorities themselves. These were successfully concluded in December 1971. Despite the increased level of fighting in Southeast Asia, the SALT talks resumed in March 1971. In April the Soviet interest in détente was articulated and legitimized by the Twenty-fourth Communist Party Congress and Secretary Brezhnev's call for eased world tensions and improved relations between the United States and the Soviet Union. In May a new area of cooperation became manifest when Soviet officials made it known that they were interested in negotiating trade agreements with the United States.

From the Soviet perspective the pressure for improved Soviet-American relations took on a new urgency with the announcement in July 1971 that President Nixon would visit the People's Republic of China the following spring. In August, President Nixon stated that his trip to China would be followed by a summit conference in Moscow.

By November 1971 it had become evident that the Soviet Union had yet another rationale for quickening the momentum of détente. Not only had American overtures to China made Soviet-American rapprochement a necessary counterweight to an increasing Chinese role, but shortages in vital sectors of the Soviet economy had made a rapid trade expansion with the United

States most advantageous. Arrangements were made for the sale of three million tons of feed grain to the Soviet Union to cover the short-fall resulting from a poor harvest. In November, Secretary of Commerce Maurice Stans visited Moscow and announced that the United States might buy oil and natural gas from the Soviet Union. From the Soviet viewpoint, the remaining barriers to an even faster acceleration of bilateral trade between the two countries were the absence of most-favored-nation status, the lack of export credits, and the extensive list of strategic goods blocked for sale to Communist countries. On the American side, the question of Soviet Jewry and the outstanding World War II lend-lease debt served as inhibiting factors. Nevertheless, limited trade continued when contracts were signed for the sale of $65 million of American mining and oil drilling equipment and for the purchase of $60 million of nonferrous metals from the Soviet Union.

The year 1972 represented a high-water mark in Soviet-American détente. During that year more agreements were concluded than at any time since diplomatic relations had begun in 1933.[13] In February the Soviet Union informed the United States that it was willing to reopen negotiations, suspended for twelve years, on the repayment of the outstanding Soviet World War II lend-lease debt. The talks opened in Washington in April. At the same time, a series of arms-control negotiations took place, ranging from measures to prevent incidents at sea to the SALT talks. Moreover, the loss of much of Russia's winter grain crop made imminent the prospect of substantial Soviet purchases of American grain.

Despite Soviet displeasure with President Nixon's trip to China and American dissatisfaction with Moscow's role in the massive North Vietnamese offensive, it was announced in April that the Soviet Union was ready to approve plans for a joint earth-orbiting mission by Soviet and American astronauts. In May President Nixon visited Moscow, highlighting the progress reached thus far. The trip raised cooperation between the two countries to the highest level since the wartime alliance of the 1940s. The summit was indicative of the "momentum of achievement" on which both leaderships were banking. The commitment of each side to détente was symbolized by the signing of a declaration embodying twelve basic principles of relations between the United States and the Soviet Union. Recognizing the necessity of coexisting, the two nuclear powers undertook to prevent the development of situations capable of dangerous exacerbation and agreed to do their utmost to avoid military confrontations. Both pledged to exercise restraint in their mutual relations, to recognize the sovereign equality of all countries, and to promote conditions in which no country would be subject to outside interference in its internal affairs.

The 1972 summit also resulted in a number of specific agreements. Foremost among these was a treaty on the limitation of Antiballistic Missile Systems and an Interim Agreement with Respect to the Limitation of Strategic Offensive Arms, which effectively terminated phase one of SALT. These agreements, for the first time, placed limits on the growth of American and Soviet strategic nuclear arsenals. A ceiling of two hundred launchers was established for each side's defensive missile system and both countries committed themselves not to build nationwide systems of antimissile defenses. The interim accord on offensive systems froze land-based and submarine-based intercontinental missiles at the level then in operation or under construction, though it placed no limitations on qualitative improvements, on the number of warheads each missile could carry, or on the number of strategic bombers. Agreements were also signed on environmental cooperation, on joint medical research, and on the formation of a joint commission to devise a comprehensive trade agreement. In late June 1974, a few weeks before his resignation, President Nixon visited the Soviet Union for yet another summit meeting.

President Gerald Ford and Soviet Party Chairman Leonid Brezhnev met for the first time in November 1974 in Vladivostok. On that occasion the two leaders reached tentative agreement on an overall ceiling of about twenty-four hundred nuclear missiles and bombers for each side. About thirteen hundred of these on each side would be missiles with multiple atomic warheads (MIRVs). The ceilings, however, were quantitative, rather than qualitative. No restrictions were set on missile flight tests to increase accuracy, nor on the development of land-mobile and air-mobile intercontinental ballistic missiles, nor on cruise missiles launched from submarines.

Even though the ceilings were high, Secretary Kissinger expressed the hope that the accord would "put a cap on the arms race" for ten years between 1975 and 1985.[14] In that sense, the Vladivostok meeting signified a modest new impulse to the momentum of détente and showed that a minimum of trust had been attained at last in the tensely guarded realm of arms control: both sides considered it more important to agree on a broad formula of strategic parity than to press for specific numerical advantages. On balance, the "cap on the arms race" meant a quantitative limitation on further arms development, not a reduction of existing stockpiles. In that sense, the agreement reached at Vladivostok was a meaningful, though not historic one.

President Jimmy Carter, despite a new emphasis on human rights, continued to pursue détente and the limitation of strategic arms. In a far-ranging speech on foreign policy, delivered at the United Nations two months after his inauguration in January 1977, the new President called for sweeping reductions in nuclear arms and for a freeze on new kinds of weapons. In the same speech, however, President Carter placed great importance on human rights and asserted that "no member of the United Nations [could] claim that mistreatment of its citizens [was] solely its own business."

This new accent on human rights, which included statements of support on behalf of Russian dissidents, irritated the Soviet leaders, who accused the United States of hypocrisy and "selective morality." The President, the Soviet leaders claimed, ignored violations of human rights in fascist dictatorships, such as South Korea, Chile, and Iran, which the United States considered to be of vital strategic value. The United States declared that SALT II would not be made contingent upon internal changes in the Soviet Union. Evidently, the Carter administration was convinced that it could pursue *both* détente and human rights in its relations with the Soviet Union. The Russian response was skeptical. The United States, the Soviet leadership declared, had no right to play the role of moral world police. Party Chairman Brezhnev stated that it was "unthinkable" that Soviet-American relations could develop normally on such a basis. When Secretary of State Cyrus Vance visited Moscow in March 1977 in order to pursue SALT II, the Soviet leadership flatly rejected two American plans to limit strategic weapons, without offering any new proposals of its own. Thereafter, President Carter became less vocal on human rights and Soviet dissidents and, in a surprise move in July 1977, announced that he had decided not to authorize the construction of the B-1 bomber. Protracted negotiations on SALT II resumed soon afterward, and even when, in July 1978, the Soviet government sentenced several of its leading dissidents to long prison terms, these negotiations were not interrupted. Nor did the Soviet offensive in the Horn of Africa affect this policy in any substantial way, although the rhetoric on both sides became somewhat more strident. The President was both Lion and Beaver. The Lion roared but the Beaver continued to work toward SALT II. Thus, while President Carter had denounced the policy of the "lone ranger," Henry Kissinger, it seemed that, despite the new initiatives on human rights, Secretary Kissinger's détente policy was continued, essentially unchanged. Morality in foreign policy, it seemed, would have to be balanced against strategic interests. This meant that human rights would have to be pursued more quietly. Ethics in international affairs, in other words, were subordinate to power.

On balance, it was clear that despite periodic setbacks, the Carter administration did not desire a return to the confrontation policies of the predétente era. Even when, in 1978, the Soviet Union, using Cuban proxy troops, infiltrated the Horn of Africa, Ethiopia, and Zaire and a pro-Soviet coup toppled the government of Afghanistan, the American public did not become overly excited. When one considers the fact that less than two decades earlier, Soviet Russia and the United States almost went to war against each other over missiles in Cuba, the détente achievement was enormous. War between the superpowers seemed a remote possibility in the 1970s, but had not been at all unlikely in the 1950s and 1960s. Objective changes in the global power constellation, in particular the rise of China, had provided the initial impetus to détente. But it was equally important that the leading personalities on both sides had the intelligence to seize the opportunity. Such moments are rare indeed in history. They seldom offer themselves a second time. And in their recognition lies the secret of historic statesmanship.

For an entire generation, Chinese and Americans had perceived each other through dark screens that often produced caricatures out of realities. They had fashioned images of one another that were based on their deepest fears and terrors. Political accommodation was quite impossible under such circumstances. They had met on fields of battle in Korea and had narrowly averted a catastrophic encounter in Vietnam. And then, at last, after more than twenty years of estrangement, a great desire to become reacquainted developed on both sides. Chinese and Americans once more decided to establish direct contacts and to move toward reality.

The roots of détente on the American side rested in the decision of President Nixon, upon entering the White House in 1969, to order a reexamination of America's China policy and to "Vietnamize" the war in Indochina. The new administration realized the sterility of past China policy and saw the need to deal with China on the basis of present facts, rather than old fears. Moreover, the reestablishment of relations with China would thrust the United States into the role of balancer between China and the Soviet Union as long as the hostility between the two great Communist powers continued to exist. On the Chinese side, the conviction gradually crystallized that the United States was a less formidable threat than the Soviet Union. After all, Americans were withdrawing from Asian soil while Soviet troops were massing on the Chinese border. Détente with the United States would eliminate the danger of a two-front cold war. Thus, to the Chinese leadership, détente with the United States became a matter of national security.

The American withdrawal from Vietnam took almost four years to complete. The first troop cut was announced in July 1969 and the Paris Accords were signed in January 1973. During that time China and the United States took a number of concrete steps toward rapprochement. The most important of these are well worth examining against the background of the gradually deescalating war in Indochina.

The first initiative was taken on the American side in February 1969 when Secretary of State William Rogers announced that the United States government wished to encourage scientific and cultural exchanges. In July 1969, when the peak figure of 541,500 American troops in Vietnam was reduced by a first cut of 25,000 men, American citizens were also permitted to bring into the country up to $100 worth of Chinese goods. This constituted the first loosening of a twenty-year-old embargo against goods from mainland China. In addition, the President announced the Nixon Doctrine, declaring that, in the future, the United States would avoid entanglements like Vietnam by limiting its support to economic and military aid rather than active combat participation. Peace negotiations began in earnest in Paris and a protest held in Washington against the war drew huge crowds demanding a rapid withdrawal of American troops. In January 1970, however, under the euphemism of "protective reaction" to cover air reconnaissance missions over North Vietnam, the United States renewed the bombing of North Vietnam.

In February 1970, in his message to Congress, President Nixon formally announced his objective of improving relations with Peking. Two months later, by executive order, the President authorized the selective licensing for export to China of goods produced by American subsidiaries abroad. A jarring note was struck on April 30, 1970, however, when President Nixon, in a nationally televised address, announced an American-led South Vietnamese "incursion" into Cambodia in order to eliminate Vietcong supply depots and sanctuaries and to demonstrate that the United States was "no pitiful, helpless giant."

In November 1970 a simple majority of the membership of the United Nations supported the seating of mainland China. While insufficient for action, the vote was significant because of its psychological importance. One month later, on December 18, in an interview with Edgar Snow, Mao Tse-tung declared that he was ready to receive President Nixon in Peking. The President responded to this invitation in his message to Congress on February 25, 1971, by affirming his intention to establish a dialogue with the Peking government without, however, breaking off relations with Taiwan. Restrictions on the travel of American citizens to mainland China were lifted in March and, one month later, in the first concrete response to these American moves, the United States table tennis team was invited to China.

The United States government immediately responded to this Chinese gesture in four specific moves. In the first place, it conveyed to American oil companies the objections of the Chinese government to their search for petroleum deposits off the China coast. Second, President Nixon announced the termination of a twenty-one-year ban on direct trade with China. Third, the Lodge Commission Report supported a system of dual Chinese representation in the United Nations. Finally, Mr. Nixon declared that he would be happy to visit China.

In July 1971 it was revealed that Dr. Henry Kissinger, the President's Special Assistant for National Security Affairs, was in Peking. On this historic occasion, Dr. Kissinger held lengthy consultations with Premier Chou En-lai and the two men developed an excellent rapport. Dr. Kissinger stated that Chou En-lai was one of the greatest statesmen of the time and the Chinese premier returned the compliment by declaring that his American visitor had a "Chinese mind." Shortly after the meeting, it was announced that President Nixon would visit China in early 1972. In August, Secretary of State Rogers declared that the United States would fight for a system of representation in the United Nations under which both Chinas would be in the organization. This plan did not succeed. On October 25, 1971, on the last day of Dr. Kissinger's second visit to China, the General Assembly voted for the seating of mainland China and the exclusion of Taiwan. On November 30, Dr. Kissinger stated that the problem of Taiwan should be resolved by direct contact between Peking and Taiwan. The road was now clear for a summit meeting between the top leadership of China and the United States.

President Nixon's visit to Peking in February 1972 was the occasion of the first substantive bilateral agreements between the two countries in more than twenty years. In the Shanghai Communiqué of February 24, it was agreed to facilitate bilateral trade and cultural exchanges. Senior United States representatives would be sent to China from time to time to further the normalization of relations. In March the Chinese table tennis team visited the United States, and in April the first American businessmen were invited to visit the Canton spring trade fair.

Détente underwent a serious test in mid-1972 when President Nixon decided to mine the port of Haiphong in North Vietnam ten days before he was scheduled to visit Moscow. However, Moscow and Peking apparently placed a higher priority on their relationship with the United States than on their alliance with North Vietnam. The Nixon visit took place on schedule. Hanoi now realized that it could not depend too much upon Soviet and Chinese support.

The United States, in turn, found itself in the anomalous position of having reached détente with one billion Communists—800 million Chinese and 200 million Russians—and yet pursuing a relentless war against a small Communist peasant country which it accused of aggression against its neighbors. Thus, so far as the United States was concerned, the Vietnam war now increasingly seemed like an anachronism. History had simply passed it by. On January 23, 1973, a cease-fire was reached in Paris which extricated the United States from combat participation in the Vietnam war.

On February 15, less than a month after the Paris agreement, Dr. Kissinger once again visited Peking. This time, the United States and China agreed to open liaison offices in Washington and Peking. At the same time, China agreed to release two captured American pilots and to review the sentence of John Downey, a CIA agent held prisoner in China since the Korean war. It was also decided to negotiate the settlement of American claims against China and of Chinese assets "blocked" in the United States since Korea.

In March 1973 David Bruce was appointed to head the United States liaison office in Peking, and Huang Chen, China's former ambassador to France, was named to fill the Washington post. The liaison offices were formally opened in May 1973.

Under the impact of political détente, trade between the two countries expanded considerably, despite the fact that China was not granted most-favored-nation status. A National Council for U.S.–China Trade was established and a delegation was sent to Peking for the first formal meeting between an American business group and Chinese trade authorities in almost twenty-five years.

In November 1973, Dr. Kissinger once again visited China. At that meeting, it was agreed to expand the functions of the liaison offices. Premier Chou En-lai stated that the full normalization of relations between China and the United States could be realized only on the basis of confirming the principle of one China. But each side decided to remain ambiguous on just how this goal of a single China was to be attained. It seemed clear, however, that a solution by force was ruled out by both sides. Thus, the delicate issue of Taiwan was neatly transformed from a problem to be solved immediately into a process to be managed over a longer period of time.

The trade pattern followed an erratic course. Two-way Chinese-American trade approached the $1 billion mark in 1974. During that year, the United States became China's second-most-important trading partner. In 1975, however, the figure was slashed in half and the Chinese abruptly canceled a large order for American wheat and corn. Taiwan's trade with the United States in 1975 was almost ten times as large, and Hong Kong's was four times as large. The evidence suggests that the Taiwan issue inhibited a more rapid expansion of commercial contacts. Financing problems, the American refusal to grant China most-favored-nation status, and the lack of a formal trade agreement could all be traced back to the absence of full diplomatic relations. Thus, Kissinger's liaison-office solution did not resolve the Taiwan problem, but merely circumvented it. By 1975 rapprochement between China and America had reached a fairly stable plateau. There was little, if any, forward movement. Even a trip to Peking by Secretary Kissinger and President Gerald Ford in the fall of 1975 did not restore the old momentum.

After the deaths of Mao Tse-tung and Chou En-lai in 1976, a power struggle erupted in China over the succession to the legendary chairman. Chiang Ching, Mao's widow, led a radical group that believed the United States was a greater threat to China than was the Soviet Union. She lost the fight to Teng Hsiao-Ping and a more moderate faction that believed the Soviet Union posed a greater danger to China than did the United States. Chiang Ching was purged from the Chinese leadership, and the successors of Chou En-lai took over the reins of power.

In the United States, the administration of President Jimmy Carter and Secretary of State Cyrus Vance decided not to deviate in any significant way from the China policy of their predecessors. In 1977, Secretary Vance visited China to underline this continuity and, in 1978, Zbigniew Brzezinski, Jimmy Carter's National Security Adviser, during a visit to Peking, emphasized the cordial relations that existed between China and the United States. The fact that this statement was made at a time of Soviet-Cuban initiatives in the Horn of Africa was not lost upon the Soviet government. It was clear that Henry Kissinger's triangular policy was still in operation. This trend was the result of objective changes in the global power constellation. America's withdrawal from Vietnam, the Soviet presence on the Chinese border, and the American decision to balance its relations with China and the Soviet Union but to remain equidistant from them both were primarily responsible for this great turning. Yet it was also true that both China and America had been fortunate to have as diplomatic leaders men of the caliber of Henry Kissinger and Chou En-lai, both equipped with realistic perceptions of themselves and of each other, a rare knowledge of history, and an even rarer gift for empathy. This personal dimension no doubt accelerated the movement away from fantasy and fiction toward reality and rapprochement. Henry Kissinger and Chou En-lai had recognized the objective conditions necessary for a turn for the better in the relations between China and America. They had seized the crucial moment at one of history's great junctions and helped to make it happen.

One other common element in the personalities of the four main architects of Sino-American détente seems significant. Each of these men was a survivor. Mao Tse-tung and Chou En-lai had survived decades of adversity. Kissinger had been a refugee from the Nazi holocaust, and Nixon had made several comebacks from political defeat. Perhaps this common theme helped to fashion a rapport among these men and helped them turn away from hatred toward a measure of acceptance.

During the opening days of 1980 the Soviet Union did something it had never done before: it used its own troops to invade a neutral country.

As close to a hundred thousand troops smashed into Afghanistan, President Carter announced that his "opinion of the Russians [had] changed more drastically in the last week than in the previous two and a half years." Describing the invasion as a "quantum jump in the nature of Soviet behavior," and the most serious crisis since World War II, the President announced an embargo on grain and high-technology products against the Soviet Union. In his State of the Union address in January 1980, he declared that the United States would use armed force, if necessary, to repel any Soviet assault on the Persian Gulf region. This new "Carter Doctrine" thus extended the NATO alliance concept to the Middle East. Containment now included all regions of vital strategic or economic interest to the United States. The SALT II negotiations were suspended and, by year's end, had become a casualty. Suddenly, all the détente efforts of the 1970s seemed in jeopardy. Nineteen eighty seemed more like 1950. What was behind these shattering events?

The evidence suggests that the Soviet leadership made its move based partly on objective considerations of strategy and power balance, but also partly on its perceptions of what the United States might or might not do.

The "objective" factors apparently were the following: Moscow's primary purpose was probably to tighten its control over a rebellious border state. The tide of Islamic fervor which had already shaken Iran was now threatening Afghanistan. Unless it was checked quickly, it might spread across the border into Soviet Central Asia and stir unrest among the Soviet Union's fifty million Moslems. Second, the invasion was probably part of a long-range strategy to gain influence over Pakistan, Iran, and other Persian Gulf nations. It might ultimately place the Soviet Union in the strategic position of controlling Western oil supplies. Finally, Moscow probably intended to send a message to Peking that it was prepared to resort to force if its border interests were threatened.

Perceptions of American intent probably also played a role. In the first place, the Soviet leadership had apparently concluded that SALT II had little chance of winning approval during an election year. Moreover, since NATO had decided in December 1979 to deploy in Western Europe, by the mid-1980s, new atomic-tipped missiles capable of striking targets in the Soviet Union, SALT was simply not all that important any longer. Second, Moscow may have reached the conclusion that the United States was so distracted by Iran that it would not act strongly on Afghanistan. After all, at that point the fifty-two American hostages held captive in Teheran by Iranian militants had dominated America's attention for two months. And finally, one might venture the following speculation: When the United States, during the 1960s and early 1970s, had more than half a million combat troops fighting in Vietnam, and had mined Haiphong and bombed Hanoi, the Soviet Union had not canceled SALT I. In fact, ten days after the mining of Haiphong harbor in May 1972, Richard Nixon and Henry Kissinger arrived in Moscow to meet with Leonid Brezhnev in a summit meeting to sign the first strategic arms limitation treaty between the superpowers. Why, then, should the United States overreact if the Soviet Union took advantage of an opportunity that came its way in 1980? It is entirely possible that the Soviet leadership underestimated the American response to Afghanistan in a manner similar to the way in which Nikita Khrushchev underestimated the U.S. response to Soviet missiles in Cuba in 1962.

So far as Afghanistan itself was concerned, it was not subjugated easily. Insurgency seems to come naturally to the Afghan people. Their character is well illustrated by an episode in 1841 when an occupying army was reduced to a single survivor—a disaster without equal in British history.

In the years of British colonialism, Afghanistan was an independent buffer state between India and Tsarist Russia. In 1839, British fears about Russian influence in Kabul prompted an Afghan war. With little resistance, the British marched into Afghanistan and installed a puppet king. This British envoy was soon pleased to report from Kabul: "All things considered, the perfect tranquillity of the country is to my mind perfectly miraculous. Already our presence has been infinitely beneficial."[15]

The occupiers were unprepared for the riot that followed. Kabul's British resident was hacked to pieces. The Afghan king whom the British had deposed led an uprising. Prudently, the British commander accepted Afghan terms for a supposedly safe exodus to the Khyber Pass, ninety miles away over difficult terrain. But his entire army was destroyed. In the first week, twelve thousand were killed; by the eighth day, only twenty officers and forty-five foot soldiers remained; a day later, only a sole survivor was alive. He was Surgeon Bryden of the Army Medical Corps. When he reached the Indian frontier, a waiting British colonel, anxious for news of the Kabul army, sighed in relief: "Here comes the messenger!"

One may wonder whether the Russian occupiers had read their history.

A dispassionate Olympian view of Soviet-American relations during the 1960s and 1970s might conclude that when it comes to testing détente through intervention, the superpower score is very close to even. The United States intervened in Vietnam, Cambodia, and the Dominican Republic, and the Soviet Union intervened in Hungary, Czechoslovakia, and Afghanistan. It is true that Afghanistan was a neutral country, but Cambodia was, too. Unfortunately, however, when passions are inflamed, such Olympian views enjoy little popularity. Empathy gives way to an "us-and-them" psychology. The lessons of the Cuban missile crisis are forgotten and the arms race gathers momentum once again.

Phase Four: In and Out of Cold War

Under the first term of Ronald Reagan's presidency, the Soviet-American relationship deteriorated to a level not seen since the days of the Cuban missile crisis. During the détente years of the 1970s, there was little talk of nuclear war. Instead, the two nations pursued a pragmatic, businesslike relationship. Ten years later, however, in 1983, a television version of nuclear holocaust was watched by one hundred million frightened Americans. In my university classes in New York City more than half of the students expected to perish in a nuclear war before the year 2000. The unthinkable had become possible once again. What had happened? And who was to blame?

In the first place, President Reagan brought to the presidency an extremely negative view of the Soviet Union. Of all American presidents, his perception was probably the darkest and his rhetoric the harshest. A few examples will serve to make the point. In his first press conference in 1981, President Reagan called the USSR a nation ruled by men who "reserve unto themselves the right to commit any crime, to lie, to cheat." A few months later, he told an audience of West Point cadets that the Soviet Union was an "evil force." And in March 1983, in an address to a conference of Christian fundamentalists in Orlando, Florida, the President referred to the USSR as the "focus of evil in the modern world . . . an evil empire."[16]

Not only did he label the Soviet Union evil, but he predicted it would not last much longer. "The West won't contain Communism, it will transcend Communism," the President told the graduating class of the University of Notre Dame in 1981. "Communism is a bizarre chapter in human history whose last pages are even now being written." And in June 1982 President Reagan declared before the British Parliament that "the march of freedom and democracy [would] leave Marxism-Leninism on the ash heap of history." The Soviet experiment was in the process of full decay.

Ronald Reagan seemed more interested in seeing the USSR in the dustbin of history than seeing it for himself. When Leonid Brezhnev died in 1982, after eighteen years of rule, the President did not see fit to attend his funeral. And when his successor, Yuri Andropov, died in 1984, once again Ronald Reagan chose not to put in an appearance in Moscow. At age 74 he had yet to visit the Soviet Union for the first time in his life.

Not only did the American President perceive the Soviet Union as an "evil empire," but he tended to regard leftist movements in the Third World as tentacles of the USSR. Guerrillas in El Salvador and the Sandinistas who ruled Nicaragua were both seen as direct extensions of Soviet ambition. Poverty and social inequality were seen as far less important causes than Soviet revolutionary subversion. Hence, in El Salvador, President Reagan supported the government against guerrillas, and in Nicaragua he supported guerrillas against the government. The President's perceptions of communism did not allow for nuances and shadings. It was "us against them," good against evil. In Ronald Reagan's universe, Joseph Stalin had never died.

The Soviet leadership probably hoped at first that Ronald Reagan would turn out to be another Nixon: tough in his rhetoric but pragmatic in his actions. Brezhnev, in his final year, was quickly disabused of this notion. Hence, fearful that the United States might try to detach Poland from the Soviet orbit in a "rollback policy" reminiscent of John Foster Dulles, Brezhnev used a Soviet-trained Polish general to declare martial law in Poland and to outlaw the Solidarity Union.

On September 1, 1983, a dreadful tragedy occurred that no doubt confirmed the perceptions of the American President. The Soviets shot down a Korean airliner on a night flight to Seoul with a loss of 269 civilian passengers. Even though the plane had overflown Soviet air space for more than an hour, and the decision to destroy it had apparently been taken by a regional Soviet commander without Politburo authorization, the barbarism of this act poisoned Soviet-American relations even further. Self-righteous "explanations" about "American spy planes" and "sanctity of Soviet air space" only increased American wrath. Name-calling reached a peak after this catastrophe. President Reagan and Secretary of State George Shultz both described the USSR as an international outlaw. Andrei Gromyko, a senior Soviet diplomat, not only failed to apologize for this example of mass murder but announced that the Soviet Union would do it again if its air space were violated. Thus, the American leader's devil image and the Soviet leadership's wooden-headedness combined to drag the relationship to its lowest ebb since the bleakest days of the cold war.

Three weeks after the Korean disaster, Yuri Andropov, the former KGB boss who now ruled the Soviet Union, delivered a major policy statement. In this document Andropov in effect accused Reagan of killing détente. "Even if someone had any illusions about the possible evolution for the better in the policy of the present U.S. Administration," Andropov declared, "the latest developments have actually dispelled them."[17] A few weeks later, Soviet diplomats and "Americanologists" such as Georgi Arbatov began to compare Ronald Reagan to Adolf Hitler. The door-slamming and bridge-burning rhetoric continued on both sides, almost to the time of Andropov's death in February 1984.

Beginning in early 1984 the President, apparently for domestic and political reasons, adopted a somewhat more conciliatory tone. In his State of the Union address in January 1984 he "reached out" to the Soviet Union. Yet, he made a gross historical error. "Our two countries have never fought each other," he declared. Apparently he had never heard of the American intervention in 1918, designed to bring down the new Soviet regime of V. I. Lenin. And again in May, in a speech before the Irish Parliament, he appealed to Moscow to reduce tensions.

Yet a great deal of damage had been done. Neither side had found the courage to say "I am wrong" on a single issue. It was as if two nasty cross-eyed men, both armed to the teeth, were continuing to bump into one another, the first one shouting at the second, "Why don't you look where you are going?" and the second one shouting back "Why don't you go where you are looking?" Worst of all, both sides were to blame for endangering the future of the planet and of generations yet unborn, for this breakdown in diplomacy had spilled over into the vital area of arms control.

When two countries despise and distrust each other as thoroughly as the United States and the Soviet Union did in the early 1980s, diplomacy itself becomes militarized. Arms control then becomes not a genuine search for reductions, but a competitive jockeying to gain an advantage over the adversary. Every proposal contains a "joker" which makes the package unacceptable to the other side. The result is not reduction, but mutual escalation.

The Soviet Union's greatest fear during the early 1980s was that the United States would implement a 1979 NATO decision to place more than five hundred Pershing and Cruise missiles into Western Europe in order to balance Soviet SS-20 missiles which were aimed at Western European targets. In late 1981 President Reagan proposed the so-called "zero option," offering not to deploy the American missiles if the Soviets dismantled theirs. After two years of intensive bargaining, the Soviets rejected the "zero option," claiming that it would still leave French and British nuclear missiles aimed at the Soviet Union and thus give NATO a net advantage. Even a much publicized "walk in the woods" near Geneva in late 1982, by Paul Nitze and Yuli Kvitsinsky—the two main arms negotiators—was not able to break the impasse.

In early 1984 the United States began to deploy the Pershings and Cruises in several European countries. President Reagan declared that the United States had to have something to bargain with, apparently expecting the Soviets to negotiate more intensively at the table. Instead, the Soviet team simply walked out and broke off all negotiations.

In the matter of strategic intercontinental missiles, the President regarded the SALT II treaty as "fatally flawed." Instead, he proposed his own START program, which stalled almost immediately. Reagan pushed vigorously for two new initiatives: first, the MX missile, which he named the "peacekeeper." The MX was an intercontinental missile equipped with ten warheads, each of which carried several hundred times the explosive power of the Hiroshima bomb and each of which could be released in flight at different times and at different targets. It was difficult for the Soviets not to perceive the MX as a first-strike weapon. Second, in early 1983, the President gave an address, quickly dubbed the "Star Wars" speech, in which he advocated laser beam stations in space designed as shields to abort a possible Soviet missile attack. Reagan described this "Strategic Defense Initiative" as purely defensive. His hope was that it would ultimately render nuclear weapons obsolete. Scientists were divided over whether the SDI was technologically feasible. The concept was immediately attacked by the Soviet leadership, which perceived the "shield" as a thinly disguised American plot to hit the USSR first without suffering a retaliatory strike. Yet another Reagan plan to "build down" nuclear arms by trading in two obsolete weapons for each new one was rejected by the Soviet Union as a design to modernize the American arsenal, not to reduce it.

By 1984 there were no negotiations between the two superpowers on virtually anything, including arms control. Konstantin Chernenko, Andropov's successor, apparently remembering the American boycott of the Moscow Olympics in 1980, decided to boycott the American Olympics in Los Angeles in 1984. The atmosphere was as icy and dangerous as it had been in the darkest days of the cold war.

Neither side had reason to be proud of its record in the early 1980s. The American President was a crusader who shunned the pragmatism and more businesslike approach of most of his predecessors. All three Soviet leaders—Brezhnev, Andropov, and Chernenko—responded with a good deal of sanctimonious wooden-headedness. Neither side was able to say the liberating phrase: "You have been wrong, but I too have made mistakes," or to echo the words of President John F. Kennedy of a quarter century before: "Let us begin." At long last, after his landslide electoral victory in November 1984, the President, apparently with an eye on the history books, declared that arms control negotiations with the Soviet Union were now a top priority.

In late 1984, President Reagan and Foreign Minister Andrei Gromyko met and agreed that the stalled arms negotiations should resume. At a preliminary meeting in January 1985, the two negotiating teams decided to divide the talks into three interrelated groups: strategic weapons, intermediate weapons, and weapons in space.

The first substantive meeting took place in Geneva in mid-March 1985, after a fifteen-month pause. That meeting coincided with the death of Konstantin Chernenko and the ascendancy to power in the Soviet Union of fifty-four-year-old Mikhail Gorbachev. The new Soviet leader placed top priority on the arms talks and expressed the hope that Soviet-American relations might return to the more cordial days of détente. Both teams agreed, however, that a significant breakthrough might be a long time away.

Under the administration of President Ronald Reagan, Sino-American perceptions warmed to the point of friendship. The United States redefined China as a "friendly nonaligned country," and the President visited it in 1984. China, in turn, instituted English as the official second language to be taught in all Chinese schools. The reason for this increasing closeness was not only the obvious negative bond forged by the iciness that prevailed in U.S.–Soviet relations, but the equally important positive bond created by China's decision to modernize and to move toward a mixed economy. For this modernization program, China needed America's help.

The China that Ronald Reagan saw was no longer a Maoist country. Teng Hsiao-Ping, the eighty-year-old leader and survivor of the Long March, had dismantled most Maoist institutions. Most important, the new leadership had virtually decollectivized agriculture. While it was still illegal to buy or sell land, peasants now signed long-term contracts with the government. These obligated them to meet certain production quotas. Beyond these quotas, however, peasants disposed of surpluses in any way they saw fit. Many began to amass considerable wealth by working above and beyond the demands of the state quotas. Teng commented approvingly that it was correct "to make some people rich first so as to lead all the people to wealth."[18] The "supply-side" flavor of this economic philosophy may have appealed to Ronald Reagan. In addition, private plots on rural communes were expanded and prices of produce from these plots were determined by supply and demand. As a result of this increase in "free enterprise," agricultural output in China rose dramatically during the 1980s. While, under Mao, probably one hundred million peasants did not have enough food to eat, under his successors, starvation became virtually a thing of the past.

The increase in disposable income sparked a consumer revolution in China. A growing middle class indulged itself in television sets, refrigerators, and washing machines. In towns and cities, individuals could open restaurants and motels. Wealthy families were even permitted to hire cooks and nannies.

One scholar, in a perceptive essay, has compared this Chinese modernization to the Soviet system in the 1920s under Lenin's New Economic Policy.[19] While this may be correct, it must not be forgotten that the NEP period in

Russia was eclipsed by Joseph Stalin. It is most unlikely that a Chinese Stalin will succeed Teng Hsiao-Ping. Far too many of his reforms have become irreversible.

Tens of thousands of Chinese students were studying abroad during the 1980s. In the United States alone, there were more than ten thousand. These are almost certain, over time, to constitute a group committed to keep China's door open to the outside world. Dozens of new universities sprang up all over China. In Shanghai alone, there were over fifty institutions of higher learning.[20] In 1984 the Chinese Ministry of Education purchased $4 million worth of scientific books from the United States in order to help China overcome the "dark age" of the Cultural Revolution. Christian churches and Buddhist temples were reopened. Foreign trade with the United States went up from $1 billion in 1978 to $5 billion in 1984. In that year alone, over a thousand contracts were signed to import advanced Western technology and equipment.[21]

The political system, too, was liberalized. While there were no free elections and no civil liberties in the American sense, political controls were loosened and people were less afraid to voice their opinions. Economic decision making was decentralized, and it became possible for provinces and municipalities to sign contracts with foreign governments without having to get Peking's approval. Tourist trips to Hong Kong were organized and visits to the United States were no longer an impossible dream.

President Reagan's visit to China in April 1984 was very successful. Even though the Chinese deleted some passages about God, capitalism, and freedom from the President's speeches, the encounter between the two leaders was warm and cordial. A number of agreements were signed, including one pertaining to the development of nuclear reactors in China. Even the Taiwan issue no longer appeared as an insurmountable problem. President Reagan left with good feelings about his first trip in a Communist country, albeit one in which Russians were no longer popular and where millions of little children were busily studying English.

What is the explanation for China's amazing about-face under Mao's successors?

One clue may be found in the fact that Mao's widow remained in prison under a commuted death sentence. She continued to symbolize the horrors of the Cultural Revolution that almost tore China apart in the 1960s and 1970s. During those years, probably close to a million people were killed or driven to suicide. Millions of others were sent to labor camps or remote rural areas. Universities were closed, intellectuals were harassed, and science and technology were set back by at least two decades. The Chinese people, embittered and exhausted, began to question the very legitimacy of Communist party rule. Respect for the socialist system was at an all-time low.

Mao's successors realized that only drastic changes could ensure their political survival. They had no desire to return to the repression of the Mao era, and began to regard the "Great Helmsman" with the kind of ambivalence with which the Russians regarded Joseph Stalin. Gradually, the Soviet model became associated in Chinese perceptions with the horrors of the Cultural Revolution. The Americans, on the other hand, did not trigger too many bitter memories. The Korean war, after all, was a generation removed by now. Besides, the Americans, too, mistrusted and despised the Soviet Union's domestic repression and imperialist foreign policy. Hence, Mao's Cultural Revolution served as the catalyst which triggered China's modernization program and the friendship with the United States. The founder of Chinese Communism also became the architect of its ultimate undoing. History is a great teacher of irony.

Thus, two nations that had lived in enmity for a generation were gradually drawn together by perceptions of a common danger and of a common opportunity. Afghanistan was probably the watershed event that moved the United States from a position of dead center between Russia and China clearly to the side of China. And the decision to modernize China, taken by Mao's successors, accelerated this trend. Once again, as in bygone days, Chinese students came to the United States to acquire science and technology. Once again, they wanted to capture the "foreign fire" for themselves. But this time China was determined to use the American "barbarians" against the Russian "barbarians." After all, since 1949 China had managed to throw out all barbarians except the Russians. What could be more logical than using the American "fire" against the only other Western nation that refused to leave territories that China considered to be its own? And what, from the American perspective, could be more logical than using China in its new hard-line policy against the Soviet Union?

This is the melancholy course by which Russia, China, and America have changed positions over the decades. Each has tried to gain the pivotal position in an ever-shifting triangle. None has succeeded permanently. Perhaps in world politics, as in love, triangles are inherently unstable. And when at least two of the players have the power to incinerate the earth, the game is far too deadly. By the mid-1980s, all three countries were ruled by aging men. Will a new generation that must assume power before long play by the old rules? Or is it possible to temper new relationships with a new humanity? The answer to these questions may determine whether our planet has a future.

REFERENCES

1. Barrington Moore, Jr., *Soviet Politics—The Dilemma of Power*. Cambridge, Mass.: Harvard University Press, 1950, p. 392.
2. *Ibid.*
3. John Lukacs, *A History of the Cold War*. New York: Doubleday, 1961, pp. 18–19.
4. Moore, *op. cit.*, p. 392.
5. Merle Fainsod, *How Russia Is Ruled*. Cambridge, Mass.: Harvard University Press, 1953, p. 285.
6. For a perceptive analysis of the Soviet-Yugoslav dispute, see Adam B. Ulam, *Titoism and the Cominform*. Cambridge, Mass.: Harvard University Press, 1952.
7. Robert Strausz-Hupé, et al., *Protracted Conflict*. New York: Harper, 1959, p. 188.
8. *Ibid.*

9. John Foster Dulles, "Thoughts on Soviet Foreign Policy," *Life*, June 3, 1946, p. 124.
10. Allen S. Whiting, *China Crosses the Yalu: The Decision to Enter the Korean War.* New York: Macmillan, 1960, *passim.*
11. Zbigniew K. Brzezinski, "Pattern and Limits of the Sino-Soviet Dispute," *The New Leader*, September 19, 1960, p. 5.
12. Arthur Schlesinger, Jr., "Origins of the Cold War," *Foreign Affairs*, October 1967, p. 52.
13. "The Danger of Détente," *The New Leader*, October 1, 1973.
14. *The New York Times*, November 25, 1974.
15. Quoted in *The New York Times*, December 27, 1980.
16. Strobe Talbott, *The Russians and Reagan.* New York: Vintage Books, 1984, p. 32.
17. Foreign Policy Statement by Yuri Andropov, September 28, 1983.
18. Donald S. Zagoria, "China's Quiet Revolution," *Foreign Affairs*, Spring 1984, p. 883.
19. *Ibid.*, p. 880.
20. *The New York Times*, July 1, 1984.
21. Zagoria, *op. cit.*, p. 889.

BIBLIOGRAPHY

Adomeit, Hannes. *Soviet Risk-Taking and Crisis Behavior.* Winchester, Mass.: Allen & Unwin, 1982.

Andrén, Nils, and Birnbaum, Karl E., eds. *Beyond Détente: Prospects for East-West Cooperation and Security in Europe.* Leiden: Lijthoff, 1976.

Arbatov, Georgi, and Oltmans, Willem. *The Soviet Viewpoint.* New York: Dodd, Mead, 1983.

Armstrong, Hamilton F. *Tito and Goliath.* New York: Macmillan, 1951.

Arnold, Anthony. *Afghanistan: The Soviet Invasion in Perspective.* Stanford, Calif.: Hoover Press, 1981.

Barnet, Richard J. *The Giants: Russia and America.* New York: Simon and Schuster, 1977.

Barnett, A. Doak. *China's Economy in Global Perspective.* Washington: Brookings Institution, 1981.

————. *Communist China and Asia: Challenge to American Foreign Policy.* New York: Harper, 1960.

Bass, Robert H., ed. *The Soviet-Yugoslav Controversy, 1948–1958: A Documentary Record.* London: Prospect Books, 1959.

Bertram, Christoph, ed. *Prospects of Soviet Power in the 1980s.* Hamden, Conn.: Ardron Books, 1980.

Bialer, Seweryn. *Stalin's Successors.* New York: Cambridge University Press, 1980.

Blackner, Donald L., and Tarrow, Sidney. *Communism in Italy and France.* Princeton, N.J.: Princeton University Press, 1976.

Blazynski, George. *Flashpoint Poland.* Elmsford, N.Y.: Pergamon Press, 1980.

Bornstein, Morris, et. al., eds. *East-West Relations and the Future of Eastern Europe.* Winchester, Mass.: Allen & Unwin, 1981.

Bradsher, Henry S. *Afghanistan and the Soviet Union.* Durham, N.C.: Duke University Press, 1983.

Brzezinski, Zbigniew K. *The Soviet Bloc: Unity and Conflict.* Rev. ed. Cambridge, Mass.: Harvard University Press, 1967.

————, and Huntington, Samuel P. *Political Power: U.S.A.–U.S.S.R.* New York: Viking, 1964.

Byrnes, Robert F. *Soviet-American Academic Exchanges 1958–1975.* Bloomington: Indiana University Press, 1976.

Campbell, John C. *Tito's Separate Road.* New York: Harper & Row, 1967.

Chung, Chin O. *Pyongyang Between Peking and Moscow.* University: University of Alabama Press, 1978.

Clubb, O. Edmund. *China and Russia: The "Great Game."* New York: Columbia University Press, 1971.

Davidson, Walter P. *The Berlin Blockade.* Princeton, N.J.: Princeton University Press, 1958.

Davis, Lynn Etheridge. *The Cold War Begins: Soviet-American Conflict Over Eastern Europe.* Princeton, N.J.: Princeton University Press, 1974.

Divine, Robert A. *Eisenhower and the Cold War.* New York: Oxford University Press, 1981.

Dornberg, John. *Brezhnev: The Masks of Power.* New York: Basic Books, 1974.

Feis, Herbert. *Between War and Peace: The Potsdam Conference.* Princeton, N.J.: Princeton University Press, 1960.

————. *The China Tangle.* Princeton, N.J.: Princeton University Press, 1953.

————. *Churchill, Roosevelt, Stalin.* Princeton, N.J.: Princeton University Press, 1957.

————. *From Trust to Terror: The Onset of the Cold War.* New York: Norton, 1970.

Fischer-Galati, Stephen, ed. *Eastern Europe in the 1980's.* Boulder, Colo.: Westview Press, 1981.

Fontaine, André. *History of the Cold War: From the Korean War to the Present.* New York: Pantheon, 1969.

Franck, Thomas M., and Weisband, Edward. *World Politics: Verbal Strategy Among the Superpowers.* New York: Oxford University Press, 1971.

Gaddis, John Lewis. *Russia, the Soviet Union, and the United States: An Interpretive History.* New York: Wiley, 1978.

————. *Strategies of Containment.* New York: Oxford University Press, 1982.

Goldman, Marshall I. *Détente and Dollars: Doing Business with the Soviets.* New York: Basic Books, 1975.

Halle, Louis J. *The Cold War as History.* New York: Harper & Row, 1967.

Herken, Gregg F. *The Winning Weapon: The Atomic Bomb in the Cold War.* New York: Knopf, 1981.

Harriman, W. Averell. *America and Russia in a Changing World: A Half Century of Personal Observation.* Garden City, N.Y.: Doubleday, 1971.

Harvey, Dodd L., and Ciccoritti, Linda C. *U.S.–Soviet Cooperation in Space.* Washington, D.C.: Center for Advanced International Studies, University of Miami, 1974.

Hollander, Paul. *Soviet and American Society: A Comparison.* New York: Oxford University Press, 1973.

Hillenbrand, Martin J., ed. *The Future of Berlin.* Montclair, N.J.: Allanheld, Osmun (for the Atlantic Institute for International Affairs), 1981.

Hough, Jerry F. *Soviet Leadership in Transition.* Washington, D.C.: Brookings Institution, 1980.

————, and Fainsod, Merle. *How the Soviet Union Is Governed.* Cambridge: Harvard University Press, 1979.

Ionescu, Ghita. *Communism in Rumania, 1944–1962.* New York: Oxford University Press, 1964.

Jacobsen, C. G. *Sino-Soviet Relations Since Mao: The Chairman's Legacy.* New York: Praeger, 1981.

Kanet, Roger E., ed. *Soviet Foreign Policy in the 1980's.* New York: Praeger, 1982.

Kaplan, Morton, ed. *The Many Faces of Communism.* New York: Free Press, 1978.

Kennan, George F. *American Diplomacy, 1900–1950.* Chicago: University of Chicago Press, 1953.

————. *Memoirs: 1925–1950.* Boston: Atlantic-Little, Brown, 1967.

————. *Memoirs: 1950–1963.* Boston: Atlantic-Little, Brown, 1972.

————. *Russia and the West under Lenin and Stalin.* Boston: Atlantic-Little, Brown, 1960.

————. *Soviet Foreign Policy, 1917–1941.* Princeton, N.J.: Van Nostrand, 1960.

Kennedy, Paul. *The Rise of the Anglo-German Antagonism.* London and Winchester, Mass.: Allen & Unwin, 1980.

Khrushchev, Nikita S. *Khrushchev Remembers.* Boston: Little, Brown, 1970.

————. *Khrushchev Remembers: The Last Testament.* Boston: Little, Brown, 1974.

Kissinger, Henry A. *The Necessity for Choice.* New York: Harper, 1961.

Leebaert, Derek, ed. *European Security: Prospects for the 1980s.* Lexington, Mass.: Lexington Books, 1979.

Liska, George. *Imperial America.* Baltimore: Johns Hopkins Press, 1967.

————. *Russia and World Order.* Baltimore: Johns Hopkins Press, 1980.

Loewenthal, Richard. *World Communism: The Disintegration of a Secular Faith.* New York: Oxford University Press, 1964.

London, Kurt, ed. *The Soviet Impact on World Politics.* New York: Hawthorn, 1974.

Low, Alfred D. *The Sino-Soviet Dispute.* Madison, N.J.: Fairleigh Dickinson Press, 1978.

Maier, Charles S., ed. *The Origins of the Cold War and Contemporary Europe.* New York: New Viewpoint, 1978.

McGeehan, Robert. *The German Rearmament Question: American Diplomacy and European Defense After World War II.* Urbana: University of Illinois Press, 1971.

McInnes, Neil. *The Communist Parties of Western Europe.* New York: Oxford University Press, 1975.

Middleton, Drew. *The Duel of the Giants: China and Russia in Asia.* New York: Scribner's, 1978.

Mitchell, R. Judson. *Ideology of a Super Power: Contemporary Soviet Doctrine on International Relations.* Stanford: Hoover, 1982.

Moore, Barrington, Jr. *Soviet Politics: The Dilemma of Power.* Cambridge, Mass.: Harvard University Press, 1950.

Morgenthau, Hans J. *A New Foreign Policy for the United States.* New York: Praeger, 1969.

————. *Truth and Power.* New York: Praeger, 1970.

Murphy, Paul. *Brezhnev: Soviet Politician.* Jefferson, N.C.: McFarland, 1981.

Nixon, Richard M. *The Real War.* New York: Warner Books, 1980.

Pipes, Richard. *U.S-Soviet Relations in the Era of Détente.* Boulder, Colo.: Westview Press, 1981.

Podhoretz, Norman. *The Present Danger.* New York: Simon and Schuster, 1980.

Quester, George H. *Nuclear Diplomacy: The First Twenty-Five Years.* New York: Dunellen, 1971.

Rapoport, Anatol. *The Big Two: Soviet-American Perceptions of Foreign Policy.* New York: Pegasus, 1971.

Remington, Robin Alson. *The Warsaw Pact: Case Studies in Communist Conflict Resolution.* Cambridge: Massachusetts Institute of Technology Press, 1971.

Revel, Jean-François. *The Totalitarian Temptation.* New York: Doubleday, 1967.

Ridgway, General Matthew B. *The Korean War.* Garden City, N.Y.: Doubleday, 1967.

Sakharov, Andrei D. *Alarm and Hope.* New York: Knopf, 1978.

Salisbury, Harrison E. *War Between Russia and China.* New York: Norton, 1969.

Schelling, Thomas C. *The Strategy of Conflict.* Cambridge, Mass.: Harvard University Press, 1960.

Schram, Stuart. *Mao Tse-tung.* New York: Simon and Schuster, 1967.

Schwartz, Benjamin I. *Chinese Communism and the Rise of Mao.* Cambridge, Mass.: Harvard University Press, 1951.

Schwartz, Morton. *Soviet Perceptions of the United States.* Berkeley: University of California Press, 1978.

Shanor, Donald R. *The Soviet Triangle: Russia's Relations with China and the West in the 1980s.* New York: St. Martin's Press, 1980.

Solzhenitsyn, Alexandr I. *The Mortal Danger.* New York: Harper, 1980.

Steele, Jonathan. *Soviet Power: The Kremlin's Foreign Policy—Brezhnev to Andropov.* New York: Simon and Schuster, 1983.

Talbott, Strobe. *The Russians and Reagan.* New York: Vintage Books, 1984.

Taubman, William. *Stalin's American Policy: From Entente to Détente to Cold War.* New York: Norton, 1982.

Thompson, Kenneth W. *Interpreters and Critics of the Cold War.* Washington, D.C.: University Press of America, 1978.

Tökés, Rudolf L., ed. *Eurocommunism and Détente.* New York: New York University Press, 1979.

Truman, Harry S. *Memoirs.* Vols. I and II. New York: Doubleday, 1955.

Ulam, Adam B. *The Rivals: America and Russia Since World War II.* New York: Viking, 1971.

———. *Stalin: The Man and His Era.* New York: Viking, 1973.

———. *Titoism and the Cominform.* Cambridge, Mass.: Harvard University Press, 1952.

———. *Dangerous Relations: The Soviet Union in World Politics.* New York: Oxford, 1983.

United Nations. *Report of the Special Committee on the Problem of Hungary.* 1957.

Weintal, Edward, and Bartlett, Charles. *Facing the Brink.* New York: Scribner's, 1967.

Werth, Alexander. *Russia at War 1941–1945.* New York: Dutton, 1964.

Wesson, Robert. *The Aging of Communism.* New York: Praeger, 1980.

Wheeler-Bennet, John W. *Munich: Prologue to Tragedy.* New York: Duell, Sloan, and Pearce, 1948.

Whetten, Lawrence L. *Germany's Ostpolitik: Relations Between the Federal Republic and the Warsaw Pact Countries.* New York: Oxford University Press, 1971.

Whiting, Allen S. *China Crosses the Yalu.* New York: Macmillan, 1960.

Wolfe, Bertram D. *Revolution and Reality: Essays on the Origin and Fate of the Soviet System.* Chapel Hill: University of North Carolina Press, 1981.

Wolfe, Thomas W. *Soviet Power and Europe, 1945–1970.* Baltimore: Johns Hopkins Press, 1970.

Yergin, Daniel. *Shattered Peace: The Origins of the Cold War and the National Security State.* Boston: Houghton Mifflin, 1977.

Young, Kenneth T. *Negotiating with the Chinese Communists: The United States Experience, 1953–1967.* New York: McGraw-Hill, 1968.

Chapter 4

The North-South Struggle

The day of small nations has passed away; the day of empires has come.

JOSEPH CHAMBERLAIN *Birmingham,* 1904

Empires have fallen on evil days and nations have risen to take their place.

RUPERT EMERSON *Cambridge, Massachusetts,* 1960

THIRD WORLD NATIONALISM

During the lifetime of a person born at the midpoint of this century, more new nations were born than in the entire history of the nation-state system put together. Most of these nations have emerged in the Third World—Asia, the Middle East, and Africa. Almost all of them rose from the ashes of dying European empires upon which the sun finally set after centuries of colonial rule. This new Third World nationalism has altered the world map more profoundly than any other phenomenon in this century.

A word of caution is in order before we begin our analysis. The term "Third World," though widely used, is an unfortunate cliché. It implies that there is a "first" and a "second" world, presumably the Western and Communist worlds respectively. The "Third World" concept, therefore, assumes an East-West division of the world and it is precisely this perspective that is *not* shared by most of the new nations. They see a world divided less between Communists and anti-Communists, and more between rich and poor, whites and nonwhites, people starving and people on a diet. They regard the phrase *Third World*—not entirely unjustly—as prejudicial and condescending.

We have tentatively defined nationalism as a people's vision of a common past and a common future. This definition of nationalism provides a general form, but is still lacking in content. We shall now attempt to build a more complete definition of nationalism in our time by analyzing those attributes that the new nations seem to hold in common. After examining the anatomy of the new nationalism in this manner, we shall subject its great adversary—colonialism—to a similar analysis. Only if we are clear about the nature of the two antagonists can we understand the pattern of their interaction.

81

The first striking fact about the new nationalism is its peculiar vision of a common past. Its birth took place in the crucible of the declining Western empires. In the words of Rupert Emerson, "empires have fallen on evil days and nations have risen to take their place."[1] The fight that these new nations waged against Western powers was their great formative experience. As the adult person is conditioned by the conscious and unconscious memories of his childhood and adolescence, the nation-state is also conditioned by its memories—in other words, its history. This explains the fact that the world view of the new nationalism is oriented toward anticolonialism rather than anticommunism.

This common colonial heritage of the new nations has resulted in their extreme ambivalence toward all things Western. Most of the new nationalist leaders harbor great admiration for many of the Western institutions and mores which they absorbed during the days of colonialism, but in their fight for national identity they are psychologically compelled to reject too close an identification with the West. It is not an accident that many of the leaders of independence movements were educated in Western universities as well as Western jails. Gandhi of India, Sukarno of Indonesia, and Nkrumah of Ghana are cases in point.

The psychological dependence on the colonial past sometimes reaches a point of fixation. A good example of this was Indonesia's insistence on annexing West New Guinea. The Indonesians had nothing in common with Guinea either ethnically or culturally. The only link that united them was the fact that both Indonesia and Guinea were parts of the Dutch empire. For this reason alone, it was felt, Guinea must belong to the new state of Indonesia. The hypnotic effect of the colonial past thus continues to play a vital role in the political policies of the new nationalism.

A final aspect of this psychological phenomenon is the paradoxical fact that in the very name of independence the new nationalism often tends to claim as its own many Western institutions that it absorbed during the colonial period. The following report from Nigeria shortly before independence will make this point clear:

> With Nigerian independence approaching, government officials are pleading with Africans to wear clothes. Abakaliki Province officials said it would not be dignified for nature-loving Nigerians to go naked in independence as they did under British colonialism. In other provinces the people have donned clothes. But in Abakaliki not even a fig leaf, much less loin cloth is worn. Provincial secretary J. W. Leach said Abakaliki residents must get clothes in thirty days. Any person found naked or scantily clothed will be prosecuted, the secretary said.[2]

In sum, the colonial heritage has left a deep and lasting impression. Even though sovereign national status is in the process of superseding Western colonialism almost everywhere in our time, the distinctive psychology of the former colonies, especially their emotions of "independicitis," are certain to persist for a long time to come. When one considers the fact that virtually everything that shaped colonial peoples was determined by the white West, this prediction should surprise no one. Their god was an alien god, their language was foisted upon them, and even their territorial boundaries, as in Africa, were drawn arbitrarily by Western hands.

The "colonial hangover," therefore, echoes down from the past into the twentieth century. We can say many critical things about the Soviet Union, but we cannot say that Russians colonized Africa. The Western nations did, and hence Africans often fear Westerners more than they fear the Soviet Union or China. One cannot free oneself from the colonial past easily or without great pain.

Turning to the vision of a common future, a second important attribute of the new nationalism is the determined quest for racial equality. All the major colonial powers practiced the color bar with varying degrees of rigor. It was an inexpensive, rapid, and reliable instrument that enabled the white man to establish his political, economic, and psychological domination. There was a relative permanence in the racial line of demarcation that was absent from other lines of demarcation, such as economic status, occupation, language, or religion. It is probably not an exaggeration to maintain that the color bar, of all the attributes of colonial rule, was the one most fiercely resented. Until the end of World War II, the alleged inherent superiority of the white man was accepted almost as an axiom by the peoples under colonial dependency. This superiority, rationalized by various concepts, such as "the white man's burden" or *la mission civilisatrice*, was frequently impressed upon the African and Asian peoples by force. There is a poignant account in Gandhi's *Autobiography* of an episode in South Africa which left a lasting impression on the young man's life. The scene took place on a train to Pretoria. In Gandhi's words:

A passenger came next and looked me up and down. He saw that I was a "coloured" man. This disturbed him. Out he went and came in again with one or two officials. They all kept quiet, when another official came to me and said, "Come along, you must go to the van compartment."

"But I have a first class ticket," said I.

"That doesn't matter," rejoined the other. "I tell you, you must go to the van compartment."

"I tell you, I was permitted to travel in this compartment at Durban, and I insist on going on in it."

"No, you won't," said the official. "You must leave this compartment, or else I shall have to call a police constable to push you out."

"Yes, you may. I refuse to go out voluntarily." The constable came. He took me by the hand and pushed me out. My luggage was also taken out. I refused to go to the other compartment and the train steamed away.[3]

Once nonwhite peoples began to win battles, the myth of the white man's invincibility began to disintegrate. This writer witnessed the process of disintegration in Asia, at a time when the Japanese war machine swept the continent and forced the English from Burma, the French from Indochina, and the Dutch from the East Indies. Although the Japanese victory was short-lived, the lesson was clear: the white man could be beaten. And when the colonialists returned in 1945, they found to their bitter surprise that they could not go home again, that indeed a relentless demand for equality rang in their ears and would not be silenced. The Japanese invasion had served as a kind of catalyst, which demonstrated that the white man could be challenged successfully. In the case of the former British colonies, sovereignty was won with relatively little bloodshed: India, Pakistan, Burma, and Malaya gained their independence through legal transfers of power. Indonesia, however, emerged from Dutch colonialism only after four years of bloody conflict; and the French colony of Indochina was liquidated only after a decade of terrible jungle warfare culminating in the disastrous battle of Dienbienphu in 1954. This battle was a major landmark in the rise of the new nationalism: it signified the first great military encounter since the Russo-Japanese war of 1904 in which a nonwhite people was victorious over the white man and made its victory stick.

The importance attached to racial equality in the new nationalist countries may also be seen in their reactions to racial problems outside their own boundaries. Preoccupation with this problem frequently distorts their perception of conditions elsewhere. The view held of the United States, for example, was never more favorable than in 1954 when the United States Supreme Court in a unanimous decision declared segregation in public schools unconstitutional. But when this decision subsequently had to be enforced at Little Rock, the United States stood condemned in the eyes of the new nationalist world. Similarly, the passage of comprehensive civil rights legislation in the United States a decade later was widely hailed, but the simultaneous racial crises were seen by many Africans as virtually a civil war. Hence, the understandable though often single-minded quest for racial equality motivating the African and Asian peoples makes it difficult for them to arrive at an objective appraisal of political forces in those parts of the world where different conditions apply. It is clear that in the perspective of the new nationalist powers, racial equality is the most important single principle of their new-found sovereignty.

The quest for equal status with the Western powers is also expressed in the economic goals of the new nationalism. Almost all of the new nations have adopted programs of industrialization, their leadership being convinced that industrialization is an essential precondition for economic development in general. As a rule, this new "industrial revolution" works in favor of centralization in both government and economy. In fact, a case may be made that rapid industrialization leads to the development of elites inimical to the democratic process. Severe splits have arisen in African and Asian societies between those who favor industrialization and those who oppose it in the name of tradition. Indeed, since such circumstances as the overpopulation of urban centers, the breakdown of kinship systems, and the breakdown of traditional handicraft economies tend in many ways to conflict with the official goal of industrialization, there is generally a great deal of such opposition. And not infrequently, the new national leadership does not shrink from resorting to undemocratic means to eradicate those who oppose it. In this struggle, there often emerge one-party machines and various other arrangements of an authoritarian nature. Former Prime Minister Nkrumah of Ghana, for example, simply sent the opposition into exile when it challenged his authority, and

President Sukarno of Indonesia frankly announced the institution of "guided democracy" shortly after he came to power.

It must, of course, be admitted that the end of political colonialism does not always necessarily mean the end of economic dependency upon the former colonial power. In many cases, a new nation's financial and trading patterns are still heavily influenced by the colonial past. Ghana's cocoa crop, for example, is still marketed primarily through London, and the price of cocoa is largely determined by the demand picture in Western countries. These vestiges of colonial dependency, described by the new nationalist leaders as "neo-colonialism," are likely to persist for a considerable time, even though it is the declared policy of most of the new nations to become self-sufficient as rapidly as possible.

A third and somewhat disturbing generalization concerns the political structures that seem to be evolving in the new nationalist countries. The trend is clearly not in the direction of democratic parliamentary regimes. Most of these new nations are leaning toward some kind of authoritarian political organization. One-party governments, weak legislative bodies, and military elites are common to most. This fact simply demonstrates that the fight for national self-determination is not necessarily synonymous with a struggle for democracy. It is a curious fact that the Western conception of the new nationalism has not sufficiently grasped this truth. Instead, many Westerners have continued to expect that, after a period of tutelage in the arts of self-government under one or another of the Western powers, the new nations of Asia and Africa would quickly develop into sound and sophisticated democracies. Yet in view of the fact that most of the new nations have a centuries-long heritage of tribalism, feudalism, or autocracy, the authoritarian trend of the new nationalism is entirely consistent with their historical tradition. One cannot expect that a single generation of political independence can quickly erase centuries of political domination.

A fourth characteristic of the new nationalism is its reluctance to ally itself with either of the two superpowers. Most of the new nations desire to stay aloof from the East-West struggle. That is the reason why Westerners have developed the habit of referring to the new non-Western nations as the Third World. In Asia, India for many years considered itself the leader of this policy of nonalignment before Prime Minister Indira Gandhi in 1971 concluded a twenty-five-year treaty of friendship with the Soviet Union. The Indians' reasoning regarding this early stand was that since their own experience had been such a unique synthesis of Asia's past and the West's present, their country might be better suited than most others to act as a mediator in the East-West struggle. In Africa, Nigeria took the lead in the adoption of such a bridge-building policy before it was convulsed by civil war in the late 1960s.

We must remind ourselves here that the term "uncommitted," when applied to the new nationalism, refers only to the East-West struggle. In the other struggle, that against colonialism, the movement is very much committed. Even in the East-West conflict, the policy of nonalignment is applied, strictly speaking, only in the avoidance of military alliances. In their political sympathies most of the so-called uncommitted nations are much less scrupulously impartial, but tend, in fact, to lean in either one direction or the other. Liberia, for example, inclines toward the West, whereas Guinea, through its late leader, Sekou Touré, was deeply influenced by Marxism. Others of the new nations, such as Indonesia and Burma, have flirted with both sides in the course of their brief histories. Cambodia presents a particularly tragic case. After many years of nonalignment during which Cambodia enjoyed a relatively prosperous economy, the nation was pulled into the vortex of the war in Indochina and was virtually devastated as a result.

In its attempts to gain the allegiance of the new nationalism in the struggle with communism the West has consistently pointed out that Western colonialism is a phenomenon of the past that is today in rapid process of dissolution. The West maintains that a far more threatening and virulent form of colonialism than that of the dying Western empires is that posed by communism. The Soviet invasion of Afghanistan in 1980 is cited as a case in point. Yet, while most of the new nations were deeply disturbed by the events of Afghanistan, they find it difficult to forget the experiences of their own history, which is the history of Western domination. And the fact remains—historical accident though it undoubtedly was—that there were no Russian colonizers in Africa and in the Middle East. The absorption of Eastern Europe and Soviet military interventions in Hungary and Czechoslovakia have been geographically too far removed from most of the African and Asian nations to arouse the indignation and concern that they have in the West.

Fifth, many of the new nations want to go back to their religious roots: Islam. The Arab nations, of course, are Moslem, but so are many Asian and African states. Indonesia and Somalia are only two examples. Christianity was identified in many of these nations with colonial oppression and Islam with freedom and resurgence. When the Ayatollah Khomeini decreed in 1980 that Iran return to Moslem fundamentalism, he did not perceive this as a backward step. After all, Islam in the eighth century had been a flourishing civilization and Moslem warriors had conquered half of Europe. By the 1980s, Islam was the only one of the world's great religions that was growing rapidly. It was estimated that there were 750 million Moslems in the world and that by the year 2000, Islam would match the one billion adherents of the Christian faith.

Finally, most of the Third World nations, with the exception of the oil-rich Arab states, are poor, some desperately so. They see an oil cartel on one side and a food cartel on the other, and they generally have few resources left to purchase either oil or food. Most Third World countries also have far too many mouths to feed. And many now angrily demand their seat at the world's banquet table. Growing access to technology, particularly nuclear technology, has made these demands more strident and more dangerous. The West will have to learn to share its wealth, or else there may be more violence and random terrorism. It is not likely that nations that are starving will watch idly while others are so overfed that they must go on reducing diets. The world, to adapt Abraham Lincoln's telling phrase, cannot endure one-quarter glutted and three-quarters hungry.

The new nationalism, then, may be defined as a movement profoundly conditioned by a Western colonial past, leaning toward authoritarian political organization, and declaring as its goal political, economic, and social equality with the West—that is, sovereignty, racial equality, and a modern industrial economy.

We shall now turn to an analysis of the great antagonists of the new nationalism.

IMPERIALISM AND COLONIALISM

Among the nations of Africa and Asia, imperialism and colonialism are generally viewed as monopolies of the white man. This view has become so widespread that the terms *imperialism* and *colonialism* have assumed a pejorative connotation in the West itself. To call a nation imperialistic has come to be an indictment, and to describe a dependent territory as a colony is likely to be construed as an insult. In effect, the two concepts have in the Western world become the symbols of a kind of collective guilt complex. Yet as a noted historian has pointed out, the West's record in this regard is by no means as unqualifiedly deserving of condemnation as is often alleged or felt to be the case. For,

> Though the brief history of Western imperialism has witnessed many injustices and cruelties, which however were in no way worse than the normal happenings in Asia and Africa before the advent of the white man, it has been on the whole a period of which the West, and especially Britain, has not to be ashamed. It would be wrong to apply twentieth century standards and principles of international law to preceding centuries. By doing that—and it should not be forgotten that these new twentieth century standards were developed by the Western world— the West suffers a bad conscience.[4]

Actually, the terms *imperialism* and *colonialism* simply denote a power relationship of one political entity over another. Imperialism describes the process of establishing that power relationship, and colonialism has to do with the pattern of domination and rule once the relationship has been consolidated. Neither is a monopoly of the white man or an exclusively modern phenomenon. Yellow peoples have dominated each other for centuries; black peoples are known to have exercised power over one another many centuries before the white man set foot on the African continent; and the history of political evolution in the West is the story of white men dominating other white men.

Historical perspective shows that these two terms have not always been in disrepute. The imperialist or colonizer of the nineteenth century was a hero to his contemporaries. Today a very different view is taken of Cecil Rhodes, for example, in both the West and in the new nations, than was taken of him two or three generations ago. The concept of colonialism has undergone a radical transformation in both time and space. The truth is, of course, that as concepts the terms *imperialism* and *colonialism* are neutral. Whether the relationship of domination they refer to is good or bad depends entirely on the values of the beholder. Power always remains power, but the values regarding what constitutes desirable or undesirable power relationships are ever changing.

It is clear that, in our day, the new nationalism sees Western colonialism as its great antagonist and directs most of its energies toward destroying it. This tendency to place colonialism and the new nationalism at opposite poles may be somewhat misleading. Actually, when viewed in historical perspective, the relationship between imperialism and nationalism has not been one essentially of antagonism, but of dialectical interrelation. Frequently, as in the course of the French Revolution, imperialism has grown out of nationalism; and such imperialism, in turn, has spawned new nationalist movements, as witness the rise of nationalism against the Napoleonic Empire. Indeed, the germs of imperialism are already in evidence in the nationalism of some of the new countries. Former Premier Nkrumah's aim to create a Pan-African movement under the leadership of Ghana was a case in point. President Nasser's Pan-Arab ambitions were another. And the war between Iraq and Iran in 1980, too, was fueled by nationalist passions. In the words of one thoughtful observer, "Nations have arisen from the ashes of empire. Must they follow the ruinous course of their cantankerous predecessors?"[5]

Imperialism and colonialism in our time cannot be understood without reference to their historical development. We shall therefore begin by examining the origins of Western imperial expansion and then compare the policies of the Western colonial nations in their respective empires.

Imperialism, like most things human, cannot be explained by a single factor, although the attempt is persistently made. The Soviet explanation of Western colonialism, for example, is based on an exclusively economic interpretation. Third World leaders, too, as a rule, fail to see the complexity of the truth.

Imperialism was, first of all, a function of the struggle for prestige and power among nations. During the nineteenth century the possession of colonies was a major criterion of national power. It is a remarkable fact that only a century ago over half the world's territory was ruled by European nations. Hence, when war broke out between two or more European powers, the hostilities held with them the seeds of world conflagration. The intense competition among Britain, France, and Germany for colonies in the nineteenth century was essentially the expression of a struggle for preponderance of power.

A second source of Western colonial expansion lay in the kind of secularized missionary zeal represented in Rudyard Kipling's concept of "the white man's burden." The stated purpose of this sense of mission was to bring the blessings of an allegedly more advanced civilization to the non-European areas of the world. And, frequently, genuine humanitarianism did indeed play a significant part. Yet nearly always there were important less altruistic motives. At times the Europeans' civilizing zeal largely expressed itself in a claim of self-styled superiority. On other occasions it served as a cover for what was chiefly a desire to export some particular religious cause. And not infrequently, as in the case of Cortes in Mexico, it stood simply for the universal human urge for adventure.

A further ingredient in "the white man's burden" attitude, as well as a factor of the greatest importance in itself as a contributor to the development of Western imperialism and colonialism, was the motive of economic self-interest. In its early form, this was usually referred to as "mercantilism." The primary reason for colonization by Spain, for example, was the mercantilist quest for gold—the quest for the riches of an overseas empire to strengthen the mother country's standing and power at home and among the other nations of Europe. As has already been pointed out, the Communist explanation of the genesis and dynamics of imperialism and colonialism limits itself to the various ramifications of this economic factor.

The principal Communist work on this subject is Lenin's *Imperialism, the Highest Stage of Capitalism*. This treatise, heavily influenced by J. A. Hobson's *Study of Imperialism*, published in 1902, still provides the official Soviet interpretation of Western imperialism and has gained wide currency in the newly emerged countries of Asia and Africa. It therefore deserves careful analysis. Lenin's thesis is based on the Marxist view that the economic struggle in the highly industrialized societies in Europe necessarily leads toward monopoly capitalism. As this state of affairs develops, there occurs a concentration of more and more wealth in the hands of fewer and fewer people, with an ever-growing group of dispossessed swelling the ranks of the proletariat. At the point of "capitalist concentration," the few remaining monopolists have no choice but to turn upon each other. When this stage in the struggle is reached, Lenin maintained, the capitalists discover a reprieve for themselves to stave off the inevitable doom that faces them at the hands of the masses of dispossessed. This reprieve is imperialism. The capitalists, instead of turning upon each other, now proceed to annex colonies overseas, which afford them vast new outlets for the export of capital, thus relieving their highly saturated markets and giving them a new lease on life. But this is a reprieve only, Lenin claimed, not an amnesty; imperialism is merely a last desperate maneuver by the capitalists to avert their inevitable collapse. All that this maneuver can accomplish is postponement of the inevitable. Hence, in Lenin's view, an imperialist policy pursued by a highly industrialized nation was a sure sign that capitalism in that nation had reached its final stage before decomposition.

Lenin's case is not to be dismissed lightly; it is the most important single weapon used by the Soviet Union to gain the adherence of the new Third World countries. In an objective appraisal, it is evident that there is much truth in Lenin's view. It is true, for example, that the quest for colonies was pursued largely by the highly industrialized powers: Britain, France, Belgium, Germany, and, to a lesser extent, the United States. On the other hand, it must be pointed out that the rule of one people over another is not the monopoly of capitalist countries. The United States granted the Philippines their freedom; some industrialized countries like Sweden never actively sought colonies. In our time, in fact, Lenin's thesis could be turned with some validity even against the major noncapitalist power, the Soviet Union.

Lenin's thesis, while a brilliant tour de force, points up the dangers inherent in any one-factor analysis. For the fact is that the causes of imperialism and colonialism must be seen in terms of a subtle interplay among many factors, of which the economic, albeit the most significant, is only one. Nevertheless, the view of Western colonialism most often held in the new nationalist countries still closely resembles the single-factor interpretation first created by Lenin. Moreover, it is applied almost indiscriminately to all the varied forms of the Western colonial experience in Africa and Asia. All Western colonialism is thus lumped together and roundly condemned. And yet, in actual fact, there have been wide divergencies among the different types of Western colonialism. Each of the major Western powers—Britain, France, Holland, Belgium, and Portugal—evolved its own special colonial techniques. If the subject of colonialism is to be done justice, these differing techniques, and the philosophies behind them, deserve careful comparative analysis.

To begin with, the differences between the colonial policies of the two greatest Western empires, those of Britain and France, have been striking indeed. The British, as a general rule, exercised a form of indirect control over their possessions. The government operated through the existing local administrative patterns and usually permitted some degree of local participation. A viceroy usually symbolized the might of the British Empire; but this viceroy, though resplendent in the pageantry of his office, made it a point not to interfere in local customs and mores unless these jeopardized the interest of the empire. This policy of indirect rule stood in sharp contrast to the French concept of direct rule from Paris, which in the early period of colonization permitted no local self-government whatever. Overseas colonies were considered as much a part of France as were Normandy or Brittany. As the British developed their concept of the Commonwealth, which in our time was gradually to supersede the empire, they began to prepare their dependencies for ultimate self-government. As happened most notably in India, for example, the ground was laid for the eventual peaceful transfer of power by absorbing into the colonial administration more and more indigenous talent. The ultimate goal of the French colonial government, on the other hand, was the exact opposite: assimilation to the French way of life, in other words, "Frenchification." While for the British the political advancement of their dependent territories qualified them for secession and independence, similar advancement in the French colonies meant closer integration into the French way of life and greater participation in the French government. In practice, only a small group of the indigenous elite were "Frenchified" under this system. The vast majority continued to live under their own customs, recognized by the French under a separate legal code, and, as a rule, very much underrepresented in the French government. The British tended to emphasize the color bar more strongly than the French; the French might be said to have observed a "culture bar" more than a color bar. Hence, the masses tended to fare better in the British colonies but the educated elite had greater opportunities under the French system.

After the battle of Dienbienphu in 1954, French colonial policy began to emulate the British. The French Community under General de Gaulle's Fifth Republic sought to pattern itself after the British Commonwealth as a voluntary grouping no longer postulating assimilation as a necessary goal but aiming at a more flexible association. In 1958 President de Gaulle in effect offered the possibility of secession to all French dependencies save Algeria, and only one colony—Guinea—elected to sever all its ties with France. Virtually all the others elected to become independent states within the French Community. Six of these—Chad, Gabon, Senegal, the Central African Republic, the Malagasy Republic, and the Congo Republic—have participated in the community, while the nine others have remained fairly inactive. Considering the community's late start, it has been a moderate success.

There was, as noted above, one exception to the new French policy: Algeria. Algeria's legal status was never that of a dependency; it was always considered an integral part of France. Moreover, almost one tenth of the ten million people of Algeria were Frenchmen, known as _colons,_ with large holdings and vested interests in North Africa. For these reasons, Algeria could not be neatly fitted into the emerging pattern of the French Community. The majority of the _colons_ persistently demanded continued integration with France, while the indigenous population fought with equal insistence for independence. The Fourth Republic of France fell as a result of this apparently insoluble dilemma. It continued to be a severe irritant to the Fifth Republic as well, since protracted warfare over the issue steadily drained the resources of the mother country. In a bold and dramatic move, President de Gaulle in 1959 attempted to break the impasse by offering three alternatives to Algeria: integration, eventual complete independence, or voluntary association in the French Community. A year later, in a popular referendum on the Algerian question, a large majority of the population of France and its overseas territories supported the President in his offer. Himself favoring a voluntarily associated Algeria with the French Community, De Gaulle consistently attempted to use his great prestige to bring about a compromise between the demands of the long-embattled French _colons_ and the indigenous Algerian peoples. At first this policy achieved only slow and halting success. Extremism on both sides repeatedly stalled all progress. But in 1962 De Gaulle's solution prevailed and Algeria received its independence. Shortly thereafter, a mass exodus of _colons_ from Algeria fundamentally changed the internal political complexion of that newly independent country.

The Netherlands, Belgium, Portugal, and Spain are known as the lesser colonial powers of the West. On the whole, their record is less enlightened than that of the major powers. For three hundred years the East Indies were one vast sugar plantation yielding enormous revenues for the Dutch government. The indigenous population was compelled to give up its land, volunteer its labor, and generally devote itself to the improvement of the economy on behalf of the Netherlands. Severe famines, a sharp population decline in the colony, and primitive labor conditions characterized the period from 1600 to 1900. Not until the twentieth century were somewhat more enlightened welfare and educational policies adopted and the rudiments of self-government introduced through advisory councils. But even this paternalism came too late. When the Japanese forced the Dutch from the Indies, they were welcomed in many parts as liberators. And even when it became clear that the Japanese form of imperialism was even harsher than that of the Netherlands, the Indies refused to join the Dutch in their struggle to get the colony back. A determined independence movement denounced both the Dutch and the Japanese with a "plague on both houses," and insisted on a sovereign state of Indonesia. This goal was realized in 1949 and motivated a major policy change on the part of the Netherlands in what remained of its colonial empire. The new concept, which evolved and was applied in Dutch island possessions in the Caribbean, was in essence the commonwealth concept: voluntary association with political autonomy in the local affairs of the dependencies. In effect, the Netherlands has emulated the British example.

The Belgian experience again is unique. From 1908 to 1960 the Congo was a major source of revenue. Until 1957 all authority over the Congo was in the hands of the Belgian government, which appointed a resident governor-general who had the power to rule by decree. The distinctive aspect of the Belgian colonial experience was its enlightened economic and social policy. Minimum wage laws, housing and medical provisions, and a relatively high standard of living—among the highest in Africa—combined to give the colonial subjects of Belgium many benefits. Yet in the realm of government, the Belgian authorities were much less liberal. They insisted, in fact, on a policy of complete and uncompromising political paternalism. In 1959 this policy began to be confronted with rapidly spreading demands for independence. The Belgians, reversing their former policy, were quick to grant the formation of elective municipal and territorial councils. But this proved not enough, for with each new concession the Belgians made, Congolese demands increased and widened. The tide of new nationalism could not be stemmed and in mid-1960 Belgium withdrew from its colonial position altogether. Their social and economic advantages notwithstanding, the Congolese—wisely or unwisely—had insisted on complete sovereignty.

One Western colonial empire continued to live on with relatively little disturbance for almost five hundred years—at least until recently. That last stronghold of colonialism was Portugal, the first of the European states to acquire overseas territories and the last one to give them up. Angola, Portuguese Guinea, and Mozambique were considered integral parts of the mother country and were tightly controlled from Lisbon. A small indigenous elite was considered "assimilated," but the vast majority remained illiterate. The Portuguese practiced conscription of labor and, for control purposes, maintained a strict system of internal passports. Their forced-labor prison colonies were notorious throughout Africa.[6] While it lasted, Portuguese Africa was without a doubt the most rigid Western colonial regime of our time. Finally, in early 1974, the lid blew off. A dissident general, Antonio de Spinola, assumed power in Lisbon through a military coup. Spinola had been profoundly critical of his country's colonial policy in Africa and promptly began to explore ways in which Angola, Portuguese Guinea, and Mozambique could be prepared for independence with the least amount of turbulence both in Lisbon and in the colonies. In view of Portugal's five-hundred-year rule over these territories, this was not an easy task. It was obvious, however, by the mid-seventies, that Portugal's long career as a colonial power was near an end, and that it would follow in the footsteps of Britain, France, Belgium, and Holland. In August 1974, Guinea-Bissau, formerly Portuguese Guinea, was admitted as a sovereign state to the United Nations, and one year later, Angola and Mozambique achieved their freedom. Western colonialism in Africa was rapidly passing into the pages of history.

In reviewing the Western colonial record, one is able to make several interesting generalizations. First, most of the Western empires have adopted the commonwealth concept of voluntary association and all have come to terms with the prospect that sooner or later their colonial holdings must be liquidated altogether.

Second, it is significant that at first the new nationalism was most vociferous and insistent in its demands in those dependencies, like the British, that had enjoyed the most liberal colonial regimes. The more the colonial administrators taught the colonial elite about democracy, the more the demand for democracy made itself heard. It is not an accident that the most repressive colonial regime, that of Portugal, was the last to be troubled by political unrest. In part this may be explained by the fact that Portugal, itself an authoritarian regime, managed so ruthlessly to insulate its African population and, hence, to deprive it of outside contacts and standards of comparison. This observation might lead a Machiavellian observer to the paradoxical conclusion that the virtues rather than the vices of the West led to the graveyard of Western colonialism. Yet this would be very shortsighted. For if, as seems the case, the disappearance of colonialism is sooner or later inevitable, there are far greater advantages—at least in the long run—in a policy of meeting the demands of colonial peoples gradually and while a spirit of mutual respect still remains. The Belgians, for example, by seeking to control and hold on to their colonial positions too uncompromisingly, in the end not only lost out completely in the Congo but reaped widespread international ill will as well. The British, in contrast, have been rewarded for their more liberal policies in India by the continuation of valuable political and economic bonds between the two countries as well as by deep admiration on the part of Western and non-Western peoples alike. The world's last colony may well be British: the crown colony of Hong Kong. But even that possession is scheduled to revert to China by 1997.

The third observation that can be noted about Western colonialism is that, though it is in fact in the process of liquidation, it continues to be denounced as the new nations' most mortal threat. Although, as we have seen, there have been very different types of Western colonialism, it tends to be represented and reacted to as one and the same reprehensible phenomenon. Communist expansion, on the other hand, has so far largely escaped this kind of wariness and opposition. Most of the representatives at the Bandung Conference, held in April 1955 by twenty-nine Asian and African nations in Bandung, Indonesia, had the West in mind when the Conference resolved that "colonialism in all its manifestations is an evil which should speedily be brought to an end." The suggestion by the delegate from Ceylon that the Soviet Union was practicing colonialism in Eastern Europe was rejected by Prime Minister

Nehru of India—the major spokesman at the conference—who declared that there was no such thing as Soviet colonialism. There has been some modification of this attitude since the Soviet invasion of Afghanistan, but the primarily Western connotation of colonialism has persisted. The United Nations, too, has been a major arena for the colonial struggle. Relentlessly, the new nationalist powers, steadily growing in numbers and strength, have demanded the "speedy and complete end of Western colonialism" in all organs of the world organization. The United Nations was unwilling to stop India from annexing the Portuguese enclave of Goa and was actually used as the vehicle for effecting the transfer of West New Guinea from Holland to Indonesia. These precedents seem to indicate that the world organization is unlikely to interfere with the liquidation of colonialism even if that liquidation may at times be accompanied by a show of force.

Finally, no discussion of colonialism would be complete without reference to the last "white redoubt" in Africa: the Republic of South Africa. This case merits special consideration.

To the one-fifth of the South African population that is white, South Africa is a "white man's country." In their view, they settled it and developed it and are therefore unwilling to yield their control of it to the black man. Through the policy of apartheid, the whites have kept the African majority apart and subordinate in education, politics, economic opportunity, and social status. Twenty percent of the population has controlled 80 percent of the land and most of the nation's wealth. No black man has ever been allowed to vote in a national election. A succession of *Afrikaner* prime ministers has insisted on absolute separation between the races. Militarily and economically, South Africa has been the most powerful nation on the African continent. Ever since the decolonization process began in earnest, however, growing majorities in the United Nations General Assembly have spurred resolutions branding apartheid as a threat to international peace and security and as a crime against humanity. The South African government has consistently ignored these resolutions as unwarranted intrusions into the domestic affairs of a sovereign state. In 1974 a concerted effort to expel South Africa from the United Nations had to be blocked by a triple veto cast in the Security Council by the United States, Britain, and France.

In 1976, after a Communist-backed faction emerged triumphant in Angola, Henry Kissinger reversed twenty years of American policy in Africa and announced that the United States would support majority rule in white-dominated Africa. Since majority rule in effect meant black rule, the South African reaction was prompt and predictable: Prime Minister John Vorster declared that there would be no easing of bars against blacks, and in 1977 South African police arrested scores of black leaders and banned their organizations and newspapers. The Carter administration continued Kissinger's African initiative. In November 1977 its new ambassador to the United Nations, Andrew Young, supported a mandatory arms embargo against South Africa in the UN Security Council, though he joined Britain and France in vetoing economic sanctions. A racial collision seemed to be in the making. The whites declared that they would fight and, if necessary, "go down first class." A black liberation fighter responded that the blacks, too, would fight: "If we clash," he said, "half of us would die but the other half would be free."[7]

In 1984 the government of Pieter W. Botha took two significant steps toward conciliation. It permitted a small number of "coloureds" and Asians to sit in the newly constituted South African Parliament, and it made peace with Angola and Mozambique on its borders. So far as the blacks of South Africa were concerned, however, there was to be no compromise.

Thus, by the 1980s the defenders of apartheid were preparing for a final epic stand against black nationalism. Like their forebears who survived by drawing their ring of ox wagons, wheels locked, against the fearful onslaught of the blacks, the whites of South Africa now stand almost alone against the world. They must ponder the choice between compromise and Armageddon.

NATIONALISM AND COLONIALISM: PATTERNS OF INTERACTION

Democratic and Authoritarian Nationalism: India and Pakistan

The unique character of modern Indian nationalism has its roots in the tremendous power of the religions that shaped the nature of ancient Indian society. Any analysis of Indian nationalism must therefore begin with an examination of the three great religions of India: Hinduism, Buddhism, and Islam.

Ancient Hinduism was an austere doctrine subscribing to the view that the cause of all evil in the world was human desire. The path toward redemption, therefore, lay in man's capacity to extinguish desire within himself through an act of will, and thus reach a state of Nirvana. Hinduism conceived of life as a never-ending cycle, or karma. Death simply meant passage into another incarnation of life. The form this new incarnation would take depended on performance in the previous one. Hence, it was quite possible for a man to pass into a lower or a higher form of life. The standard of excellence toward which the Hindu was to aspire was the attainment of Nirvana, or renunciation of desire. Since men were by nature unequal, only a few could attain this goal. This concept of the inequality of men was expressed in the social structure of ancient India, the caste system. Society was divided into four rigidly separated castes: The Brahmins, or priests, who had come closest to the Hindu ideal; the warriors who were to defend the society; the merchants; and the laborers. Actually, the social system was even more complex, since each caste had numerous subdivisions. At the bottom of the social pyramid were the outcasts, or pariahs, also known as "untouchables."

The great inroads made by Buddhism in ancient India may be explained largely in terms of the austerity of the Hindu doctrine. While Buddhism, too, was directed toward the afterlife, its view of man was much more optimistic.

Under its influence, the Nirvana concept gradually changed from a doctrine of extinction and renunciation to a goal not unlike the Christian paradise. The figure of the Bodhisattva entered Indian life—the priest who, though entitled to enter Nirvana, has decided to postpone his own entrance in order to show the way to others. Late Buddhism, in fact, steered away more and more from the austerity of the Hindu faith. Sometimes only a few invocations would suffice to gain entrance to Nirvana, and Bodhisattvas frequently became deities who played the role of "social workers," assisting their less fortunate brethren. Despite this radical transformation of Hinduism, it must be remembered that Buddhism was able to grow out of Hinduism because the latter lent itself to the absorption of new forms of faith quite readily.

The third major religion of ancient India—Islam—stands in striking contrast to the other two. It came to India around 1000 A.D. Unlike Buddhism, Islam was never absorbed by the Hindus. The only attribute that Islam shares with its predecessor is its accent on the hereafter; there the similarity ends. While the Hindu worships a pantheon of gods, Islam is strictly monotheistic. When the Moslems first came to India, they destroyed all the Hindu temples and sculptures they found because they considered them idolatrous. The Hindu made no effort to convert others to his faith; Islam, like medieval Christianity, tended to proselytize by the sword. Even the social customs differed sharply. The Hindu was forbidden to eat beef, the Moslem was enjoined from eating pork. Worship in Hindu temples was often accompanied by music, whereas the Moslem in his mosque insisted on strict silence. The two religions were virtually irreconcilable. After sections of India in the northeast and the northwest were conquered by Moslems, the Hindus tended to regard them as another caste to be kept rigidly separate. The religious conflict between Hinduism and Islam still exists and is at the root of the struggle between India and Pakistan. Thus, by the time the West arrived there, India was a society politically divided, a society in which two radically different ways of life competed for the allegiance of the population: Hinduism, which was tolerant of dissension and absorptive; and Islam, which was militant, exclusive, and dogmatic.

British rule in India was established in the early seventeenth century through the instrument of the East India Company. In their campaigns to gain control of the subcontinent, the British followed a strategy of "divide and rule." The many satraps were played against each other until, by the late eighteenth century, most of India was in British hands.

The administration of British India presents a story full of contradictory harmonies and conflicts. The coming of the British added yet another element to the already highly complex Indian society. Christianity was brought to India, and yet the materialism of the Christian colonizers stood in stark contrast to the spiritualism of the Hindu. The individualism of the British differed sharply from the group-centered culture of India. The democratic ideal of equality seemed strange to the caste-conscious Hindu. The British tried very hard, on the whole, to harmonize these many conflicts, and generally succeeded.

In the pattern of indirect rule initiated by the British, a viceroy was put in charge of colonial administration. Local customs were left intact so long as they did not present a direct threat to the British presence or radically offend the British social ethos. Thus, the British did not interfere much with the caste system, although they did insist on the abolition of the Hindu custom of suttee, the immolation of widows on the funeral pyres of their husbands. They also outlawed infanticide and "thuggee," the practice of sacrificing unsuspecting travelers in lonely mountain passes to the goddess Kali.

The British made every effort to teach the Indians about British democracy, thus shaping the thinking that later was to result in the Indians' demand for self-rule. Imported British law and contractual relationships were often superimposed upon the Indian culture. Especially in the later colonial period, indigenous talent was admitted into the civil service. On the other hand, the British often exhibited extreme insensitivity. For example, in 1857 a full-dress rebellion was started by the rumor that pig and cow fat were being used to grease cartridges in rifles to be employed by Hindu and Moslem recruits in the army. The Sepoy Rebellion of 1857 that was touched off by this incident was crushed by the British with extreme cruelty.

The economic side of the Indian colonial experience presents a similarly mixed record. The early profits made by the East India Company were enormous. The British flooded India with manufactured goods and in turn compelled the indigenous population to concentrate on the production of raw materials, thus causing an imbalance in the economy and a decline in Indian industry. On the other hand, the industrial development of India meant the development of modern roads, telegraphs, harbors, mails, and railroads. Some aspects of this industrialization did not conflict with traditional customs, but at times even helped to revive them. For example, a modern network of railroads made religious pilgrimages easier for many Hindus. Another important byproduct of British colonialism was the rise of a whole new class of bankers, traders, educators, and lawyers who were to play a major role in the rise of the new India.

It is impossible to say whether modern India has benefited or suffered more as a result of its experience with British colonialism. To be sure, colonialism had many unfortunate effects. It frequently meant the exploitation of indigenous labor in order to develop the natural resources of the colony. And it resulted in the dislocation of the economy by turning the colony into a raw-material-producing area—a condition of "economic colonialism" that was to last much longer than its political counterpart. On the other hand, the British also did much to prepare India for the modern world: they bestowed upon the country an enlightened health and education program; they provided at least the foundations for a higher standard of living; and they educated an elite of future leaders.

In sum, then, India's experience with Western colonialism was by no means entirely negative. In view of this fact, combined with the tolerant faith of the Hindu religion, it is not surprising that when the nationalist reaction in India came, it followed an essentially nonviolent and democratic path.

The Indian nationalist movement was marked by the overwhelmingly

powerful personality of Mahatma Gandhi. Gandhi was the spiritual father of
the Indian Congress, the nationalist resistance organization under the British,
which, without his unifying influence, would have been destroyed by faction-
alism. Indeed, without the charismatic leadership of Gandhi, Indian nationalism might well have run a very different and far more violent course.

Gandhi's nationalism was rooted in the Hindu doctrine of *ahimsa*, or non-
injury to any living being. This concept was translated into the political doctrine of passive resistance, or "civil disobedience," a technique of nationalist
assertion that the British found very embarrassing. Gandhi, himself of humble
origins, lived most unpretentiously. He used a spinning wheel to produce his
few garments. He denied himself all comforts and often endured long fasts in
order to find support for his causes. When, in 1930, the British imposed a
heavy tax on salt, Gandhi walked 165 miles to the sea to make his own salt. His
example of employing a spinning wheel led to a widespread boycott of foreign
cloth. Rather than cooperate with the British, he exhorted the population to go
to jail. He himself was frequently imprisoned. But always, he emphasized the
nonviolent character of Indian nationalism. His rejection of bloodshed as a de-
plorable aberration was, indeed, the movement's most basic moral and political principle. The steady advance toward independence made by India
between 1900 and 1947 was due in large measure to Gandhi's insistence on
spiritual rather than physical power.

Despite his enormous influence, Gandhi was unable to forge Indian nationalism into a cohesive whole. The Congress was always viewed with suspicion by the Moslems of the colony who feared persecution at the hands of a
Hindu majority once India became independent. Though he tried his utmost
to do so, Gandhi never succeeded in composing the differences between the
two faiths. In the end, in 1948, he was assassinated by a Hindu fanatic who
found the Mahatma's dogged attempts at reconciliation unbearable.

The Moslems early developed their own nationalist organization, the
Moslem League. Its leader, Mohammed Ali Jinnah, insisted on the creation of
a separate state of Pakistan for the Moslem minority. The great chasm between Hinduism and Islam robbed the Indian nationalist movement of much
of its effectiveness. Often the two antagonists feared each other more than
they did the colonial rule of Britain. The depth of the conflict may be seen
from the fact that not even the unparalleled prestige of Gandhi was able to
persuade his Hindu followers to make common cause with Islam. Nor did the
Moslems feel any less strongly. As their view was expressed by Jinnah:

How can you even dream of Hindu-Moslem unity? Everything pulls us apart: We
have no intermarriages. We have not the same calendar. The Moslems believe in
a single God, and the Hindus are idolatrous. Like the Christians, the Moslems
believe in an equalitarian society, whereas the Hindus maintain their iniquitous
system of castes and leave heartlessly fifty million Untouchables to their tragic
fate, at the bottom of the social ladder.[8]

It is quite possible that this intense communal strife would have enabled
the British to maintain control over India for an indefinite period. But World

War II forced the British to make their peace with the prospect of Indian sovereignty. As a condition of India's collaboration in the war, Gandhi demanded a promise of immediate independence. When the British hedged, the Indian leader stated caustically that he was unwilling to accept "a post-dated check on a bank that was obviously failing." Even a British guarantee of speedy independence did not prevent some Indian nationalist leaders, like Subhas Chandra Bose, from throwing in their lot with the Japanese. After the conclusion of the war, it fell to the British Labour government, which itself had always been severely critical of Conservative policy toward India, to honor Britain's pledge. But when, in 1947, Indian nationalism finally triumphed, it left the country a house divided. In spite of Gandhi's repeated fasts and prayer meetings against it, partition seemed the only practicable solution. Hence, India and Pakistan emerged from British colonial rule as two separate sovereign states.

The triumph of nationalism in India was thus severely marred by the tragedy of partition. Three staggering problems were the direct result of this tragedy. The first aftermath of partition was a gigantic population exchange, one of the most massive in history. Over seven million Hindus, fearful of persecution in Pakistan, frantically sought refuge in India, and a similar number of Moslems fled to safety from India to Pakistani soil. The integration of these millions of refugees presented an almost insurmountable problem to both of the new states.

The second problem was economic in nature. Colonial India had been an economic unit for centuries and now suddenly found itself divided into three parts: India, East Pakistan, and West Pakistan. East Pakistan, formerly East Bengal, was separated from West Pakistan by almost one thousand miles of Indian territory. These two Moslem enclaves, dating from the Moslem conquest, had in common their religion but almost nothing else—not even language. Regional jealousies and economic competition immediately rose to the surface between the two Pakistans. Worse, Pakistan and India almost at once began economic warfare. India devalued her rupee, but Pakistan refused to follow suit. Jute, an important raw material grown mostly in Bengal, now became prohibitively expensive in India. In short, the three parts of the Indian subcontinent, which for centuries had been operating as an economic entity, now found themselves in the throes of a destructive economic feud. Overshadowing all the other disputes between the two new nations was the struggle for contested territory, especially the princely state of Kashmir. India demanded Kashmir on the ground that its ruler had been a Hindu, but Pakistan claimed the state on the basis that over three fourths of the population of Kashmir was Moslem.

The political structures of Hindu and Moslem nationalism also diverged sharply after independence. India, under the leadership of Jawaharlal Nehru, Gandhi's successor, immediately embarked on the ambitious and unprecedented experiment of shaping an overwhelmingly illiterate country into an advanced democracy. The Indian national elections of 1951–1952 were indeed an impressive performance. The new Indian government spared no effort to make this election a truly democratic one, and, on the whole, succeeded admirably. The Congress party, now pursuing a policy of gradual socialism patterned after the example of the British Labour party, became the dominant political power, with Nehru as its undisputed leader. In foreign affairs, the new India began at once to pursue its policy of nonalignment in the conflict between East and West and continued its primary emphasis on the struggle against colonialism. Pakistan set out on a very different road. It followed the general pattern of the new nationalism by developing its political structure along authoritarian lines; yet it departed from that pattern in its foreign policy by almost immediately embracing the side of the West in the East-West struggle.

The death of Nehru in 1964, however, marked the end of the postcolonial era in India. In the elections of 1967, the Congress party, now no longer associated by the opposition with the independence movement but rather with a stagnant status quo, suffered severe setbacks. Pakistan, too, changed course. While technically remaining a member of two Western alliances, SEATO and CENTO, the policies of its president, Ayub Khan, tended to remove it from the Western orbit. Relations between the two countries remained bitterly hostile. In 1965 fighting broke out along the Kashmir cease-fire line, ending later that year with another UN cease-fire. In January 1966 Soviet Premier Kosygin, at a meeting in Tashkent, persuaded both Pakistani President Ayub Khan and Indian Prime Minister Lal Bahadur Shastri to withdraw to the pre-1965 cease-fire lines in Kashmir. In 1966, Indira Gandhi, Nehru's daughter, was elected Prime Minister of India in a democratic election, while in 1969, President Ayub Khan turned Pakistan over to General Yahya Khan who placed the country under martial law.

In 1970, conditions on the Indian subcontinent deteriorated dramatically when severe tensions between East and West Pakistan erupted into open conflict. The catalyst was the worst cyclone of the century, which swept through East Pakistan, killing almost half a million people. In the aftermath of the storm, the Bengalis of East Pakistan felt that West Pakistan did not respond adequately to the needs of the victims. This sentiment led to increasingly insistent demands by the Bengalis for regional autonomy, articulated by their leader, Sheik Mujibur Rahman. During 1971, the West Pakistan government resorted to extremely repressive measures to deal with Bengali demands for autonomy. Severe fighting broke out and massive waves of Bengali refugees fled for their lives into the territory of their former enemy, India. By late 1971 the number of refugees approached the ten million mark. This flood of homeless and dispossessed people imposed a severe strain on the Indian economy and pressure mounted on Mrs. Gandhi to move toward a showdown with Pakistan.

In August 1971 India signed a defense treaty with the Soviet Union and shortly thereafter its forces crossed into East Pakistan, now renamed Bangladesh by the Bengalis. India's objective was to sever Bangladesh from West Pakistan, stop the flow of refugees into India, and dismember its old enemy. Indian soldiers were welcomed as liberators by the Bengalis, Pakistan was divided in half, Sheik Mujibur Rahman returned to Dacca in triumph, and

Bangladesh became a political reality. At the United Nations, the Security Council met, but repeated Soviet vetoes prevented a cease-fire until the Indian forces had attained their military objectives. China supported West Pakistan, but with little more than rhetoric. By 1972 the political complexion of the Indian subcontinent had fundamentally changed.

The above analysis suggests that independence is no unmixed blessing. The two nations that emerged from British colonialism never really managed to live in peace with one another. When, moreover, West Pakistan decided to persecute its Moslem brethren in the East, India used this event as a pretext for a war that ended in the dismemberment of Pakistan. The great powers were also drawn into the vortex of this confrontation in the Third World. The Soviet Union backed India and thus increased its influence on the subcontinent. China backed Pakistan, largely as a function of its split with the Soviet Union, and the United States "tilted" toward Pakistan, since President Nixon, on the eve of his visit to China, found it tactically advisable to do so. Neither India nor Pakistan, during its thirty years of independence, made any radical changes in its political structure. India's government, except for two years of an authoritarian rule by Indira Gandhi in the mid-1970s, remained a constitutional democracy while the two Pakistans preferred authoritarian rule. For both countries, nationalism had been a bulldozer that had pushed them into the twentieth century. They now enjoyed the blessings of self-determination, but also inherited all the travails and turbulence of the modern world.

Strife between Hindus and Moslems still erupts periodically. In 1984, for example, major riots took place in several Indian cities. In addition, the Sikhs, followers of a monotheistic blending of Hinduism and Islam that began about 1500, waged a campaign for self-determination against the Indian government. Prime Minister Gandhi ordered the military suppression of the Sikh insurrection. In November 1984 she was assassinated by Sikhs who resented her strong-arm methods. Her death, in turn, triggered new outbursts of violence against the Sikh community in India.

When one surveys the histories of India and Pakistan since the end of British colonial rule, it is difficult to avoid the conclusion that, in terms of human suffering, a high price has been paid for independence.

Nationalism in Africa: From Rhodesia to Zimbabwe

The most dynamic arena of nationalism in our time is the continent of Africa. In the course of a single generation, the mounting discontent and will to independence of the peoples of Africa have resulted in the liquidation of several massive Western empires whose imperial rule had lasted for centuries. The pacemaker of the new African nationalism was the state of Ghana, formerly known as the British Gold Coast, the first African colony to receive its independence in the twentieth century. When Ghana became a sovereign state in 1957, the frenzied shouts of jubilation celebrating its triumph sounded the death knell of the Western empires in all of Africa. Thereafter, the birth of a new African nation became an annual—at times even monthly—event. In

April 1980, the continent's last white-dominated colony, Southern Rhodesia, emerged as Zimbabwe, Africa's fifty-first independent state. The present case study will trace the painful, often violent, transition from Southern Rhodesia to Zimbabwe.

Cecil Rhodes, the founder of Southern Rhodesia, was a classical British empire builder of the nineteenth century. He had gone to Africa as a teenager and was immediately successful with claims in the newly discovered diamond fields in Kimberley. Before the age of thirty, he controlled most of the world's diamond production. Believing that the Anglo-Saxon race was the highest to be evolved in a divine plan and eager to secure its predominance, Rhodes assembled a "Pioneer Column" in 1890 which shattered numerous black tribes and established the British South Africa Company. Under Rhodes' philosophy, which was a mixture of Adam Smith's *laissez faire* and Charles Darwin's survival of the fittest, the conquered territory was quickly transformed into a white man's colony. Its diamond mines were taken over and blacks were regarded as children unfit to govern themselves. In 1897 Rhodes faced and defeated bloody rebellions by the blacks whose lands had been usurped. Still striving to annex yet more land and gain more wealth for himself and the British Empire, Rhodes died in 1902 with the words: "So little done, so much to do!" In 1923 Britain formally annexed the territory and granted internal self-rule to its white settlers. The blacks, who outnumbered the whites by a ratio of thirty to one, were given no voice in the shaping of their destiny.

Southern Rhodesia, with its capital at Salisbury, experienced relatively little unrest until the tide of liberation began to sweep across Africa in the 1960s. In 1961, when Britain approved a new constitution that completely disfranchised the blacks, an angry nationalism began to gather momentum. The following year, the United Nations General Assembly, in an increasingly anticolonial mood, demanded that Southern Rhodesia be placed under UN supervision and that the 1961 constitution be abrogated in favor of universal adult suffrage. Britain, which had granted independence to Ghana in 1957, began to counsel compromise to the whites in Salisbury. In 1965, however, Ian Smith, the leader of the ruling white minority, broke away from Britain in a defiant unilateral declaration of independence. The whites now were not only in revolt against their motherland, but also faced rising black guerrilla warfare and angry condemnations by the United Nations. In 1966, for the first time in UN history, the Security Council, in a vote of 11 to 0, imposed selective economic sanctions against the Smith regime. The following year, Secretary-General U Thant reported that, although ninety-two nations had complied with the resolution, the sanctions were not sufficient to bring down the Salisbury government. The United States, for example, continued to import chromium from Rhodesia. In 1968 the Security Council resolved to extend the sanctions to all imports and exports except for emergency food and medical supplies. Despite this growing hostility from abroad and increasing violence at home, the white minority government continued to stand fast.

In 1976 Secretary of State Henry Kissinger, alarmed by the emergence of a new, pro-Marxist government in Angola and convinced that the tide of black liberation in Africa had become irresistible, placed the prestige of the United States behind majority rule in Southern Rhodesia. He announced that the United States would give no further material or diplomatic support to the Smith regime in its conflict with black Africa. Together with Britain, Kissinger worked out a plan whereby Rhodesia's white minority would be compensated for acquiescing to black majority rule. Confronted with the stark choice of adapting to the inevitable or leaving the country, the whites tried to stall for time. Yet it seemed a losing battle. Black guerrilla attacks intensified in ferocity and scope, and neighboring Mozambique—formerly a white ally—had now become a nationalist staging center. In November 1977 Ian Smith finally bowed to the inevitable and accepted the one-man-one-vote rule as a basis for negotiations. However, pressures for immediate reform continued to rise because of the Soviet Union's increasing support for the black guerrillas. By 1978 the cost of fighting these guerrillas constituted more than half of Rhodesia's national budget. Later that year, Ian Smith, in an effort to achieve an interim solution, made an agreement in Salisbury with three black leaders. In 1979 a moderate black leader, Bishop Abel Muzorewa, became prime minister, retaining Ian Smith in the cabinet as a minister without portfolio. Shortly afterward, however, the heads of the governments of the British Commonwealth met in Lusaka, Zambia, and declared that the compromise settlement was defective. Nothing short of free and universal elections would do. The United States supported the Lusaka agreement and refused to lift the sanctions against Rhodesia. After prolonged negotiations punctuated by increasing guerrilla violence, agreement was finally reached to hold elections in February 1980. As whites and blacks went to the polls that month, the nation held its breath. Out in the bush, a white soldier said grimly: "Now I know what it's like to be waiting for the end of the world."[9] The election results were stunning: a landslide victory for the black guerrilla leader, Robert Mugabe. The whites were horrified and talked bitterly of "gapping it"—their Rugby-derived term for emigrating. The blacks, needless to say, were overjoyed. On April 18, 1980, the Union Jack was lowered for the last time in what had been Rhodesia for ninety years. In its place rose the multistriped banner of newly born Zimbabwe. In neighboring Tanzania, President Julius Nyerere, who had suspected that the election would be rigged in favor of the moderate, Bishop Muzorewa, celebrated Mugabe's victory with a champagne toast. "This is not the first time I have been proven wrong," Nyerere declared with a broad smile, "and it is not the first time that I'm very pleased that I'm wrong."[10]

Mugabe's victory had been the climax of twenty years of struggle. The son of a poor laborer, Mugabe had been educated in Roman Catholic mission schools. After earning degrees from two South African universities, he had embarked on a career as schoolteacher, but ultimately immersed himself in Rhodesian nationalist politics during the 1960s. He was repeatedly arrested for his political activities and spent more than ten years in jail. As a prisoner, he completed three more university degrees by correspondence. Released in 1974, Mugabe went into exile in Mozambique. There, sheltered by Marxist President Samora Machel and armed largely by Communist China, he organized his Zimbabwe African National Liberation Army and launched a full-scale guerrilla war against the Smith regime. In 1976 Mugabe formed a Patriotic Front Alliance with Joshua Nkomo, another guerrilla fighter, whose smaller, Soviet-armed Zimbabwe People's Revolutionary Army was operating out of bases in Zambia. Based on Mugabe's history, therefore, whites and blacks alike expected that this pro-Marxist guerrilla leader would carry his radical principles with him into independence. They were to be mistaken.

In a speech to the new nation shortly after an eternal flame commemorating 27,000 dead guerrillas had been lit, Prime Minister Mugabe vowed his commitment to a policy of peace and reconciliation. "Tomorrow we are born again," he said, "born collectively as a nation of Zimbabweans." Addressing the nation's 200,000 whites, he said: "If yesterday I fought you as my enemy, today you have become a friend and ally with the same national interest."[11]

The task of national conciliation was not an easy one and the scars of war were deep indeed. In December 1980 Edgar Tekere, Minister of Manpower, Planning, and Development in Mugabe's cabinet, was found guilty of murdering a white farm manager. However, the court accepted Tekere's claim that he had acted to suppress terrorism. Tekere was set free.

Ironically, the law that permitted such justice was not the product of the country's new black leadership. It had been enacted in 1975 as a protection for whites, under the leadership of Ian Smith, when the "terrorists" the whites had sought to suppress had included Edgar Tekere and Robert Mugabe. By 1980 the "terrorists" were whites.

The challenge was clear. A black-ruled Zimbabwe would have to be more than a white racist Rhodesia in reverse. If law is not to be blind, it must be color-blind.

Zimbabwe in 1980 was virtually bankrupt and in debt to white-ruled South Africa for $350 million. The war had turned 850,000 people into homeless refugees and another 70,000 remained in Mozambique and Zambia. Two hundred thousand people were dependent on Red Cross food shipments. Britain, the United States, and the United Nations provided disappointingly modest sums for refugee aid. Mugabe nonetheless pursued a policy of nonalignment and refused to depart from his moderate conciliatory course. One senior government official, angered by the small amounts of aid, commented ironically: "If we had turned to Moscow after the election, we would be drowning in dollars and pounds now."[12]

The birth of Mugabe's Zimbabwe increased anxiety in neighboring South Africa, the continent's last bastion of white minority rule. Prime Minister Botha issued a stern warning to Zimbabwe-style liberation fighters: "Anyone planning violence had better not try it. You will rue it." Tensions were particularly high in Namibia, formerly known as Southwest Africa. This large, uranium-rich territory was administered by a South African-backed minority regime in defiance of United Nations demands for black majority rule. There was little doubt, however, that in the long run, Namibia would follow Zimbabwe's example. The only question was whether the ultimate victory of the blacks would be attained through peaceful elections or by a bloody, possibly ruinous, struggle.

The birth of Zimbabwe suggests that nationalist revolutionaries, once in power, may often become moderates. Managing power may be more challenging than seizing it. Mugabe demonstrated considerable talent in both areas. After 1980 he worked hard at the impossible: to satisfy black aspirations, retain white confidence, and keep the peace. And he did well in reconciling opposites. Bernard Miller, the white editor of the monthly *Rhodesian Farmer,* declared: "We were all wrong about him. Everyone's got egg on his face."[13] Independence thus did not separate the people from their leader, nor the leader from the hope for moderate solutions. Sporadic violence, of course, continued. But as Joshua Nkomo, Mugabe's former guerrilla rival and new Home Affairs Minister, put it in late 1980: "What is happening is what takes place after a veld fire. You see small areas where the wood is still smoldering and burning off. That's what we have in Zimbabwe today. The smolderings are burning themselves out." Most Zimbabweans profoundly shared that hope.

The name "Zimbabwe," which now supplants Rhodesia as the name of the nation, derives from stone ruins in the southeastern part of the country believed to date from about the ninth century. Although the origin of the Zimbabwe ruins is in dispute, black nationalists see them as evidence of an advanced civilization in the region long before the domination of Cecil Rhodes and the white colonizers began.

Competitive Nationalism: The Middle East

The Iran-Iraq War. Perhaps the most perplexing problems raised by Third World nationalism occur when it takes different and hostile forms in the same geographic area. This has most notably been the case in the Middle East, which has, in fact, been undergoing a twofold nationalistic struggle: Moslems versus Moslems and Arabs versus Israel.

Ever since the end of World War II, the Arab world has been divided against itself. Despite efforts by leaders with pan-Arabic ambitions, such as President Gamal Abdel Nasser of Egypt, to unite the Arab world in a resurgence of past greatness, these initiatives have foundered on the rocks of nationalism and religious warfare. As a result, alliances in the Arab world have shifted over the years in almost kaleidoscopic fashion. Not even the common hostility against the state of Israel was able to give substance to the ancient dream of Arab unity. Perhaps the best example of this complex rivalry within the world of Islam was the war between Iraq and Iran.

In the fall of 1980 Iraqi infantry punched across five hundred miles of desert front and Iraqi pilots flying Soviet-built Migs bombed military targets and oil facilities. Caught by surprise at first, the Iranians soon responded with attacks of their own, and American-made Phantom F-11 fighter bombers streaked toward Iraqi cities and military installations. A nightmare had become reality. An area that was crucial to the Western world's oil supply was aflame. Moreover, there was the dire possibility that the Strait of Hormuz might be closed by the Iranians. Forty percent of the West's oil passed through this vital shipping lane and, hence, the war quickly assumed global implications. The United States and the Soviet Union had contributed to the problem by heavily arming Iran and Iraq in the 1970s when Washington had close relations with the Shah and Moscow had equal influence in Baghdad.

There were several reasons for the outbreak of this dangerous conflict. In the first place, the war between Iraq and Iran had the earmarks of a religious conflict between two major sects of Islam. The Shi'ite Moslems, under the leadership of the Ayatollah Khomeini of Iran, believed that there were intermediaries between Allah and man. These deputies of God were "ayatollahs," an Arabic term signifying "reflection of Allah." The Sunni Moslems, who were dominant in the Iraqi leadership of President Saddam Hussein, believed that there should be no such intermediaries and that each man had a personal relationship with Allah. To some degree, the conflict was reminiscent of the religious wars in seventeenth-century Europe between Catholics, who believed in a papacy, and Protestants, who did not. It may be significant, in this connection, that when Christianity was torn apart by these internal struggles, it was fifteen hundred years old, which is the age of Islam today. So fierce was the religious nature of the struggle that the Iraqi president, in a national broadcast in November 1980, declared the conflict a *jihad,* a holy war to defend the ideals of the Prophet Mohammed. Khomeini reciprocated by pronouncing the Iraqis enemies of God and Islam. Iraqis and Iranians alike believed that, if they died in battle, they would go directly to paradise. Death in a *jihad* assured the Moslem warrior of immortality.

Nationalism has been at least as strong a force as religious fanaticism. Although more than half of Iraq's population is Shi'ite, the Iranians were unable to incite them against the Sunni leadership of Saddam Hussein. However, Iraq's appeals to fellow Arabs in Iran's embattled Khuzistan province provoked an uprising there against Persian rule. Territorial ambitions further fueled nationalism. The Iraqi war plan apparently hinged on seizing enough territory in an initial strike to use as a bargaining counter to regain sovereignty over the Shatt-al-Arab waterway, which Iraq had agreed to share with Iran in a 1975 agreement with the Shah. Iran, however, rebounded from the Iraqi attack and, fighting with fanatical zeal, turned the war into a prolonged and bloody stalemate.

Personal ambitions also played a role. The Ayatollah Khomeini, the self-appointed prophet of Islam, had spent thirteen years in exile in Iraq, preparing for the uprising that eventually ousted his enemy, the Shah. But in 1978 Iraq's government asked him to leave the country, thereby obliging him to spend the final months of his exile in France. The Ayatollah never forgave nor forgot that insult. Saddam Hussein, on the other hand, eager to replace Anwar Sadat of Egypt as the most powerful leader in the Arab world, was convinced that a "blitzkrieg"-type victory over Iran would vastly enhance his status and prestige. He was eulogized in the Iraqi press as "the awaited, the promised one" to destroy the Persian tyrant. His portrait was prominently displayed all over Iraq, from coffeehouses to supermarket checkout counters. Both leaders thus had exalted perceptions of themselves while entertaining devil images of one another.

Other Arab countries chose sides in the Iraq-Iran conflict. Colonel Muammar el-Qaddafi of Libya declared that it was his Islamic duty to fight on the side of the Moslems in Iran. Syria's President Hafez el-Assad, too, supported the Iranian cause. King Hussein of Jordan, on the other hand, gave his support to Iraq as did Egypt, Saudi Arabia, and the rulers of the smaller emirates in the Persian Gulf. Yassir Arafat, the leader of the Palestine Liberation Organization (PLO), on good terms with both Iraq and Iran, stood only to lose from the conflict. His attempts to mediate were rebuffed, as were the good offices of Olof Palme, Sweden's former prime minister.

By the mid-1980s the Iran-Iraq War escalated to new levels of ferocity. Saddam Hussein of Iraq, having started a war he could not win, resorted to the use of poison gas and chemical warfare. Khomeini responded by using "human-wave" tactics. Ten-year-old Iranian boys would blow themselves up in Iraqi minefields to make way for Iranian tanks. In return they were promised immediate access to paradise by the Ayatollah.

The superpowers and their allies were not left unaffected by this terrible conflict. In its desperation Iraq began to bomb Kharg Island, Iran's major oil terminal, with French-supplied missiles. It also resorted to attacks on oil tankers in the Persian Gulf in order to bring international pressure on Iran to accept a peace settlement. Khomeini, in his single-minded zeal to destroy Saddam Hussein and to create an Islamic theocracy in Iraq, retaliated by engaging in devastating tanker attacks of his own. "If we are not safe," Khomeini declared, "then no one will be."

While oil prices climbed for a few weeks, and Lloyd's of London raised its insurance rates for ships venturing into the Gulf, the war's implications for other nations remained relatively minor. Only Japan, whose dependency on imported oil was the heaviest, showed concern. The United States, having no love for either Iran or Iraq, observed a posture of neutrality. As for the combatants, casualties by the mid-1980s had reached the half-million mark. The Iran-Iraq war had become one of the major wars of the century.

An Israeli academic, Yehezkol Dror, in a book called *Crazy States*, published in 1971, had warned of the danger of military conflicts in the Third World. "Thanks to the advancement of modern technology," Mr. Dror had written, "the capabilities of crazy states and their potential impact are increasing on a very steep curve."[14] Put a bit more objectively, it is true that former colonial nations, armed to the teeth by the two superpowers, have, over the years, acquired imposing military arsenals. Hence, the temptation to resort to force has often been irresistible, especially when power, prestige, and religious fanaticism have been heavily involved. In that sense, Iraq and Iran may be harbingers of a new era of Third World conflicts in which new states may adopt the bad habits of the old.

The Arab-Israeli Struggle.   There is little doubt, of course, that Arab nationalism and Zionism remained the major adversaries on the Middle East scene. The founder of the Zionist movement was Theodor Herzl, a nineteenth-century Austrian journalist, who was convinced that in a world of recurrent anti-

Semitic pogroms only the establishment of a national Jewish home could safeguard the rights of the Jewish people. Herzl and the Zionists based their case
primarily on the ancient Hebraic Biblical claim to the Promised Land from
which the Jews had been driven into the Diaspora. In 1917, when Palestine
was a British Mandate, the British issued an ambiguously worded document,
the Balfour Declaration, in which they stated that the British government
"looked with favor upon the establishment of a national Jewish home in Palestine." The Zionist movement was much encouraged by this half-promise; the
Arabs, on the other hand, feeling that Palestine was Arab territory that the
British did not have the right to promise to anybody, were incensed. However,
the destruction of six million Jews by the Nazis lent new vigor to the Zionist
movement and finally, on May 15, 1948, Theodor Herzl's dream came to be
realized. The new State of Israel was proclaimed a sovereign national entity.

Thereafter, the Arab-Israeli dispute turned into what was in essence a
struggle between two competing forms of nationalism. It had, however, the
elements of a genuine tragedy, since each side's case, though containing points
of merit, did not invalidate the case of the other. For example, the Palestinian
problem, which has been the most important single issue in the struggle, originated in two different interpretations of the same event. When the new state
of Israel was established, over eight hundred thousand Arabs left their homes.
The Arab position in the matter was that these refugees were forced to flee by
the Zionist troops in order to make room for Jewish settlers. The Zionists, on
the other hand, maintained that the refugees fled as a result of exhortation by
their own leaders, who wanted to use them as a political tool in the struggle
against Israel. Approaches to a solution differed radically. The Arabs insisted
on the Palestinians' right to their own state. The Jews, on the other hand, fearing that if such a state were created it would become a dagger pointed at
the heart of Israel, urged that the Palestinians be resettled in adjacent Arab
lands.

Similar intransigence frustrated the resolution of every other Arab-Israeli
dispute. Not surprisingly, therefore, the conflict resulted in four major wars,
countless Arab-Israeli border clashes, raids and counterraids, and spilled over
into the religious sphere in the division of the city of Jerusalem.

In June 1967 open war erupted between Israel and three of her Arab
neighbors—Egypt, Jordan, and Syria. In six days of lightning warfare, Israel
defeated her three antagonists and captured the Sinai peninsula, the Gaza
Strip, the West Bank of the Jordan River, the Old City of Jerusalem, and borderlands in Syrian territory. As a condition of withdrawal Israel now insisted
on direct peace negotiations with the Arab states and an end to belligerency.
The Arab states, on the other hand, insisted that Israel withdraw first before
any meaningful negotiations could take place. The war seemed to be but another battle in a protracted conflict.

Israel's swift and decisive victory in 1967 had left a legacy of shame and
bitterness on the Arab side. Diplomacy had not been able to dislodge the Israelis from the territories they had captured from the Arab countries in June
1967. Israel seemed bent on de facto annexation and the Arabs seemed equally
determined to prevent it.

On Yom Kippur, the Jewish Day of Atonement, in October 1973, Syria and Egypt launched a well-coordinated surprise attack that sent Israel's defenders backward into the desert. By the end of the first week of war, Israel had stemmed the Arab onslaught, but the myth of its invincibility had nevertheless been shattered. During the second week, Israel gradually gained the upper hand and on the seventeenth day of the war, a cease-fire was reached. The fragile superpower détente held and prevented a fateful escalation with dire consequences for mankind.

Chastened by four inconclusive wars, Arabs and Jews alike began to feel that, unless wisdom and reason ultimately prevailed, the only alternative seemed mutual exhaustion. Under American and Soviet pressure, Israelis and Arabs did agree to meet in a peace conference in Geneva in December 1973. This was their first face-to-face diplomatic encounter in a quarter of a century. A compromise agreement over Sinai hammered out by Dr. Kissinger between Israel and Egypt in 1975 was widely interpreted as an important milestone on the long and arduous road toward a Middle Eastern peace.

In November 1977, the world held its breath when, in a spectacular and unprecedented move, Egypt's President Anwar Sadat visited the Jewish state and addressed the Israeli Parliament. While neither he nor Prime Minister Menachem Begin made any substantive concessions during that first dramatic face-to-face encounter in Jerusalem, both leaders made a solemn pledge never again to go to war with one another. While peace, unlike war, does not simply break out, the Sadat mission was widely heralded as a major turning point in the thirty-year-old conflict. At last an Arab statesman had openly recognized the Jewish state. Two old enemies suddenly seemed to have become friends.

The euphoria, however, was short-lived. In early 1978 Begin offered to return Sinai in exchange for a separate peace with Egypt, but refused to relinquish Israeli jurisdiction over the West Bank of the Jordan River. All he was prepared to offer was "home rule" for the Palestinian population. Sadat turned down the offer and was particularly critical of Israel's policy of establishing new Jewish settlements on the West Bank. Relations deteriorated once again, and the Palestine Liberation Organization staged a commando raid near Tel Aviv, which triggered a massive Israeli invasion of southern Lebanon. Begin now intended to "cut off the evil arm of the PLO." The United Nations, under American pressure, quickly established a small peace force to supervise Israeli withdrawal, but the Israelis, fearful that the PLO guerrillas would return to southern Lebanon, complied only very slowly. Thus, by 1978 Lebanon had become yet another Arab "confrontation state" with Israel.

The Sadat peace initiative had one significant effect, however: it changed the American perception of the Middle Eastern conflict. Sadat's prestige had soared and Begin's had declined. While the United States was still willing to stand by Israel, it was no longer prepared to defend Israel's 1967 conquests. And when, in May 1978, the United States Senate endorsed a proposal by President Carter to sell jet aircraft not only to Israel, but *also* to Saudi Arabia and Egypt, the Israeli government was desperately concerned that its "special relationship" with the United States was seriously threatened. It perceived, correctly, that the United States was now pursuing a two-track policy of supporting *both* Israel and moderate Arab governments, such as Egypt, Jordan, and Saudi Arabia. Israel, in the view of its American ally, would have to make a choice between peace and territory. Clearly, Israel would not be able to have both. Sooner or later, some territorial compromises would have to be hammered out. The hope was that these could be achieved without the tragedy of yet another war.

In September 1978 President Carter, in a desperate attempt to rescue the stalled peace talks between Begin and Sadat, invited the two leaders to a "summit" at Camp David. After two weeks of intense and secret deliberations, two important agreements were hammered out. First, Begin and Sadat agreed on a "Framework for Peace between Egypt and Israel," which provided for the phased withdrawal of Israeli forces from Sinai and the signing of a full-fledged peace treaty. Secondly, the two leaders agreed on a broader "Framework for Peace in the Middle East," which was designed to permit the progressive resolution of the Palestinian issue and of the West Bank problem over a five-year period. At that very moment, however, the Shah of Iran was driven into exile by the fundamentalist Islamic forces of the Ayatollah Khomeini. As Iranian oil exports dried up, the United States became increasingly dependent on Saudi Arabia. The Saudis, realizing their advantage, insisted on a linkage between the separate Egyptian-Israeli peace treaty and progress toward the far more difficult issues of the West Bank, the Palestinians, and the status of Jerusalem. Carter, under the pressure of American energy needs, in turn exerted greater pressure on Israel to be more flexible. Then at last, in March 1979, Begin and Sadat, after yet another Carter visit to the Middle East, signed a separate peace treaty. The President's tenacity and faith had finally borne fruit. After thirty years of war, the Middle East had taken a large step toward peace.

Three years after the Israeli-Egyptian peace-treaty, Anwar Sadat was assassinated by Moslem fanatics. Under his successor, Hosni Mubarak, relations with Israel began to cool. In 1982 Israel, responding to shellings of its settlements by Syrians in Lebanon, launched an invasion of that country that brought its forces to the very gates of Beirut. That fateful decision involved Israel in a long war of attrition. In order to prevent Lebanon from falling into Syrian hands, Israel committed itself to the military occupation of much of southern Lebanon. This latest expansion into neighboring territory virtually isolated Israel from the Arab world. Palestinian terrorist attacks in the occupied territories increased in ferocity, and the fifth anniversary of the Egyptian-Israeli peace treaty was observed in 1984 in an icy atmosphere. Israel's only friend in the Middle East—the United States—played an ambiguous role. At first it asked Israel to leave Lebanon, then it requested its help there, and finally it pulled out, leaving Israel to fend for itself in Lebanon. In early 1985, Israel, in complete frustration, began a phased withdrawal of its own troops from Lebanon. Thus, Israel's fifth war was not only its longest, but probably also its most indecisive.

Historical tragedies do not arise from encounters in which right clashes with wrong. They occur when right clashes with right. This is the heart of the conflict between Israel and the Arab states in Palestine. A large number of Jews, responding to Hitler's systematic policy of extermination, attempted to save themselves by creating a state of their own. They established it in a land that had been occupied by Arabs for centuries, at the precise moment when the Arab peoples were emerging from the crucible of Western colonialism and were rediscovering their own national destinies. Thus, Jewish nationalism clashed head on with Arab nationalism in Palestine.

The five wars between Israel and its Arab neighbors have been the result of this collision. The modern Middle East has been the scene of both irreconcilable hopes and aspirations and bitter hatreds and violent passions. The wars were fought with the deepest emotion. Each contestant regarded his rights as self-evident and firmly based upon the will of God, morality, reason, and law. As passions rose, irrationality became commonplace. Desperate deed was heaped upon desperate deed until right and wrong, responsibility and guilt could no longer be distinguished. Each side had done things that the other could neither forgive nor forget.

The struggle between Jewish and Arab nationalism has the dimension of a Thirty Years' War. More than three hundred years ago, in 1648, Catholics and Protestants finally made peace at Westphalia after thirty years of war. They settled for a peace without victory or defeat. In the Middle East today, nationalism and religion are joined in fateful fusion, which has made the struggle even more ferocious. And so, five times in short succession, Israel and the Arab states, each invoking its gods and its secular claims, have met on fields of battle under empty skies from which the gods had departed. It seems most unlikely that either Arabs or Jews can win a decisive victory in the Middle East. The only rational alternative to further protracted and inconclusive conflict seems to be a modern peace of Westphalia in the Holy Land.

If one considers the Arab-Israeli dispute in psychological terms, it becomes clear that, in the eyes of the Arab nationalists, Israel has become the successor to Western imperialism. Like Britain and France, Israel is an advanced Western-type democracy. It is, moreover, the only modern industrial state in the Middle East. Hence it can quite correctly be regarded as the only representative of democratic nationalism in the region. The Arab world's antipathy to the new Jewish state on these grounds was strongly reinforced when, in 1956, Israel joined Britain and France in a punitive military expedition against Egypt and when, in 1967, 1973, and 1983, the United States tended to favor Israel in its confrontation with the Arabs. As a result Israel is not only opposed as a competing form of nationalism; it is also felt to be in league with Western imperialism. This double resentment of Israel goes a long way in explaining why Arab hostility continues to be intense.

An objective assessment of the record shows that Western colonialism in the Middle East is no longer a reality. Each of the great powers, however, has its own views on how the Middle East problem should be resolved, and it is precisely this which has made the impasse so intractable. The United States, until recently, has leaned toward Israel. The Soviet Union has supported the Arab side and signed "friendship treaties" with several Arab states. And China, fearful of Soviet-American détente, has thrown its support to the most radical of the Arabs, the Palestinians. By 1980 Palestinian nationalism had become the single most explosive force in the Middle East. There were over three million Palestinians and over three million Israelis. Neither side would go away. Sooner or later, there would have to be a compromise.

In order to regain a sense of unity and drive, the Arab world needs the continued existence of its adversary, the state of Israel. Indeed, with Western colonialism in the Middle East now a thing of the past, the role assigned to the new Jewish state as a common enemy is undoubtedly the most crucial factor making it possible for Arab nationalism to survive at all. Ironically, therefore, if the avowed aim of the "rejectionist" Arabs—the destruction of Israel—were actually realized, it might also mean the end of a united Arab nationalism.

As diverse as the above four case studies of the interaction between nationalism and colonialism are, they permit several general conclusions. First, it is clear that the patterns of colonial rule have varied widely, that the results for the colonies have been both beneficial and harmful, but that Third World nationalism continues to view the entire Western colonial experience as a monolithic and unmitigated evil. Similarly, while the record indicates that Western colonialism is in a state of irreversible liquidation, Third World nationalism acts as though it remained a living and ever-menacing threat. Second, it is evident that nationalism has been strongest and most successful in those areas where colonial rule was least repressive and most enlightened politically. Third, it appears from our cases that Third World nationalism, in its battle against colonialism, is seldom a cohesive force; indeed, it seems to be able to draw its life-force not only from being an "anti-movement" directed against colonialism, but also from its confrontation with other and competing forms of nationalism. The war between Iraq and Iran is a case in point. Fourth, there would seem to be a very real danger that once the new nationalism reaches its goal, it may spawn a new imperialism of its own. Many of the new nations have begun to subscribe to the principle of *Realpolitik* and have engaged in military adventures reminiscent of the Balkan wars in Europe in an earlier era. Fifth, as colonialism passes into the pages of history, it may well be seen as the vehicle that brought the non-European peoples into the modern world, for better or worse. Herbert Lüthy had made this point well:

> Europe's colonization of the world was neither a chain of crimes nor a chain of beneficence; it was the birth of the modern world itself. Not one of the former colonial peoples remembers it with gratitude, for it was an alien rule, but none wishes to turn back the clock and this perhaps is colonialism's ultimate historical justification.[15]

Finally, the axis of the world's greatest power struggle is slowly shifting from East-West to North-South. While our generation has been obsessed with the conflict between Communism and democracy, our children may well confront another global tug-of-war: that between the rich and poor, the whites and nonwhites, the haves and have-nots of this earth.

REFERENCES

1. Rupert Emerson, *From Empire to Nation.* Cambridge, Mass.: Harvard University Press, 1960, p. 3.
2. *The New York Times,* July 4, 1960.
3. Mohandas K. Gandhi, *An Autobiography.* Boston: Beacon Press, 1971, p. 111.
4. Hans Kohn, *Is the Liberal West in Decline?* London: Pall Mall Press, 1957, pp. 69–70.
5. Emerson, *op. cit.,* p. 419.
6. For further reference, see the perceptive book by James Duffy, *Portuguese Africa.* Cambridge, Mass.: Harvard University Press, 1959.
7. *The New York Times,* November 13, 1977.
8. Quoted in George McT. Kahin, *Major Governments of Asia.* Ithaca, N.Y.: Cornell University Press, 1958, p. 268, fn. 35.
9. "Mugabe Takes Charge," *Time,* March 17, 1980, p. 42.
10. *Ibid.*
11. "Festive Birth of a Nation," *Time,* April 28, 1980, p. 28.
12. *Ibid.,* p. 29.
13. *Ibid.*
14. Cited in *The New York Times,* October 7, 1980.
15. Herbert Lüthy, "The Passing of the European Order," *Encounter,* November 1957, p. 12.

BIBLIOGRAPHY

Ajami, Fouad. *The Arab Predicament.* New York: Cambridge University Press, 1981.

Almond, Gabriel A., and Coleman, James S., eds. *The Politics of the Developing Areas.* Princeton, N.J.: Princeton University Press, 1960.

Amin, Samir. *Neo-Colonialism in West Africa.* New York: Monthly Review Press, 1975.

Amos, John W. II. *Palestinian Resistance: Organization of a Nationalist Movement.* Elmsford, N.Y.: Pergamon Press, 1981.

Arnon-Ohanna, Yuval, and Yodfat, Aryeh Y. *PLO Strategy and Tactics.* New York: St. Martin's, 1981.

Astiz, Carlos Alberto, with McCarthy, Mary F. *Latin American International Politics.* Notre Dame, Ind.: University of Notre Dame Press, 1969.

Ayoob, Mohammed, ed. *The Politics of Islamic Reassertion.* New York: St. Martin's, 1981.

Ayubi, Shaheen, and Tahir-Kheli, Shirin, eds. *The Iran-Iraq War: New Weapons, Old Conflicts.* New York: Praeger, 1983.

Badeau, John S. *The Middle East Remembered.* Washington: Middle East Institute, 1983.

Baker, Raymond William. *Egypt's Uncertain Revolution Under Nasser and Sadat.* Cambridge, Mass.: Harvard University Press, 1978.

Barber, James. *Rhodesia: The Road to Rebellion.* New York: Oxford University Press, 1967.

Beeson, Irene, and Hirst, David. *Sadat.* London and Winchester, Mass.: Faber & Faber, 1982.

Begin, Menachem. *The Revolt.* New York: Nash, 1977.

Benvenisti, Meron. *Jerusalem: The Torn City.* Minneapolis: University of Minnesota Press, 1977.

Bhatia, Krishnan. *Indira: A Biography of Prime Minister Gandhi.* New York: Praeger, 1974.

Black, C. E. *The Dynamics of Modernization.* New York: Harper & Row, 1966.

Blake, Robert. *A History of Rhodesia.* New York: Knopf, 1978.

Bovis, H. Eugene. *The Jerusalem Question, 1917–1968.* Stanford, Calif.: Hoover Institution Press, 1971.

Bozeman, Adda. *Conflict in Africa.* Princeton, N.J.: Princeton University Press, 1976.

Campbell, John C. *The Defense of the Middle East.* New York: Praeger, 1961.

Carmichael, Joel. *The Shaping of the Arabs: A Study in Ethnic Identity.* New York: Macmillan, 1967.

Carter, Gwendolen M., ed. *National Unity and Regionalism in Eight African States.* Ithaca, N.Y.: Cornell University Press, 1966.

————. *Which Way Is South Africa Going?* Bloomington: Indiana University Press, 1980.

————, and O'Meara, Patrick, eds. *Southern Africa: The Continuing Crisis.* Bloomington: Indiana University Press, 1979.

————, and O'Meara, Patrick, eds. *International Politics in Southern Africa.* Bloomington: Indiana University Press, 1982.

Chaliand, Gerard. *Revolution in the Third World.* New York: Viking, 1977.

Chinweizu. *The West and the Rest of Us.* New York: Random House, 1975.

Cleron, Jean Paul. *Saudi Arabia 2000: A Strategy for Growth.* New York: St. Martin's Press, 1978.

Clough, Michael, ed. *Changing Realities in Southern Africa: Implications For American Policy.* Berkeley: University of California Institute of International Studies, 1982.

Cobban, Helena. *The Palestinian Liberation Organization: People, Power and Politics.* New York: Cambridge University Press, 1984.

Coleman, James S. *Nigeria, Background to Nationalism.* Berkeley: University of California Press, 1958.

Collier, David, ed. *The New Authoritarianism in Latin America.* Princeton, N.J.: Princeton University Press, 1980.

Crawley, Edwardo. *Dictators Never Die: A Portrait of Nicaragua and the Somozas.* New York: St. Martin's Press, 1979.

Cremeans, Charles D. *The Arabs and the World.* New York: Praeger, 1963.

Crowder, Michael. *West Africa Under Colonial Rule.* Evanston, Ill.: Northwestern University Press, 1968.

Curtis, Michael, and Gitelson, Susan A., eds. *Israel in the Third World.* New Brunswick, N.J.: Transaction Books, 1976.

Davidson, Basil. *The African Genius.* Boston: Atlantic-Little, Brown, 1970.

————. *Black Star: A View of the Life and Times of Kwame Nkrumah.* New York: Praeger, 1974.

Dayan, Moshe. *Breakthrough.* New York: Knopf, 1981.

Decalo, Samuel. *Coups and Army Rule in Africa: Studies in Military Style.* New Haven, Conn.: Yale University Press, 1976.

De Lusignan, Guy. *French-Speaking Africa Since Independence.* New York: Praeger, 1969.

Douglas-Home, Charles. *The Arabs and Israel: A Background Book.* Chester Springs, Pa.: Dufour Editions, 1969.

Dugard, John. *Human Rights and the South African Legal Order.* Princeton, N.J: Princeton University Press, 1978.

Emerson, Rupert. *From Empire to Nation.* Cambridge, Mass.: Harvard University Press, 1960.

Erikson, Erik H. *Gandhi's Truth: On the Origins of Militant Nonviolence.* New York: Norton, 1969.

Fairbank, John King. *Chinabound: A Fifty-Year Memoir.* New York: Harper & Row, 1982.

Feis, Herbert. *The Birth of Israel: The Tousled Diplomatic Bed.* New York: Norton, 1969.

Feit, Edward. *African Opposition in South Africa: The Failure of Passive Resistance.* Stanford, Calif.: Hoover Institution Press, 1967.

First, Ruth. *Power in Africa.* New York: Pantheon, 1971.

Fitzgerald, C. P. *China and Southeast Asia Since 1945.* New York: Longman, 1974.

Forsyth, Frederick. *The Biafra Story.* Baltimore: Penguin, 1969.

Fox, Anette B. *The Power of Small States: Diplomacy in World War II.* Chicago: University of Chicago Press, 1959.

Fredrickson, George M. *White Supremacy: A Comparative Study in American and South African History.* New York: Oxford University Press, 1981.

Gann, L. H., and Duignan, Peter. *Burden of Empire: An Appraisal of Western Colonialism in Africa South of the Sahara.* New York: Praeger, 1967.

Gerard-Libois, Jules. *Katanga Secession.* Madison: University of Wisconsin Press, 1966.

Gerhart, Gail M. *Black Power in South Africa.* Berkeley: University of California Press, 1978.

Gibney, Frank. *Japan: The Fragile Superpower.* New York: Norton, 1975.

Gifford, Prosser, and Louis, Wm. Roger. *Britain and Germany in Africa: Imperial Rivalry and Colonial Rule.* New Haven, Conn.: Yale University Press, 1971.

Goldberg, Glen; Hauck, David; and Voorhes, Meg. *Two Decades of Debate: The Controversy Over U.S. Companies in South Africa.* Washington: Investor Responsibility Research Center, 1983.

Goldman, Nahum. *The Jewish Paradox.* New York: Grosset & Dunlap, 1978.

Good, Robert C. *U.D.I. The International Politics of the Rhodesian Rebellion.* Princeton, N.J.: Princeton University Press, 1973.

Gordon, David C. *Self-Determination and History in the Third World.* Princeton, N.J.: Princeton University Press, 1971.

Grimal, Henri. *Decolonization: The British, French, Dutch, and Belgian Empires, 1919–1963.* Boulder, Colo.: Westview Press, 1978.

Gurtov, Melvin. *The United States Against the Third World: Antinationalism and Intervention.* New York: Praeger, 1974.

Haber, Eitan. *Menachem Begin: The Legend and the Man.* New York: Delacorte, 1978.

Halberstam, David. *Ho.* New York: Random House, 1971.

Hansen, Roger D. *Beyond the North-South Stalemate.* New York: McGraw-Hill, 1979.

Hatch, John. *Africa Emergent: Africa's Problems Since Independence.* Chicago: Regnery, 1974.

Hermassi, Elbalei. *The Third World Reassessed.* Berkeley: University of California Press, 1980.

Herzog, Chaim. *The Arab-Israeli Wars.* New York: Random House, 1982.

Hobson, John A. *Imperialism.* London: Allen and Unwin, 1938.

Hopkins, Harry. *Egypt, The Crucible: The Unfinished Revolution in the Arab World.* Boston: Houghton Mifflin, 1970.

Howe, Russel Warren. *Black Africa: Africa South of the Sahara from Pre-History to Independence.* New York: Walker, 1967.

Hudson, Michael C. *Arab Politics: The Search for Legitimacy.* New Haven, Conn.: Yale University Press, 1977.

Huntington, Samuel P., and Nelson, Joan M. *No Easy Choice: Political Participation in Developing Countries.* Cambridge, Mass.: Harvard University Press, 1976.

Hussein, Saddam. *Social and Foreign Affairs in Iraq.* London: Croom Helm, 1979.

Isaacman, Allen, and Barbara. *Mozambique: From Colonialism to Revolution.* Boulder, Colo.: Westview Press, 1983.

Issawi, Charles. *The Arab World's Legacy.* Princeton, N.J.: Darwin Press, 1981.

Jansen, G. H. *Militant Islam.* New York: Harper, 1980.

Jessup, Philip C. *The Birth of Nations.* New York: Columbia University Press, 1974.

Jones, Charles A. *The North-South Dialogue: A Brief History.* New York: St. Martin's Press, 1983.

Jordan, Robert S. *Government and Power in West Africa.* New York: Africana, 1970.

Kautsky, John H. *Political Change in Underdeveloped Countries: Nationalism and Communism.* New York: Wiley, 1963.

Kilson, Martin, ed. *New States in the Modern World.* Cambridge, Mass.: Harvard University Press, 1975.

Kurian, George Thomas, ed. *Encyclopedia of the Third World.* New York: Facts on File, 1978.

Kürnan, Thomas. *Arafat: The Man and the Myth.* New York: Norton, 1976.

La Feber, Walter. *The Panama Canal: The Crisis in Historical Perspective.* New York: Oxford University Press, 1978.

Lacouture, Jean. *The Demigods: Charismatic Leadership in the Third World.* New York: Knopf, 1970.

————. *Nasser.* Paris: Editions du Seuil, 1971.

Lall, Arthur. *The Emergence of Modern India.* New York: Columbia University Press, 1981.

Lamb, Alastair. *The Kashmir Problem.* New York: Praeger, 1967.

Lamb, David. *The Africans.* New York: Random House, 1982.

Lambley, Peter. *The Psychology of Apartheid.* Athens: University of Georgia Press, 1981.

Leonard, Richard. *South Africa at War.* Westport, Conn.: Lawrence Hill, 1983.

Lichtheim, George. *Imperialism.* New York: Praeger, 1971.

Llerena, Mario. *The Unsuspected Revolution: The Birth and Rise of Castroism.* Ithaca, N.Y.: Cornell University Press, 1978.

Magdoff, Harry. *Imperialism: From the Colonial Age to the Present.* New York: Monthly Review Press, 1978.

Marquard, Leo. *A Short History of South Africa.* New York: Praeger, 1968.

Masani, Zareer. *Indira Gandhi: A Biography.* London: Hamish Hamilton, 1975.

Mates, Leo. *Nonalignment: Theory and Current Policy.* New York: Oceana, 1972.

Matthews, Herbert L. *Fidel Castro.* New York: Simon and Schuster, 1969.

May, Brian. *The Third World Calamity.* Boston: Routledge & Kegan Paul, 1981.

Mazrui, Ali A. *Cultural Engineering and Nation-Building in East Africa.* Evanston, Ill.: Northwestern University Press, 1972.

Mboya, Tom. *The Challenge of Nationhood.* New York: Praeger, 1970.

McAlister, John T. *Vietnam: The Origins of Revolution.* New York: Knopf, 1969.

Mehta, Ved. *A Family Affair: India Under Three Prime Ministers.* New York: Oxford University Press, 1982.

Migdal, Joel, et al. *Palestinian Society and Politics.* Princeton, N.J.: Princeton University Press, 1980.

Miller, J. D. B. *The Politics of the Third World.* London: Oxford University Press, 1967.

Minter, William. *Portuguese Africa and the West.* New York: Monthly Review Press, 1974.

Mommsen, Wolfgang J. *Theories of Imperialism.* New York: Random House, 1981.

Moore, Clement Henry. *Politics in North Africa: Algeria, Morocco and Tunisia.* Boston: Little, Brown, 1970.

Moraes, Dom. *Indira Gandhi.* Boston: Little, Brown, 1980.

Mortimer, Edward. *France and the Africans 1944–1960: A Political History.* New York: Walker, 1969.

Nevakiki, Jukka. *Britain, France and the Arab Middle East, 1914–1920.* New York: Oxford University Press, 1969.

Niven, Sir Rey. *Nigeria.* New York: Praeger, 1967.

Nye, Joseph S., Jr. *Pan-Africanism and East African Integration.* Cambridge, Mass.: Harvard University Press, 1965.

Osia, Kunirum. *Israel, South Africa and Black Africa.* Washington: University Press of America, 1982.

Ottaway, Marina, and David. *Afrocommunism.* New York: Africana, 1981.

———. *Soviet and American Influence in the Horn of Africa.* New York: Praeger, 1982.

Pahlevi, Mohammad Reza, the Shah of Iran. *Answer to History.* Briarcliff Manor, N.Y.: Stein and Day, 1980.

Penrose, Edith and E. F. *Iraq: International Relations and National Development.* Boulder, Colo.: Westview Press, 1978.

Polk, William R. *The Elusive Peace: The Middle East in the Twentieth Century.* New York: St. Martin's Press, 1980.

———. *The Arab World.* Cambridge: Harvard University Press, 1980.

Reischauer, Edwin O. *The Japanese.* Cambridge, Mass.: Harvard University Press, 1977.

Roberts, Samuel J. *Survival or Hegemony? The Foundations of Israeli Foreign Policy.* Baltimore: Johns Hopkins Press, 1973.

Rotberg, Robert I. *Suffer the Future: Policy Changes in Southern Africa.* Cambridge, Mass.: Harvard University Press, 1980.

———, and Mazrui, Ali A. *Protest and Power in Black Africa.* New York: Oxford University Press, 1970.

Rothenberg, Morris. *The U.S.S.R. and Africa: New Dimensions of Soviet Global Power.* Washington, D.C.: Advanced International Studies Institute, 1980.

Rubin, Barry. *Paved With Good Intentions: The American Experience in Iran.* New York: Oxford University Press, 1980.

Ruiz, Ramon Eduardo. *Cuba: The Making of a Revolution.* Amherst: University of Massachusetts Press, 1968.

Sachar, Howard M. *A History of Israel: From the Rise of Zionism to Our Time.* New York: Knopf, 1976.

Sadat, Anwar El. *In Search of Identity: An Autobiography.* New York: Harper, 1978.

Said, Edward W. *The Question of Palestine.* New York: Times Books, 1979.

Shafer, Boyd C. *Faces of Nationalism: New Realities and Old Myths.* New York: Harcourt Brace Jovanovich, 1972.

Sigmund, Paul E. *The Overthrow of Allende and the Politics of Chile, 1964–1976.* Pittsburgh: University of Pittsburgh Press, 1977.

Silvert, Kalman, ed. *The Americas in a Changing World.* New York: Quadrangle Press, 1975.

Snetsinger, John. *Truman, the Jewish Vote, and the Creation of Israel.* Stanford, Calif.: Hoover Institution Press, 1974.

Stevens, Richard P. *Lesotho, Botswana and Swaziland: The Former High Commission Territories in South Africa.* New York: Praeger, 1967.

Stone, Julius. *Israel and Palestine: Assault on the Law of Nations.* Baltimore: Johns Hopkins Press, 1981.

Suchlicki, Jaime. *Cuba: From Columbus to Castro.* New York: Scribner's, 1974.

Thompson, Scott W. *Ghana's Foreign Policy 1957–1966. Diplomacy, Ideology, and the New State.* Princeton, N.J.: Princeton University Press, 1969.

Thompson, Virginia. *West Africa's Council of the Entente.* Ithaca, N.Y.: Cornell University Press, 1972.

Thornton, A. P. *Imperialism in the Twentieth Century.* Minneapolis: University of Minnesota Press, 1978.

Tötemeyer, Gerhard. *Namibia Old and New.* New York: St. Martin's Press, 1979.

Treger, Peter, and Burley, John. *African Development and Europe.* New York: Pergamon, 1970.

Trevelyan, H. *The Middle East in Revolution.* Boston: Gambit, 1970.

Vogel, Ezra F. *Japan As Number One.* Cambridge, Mass.: Harvard University Press, 1979.

Wallerstein, Immanuel. *Africa: The Politics of Independence.* New York: Vintage, 1961.
———. *Africa: The Politics of Unity.* New York: Random House, 1967.
Ward, Richard; Peretz, Don; and Wilson, Evan M. *The Palestine State: A Rational Approach.* Port Washington, N.Y.: Kennikat Press, 1977.
Wheeler, Richard S. *The Politics of Pakistan: A Constitutional Quest.* Ithaca, N.Y.: Cornell University Press, 1970.
Willetts, Peter. *The Non-Aligned Movement.* New York: Nichols, 1978.
Xydis, Stephen G. *Cyprus: Conflict and Conciliation.* Columbus: Ohio State University Press, 1967.
———. *Cyprus: Reluctant Republic.* The Hague: Morton, 1973.

Chapter 5

The Two Political Power Struggles of Our Time

When sorrows come, they come not single spies, but in battalions.

SHAKESPEARE *Hamlet*, IV, 5

THE LINKAGE BETWEEN THE TWO STRUGGLES

The most significant characteristic of the international struggle for power in our time lies in the fact that its two principal conflicts—the struggle between East and West and that between North and South—are very closely and inseparably intertwined. At least potentially, every nation is today to a greater or lesser degree involved in both these struggles.

This linkage between the two struggles has steadily increased as each of them has intensified. In an earlier phase, the nations' energies tended to be directed to only one of the two conflicts, with their involvement in the other remaining obscured or unemphasized. Immediately after World War II, for example, the United States was inclined to perceive world affairs largely in terms of a division between East and West, between the democracies and the Communist powers. The Soviet Union, tending to share this chiefly East-West orientation, also paid comparatively little attention to the developing areas of the world. India, on the other hand, was above all concerned with the conflict between nationalism and colonialism, regarding the East-West struggle as of distinctly secondary importance.

The most dramatic expression of this limited perception of world affairs by the major nations involved came to center around the term "neutralism." The United States, for its part, frequently became impatient with the "neutralism" shown by the new nations toward the issues of the East-West struggle. It viewed their reluctance to join the American-led system of alliances as less than responsible and saw their inclination to abstain in voting on East-West issues in the United Nations as, at best, blindness to what was really at stake in

119

international relations. The new nationalist countries, on the other hand, felt strongly critical of the United States' attitude of seeming detachment—politically as well as in the United Nations—in regard to the issues of the colonial struggle. India, for example, failed to understand the "neutralism" of the United States in the disputes between France and Algeria, the Netherlands and Indonesia, or Portugal and India over the disposition of Goa. It could not understand how the United States, itself once a revolutionary power, could fail to sympathize with the new nationalism against the colonial threat. From India's point of view, the colonial struggle was paramount. The United States wanted to enlist the support of India and India wanted to enlist the support of the United States. But their causes, and therefore their perceptions of the struggle, differed sharply. Each was quick to accuse the other of indifference in the battle that really mattered. In other words, the perception of each remained limited to one of the two great power struggles.

As Third World nationalism continued to gain ground during the 1950s and 1960s, both East and West became increasingly aware that the objectives of the new nations could no longer be ignored. Recognizing the need for allies in the prosecution of the East-West conflict, the United States and the Soviet Union alike found it in their self-interest to pay greater and greater heed to the colonial struggle. And as each searched for friends and prospective allies among the new nations, the involvement of each in the colonial struggle became more extensive. At the same time, the new nationalist powers took increasing cognizance of the East-West struggle and began wherever possible to exploit it to gain advantages in their fight against colonialism. Thus the international power struggle came more and more to resemble a game of three-dimensional chess.

In a dramatic reversal of its traditional foreign policy, the United States surrounded itself with a ring of defensive alliances against Communist expansion. It was instrumental in the forging of NATO, OAS, SEATO, and ANZUS—all of them regional military alliances. In addition, it concluded bilateral defense agreements with Japan, South Korea, Formosa, and the Philippines. Altogether, the United States became allied with forty-two nations. Moreover, though not technically a member, it pledged its support to the Central Treaty Organization (CENTO), linking Britain, Turkey, Iran, and Pakistan in the common defense of the Middle East. (For an analysis of these military alliance systems, see Chapter 6.)

In its quest for allies, the United States thus made it its policy to woo both nationalist and colonial powers. On the one hand, through NATO, it found itself allied with all the great Western colonial powers—Britain, France, Belgium, the Netherlands, and Portugal. On the other, it simultaneously courted the newly emerged nations that were in, or had recently been engaged in, all-out conflict with the colonial powers. As a result, prospective allies against communism frequently tended to be incompatible and to be more fearful of each other than of the alleged common enemy, the Soviet Union. This was the situation when the United States attempted to persuade India, Indonesia, and Burma to join SEATO. These nations rebuffed the United States' overtures, in large part because they suspected the United States of sympathizing with the colonial powers in view of its alliance with them in NATO. Only in the mid-1970s was this policy of equivocation finally modified when the United States, for strategic reasons, gave its support to the cause of black majority rule in Southern Africa.

Most of the new nations pursued a policy of remaining uncommitted in the East-West struggle. They have felt that such a "nonaligned" course mitigated East-West tensions and, most importantly, netted them the greatest advantages in gaining their own objectives. The United States, attempting to attract both colonial and anticolonial powers into its anti-communist defense system, found it in its interest to pursue an equally nonaligned policy toward the colonial struggle. For if it supported the new nationalism too strongly, it would jeopardize its alliance with its partners in NATO, and if it identified itself too closely with the colonial powers, it would incur the certain hostility of the new nationalism. Since either eventuality would accrue to the benefit of the Soviet Union, the United States confronted most of the major colonial disputes with a Hamlet-like posture, refusing to commit itself or indicate its unqualified support for either side. It pursued a similarly detached strategy—for similar reasons—in the struggles that occurred among various of the new nations themselves. On the one hand, to assure the flow of essential oil to its NATO allies, it supported such old monarchical forms of nationalism as that of Saudi Arabia. On the other, wanting above all to prevent its absorption into the Communist orbit, it also maintained a measure of commitment to the more modern nationalism of Egypt. At the same time, Arab hostility notwithstanding, it recognized and supported the new Jewish state of Israel. In each case, the United States did its utmost to prevent the anticolonial nations from feeling it necessary to align themselves with the Soviet Union, and to secure the pacification of whatever disputes existed among them. The logic of the policy of pacification was that only when differences among the new nations were reconciled could they be persuaded to turn their attention to the East-West struggle.

The United States' desire to keep itself as attractive as possible to as diverse a group of nations as possible has not been the only obstacle standing in the way of a more consistent and forceful anticolonial posture. A further complicating factor has been America's own historical tradition in the matter of colonialism. For the fact is that the United States finds itself in the unique position of having been both an anticolonial and a colonial power. In its successful battle for independence from Britain in 1776, the United States waged the first major anticolonial struggle in modern history. This American example, along with the Declaration of Independence in which it was proclaimed, has inspired and guided nationalist leaders throughout the world and has made it difficult for them to understand American nonalignment on the question of colonialism in our time. Yet it is no less a fact that in the late nineteenth century the United States became involved in an experience of its own as a colonial power, albeit reluctantly and with an exceedingly bad conscience. For in the wake of the Spanish-American War, the Philippines were annexed and

Puerto Rico, Guam, Hawaii, and the Samoan islands became American territories. Nevertheless, official American terminology never referred to these possessions as "colonies" nor to the United States itself as an "empire." Indeed,
the effect of this bad conscience was an attempt to humanize the United
States' venture into colonialism and to establish as its eventual goal the giving
of self-government and independence to the areas concerned. Just how ambivalent American feelings were upon becoming a colonial power may be gathered from President McKinley's report of his reflections on his decision in 1898
to keep the Philippines:

> The truth is I didn't want the Philippines and when they came to us as a gift from
> the gods, I did not know what to do about them. . . . I sought counsel from all
> sides—Democrats as well as Republicans—but got little help. I thought first we
> would take only Manila; then Luzon; then other islands, perhaps, also. I walked
> the floor of the White House night after night until midnight; I am not ashamed
> to tell you, gentlemen, that I went down on my knees and prayed to Almighty
> God for light and guidance more than one night.
>
> And one night late it came to me this way, I don't know how it was, but it
> came: (1) that we could not give them back to Spain—that would be cowardly
> and dishonorable; (2) that we would not turn them over to France or Ger-
> many—our commercial rivals in the Orient—that would be bad business and dis-
> creditable; (3) that we could not leave them to themselves—they were unfit for
> self-government—and they would soon have anarchy and misrule over there
> worse than Spain's was; and (4) that there was nothing left for us to do but to take
> them all, and to educate the Filipinos, and uplift and civilize and Christianize
> them and by God's grace do the very best we could by them, as our fellow-men
> for whom Christ also died. And then I went to bed, and went to sleep and slept
> soundly. . . .[1]

By the end of the first half of the twentieth century, the United States had
almost ended its entire colonial experiment. Franklin Delano Roosevelt's
"Good Neighbor Policy" had replaced American intervention in Latin
America; Puerto Rico had been prepared for limited self-government; and
Hawaii and Alaska were ready to be absorbed as states into the Union. The
Philippines received their political independence in 1946, although a high
degree of economic dependence on the United States continued. The distinc-
tive aspect of the American colonial experience was the fact that, unlike the
British, French, or Dutch colonies, most American possessions, save for the
Philippines, came to see as their ultimate goal not independence from the
United States but full-fledged and permanent membership in the American
union.

In contrast to the dilemmas faced in regard to the "colonial-anticolonial"
struggle by the United States, the Soviet Union has had a comparatively easy
time of it and has benefited accordingly. Communism has not had to contend
with a choice between nationalism and colonialism. It has clearly and almost
without exception been in the Soviet Union's interest to give unqualified support to the new nationalism in its conflict with the Western colonial powers.
This policy has served the twofold purpose of winning the new nations' good

will for the Soviet Union and, at the same time, of weakening NATO by hastening the dissolution of the Western empires.

Nor were the Third World powers any less advantage-minded in their conduct vis-à-vis the East-West struggle. They showed themselves prepared to use whatever opportunities came their way to utilize this struggle to enhance their own positions, both in the competition among themselves and in their conflicts with Western colonialism. In July 1960, for example, Premier Patrice Lumumba of the new Republic of the Congo threatened to request the intervention of Soviet troops in order to expel the Belgians. The Soviet Union immediately responded by denouncing "Belgian imperialism," hoping thereby to widen the gulf between Belgium and the Congolese. This in turn compelled the United States to respond, though in line with its own national interest it brought its power to bear for a conciliation of the dispute. In any case, here as in numerous similar situations, the superpowers became involved in the colonial struggle less of their own initiative than as a result of the conscious designs of the new nations themselves. Indeed, the existence of the East-West struggle was in many instances a great boon to the newly sovereign states. Ready to be wooed by either side, and sometimes by both simultaneously, they often acquired much greater international bargaining power than would have been possible on the basis of their own national capabilities alone. The position of the Arab states in the wars with Israel in 1967 and 1973, for example, demonstrated this truth.

While it may appear from the above discussion that the Soviet Union is in an incomparably better position to gain the allegiance of the Third World powers than is the United States, this is not entirely true. For though the Soviet Union has consistently supported Third World nationalism, the record indicates that communism—once in power—is itself inclined to look with hostility upon the politics of national self-determination. It attempted to destroy Yugoslav nationalism; it crushed the Hungarian revolt for national independence; it was unwilling to tolerate political liberalization in Czechoslovakia; it smashed into Afghanistan; and it threatened Poland with invasion. Though, as we have seen earlier, the new nationalism is still hypnotized by the specter of Western colonialism, the lessons of Soviet intervention have not failed to make a deepening impression.

In order to illustrate the complex linkage patterns of the East-West and North-South struggles, we shall once again employ the case study approach. Probably the best example of this linkage in Asia may be seen in the rise of nationalism and communism in China, the subject of our first case study. Second, we have selected the three Middle Eastern crises of 1956, 1967, and 1973. Our third case will deal with the Iranian-American crisis of 1980, and our final one with Lebanon. These four studies show clearly how extensively and inextricably the two great power struggles of our time interpenetrate—to the point, indeed, of being essentially merely two different aspects of a single global political drama.

THE LINKAGE PATTERN

The Case of China

Napoleon was once reported to have said, "Let China sleep; when she awakens, the world will be sorry." These were prophetic words. During the last century the impact of the colonial West first awakened China from its traditional past. That awakening has resulted in the modern Communist regime of Peking today. The events in this development excellently illustrate how closely the two great political conflicts of our time are connected.

It is a significant fact, frequently not realized in the West, that ours is the first century in over four thousand years in which China does not consider itself to be at the center of the universe. The Chinese Empire was also known as the Middle Kingdom. For over four millennia it conceived of itself as the hub of civilization, the great school of the world—much as Athens had once considered itself to be the school of the ancient Mediterranean world. Although dynasties came and went, the political structure of the empire remained essentially static. The emperor, aided by a small intellectual elite, controlled the government. Insofar as the large mass of the population was concerned, this government was an amorphous force, inscrutable and unpredictable. The emperor ruled by the Mandate of Heaven, and his edicts had the authority of the philosopher-king. The Socratic dictum "virtue is knowledge" could have been the motto of the Confucian scholars, or "mandarins," whose major qualification for government office was a knowledge of the great literary classics of the empire. Admission to government posts was not decided by imperial fiat or arbitrary violence, but through the institution of a highly formalized system of civil service examinations held in the capital. These examinations, open to all, were the first of their kind in history.

The world beyond the Great Wall of China did not hold much interest since, in the eyes of the Chinese, it was populated by barbarians. Hence, the foreign relations of the empire were in essence tributary relationships: long caravans laden with gifts for the emperor would weave their way across the land to the Imperial Court at Peking; the envoy would kowtow before the Son of Heaven, present the tribute, and hope for the favor of being permitted to trade with the great empire. The arts of war and the use of violence were not held in high esteem in the Confucian ethos. The Chinese believed that since it was perfectly evident that their empire was a superior civilization, it would be in the interest of all barbarians to learn from it rather than destroy it. The military preparedness of the empire was therefore limited to defense against intermittent incursions by barbarians into China's territory.

This self-sufficient and almost static society had virtually no contact whatsoever with the West. The travels of Marco Polo in the twelfth century and the Jesuit mission of Father Matthew Ricci in the sixteenth were of too brief duration to create a lasting impression. The first massive Western impact occurred in the eighteenth century, when the British in their quest for more lucrative trade became intent upon establishing trade relations with the empire. The Chinese, significantly enough, attempted to fit these British overtures into their traditional tributary framework. When, in 1793, a British trade mission led by Lord Macartney arrived at Peking, it was labeled as a tributary mission from the King of England. In exchange for the privilege of presenting his gifts, Lord Macartney was expected to kowtow, that is, to perform three kneelings and nine prostrations before the emperor. When the British Lord objected to this procedure, he was politely requested to go home, although his tribute was graciously accepted. Shortly thereafter the emperor sent an Imperial Edict to the King of England. This document is so significant that parts of it deserve to be quoted:

> You, O King, are so inclined toward our civilization that you have sent a special envoy across the seas to bring to our Court your memorial of congratulations on the occasion of my birthday and to present your native products as an expression of your thoughtfulness. On perusing your memorial, so simply worded and sincerely conceived, I am impressed by your genuine respectfulness and friendliness and greatly pleased.
>
> The Celestial Court has pacified and possessed the territory within the four seas. Its sole aim is to do its utmost to achieve good government and to manage political affairs, attaching no value to strange jewels and precious objects. The various articles presented by you O King, this time are accepted by my special order to the office in charge of such functions in consideration of the offerings having come from a long distance with sincere good wishes. As a matter of fact, the virtue and prestige of the Celestial Dynasty having spread far and wide, the kings of the myriad nations come by land and sea with all sorts of precious things. Consequently there is nothing we lack, as your principal envoy and others have themselves observed. We have never set much store on strange or ingenious objects, nor do we need any more of your country's manufactures. . . .[2]

There was one commodity, however, for which the British did find a market in China, and a lucrative one indeed: opium. Large quantities of opium were brought into China by traders of the British East India Company and in the early nineteenth century over one million Chinese became addicted to the poison. The emperor became increasingly perturbed and authorized one of his mandarins to appeal to the conscience of the British ruler to discontinue the smuggling of opium into China. One of his officials, Commissioner Lin, sent a poignant note of protest to Queen Victoria in 1839, at a time when the use of the drug threatened to undermine the health of the entire population. This protest is an historic document:

> We find that your country is sixty or seventy thousand li [three li make one mile, ordinarily] from China. Yet there are barbarian ships that strive to come here for trade for the purpose of making a profit. The wealth of China is used to profit the barbarians. That is to say, the great profit made by barbarians is all taken from the rightful share of China. By what right do they then in return use the poisonous drug to injure the Chinese people? Even though the barbarians may not necessarily intend to do us harm, yet in coveting profit to an extreme, they have no regard for injuring others. Let us ask, where is your conscience? I have heard that the smoking of opium is very strictly forbidden by your country; that is because the harm caused by opium is clearly understood. Since it is not permitted

to do harm to your own country, then even less should you let it be passed on to the harm of foreign countries—how much less to China! Of all that China exports to foreign countries, there is not a single thing which is not beneficial to people; they are of benefit when eaten, or of benefit when used, or of benefit when resold; all are beneficial. Is there a single article from China which has done any harm to foreign countries? Take tea and rhubarb, for example; the foreign countries cannot get along for a single day without them. If China cuts off these benefits with no sympathy for those who are to suffer, then what can the barbarians rely upon to keep themselves alive?[23]

The request went unheeded and finally Commissioner Lin decided to take strong action. He issued orders to blockade British merchants at Canton and to destroy their opium. The British interpreted this seizure as an interference with freedom of trade and as an act of aggression. Instead of ending the smuggling of opium, Commissioner Lin precipitated the Opium war. This war was little more than a skirmish, settled by the Treaty of Nanking in 1842. The war itself, which signified the first violent contact between China and the West, showed how distorted were the perceptions that the two sides held of each other. The British, surprised by the weak show of resistance exhibited by the Chinese, interpreted this weakness as a surrender and proceeded to advance up the coast to occupy all the major coastal ports of China. The Chinese, on the other hand, with a few exceptions like Commissioner Lin himself, firmly believed that the British, like other barbarians before them, would recognize the self-evident superiority of Chinese civilization and behave accordingly. The Treaty of Nanking, marking the beginning of Western imperialism in China, was thus a surprise to both sides: to the Chinese because they found themselves unable to eject the "barbarians" by moral persuasion; to the British because they encountered almost no effective military resistance.

The first massive Western influence on China, therefore, was one of violent intrusion. It now remained for the West to consolidate its position in the empire. This was accomplished through a series of arrangements known as the "unequal treaties," which gradually divested the Chinese Empire of its territorial integrity. The British were quickly followed by other Western nations, who were lured to China by the British example: French, Portuguese, and German colonizers attempted to negotiate similarly advantageous treaties with the empire. The empire had little choice but to grant the foreigners extensive concessions, with the result that by the mid-1840s China's sovereignty was little more than a fiction. The ominous and omnipresent threat of Western gunboats and superior military techniques were simply more than the old China could effectively resist.

The treaties which carved up China among the Western powers all had certain elements in common. First, there was the legal device of extraterritoriality. Under this system, foreigners in China were not subject to Chinese law but remained under the jurisdiction of their own governments. Many desirable sites on Chinese soil, including most residential areas in the large Chinese cities, were made inaccessible to the Chinese. Thus the Chinese suddenly found themselves in the incredible position of not being permitted to enter the choicest buildings and parks in their own cities unless permitted by a "barbarian" to do so. China's foreign trade and its customs and tariff policy were placed under the control of an Englishman, Inspector General Sir Robert Hart. One of the most anomalous consequences of this one-sided treaty system was the influx of Christianity into China. The picture of Christian missionaries attempting to repair the ravages of opium addiction caused by their conationals became a source of additional confusion.

The most important single feature of the unequal treaty system was the so-called "most-favored nations clause." Professor John K. Fairbank, a leading American authority on China, has called this "the neatest diplomatic device of the nineteenth century." The clause simply meant that all Western nations would participate in whatever any one of them could obtain. For example, if Germany was able to persuade China to give it a ninety-nine-year lease on an important port, all of the other Western powers had the automatic right to similarly favorable leaseholds. This rule of the "highest common denominator" made it a foregone conclusion that by mid-nineteenth century the entire coastal area of China, including its most important cities, were virtually in the hands of the West.

The rise of Chinese nationalism, including its culmination in the Communist Revolution, must be understood in terms of this initial Western impact. During the past century, China has undergone five major convulsions: the Great Peasant Rebellion, the Boxer Rebellion, the Self-Strengthening Movement, the Nationalist Revolution, and the Communist Revolution. Each of these has been in essence a desperate attempt to regain national status, and each has its roots in the Western policy of imperialism mounted against China a little over a century ago. We shall now analyze each of these five nationalist movements.

The Great Peasant Rebellion of 1851 was one of the great social upheavals of modern times. It marked the first time in the history of the empire that the Chinese population was politically activated en masse. An estimated twenty million people lost their lives in the course of this fifteen-year rebellion. Its leader, Hung, was a disappointed office-seeker. He claimed to have experienced a vision in which a venerable sage exhorted him to save humanity. Hung began to play on the population's fear of the "foreign devils" and its impatience and disgust with the tottering empire which seemed to be at the mercy of the "barbarians." Hung vowed to unseat the bankrupt Manchu government and ultimately to eject the foreigners. He began to describe himself as "the younger brother of Jesus" and developed a philosophy incorporating tenets of Christianity and an ambitious program of agrarian reform. Millions of peasants supported his cause. Many believed that Hung had the Mandate of Heaven for a new dynasty that would displace the weak and discredited Manchus. Many peasants were also deeply fearful of the foreigners. For example, the foreigners built railroads and suspended wires in the air; when it rained, these wires would rust and reddish drops would fall onto the ground; the Chinese peasants believed that these reddish drops were the blood of the good spirits which had impaled themselves on the wires cunningly placed there by the foreign devils. A terrible famine gave the rebellion its final impetus. Millions of peasants began to advance rapidly toward Peking, led by Hung, who vowed to establish his strange theocracy. By the mid-1850s, the rebels were in control of half of China. The Manchu government as well as the Western powers on the coast became increasingly terrified. In desperation the Manchus formed an alliance with the foreigners in order to present a united front against the rebels. The battle seesawed back and forth for an entire decade. Finally, the imperial forces, buttressed by modern arms and aided by foreign military leaders, were able to stem the rebellion. Hung committed suicide in 1864 and his death marked the defeat of the Great Peasant Rebellion.

This first reaction to the impact of Western imperialism is interesting for several reasons. The rebellion was the first example of popular nationalism in China and proved so powerful that only an alliance between the Manchu government and its worst enemy was able to crush it. It was in effect the first mass movement in China's history and, in historical perspective, was clearly a forerunner of the Communist Revolution.

China's second attempt to rid herself of the West was the pathetic and ill-fated Boxer Rebellion of 1900. The Manchu dynasty, which had received a new lease on life, decided on a show of force. The Boxers, fanatical members of anti-Western secret societies who believed themselves to be invulnerable, decided to besiege the foreign community in its own legations in Peking. For two months in the summer of 1900 most foreign officials were the prisoners of the Boxers. The suicidal futility of this venture became apparent when reinforcements arrived and the Western plenipotentiaries and their families were liberated. Retribution was swift: the leaders of the rebellion were executed and a heavy indemnity was exacted from the Chinese treasury. This second attempt at nationalist revolt was an utter and dismal failure.

During the second half of the nineteenth century it became increasingly clear to many Chinese intellectuals that their entire way of life was being undermined by the firepower of foreign arms and by superior Western technology. The Peasant and Boxer rebellions, though very different, had proven equally futile because of China's backward state of military development. As a typical example of this state of affairs, in Fairbank's words, "the British had used on the coast of China a shallow bottomed paddle-wheel iron steamer called the *Nemesis*. It carried swivel cannon fore and aft and was capable of moving into the wind and against the tide in a manner disastrous to China's fortunes."[4] The realization of China's inadequacy vis-à-vis the West led to the development of the so-called Self-Strengthening Movement, which spanned the latter half of the nineteenth century. The premise of the movement was a simple one: "Chinese learning as the fundamental structure, Western learning for practical use."[5] Its leaders felt that the only way of restoring the national status of China was for the Chinese themselves to utilize Western science and military techniques. In short, some of the ways of the foreigner would have to be copied in order to get rid of him. Accordingly, shipyards, arsenals, and science academies began to flourish. The Self-Strengtheners emphasized, over and over again, that this Western technology must be used to preserve Chinese values, not to destroy them. Thus, for example, Chinese students were sent to the West but were always accompanied by Confucian chaperones who made sure that these future leaders of China would not be infected by Western ideas. The fallacy of the Self-Strengthening Movement lay in its assumption that knowledge and life could be neatly compartmentalized, that one could adopt the tools of the West but totally ignore its values, that one could leap into the modern world only halfway. Inevitably, "one Western borrowing led to another, from machinery to technology, from science to all learning, from acceptance of new ideas to change of institutions, eventually from constitutional reform to republican revolution."[6] In the last analysis, the principal net effect of the Self-Strengthening Movement was to prepare the ground for the Nationalist Revolution of 1911.

One of the outstanding leaders of the Self-Strengthening Movement was Dr. Sun Yat-sen, destined to become the leader of the Nationalist Revolution. The life of Dr. Sun affords a fascinating case study of a revolutionary. He was born in Portuguese Macao, received his education in an English school, and was converted to Christianity early in life. He decided to study medicine in Hong Kong, where he came under the influence of a British missionary doctor, Sir James Cantlie. Cantlie acquainted the young Sun Yat-sen with Western ways ranging from the study of physics to the playing of cricket. Sun received his medical degree and hoped to set up practice as a surgeon in Macao. The Portuguese, however, debarred him from practice in his own country. Subsequently Dr. Sun abandoned his new profession and embarked on a revolutionary career. Between 1894 and 1911 he organized revolutionary sentiment against both the tottering Manchu dynasty and the Western powers. Like Lenin, he lived in exile with a price upon his head and relentlessly worked for the cause of revolution. At one point, in 1896, during a stay in London, he was abducted and imprisoned in the Chinese Legation for shipment back to China and certain death. He managed to inform Sir James Cantlie, who lived nearby, of his plight. Cantlie mobilized Scotland Yard and Sun was saved through British intervention. From this time onward, Sun was recognized as the undisputed leader of the Nationalist Revolutionary Movement.

It was during this incubation period of the revolution that Dr. Sun developed his philosophy of the "Three Principles of the People": Nationalism, Democracy, and the People's Livelihood. This concept went beyond the philosophy of the Self-Strengthening Movement; Sun insisted that in order to become free, China would have to borrow not only science but ideas as well. Sun's first principle of Nationalism simply meant "China for the Chinese." Democracy, as conceived by him, was to be an amalgam of American, British, and Swiss constitutional principles. And the People's Livelihood stood for a gradualist program of socialism patterned after the example of the Fabians in Britain. Armed with this synthesis of Western political thought, Dr. Sun Yat-sen engineered ten revolutionary attempts against the Manchu government, all of which failed. Finally, in October of 1911, Sun went to the United States to raise funds for his cause. During his campaign he received a coded cable which he was unable to decipher because he had shipped his code book ahead. As it turned out, the cable contained news of yet another plot. This time the plot was successful. A few days later, on October 10, 1911, Sun Yat-sen read in the newspapers that a Nationalist Revolution had broken out in China and that he was to be the first president of the new Republic.

It now remained for Sun to consolidate the Nationalist Revolution. This was by no means an easy task. With the collapse of imperial authority, China was now controlled by numerous warlords who were unwilling to yield to Sun Yat-sen's demand for unification under the Nationalist banner. The revolution seemed abortive. The warlords were not receptive to Sun's new ideas of parliamentary democracy, for these were wholly alien to the authoritarian tradition in which the empire had been ruled for centuries. Moreover, they refused to reconcile their parochial interests with the national programs of the revolution. In 1912, as a result, Sun resigned as president and it seemed that the Nationalist Revolution had foundered on the rock of warlordism. Yet Sun continued to work for his ideal and, in desperation, approached the Western powers, pleading with them for aid in his struggle for national unification. The response, however, was negative, partly because a divided China was preferred by the West and partly because the energies of the great powers were primarily engaged in Europe, which was drifting toward the brink of war.

Western indifference to Sun Yat-sen during this period helped to direct the course of Chinese nationalism toward authoritarianism. Sun turned away from the West in disappointment and became increasingly disillusioned with parliamentary democracy as a way toward unification. It was no accident that when, at this critical moment in the fortunes of Chinese nationalism, another vast revolution took place—that in Russia in 1917—Sun looked toward the newly formed Soviet Union. To his amazement he saw that the Bolsheviks were able to subdue a country larger than China in a relatively short space of time, whereas China, a decade after the revolution, still lay prostrate at the mercy of the warlords. It was at this moment that Chinese nationalism began to look to communism for inspiration. Sun Yat-sen had found Lenin.

Both Lenin and Sun Yat-sen were professional revolutionaries, yet no two men could have differed more. Sun Yat-sen was a Christian and by temperament inclined toward parliamentarianism rather than the use of violence; Lenin was a tough, shrewd revolutionary strategist who firmly believed that only a tightly organized, blindly obedient party could accomplish the goals of revolution.

The Bolshevik success induced Sun Yat-sen to accept Lenin's advice and organize a Nationalist party, the Kuomintang, patterned on authoritarian principles. Soviet advisors, most prominent among whom was the Comintern agent Michael Borodin, helped in the organization of the new Nationalist party at Nanking. By 1924 the Nationalist party apparatus was sufficiently permeated with Communists that China could have been absorbed into the Communist orbit without much difficulty. But in that year Lenin died and during the remainder of the 1920s the energies of Soviet leaders were absorbed in a brutal struggle for succession.[7] As a result, though China seemed to lie within their grasp, none of the Soviet leaders gave it much attention. As Stalin put it, when the time came, the Soviet Union would "squeeze the Chinese Nationalists like a lemon."

In 1925 Dr. Sun Yat-sen died. Unlike Lenin, who had not groomed a successor for his mantle, Sun had prepared one of his most brilliant disciples to follow in his footsteps. This man was Chiang Kai-shek, a young military leader who had been sent by Sun to the Soviet Union for study, to acquaint himself with Soviet political and military techniques. When Chiang Kai-shek took over the leadership of the Nationalist Revolution, he was quite aware of the Comintern's plans to absorb China. He decided to "squeeze the lemon" first. Using techniques that he had learned from the Communists, Chiang Kai-shek decided to stage a workers' strike. He then blamed this strike on the Communists in his own party and used it as an excuse to purge them ruthlessly from the Kuomintang, forcing them on the famous "Long March," which was to last seven years and was to take them to the other end of China.

By 1930 Chiang Kai-shek, having assumed the title of generalissimo, was at the zenith of his power. He had expelled the Communists and was now able to embark on his goal of unification of all of China, the first aim of the Nationalist Revolution. He announced that China was to be under the political tutelage of the Nationalist party until conditions became stable enough to make possible the transition to constitutional democracy.

Under the leadership of the generalissimo, the new Nationalist government made a determined effort to rid itself of the unequal treaties with the West. Chiang Kai-shek mapped out his program in his book, *China's Destiny*, in which he blamed most of the ills of China on Western imperialism. He announced a "Rights Recovery Movement" and a "New Life Movement." The former was a plan gradually to wipe out extraterritoriality, Western customs control, and the foreign concessions in the major Chinese cities. The latter was an attempt to restore the old Confucian virtues which had been displaced by the West. The Kuomintang was to serve as the instrument of the generalissimo's will.

Chiang Kai-shek's nationalism was in essence an attempt to revive the past and the tradition of the empire. It was a somewhat modernized version of the old imperial hope that government by Confucian precept and example would restore China to its rightful place of centrality in the comity of nations. The party ruled in an almost completely authoritarian manner, providing little opportunity for popular participation in government. The lesson of the Great Peasant Rebellion was forgotten; once more the peasant was virtually disfranchised and little attempt was made to ease his lot through land reform. The New Life Movement was symbolic of the Kuomintang approach: the anomalous picture of old greybeards preaching the restoration of Confucius to impatient university students brimming with the excitement of new ideas and yearning for a whole new way of life.

Moreover, Chiang Kai-shek's conservative nationalist program was never really tested in time of peace. In 1931 the country was attacked by Japan and after 1937 the Nationalist government had to bear the brunt of the full fury of the new Japanese imperialism. In the face of this deadly threat, Chiang Kai-shek was compelled to suspend his domestic programs and to employ almost his entire resources in the battle for national survival. Even so, the invaders succeeded in capturing the capital at Nanking and forcing Chiang Kai-shek to relocate the seat of his government in the mountains of the interior, at Chungking.

Meanwhile, the few thousand Chinese Communists who arrived exhausted in Yenan in 1934 appeared destined for oblivion. Chiang Kai-shek had turned his attention to the Japanese and the Comintern had written them off as hopeless. But during the Long March a new and tenacious leadership had emerged which was ultimately to bring the Communists to a complete national victory. Mao Tse-tung, surely one of the most complex figures of our time—a mixture of scholar, poet, party organizer, and military strategist—took command. The redoubtable leader Chu Teh became responsible for military operations; and Chou En-lai, the most cosmopolitan of the three, took charge of the Chinese Communists' foreign relations.

Yenan in the mid-1930s provided a privileged sanctuary to the Communists. The first American reporter to visit them there in 1936 described the startling contrast between the electric atmosphere of optimism prevailing in Yenan and the dank smell of defeat in Chiang Kai-shek's wartime capital.[8] It was during this period that Mao Tse-tung worked out the program whereby his Communist forces were to take over the leadership of Chinese nationalism. For one thing, the Chinese Communist party completely emancipated itself from control by Moscow and thereby became the only Communist party in the world that was independent of the Soviet Union from the very beginning of its rise to power. Mao Tse-tung embarked on an important ideological deviation by declaring that in China, communism would have to be built on an agrarian rather than an industrial base. "Just as fish cannot live without water," he said, "communism in China cannot survive without the support of the peasants."

The second significant aspect of Mao's program was his strategy of attempting to win the allegiance of the peasantry by capitalizing on the economic and social inadequacies of the Chiang Kai-shek government. Mao Tse-tung promised an extensive land reform program and pledged that no Communist soldier would be permitted to live off the land, that indeed the Communist soldier should be considered as the friend of the peasant. The Communists organized festivals and dances to woo the peasantry and gained thousands of recruits. Their great opportunity came in 1936. Chiang Kai-shek, badly pressed by the Japanese, was being beseeched by his officers to form a United Front with the Chinese Communists against the common enemy. When he refused, he was kidnapped by some of his own military leaders and forced to ask the Communists to join in the battle. As soon as he had reluctantly agreed, the Communists sallied forth from their sanctuary and swept across the countryside, picking up nearly a half million new recruits on the way. As Chiang Kai-shek had suspected, the United Front was for the Communists largely a project in self-aggrandizement. Given minimal help by the Communist Chinese Eighth Route Army, he had to fight the Japanese alone until the entrance of the Allies into the war.

This writer witnessed the liberation of Shanghai from the Japanese by Chiang Kai-shek's forces in 1945. Seldom was there a more Pyrrhic victory; the Nationalist soldiers entered the city tattered, exhausted, and demoralized, while the Communist forces stood poised only a few hundred miles away, fresh and ready for the decisive encounter. Hence the defeat of Japan did not bring peace to Chiang Kai-shek's government. Instead of being free to implement his long-postponed programs, he was compelled to mobilize his resources to attempt to block the steadily advancing armies of the Communists. In the ensuing four years of civil war, the generalissimo's fortunes steadily declined. Mediation attempts by the United States—first through Ambassador Patrick Hurley and then through General George C. Marshall—proved to be of no avail. Chiang Kai-shek refused to form a coalition government with the Communists because he feared their techniques of infiltration. Mao Tse-tung was equally unwilling to agree to a compromise because he was certain of ultimate victory. In addition to his program of economic and social reform, Mao Tse-tung now bitterly attacked the rampant corruption of the Nationalist government and proceeded to portray Chiang Kai-shek as a lackey of Western imperialism. The Nationalists, corroded by inflation, corruption, and defeat, finally had to quit the mainland in 1949 in a desperate scramble for refuge on the island of Formosa. The Mandate of Heaven passed from their hands. It was now the Communist party that assumed leadership of the new nationalism in China.

The course of these Chinese developments affords some interesting insights into the linkage of the East-West and the North-South struggles. It is clear that both the Nationalist and the Communist revolutions in China were in essence reactions against Western imperialism. The five upheavals in which this reaction became manifest were not isolated events but consecutive expressions of a continuing development. Indeed, so far as China is concerned, the East-West conflict was a direct outgrowth of the long struggle of Chinese nationalism against Western imperialism.

In the United States, which consistently supported Chiang Kai-shek, the struggle between the Nationalist government and the Chinese Communists has received much attention and aroused a great deal of emotion. It was widely believed that the two sides represented completely opposite motives and aspirations. Few Americans perceived the complex truth that the Nationalist and Communist revolutions were *both* in essence anti-Western movements and that the struggle between them was more a struggle for power between competing forms of authoritarian nationalism than a conflict between radically different ideologies. It was a measure of the extent to which Americans had failed to recognize this basic fact that during the 1950s so many people in the United States were prepared to accept the allegation that the United States had "lost" China as a result of the machinations of subversives in the American government. Though it is not within the purview of this case study to examine the problem of subversion, it must be noted that underlying this "explanation" of the recent course of Chinese history is the assumption that a handful of Americans actually had it in their power to determine the fate of the one billion people of China.

During the quarter century of nonrelations between the United States and China, most Americans regarded Chiang Kai-shek as a soldier-saint who could do no wrong. After all, he had fought the Japanese and the Communists and was a Christian. Mao Tse-tung, on the other hand, was perceived as the Communist devil in league with Stalin. This devil image of Mao Tse-tung, so prevalent in America, helps to explain why a détente between the two nations was so long in coming. When in 1954 Secretary of State John Foster Dulles refused to shake hands with Chou En-lai in Geneva, he expressed the feelings of most Americans at the time: one does not engage in commerce with the devil. Another eighteen years had to elapse before an American President shook hands with the Chinese premier, this time on Chinese soil. In truth, the similarities between Chiang Kai-shek and Mao Tse-tung over half a century had always been greater than the differences.

In conclusion, our case study demonstrates the continuity between the Nationalist and the Communist revolutions. The pattern is, in fact, a continuum: China's role in the East-West conflict actually grew out of the struggle between nationalism and Western imperialism. In this struggle for national self-assertion against the West, Communist China used the Soviet Union as an ally. There were, after all, striking elements of similarity between the old authoritarian nationalism of the Chinese Empire and the new authoritarian nationalism of the Russian Communists. Communism, like the empire, saw itself as occupying a central position in the world, almost messianic in character. And communism, too, had its "barbarians"—the West—to be treated with contempt and derision. Communist ideology was the anti-Western cement that temporarily bound the two nations together. But once China had demonstrated its new prowess to the West, it turned against the East as well. The alliance with the Soviet Union had now outlived its usefulness. Remembering that Russia, too, had in the nineteenth century joined in the predatory policies of the Western powers, China now pressed territorial claims along the Sino-Soviet border. And by the 1980s, China had become so fearful of the Soviet Union that she forged a de facto alliance with the United States. America once more became the model and China's major hope against the Russian "barbarians." Things had come full circle.

It is perhaps well to remind ourselves again that ours has been the only century in the past four thousand years in which China has not seen itself as the center of the universe. Is it possible that communism may turn out to be the instrument that the new nationalism in China has forged for itself to restore China to the central place that she considers to be rightfully hers by the verdict of history? This may yet be the ultimate bearing that the two great power struggles of our time have on the fate of China.

The Suez Crisis of 1956 and the Arab-Israeli Wars of 1967 and 1973

Our second case study focuses upon three wars: the Suez crisis of 1956 and the Arab-Israeli conflicts of 1967 and 1973. A comparative analysis of these three events affords dramatic insights into the complexities and ambiguities of the political struggle of our time. For not only did these three crises involve the two general global struggles of East versus West and nationalism versus colonialism; in addition, they generated sharp conflicts among the Western powers and among the new anticolonial nations themselves.

The Suez crisis was precipitated in the summer of 1956 when President Gamal Abdel Nasser of Egypt nationalized the Suez Canal, abrogating, in the view of Britain and France, the International Convention of Constantinople of 1888, which had provided that "the Suez Maritime Canal shall always be free and open, in time of war as in time of peace, to every vessel of commerce or of war without distinction of flag." The Egyptian leader defended his act by stating that the canal was within Egyptian territory and that the time had come to announce Egypt's "Declaration of Independence from Imperialism." In an emotional speech, he hailed nationalization as a symbolic act which would set Arab nationalism on its course from the Atlantic to the Persian Gulf. Britain and France, aghast at this unexpected move, lodged a strong protest against the seizure of "an international waterway" and against the violation of what the two Western nations considered to be their legal rights in the area. For Britain, as well as for Egypt, the Suez Canal was a symbol. While for Egypt it represented the growing power of the new nationalism, for Britain, control of the canal symbolized its status as an empire and as a world power. To the French, who blamed Egypt for supporting the Algerian rebellion against France, seizure of the canal served as a kind of last straw. For Britain and France alike, the issue at stake was therefore not merely the rational one of safeguarding the economic rights of their shareholders in the Suez Canal Company. Far more important was their emotional reaction to the seemingly insolent and irresponsible nationalism represented by the Egyptian move. The highly emotional nature of the conflict thus set the stage for a violent encounter between nationalism and colonialism.

During the weeks that followed Nasser's action the conflict broadened. Britain and France sounded out the official American reaction to the situation. Prime Ministers Eden and Mollet, contemplating the use of force against Nasser, were partially reassured by the fact that Secretary of State John Foster Dulles also appeared outraged by Egypt's action. The British and French foreign ministers compared Nasser's action to Hitler's behavior at Munich and stated in the strongest terms that this type of Western appeasement must not be allowed to occur again. Secretary Dulles replied that "force was the last method to be tried, but the United States did not exclude the use of force if all other methods failed."[9] From this statement Mr. Eden inferred that the United States would, at best, present a united front with Britain and France in a show of force against Nasser and, at worst, remain benevolently neutral. Thus it seemed in the late summer of 1956 that the United States would side with the colonial powers against the new nationalism.

Britain and France now prepared for military action. They hoped to mount a lightning attack against Egypt, occupy the canal, depose Nasser, and then negotiate with his successor from a position of strength. In the course of these preparations, it became increasingly evident to the two Western powers that they shared a common interest with Israel. The new Jewish state, harassed by border clashes and made increasingly insecure by Nasser's pronouncements "to drive Israel into the sea," could be used as the cutting edge of the Anglo-French punitive expedition against Egypt. "Collusion" between Britain and France on the one hand and Israel on the other has not been substantiated, but a great deal of circumstantial evidence points in that direction. At any rate, Israel penetrated Egyptian territory on October 29, 1956, and rapidly advanced toward the Suez Canal. On the following day the British and French bombarded Cairo. What had thus begun as an armed conflict between the two new Middle Eastern nations now assumed the proportions of a large-scale Western onslaught against the new nationalism. The United States, instead of observing a benevolent neutrality toward the British, French, and Israeli actions, took a leading role in the United Nations General Assembly in calling for a cessation of fighting and the immediate withdrawal of the Anglo-French-Israeli forces from Egypt. To the consternation of most of its allies in NATO and to the delight of Egypt, the United States upheld the United Nations Charter against the NATO alliance. On the same day, the Soviet Union took up the Egyptian cause, and threatened to send "volunteers" to Egypt and to bomb London and Paris with rocket missiles. Thus the United States found itself in the paradoxical position of being allied in the United Nations with its great antagonist in the East-West struggle, the Soviet Union, and of being at odds with its closest friends and allies, Britain and France. By November 6 Britain had to yield. Confronted by United Nations resolutions charging Britain with aggression, dismayed by the action of the United States, and troubled by an increasingly hostile opposition at home, Prime Minister Eden terminated his abortive venture. France had no choice but to follow suit, and the "gentle persuasion" of the United States resulted in the withdrawal of Israeli forces shortly thereafter. A world conflagration had narrowly been averted.

Of all the roles in the drama, that of the United States was undoubtedly the most problematical. Confronted in the most acute way possible with the old dilemma of whether to support the colonial powers or the new nationalism, the United States was bound to lose either way. The actual decision to side with Egypt inevitably alienated Britain and France and put the most severe strains on the NATO alliance. Sir Anthony Eden was compelled to resign, and throughout Britain as well as France a growing body of "neutralist" sentiment became articulate. Indeed, in the view of a number of observers, for example former Secretary of State Dean Acheson, American policy in the crisis came close to losing the United States its two most trusted allies and thus exposing Western Europe to the domination of communism. On the other hand, if the United States had sided with Britain and France against Egypt, its risks would have been no less heavy. The new nations of Africa, Asia, and the Middle East would have quickly concluded that when the chips were down the United States was at heart no less a colonial power than its Western European allies. In disillusionment, the new nationalism would almost certainly have veered sharply away from the United States toward the Soviet Union. Probably the least amount of animosity would have resulted if the United States had followed its more typical pattern in such situations and abstained from the conflict altogether. Yet even in this case both sides would likely have found reason for objecting to America's role.

As one observer has pointed out, "the criticism of the American stand came essentially to this point: the United States had chosen to behave like a collective security power, not like an ally. In the Middle Eastern situation, 'Uniting for Peace' had prevailed over NATO."[10] Yet the American rejection as "unthinkable" of a Soviet proposal for joint superpower intervention in the Middle East suggests strongly that the American position was not determined by the abstract considerations of the collective security ideal. There was, first, the sense of outrage that the President and Secretary of State both felt because the British and French had not bothered to consult their NATO ally on a matter as important as military action in the Middle East at a time when a national election was imminent in the United States. Second, from a purely military standpoint, the Anglo-French punitive expedition seemed to be foundering and thus could not be presented to the General Assembly as a *fait accompli*. The United States, by supporting the Anglo-French venture or even by taking a neutral view of it, would have risked the ill will of a large majority of the UN membership and, in addition, might have had to look on helplessly while the military action failed or bogged down. Moreover, such an American response might have persuaded many neutralists that the United States, by countenancing aggression in the Middle East, differed little from the Soviet Union, which was practicing aggression by crushing a rebellion in Hungary with military force. Most important, the United States feared the possibility of Soviet intervention in the Middle East through "volunteers" and the risk of sparking a major war through direct superpower confrontation in the contested area.

All this does not exclude the possibility that some of the reasons motivating the United States were of a genuinely moral nature. As stated by the American government, the United States acted as it did because it insisted on the principle that the same standard of international law and morality should apply to all nations, friends and foes alike. Yet even this seemingly unassailable moral reason rested upon ambiguities. It could be argued, for example, that a "moral" action might under certain circumstances eventuate in "immoral" consequences. Thus the "moral" behavior of the United States in the Suez crisis ran the risk of leading to the disintegration of NATO and the "immoral" result of opening Western Europe to Soviet domination. Conversely, if the United States had decided upon the "immoral" step of supporting the British and French military expedition against Egypt, the outcome might have been the quite "moral" one of restoring the legal economic rights of the Western powers and of reestablishing the Suez Canal as an international waterway. The point here is *not* that the United States acted either morally or immorally. It is, rather, that among other things, the Suez affair demonstrated how subtle and indeterminate the relationship between ethics and power in international relations can be. The most "moral" intentions may lead to highly "immoral" consequences, whereas on other occasions and in different circumstances the very reverse may be true.

The Soviet Union's role in the Suez crisis was much simpler. From its point of view, the only unusual aspect was its strange alliance with the United States in the United Nations. In order to dissociate itself from this somewhat unwelcome association, the Soviet Union interpreted the action of the United States not as being helpful to Arab nationalism, but, rather, as a nefarious scheme to replace British and French imperialism with American imperialism. In contrast, it pointed to itself as the only true champion of the new nationalist cause. Its threat of rocket retaliation against Britain and France was designed to underline how firm its commitment to the new nationalism in fact was. From the Soviet Union's point of view, indeed, the Suez crisis constituted a great windfall in the East-West struggle: the British and French appeared to be digging their own graves in the Middle East and the United States seemed to be doing its best to help them. Thus, by appealing to the cause of Arab nationalism, the Soviet Union saw its opportunity to eject all Western influence from the Middle East and gain a foothold of its own. The fact that Israel was allied with the two colonial powers also played into Soviet hands. Typically, therefore, the Soviet Union showed itself ready to use every facet of this colonial struggle to advance its own cause in the East-West battle. And, from the melee, communism emerged with a clear-cut gain.

The main losers in the Suez affair were clearly the two colonial powers, Britain and France. In humiliation, they had to watch Nasser snatch a political victory from a military defeat. Abandoned by their closest and oldest ally, they had to admit that they could no longer act like great powers and that, in the last analysis, their initiative in international politics depended upon the decisions of the United States. The new nationalism had inflicted a painful defeat upon them and the very issue that they had set out to rectify by force of arms—the internationalization of the Suez Canal—now seemed beyond redemption. For all practical purposes, the Suez crisis terminated Anglo-French authority in the Middle East. Suez had become another Dienbienphu.

The greatest victory in the Suez crisis was won by Arab nationalism. Nasser was now clearly master of the Suez Canal. The two great superpowers had both supported him. The prestige of the Egyptian leader reached its zenith immediately after the Suez affair. Not only did Nasser triumph in the showdown with Western colonialism, but his other great foe, Israel, had also been compelled to withdraw as a result of American pressure. The political logic of the East-West struggle, by becoming the decisive factor in the crisis, thus operated to advance the cause of Arab nationalism to greater strength and prestige than it had ever possessed or than Nasser could ever have hoped to gain on his own.

Only Israel emerged relatively unchanged from the turmoil of the Suez affair. To be sure, it had demonstrated its military superiority over the competing nationalism of Nasser, yet it was prevented from capitalizing on its advantage by strong United States pressure to withdraw. In the end, nearly all the territories it had occupied had to be given up.

When the Suez crisis was over, the world's power configuration had definitely altered. In the East-West struggle, the Soviet Union clearly had come off best. It had created a more attractive image of itself in the Arab world and had won its first foothold in the Middle East. The promulgation by the United States of the Eisenhower Doctrine in March 1957—pledging American assistance to Middle Eastern countries against communism—was testimony to increasing American awareness of this latest Soviet gain. In the second struggle, that of nationalism versus colonialism, the winner was clearly the new nationalism. After Suez, the great-power role of Britain and France in the Middle East was clearly at an end. The Eisenhower Doctrine attempted to salvage what was left of Anglo-French influence. In the third struggle, that of nationalism versus nationalism, no appreciable change occurred in the distribution of power between Arab nationalism and Zionism. Both emerged stronger from the crisis, Israel because of its formidable military prowess and Egypt owing to its political triumph over Britain and France.

One question still remains about the Suez crisis that cannot be answered with certitude but that nevertheless ought to be raised. It is quite conceivable that the events in Suez determined the course of another political struggle, thousands of miles away—that of the Hungarian revolutionaries against the Soviet Union. The simultaneity of the two upheavals may have been more than accidental. The first stage of the Hungarian revolution was completed when Imre Nagy assumed complete control of Hungary and announced on November 1, 1956, that Hungary would be "free, independent, democratic, and neutral." Soviet forces were withdrawing from Hungary and agreement seemed to be near between the Soviet Union and the new Hungarian government. On that same day, however, the British and French mounted their invasion of Egypt, which reached its climax on November 3. On that day Nagy was informed that Soviet forces, in battle formation, were steadily advancing on the capital. On the following day, Soviet armored units had broken through the defenses of Budapest and the Hungarian revolution was drowned in blood.

Is it possible that the Soviet Union, in addition to the other advantages which it derived from the Suez crisis, decided to use the Anglo-French invasion of Egypt as a pretext for deflecting attention from events in Hungary? Or, to put it in other words, would the Soviet Union have decided to let Hungary escape from communism into a position of international neutrality if the Suez crisis had not occurred? Should we ask ourselves the somewhat ironical question of whether, because of the actions of Britain and France, the West itself was responsible for the failure of the Hungarian revolution? It is very doubtful that, in our own generation at least, we shall have the answers to these questions. What the Suez crisis did make dramatically clear, however, is that both in its origins and in its consequences the struggle for power among nations in our time has become one continuous, global, and indivisible process.

Interdependence again was the keynote of the Arab-Israeli war of 1967, although the specific alignment of forces was quite different. This time the two superpowers took opposing sides, while Britain tended to favor Israel and France leaned toward the Arabs.

The decade between the two crises had seen a bevy of border incidents but no major eruption. In early 1967, however, tension began to mount. President Nasser's Arab neighbors accused the Egyptian leader of hiding behind the United Nations Emergency Force in order to avoid a confrontation with Israel. Sensitive to this charge, Nasser demanded on May 18 that UNEF leave the positions in Sinai that it had occupied for more than ten years. It is not certain whether the Egyptian leader initiated this move primarily to assuage his Arab critics or whether he really intended to clear the field for military action. At any rate, Secretary-General U Thant complied with the demand, reasoning that UNEF could no longer remain in the area if the consent of the host government were withdrawn. Hence, the UNEF contingents were removed from Sinai, the Gaza Strip, and from Sharm El-Sheik overlooking the Straits of Tiran. Almost simultaneously, Israel, Syria, and Jordan began to mobilize their armed forces and mass them on their respective borders. On May 20, military control over the Gaza Strip reverted to Egypt and the Arab League issued a joint declaration signed by twelve of its members with only Tunisia abstaining, stating that an attack on one would be considered as an attack on all. Israel responded by calling up the reserves and on May 22 Egypt ordered total mobilization. During this early phase of the crisis the superpowers indicated their positions, but refused to become vitally involved.

The second phase of the crisis began when, on May 23, President Nasser announced a blockade of the Gulf of Aqaba, thus cutting off Israel's only southern port, at Elath. Israel immediately responded by defining the blockade as an act of war that entitled it to take appropriate action. Egypt, for its part, maintained that the Straits of Tiran were within its territorial waters and therefore could be closed to states with which it was at war.

At this juncture, the East-West struggle was superimposed upon the two competing nationalisms of Israel and the Arab states. On May 23, President Lyndon B. Johnson presented the American position. He described the blockade as "illegal and potentially disastrous to the cause of peace" and affirmed that "the right of free, innocent passage through the international waterway [was] a vital interest of the international community." The American President supported the settlement that had been reached after the Suez crisis of 1956. Since Egypt was determined to overthrow that settlement, the American position in effect came down on the side of Israel.

On the following day, the Soviet Union declared that Israel was to blame for the dangerous aggravation of tensions in the Middle East. The forces of imperialism represented by "a handful of colonial oil monopolies" and backed by commercial interests in the United States and Britain were the chief culprits behind the scene, in the Soviet view. The USSR further proclaimed its support for the Arab states in their "just struggle for national liberation against colonialism."

The other major powers—Britain, France, and China—also took stands in the escalating crisis. Britain supported the United States on the right of free passage of all nations through the disputed straits; France declared itself to be "not committed in any way and on any subject" on the side of "any of the states involved"; and China, supporting the Arab cause, also accused both the

United States and the Soviet Union of "strangling the just struggle of the Palestinian people."

In the meantime, the two main protagonists edged closer to the brink. On May 25, Israel's chief delegate to the United Nations, Abba Eban, flew to London and Washington in order to ascertain what the two Western powers would do to end the blockade. Both offered vague assurances but counseled restraint. On May 28, Syria and Iraq signed a military agreement calling for the cooperation of their armies against Israel—and on the following day, President Nasser announced that Soviet Premier Aleksei Kosygin had sent him a pledge to guarantee the Egyptian blockade. On May 30, King Hussein, described several weeks earlier as a "Hashemite Harlot" by President Nasser, placed Jordan's armed forces under Egyptian control in the event of war with Israel. Thus, by the end of May, the brink was reached and Israel confronted the armies of Egypt, Syria, and Jordan.

On the morning of June 5 heavy fighting broke out between Israel and Egypt. In four days of lightning warfare, Israel defeated the armies of her three main Arab antagonists. In Egypt, she captured the Sinai up to the east bank of the Suez Canal and also lifted the blockade of Aqaba by capturing Sharm El-Sheik. The Gaza Strip also fell into Israeli hands. In bloody fighting with Jordan, Israel occupied the Old City of Jerusalem and all of Jordan west of the Jordan River. Finally, Israel also captured portions of Syrian borderlands from which Arab guns had harassed Israeli settlements. On June 9 the short but violent war came to a halt with the cease-fire resolution passed by the UN Security Council.

During the next phase, the conflict moved from the military arena of the Middle East to the political forum of the United Nations. Both the Security Council and the General Assembly debated the issues, the latter in a four-week emergency special session. In the world forum, Israel insisted on recognition by the Arab states and an end to belligerency as conditions of withdrawal from the occupied Arab territories. Israel was supported in this view by the United States. The Arab states demanded unconditional withdrawal and full reparations, and insisted that Israel be condemned as an aggressor. Soviet Premier Aleksei Kosygin supported the Arab demands from the rostrum of the General Assembly. France inclined toward the Arab position and the small nations were about evenly divided. Neither superpower was able to muster a two-thirds majority for its respective position and hence the General Assembly adjourned in a mood of frustration after two resolutions calling upon Israel to rescind its annexation of Old Jerusalem were ignored. The one concrete UN measure was the dispatch of a small number of cease-fire observers to the Suez Canal.

An analysis of the changes in power constellations after the war reveals some suggestive comparisons and contrasts with the 1956 crisis. In the first place, the Soviet Union had backed a loser this time, while it had been on the winning side a decade earlier. Most of the military hardware that the USSR had shipped to the Arab states had been destroyed in the six days of war. Nor was the Soviet Union able to turn anticolonial sentiments to its advantage in the United Nations, since many of the smaller nations also identified with Israel. On the other hand, their defeat now made the Arab states more than ever dependent upon the USSR, which promptly resumed arms shipments to them.

The role of the United States was once again problematical. It was on the winning side and, superficially, its policy seemed successful. But on a deeper level, it was clear that the swiftness of Israel's victory had saved the United States from having to make some very difficult decisions. Had the war gone badly for Israel, the United States might have been forced to intervene and risk a confrontation with the Soviet Union.

Britain and France, the two main losers in the 1956 affair, this time were only marginally involved. A new power factor in the equation, however, was China, which accused the United States and the Soviet Union of conspiring together in the Middle East.

Israel, which had to withdraw in 1956, this time was determined not to yield its military gains, except in exchange for an end to belligerency. This the Arabs were unwilling to concede and thus, in the view of many observers, the 1967 war had not resolved and perhaps had even exacerbated the deeper causes of the conflict.

Thus, by mid-1967, the balance of power in the Middle East had definitely altered. Although Israel had won its military victory essentially unaided, the political constellation clearly showed once again the interdependence of the two great struggles of our time. One superpower tried to exploit the Arab-Israeli war by describing it as a struggle between Arab nationalism and Western imperialism. In this effort the USSR failed where it had succeeded in 1956 when the two superpowers found themselves on the same side. And the United States, eager to pacify the struggle, was saved by Israel's arms from the decision to intervene. Thus, the connection between the two world struggles might have widened the theater of war had the conflict between the two main antagonists been inconclusive or gone the other way.

The years between the Six-Day War of 1967 and the October War of 1973 saw a developing détente between the United States and the Soviet Union. The October War strained that détente to the limit, but did not shatter it. In the wake of that war, the Arab states discovered a powerful new weapon against the United States and the former colonial powers of the West: the oil embargo. This weapon worked so well that it compelled the United States to change from a stalwart supporter of Israel to a balancer between Israel and the Arabs in the Middle East. Thus, Soviet and American power contained the conflict and kept it from escalating, but the oil embargo gave the Arab states a measure of real power that they had never enjoyed before. This unprecedented global constellation showed up the linkage between the two world struggles in an entirely new light.

After the Israeli victory of 1967 the Soviet Union gradually replaced the military hardware that the Arabs had lost in the Six-Day War. The Soviets also trained Egyptian and Syrian commanders in Soviet military strategy and tactics in order to prevent a repetition of the 1967 debacle. By 1973 the Arabs were encouraged to believe that at least some of the lost territories could be regained by force of arms. Thus, the stage was set for another violent encounter.

The Arab attack on October 6 did not come as a complete surprise to the Israeli leadership. Defense Minister Moshe Dayan claimed several days later that he had advance information that some sort of attack was imminent but had decided against a preemptive strike. Secretary of State Henry Kissinger had warned the Israelis repeatedly not to "preempt" and this admonition weighed heavily in their calculations. The Israeli leadership feared that the United States might abandon the Jewish state if it started the war. Thus, the decision was made to have the political advantage of not having attacked first, even at the expense of the military advantage. Kissinger did not believe that the Soviets would risk détente by encouraging an Arab attack. Actually, the Soviets calculated that they could encourage such a war and still preserve détente. This was similar to Nixon's and Kissinger's calculation in 1972, when the President decided to mine Haiphong several days before the Moscow summit was scheduled to take place. The Americans hoped that they could escalate the war and yet preserve the summit. The American gamble worked in 1972 just as the Soviet gamble paid off in 1973.

The price that Israel paid for its self-restraint in October 1973 was heavy. On the Suez front the Egyptians swarmed across the canal in large numbers, laid down bridges, and landed hundreds of tanks and other war materiel. They managed to overrun the famous Israeli defense installation, the Bar-Lev line, with heavy air and artillery assaults. The lightly defended Israeli positions had to be abandoned. On the Golan Heights an enormous Syrian force equipped with eight hundred tanks plunged across the cease-fire lines at four points. Commando units landed by helicopter on Mount Hermon and seized a major Israeli position. Overwhelmed by the force of the attack, Israeli defenders had to evacuate several outposts.

One explanation of these early Arab successes may be found in Israel's perception of its own military superiority and of the Arabs as notoriously poor and bumbling soldiers. The Israeli leadership had convinced itself of its own superiority to such an extent that it believed that an Arab attack would be suicidal. Israel, in short, was suffering from a case of military hubris.

By the end of the first week of war, Egypt had managed to insert almost one hundred thousand men on the East Bank of the Suez Canal and the fiercest tank battles since World War II were raging in the Sinai desert and the Golan Heights. Casualties were heavy on both sides, and new Soviet ground-to-air missiles presented a grave threat to the Israeli air force. Buoyed up by the successes of Syria and Egypt, other Arab countries joined in the battle. Iraq and Jordan supplied troops for the Syrian front, and Saudi Arabia and other oil-rich Arab sheikdoms placed increasing pressure on the United States to abandon its support of Israel.

As casualties mounted and both sides suffered staggering losses in war materiel, the superpowers entered the arena. The Soviet Union began to resupply the Arab states with ammunition and light weapons. When the United States decided to do the same for Israel, the Soviet Union escalated its supply operations to tanks and planes. This, too, was matched by the United States. Thus, by the end of the first week, the war had reached a new and dangerous plateau. Not only was the armor of both sides locked in a death struggle, but the fragile détente between the Soviet Union and the United States hung in the balance.

During the second week of war, Israel gradually gained the upper hand on both the Syrian and Egyptian fronts. After fierce tank battles in the Golan Heights, the Israelis not only threw back the Syrians but embarked on the road to Damascus. The Israeli advance into Syria came to a standstill at the village of Sasa, twenty miles from the Syrian capital. On the Egyptian front, the Israelis, in a daring tactical maneuver, inserted troops on the West Bank of the Suez Canal on Egyptian territory. Their aim was to encircle the Egyptian troops on the East Bank in Sinai and to cut off their retreat across the canal back to Egypt. After massive air and tank battles, the Israeli objectives were attained. The Egyptian troops were trapped in two large pockets in Sinai and the Third Army was at Israel's mercy for its supply of food and water. At this juncture, with the balance shifting rapidly in Israel's favor, the superpowers once again intervened.

On October 21, acting with great urgency to protect its Egyptian ally, the Soviet leadership agreed on a formula for a cease-fire resolution with Secretary of State Henry Kissinger. This resolution, which was rushed through the UN Security Council on the following morning under joint Soviet-American sponsorship, provided for a cease-fire in place and called on all parties to start immediate negotiations. The cease-fire began shakily, with the Egyptian forces trapped behind Israeli lines trying to break out and Israel seeking to destroy the Egyptian forces once and for all. A second cease-fire call still did not end the fighting. As a result, the Soviet Union proposed that a joint Soviet-American peace force be dispatched to the Middle East. This proposal was rejected by the United States, which feared the possibility of a military confrontation in the area. The Soviet Union then declared that it would introduce its own troops into the area unilaterally. To this Soviet threat, President Nixon responded by placing the armed forces of the United States on military alert.

During the "alert" crisis, a compromise was worked out. The UN Security Council approved a third resolution sponsored by the nonaligned countries that authorized the Secretary-General to send a UN buffer force to the area. This 7,000-man emergency force would be patterned after the old UN Emergency Force that had been created by Dag Hammarskjöld in 1956. It was to exclude the permanent members of the Security Council from active participation. To save face, however, the two superpowers insisted on sending a small number of observers into the cease-fire area. The first UN troops began to arrive from Cyprus on October 27. By then, all fronts were quiet. The precarious Soviet-American détente had held after all.

All during 1973 the Arab states had threatened to use the oil weapon in their struggle against Israel. The American airlift of tanks and planes to the Jewish state converted this threat into a reality. On October 17 the Arab oil-producing states voted to reduce their production by 10 percent. On October

18 Abu Dhabi imposed an oil embargo against the United States. On October 19 Libya followed suit. On October 20 the world's largest oil-producing country, Saudi Arabia, announced a similar embargo, to be followed on October 21 by Kuwait and Algeria. During the months ahead, this concerted Arab policy had a damaging effect on the American economy and forced Secretary Kissinger to accelerate his diplomatic peace-making efforts in order to persuade the Arabs to lift their embargo.

As the October war drew to a close after seventeen days of violent fighting, Arabs and Israelis were locked in an inconclusive military stalemate. Although the two superpowers backed different sides, détente between them held. The relationship that they had built so painstakingly over the past few years had already become more valuable to them than their respective allies in the Middle East. The largest diplomatic gain in the overall picture, however, was made by the Arab states, which, for the first time in their histories, managed to agree not only on a common military policy against Israel, but on a common economic policy vis-à-vis the West as well. Thus, the linkage between the world's two great power struggles was demonstrated once again, but this time the Arabs played a pivotal role. On the one hand, they had real power over the United States through their oil. But, on the other hand, they knew that they could regain their territories only with the help of the United States. This new element in the Middle East kaleidoscope, more than any other, explained the new Arab-American rapprochement that evolved in the wake of the October War.

The Shah of Iran, Khomeini, and America

On January 16, 1979, after thirty-seven years of autocratic rule, Muhammad Reza Pahlevi, the Shah of Iran, left his country never to return. From exile he watched his mortal enemy, the Ayatollah Khomeini, establish an Islamic theocracy which demanded his execution, called Iran's old ally, the United States, the "Great Satan," and turned more than fifty American embassy personnel into hostages in their own embassy. The Shah's death in Egypt in July 1980 unleashed a frenzied orgy of jubilation in Teheran, capped by executions of "enemies of the Islamic Revolution." Khomeini, now leader of Iran "for life," predicted the destruction of "satanical" America. A tyrant friendly to the West had been replaced by a fanatical adversary. How did these shattering events come about?

The Shah of Iran had been a complex man. Austere and remote in his demeanor, he had nonetheless been a man of vision. For thirty-seven years, he had pursued a grand design with single-minded zeal: under his tutelage, Iran was to become a powerful industrial state. This modern Persian renaissance was to be achieved through the Shah's "White Revolution," a "shock program that would allow Iran to overcome in 25 years its centuries of suppression."[11] In the Shah's own words, this march toward a "Great Civilization" would turn Iran into "one vast workshop in which all the elements indispensable to modernization would spring up: universities, school groups, professional institutes, hospitals, roads, railroads, dams, electric plants, pipelines for gas and oil, factories, industrial, cultural, artistic and sports complexes, cooperatives, metropolitan areas, and new villages."[12] Within a single generation, Iran would wrest its oil resources from foreign ownership and use its new-found wealth in the service of modernity and power. In this quest, the Shah had found a natural ally: the United States. For decades, American firms supplied the Shah's Iran with the technology and weapons that were the instruments of his "White Revolution." And the Shah, in return, supplied the United States with badly needed oil and an unconditional fidelity in the struggle against Communism. Friendship and foreign policy thus went hand in hand.

Unfortunately, the Shah exacted a high price for his modernization program. In the first place, he had created a secret police, the "Savak," to deal with enemies of the state. Savak's net was wide and its techniques ruthless. Torture and abuse were commonplace in Savak prisons. It is estimated that over a hundred thousand Iranians died in Savak's dungeons. Even the Shah himself admitted that "there were people arrested and abused," and that his country "fell victim to excesses."[13] "To let saboteurs act freely," the Shah explained, "would not have permitted the program's realization."[14] In other words, terror was essential for the attainment of the "Great Civilization." Who, then, were the saboteurs?

Khomeini and his Islamic fundamentalists considered the Shah an arch-traitor to his country. According to the Moslem Shi'ite clergy, the Shah had sold Iran out to the West and stolen its resources, all for the sake of personal wealth and glory. Islam, in the fundamentalists' opinion, had to cut loose from the United States and return to its historical tradition. The Shah's program had led only to sinfulness and atheism. Women would have to wear the veil again, as they did before the Shah's emancipation program. Justice would be meted out according to the Koran, including the stoning of adulterous women. Secular government officials would be subject to "spiritual leadership" by members of the Shi'ite clergy. These "mullahs" were the Shah's bitterest enemies and, together with victims of Savak, Communists, and "student" militants, prepared the ground for the Iranian monarch's fall.

Until the advent of Jimmy Carter in 1977, the alliance between Iran and the United States had continued relatively undisturbed. The new American president, however, deeply committed to the cause of human rights, criticized the Shah and pressed him to institute reforms. Political prisoners, the President demanded, should be given a fair trial and set free if found not guilty. Human rights abuses, President Carter declared in the United Nations, would no longer be the offending nation's exclusive domestic business. The United States would punish the offenders by cooling off relations. Iran was one of many nations that Amnesty International had described as "serious violators of human rights." The Shah, shaken by these criticisms emanating from his ally, embarked on a program of liberalization. By November 1977 "the police-state atmosphere had altered drastically to a mood of vastly greater individual freedom and relaxation."[15] This very loosening of controls, however, emboldened the Shah's enemies and prepared the ground for revolution.

The American President did not seem to be aware of the coming revolution in Iran. No one in Washington, including the Central Intelligence Agency, expected the Shah to fall. It was generally assumed that the liberalization moves would save and strengthen the regime. Besides, Carter had begun to realize the Shah's importance as an ally. Muhammad Reza Pahlevi had been an unconditional friend of the United States for thirty-seven years. He had sold the Americans oil during the Arab embargo of 1973; he had even sold Israel oil; he had provided the United States a listening post on the Soviet border; he had refueled the American fleet without question; he had bought aircraft and technology from American firms and paid cash; and he had been a staunch anti-Communist. Accordingly, Jimmy Carter, on New Year's Eve 1978, visited the Shah in Teheran and made the following statement: "Iran, because of the great leadership of the Shah, is an island of stability in a turbulent sea."[16] He also spoke effusively about the "love and admiration" which the Iranian people apparently gave to their leader. A week later, on January 7, 1978, the first riots erupted that, one year later, were to seal the doom of the Pahlevi dynasty.

During most of 1978, the year of the Shah's slide to oblivion, Jimmy Carter temporized. Had he remained consistent and continued to press on for human rights, the new revolutionary government might have been more friendly when it came to power. Alternatively, a show of force by the United States including military aid might just possibly have saved the Shah. As it turned out, Carter's policy of vacillation got him the worst of both worlds. It did not save the Shah nor did it save his victims while he ruled Iran. Henry Kissinger, in early 1979, added the final touch: "A foreign policy that makes human rights its cornerstone, invites revolution." Jimmy Carter did not have an answer. The Iranian tragedy, more starkly perhaps than any other case, showed up the dilemma of human rights and naked power. By year's end, desperate emotions had swept events beyond the possibility of compromise.

On November 4, 1979, with the Shah mortally ill in a New York hospital, the United States endured one of the worst humiliations in its history. Iranian militants seized the American embassy in Teheran and held ninety-eight persons hostage, demanding that the United States return the deposed Shah and make restitution on the wealth that he had "stolen" from Iran. The seizure of embassy personnel in their own compound had few precedents in the annals of diplomacy and was in clear violation of all established norms of international law. As anti-American fervor rose to a fever pitch in Teheran, with President Carter burnt in effigy as the "Great Satan," the Ayatollah Khomeini gave his blessing to the seizure of the hostages. Under the new Islamic Constitution, Khomeini had just been given "supreme power for life" over Iran. The eyes of the world now were on the United States.

President Carter responded cautiously. Unwilling to risk the lives of the hostages, he took no military action. Instead, he halted oil imports from Iran, froze Iranian assets in the United States, and called on the United Nations for assistance. Khomeini decided to release women and blacks, leaving fifty-three Americans held captive. In January 1980 the UN Security Council, by a vote of

11 to 0, demanded the release of the hostages without delay. One of the four abstaining nations was the Soviet Union, which complained that the tone of the resolution was "too belligerent." The Soviet delegate failed to note that, while he spoke, Russian tanks were rolling into Afghanistan.

The geopolitical effects of the Shah's demise were now becoming evident. The loss of Iran as a reliable Western ally had no doubt emboldened the Soviet Union when contemplating the possible costs of the invasion of Afghanistan. If the United States would not move to save a valuable friend, why should it move to save a neutral country? The conviction of the Shah that the United States would not permit events in Iran to run out of control had been shared widely by friends and enemies alike. Now that this assumption had proved to be completely wrong, the Soviet Union drew the logical conclusion. It began to lean toward Iran in its test of wills with the United States. In short, it began to support nationalism—even Moslem fundamentalism—against the "imperialism" of America. When, in late January 1980, the United States asked for economic sanctions against Iran by the UN, the Soviet Union cast a veto, thus preventing any forceful action. The Shah, before his fall, had predicted an "unholy alliance" between the mullahs and the Communists.[17] It seemed that, by 1980, he was not altogether wrong.

The year 1980 was dominated by the hostage crisis. Hopes were in turn raised and dashed. UN Secretary-General Kurt Waldheim went to Teheran only to return empty-handed. "I do not trust this man," Khomeini had said about the Secretary-General. Nor did the Ayatollah agree to see a UN commission of five men who had flown to Teheran. The United States brought its complaint against Iran to the International Court of Justice at The Hague. The Court ordered the captors to release the hostages, but Iran ignored the ruling. Finally, in April 1980, President Carter ordered a helicopter rescue mission, which ended in a debacle in the Iranian desert. The Soviet Union, eager to exploit America's discomfort, accused the President of an "abortive provocation" that could have caused "mass bloodshed and the death of the hostages," lives the Soviets claimed "the president was willing to sacrifice for his election interests." Carter's misadventure not only lowered the United States' esteem throughout the world, but also shifted international attention away from the Soviet Union's invasion of Afghanistan.[18] Once again, the Soviet Union had exploited the struggle between Iran and the United States for it own purposes.

The Shah's death in July 1980 had no effect upon the situation. One of the hostages had been released by Khomeini for reasons of health, leaving fifty-two captives. Economic sanctions had no impact nor did the war between Iraq and Iran that broke out in the fall. In October there seemed to be some progress. Khomeini announced four conditions for the release of the hostages who, since the rescue attempt, had been dispersed throughout Iran: an American pledge not to interfere, "either directly or indirectly, politically or militarily, in the affairs of the Islamic Republic of Iran"; return of the fortune of "the cursed Shah"; unfreezing of Iranian assets in American banks; and cancellation of U.S. legal and financial claims against Iran.

On November 4, 1980, Jimmy Carter lost the presidential election to

Ronald Reagan. An Iranian offer, made shortly afterward via Algeria, to release the hostages for a payment of $24 billion did little to alleviate the situation. President Carter turned the offer down and Ronald Reagan, the President-elect declared that "the United States would not pay ransom to barbarians."[19] Finally, after a frenzy of negotiations, a deal was struck: the Iranians were to receive their money and the Americans were to get their people back. After $3 billion of Iran's assets were transferred to that nation's central bank, the fifty-two hostages made their flight to freedom on January 20, 1981, Ronald Reagan's Inauguration Day as President. Apparently, the Iranians did not wish to deal with a new American administration that might have taken a much tougher line than that of President Carter.

In retrospect, it became clear how deep the chasm of misunderstanding had been between the United States and Khomeini's Iran. The Americans, basing their claim on the sanctity of embassies and international law, had forgotten that these concepts had their origin in the Judeo-Christian tradition and that revolutionary Iran had not participated in their formulation. Moreover, the Americans had tended to negotiate with their Western-educated counterparts in Iran, overlooking the fact that the real power rested with the Islamic clergy. They had also underestimated the Iranians' fury when the United States admitted the deposed Shah into the country. The Iranians, in turn, had failed to appreciate the United States' commitment to principles of Western diplomacy. Their leaders had little understanding of the way the American government worked. The prime minister, for example, believed that Jimmy Carter's power in the United States was as absolute as that of Khomeini in Iran. Finally, it took several months before the Iranians believed that the United States had not instigated the Iraqi invasion of Iran. Thus, misperception and ignorance of each other's cultures were the real villains in the tragedy of the encounter between Iran and the United States.

Strategically, there was no doubt that the Iranian crisis had weakened the United States and strengthened the Soviet Union. An unconditional ally had become a bitter enemy. Quite suddenly, the United States was compelled to reconsider its strategic posture in the Persian Gulf and to compensate for the loss of Iranian power with American military strength. Terrorists the world over took heart from the example of Iran. The radical Islamic movement, too, gathered momentum. The Soviet Union was probably the biggest winner. Iran had deflected attention from Afghanistan, and Khomeini might have unwittingly prepared the ground for Soviet penetration of his country. The Iraqis, friendly to the Soviets, might be induced to make a common front with the Iranian Communists, the Tudeh party, to prepare the ground for Soviet action. Besides, the Persian Gulf region was in Russia's strategic backyard, with American military might far away and apparently ineffectual. Thus, radical nationalism in Iran had played into the hands of Soviet Russia.

Could the United States have prevented the Iranian fiasco? Possibly. On the one hand, it could have placed strategic power interests above human rights and tried to save the Shah by a show of military force. Conversely, it might have made human rights its cornerstone, refused to embrace the Shah, and welcomed the Islamic revolution. Either way, the United States might have succeeded. But by a policy of vacillation, the United States lost an old ally and had to face a new relentless enemy. Not to choose, as Albert Camus had once said, too, was a choice.

The Lebanese Tragedy

There was a time when Lebanon was a peaceful, happy land, a kind of Middle Eastern Switzerland, with its graceful seaport capital, Beirut, a major tourist attraction. This tranquillity depended on a fine balance between the Moslem and Christian populations of the country. When that balance came unstuck, Lebanon gradually descended into an abyss of devastation. Jealous factions fighting for turf dismembered it piece by bloody piece until it became a country without an effective government. Unable to control its own destinies, Lebanon was drawn into the vortex of both major power struggles in world politics. It became a bitterly divided country, with Beirut a divided city.

After Israel occupied the West Bank in 1967, hundreds of thousands of Palestinians moved to Lebanon over the years, gradually upsetting the country's fragile balance between Moslems and Christians. In 1975 the country erupted in civil war triggered by a round of local murders which were to become typical of the Lebanese scene. Beirut was devastated for the first time. Syria's President Assad, seeing an opportunity for expansion, sent a "peacekeeping" force into Lebanon which became the beginning of the Syrian occupation of central Lebanon. Israel's Premier Begin, apprehensive about Syrian intervention, carved out for Israel a "security strip" in southern Lebanon in 1978. Four years later, in June 1982, Israeli forces invaded Lebanon in full force, all the way to Beirut. Their goal was to drive the Palestinian guerrillas out of southern Lebanon and to counter Syria's growing influence in the wartorn country.

The descent into violence quickened in August when Lebanon's President-elect Bashir Gemayel, head of the Maronite Christian faction, was assassinated by Palestinian terrorists. A few days later, the Christians revenged themselves by killing hundreds of Palestinian civilians in two refugee camps in Sabra and Shatila, with the Israeli army apparently acquiescing in the massacre. Two days after this bloodletting, Amin Gemayel, the brother of the assassinated head of state, was elected President by the Lebanese Parliament.

At this juncture, the United States, fearful that the apparent disintegration of Lebanon might play into Soviet hands, decided to become involved. The Reagan administration worked out an agreement with three of its allies—Britain, France, and Italy—to send about five thousand marines into Lebanon. The objective of this "multinational peace-keeping force" was to monitor the withdrawal of PLO forces from Lebanon and, hopefully, to persuade Israel to pull out so that Syria, too, might withdraw. The United States hoped, in short, that it might be helpful in returning Lebanon to the Lebanese. Unfortunately, this was not to be.

As the Palestinians were evacuated and the Israelis returned West Beirut to Amin Gemayel's forces, the mission of the four-power peace-keeping force became somewhat unclear. Gradually it was redefined as providing support for the Gemayel government. But the young president acted more like the head of the Christian faction than the leader of the entire country and thus the force quickly became identified as pro-Christian and anti-Moslem. A new tragedy was in the making.

In October 1983 a Moslem fanatic drove a truck loaded with explosives, kamikaze-style, into the sleeping quarters of the American marines in Beirut. The vehicle exploded with such force that the structure collapsed in seconds, killing 241 American servicemen. Simultaneously, another suicide mission killed fifty-eight French soldiers, also asleep in their compounds. For the United States this was the highest death toll since Vietnam; for France, the heaviest since the Algerian War.

When looked at in the cold light of political analysis, this dreadful tragedy had all the overtones of the North-South struggle. The Moslem fundamentalists who committed these murders probably perceived the American, British, French, and Italian soldiers not only as partial to the Christian cause in Lebanon but also as the vanguard of a new Western imperialism. After all, these were the very four nations that had engaged in colonial adventures not all that long ago. Lebanon had been a French colony, Libya had belonged to Italy, much of the Middle East to Britain, and the United States was, of course, the main instigator of this renewed colonial intrusion. Islam, especially Shi'ite Islam inspired by Iran, perceived itself as the main bulwark against Western aggression. The murderers were thus not really murderers. They were freedom fighters and their reward would be immediate entry into paradise.

After this catastrophe, the days of the multinational peace-keeping force were numbered. Senator Ernest Hollings of South Carolina put it well when he called on the President to withdraw the marines within sixty days: "If they've been put there to fight then there are far too few," he said, "but if they've been put there to be killed, there are far too many."[20] Accordingly, after some fruitless shellings by the battleship U.S.S. *New Jersey*, the American soldiers were withdrawn from Lebanon in February 1984. Shortly thereafter, their French, British, and Italian fellow-marines too were removed. Lebanon by now was a carcass, and a dismembered one at that. For all practical purposes, by mid-1984, Lebanon was a divided country, with Beirut a divided city. Within these divisions, there were further factions which made the country look like a crazy quilt or Chinese puzzle. Nevertheless, in a very rough sort of way, these factions tended to fall, either directly or indirectly, along East-West lines. On the Western side were the Israeli forces stationed in southern Lebanon, now left to fend for themselves after the American withdrawal. The Maronite Christians and, to a somewhat lesser extent, the Sunni Moslems, were not unfriendly to Israel and the Western cause. On the other side, Druze and Shi'ite Moslems, supported the Syrian presence, which in turn was backed by the Soviet Union. President Gemayel, virtually powerless after the pullout of the Western forces, had to accept the indefinite presence of the Syrians and even felt compelled to host a Soviet delegation in Beirut. When, in early 1985,

Israel began to withdraw its troops from Lebanon, Gemayel's hold on power became even more precarious and the Syrian threat even more ominous.

After the American fiasco in Beirut, it appeared that Lebanon, not unlike Germany and Korea, might have to settle for a permanent partition, with that partition probably congealing along East-West lines. Thus, once again the linkage between the two great power struggles in the world became manifest: a North-South collision led to an East-West partition in a tragic and dismembered land.

Our analysis has shown that the two paramount political struggles of our time are being waged between the old and the new nations and between the Communist and the Western nations. Most of the world's nations are engaged in one of these two conflicts, many in both. Hence, there has emerged a web of global political interdependence, though each specific issue has produced its own alignment of forces.

The revolutionary upheavals in China during the last hundred years demonstrate that the Chinese struggle against Western imperialism during the nineteenth century provided the seedbed for the Communist Revolution. Indeed, in historical perspective, it becomes clear that Chinese communism is but the most recent phase of the Chinese nationalist reaction against the coming of the West. It was the end product of the Chinese struggle for self-assertion. In China, therefore, the pattern of interdependence appears as a continuum: the East-West conflict actually grew out of the struggle between Chinese nationalism and Western imperialism.

The Middle East crises also exhibit the continuum pattern, though over a much shorter interval of time. They began as local conflicts between competing forms of nationalism: the Arab states and Israel in the Middle East. This conflict between competing forms of nationalism ushered in the next stage: nationalism versus colonialism. The 1956 Suez Canal crisis precipitated a violent eruption between Arab nationalism and the two colonial powers, Britain and France. During the 1967 war, the Arabs tended to perceive Israel as the vanguard of Western imperialism backed by the United States and Britain. And in 1973 they punished the United States with a political weapon of nationalist self-assertion: the oil embargo. Finally, the East-West conflict entered the picture as the last of three widening concentric circles: the Soviet Union gained influence in the Middle East by taking the Arab side while the United States, caught between its oil dependency on the Arabs and its allegiance to Israel, adopted a policy of balance.

Once both political struggles were involved, the linkage pattern became one of mutual exploitation. Nationalists used the East-West struggle to shore up their position, and the Soviet Union used the new nationalism to further its own ends. Nevertheless, the very conditions that gave rise to this multifaceted struggle for power also provided the opportunity for the strengthening of international order. The two superpowers, despite their divergent interests in the Middle East, permitted the establishment of United Nations peace forces in the Middle East after the Suez crisis of 1956 and the October War of 1973.

The struggle for power and the struggle for order both found their nourishment in the same soil.

In the Iranian events of 1980, the Soviet Union used the resurgence of Islam for its own benefit. It is very likely that American acquiescence in the Shah's destruction weighed heavily in Soviet plans to smash into Afghanistan. The Soviet leadership may have reasoned, quite correctly, that if the United States failed to sustain an ally, it would certainly not help a neutral nation. Subsequently, in the tug of war between Carter and Khomeini over the hostages, the Kremlin leaned more and more toward the latter. It did so because it may have perceived yet another opening. Iran might be so weakened by Western economic sanctions and by the war with neighboring Iraq that it could be ripe for Soviet penetration and ultimate absorption. The United States, not having helped the Shah, would probably not risk a war over Iran. The lesson seemed quite clear. It was not written in the stars that Third World countries would necessarily favor the Soviet Union over the United States, but a policy of drift by America in its relations with Third World countries played into Russian hands. This may yet be the central lesson of Iran.

And in Lebanon in the 1980s, the linkage once again appeared as a continuum. The United States, fearful of Syrian and Soviet intentions, injected itself into the picture and thus precipitated a suicide mission of anti-Christian, anti-Western fanatics. The subsequent American decision to withdraw left Lebanon temporarily divided between Israeli and Syrian occupation troops, that is to say, proxies of the United States and the Soviet Union. Thus, Lebanon became the stage for both power struggles that make up the great global political drama.

As the twentieth century nears its end, the web of interdependence between the two great political struggles has become truly universal. The 1950s saw it expand into Asia; the 1960s and 1970s saw it move into the Middle East and Africa; and in the 1980s, it reaches into the remotest corners of the globe. The international struggle for power among nations in our time has indeed become a one-world struggle.

One important difference between the two struggles may suggest something about their ultimate resolution. In the East-West conflict the two sides have fought to a kind of stalemate, whereas in the North-South struggle the forces of anticolonialism have virtually achieved victory. It is quite conceivable that the East-West conflict will still be with us in the next generation, but it is almost certain that the struggle over colonialism is about to become history.

REFERENCES

1. Thomas A. Bailey, *A Diplomatic History of the American People.* 4th ed. New York: Appleton-Century-Crofts, 1950, p. 520.
2. John K. Fairbank and Ssu-yu Teng, *China's Response to the West.* Cambridge, Mass.: Harvard University Press, 1954, p. 19.

3. *Ibid.*, p. 25.
4. John K. Fairbank, *The United States and China.* Cambridge, Mass.: Harvard University Press, 1958, p. 142.
5. *Ibid.*, p. 143.
6. *Ibid.*
7. For an excellent description and perceptive analysis of this period, see Conrad Brandt, *Stalin's Failure in China.* Cambridge, Mass.: Harvard University Press, 1958.
8. Edgar Snow, *Red Star Over China.* New York: Random House, 1938, *passim.*
9. *Full Circle: The Memoirs of Anthony Eden,* quoted by Herbert Feis in *Foreign Affairs,* July 1960, p. 600.
10. Inis L. Claude, Jr., *Swords into Plowshares.* 2nd ed. New York: Random House, 1959, p. 460.
11. Mohammed Reza Pahlevi, *Answer to History.* Briarcliff Manor, N.Y.: Stein and Day, 1980, p. 175.
12. *Ibid.*, p. 176.
13. *Ibid.*, p. 158.
14. *Ibid.*
15. *Time,* November 15, 1977.
16. *The New York Times,* January 1, 1978.
17. Pahlevi, *op. cit.*, pp. 145–174.
18. *Time,* May 5, 1980, p. 14.
19. *The New York Times,* December 29, 1980.
20. *Time,* October 31, 1983, p. 18.

BIBLIOGRAPHY

Abrahamian, Ervand. *Iran: Between Two Revolutions.* Princeton, N.J.: Princeton University Press, 1982.
Badri, H.; Magdoub, T.; and Zohdy, M. D. *The Ramadan War, 1973.* Dunn Loring, Va.: Dupuy, 1978.
Barnds, William J. *India, Pakistan and the Great Powers.* New York: Praeger, 1972.
Barnett, A. Doak. *Communist China and Asia: Challenge to American Foreign Policy.* New York: Harper, 1960.
————. *Communist China: The Early Years, 1949–55.* New York: Praeger, 1964.
Baum, Richard, ed. *China's Four Modernizations: The New Technological Revolution.* Boulder, Colo.: Westview Press, 1980.
Beal, John R. *Marshall in China.* Garden City, N.Y.: Doubleday, 1970.
Bonavia, David. *The Chinese.* New York: Lippincott and Crowell, 1980.
————. *Verdict in Peking: The Trial of the Gang of Four.* New York: Putnam, 1984.
Braddon, Russell. *Suez: Splitting of a Nation.* London: Collins, 1973.
Breacher, Michael. *Decisions in Crisis: Israel, 1967 and 1973.* Berkeley: University of California Press, 1980.
Brzezinski, Zibigniew. *The Fragile Blossom: Crisis and Change in Japan.* New York: Harper & Row, 1972.
Butterfield, Fox. *China: Alive in the Bitter Sea.* New York: Times Books, 1982.
Buttinger, Joseph. *Vietnam: A Dragon Embattled,* Vols I and II. New York: Praeger, 1967.
Chalaind, Gerard. *The Struggle For Africa: Conflict of the Great Powers.* New York: St. Martin's, 1982.
Choudhury, G. W. *India, Pakistan, Bangladesh and the Major Powers: Politics of a Divided Subcontinent.* New York: Free Press, 1975.

Chung, Chin O. *Pyongyang Between Peking and Moscow*. University: University of Alabama Press, 1978.

Cleveland, Harlan, and Goodpaster, Andrew J. *After Afghanistan—The Long Haul: Safeguarding Security and Independence in the Third World*. Boulder, Colo.: Westview Press, 1980.

Clissold, Stephen, ed. *Soviet Relations with Latin America 1918–1968*. New York: Oxford University Press, 1970.

Clough, Ralph N. *Island China*. Cambridge, Mass.: Harvard University Press, 1978.

Clutterbuck, Richard. *Kidnap and Ransom: The Response*. London and Boston: Faber, 1978.

Copper, John Franklin. *China's Global Role*. Stanford, Calif.: Hoover Institution Press, 1980.

Crawshaw, Nancy. *The Cyprus Revolt*. London and Boston: Allen and Unwin, 1978.

Crosbie, Sylvia K. *A Tacit Alliance: France and Israel from Suez to the Six Day War*. Princeton, N.J.: Princeton University Press, 1974.

Dawisha, Adeed, ed. *Islam in Foreign Policy*. New York: Cambridge University Press, 1984.

Donaldson, Robert H., ed. *The Soviet Union in the Third World: Successes and Failures*. Boulder, Colo.: Westview Press, 1981.

Dupuy, Trevor N. *Elusive Victory: The Arab-Israeli Wars, 1947–1974*. New York: Harper, 1978.

Esherick, Joseph W., ed. *Lost Chance in China: The World War II Dispatches of John S. Service*. New York: Random House, 1974.

Fairbank, John K. *China Perceived: Images and Policies in Chinese-American Relations*. New York: Knopf, 1974.

———. *The United States and China*. 4th ed. Cambridge, Mass.: Harvard University Press, 1978.

Fall, Bernard B. *The Two Vietnams*. New York: Praeger, 1967.

Fitzgerald, C. P. *Mao Tse-tung and China*. New York: Holmes and Meier, 1976.

Freedman, Robert O. *Soviet Policy toward the Middle East since 1970*. New York: Praeger, 1975.

Gittings, John. *The Role of the Chinese Army*. New York: Oxford University Press, 1967.

———. *The World and China, 1922–1972*. New York: Harper & Row, 1974.

Gordon, King. *UN in the Congo*. New York: Carnegie Endowment for International Peace, 1962.

Gouré, Leon, and Rothenberg, Morris. *Soviet Penetration of Latin America*. Miami: University of Miami Press, 1975.

Grose, Peter. *Israel in the Mind of America*. New York: Knopf, 1983.

Guillermaz, Jacques. *A History of the Chinese Communist Party*. New York: Random House, 1972.

Gurtov, Melvin. *The First Vietnam Crisis*. New York: Columbia University Press, 1967.

Haley, Edward P. *Qaddafi and the United States Since 1969*. New York: Praeger, 1984.

Heikal, Mohamed. *Iran: The Untold Story*. New York: Pantheon, 1982.

Hsu, Immanuel C. Y. *China Without Mao: The Search for a New Order*. New York: Oxford University Press, 1983.

Hurewitz, J. C. *Soviet-American Rivalry in the Middle East*. New York: Praeger, 1969.

Jackson, D. Bruce. *Castro, the Kremlin and Communism in Latin America*. Baltimore: Johns Hopkins Press, 1969.

Jackson, Robert. *South Asian Crisis: India, Pakistan and Bangladesh*. New York: Praeger, 1975.

Johnson, Cecil. *Communist China and Latin America, 1959–1967*. New York: Columbia University Press, 1970.

Kahn, E. J., Jr. *The China Hands: America's Foreign Service Officers and What Befell Them.* New York: Viking, 1975.

Kanet, Roger E., ed. *The Soviet Union and the Developing Nations.* Baltimore: Johns Hopkins Press, 1974.

Kautsky, John H. *Political Change in Underdeveloped Countries: Nationalism and Communism.* New York: Wiley, 1962.

Keyserlingk, Robert Wendelin. *The Dragon's Wrath.* New York: Vantage Press, 1982.

Klieman, Aaron S. *Soviet Russia and the Middle East.* Baltimore: Johns Hopkins Press, 1970.

Klinghoffer, Arthur Jay. *The Angolan War: A Study in Soviet Policy in the Third World.* Boulder, Colo.: Westview Press, 1980.

Kohler, Troy D.; Govre, Leon; and Harvey, Mose L. *The Soviet Union and the October 1973 Middle East War: The Implications for Detente.* Washington, D.C.: Center for Advanced International Studies, University of Miami, 1974.

Lacouture, Jean. *Vietnam Between Two Truces.* New York: Random House, 1965.

Laqueur, Walter. *Confrontation: The Middle East and World Politics.* New York: Quadrangle, 1974.

———. *The Pattern of Soviet Conduct in the Third World.* New York: Praeger, 1983.

———. *The Soviet Union and the Middle East.* Baltimore: Johns Hopkins Press, 1970.

Ledeen, Michael, and Lewis, William. *Debacle: The American Failure in Iran.* New York: Knopf, 1981.

Legum, Colin; Zartman, I. William; Mylelka, Lynn K.; and Langdon, Steven. *Africa in the 1980s: A Continent in Crisis.* New York: McGraw-Hill, 1979.

Legvold, Robert. *Soviet Policy in West Africa.* Cambridge, Mass.: Harvard University Press, 1970.

Leys, Simon. *Chinese Shadows.* New York: Viking, 1977.

Lilienthal, Alfred M. *The Zionist Connection: What Price Peace?* New York: Dodd, Mead, 1978.

Lloyd, Selwyn. *Suez 1956: A Personal Account.* London: Jonathan Cape/New York: Mayflower Books, 1979.

Loh, Pichon P. Y. *The Early Chiang Kai-shek.* New York: Columbia University Press, 1971.

Lustik, Ian. *Arabs in the Jewish State: Israel's Control of a National Minority.* Austin: University of Texas Press, 1980.

Mancall, Mark. *China at the Center.* New York: Free Press, 1984.

Maxwell, Neville. *India's China War.* New York: Pantheon, 1971.

McLaurin, R. D. *The Middle East in Soviet Policy.* Lexington, Mass.: Lexington Books, 1976.

Meisner, Maurice. *Mao's China: A History of the People's Republic.* New York: Free Press, 1977.

Neff, Donald. *Warriors at Suez: Eisenhower Takes America into the Middle East.* New York: Linden Press/Simon and Schuster, 1981.

Nutting, Anthony. *No End of a Lesson: The Story of Suez.* New York: Potter, 1967.

Palmer, Norman D., and Shao Chuan Leng. *Sun Yat-sen and Communism.* New York: Praeger, 1960.

Pennar, Jaan. *The U.S.S.R. and the Arabs: The Ideological Dimension.* New York: Crane, Russak, 1973.

Pipes, Daniel. *In the Path of God: Islam and Political Power.* New York: Basic Books, 1983.

Ponchaud, François. *Cambodia Year Zero.* New York: Holt, Rinehart and Winston, 1978.

Quandt, William B. *Decade of Decisions: American Policy Toward the Arab-Israeli Conflict, 1967–1976.* Berkeley: University of California Press, 1977.

Ramazani, R. K. *The Persian Gulf and the Strait of Hormuz.* Alphen aan den Rijn, Netherlands: Sijthoff, 1979.

Rawski, Thomas G. *China's Transition to Industrialism.* Ann Arbor: University of Michigan Press, 1980.

Roosevelt, Kermit. *Countercoup: The Struggle for the Control of Iran.* New York: McGraw-Hill, 1980.

Rubin, Jeffrey Z., ed. *Dynamics of Third Party Intervention: Kissinger in the Middle East.* New York: Praeger, 1981.

Rubinstein, Alvin Z. *Soviet Policy Toward Turkey, Iran, and Afghanistan.* New York: Praeger, 1982.

———, ed. *The Great Game: Rivalry in the Persian Gulf and South Asia.* New York: Praeger, 1983.

———. *Red Star on the Nile: The Soviet-Egyptian Relationship Since the June War.* Princeton, N.J.: Princeton University Press, 1977.

Safran, Nadav. *Israel: The Embattled Ally.* Cambridge, Mass.: Harvard University Press, 1978.

———. *The United States and Israel.* Cambridge, Mass.: Harvard University Press, 1963.

Sainteny, Jean. *Ho Chi Minh and His Vietnam.* Chicago: Cowles, 1972.

Schwartz, Benjamin I. *Chinese Communism and the Rise of Mao.* Cambridge, Mass.: Harvard University Press, 1951.

Selden, Mark. *The Yenan Way in Revolutionary China.* Cambridge, Mass.: Harvard University Press, 1971.

Sheehan, Edward R. *The Arabs, Israelis and Kissinger: A Secret History of American Diplomacy in the Middle East.* New York: Reader's Digest Press, 1976.

Short, Philip. *The Dragon and the Bear: Inside China and Russia Today.* New York: Morrow, 1983.

Shwadran, Benjamin. *The Middle East, Oil, and the Great Powers.* 3rd ed., rev. New York: Halsted Press, 1973.

Singh, Lalita Prasad. *Power Politics and Southeast Asia.* Atlantic Highlands, N.J.: Humanities Press, 1980.

Stevens, Christopher. *The Soviet Union and Black Africa.* New York: Holmes and Meier, 1976.

Sullivan, William H. *Mission to Iran.* New York: Norton, 1981.

Thomas, Hugh. *Cuba: The Pursuit of Freedom.* New York: Harper & Row, 1971.

———. *Suez.* New York: Harper & Row, 1967.

Thomas, Raju G. C., ed. *The Great-Power Triangle and Asian Security.* Lexington, Mass.: Lexington Books, 1983.

Tillman, Seth P. *The United States in the Middle East.* Bloomington: Indiana University Press, 1982.

Tuchman, Barbara W. *Stilwell and the American Experience in China, 1911–45.* New York: Macmillan, 1971.

Whiting, Allen S. *China Crosses the Yalu.* New York: Macmillan, 1960.

Wiles, Peter, ed. *The New Communist Third World.* New York: St. Martin's, 1982.

Wilson, Dick. *The Long March 1935: The Epic of Chinese Communism's Survival.* New York: Viking, 1972.

Yahuda, Michael. *Towards the End of Isolationism: China's Foreign Policy After Mao.* New York: St. Martin's, 1984.

Zagoria, Donald, ed. *Soviet Policy in East Asia.* New Haven, Conn.: Yale University Press, 1982.

Chapter 6

The Military
Struggle for Power

Blood and destruction shall be so in use,
And dreadful objects so familiar,
That mothers shall but smile when they behold
Their infants quartered with the hands of war.

SHAKESPEARE *Julius Caesar*, III, 2

THE EAST-WEST MILITARY STRUGGLE

Since the coming of the nuclear age, it has sometimes been said that war has become rationally unthinkable and therefore impossible. This assertion is untrue. It is based on the false premise that whatever is too horrible cannot happen. And it erroneously assumes that men always act rationally and that pathological behavior—like that of Hitler—was abruptly ended with the discovery of atomic power. The truth is that atomic warfare *is* a possibility. Atomic power, like other discoveries of genius, is inherently amoral. It is merely an instrument that in itself in no way guarantees human progress. How it is used—whether for welfare or for warfare—depends entirely on human choice and direction.

The founders of the United Nations did indeed nurture the hope that the birth of the world organization would usher in a brave new world in which alliances and counteralliances, power politics and aggressive war could at last be thrown into the garbage can of history. It was widely believed that the principle of collective security, if rigorously applied, would at last render these age-old international maneuvers superfluous. The meaning of this principle was nothing less than that international relations should henceforth be governed by "the rule of all for one and one for all." There would be no more Ethiopias and no more Munichs. The overwhelming military power of the world community would be arrayed against aggression. Collective security was to be indifferent to traditional alliances, friendships, or animosities. It was to act impartially and anonymously. Indeed, it was hoped that the collective security principle would completely supersede all old-fashioned alliances.

Actually, these hopes were never realized. The Great Power veto in the

UN Security Council served as a clear reminder that the United Nations was not to have the function of mobilizing collective security against major aggressors. The intensification of the East-West struggle and the post–World War II gains made by the Soviet Union in Eastern Europe starkly pointed up this limitation. By 1947 the West had found to its dismay that the principle of collective security could not in practice be applied to check further Communist expansion. In the absence of real unanimity among the Great Powers, the Security Council unanimity rule threatened to make a mockery of the collective security ideal. As a result of this blighting of the great hopes earlier entertained for the UN, there occurred a return to "selective security," a devolution of military responsibility for keeping the peace from the United Nations to regional and bilateral arrangements. A military struggle of unprecedented magnitude began to take shape between East and West. And in this struggle for preponderance there soon emerged a vast network of alliances and counteralliances. We shall now turn to a description and analysis of these alliance systems.

Until 1947 the United States had consistently avoided "entangling alliances," heeding the warning of its first President. But the absorption of most of Eastern Europe into the Soviet orbit elicited in the United States a profound fear of Soviet domination of all Europe. The growing conviction that the American national interest lay in the defense of Europe against communism led to the abandonment of the "go it alone" policy. In March 1947 the President proclaimed the Truman Doctrine, offering American support to "free peoples who [were] resisting attempted subjugation by armed minorities or by outside pressures."[1] This doctrine was applied immediately in the cases of Greece and Turkey, which were threatened by Soviet infiltration. The successful Communist coup in Czechoslovakia in the following year resulted in the traditional American policy of nonalliance being reversed altogether. In April 1949, in the North Atlantic Treaty, the United States committed itself to the proposition that a military attack upon any one of ten Western European countries or on Canada would be considered as an attack on the United States. The NATO Treaty became the first expression of a revolutionary American policy of collective defense. In the words of President Truman, it was "the first peacetime military alliance entered into by the United States since the adoption of the Constitution."[2] Thus, ironically enough, the age of collective security ushered in for the United States an age of alliances, of checking power with counterpower. The Rio Treaty, or Inter-American Treaty of Reciprocal Assistance, which the United States had signed in 1947 with her sister republics in Latin America, was not, strictly speaking, a military alliance although it was alliancelike in its external orientation. It served to transform the traditional Monroe Doctrine into a multilateral arrangement and established machinery for the settlement of hemispheric disputes.

Communist activity in the Far East, especially the outbreak of the Korean War, resulted in a quest for further allies. In 1951 the United States entered into bilateral security arrangements with Japan and the Philippines. In the same year, the ANZUS Treaty linking the United States to Australia and New

Zealand was concluded. After the end of hostilities in Korea, a treaty of mutual defense with the Republic of Korea was added. The French loss of Indochina and Communist absorption of North Vietnam caused the extension of the Western alliance system to Southeast Asia in the form of the Southeast Asia Treaty Organization (SEATO), signed at Manila in 1954. SEATO included the ANZUS countries, two NATO countries (Britain and France), and three Asian countries (Pakistan, the Philippines, and Thailand). Vietnam, Laos, and Cambodia did not become signatories but were given SEATO "protection." In December 1954 the United States concluded a mutual defense treaty with the Nationalist Chinese government on Formosa.

By then, only the Middle East was excluded from the Western alliance system. In 1955 Britain, Turkey, Iraq, Iran, and Pakistan joined in the Baghdad Pact. The United States did not technically become a member, since many Arab states considered the pact an oblique attack on Arab unity, but in effect the United States was a mainstay of the new alliance. When, as a result of the Suez fiasco, British and French authority in the Middle East reached a new nadir and communism gained its first foothold in the Arab world, the Eisenhower Doctrine, promulgated in March 1957, attempted to salvage Western interests in the Middle East. This doctrine suggested that the United States might "use armed force to assist any nation or group of nations requesting assistance against armed aggression from any country controlled by international Communism."[3] In the words of Secretary of State Dulles, the doctrine had "as much effectiveness as membership in the Baghdad Pact."[4] In July 1958 Iraq seceded from the pact as a result of an internal revolution. The alliance continued to exist, however, under the new name of Central Treaty Organization (CENTO).

By the mid-1960s the United States had bilateral or regional military alliances with forty-two nations: the Organization of American States (OAS) had twenty-one members; NATO, with the addition of West Germany in 1955, comprised fifteen signatories; SEATO included eight nations; and finally, the bilateral arrangements with Japan, South Korea, and Formosa complete the list. In addition to these formal military commitments, SEATO extended its "protection" to three Southeast Asian countries, and the Eisenhower Doctrine offered assistance to the nations of the Middle East. In a little over a decade the United States had thus changed from a "go it alone" policy to an alliance system of "going it with forty-two others."

Like the West, the Soviet Union also sought military allies. During the years following World War II it entered bilateral security arrangements with the seven Eastern European countries that had been absorbed into the Soviet orbit. It also became a party to a multilateral alliance, the Conference of European Powers for the Assurance of Peace and Security in Europe, better known as the Warsaw Pact. This union, established in 1955, linked the Soviet Union in a military pact with its seven Eastern European allies. It was intended as a riposte to the North Atlantic Treaty and, indeed, was practically a carbon copy of NATO. Both provided that an armed attack upon one nation was an attack upon all; and in both, the commitment was to render such assistance, including armed assistance, as was deemed necessary. The Soviet rationale for the Warsaw Pact was that the inclusion of a rearmed West Germany in NATO made a Soviet defensive alliance absolutely essential. In 1950 the Soviet Union concluded another bilateral mutual assistance treaty, this one with the new Communist government on mainland China.

Both East and West consistently described their respective military alliance systems as purely defensive in character. Thus, in the West's view, NATO was conceived as a reaction to Communist expansion, with no aggressive designs whatsoever. In the Soviet view, however, NATO was an "aggressive, imperialist bloc" of hostile nations whose military alliances extended over most of the world and who—most terribly of all from the viewpoint of the Soviet Union—went so far as to rearm West Germany. Conversely, the West tended to think of the Warsaw Pact as a "collective Communist menace," the military arm of the aggressive design of international communism.

By the mid-1960s two military blocs of unprecedented power and destructive capacity faced each other across a chasm of apparently unbridgeable political differences. Each claimed to be a purely defensive instrument against a war that neither wanted. Each was engaged in a gigantic arms race which was to deter the other from starting such a war. And, most important, each of the two superpowers leading the respective alliance systems had at its disposal an arsenal of atomic weapons powerful enough to devastate most of the civilized world. We shall now turn to a specific analysis of the Western and Soviet alliance systems and the relationship between them.

NATO: The West's Main Military Alliance in the Nuclear Age

The North Atlantic Pact, concluded in 1949, bound together twelve states of the Atlantic community: the United States, Britain, France, Canada, Italy, Portugal, Norway, Denmark, Iceland, Belgium, Holland, and Luxembourg. Greece and Turkey joined the alliance in September 1952 and West Germany's accession in 1955 brought the total membership to fifteen. The chief political arm of NATO has been its Permanent Council, composed of representatives of all the member states at the ministerial level. Its military organization consists of a Military Committee made up of the Chiefs of Staff of all NATO members. NATO's principal purpose has been the defense of Western Europe, which has been the responsibility of the Supreme Headquarters Allied Powers Europe (SHAPE). The secretariat of NATO, like the United Nations Secretariat, has employed an international staff headed by a Secretary-General.

The United States has clearly been the leading member of the alliance. Arnold Wolfers has aptly applied the analogy of a wheel to describe the relationship of the United States to its partners in NATO. "The friends and allies of the United States are spread out along its rim each occupying the end of a spoke, while the United States is located at the hub of the wheel."[5] Thus, danger to any allied country, Denmark or Turkey for example, would be communicated to the United States at the center but not necessarily to other states on the rim. Any action emanating from the hub, however, would affect the entire wheel. The United States had consistently viewed itself as the main "producer" of security, while casting most of its allies in NATO into the role of "consumers."

While NATO had doubtless been the most powerful of the Western military alliances, there have been problems and tensions which, at times, have seriously threatened the cohesion of the pact. These problems have tended to fall into three categories: political, military, and economic. The political tensions have arisen from divergent national aims and policies pursued by the chief members of the alliance; the military problems have been primarily of a strategic nature raised, above all, by the unprecedented dilemmas posed by the discovery of nuclear power; and new economic challenges confronted NATO as a direct result of the energy crisis.

The struggle over colonialism was responsible for some political schisms in NATO. As we have seen earlier, the United States considered the East-West struggle as paramount, but this view was not always shared by all of its NATO allies. The Suez crisis of 1956 illustrated this dilemma in all its stark contours. The United States voted against its two closest military allies, Britain and France, and paradoxically found itself aligned in the United Nations with the very power against which it had called NATO into existence. By preferring collective security through the United Nations to selective security via NATO, the United States seriously jeopardized the unity of the alliance. Although Britain and France in effect had no choice but to remain in NATO, Anglo-French resentment was so considerable that a major operation had to be launched in order to retighten the bonds of the pact. Indeed, the Suez crisis might well have led to NATO's disintegration. What if the British and French had not recoiled before the fact of a united world public opinion and had persisted—against the will of the United States—in their attempt to destroy the Egyptian government by force? Such a course might have left Britain and France no choice but to withdraw from the alliance.

The colonial struggle, like a hydra-headed monster, also tended to rise in other parts of the world to haunt the American leadership of NATO. Thus the United States found itself embarrassed by a protracted dispute between India and Portugal over Goa, and by another longstanding quarrel between the Netherlands and Indonesia over the disposition of West New Guinea. In both cases, NATO allies were involved. When India annexed the Portuguese enclave by force in 1961, the United States did protest, but was severely criticized by India for doing so. And when in the same year the United States voted against Portugal in the United Nations on the issue of Angola, Portugal threatened to evict the United States from its base in the Azores. Similarly, the United States was caught in the middle of the Dutch-Indonesian dispute, though in this case conciliation attempts of an American intermediary and the peaceful transfer in 1963 of West New Guinea to Indonesia with the help of the United Nations prevented an actual outbreak of hostilities.

Two military conflicts with colonial overtones in the Third World caused the United States particular embarrassment in its role as alliance leader.

In 1982 Argentina, under the leadership of a military junta, invaded the Falkland Islands in the South Atlantic. These bleak wind-swept islands off the Argentine coast were a British possession, but had long been claimed by Argentina as the "Malvinas Islands." The junta hoped to deflect the Argentinians' attention from inflation and other domestic miseries by whipping up patriotic fervor against "British colonialism."

To the junta's surprise and dismay, the British decided not to be humiliated once again. Prime Minister Margaret Thatcher, in a show of force, dispatched the fleet from Plymouth on an eight-thousand-mile voyage to reconquer the Falkland Islands.

The United States, caught in the middle between its NATO ally, Britain, and its OAS ally, Argentina, found itself dreadfully embarrassed. While the British fleet was steaming toward the South Atlantic, Secretary of State Alexander Haig shuttled between London and Buenos Aires in a desperate effort to find a compromise solution. The mission was a failure and the United States finally had to take a stand. Responding to Mrs. Thatcher's statement that "if the United States did not support its ally, although its cause was just, then the alliance was useless," the Reagan administration decided to tilt toward Great Britain. Shortly thereafter, British marines landed on the two islands and, after some brief though bloody fighting, overcame the Argentinians and restored British rule. The sun had not yet set completely on the Empire after all.

The United States, needless to say, was loudly cheered in London and roundly cursed by the junta in Buenos Aires, which, not surprisingly, fell from power soon afterward. Secretary Haig, haunted by his failure, resigned in 1983 and was replaced by George Shultz. Even thirty-five years after the birth of NATO and OAS, the United States found it difficult to keep the peace between its squabbling allies.

A somewhat different colonial dilemma arose in the Caribbean not too long after the Falklands crisis. On March 23, 1983, President Reagan showed a reconnaissance photo of a runway on an airfield in Grenada and warned the American people:

> On the small island of Grenada ... the Cubans, with Soviet financing and backing, are in the process of building an airfield with a 10,000 foot runway. Grenada doesn't even have an air force. Who is it intended for? ... More than half of all American oil imports now pass through the Caribbean. ... The Soviet-Cuban militarization of Grenada can only be seen as a power projection into the region.[6]

Seven months later, the United States invaded Grenada. Ostensibly, the administration claimed that the action was a rescue mission to extricate a thousand medical students who might have become hostages of an unsavory junta whose leader had just murdered Grenada's Prime Minister Maurice Bishop. Fearful of this violent turn of events, several members of the Organization of Eastern Caribbean States appealed to the United States to act at once.

Even though the military operation was a complete success, several NATO and OAS allies expressed strong objections. Margaret Thatcher, who learned of the invasion only after it was well under way, was incensed. Many European leaders expressed deep concern about the "trigger-happiness" of the American President. Latin Americans talked of "Yankee imperialism and gunboat diplomacy."

After the United States marines established control over Grenada, they discovered substantial Soviet and Cuban military equipment. Moreover, a 750-man Cuban "labor" force had shown considerable fighting ability against the marines. On the whole, the Reagan administration was able to present a fairly convincing picture of Grenada as an imminent victim of Cuban and Soviet subversion. Nonetheless, NATO and OAS suspicions lingered for quite some time and outcries against "colonialism" and "gunboat diplomacy" resounded in numerous capitals. While the invasion could not be faulted in practice, America's allies did criticize it in principle. It took several months before the Latin Americans and Europeans calmed down, and then probably only because the last American marines were withdrawn from Grenada by December 1983. The "colonial" action had not only succeeded, it had succeeded quickly, and Grenada was restored to self-rule after two months.

The second set of problems confronting the American leadership of NATO has been concerned with the challenge of nuclear power. The problem may be divided into the two related issues of atomic sharing and devising a viable nuclear strategy. So long as the United States possessed a monopoly of nuclear power, most American military thinkers tended to base NATO's primary defense against the Soviet Union upon the concept of atomic deterrence. Fear of atomic retaliation, it was hoped, would prevent Communist aggression. Sir Winston Churchill expressed this early view when he said in March 1949: "It is certain that Europe would have been communized like Czechoslovakia and London under bombardment some time ago but for the deterrent of the atomic bomb in the hands of the United States."[7]

Secretary of State Dulles, speaking for the United States in January 1954, also placed most of his faith in the Great Deterrent, although he admitted the necessity of local defense with conventional weapons as an auxiliary factor:

> Local defense will always be important. But there is no local defense which alone will contain the mighty landpower of the Communist world. Local defenses must be reinforced by the further deterrent of massive retaliatory power. A potential aggressor must know that he cannot always prescribe battle conditions that suit him. Otherwise, for example, a potential aggressor, who is glutted with manpower, might be tempted to attack in places where his superiority was decisive.
>
> The way to deter aggression is for the free community to be willing and able to respond vigorously at places and with means of its own choosing.[8]

This policy of the Great Deterrent, or reliance upon "massive retaliation" as it came to be called, suggested that a Soviet military attack upon any member of the alliance might be countered with a crippling atomic attack. The essence of this policy was not the stationing of American troops in NATO countries nor even the presence there of American bases, but the commitment itself. The United States intended to spread the strength of its atomic shield over the weakness of its allies and thus place them under virtually invulnerable protection.

For a time this tying of NATO to the American atomic monopoly seemed to give the West a decisive edge in its confrontation with the Soviet Union. But haunting doubts once more began to torment NATO planners. For one thing, it seemed that the massive retaliation strategy was highly inflexible and tended to commit the United States to a kind of "all or nothing" policy. The Great Deterrent seemed an efficient instrument in case of an all-out Soviet attack, but what if the Soviet Union should choose to provoke some more local conflict? Or if it should limit itself to aggression through infiltration? In such cases the Great Deterrent seemed to be a disproportionate application of military force. This in turn raised the question of credibility. If a threat is to be effective, it must be believed or at least considered within the realm of the possible. Would the Soviet Union believe that the United States and NATO would unleash massive retaliation with atomic weapons in case of an East German attack on West Berlin, or of a Soviet attack on Britain? Or would this strategy be invoked only in case of a Soviet attack on the United States itself? Might not the Soviet Union assume that in a showdown the United States would not be able to bring itself actually to use the Great Deterrent? The problem was that the strategy of massive retaliation tended to leave the West too exclusively prepared for a total war—which might seem unwarranted—and too little prepared for aggression of the "nibbling" variety, which was the kind most likely actually to be encountered.

The validity of such fears as to the adequacy of massive retaliation strategy became apparent on three different occasions during the 1950s. Encouraged by the high hopes of the massive retaliation policy, Secretary Dulles announced that NATO's aim of containment of communism was no longer sufficient. To win the East-West struggle, the secretary declared, the United States would embrace a policy of "liberation" toward the Eastern European satellites of the Soviet Union. Whether liberation meant military or political or merely moral support by the United States and NATO was never clearly spelled out. The first test of the new policy occurred in June 1953 when, in a spontaneous revolutionary outbreak, East German workers and students rose against their Communist government. When Chancellor Konrad Adenauer asked the United States government whether it planned to intervene on the basis of the liberation policy, the answer was negative. The second test took place during the Polish uprising of October 21 where, in case of Soviet military intervention, the United States would take no action.[9] The most dramatic test of the liberation formula, of course, was the Hungarian revolution of October 1956. In this case the United States' attitude proved to be one of complete paralysis, with the liberation policy petering out in only a lame American recommendation in the United Nations to "study suitable moves."[10] These three events amply showed that since the liberation policy, coupled with the strategy of massive retaliation, could too easily lead to World War III, it was in fact felt to be too risky to be invoked.

The possible consequences of the Great Deterrent began to cause the

United States' allies concern. Of particular worry was the fact that if American protection through massive retaliation were to serve its purpose, it would have to be premised on the continuing atomic monopoly of the United States. The grounds for this fear became a reality when in August 1953 the Soviet Union exploded its first hydrogen bomb. The promulgation of the American massive retaliation doctrine five months later seemed anachronistic to most European military planners. Their thinking began to run something like this: "If the Americans mean what they say and unleash the Great Deterrent, we shall become an atomic rubble heap; but if they do not mean what they say and are bluffing, the Red Army will take over Western Europe without a shot. Either way, we are the losers." Thus, many NATO allies became almost as fearful of American protection as of Soviet aggression. As a result, most of America's allies began to raise their voices for "no annihilation without representation."

With the development of the new nuclear stalemate between East and West, the NATO allies' attitude toward the United States changed sharply. Suddenly, membership in the alliance seemed a provocation to the Soviet Union and hence fraught with danger. The fate of each member of the pact seemed to hinge upon decisions of the United States. To free themselves from this situation and possible danger, most of the powers became intent on developing their own defense policies independent of the United States. But sharp disagreement arose among members of the Western Alliance and within each country as to the most effective methods for establishing such policies. Some observers felt that their nations should join the "nuclear club" as rapidly as possible and thus be in a position to develop their own atomic defense policies. This could be done by stepping up the pace of national atomic research, or by appealing to the United States to share the secrets of the atom. Other observers were convinced that the road to safety lay not in the quest for atomic weapons but in a retreat from power. Since membership in NATO was now a policy entailing great risk, it was argued that the best way of enhancing the chances of survival was to withdraw from NATO and pursue a policy of neutrality.

This process of reappraisal in the capitals of Western Europe confronted the United States with renewed dilemmas of power and responsibility. While some of the NATO nations, such as Britain and France, succeeded in joining the "nuclear club," others counted on the United States to supply them with technical knowledge and materials with which to develop independent atomic arsenals. Yet for the United States to grant this request entailed serious responsibilities. It meant the dispersion of atomic power to many countries, with unforeseeable consequences. Although under the terms of the Atlantic Pact all partners were equal, in the American view some were "less equal than others"—that is, less dependable. If the United States were to decide to give atomic weapons to Norway, a democracy, would she be in duty bound to grant them also to Portugal, a dictatorship? In any case, the dissemination of atomic weapons throughout NATO might increase the mathematical chances of a war through inadvertence. This fact had to be weighed against the opposing claim that independent atomic arsenals for each member nation would strengthen the alliance as a whole. Furthermore, if the United States were to vest nuclear power in its NATO allies, could it refuse similar requests from OAS, and if so, on what grounds? But if the United States refused to furnish any atomic weapons at all to its allies, would the Soviet Union believe the American claim that it would protect a European ally even at the risk of exposing the United States to Soviet atomic attack? For example, if the Soviet Union were to threaten the "liberation" of West Berlin and were to warn the United States of atomic retaliation if Washington interfered, would the United States then honor its obligation to its West German partner in NATO? Or would the Soviet Union only take seriously a threat from the country that it intended to attack, in this case West Germany itself? Many observers were convinced that the Soviet Union would find only those threats of nuclear reprisal credible that came from the nation whose own survival was at stake. Hence the biggest dilemma that the United States now faced was how to respond to a Soviet attack that was limited to a particular member of NATO.[11]

The United States has continued to agonize over the dilemma of whether or not to share nuclear weapons with its NATO allies. In 1960 the first proposals to convert the entire alliance into a nuclear striking force were put forward: General Lauris Norstad, Supreme Commander of NATO, suggested a NATO atomic force, based on an allied pool of atomic power but separate from the American, British, and French forces of the same kind. This plan was to provide an added deterrent against the Soviet Union; it was to meet allied demands for a share in the control of nuclear arms in Europe; and it was to give assurance to the NATO allies that they would have atomic arms of their own, thereby allaying suspicions that the United States might withhold nuclear defense of Europe for fear of nuclear retaliation by the Soviet Union on its own soil. A "fire brigade" of highly mobile forces equipped with tactical nuclear weapons was also proposed to deal with "brushfire" conflicts.

The administration of President John F. Kennedy reexamined the entire problem of nuclear sharing. It came to the conclusion that, in the light of the mutually deterrent effect of Soviet and American nuclear power, the importance of conventional forces was increasing. Hence American proposals now sought to trade United States nuclear commitments for conventional build-ups on the part of the Europeans. For example, the United States offered to commit five Polaris missiles to NATO in return for an increase of European conventional forces to thirty divisions. Many European military thinkers were hesitant, however, and pointed out that such arrangements were too one-sided, since the United States would keep its finger on the atomic trigger. President de Gaulle of France, for example, declared that an independent national nuclear force was now more important than ever, since no one could be sure that an American President would always be willing to risk nuclear devastation by defending Europe. The United States, in turn, strongly opposed the development of national nuclear forces in Europe for fear of being drawn into a nuclear war against its will.

The dialogue continued with an American proposal, made in 1961, to create "a NATO seaborne force which would be truly multilateral in ownership

and control."[12] While the Europeans were invited to participate in the establishment of policy guidelines, the United States insisted on maintaining a veto
power over the use of the nuclear weapons. Hence European suspicions were
far from allayed, even though in 1963 the United States proposed a multilateral NATO force of mixed crews. The Europeans' own quest for nuclear independence met with mixed results, however: in 1962 the British had to
eliminate their plans for a "Skybolt missile" for technical reasons; and the
French *force de dissuasion*, while of some limited military value, was widely
regarded as primarily a status symbol.

The continuing dialogue over nuclear sharing forced the United States
continuously to reexamine its fundamental thinking with regard to the even
more basic problem of evolving a viable strategic doctrine. After 1956 there
was almost unanimous agreement in the United States that the concept of
massive retaliation had become obsolete. Leading military thinkers in the
United States began to feel that the United States had added the hydrogen
bomb to its arsenal in the East-West struggle without making room for its implications in American strategic thinking. Since massive retaliation was an all-
or-nothing posture, the Soviet Union would be able to win the military struggle by installments. As Henry Kissinger put it in 1957:

> If the Soviet bloc can present its challenges in less than all-out form it may gain a
> crucial advantage. Every move on its part will then pose the appalling dilemma
> of whether we are willing to commit suicide to prevent encroachments, which do
> not, each in itself, seem to threaten our existence directly but which may be steps
> on the road to our ultimate destruction.[13]

Kissinger pointed out that the United States' capacity for massive retaliation
had created a "psychological gap," a situation in which America's NATO
allies had become convinced that they had nothing to gain from it and the Soviet leaders had begun to feel that they had nothing to fear from the threat of
it. In Kissinger's words, "the dilemma of the nuclear age reside[d] in the im-
possibility of combining maximum horror with maximum certainty."[14]

It was from this type of thinking that the new strategic concept of "graduated deterrence" emerged. This concept was based on the simple assumption
that to make the threat less horrible would render it more credible. The
United States would not have to place itself in a position of risking its national
substance every time a stand had to be taken against aggression. Instead
NATO would inform the Eastern military bloc that the West was determined
to exact a price for Soviet aggression that would exceed the benefits to be
gained from the act, but that such retaliation would not aim at the total destruction of the Soviet Union itself. Thus, by a kind of Benthamite calculus,
each crime would be punished in proportion to its seriousness. The United
States would not say to the Soviet Union: "If you march into West Berlin, we
may do something terrible to you, even use massive retaliation." It would
warn, rather: "If you march, we *shall* make you pay a price that will exceed
the prize gained from your act." Exactly how and in what magnitude the more
limited wars of this strategy of graduated deterrence would be fought of
course raised many further problems of far-reaching complexity.

The great hope of the strategy of graduated deterrence among the members of NATO was that it should combine a minimum threat with a maximum of credibility. Thus, they looked to a wide range of weapons, including nuclear arms, in order to achieve as wide a variety of choices of retaliation as possible. This strategy, it was held, would make NATO much more flexible than it had been. For so long as every war threatened to mushroom into an all-out war, NATO allies were naturally inclined to do their best to prevent *any* action by the United States that would involve them. But with the availability of a variety of strategic alternatives, it was reasoned, this reluctance would be overcome and the Atlantic Alliance could once again function as a truly effective instrument of deterrence.

Critics of this new strategic doctrine, however, pointed out that it rested on the dubious assumption that the actions of the opposing military bloc would always be governed by rationality. They admitted that massive retaliation had purchased deterrence at an exorbitant risk, but expressed serious doubt as to whether a limited war in the atomic age—especially one fought with nuclear weapons—would *remain* limited. The premise of graduated deterrence was almost a medieval one—a kind of chivalry imposed by necessity upon the two opponents not to unleash the ultimate weapon against one another. But how would NATO know what "the other side" would actually do, and whether it would always react rationally? Even if its rationality could be counted on, would it believe NATO's "guarantee" to make the punishment fit the crime? And, most important, would not the use of "tactical" nuclear weapons by NATO result in the use of similar or more powerful "tactical" weapons by the other side, until one of the two antagonists would decide to use "strategic" atomic weapons, from which it would only be a short step to massive retaliation? In other words, the critics of a graduated deterrence strategy for NATO felt that a war in the nuclear age could *begin* as a limited war, but was likely to *end* as an all-out war. Hence, graduated deterrence would, sooner or later, lead to massive retaliation by both sides, and total destruction.

The problem of targeting also caused major concern. It was quickly realized that a "second strike counter-city" doctrine would be ineffective, since destruction of Soviet cities would still leave the Soviet striking force intact. Nor was a "second strike counter-force" strategy completely satisfactory, since even the most careful targeting of the enemy's missile sites could not ensure the complete elimination of its nuclear bases. In the absence of any one completely adequate strategic doctrine, the United States decided to emphasize a maximum of flexibility in its defense posture, ranging from guerrilla warfare all the way up to nuclear war.

The United States leadership in NATO was not able to resolve the fearful dilemmas created by the condition of mutual atomic deterrence that has prevailed between the two superpowers. The uncertainties and ambiguities of alliance strategy in the nuclear age created an extreme ambivalence between the United States and its partners, a kind of love-hate relationship, a "dialectic of dependence and counterdependence," a constant process of asking "who needs whom most and who will defend whom?"[15] As long as the United States was safe from Soviet atomic attack, it tended to doubt the readiness of its

NATO partners to fulfill their obligations in a war which would involve the two superpowers. Would France "come through" if the Soviet Union were to launch an attack upon the United States and threaten France with complete destruction unless it remained neutral? But even while the United States still possessed an atomic monopoly, some of its NATO allies feared the opposite, namely that the United States would not "come through" in case of a Soviet attack on a NATO country that was not considered "vital" to America's defense. With mutual deterrence a fact of life between East and West, the mutual suspicions between the United States and its NATO partners grew apace. Would the United States stand by the defense of France if this might mean the destruction of its own national substance? President de Gaulle believed that no American president would do this. In February 1966 the French president, in a dramatic move, announced his intention to withdraw French units progressively from the integrated NATO command. He implied that France would withdraw from NATO altogether when the Treaty would permit such action in 1969. He declared that the American deterrent was at best "indeterminate," that American military involvements in other parts of the world might drag France into an undesired war, and that, for all these reasons, the reestablishment of normal sovereign relations between France and the United States was a "necessary adaptation." While De Gaulle, in a letter to President Johnson in March, reaffirmed France's intention to fight on the side of its allies in case of attack, he nevertheless began the process of troop withdrawal. The United States deplored the French move and President Johnson found it "difficult to believe that France [would] long remain withdrawn from the common affairs and responsibilities of the Atlantic." However, in March 1967, NATO Headquarters were shifted from Paris to Brussels. The disengagement of France from NATO was now a physical reality.

The French move served to underline the fact that the world power constellation had changed. More specifically, it was an expression of French dissatisfaction with the fact that the problem of nuclear sharing was not resolved so long as the United States retained its veto over the use of nuclear weapons. All other concessions were regarded by France—and to a lesser extent Britain and West Germany—as peripheral and insufficient. The Europeans, encouraged by the French example, began to demand participation in the entire NATO decision-making process, ranging from the creation of forces to the use of ultimate weapons. Nothing short of this was likely to satisfy them.

By the early 1980s, despite these discordant notes, NATO nonetheless remained the West's only effective military alliance. President Carter, in particular, who believed that Henry Kissinger had neglected America's allies and concentrated too much on its adversaries, had made the NATO countries a more central focus of his foreign policy. Yet as the Treaty passed its thirtieth anniversary, NATO's inner cohesion still seemed in serious jeopardy. A NATO decision taken in 1979, to deploy United States missiles in Europe unless the Soviet Union removed SS-20 missiles that were aimed at Western Europe had made the Europeans nervous. They remembered American behavior in Suez in 1956, the "derecognition" of Taiwan in 1979, and the indecision on Iran in

1980. Some of the Europeans seemed prepared to follow the example of Finland and observe neutrality. Although German Chancellor Helmut Schmidt remained a loyal advocate of NATO membership, discordant voices were heard even in Germany. "In the age of the atom," wrote Rudolf Augstein, editor of *Der Spiegel*, in 1980, "the Germans can only hope—and also be certain—that the Americans will not meet their NATO commitments in a war."[16] Even more important than such "Finlandization" was a mood of "Denmarkization." This was a term applied to a NATO country that, like Denmark in recent years, had decided that there was no need to spend more money on its defense because the United States would be forced to defend it anyway.[17] Thus, the fundamental question asked in the 1950s, "Who will come through for whom and under what conditions?" was still asked in the 1980s.

In 1983, after President Reagan's "zero option" proposal had been rejected with finality by the Soviets, the United States began the deployment of over five hundred Pershing and Cruise missiles in Western Europe. The Soviets, who had lobbied intensively against this move, walked out of all arms control negotiations as a result. The NATO alliance, too, was somewhat shaken. Right-wing groups suspected that American missiles might become a substitute for American troops. Left-wing groups reasoned that these missiles, especially if deployed in Germany, might be an unacceptable provocation to the Soviet Union, which had lost twenty million men in a war with that country. Nonetheless, the Pershings and Cruises were deployed and the alliance held fast. Yet, a profound malaise continued to prevail between America and Europe in the mid-1980s.

On perhaps the deepest level, the Europeans asked the question whether nuclear deterrence between the two great powers had not in itself become sufficient for the prevention of aggression. In short, were military alliances becoming obsolete? Thus NATO, though effective as a military bulwark for more than thirty years, was gradually becoming an alliance in search of a new cause. Perhaps the time had come to knit the bonds of solidarity not only on the basis of defense but on the more lasting values of building a larger Atlantic Community between North America and Western Europe.

The East's Military Alliance System

The two major pillars of the East's military alliance system have been the Warsaw Pact and, until the late 1950s, the Sino-Soviet Alliance.

The Warsaw Pact, concluded in 1955 as a counterpoise to NATO, committed the Soviet Union to the defense of its seven Eastern European allies. Its Article 4—virtually a carbon copy of NATO's Article 5—commits the Soviet Union to such armed assistance as it might "deem necessary." Yet in other respects the Warsaw Pact has differed significantly from its Western counterpart. For one thing, while the former has been geographically compact, the membership of the latter extends over a great distance. Moreover, the main difference between the two alliances lies in the fact that the Soviet Union insisted on fairly tight political bonds within the alliance, whereas the United

States was content with quite loose ones. All NATO partners have been relatively free agents, but it would be difficult to speak of Bulgaria as a sovereign
equal in the Warsaw Pact. The United States has never compelled a NATO
ally to remain within the alliance by force. But what kept Hungary in the
Warsaw Pact after 1956 was clearly not its freely given consent. Whereas
NATO military policy has admittedly been strongly influenced by American
leadership, the Warsaw Pact has been almost completely dominated by the
Soviet Union. Whereas the NATO powers' share in Western security has been
the subject of multilateral negotiations, Eastern Europe's contributions to Soviet security have in effect been determined by unilateral decision of the Soviet Union. Finally, the American military leadership in NATO has not been
accompanied by the export of ideology, while the Soviet Union has attempted
to cement the military bonds of the Warsaw Pact with the unifying mortar of
the Communist creed. The invasion of Czechoslovakia in 1968 by the Soviet
Union and four other members of the Warsaw Pact was an effort to impose this
creed by force of arms even though Czechoslovakia, unlike Hungary, had
never declared its intention to give up membership in the pact.

Though the structural differences between the two military blocs have
thus been great, the stategic problems they have faced have been fairly similar. Ironically enough, the coming of mutual deterrence has confronted the
Soviet Union with strategic agonies analogous to those tormenting the United
States. Dilemmas of "massive retaliation" and "graduated deterrence" have
also been plaguing the Warsaw Pact nations. More specifically, the Soviet
Union's problem of whether or not to give nuclear weapons to its allies has
been no less difficult than the same issue confronting the United States. There
has been pressure on Moscow to share its nuclear monopoly. Western rearmament of West Germany has given rise to great fears, particularly in Poland and
East Germany. If they possessed atomic weapons, these nations have argued,
their security would be restored. In this decision the Soviet Union, like the
United States, has seen "its native hue of resolution sicklied o'er with the pale
cast of thought." On the one hand, could the Soviet Union refuse atomic weapons to East Germany if the West Germans should be so equipped by the
United States? On the other, what if another Tito, equipped with nuclear
weapons, were to decide to leave the Warsaw Pact? And what if the Hungari-
ans had had atomic weapons in 1956? Moreover, nationalist tendencies and
de-Stalinization programs in most of the Eastern European countries have
greatly reduced the degree of Soviet control over Eastern Europe. The
Czechoslovak crisis of 1968 did not reverse but probably only slowed this overall trend. In fact, some of the Eastern European countries, particularly Rumania, have tended to pursue policies fairly independent of the Soviet Union.
Rumania even suggested the dissolution of the Warsaw Pact in the context of a
United States–Soviet agreement on troop withdrawal from the European continent. And the Polish workers' strike in 1980 weakened the bonds of the War-
saw Pact even in Warsaw. In fact, by the mid-1980s, the heroes of Communist
Poland were three Catholics: Pope John Paul II, the Archbishop, and Lech
Walesa, the leader of the outlawed Solidarity Union. In 1983 Walesa was

awarded the Nobel Peace Prize. Karl Marx would hardly have approved of these developments, had he lived to see them.

On the whole, the cohesion of both NATO and the Warsaw Pact has loosened. One expert has described this loosening process as follows:

> Considering the over-all picture of the alliances . . . one is impressed by the similarity of the changes that have occurred in the structure of the European alliances on both sides of the Iron Curtain. The seemingly irreversible trend toward a two-bloc system that marked the immediate postwar era has been arrested, if not reversed. The uncommitted nations not only want to remain uncommitted but have, with a few exceptions, also shown the ability to do so. On the other hand, many of the European nations that are committed as allies of one or the other of the superpowers would like to join the ranks of the uncommitted nations but have, with the exception of Yugoslavia, been unable to do so. They have at best been able to move to the outer confines of the blocs to which they belong, but have had to stop there. In consequence, the two-bloc system is in the process of loosening but not of breaking up.[18]

The most formidable military instrument of the East used to be the Sino-Soviet Alliance concluded in February 1950. In this treaty the two parties had agreed that, in case of attack on one, the other would use all means available to provide immediate military and other assistance. We have seen earlier that the Chinese Communist party reached power without Soviet assistance and that Stalin obviously sacrificed ideological uniformity on the altar of coalition unity when he recognized the new regime upon its accession to power. This relationship had made of the Sino-Soviet Pact a genuine alliance between two equals, held together by joint interests and coordinated policies—unlike the Warsaw Pact, which was dominated by the Soviet Union.

The Sino-Soviet Alliance held fast into the late 1950s, but then began to disintegrate in the context of the widening ideological rift. As late as 1957 the Soviet Union made an agreement with Communist China providing its ally with technical atomic assistance in order to speed China's entry into the nuclear club, and in 1958 Premier Khrushchev fully endorsed the Chinese Communist claim to Formosa, pledging that "an attack on the People's Republic of China was an attack on the Soviet Union."[19]

In 1959, however, China's aggressive attitude over the Taiwan question and its incursions into Indian territory forced the Soviet Union to reconsider its policy of equipping its ally with nuclear teeth. Moreover, China's claim that "after the next war there would be twenty million Americans, five million Englishmen, fifty million Russians, and three hundred million Chinese left," no doubt gave the Soviet Union food for thought.[20] At any rate, Russia abrogated its nuclear assistance treaty with China in 1959 and had withdrawn most of its technicians from China by 1960. There is little doubt that this action was one of the major factors contributing to the rising temperature of the Sino-Soviet dispute. It also demonstrated that the dispute was shifting from an ideological disagreement over the best method of "burying" the West to a power struggle between two competing national states. After all, ownership of the bomb by one Communist state would have been sufficient to advance the cause of world communism. But the fact that the Chinese wanted atomic power in their own right and attained it in 1964 showed that they were eager to demonstrate their national power too—vis-à-vis Russia as well as the West. By the 1970s little if anything remained of the Sino-Soviet Alliance of 1950. And by the 1980s the two colossi of the Communist world were bitter enemies.

The East-West Military Confrontation

During the 1950s the discussion of East-West problems increasingly shifted from the political to the military realm. Evidence of this development could be seen in the growing preoccupation of the two superpowers not with matters of diplomatic substance but with propagandistic flourishes of military power. Some leading military thinkers on both sides continued to profess their desire to see the arms race ended. For example, General Lauris Norstad, Supreme Commander of NATO, said in 1957: "No military man is pleased with the present *status quo*—two armed camps sitting opposite each other. That would be a hell of a state of affairs to perpetuate."[21] Other military leaders, however, fatalistically concluded that, like other arms races before it, the East-West weapons build-up would sooner or later lead to war and that the only open question was therefore the question of what kind of war it was necessary to be prepared for: all-out, limited conventional, or limited nuclear. This vacillation between statements of hope for the best and fears for the worst tended to characterize the Eastern and Western alliance systems alike during the 1950s.

This confrontation of two opposing military blocs was commonly referred to as "biopolarity" before it was transformed in many important ways in the 1960s. In itself such a political division of the world was by no means unprecedented. Athens and Sparta, Rome and Carthage provide classic illustrations of bipolar relationships. The U.S-Soviet bipolarity was unique, however, in that the two protagonists were equipped with weapons that in case of war would, for the first time in history, threaten the survival not only of entire populations but of the species itself. Though it has occurred before, bipolarity has not been the normal pattern in history. More typically, the power configuration among nations has been that of a multiple equilibrium, known as "balance of power." This multiple equilibrium provided a flexible framework in which a number of nations sought to maximize their power and, at the same time, frequently switched sides so as to prevent any one from attaining preponderance. This traditional balance of power in our time gave way to what Sir Winston Churchill so aptly called the "balance of terror," a precarious balance between two superpowers, each equipped with the weapons of nuclear mass destruction. In this new situation room for maneuvering steadily lessened, with the result that there was no longer a flexible balance but, in effect, two virtually frozen and uncompromising blocs. The superpowers could only

> . . . advance and meet in what is likely to be combat, or they can retreat and allow the other side to advance into what to them is precious ground. Those manifold and variegated maneuvers through which the masters of the balance of power tried to either stave off armed conflicts altogether or at least make them brief and decisive, yet limited in scope—the alliances and counteralliances, the

shifting of alliances according to whence the greater threat or better opportunity might come, the sidestepping and postponement of issues, the deflection of rivalries from the exposed frontyard into the colonial backyard—these are the things of the past.[22]

Military thinkers in the West disagreed on what kind of "balance" between the two blocs would most effectively deter them from attacking one another. Some claimed that as exact an equilibrium as possible would afford the best chance for peace. Others maintained that war would be less likely if one bloc were far stronger than the other. But almost all were agreed that the threat of war was greatest in the case of a slight imbalance. As Organski pointed out, most major wars of recent history occurred when the challenger had grown rapidly, but before he was quite as powerful as the dominant nation and its allies.[23]

It is clear that the atomic balance of terror greatly inhibited the traditionally almost casual resort to war as "a continuation of policy by other means." Sir Winston Churchill even suggested that "It may well be that we shall, by a process of sublime irony, have reached the stage in this story where safety will be the sturdy child of terror, and survival the twin brother of annihilation."[24] Sir Winston's optimism, however, seemed somewhat exaggerated. For while it is true that mutual deterrence operates as a safeguard to some extent at least, it is equally true that the closeness of the arms race between East and West meant repeated passage through the most dangerous power configuration of all, namely that of a slight imbalance.

There was a further danger inherent in the condition of mutual deterrence. The Churchillian balance of terror was based on the assumption that both East and West were protected through weapons that were never actually to be used. There was a serious flaw in this reasoning. Its ultimate premise involved a gigantic bluff. For on the one hand, if the nuclear weapons should actually be used, they might well end up destroying most of what they were intended to protect. On the other hand, if everyone assumed that they would never be used, they could not offer adequate protection, since the opponent could feel free to act as if they did not exist. In order to protect itself, therefore, each superpower had to be determined to use nuclear arms if necessary, and this meant that they might indeed one day be used.

Perhaps the greatest peril of all inherent in the relationship of nuclear parity between the two blocs was that a nuclear war could be triggered through irrationality or inadvertence. Each side, assuming that the other intended to behave rationally, was nevertheless compelled to include in its calculations the possibility of irrational behavior by the other side. The Western bloc's view of "the Communist menace" and the Soviet bloc's conception of "the imperialist camp of the West" tended to heighten expectations of irrational behavior. Hence, policies might be based on what one side believed the other side believed, with the danger of an outcome desired by neither. Thomas C. Schelling described this problem well in the following analogy:

If I go downstairs to investigate a noise at night, with a gun in my hand, and find myself face to face with a burglar who has a gun in his hand, there is danger of an outcome that neither of us desires. Even if he prefers just to leave quietly, and I wish him to, there is danger that he may *think* I want to shoot, and shoot first. Worse, there is danger that he may think that I think *he* wants to shoot. And so on. "Self-defense" is ambiguous when one is only trying to preclude being shot in self-defense.[25]

If war through irrationality could be caused by incorrect expectations of what the other side may or may not do, war through inadvertence could result from a mere technical error. A misunderstanding of orders; a misinterpretation of a situation; a speck on a radar screen caused by a meteorite or a swarm of birds could be mistaken for a plane or a missile—all these could set off atomic retaliations almost automatically. This danger was increased by the fact that modern means of weapons delivery made a great many types of military errors irrevocable. Planes could be called back from a bombing mission, but intercontinental ballistic missiles could not. In other words, there now existed the real possibility of world destruction by mistake. Whereas war was traditionally regarded as "the continuation of diplomacy by other means," the atomic age had transformed diplomacy between the two superpowers into a variety of warfare.

The problem of somehow stabilizing the precarious balance of terror became the overriding concern of responsible military thinkers on both sides of the Iron Curtain. Yet in view of the numerous difficulties, the task seemed almost insurmountable. Perhaps the greatest difficulty was to make the nuclear balance work even though trust and good faith were lacking and there was no recourse to a higher authority. Schelling astutely pointed out that in having to live with this problem, our generation was at a disadvantage when compared with that of Machiavelli, for example. In the days of Machiavelli—as in many other historical periods—peace was not felt to be dependent on trust, good faith, and mutual respect in interstate relations. It was recognized as resulting no less frequently from hard and often ugly political realities. Perhaps, Schelling suggested, we too must become accustomed to such situations.

> We may wish to solicit advice from the underworld, or from ancient despotisms. The ancients exchanged hostages, drank wine from the same glass to demonstrate the absence of poison, met in public places to inhibit the massacre of one by the other, and even deliberately exchanged spies to facilitate transmittal of authentic information.[26]

There was good sense in this argument. For it seemed, ironically enough, that the balance of terror would not really be stabilized until both sides had invulnerable retaliatory power. Once this condition prevailed, neither side—even if it struck first—could then destroy the other's ability to strike back. The "ancient wisdom" of the proposition rested on the somewhat Machiavellian assumption that the safety of weapons would increase the safety of people. Once each side knew that no blow, however massive, could destroy the other's capacity to return the blow, a greater stability would result.

The conception each side in the East-West struggle tended to hold of its own camp was one of defense against the other. The tragedy of this phase of the military struggle between East and West was in the possibility that these images could *become* reality and that the circle of suspicion and countersuspicion could precipitate a "preventive" war. If each side continued to believe that the other was its mortal enemy, this could influence behavior to such a point of rigidity and compulsiveness that the "inevitable conflict" could end up becoming a self-fulfilling prophecy.

The 1960s saw the beginning of the breakup of the bipolar system. The Sino-Soviet rift spelled the end of a monolithic Soviet bloc and the policies of President de Gaulle of France introduced powerful centrifugal tendencies into the Western camp. Most important, in 1962 a dramatic military confrontation took place between the Soviet Union and the United States that changed the entire complexion of the cold war. This turning point deserves close analysis as a case study.

The Cuban Missile Crisis of 1962

This crisis was the climax to the rising tensions between the superpowers during 1961. The Soviet Union's action in testing nuclear weapons of unprecedented explosive force had triggered off a major debate over fallout shelters in the United States; the erection of the Berlin Wall had made the tension almost palpable; and the memory of the abortive American-sponsored invasion of Cuba was still fresh. But as yet there had been no "eyeball-to-eyeball" confrontation. The Cuban missile crisis was a confrontation.

In mid-October 1962 hard evidence that the Soviet Union was secretly building offensive missile bases in Cuba with headlong speed had been gathered by United States intelligence services. High-altitude photographs had disclosed a medium-range ballistic missile site near San Cristóbal and one near San Diego de los Banos. Tanker trucks, power and instrument installations, missile guidance stations, and erector launchers were clearly visible. And pictures of cylindrical shapes on incoming Soviet freighters confirmed the worst.

It is difficult to determine with certitude why the Soviet leadership made the decision to try to make Cuba an offensive missile base. First, it has been suggested that Premier Khrushchev intended to use the bases as a psychological lever to make more effective his demands for Berlin. Indeed, in the summer of 1962 Khrushchev had announced that he would postpone the Berlin issue until after the American elections. He may have hoped that President Kennedy would not dare to disclose a missile build-up during an election campaign and that he could therefore confront the United States over Berlin with the Cuban bases as a *fait accompli*. Second, the Soviet leader probably underestimated the will of the American President. The Berlin Wall, Laos, and especially the fiasco in the Bay of Pigs may have suggested to Khrushchev that Kennedy lacked resolve and would not take determined action. Third, successful installation of the weapons would give the Soviet Union an important temporary military advantage; rockets launched from Cuba could destroy American cities and knock out United States missiles and bombers on the ground in a first-strike attack, since the warning time would be critically reduced. The American weapons lead over the Soviet Union would not be canceled but would be seriously weakened. Fourth, neo-Stalinist pressures on Khrushchev may have played a role, although this is unlikely, since Stalinism was very much on the defensive in Russia at the time and the Soviet leadership was emphasizing its policy of "peaceful coexistence" against the harsher line of Communist China. Nor is it likely that Cuban Premier Fidel Castro had persuaded the Soviet leader to install the missiles in order to prevent an American invasion of Cuba. On balance, Khrushchev probably calculated that, at best, a frightened America would go down on its knees, lose the confidence of its military allies in Europe, Asia, and Latin America, and thus give the Soviet Union a new opportunity to resume the offensive in the cold war. If the United States insisted on the removal of the bases, perhaps a barter deal could be worked out over bases in Greece and Turkey. And, even if the United States took a resolutely uncompromising stand, Khrushchev could gain favor in world public opinion by a policy of withdrawal. At the very worst, then, the *status quo ante* would be maintained, with Soviet control over Cuba intact.

The American leadership, which had hard evidence of the missile sites by October 15, now weighed its decision silently. For one week the President and his closest associates constituted themselves as an Executive Committee of the National Security Council and pondered the alternatives. The President continued his preparations for the forthcoming political campaign, and as late as October 18 met with Soviet Foreign Secretary Andrei Gromyko, who professed ignorance of the offensive nature of the missile sites in Cuba.

Inside the White House and Pentagon, the war council considered the alternatives along a kind of "escalation ladder." There developed seven possible responses in ascending order of severity: first, a sharp protest note to the Soviet government; second, an American appeal to the United Nations Security Council; third, some form of economic retaliation against the Soviet Union; fourth, a naval blockade of Cuba; fifth, a "surgical air-strike" to eliminate the bases; sixth, invasion of the island; and seventh, direct nuclear retaliation against the Soviet Union. The war council immediately eliminated the first three alternatives as ineffective and the last as unwarranted. The discussion centered around the alternatives in the middle range. The problem confronting the American planners was the classic one of deterrence strategy: so to combine the twin demands of capability and credibility that the Soviet leader would be checked by the actual and potential display of American power. Too little power could be interpreted as surrender, too much power as a bluff. Only controlled and flexible use of power at every step would make deterrence effective in the mind of the opponent.

An immediate invasion of Cuba was ruled out because that might have provoked the war which deterrence was designed to prevent. An air-strike at the missile bases was also rejected since Russian personnel would have been killed at the sites and such an action would have been difficult to justify by a nation that had made Pearl Harbor a symbol of infamy. A quarantine seemed to hold out the best hope for a solution. It would entail the requisite amount of strength by throwing a naval ring around Cuba, especially if it were coupled with a demand that the Soviet Union dismantle its bases there. Yet it offered the Soviet Union a way out: Khrushchev could avoid a direct confrontation by ordering his ships to change their course. Also, a quarantine would entail no violence, at least not immediately. Thus, on the evening of October 22, President Kennedy announced the American decision to impose a quarantine and added that "any nuclear missile launched from Cuba against any nation in the Western Hemisphere" would be regarded "as an attack by the Soviet Union on the United States requiring a full retaliatory response on the Soviet Union."[27] The issue was now squarely joined between the superpowers in the most dramatic military confrontation of the cold war. It was clear to participants and onlookers alike that Castro's Cuba was by now only a pawn. The United States had announced a check to the king, and the King was Premier Khrushchev.

The quarantine announcement was accompanied by an unprecedented peacetime mobilization of military power in the United States. The Polaris fleet was moved within striking range of the Soviet Union and for the first time Strategic Air Command bombers were dispersed to civilian airfields. Half of the SAC force was on airborne alert. If necessary, the United States was ready to deliver an equivalent of thirty billion tons of TNT upon the Soviet Union. An atmosphere of impending showdown also pervaded the Soviet Union, where all military leaves were canceled. The next seven days took the world to the brink of war.

On October 23, the Organization of American States supported the quarantine in a unanimous vote. The NATO allies came to the support of the United States, though with misgivings and not without reminding the United States of its behavior during the Suez crisis. The UN Security Council met in the afternoon. The United States demanded the immediate withdrawal, under international inspection, of the offensive weapons; the Soviet Union condemned the blockade as piracy and asked for its immediate termination. Neither resolution was voted on and the Security Council presented a spectacle of complete helplessness. Toward evening the Russian tanker *Bucharest* approached the blockade zone and the American destroyer U.S.S. *Gearing* steamed to meet it. Since the Russian vessel carried no contraband, it was allowed to proceed. Khrushchev claimed that the ship had not stopped; the United States claimed that the captain had acknowledged inspection. Neither side had backed down. October 24, United Nations Day, took the world a step closer to the brink. Secretary-General U Thant advanced a plan for a two-week cooling-off period to explore the issues. Khrushchev accepted the proposal at once but Kennedy rejected it on the ground that the issue of removing the missiles was not negotiable. An appeal by Premier Khrushchev to the British pacifist leader Bertrand Russell to use his influence to effect a general lowering of temperatures was also rejected as irrelevant by the United States. On October 25 Ambassador Stevenson challenged Soviet Ambassador Valerian Zorin to admit the existence of the missiles, stating that he was ready to wait for his answer "until hell freezes over."

On October 26 it was learned that several Soviet ships bound for Cuba were changing their course. But on the other hand, continued photo scrutiny of the missile bases indicated a speed-up in their construction since the announcement of the quarantine. The American offensive had to gather speed before the sites were ready and the missiles operational. President Kennedy spoke of possible "further measures" and did not rule out an air-strike at the bases. He also pointed out the numerous possibilities for accidental war if the Soviet Union would not comply. That evening a telegram from Premier Khrushchev arrived, which looked like a conditional surrender. In it the premier indicated his willingness to withdraw the missiles provided Cuba was guaranteed against invasion. This seemed like a fair offer.

On the morning of the following day, however, the White House received a second telegram from the Soviet leader which was much tougher in tone and more demanding in content. This time a deal was suggested: The United States was to dismantle her missile bases in Turkey and the Soviet Union would withdraw her missiles from Cuba.

The war council now had to make a crucial decision. Superficially the Soviet proposal seemed reasonable. It expressed a widespread feeling among neutralists that both sides should compromise and sacrifice something. It was generally approved in the United Nations, and several distinguished Western commentators like Walter Lippmann supported it. Nevertheless, the war council turned down the proposal. In the first place, President Kennedy felt that the first Soviet telegram reflected more clearly than the second the Soviet leader's real feelings. And second, to bargain away NATO bases under pressure would be to undermine the entire alliance and engender a Munich psychology. Each time the Soviet Union would gain a strategic advantage in the cold war, it might offer to give it up in exchange for an existing NATO base until the alliance would be totally dismantled. Thus, by turning down the barter offer, the United States in effect presented the Soviet Union with an ultimatum: Remove the bases or "further measures" will be taken. The brink had been reached.

On Saturday morning, October 27, the Soviet Union "blinked" and the eyeball-to-eyeball confrontation came to an end. Kennedy's gamble on the first Soviet telegram had paid off. The Soviet leader reiterated his offer of withdrawing the missiles in return for an American "no-invasion" pledge. The American President accepted immediately and welcomed Khrushchev's "constructive contribution to peace." Other differences were settled in short order. Castro refused to admit on-site inspection by the United Nations to survey the dismantling of the bases, but the United States decided to forego such inspection and continued to rely upon its own aerial surveillance. The missile sites were completely stripped within a few weeks and outgoing Soviet ships laden with shrouded shapes that everyone took to be missiles brought the crisis to an end. The world had gone to the brink of nuclear hell and come back.

An analysis of the Cuban missile crisis reveals all the strengths and weaknesses of deterrence strategy. A strong case can be made for the American President's action on several grounds. Diplomatically, the action exhibited a combination of toughness and flexibility worthy of a great chess player. It never lost sight of the ultimate goal: the removal of the bases. Yet it at all times offered the Soviet leader the possibility of a retreat with dignity. Militarily, it prevented a serious upset of the distribution of power by forcing the removal of medium-range ballistic missile bases ninety miles from American shores. And historically, it was based on the bitter lesson of Munich that appeasement under pressure is the road to war.

Yet there is a case to be made against deterrence. First, it is accident-prone. Many times during those crucial days in October 1962 the world could have been destroyed by accident. The sinking of an American or Soviet ship could have triggered off a naval war. Indeed, an accident almost did occur. An American U-2 plane on a routine mission over Alaska on October 26 lost its bearings and headed for Siberia. Khrushchev hesitated, but in the atmosphere of crisis *might* have ordered a full retaliatory blow.[28] Second, the quarantine demonstrated that when power speaks, international law declines in importance. It is not difficult to see that a blockade, traditionally regarded as an act of war, does not advance the cause of world law in international relations. And finally, one should not lightly assume that deterrence will always work because it once did in a major showdown.

On balance, deterrence strategy was applied with consummate skill in the Cuban crisis. All things considered, the American President's determination was matched only by his prudence. He merely demanded the restoration of the status quo. Any additional demand, such as the withdrawal of Russian forces from Cuba, might have been intolerable to the Soviet Union and provoked a thermonuclear war. This feeling for nuance seems to be one of the integral requirements for a successful deterrence strategy. After all, the world's two most powerful statesmen had to make decisions that no mortal man before them ever had in his power to make. Hence, they had to speak to each other in a language the grammar of which they had to learn in action. Advisers on both sides could *clarify* the choices, but the two leaders had to *make* them. This truth was well expressed by President Kennedy when he cited the following poem:

> Bullfight critics ranked in rows
> Crowd the enormous Plaza full;
> But only one is there who *knows*
> And he's the man who fights the bull.[29]

Even Premier Khrushchev paid a grudging compliment to his opponent when he admitted to a Western diplomat: "Had I been in the White House instead of the Kremlin, I would have acted like Kennedy."[30]

A good case may be made for the proposition that the successful application of deterrence strategy by the United States in 1962 ushered in a period of détente in East-West relations. The partial nuclear test-ban treaty concluded in 1963 was probably a result of it. And the installation of a "hot line" between the White House and the Kremlin reduced the chances of war through misunderstanding or accident. Thus, power, when prudently and judiciously applied, can give life to new elements of order, which in turn may soften the fierce edge of the power struggle among states.

In the past, great-power confrontations were often accompanied by large-scale physical violence such as World Wars I and II. Yet, these conflicts often led to new efforts in international order-building, such as the League of Nations and the United Nations. The Cuban missile crisis suggests the possibility that humanity may be able to fight bloodless wars and build new institutions of order without having to pay the terrible price of nuclear conflict.

The Soviet and American Military Arsenals

In 1962, when Nikita Khrushchev withdrew his missiles from Cuba, the United States enjoyed a decisive edge over the Soviet Union in virtually all categories of weapons systems. When Khrushchev was ousted in 1964 as a "harebrained schemer," the new Soviet leadership decided on a relentless effort to catch up and, if possible, surpass the United States. In this massive push, the Soviet Union has been largely successful. Since the mid-1960s, the Soviet military budget has grown by 3 to 4 percent every year. By the mid-1980s, two decades after the missile crisis, Soviet military power had grown to formidable proportions, at least equaling and, in some instances, even surpassing, that of the United States. A comparative analysis of Soviet and American military arsenals in the 1980s therefore is in order.

In the category of nuclear weapons, a rough strategic parity existed between the two superpowers. While in 1965, the Soviet Union had fewer than 500 land-based and submarine-launched missiles, by the mid-1980s it had 1,400 intercontinental missiles and 1,000 submarine-based weapons. In addition, it also had 156 long-range bombers. The United States had more than 1,000 land-based missiles: 1,000 Minutemen and 54 Titans. The American arsenal also included 656 submarine-based missiles and 338 long-range bombers. In civil defense strategy, however, there was a large gap with the Soviet program outstripping its American counterpart by a ratio of ten to one.

In conventional weapons the Soviet Union had pulled ahead of the United States by 1980. It had more than 3.5 million men in the armed services, based on conscription for two or three years and an obligation in the reserves to the age of fifty. Almost two million of these men were combat-ready. The United States, by contrast, only had two million volunteers, less than half of whom were combat-ready. Fifty thousand tanks were available to the Soviet Union with only one-fifth that number available to the United States. If one compared air forces, the Soviet Union had 5,000 fighter bombers as against 3,700 for the United States. The Soviet fleet also outnumbered the American navy with 289 major warships to 73.

This Soviet growth in military might, in both absolute and relative terms, has been the subject of sharp debate among Western students of the USSR. George Kennan, a former ambassador to Moscow, for example, perceived the Soviet build-up as motivated by defensive rather than offensive impulses. In his view, the USSR had been forced to confront a succession of real and potential threats, ranging from the German invasion in 1941 to the creation of the NATO alliance in 1949 and the emergence of a hostile China in the 1960s. Moscow's most serious concern, Kennan believed, was the emergence of a four-sided global alliance consisting of the United States, Western Europe, Japan, and China. Besides, 20 percent of Soviet military power was directed not against the West, but against China, with another 20 percent needed to keep the Soviet Union's Eastern European allies in line. Hence, Kennan thought that the dangers of the Soviet build-up easily lent themselves to exaggeration.

Other analysts, however, imputed far more aggressive designs to the Soviet thrust. A Central Intelligence research team led by Professor Richard E. Pipes of Harvard University, for example, asserted that the Soviet arms program signified an ideologically inspired drive for domination. Little had changed in Russia since Lenin, in the view of these specialists. The Soviet leadership would take one step backward if properly contained, but two steps forward if tempted by Western weakness. Deterrence through armed might therefore was the only answer.

However one views this debate, one fact is certain: we live today in a world of about fifty thousand nuclear warheads—with a destructive power one million times that of the Hiroshima bomb—divided roughly evenly between the United States and the Soviet Union. Both East and West have tended recently to militarize their diplomacies. In and by themselves, such policies are not new. When the Roman emperors saw their appeal eroding, they sent out their legions and when European kings lost popularity, they launched new wars of conquest. In those distant days, the ultimate questions of strength and weakness were decided on the battlefield. No one wants to seek the answers there today. One must hope that, as we near the year 2000, we may live to ask the questions.

THE LINKAGE PATTERN IN WAR

The Case of Vietnam

The military struggle between Western colonialism and Third World nationalism has been decided in favor of the latter. The French were forced to leave Indochina; the Dutch, Indonesia; and the Belgians, the Congo. However, in some cases the termination of the colonial presence on the soil of the new nations did not end the struggle, but only moved it into a new and even more violent phase. This tragic development occurred when a war between the forces of nationalism and colonialism gradually merged into a war between East and West. Such was the case in Vietnam, where the linkage between the two great struggles of our time brought about one of the most complex and terrible conflicts since the advent of the atomic age. Its importance in the context of our general analysis warrants a special case study.

The origins of the conflict go back to the end of World War II. The Japanese surrender in August 1945 had left a vacuum that two different forces now attempted to fill. On one side stood Ho Chi Minh, a typical product of the cross-fertilization of Vietnamese nationalism and European communism, leader of the Vietminh forces, most of whom were Vietnamese nationalists with Communist leadership cadres. Ho quickly established control over much of Vietnam. There was little effective immediate competition since the Japanese had driven out the French and the Americans had beaten the Japanese. France, however, was determined to regain its old colonial holdings in Indochina. After a number of efforts at negotiations had failed, the mounting tension culminated in November 1946 when a French naval bombardment of Haiphong touched off major hostilities. For the next eight years, France fought a bitter war against the Vietminh. With its superior firepower, France was able to hold many of the cities, but the Vietminh gained more and more of the countryside. In 1949, the French installed a Vietnamese emperor, Boa Dai, but to no avail. France was simply unable to gain the confidence of the non-Communist Vietnamese nationalists, while Ho Chi Minh organized more and more determined opposition to France under his Vietminh leadership. Thus, the Communists used nationalism more effectively against the French than the French were able to use anticommunism against the nationalists. In short, while the war in its early phase was primarily a struggle between nationalism and colonialism, gradually it tended to take on overtones of an East-West conflict.

Between 1946 and 1949 the United States remained aloof from the war in Indochina. With the victory of communism on the Chinese mainland, however, and the massive American involvement in the Korean war during the following year, the American attitude toward Indochina underwent a significant change. On February 7, 1950, the United States recognized the Bao Dai government and a few months later President Truman announced that the United States would supply substantial military assistance to the French forces. By late 1950 United States aid was flowing in support of the French war effort and by 1953, this aid had reached the $500 million mark. By 1954 the United States was deeply committed to the French cause in Indochina and was paying for 50 percent of the costs of the war.

Nevertheless, in the spring of 1954 the United States still decided against military intervention. On March 20, 1954, the French Chief of Staff, General Paul Ely, informed President Eisenhower that only massive American military intervention could save the French at Dienbienphu. This prospect touched off a vigorous debate within the American government. Vice President Nixon and the Chairman of the Joint Chiefs of Staff, Admiral Radford, favored prompt United States intervention. On the other hand, President Eisenhower's Army Chief of Staff, General Matthew B. Ridgway, and several members of the State Department's Policy Planning Staff, urged a policy of restraint. President Eisenhower finally decided not to intervene. He feared that the French had engendered too much popular antagonism to win the war and also felt that his administration would get little backing from the Congress and from Great Britain for even a limited military intervention.

The Geneva Conference of mid-1954 and the formation, a few weeks later, of the Southeast Asia Treaty Organization signified the end of French military involvement and the beginning of an American military presence in

Indochina. The Geneva Conference resulted in the signing of several agreements to cease hostilities in Indochina and to establish three independent sovereign states: Laos, Cambodia, and Vietnam. The agreement on Vietnam provided for a "provisional military demarcation line" at the seventeenth parallel. Vietminh forces were to regroup north of the line while the forces of the French Union were to regroup to the south. The line was to have military significance only and the political unification of Vietnam was to be brought about through a general election two years hence under the supervision of a neutral three-powered International Control Commission consisting of Canada, India, and Poland.

France had little choice, but its exit was made somewhat more graceful. Ho Chi Minh's Vietminh forces were dominant in more than three-quarters of Vietnam and were poised to overrun considerably more. To Ho, the terms of the agreement were acceptable since he was convinced that the general election of 1956 would win him all of Vietnam. From his point of view, the certainty of a military victory was simply replaced by the certainty of a political victory. Both the Soviet Union and Communist China, reflecting their recently adopted line of "peaceful coexistence," applied pressure on Ho to accept the terms of the agreement, reassuring him that his victory at the polls was certain.

The United States never signed the Geneva Accords. However, in a unilateral declaration at the end of the Geneva Conference, the United States government pledged to "refrain from the threat or the use of force to disturb" the settlement and added that it would view any violation of the Geneva Agreement with grave concern.

The general American position at the conference remained ambivalent since, on the eve of a congressional election campaign, the maintenance of Eisenhower's domestic appeal as peacemaker in Asia was of great importance. Moreover, to block a peaceful settlement of the Indochina war would also have jeopardized French participation in European defense plans. These conflicting considerations led the Eisenhower administration to dissociate the United States from the Geneva Agreement and to seek another solution that would prevent any further territory in Asia from falling under Communist control. The answer was the creation of SEATO. Secretary of State Dulles declared that now that the war had ended, the United States could make arrangements for collective defense against aggression and build up "the truly independent states of Cambodia, Laos, and South Vietnam." On the day the treaty was signed at Manila, by an additional protocol, its eight members designated the states of Cambodia and Laos and "the free territory under the jurisdiction of the state of Vietnam" to be under SEATO protection. The United States thus created SEATO to offset the results of Geneva. It also decided to consider South Vietnam as a separate state.

The Vietminh, on the other hand, regarded SEATO as a clear violation of the spirit of the Geneva Agreement. Ho Chi Minh saw the American position as an effort to deprive the Vietminh in the political arena of what it had gained militarily on the battlefield. Nevertheless, Ho withdrew his forces from the

South, assuming that he would get enough votes there in 1956 so that he would emerge with a clear majority on a nationwide basis at election time. After all, his election in the North would be a certainty and if only a minority would support the Vietminh in the South, his election would be assured. President Eisenhower, too, thought that elections, if held on the basis of the Geneva Agreement, would lead to a Communist victory. As he put it in 1954, "Had elections been held as of the time of the fighting, possibly 80 percent of the population would have voted for the Communist Ho Chi Minh as their leader rather than Chief of State Bao Dai."[31]

In the meantime, Ngo Dinh Diem, an American-backed Roman Catholic from a Mandarin family, began to challenge Emperor Bao Dai in the South. The United States strongly supported Diem in his bid for power and in October 1955, Diem proclaimed the establishment of a Republic of Vietnam, with himself as president.

Hence, Geneva and the SEATO Treaty meant the end of French power in Indochina and the beginnings of the American effort to enter the struggle with military might. As yet there were no significant military encounters between Vietminh and American forces. But the issue was joined. The Vietminh now saw the Americans as following the path of French imperialism and the Americans perceived Geneva as a well-laid Communist trap to engulf all of Vietnam. The end of a colonial war merely signified the beginnings of a war between Americans and Communists. Thus, once again the continuum pattern appeared: the East-West conflict simply grew out of the struggle between nationalism and colonialism.

As the East-West conflict superseded the colonial war, the pace of battle gradually intensified. A pattern of escalation emerged by which every diplomatic failure to achieve negotiations paved the way for yet another upward step on the scale of violence.

The first such discernible move after Geneva was the American effort between 1954 and 1956 to strengthen President Diem's military establishment and Ho Chi Minh's visit to Moscow and Peking in 1955 to negotiate aid and friendship treaties with the two Communist powers. Diem declared in July 1955 that, since South Vietnam had not signed the Geneva Agreements, he was not prepared to permit elections under the conditions specified by it. He also added that there was no freedom in the North to campaign for any opposition to Ho Chi Minh. The American government supported this view and July 1956, the date scheduled for general elections in the Geneva Accords, passed without elections being held. Ho, in retaliation, began to train Communist cadres for guerrilla war in the South. He also became the recipient of aid from the Soviet Union and China for the purpose of shoring up the economic base of the North Vietnamese state.

On December 20, 1960, a National Liberation Front was created in South Vietnam. The Front announced a ten-point program calling for the overthrow of the incumbent Saigon government and the removal of American military advisers.

During the remaining years of the Eisenhower administration, the United States continued to support the increasingly unpopular President Diem with military advisers. The second rung of the escalation ladder was reached in January 1961 when Hanoi announced its endorsement of the National Liberation Front in South Vietnam.

The three years of the Kennedy administration were years of gradually deepening, though always limited, American involvement. By the time of President Kennedy's death, the United States had approximately 17,000 advisers in Vietnam though there was no direct American participation in actual combat. A further complicating factor was the increasingly oppressive nature of Diem's regime, which was ultimately overthrown by a military coup in November 1963. Kennedy himself always tried to draw a distinction between American assistance to South Vietnam and Americanization of the war. "In the final analysis," he said, "it is their war. They are the ones who have to win it or lose it."[32] In the meantime, the growth of Communist insurgency in the South was rapid. The resurrected Vietminh, now called Vietcong by the Americans, infiltrated the South in increasing numbers. The National Liberation Front built a highly efficient network of political cadres which began a campaign of terror and assassination in South Vietnamese villages. By late 1963 both sides had raised the stakes and the United States, though not yet directly involved in actual combat, began to establish the necessary logistical base for further action.

Another threshold was crossed in the summer of 1964. In July the new South Vietnamese prime minister, General Khanh, delivered a major address, the keynote of which was "to the North." Two days later Nguyen Cao Ky, the commander of the South Vietnamese Air Force, announced that he was prepared to bomb North Vietnam at any time. In early August North Vietnamese torpedo boats launched attacks on two American ships in the Gulf of Tonkin. President Johnson retaliated by bombing oil depots and other facilities in North Vietnam. On August 19 the President secured the passage of the Tonkin Gulf Resolution in Congress, which authorized him "to take all necessary measures to repel any armed attack against the forces of the U.S. and to prevent further aggression." The air war had gone north of the seventeenth parallel for the first time.

The next rung on the ladder was reached in February 1965. On February 7 the Vietcong staged a night raid against American barracks at Pleiku, killing 8 Americans and wounding 126. Twelve hours later, American jets attacked North Vietnam in what was to be the first of an almost uninterrupted series of daily air attacks against the North. In the South, marines were introduced into the ground war which was now rapidly Americanized. By 1966 United States fighting units were frequently suffering higher casualty rates than their South Vietnamese allies. The Liberation Front responded to these events with its harsh five-point manifesto of March 1965 in which it refused to enter into negotiations until after American troops had been withdrawn. Three weeks later, however, Hanoi published its own "four-point program" in which it did not rule out the possibility of negotiations. In mid-May, the United States stopped its bombings of the North for five days, but no talks ensued—and the air attacks were resumed.

In February 1966, President Johnson met with the South Vietnamese leader, Air Marshal Ky, at Honolulu, where the two men underlined their solidarity against "the aggression from the North." In mid-1966 President Johnson announced that guerrilla infiltration from the North had increased at an alarming rate and that further American retaliatory action might be necessary. In June the United States bombed the North Vietnamese capital of Hanoi and its largest port, Haiphong. In the South, American manpower had risen from 17,000 to 500,000 by 1968. There was no evidence, however, that this policy of "strategic persuasion" had deterred the Hanoi regime from sending more guerrillas to the South or the Liberation Front from attempting to infiltrate the countryside. The war had escalated in ever more violent bursts but no decisive change had occurred in the balance of power among the main belligerents.

By this time, a deep division had occurred within the United States about the American commitment in Vietnam and the future course of American foreign policy in Southeast Asia. The administration defended its policy in Vietnam on the following main grounds: First, it defended the air attacks as "strategic persuasion" of the North to leave its neighbors to the South alone. Also, the bombing raids, in the view of the administration, "raised the costs of aggression" and made it more difficult to send guerrillas to the South via the "Ho Chi Minh trail." Second, a withdrawal would, in the eyes of the administration, signify a tremendous victory for the Chinese view on "wars of liberation," showing up the United States as a "paper tiger" and encouraging stepped-up aggressive moves by communism elsewhere in the world. Third, "aggression must be stopped at the source." In the view of the administration, Hanoi stood behind the National Liberation Front and China stood behind Hanoi. Hence China must be contained on her periphery as the Soviet Union was successfully contained twenty years earlier. A withdrawal, on the other hand, would produce a "row of falling dominoes" and bring to an end the American presence in Southeast Asia altogether.

Critics of the administration pointed to the experience of 400,000 French troops of Indochina and wondered whether the United States could fare better in a counterinsurgency war in which a ten-to-one troop ratio in favor of the United States might be necessary for victory over the Vietcong. Opponents of the war also accused the United States of destroying the social fabric of South Vietnam—the very nation it had set out to save from communism—through air bombardments and ground warfare. Third, the danger of Chinese or Soviet intervention on Hanoi's side took a prominent place in the view of most critics. Finally, opponents asserted that the United States still behaved as if communism were a monolithic force that had to elicit an American response whenever a Communist regime appeared. Actually, the argument continued, communism was now much more diffuse and each such regime should be evaluated in a specific and pragmatic manner by the United States rather than seen automatically as an attempt to extend the design of world communism. Hence, the argument concluded, the American involvement in Vietnam would have made sense twenty years earlier, as did the formation of NATO in Europe, but in the 1960s a strategic United States commitment in Southeast Asia was at best an anachronism and, at worst, a catastrophe. These differing perceptions of the nature of communism lay at the heart of the dialogue between "hawks" and "doves" in the United States.

By 1968, the impasse over negotiations between the NLF and North Vietnam on one side and the United States and South Vietnam on the other had crystallized into a single issue: the bombing of North Vietnam. Hanoi and the Front demanded the cessation of bombings as a precondition to talks; the United States and South Vietnam demanded an end to Communist infiltration into the South as a precondition to the cessation of air attacks on the North. On March 31, 1968, President Johnson decided to stop all bombings north of the nineteenth parallel. Shortly thereafter, peace talks began in Paris between the United States and North Vietnam. At these talks, the North Vietnamese negotiators insisted on a total halt to the bombings, but the United States in turn insisted on the simultaneous reduction of guerrilla infiltration into South Vietnam as an act of reciprocity. On October 31, President Johnson ordered the complete cessation of the bombings. The Paris peace talks were broadened to include South Vietnam and the National Liberation Front. But as in Korea, the peace talks were only a prologue to the difficult business of peacemaking.

The war continued during Richard M. Nixon's presidency. The objective of the new President was "Vietnamization," or the turning over of the ground war to the combat forces for South Vietnam. Under this policy, Nixon gradually withdrew American combat troops from South Vietnam. In March 1972, however, the North Vietnamese launched a major offensive in the most impressive show of force since the Tet assault in 1968. The North Vietnamese leadership had decided to make an all-out effort to seize what it could in the South at a time when it was facing a new form of diplomatic isolation. The latest American overtures to China and the Soviet Union threatened to separate North Vietnam from its two major Communist allies. The offensive began shortly after President Nixon's visit to Peking in February but before his trip to Moscow, scheduled for May.

In April and May of 1972, Nixon took two gambles that escalated the war to new levels of violence. In April, B-52 bombers struck Hanoi and Haiphong in saturation bombings that by far exceeded the ferocity of the Johnson raids. And in May, the President took a step that his predecessor had always ruled out as too perilous: he ordered the mining of North Vietnam's harbors to cut off the flow of tanks, artillery, and other offensive weapons supplied to Hanoi by the Soviet Union and other Communist nations. At the same time, however, he offered a total troop withdrawal from South Vietnam four months after an Indochina-wide cease-fire and the return of prisoners of war. The risk of Soviet-American confrontation at sea dominated world attention for several days, but only verbal denunciations emanated from Moscow and Peking. The Soviet Union by now placed a higher priority on the growing détente with the United States than on the interest of North Vietnam. The Soviet-American summit took place on schedule and the President's gamble paid off. North Vietnam now realized that it had been virtually abandoned by its own allies. The United States suddenly found itself in the anomalous position of having reached détente with the two colossi of communism—China and the Soviet

Union—while it continued to wage war against a small Communist peasant country which it accused of aggression.

In July the Paris peace talks resumed and troop withdrawal continued. On October 26, in a dramatic announcement, Henry Kissinger predicted that "peace was at hand." This optimism proved to be premature. Early in December, Kissinger's "final talks" with the North Vietnamese were broken off and he reported a stalemate.

On December 18, President Nixon ordered all-out bombing attacks on Hanoi and Haiphong. Millions of tons of explosives were dropped on the North. The fierce intensity and relentlessness of the attacks produced an outcry of protest against "terror bombings" from many parts of the world. The raids were halted on December 30, and the Paris talks once again resumed. On January 23, 1973, after almost three decades of war, a cease-fire was reached.

The Paris Accords provided for the withdrawal of all American troops and military advisers, an exchange of prisoners, consultations between South and North Vietnam on general elections, new supervisory machinery, and the withdrawal of all foreign troops from Laos and Cambodia.

In essence, what was achieved in Paris in 1973 was a reversion to the status of Vietnam at the time of the 1954 Geneva Accords. The United States had come full circle in Vietnam. The clock was turned back twenty years. There was an Orwellian irony to the situation. Progress was regress: 1954 by 1973.

The American hope, after the withdrawal of American troops, was that South Vietnam would be able to defend itself against the North with military and financial assistance from the United States. For two years that hope seemed justified, but then the dam broke. In the spring of 1975, the Communist insurgents in Cambodia, the Khmer Rouge, marched upon the capital, Phnom Penh, and forced Marshal Lon Nol, Cambodia's American-supported president, to flee the country. Thus, the American "incursion" of 1970 finally produced the opposite of what it had intended: a Communist instead of a neutralist Cambodia. At the same time, the South Vietnamese army lost its fighting spirit and collapsed entirely. In a matter of weeks, almost all of South Vietnam fell to the Communists. In the United States, a test of wills took place between the administration of President Gerald R. Ford, who favored continued military aid to Cambodia and to South Vietnam, and the Congress, which became increasingly reluctant to cooperate. Finally, the United States was left with the humanitarian responsibility of rescuing terror-stricken refugees who were fleeing from the advancing North Vietnamese armies. In April Saigon surrendered to the Communists and was renamed Ho Chi Minh City. Twenty years of American effort thus ended in failure. As Dean Rusk, one of the main architects of American Vietnam policy during the 1960s, put it in April 1975:

> Personally, I made two mistakes: I underestimated the tenacity of the North Vietnamese and overestimated the patience of the American people.[33]

By the mid-1970s, both the supporters and the critics of the Vietnam war in the United States tended to regard the second Indochina war as one of the most terrible episodes in the history of American foreign policy. There was a general consensus that it would take a long time for the wounds to heal, both in Indochina and in the United States.

The American involvement in Indochina had begun imperceptibly, almost like a mild toothache. At the end, it ran through Vietnam and America like a pestilence. Each President based his policies on exaggerated fears, and later on exaggerated hopes. Thus, each President left the problem to his successor in worse shape than he had found it.

The United States dropped more than seven million tons of bombs on Indochina. This is eighty times the amount that was dropped on Britain during World War II and is equal to more than three hundred of the atomic bombs that fell on Japan in 1945. The bombs left twenty million craters. After the bombardments much of Vietnam looked like a moonscape. Nothing will grow there for generations.

America, too, was in anguish over the war. Its leadership lost respect in the eyes of an entire generation, universities were disrupted, careers were blighted, and the economy was bloated with war inflation. The metal caskets in which the remains of 56,000 Americans came back from Vietnam were to symbolize the war's ultimate and only meaning.

In historical perspective, the great unanswered question will probably be: Which would have been less costly, an earlier Communist victory or the agony of this war? One cannot help but wonder what might have happened if not one single American soldier had ever come to Indochina. History does not reveal its alternatives, and thus one cannot say with certitude where this road not taken would have led. Vietnam might indeed have gone Communist much earlier. It would, however, probably have been a form of communism of the Titoist variety—with a strong dose of nationalism and a fierce tradition of independence vis-à-vis Moscow and Peking. The United States could have lived with that, it seems. Certainly, its postponement was hardly worth the sacrifice of more than 56,000 American lives and hundreds of thousands of Vietnamese lives, and $150 billion.

As the war cost more and more in blood and treasure, it tended to resolve less and less. Finally it ended in the stunned exhaustion of defeat for two American-supported regimes. Ironically, despite Indochina, the United States had reached détente with the two major Communist powers. The hopes, rather than the fears, of five presidents were borne out by long-range international developments. A calmer world had begun to emerge and the Vietnam conflict, first initiated to combat the spread of communism, had become a deadening anachronism. This, perhaps, is the bitterest lesson of this terrible war. It had begun in the world of the cold war and ended, a generation later, in a world of détente. Thus, the reasons for its outbreak had almost become irrelevant. History had simply passed it by. When considered in this perspective, the awesome logic about Vietnam is apparent: It was probably in vain that combatants and civilians had suffered, the land was devastated, and the dead had died.

The United States and Central America

President Reagan's perception of the Soviet threat resembled that of Lyndon Johnson. When it came to Communism, both men had an "us versus them," "good versus evil" attitude. Joseph Stalin, in his grave since 1953, was a kind of Frankenstein monster ready to spring to life at any moment. World conquest was still the Soviet goal, in both men's view. Hence, while objectively there was only a superficial resemblance between Vietnam and Central America, Ronald Reagan perceived the challenge to the United States in similar terms: as a test of America's resolve to turn back the Communist tide.

By the mid-1980s, the United States had not only invaded Grenada; its warships were deployed off the coast of Central America. Fifteen thousand guerrillas covertly funded by the CIA and openly endorsed by the Reagan administration were trying to bring down the Marxist Sandinista regime in Nicaragua. In addition, the CIA was engaged in the mining of Nicaraguan ports, and the administration refused to recognize the jurisdiction of the World Court in the affair. In El Salvador the administration funded the training of officers and cadets in the government's war against Marxist guerrillas. In November 1983 Undersecretary of Defense Fred C. Iklé warned in a White House-approved speech that in El Salvador "we do not seek a military defeat for our friends; we do not seek a military stalemate; we seek victory for the forces of democracy." In his appraisal of the threat from Nicaragua, Iklé was even more forceful:

> We must prevent consolidation of the Sandinista regime in Nicaragua; if we cannot prevent that, we have to anticipate the partition of Central America. Such a development would then force us to man a new military front line of the East-West conflict, right here on our continent.

In 1984 a CIA handbook detailing the art of political assassination in Nicaragua became a source of considerable embarrassment for the Reagan administration.

In other words, in order to roll back Communism, the United States supported a government against guerrillas in El Salvador and guerrillas against a government in Nicaragua. Sandinistas and Salvadoran guerrillas perceived the conflict in terms of "Yankee imperialism" versus self-determination. The Reagan administration, on the other hand, viewed it as a struggle between Communism and democracy. Thus, once again, the world's two great power struggles were inextricably linked.

By late 1983 neither the "contras" in Nicaragua nor the Salvadoran army had been particularly successful in containing, let alone rolling back, Marxist advances. On the contrary, the Salvadoran guerrillas were making major advances and the Sandinista regime seemed firmly entrenched in Nicaragua despite the mining of its harbors. The logic of the Reagan administration thus seemed open to serious question.

In January 1984 a National Bipartisan Commission on Central America, headed by former Secretary of State Henry Kissinger, presented its findings to the President. The essence of the Commission's report was that the exploitation of Central American unrest by the Soviet Union and Cuba threatened American security interests. The solution was to be found in offering pro-United States regimes military assistance to defeat externally supported insurgencies and economic assistance to overcome the poverty and misery that triggered such insurgencies. The amount of aid recommended was $8 billion over a five-year period. Failure would constitute a significant victory for the Soviet Union and a serious defeat for the United States. In short, Central America was to become an East-West military and economic battleground.

It was in the Commission's findings that a disturbing analogy to Vietnam became apparent. The United States strongly supported José Napoleon Duarte as its candidate for the presidency of El Salvador. Duarte duly won the election and thereby became America's "client." In the past, in China and Vietnam, such "clients" had lost popular support precisely because of their close association with the "imperialist" power. The title to the revolution was then captured by Mao Tse-tung and Ho Chi Minh because of their unrelenting hostility to Western imperialism. Could this be the reason why five thousand Marxist guerrillas could not be eliminated by the Duarte government in El Salvador and why fifteen thousand U.S.-supported contras could do little to weaken the Marxist regime in Nicaragua? Might the United States, in its frustration in Central America, assume a more direct military role as it did in Vietnam and try to do the job itself?

Perhaps a warning voiced by four countries far more familiar with the Central American terrain than the twelve members of the Kissinger Commission should not go unheeded. Mexico, Venezuela, Colombia, and Panama, known as the "Contadora Group," did not see the Soviet threat as apocalyptically as the Commission members who had spent only one day each in El Salvador, Nicaragua, Honduras, Guatemala, and Costa Rica. The Contadora Group urged that the problems of the region be resolved by diplomatic means rather than by military force.

Obviously, it would be most attractive for the United States if the five Central American countries were all pro-American. It would also be unacceptable if Central America were to become a Soviet base. Both of these extremes are probably beyond the power of either the United States or the Soviet Union to achieve. The United States cannot attain the first though it can prevent the second. In all probability, Central America will continue to be plagued by turbulence and civil wars. In Vietnam, Lyndon Johnson escalated a civil war into a global conflict. Ronald Reagan's views of Central America, a decade after America's defeat in Vietnam, were disturbingly similar. It is important to remember that people will insist on finding their own way to national identity. Neither the Soviet Union nor the United States has the power indefinitely to stem the course of national self-determination. "Every country," Britain's Ambassador to Washington, Lord Harlech, once said, "has a right to its own War of the Roses." History has its own logic in each country and all too often its rivers flow with blood.

WHY NATIONS GO TO WAR

"If you look deeply into the abyss," said Nietzsche, "the abyss will look into you." The face of war in our time is so awesome and so terrible that the first temptation is to recoil and turn away. Medusa-like, the face of war, with its relentless horror, threatens to destroy anyone who looks at it for long. Yet we must find the courage to confront the abyss. I deeply believe that war is a sickness, though it may be mankind's "sickness unto death." No murderous epidemic has ever been conquered without exposure, pain, and danger, or by ignoring the bacilli. But in the end, man's faculty of reason and his courage have prevailed and even the plague was overcome. The Black Death that ravaged our planet centuries ago today is but a distant memory.

It is true that the analogy between sickness and war may be open to attack. It has been fashionable to assert that war is not an illness but, like aggression, an ineradicable part of human nature. In this writer's judgment this is a dubious assumption. While aggression may be inherent in us all, war is learned behavior and, as such, can be unlearned and, ultimately, selected out entirely. There have been other habits of mankind that seemed impossible to shed. In the Ice Age, when people lived in caves, incest was perfectly acceptable; often there were no people other than father, mother, sister, or brother around. Today, incest is virtually gone. Cannibalism provides an even more dramatic case. Thousands of years ago, human beings ate each other and drank each other's blood. That, too, was part of "human nature." Even a brief century ago, millions of Americans believed that God had ordained white people to be free and black people to be slaves. Why else would He have created them in different colors? Yet slavery, once a part of "human nature," was abolished because human beings showed a capacity for growth. The growth came slowly, after immense suffering, but it *did* come. "Human nature" had been changed. Like slavery and cannibalism, war too can be eliminated from mankind's arsenal of horrors.

It seems, however, that men abandon their bad habits only when catastrophe is close at hand. The intellect alone is not enough. Men must be shaken, almost shattered, before changing. A grave illness must pass its crisis before it is known whether the patient will live or die. Most appropriately, the ancient Chinese had two characters for the word *crisis*—one connoting danger and the other, opportunity. The danger of extinction is upon us, but so is the opportunity for a better life for all men on this planet.

We must therefore make an effort to look Medusa in the face and to diagnose the sickness. Diagnosis is no cure, of course, but it is the first and the most necessary step. I shall attempt this diagnosis by suggesting certain common themes about war in this century.

The first general theme that compels attention is that no nation that began a major war in this century emerged a winner. Austria-Hungary and Germany, which precipitated World War I, went down to ignominious defeat; Hitler's Germany was crushed into unconditional surrender; the North Korean attack was thwarted by collective action and ended in a draw; in the Vietnamese war it is difficult if not impossible clearly to identify the aggressor; the

Arabs who invaded the new Jewish state in 1948 lost territory to the Israelis in four successive wars; and Pakistan, which wished to punish India through pre-emptive war, found itself dismembered in the process. In all cases, those who began a war came a cropper. The nature or the ideology of the government that started a war seems to have made little, if any, difference. Defeat came to aggressors whether they were capitalists or Communists, white or nonwhite, Western or non-Western, rich or poor.

In the nineteenth century, by contrast, most wars were won by the governments that started them. Only those like Napoleon, who aspired to the big prize, suffered ultimate defeat. War then was still a rational pursuit, fought for limited objectives. Twentieth-century aggressors, on the other hand, tended to be more demanding and more ruthless: they fought for total stakes and hence made war a question of survival. Those who were attacked had to fight for life itself. Courage born of desperation proved to be a formidable weapon. In the end, those who began the war were stemmed, turned back, and in some cases, crushed completely. In no case has any nation that began a war in our time achieved its ends.

In the atomic age, war between nuclear powers is suicidal; wars between small countries with big friends are likely to be inconclusive and interminable; hence, decisive war in our time has become the privilege of the impotent. It has become almost banal to say that the atomic age has fundamentally altered the nature of war. No nuclear power can tell another: "Do as I say or I shall kill you," but is reduced to saying: "Do as I say or I shall kill us both," which is an entirely different matter. Thus, when everybody is somebody, nobody is anybody. But it is not only nuclear countries that cannot win wars against each other. A small country with a good tie to a big ally also can no longer be defeated. The wars in Korea, Vietnam, and the Middle East all illustrate this point. The North Koreans were unable to defeat South Korea so long as the United States was willing to support the South and to neutralize the North's successes. And the South Koreans could not defeat the North so long as China and the Soviet Union were willing to render assistance. Thus, in the end, the Korean war ended with the frontiers virtually unchanged. The main difference was the large number of dead Koreans on *both* sides. In Vietnam, the Soviet Union and China sent enough supplies to offset the results of American bombings. In 1980 the deserts of the Middle East became veritable proving grounds for the testing of new superpower weapons. Iraq bombed Iran with Soviet Migs, and Iran reciprocated by bombing Iraq with American-made Phantom jets. Thus, wars between small nations with big weapons will be interminable so long as the ally of the weaker side is willing to continue its support. Neither side can win; only the casualties mount. In our time, decisive victories seem possible only for nations without big friends or for the impotent. Thus, Bangladesh was able to break away from Pakistan because none of the great powers considered the issue important enough to restore the status quo by force of arms. Nor did the genocidal violence perpetrated by the Tutsi tribe against the Hutu people in Central Africa stir the great powers into action. Thus, the paradox of war in the atomic age may be summarized as follows: The power of big states vis-à-vis each other has been reduced if not altogether canceled out,

while the power of small and friendless states vis-à-vis each other has been pro-
portionately enhanced.

In our time, unless the vanquished is destroyed completely, a victor's
peace is seldom lasting. Those peace settlements that are negotiated on a basis
of equality are much more permanent and durable. In 1918, Germany was defeated but not crushed. Versailles became the crucible for Hitler's Germany,
which was then brought down only through unconditional surrender. The Korean truce of 1953 was negotiated between undefeated equals. Both sides were
unhappy, but neither side was so unhappy that it wished to overturn the settlement and initiate yet another war. An uneasy armistice or truce was gradually
recognized as a basis for a legitimate peace settlement. The relative insecurity
of each side thus became the guarantor of the relative security of both. Israel
learned this lesson in October 1973. The victor's peace of 1967 had left the
Arabs in a state of such frustration that they were compelled to try their hand
once more at war. With their dignity restored in 1973, they found it psychologically possible to meet with Israelis in a face-to-face diplomatic encounter
for the first time in a quarter of a century.

Turning to the problem of the outbreak of war, the record indicates the
crucial importance of the personalities of leaders. One is less impressed by the
role of abstract forces such as nationalism, militarism, or alliance systems that
traditionally have been regarded as the causes of war. Nor does it seem that
economic factors played a vital part in precipitating war. The personalities of
leaders, on the other hand, have often been decisive. The outbreak of World
War I illustrates this point quite clearly. Conventional wisdom has blamed the
alliance system for the spread of the war. Specifically, the argument runs, Kaiser Wilhelm's alliance with Austria dragged Germany into the war against the
Allied powers. This analysis, however, totally ignores the role of the Kaiser's
personality during the gathering crisis. Supposing Wilhelm had had the fortitude to continue his role as mediator and to restrain Austria instead of engaging in paranoid delusions and accusing England of conspiring against
Germany? The disaster might have been averted and then the conventional
wisdom would have praised the alliance system for saving the peace instead of
blaming it for causing the war. In truth, the emotional balance or lack of balance of the German kaiser turned out to be absolutely crucial. Similarly, the
relentless mediocrity of the leading personalities on all sides no doubt contributed to the disaster. Looking at the outbreak of World War II, there is no
doubt that the victor's peace of Versailles and the galloping inflation of the
1920s brought about the rise of Nazi Germany. But once again, it was the personality of Hitler that was decisive. A more rational leader would have consolidated his gains and certainly would not have attacked the Soviet Union. And
if Russia had to be attacked, then a rational man would have made contin-
gency plans to meet the Russian winter instead of counting blindly on an early
victory. In the Korean War, the hubris of General MacArthur probably prolonged the conflict by two years, and in Vietnam, the fragile egos of at least
two American presidents who could not face the facts first escalated the war
quite disproportionately and then postponed its ending quite unreasonably. In
the Middle East, the volatile personality of Gamal Abdel Nasser was primarily

responsible for the closing of the Gulf of Aqaba which precipitated the Six-Day War of 1967. In all these cases, a fatal flaw or ego weakness in a leader's personality turned out to be of crucial importance. It may, in fact, have spelled the difference between the outbreak of war and the maintenance of peace.

Perhaps the most important single precipitating factor in the outbreak of war is misperception. Such distortion may manifest itself in four different ways: in a leader's image of himself; a leader's view of his adversary's character; a leader's view of his adversary's intentions toward himself; and, finally, a leader's view of his adversary's capabilities and power. Each of these is of such importance that it merits separate and careful treatment.

There is a remarkable consistency in the self-images of most national leaders on the brink of war. Each confidently expects victory after a brief and triumphant campaign. Doubt about the outcome is the voice of the enemy and therefore incomprehensible. This recurring atmosphere of optimism is not to be dismissed lightly by the historian as an ironic example of human folly. It assumes a powerful emotional momentum of its own and thus itself becomes one of the causes of war. Anything that fuels such optimism about a quick and decisive victory makes war more likely and anything that dampens it becomes a cause of peace.

This common belief in a short, decisive war is usually the overflow from a reservoir of self-delusions held by the leadership about both itself and its nation. The kaiser's appearance in shining armor in August 1914 and his promise to the German nation that its sons would be back home "before the leaves had fallen from the trees" was matched by similar scenes of overconfidence and military splendor in Austria, in Russia, and in the other nations on the brink of war. Hitler's confidence in an early German victory in Russia was so unshakable that no winter uniforms were issued to the soldiers and no preparations whatsoever made for the onset of the Russian winter. In November 1941, when the mud of autumn turned to ice and snow, the cold became the German soldier's bitterest enemy. Tormented by the arctic temperatures, men died, machines broke down, and the quest for warmth all but eclipsed the quest for victory. Hitler's hopes and delusions about the German superman were shattered in the frozen wastes of Russia. The fact that Hitler had fought in World War I and seen that optimism crumble in defeat did not prevent its reappearance. When North Korea invaded South Korea, her leadership expected victory within two months. The Anglo-French campaign at Suez in 1956 was spurred by the hope of a swift victory. In Pakistan, Yahya Khan hoped to teach Indira Gandhi a lesson modeled on the Six-Day War in Israel. And in Vietnam, every American escalation in the air or on the ground was an expression of the hope that a few more bombs, a few more troops, would bring decisive victory.

Thus, leaders on all sides typically engage in self-delusions on the eve of war. Only the war itself then provides the stinging ice of reality and ultimately helps restore a measure of perspective in the leadership. The price for this recapture of reality is high indeed. It is unlikely that there ever was a war that fulfilled the initial hopes and expectations of both sides.

Distorted views of the adversary's character also help to precipitate a conflict. As the pressure mounted in July 1914, the German kaiser explosively admitted that he "hated the Slavs, even though one should not hate anyone." This hatred no doubt influenced his decision to end his role as mediator and to prepare for war. Similarly, his naive trust in the honesty of the Austrian leaders prompted him to extend to them the blank check guarantee that dragged him into war. In reality, the Austrians were more deceitful than he thought and the Russians more honest. Worst of all, the British leadership, which worked so desperately to avert a general war, was seen by Wilhelm as the center of a monstrous plot to encircle and destroy the German nation. Hitler, too, had no conception of what Russia really was like. He knew nothing of the history and depth of the Russian land and believed that it was populated by subhuman barbarians who could be crushed with one decisive stroke and then be made to serve as slaves for German supermen. This relentless hatred and contempt for Russia became a crucial factor in Hitler's ill-fated assault of 1941. Perhaps the most important reason for the American military intervention in Vietnam was the misperception of the American leadership about the nature of communism in Asia. President Lyndon Johnson committed more than half a million combat troops to an Asian land war because he perceived the Vietnam War in terms of purely Western categories: a colossal shootout between the forces of communism and those of anticommunism. The fact that Ho Chi Minh saw the Americans as the successors of French imperialism whom he was determined to drive out was completely lost upon the President. Virtue, righteousness, and justice were fully on his side, he thought. America, the child of light, had to defeat the child of darkness in a twentieth-century crusade. Mutual contempt and hatred also hastened the coming of the wars between the Arab states and Israel and between India and Pakistan. In the former case, the Arab view of Israel as an alien and hostile presence was a precipitating cause of conflict. And, in the latter, the two religions of Hinduism and Islam led directly to the creation of two hostile states that clashed in bloody conflict three times in a single generation.

If a leader on the brink of war believes that his adversary will attack him, the chances of war are fairly high. If both leaders share this perception about each other's intent, war becomes a virtual certainty. The mechanism of the self-fulfilling prophecy is then set in motion. If leaders attribute evil designs to their adversaries, and if they nurture these beliefs for long enough, they will eventually be proven right. The mobilization measures that preceded the outbreak of World War I were essentially defensive measures triggered by the fear of the other side's intent. The Russian tsar mobilized because he feared an Austrian attack; the German kaiser mobilized because he feared the Russian "steamroller." The nightmare of each then became a terrible reality. Stalin, imprisoned by the Marxist dogma that capitalists would always lie, disbelieved Churchill's truthful warnings about Hitler's murderous intent—he was so blind to it that Russia almost lost the war. Eisenhower and Dulles were so convinced that the Chinese would move against the French in Indochina in the way they had against MacArthur's UN forces, that they committed the first American military advisers to Vietnam. The Chinese never intervened, but the Americans had begun their march along the road to self-entrapment in the

Vietnam quagmire. Arabs and Israelis and Indians and Pakistanis generally expected nothing but the worst from one another, and these expectations often led to war. The conviction held by Syria and Egypt after 1967 that Israel intended to hold on to the occupied territories forever was the immediate precipitating cause of the October War of 1973, in which the Arabs made a desperate attempt to reconquer their lost lands. And Yahya Khan's perception of India's intention to fight on the side of the secessionist movement in Bengal led directly to his abortive and suicidal air attack.

A leader's misperception of his adversary's power is perhaps the quintessential cause of war. It is vital to remember, however, that it is not the actual distribution of power that precipitates a war; it is the way in which a leader *thinks* that power is distributed. A war will start when nations disagree over their perceived strength. The war itself then becomes a dispute over measurement. Reality is gradually restored as war itself cures war. And the war will end when the fighting nations perceive each other's strength more realistically.

Germany and Austria-Hungary in 1914 had nothing but contempt for Russia's power. This disrespect was to cost them dearly. Hitler repeated this mistake a generation later and his misperception led straight to his destruction. One of the clearest examples of another misperception of this kind took place in the Korean War. MacArthur, during his advance through North Korea toward the Chinese border, stubbornly believed that the Chinese Communists did not have the capacity to intervene. When the Chinese did cross the Yalu River into North Korea, MacArthur clung to the belief that he was facing 40,000 men while in truth the figure was closer to 200,000. And when the Chinese forces temporarily withdrew to assess their impact on MacArthur's army, the American general assumed that the Chinese were badly in need of rest after their encounter with superior Western military might. And when the Chinese attacked again and drove MacArthur all the way back to South Korea, the leader of the UN forces perceived this action as a "piece of treachery worse even than Pearl Harbor." The most amazing aspect of this story is that the real facts were quite available to MacArthur from his own intelligence sources, if only the general had cared to look at them. But he knew better and thus prolonged the war by two years. Only at war's end did the Americans gain respect for China's power and take care not to provoke it again beyond the point of no return. Yet in the Vietnam War, the American leadership committed precisely the same error vis-à-vis North Vietnam. Five successive presidents believed that Ho Chi Minh would collapse if only a little more military pressure would be brought to bear on him either from the air or on the ground. The North Vietnamese leader proved them all to be mistaken, and only when America admitted that North Vietnam could not be beaten did the war come to an end. In both Korea and Vietnam the price of reality came high indeed. As these wars resolved less and less, they tended to cost more and more in blood and treasure. The number of dead on all sides bore mute testimony to the fact that America had to fight two of the most terrible and divisive wars in her entire history before she gained respect for the realities of power on the other side. In 1948, the Arabs believed that an invasion by five Arab armies would quickly put an end to Israel. They were mistaken. But in 1973, Israel, encouraged to the point of hubris after three successful wars, thought of Arab power only with contempt and of its own as unassailable. That, too, was wrong, as Israel had to learn in the bitter war of October 1973. And in the 1980s the Iraqi leadership discovered that its attack on Iran, far from being a knock-out blow, only served to inflame the Iranians' fanatical fighting zeal. As a result the Iraq-Iran war became a terrible war of attrition that cost each side hundreds of thousands of casualties.

Thus, on the eve of each war at least one nation misperceives another's power. In that sense, the beginning of each war is a misperception or an accident. The war itself then slowly, and in agony, teaches men about reality. And peace is made when reality has won. The outbreak of war and the coming of peace are separated by a road that leads from misperception to reality. The most tragic aspect of this truth is that war has continued to remain the best teacher of reality and thus has been the most effective cure for war.

Despite the persistence of so much human tragedy and folly, it is nevertheless possible to conclude on a note of hope. There has been a slow dawning of compassion and of global consciousness over humanity's bleak skies in our generation. This has manifested itself both in a new awareness of and even resistance to the havoc that war wreaks upon the human spirit. It is no longer quite acceptable to our sense of logic that throwing a human being into a fire is an atrocity, while throwing fire on many human beings may be designated as a military operation. We can no longer quite understand how one man who kills another is punished as a murderer while another man who murders thousands anonymously from the sky may be acclaimed as a patriot or hero. This new dawning has come through dreadful suffering, but it *has* come.

At the very moment when mankind has the power to destroy the earth, men also have begun to perceive the planet as a whole. If the most fundamental challenge of this generation was to help prevent another world war, the great challenge of the coming generation may be the preservation of the possibility of a decent life on spaceship earth. The atom bomb, through its own inexorable logic, has left no alternative to a negotiated world order. Similarly, problems of resources and environment will be surmounted on a global basis or not at all. Thus, in both cases, the brute logic of the insensate machine has dictated a modicum of world order: the terror of atomic fire in the former, and the prospect of men starving or choking in their own waste in the latter. And out of this terror has sprung the recognition of the need for flexibility and change. The bomb must not become the earth, nor must the earth become the bomb.

It is this new, slow dawning of compassion and of global consciousness that is our greatest hope. From this new spirit that is stirring deep within us we shall forge the weapons against war. Man has built both cathedrals and concentration camps. While he has descended to unprecedented depths in our time, he has also soared to greater heights than ever before. Man is not burdened with original sin alone; he also has the gift of original innocence.

REFERENCES

1. Department of State Bulletin, March 23, 1947, p. 534.
2. Harry S Truman, *Memoirs, Vol. II: Years of Trial and Hope.* Garden City, N.Y.: Doubleday, 1952, p. 241.
3. Department of State Bulletin, March 25, 1957, p. 481.
4. *The New York Times,* January 31, 1958.
5. Arnold Wolfers, "Stresses and Strains in 'Going It With Others,'" in Arnold Wolfers, ed., *Alliance Policy in the Cold War.* Baltimore: Johns Hopkins Press, 1959, p. 7.
6. Ronald Reagan, "Peace and National Security: A New Defense," delivered from the White House, March 23, 1983.
7. Address at the Massachusetts Institute of Technology, March 31, 1949.
8. Wolfers, ed., *op. cit.,* p. 119.
9. Zbigniew K. Brzezinski, "U.S. Foreign Policy in East Central Europe—A Study in Contradiction," *Journal of International Affairs.* New York: Columbia University, Vol. IX: No. 1, 1957, p. 67.
10. *Ibid.,* p. 68.
11. Wolfers, ed., *op. cit.,* p. 136.
12. President Kennedy's address to the Canadian Parliament, Ottawa, May 17, 1961, in *Documents on American Foreign Relations 1961.* New York: Harper & Row, 1962, pp. 272 ff.
13. Henry A. Kissinger, *Nuclear Weapons and Foreign Policy.* New York: Harper & Row, 1957, p. 16.
14. *Ibid.,* p. 172.
15. John Herz, *International Politics in the Atomic Age.* New York: Columbia University Press, 1959, p. 175.
16. *The Wall Street Journal,* November 20, 1980.
17. *Ibid.*
18. Hans J. Morgenthau, "Alliances in Theory and Practice," in Wolfers, ed., *op. cit.,* p. 209.
19. A. Doak Barnett, *Communist China and Asia.* New York: Harper & Row, 1960, p. 344.
20. Zbigniew K. Brzezinski, *The Soviet Bloc, Unity and Conflict.* Cambridge, Mass.: Harvard University Press, 1960, p. 403.
21. *The New York Times,* July 17, 1957.
22. Hans J. Morgenthau, *In Defense of the National Interest.* New York: Knopf, 1952, p. 50.
23. A. F. K. Organski, *World Politics.* New York: Knopf, 1958, p. 338.
24. *The New York Times,* March 2, 1955.
25. Thomas C. Schelling, *The Strategy of Conflict.* Cambridge, Mass.: Harvard University Press, 1960, p. 207.
26. *Ibid.,* p. 20.
27. U.S. Department of State, *Bulletin,* Volume XLVII, No. 1220, November 12, 1962, pp. 715–720.
28. Cited in Henry M. Pachter, *Collision Course: The Cuban Missile Crisis and Coexistence.* New York: Praeger, 1963, p. 58.
29. *Ibid.,* p. 89.
30. *Ibid.*
31. Dwight D. Eisenhower, *Mandate for Change.* New York: Doubleday, 1963, p. 372.
32. Department of State Bulletin, Washington, September 30, 1973, pp. 498–499.
33. Interview on NBC Television, April 3, 1975.

BIBLIOGRAPHY

Adelman, Jonathan R. *The Revolutionary Armies: The Historical Development of the Soviet and the Chinese People's Liberation Armies.* Westport, Conn.: Greenwood Press, 1980.
Albert, Stuart, and Luck, Edward C., eds. *On the Endings of Wars.* Port Washington, N.Y.: Kennikat Press, 1980.
Alexander, Yonah; Carlton, David; and Wilkinson, Paul, eds. *Terrorism: Theory and Practice.* Boulder, Colo.: Westview Press, 1979.
Allison, Graham T. *Essence of Decision: Explaining the Cuban Missile Crisis.* Boston: Little, Brown, 1971.
An, Tai Sung. *The Sino-Soviet Territorial Dispute.* Philadelphia: Westminster Press, 1973.
Asprey, Robert B. *War in the Shadows: The Guerrilla in History.* Garden City, N.Y.: Doubleday, 1975.
Austin, Anthony. *The President's War.* Philadelphia: Lippincott, 1971.
Bell, J. Bowyer. *A Time of Terror: How Democratic Societies Respond to Revolutionary Violence.* New York: Basic Books, 1978.
Berman, Larry. *Planning a Tragedy: The Americanization of the War in Vietnam.*
Best, Geoffrey. *Humanity in Warfare.* New York: Columbia University Press, 1980.
Betts, Richard K. *Surprise Attack.* Washington: Brookings Institution, 1982.
Blechman, Barry M., ed. *Rethinking the U.S. Strategic Posture.* Cambridge: Ballinger, 1982.
Brown, Harold. *Thinking About National Security.* Boulder, Colo: Westview Press, 1983.
Buchan, Alastair, ed. *Power and Equilibrium in the 1970's.* New York: Praeger, 1973.
Buckley, Tom. *Violent Neighbors: El Salvador, Central America and the United States.* New York: Times Books, 1984.
Cable, James. *Gunboat Diplomacy.* New York: Praeger, 1971.
Canan, James. *War in Space.* New York: Harper & Row, 1982.
Caputo, Philip. *A Rumor of War.* New York: Holt, Rinehart and Winston, 1977.
Carter, Ashton B., and Schwartz, David N., eds. *Ballistic Missile Defense.* Washington: Brookings Institution, 1984.
Churchill, Winston. *The Second World War.* Vols. I–VI. Boston: Houghton Mifflin, 1948–1953.
Clarke, Robin. *The Science of War and Peace.* New York: McGraw-Hill, 1972.
Claude, Inis L., Jr. *Power and International Relations.* New York: Random House, 1962.
Clausewitz, Karl von. *On War.* New York: Modern Library, 1943.
Collins, John M. *American and Soviet Military Trends Since the Cuban Missile Crisis.* Washington, D.C.: Georgetown University, 1978.
————. *U.S.-Soviet Military Balance: Concepts and Capabilities, 1960–1980.* New York: McGraw-Hill, 1980.
Committee for the Compilation of Materials on Damage Caused by the Atomic Bombs. *Hiroshima and Nagasaki: The Physical, Medical, and Social Effects of the Atomic Bombings.* New York: Basic Books, 1981.
Cooper, Chester L. *The Lost Crusade: America in Vietnam.* New York: Dodd, 1970.
De Raeymaeker, Omer, et al. *Small Powers in Alignment.* Leuven, Belgium: Leuven University Press, 1974.
Detzer, David. *Brink: Cuban Missile Crisis, 1962.* New York: Crowell, 1979.
Dinerstein, Herbert S. *The Making of a Missile Crisis.* Baltimore: Johns Hopkins Press, 1976.
Dismukes, Bradford, and McConnell, James M., eds. *Soviet Naval Diplomacy.* Elmsford, N.Y.: Pergamon Press, 1979.

Divine, Robert A. *Exploring the Johnson Years.* Austin: University of Texas Press, 1981.

Douglass, Joseph D., Jr. *Soviet Military Strategy in Europe.* Elmsford, N.Y.: Pergamon Press, 1980.

Dunn, Frederick S. *War and the Minds of Men.* New York: Harper & Row, 1950.

Dunn, Lewis A. *Controlling the Bomb: Nuclear Proliferation in the 1980's.* New Haven: Yale University Press, 1982.

Dyson, Freeman. *Weapons and Hope.* New York: Harper/Bessie, 1984.

Earl, Edward M. *Makers of Modern Strategy: Military Thought from Machiavelli to Hitler.* Princeton, N.J.: Princeton University Press, 1943.

Ehrlich, Paul; Sagan, Carl; Kennedy, Donald; and Roberts, Walter Orr. *The Cold and the Dark: The World After Nuclear War.* New York: Norton, 1984.

Fairhall, David. *Russian Sea Power.* Boston: Gambit, 1971.

Fallows, James. *National Defense.* New York: Random House, 1981.

Feinberg, Richard E., ed. *Central America: International Dimensions of the Crisis.* New York: Holmes & Meier, 1982.

Fitzgerald, Frances. *Fire in the Lake.* Boston: Little, Brown, 1972.

Freedman, Lawrence. *Britain and Nuclear Weapons.* London: Macmillan (for the Royal Institute of International Affairs), 1980.

———. *The Evolution of Nuclear Strategy.* New York: St. Martin's, 1981.

Gabriel, Richard A. *Operation for Peace Galilee: The Israeli-PLO War in Lebanon.* New York: Hill and Wang, 1984.

Gann, Lewis H. *Guerrillas in History.* Stanford, Calif.: Hoover Institution Press, 1971.

Gelb, Leslie H., with Betts, Richard K. *The Irony of Vietnam: The System Worked.* Washington, D.C.: Brookings Institution, 1979.

Gilmour, David. *Lebanon: The Fractured Country.* New York: St. Martin's Press, 1983.

Gompert, David C., et al. *Nuclear Weapons and World Politics.* New York: McGraw-Hill, 1977.

Gray, Colin S. *The Soviet-American Arms Race.* Lexington, Mass.: Lexington Books, 1976.

———. *American Military Space Policy.* Cambridge: Abt Books, 1983.

Greenwood, Ted. *Making the MIRV: A Study of Defense Decision Making.* Cambridge, Mass.: Ballinger, 1975.

Griffith, Samuel B. *The Chinese People's Army.* New York: McGraw-Hill, 1967.

Hackett, General Sir John, et al. *The Third World War: August 1985.* New York: Macmillan, 1979.

Harrison, Michael M. *The Reluctant Ally: France and Atlantic Security.* Baltimore: Johns Hopkins Press, 1981.

Herring, George C. *America's Longest War: The United States and Vietnam, 1950–1975.* New York: Wiley, 1979.

Herzog, Chaim. *The War of Atonement: October 1973.* Boston: Little, Brown, 1975.

Holloway, David. *The Soviet Union and the Arms Race.* New Haven, Conn.: Yale University Press, 1983.

Holsti, Ole R. *Crisis Escalation War.* Montreal: McGill-Queen's University Press, 1972.

Hosmer, Steven T; Kellen, Konrad; and Jenkins, Brian M. *The Fall of South Vietnam.* New York: Pantheon, 1980.

Howe, Russell Warren. *Weapons: The International Game of Arms, Money and Diplomacy.* New York: Doubleday, 1980.

Huntington, Samuel P. *The Soldier and the State: The Theory and Politics of Civil-Military Relations.* Cambridge, Mass.: Belknap Press of Harvard University Press, 1957.

Hurewitz, J. C. *Middle East Politics: The Military Dimension.* New York: Praeger, 1969.

Iklé, Fred Charles. *Every War Must End.* New York: Columbia University Press, 1971.

Insight Team of the Sunday Times. *Insight on the Middle East War.* London: André Deutsch, 1974.

Jasani, Bhupendra, ed. *Outer Space: A New Dimension of the Arms Race.* London: Taylor & Francis, 1982.

Jenkins, Simon, and Hastings, Max. *The Battle for the Falklands.* New York: Norton, 1983.

Johnson, Chalmers. *Autopsy on People's War.* Berkeley: University of California Press, 1973.

Kahan Commission. *The Beirut Massacre: The Complete Kahan Commission Report.* New York: Karz-Cohl, 1983.

Kahn, Herman. *On Thermonuclear War.* Princeton, N.J: Princeton University Press, 1960.

————. *Thinking About the Unthinkable.* New York: Horizon, 1962.

Kaplan, Stephen S., et al. *Diplomacy of Power: Soviet Armed Forces as a Political Instrument.* Washington: Brookings Institution, 1981.

Katz, Arthur M. *Life After Nuclear War.* Cambridge: Ballinger, 1981.

Kennan, George F., et al. *Encounters with Kennan: The Great Debate.* London and New York: Cass, 1979.

Kennedy, Gavin. *The Military in the Third World.* New York: Scribner, 1975.

Kennedy, Robert F. *Thirteen Days: A Memoir of the Cuban Missile Crisis.* New York: Norton, 1969.

Keynes, Edward. *Undeclared War: Twilight Zone of Constitutional Power.* University Park: Penn State Press, 1982.

Kissinger, Henry A. *The Necessity for Choice.* New York: Harper, 1961.

————. *Nuclear Weapons and Foreign Policy.* New York: Harper, 1957.

————. *The Troubled Partnership.* New York: McGraw-Hill, 1965.

————. *The Report of the President's National Bipartisan Commission on Central America.* New York: Macmillan, 1984.

Knightley, Phillip. *The First Casualty, from the Crimea to Vietnam: The War Correspondent as Hero, Propagandist, and Myth Maker.* New York: Harcourt Brace Jovanovich, 1975.

Kupperman, Robert, and Trent, Darrell. *Terrorism: Threat, Reality, Response.* Stanford, Calif.: Hoover Institution Press, 1979.

LaFeber, Walter. *Inevitable Revolutions: The United States in Central America.* New York: Norton, 1983.

Laqueur, Walter. *Terrorism.* Boston: Little, Brown, 1977.

————, ed. *The Terrorism Reader.* Philadelphia: Temple University Press, 1978.

Leebaert, Derek, ed. *Soviet Military Thinking.* Winchester, Mass.: Allen & Unwin, 1981.

Leiken, Robert S., ed. *Central America: Anatomy of a Conflict.* New York: Pergamon Press, in cooperation with Carnegie Endowment, 1984.

Leites, Nathan. *Soviet Style in War.* New York: Crane, Russak, 1982.

Levine, Barry B., ed. *The New Cuban Presence in the Caribbean.* Boulder, Colo.: Westview Press, 1983.

Luttwak, Edward. *A Dictionary of Modern War.* New York: Harper & Row, 1971.

————. *Strategy and Politics: Collected Essays.* New Brunswick, N.J.: Transaction Books, 1980.

Mandelbaum, Michael. *The Nuclear Revolution: International Politics Before and After Hiroshima.* New York: Cambridge University Press, 1981.

Martin, Lawrence, ed. *Strategic Thought in the Nuclear Age.* Baltimore: Johns Hopkins Press, 1980.

Martin, L. W. *The Sea in Modern Strategy.* New York: Praeger, 1967.

Mearsheimer, John J. *Conventional Deterrence.* Ithaca, N.Y.: Cornell University Press, 1983.

Midlarsky, Manus I. *On War: Political Violence in the International System.* New York: Free Press, 1975.

Milward, Alan S. *War, Economy, and Society, 1939–1945.* Berkeley: University of California Press, 1977.

Moulton, Harland B. *From Superiority to Parity: The United States and the Strategic Arms Race, 1961–1971.* Westport, Conn.: Greenwood Press, 1973.

Nash, Henry T. *Nuclear Weapons and International Behavior.* Leiden: Lijthoff, 1975.

Nef, John U. *War and Human Progress.* Cambridge, Mass.: Harvard University Press, 1950.

Neustadt, Richard E. *Alliance Politics.* New York: Columbia University Press, 1970.

Olive, Marsha McGraw, and Porro, Jeffrey D., eds. *Nuclear Weapons in Europe.* Lexington, Mass: Lexington Books, 1983.

Osgood, Robert E. *Limited War Revisited.* Boulder, Colo.: Westview Press, 1979.

Pachter, Henry M. *Collision Course: The Cuban Missile Crisis and Coexistence.* New York: Praeger, 1963.

Paget, Julian. *Counter-Insurgency Operations.* New York: Walker, 1967.

Palmer, Dave Richard. *Summons of the Trumpet: U.S.-Vietnam in Perspective.* San Rafael, Calif.: Presidio Press, 1978.

Pike, Douglas. *Vietcong.* Cambridge: Massachusetts Institute of Technology Press, 1966.

Porter, Gareth. *A Peace Denied: The United States, Vietnam, and the Paris Agreement.* Bloomington: Indiana University Press, 1976.

Ra'anan, Uri. *The U.S.S.R. Arms the Third World.* Cambridge: Massachusetts Institute of Technology Press, 1969.

Randal, Jonathan C. *Going All the Way: Christian Warlords, Israeli Adventures, and the War in Lebanon.* New York: Viking, 1983.

Randle, Robert F. *Geneva 1954: The Settlement of the Indochinese War.* Princeton, N.J.: Princeton University Press, 1969.

Ridgway, Matthew B. *The Korean War.* Garden City, N.Y.: Doubleday, 1967.

Scheer, Robert. *With Enough Shovels: Reagan, Bush and Nuclear War.* New York: Random House, 1982.

Schelling, Thomas C. *Arms and Influence.* New Haven, Conn.: Yale University Press, 1966.

———. *The Strategy of Conflict.* Cambridge, Mass.: Harvard University Press, 1960.

Schmidt, Steffen W. *El Salvador: America's Next Vietnam?* Salisbury, N.C.: Documentary Publications, 1983.

Schwartz, David N. *NATO's Nuclear Dilemmas.* Washington: Brookings Institution, 1983.

Scott, Harriet Fast, and Scott, William F. *The Armed Forces of the USSR.* Boulder, Colo.: Westview Press, 1979.

Scoville, Herbert Jr. *MX: Prescription for Disaster.* Cambridge: Massachusetts Institute of Technology Press, 1981.

Seagrave, Sterling. *Yellow Rain: A Journey Through the Terror of Chemical Warfare.* New York: M. Evans, 1981.

Shawcross, William. *Sideshow: Kissinger, Nixon and the Destruction of Cambodia.* New York: Simon and Schuster, 1979.

Sheehan, Neil, et al., eds. *The Pentagon Papers.* New York: Quadrangle Books, 1971.

Sherwin, Martin J. *A World Destroyed: The Atomic Bomb and the Grand Alliance.* New York: Knopf, 1975.

Sigal, Leon V., and Steinbruner, John S., eds. *Alliance Security: NATO and the No-First-Use Question.* Washington: Brookings Institution, 1983.

Sihanouk, Prince Norodom. *War and Hope: The Case for Cambodia.* New York: Pantheon, 1980.

Siskin, Martin, ed. *Trouble in Our Backyard: Central America and the United States.*

Snepp, Frank. *Decent Interval.* New York: Random House, 1977.

Stockholm International Peace Research Institute (SIPRI). *The Arms Trade with the Third World.* New York: Humanities Press, 1971.
————. *Tactical and Strategic Antisubmarine Warfare.* Cambridge: Massachusetts Institute of Technology Press, 1974.
————. *Tactical Nuclear Weapons: European Perspectives.* London: Taylor and Francis, 1978.
Stoessinger, John G. *Why Nations Go to War.* 4th. New York: St. Martin's Press, 1985.
Tammen, Ronald L. *MIRV and the Arms Race: An Interpretation of Defense Strategy.* New York: Praeger, 1973.
Timerman, Jacobo. *The Longest War: Israel in Lebanon.* New York: Knopf, 1982.
Van Dyke, John M. *North Vietnam's Strategy for Survival.* Palo Alto, Calif.: Pacific Books, 1972.
Wagner, Abraham R. *Crisis Decision-Making: Israel's Experience in 1967 and 1973.* New York: Praeger, 1974.
Walzer, Michael. *Just and Unjust Wars.* New York: Basic Books, 1977.
Werth, Alexander. *Russia at War 1941–1945.* New York: Dutton, 1964.
Westmoreland, General William C. *A Soldier Reports.* New York: Dell, 1980.
White, Ralph K. *Nobody Wanted War: Misperception in Vietnam and Other Wars.* Garden City, N.Y.: Doubleday, 1968.
Whiting, Allen S. *The Chinese Calculus of Deterrence: India and Indochina.* Ann Arbor: University of Michigan Press, 1975.
Wilkinson, Paul. *Political Terrorism.* New York: Halsted Press, 1975.
Willrich, Mason, and Taylor, Theodore B. *Nuclear Theft: Risks and Safeguards.* Cambridge, Mass.: Ballinger, 1974.
Wolf, Eric R. *Peasant Wars of the Twentieth Century.* New York: Harper & Row, 1969.
Wright, Quincy. *A Study of War.* Chicago: University of Chicago Press, 1942.
Zasloff, Joseph J. *The Pathet Lao: Leadership and Organization.* Lexington, Mass.: Lexington Books, 1973.

Chapter 7

The Economic Struggle for Power

My credit now stands on such slippery ground.

SHAKESPEARE, *Julius Caesar*, III, 1

As the twentieth century nears its end, the world has become the stage for a three-cornered economic power struggle: first, the "old rich" countries of the industrialized West are confronting the "new rich" nations of OPEC; second, the world's poor are confronting the world's rich; and finally, the Soviet Union is still competing with the United States for economic primacy. These struggles—deeply interwoven as they are—have profoundly changed the world's power constellation. In the space of a few years, weak states have become powerful and strong states have become vulnerable. Seldom if ever before in history did weakness become strength so quickly, and strength weakness. These upheavals will form the substance of the present chapter.

THE OLD RICH AND THE OIL RICH: THE WEST VERSUS OPEC

At the beginning of the 1970s, the United States and the industrialized world including Japan clearly controlled the international economy. For practical purposes, the global economy *was* the economy of the Western world. The West did not depend on the economic behavior of other nations in any significant way and was largely in control of what it needed.

In 1973, all this changed dramatically. A relatively small group of oil-producing countries suddenly assumed tremendous power through cartel pricing of oil. This had the effect of a huge tax on the economies of the world's oil-importing countries.

During the 1970s the world's oil-producing countries took over complete control of the oil industry in their countries. They coordinated their policies through the Organization of Petroleum Exporting Countries (OPEC). This organization consists of six Middle Eastern countries with relatively sparse populations—Saudi Arabia, Kuwait, Iraq, Libya, Qatar, the United Arab Emirates—and seven countries with large populations and large development needs—Iran, Algeria, Ecuador, Gabon, Nigeria, Venezuela, and Indonesia. Between 1970 and 1974, the OPEC cartel achieved increases in oil prices that raised the income of the Middle East producing countries from $4 billion in 1970 to $60 billion in 1974. The oil revenues of all the OPEC countries reached $100 billion in 1974. Allowing for their own foreign exchange requirements, the OPEC producing countries enjoyed surplus revenues of $60 billion in 1974.[1] The Arab oil embargo against the West, which was decided upon in late 1973, thus became a major threat to the industrialized but oil-poor nations of Western Europe and to Japan, all of which imported most of their oil from the Middle East. Even the United States, which imported only 10 percent of its energy requirements from the Arab world, found the embargo irritating enough to modify its Middle Eastern policy from a pro-Israel to a more "even-handed" posture. The control of the producing countries over the international oil companies had become so complete that American- and Dutch-owned oil companies had no choice in 1973 but to become the instruments for carrying out the embargo policy on oil shipments to their own home countries. Faced with a major "supply shock" in October 1973, the immediate reaction of practically every importing country was to engage in a competitive scramble for oil supplies, coupled with offers to adapt its Middle East policy to Arab demands, and promises of all kinds of inducements. Arab foreign petroleum ministers skillfully manipulated individual importing countries through the device of handing out oil rewards and punishments.

The oil embargo was followed by a quadrupling of oil prices. These price rises were of such magnitude that practically every importing nation was suddenly confronted with major balance-of-trade problems of immediate and continuing effect. The cost of foreign oil supplies for all importing nations exceeded $100 billion in 1974, compared with $20 billion in 1972. For the developing countries alone, it jumped from $5 billion in 1973 to $15 billion in 1974. This $10 billion increase exceeded all the foreign aid that these countries had received in 1973. Meanwhile, as noted above, during 1974 alone the OPEC countries accumulated surplus holdings of some $60 billion—or nearly two thirds of the total United States private foreign investments. Clearly, a massive transfer of wealth from oil-consuming to oil-producing nations had taken place.

In 1979 the Iranian revolution dealt a second "oil supply shock" to the Western world. Supplies from the nation that had been OPEC's second-largest exporter next to Saudi Arabia plunged and prices tripled once again, to over $30 a barrel. In 1980 the war between Iraq and Iran reduced supplies even further and drove the price of oil to over $40 a barrel in the spot market. When one considers the fact that, during the 1960s, the price of oil had held at $2 a barrel, this twentyfold increase in a decade was nothing less than shattering.

The OPEC countries did not feel defensive about the sharp increase in the price of their product. They maintained that, in the past, cheap oil had been a major factor in the growth of the industrialized countries. In that sense, the developed countries achieved their present status as a result of a parasitical relationship to the oil-producing countries. Moreover, in the opinion of the OPEC nations, oil prices simply caught up with the inflationary prices that the industrialized countries demanded for their technology and commodity products. When considered in that light, oil prices had been depressed for far too long. "Coca Cola cost a nickel not too long ago," a Saudi prince commented recently. "Now it costs fifty cents, but I don't hear anyone complaining. Why is everyone complaining about oil prices? Oil is all we've got to sell."[2]

Whatever the merits of the oil price increases, their impact was dramatic. In the West, the price increases contributed to a two-digit inflationary spiral that threatened the very fabric of Western liberal democracy. In Britain, France, Italy, and West Germany there was serious concern over whether democratic institutions could survive such economic strains.

By the 1980s a situation without precedent in history had arisen. A handful of countries which had little *but* oil managed to hold hostage most of the military and political power wielders of the modern world. Countries with almost none of the traditional elements that made up national power found themselves able to influence the policies of nations with the most formidable military arsenals. How did the Western powers meet this challenge?

No one in the Western world of 1960 would ever have dreamed what OPEC would do to the global economic power structure a little over a decade later. The Western nations, riding high from the rich 1950s, were about to embark on another decade of prosperity. In 1960 George E. Marshall, the United States Secretary of State who had initiated the postwar European recovery program, led the way in setting up the Organization for Economic Cooperation and Development (OECD). This was a forum in which the United States and its wealthy industrial partners would coordinate their economic policies. That same year, Juan Pablo Perez Alfonso, a Venezuelan, persuaded the oil-producing countries to set up OPEC. The OECD countries hardly took notice of that event. During the decade of the 1960s, they still ruled the world economy. Those days are over, apparently forever.

By the mid-1970s, the Western industrial democracies and Japan recognized the gradual but relentless shift of wealth and industry to those parts of the world that had once been their colonies. The most immediate manifestation of that shift was the disastrous combination of inflation and economic stagnation that began to gnaw at the economies of the Western nations. Growth slowed in all these countries while unemployment rose. As late as 1977, OECD still believed that the Western world could blast itself back into the 1960s through the "locomotive recovery theory." The United States, Germany, and Japan, it was hoped, would pull the West out of its recession by expanding their economies more quickly. The plan, however, did not work. The oil price rises proved to be too much for even these powerful economies. "Stagflation" buried Western hopes for quick recovery. By 1980 Western leaders were gloomy in their forecasts. Chancellor Helmut Schmidt of West Germany warned that his nation's "economic miracle" was not invulnerable to the recessionary forces loose in the world. France's prime minister, Raymond Barre, predicted that the West would have to brace itself for yet another decade of sluggish growth and high unemployment while it adapted to the "new realities" of international economic life. And former British Chancellor of the Exchequer, Denis Healey, declared that "all the evidence indicate[d] that for the foreseeable future, the average growth of output in the free world [was] not going to recover to the level which we enjoyed during those golden days from 1951 to 1973."[3] Rising oil prices, unemployment, and inflation had robbed the Western economies of the resilience and dynamism that they exhibited in earlier years.

Western efforts to confront power with counterpower did not succeed very well. In 1974 Henry Kissinger urged the Western nations to form a countercartel of consumers. His initiative produced the International Energy Agency, whose efforts to coordinate Western energy policies met with only partial success. By the 1980s pressures for a military solution to the "oil problem," including the development of a "Rapid Deployment Force" to keep open the flow of oil from the Persian Gulf and, in particular, through the Straits of Hormuz, gathered increasing momentum. Thus, the rise of OPEC increased the possibility of a superpower confrontation in the Persian Gulf.

In the meantime, the OPEC countries discovered that they had found almost unimaginable wealth, but that there was no safe haven to invest it in. The Third World was too unstable and the Western economies were ailing. Hence, OPEC surpluses were piling up on an increasingly shaky pyramid of credit that seemed more of a threat than an aid to global recovery. This had been foreseen by Juan Pablo Perez Alfonso, OPEC's founder. "A wave of money can destroy as well as create," the Venezuelan had warned in 1973. By 1980 this warning seemed prophetic.

Thus, three oil shocks—all triggered by geopolitical events in the Persian Gulf region—had created the most massive transfer of wealth in the history of the world.

By the mid-1980s, oil prices had dropped below $30 a barrel and it was OPEC's turn to be in difficulties. In the first place, a determined conservation campaign all over the Western world had begun to bear fruit. Small cars were popular, alternate fuel sources were being explored, and speed limits were lowered. Second, new oil and gas discoveries were made in non-OPEC countries, such as Britain and Mexico. Third, several OPEC countries, in particular Ecuador, Nigeria, Indonesia, and Venezuela, had spent themselves into debt and, in their eagerness to increase their share of the oil market, were shaving their prices. Fourth, oil production in the non-OPEC countries—the United States, Britain, the Soviet Union, Mexico, and Canada—exceeded that of OPEC. Finally, in 1984, the first cracks appeared in OPEC's price structure when Nigeria and Algeria lowered their prices for oil. Stated bluntly, OPEC had ceased to be an effective cartel and even the expansion of the Iran-Iraq war into the shipping lanes of the Persian Gulf resulted in only a modest temporary rise in prices. It appeared that, while the 1970s had been the decade of OPEC, the West's relative determination and OPEC's internal disunity put an end to the cartel's dominance by the 1980s. Once again, the industrial economies assumed the lead.

THE RICH-POOR ECONOMIC CONFRONTATION: OIL, FOOD, MONEY, AND PEOPLE

If the impact of oil prices on the Western world was dramatic, it was devastating on the poorer nations of the earth. In 1976, for example, when OPEC quadrupled its oil prices, the increase in the oil bill for the developing countries more than canceled out the foreign aid they were receiving. It was estimated that at least $3 billion in extra concessional aid would have to be granted to these countries to avoid economic disaster. By 1981 it was estimated that the nations of the Third World had accumulated a total debt of $500 billion.[4] Since such sums could not be repaid, a "Fourth World" emerged from the Third. Its members were those that lacked resources or economic power. Bangladesh, for example, had neither food nor oil, but did have a rapidly growing population. Such nations were more dependent and more desperate than any large segment of the world's population in history. They faced not only an oil cartel, but a food cartel as well, and had no resources to pay for either. To them, hopeless poverty in a world that had the means to stop it had become intolerable.

Oil was not the only world product that was the object of a fierce power struggle during the 1970s. Food loomed equally large as an object of competition. Here the United States has been in a commanding position. The United States has controlled a larger share of the world's exportable food than the Arab countries' share of oil. The world of the 1970s had become dependent upon American agriculture for its well-being. However, the surge in world food demand and huge Soviet grain purchases directly affected food prices in the United States. Crop failures in the Soviet Union and in India sent foreign buyers to the United States to compete directly with American bakers, cattlemen, and other food processors for increasingly more expensive products. The relationship of much of the world to the United States in food terms began to resemble the relationship of much of the world to the OPEC countries in energy terms.

The more than a hundred nations that gathered in Rome in November 1974 for the first World Food Conference in history tended to regard the global food situation not merely as an acute crisis, but as the beginning of a chronic global condition that called for unprecedented cooperative measures. Famines in India, Bangladesh, and several sub-Saharan African countries had claimed hundreds of thousands of lives. World food reserves were the lowest in a twenty-year period that saw world population grow by one billion. The rampant inflation of food prices everywhere threatened the livelihood of millions of people who literally could no longer afford to eat. Economic disasters tended to have far-reaching political repercussions. The experience of flood in Pakistan in 1970, for example, had contributed directly to the secession of Bangladesh in 1971.

The position of the United States was beset by dilemmas. On the one hand, in the interest of détente, the United States had sold large quantities of grain to the Soviet Union at relatively cheap prices. On the other hand, these sales made food more expensive for the American consumer and made the government more reluctant to ship grain at reduced prices to famine-stricken India. Thus, after President Gerald Ford approved the sale of 2.2 million tons of wheat to the Soviet Union in 1974, Secretary of State Kissinger informed Indian officials that the United States would be able to supply only 500,000 tons of low-priced grain to India, even though India needed at least seven million tons of grain to overcome its 1974 food deficit.

The United States recognized the long-term need to increase the world's food supply through helping to stimulate improved farming techniques in the poor countries and, in desperate short-term cases, to supply food relief on a humanitarian basis. The severe inflation in food prices in the United States itself, however, made it difficult to meet these needs. The peoples of the rich, industrialized countries became increasingly reluctant to make sacrifices for the benefit of starving Asians and Africans when their own high living standards were threatened by rapidly rising prices. Economic interdependence had not yet become enough of a "gut reality" for the rich countries to justify that kind of sacrifice.

Two points emerged with great clarity from the world food crisis of the mid-1970s: first, the need for a global food reserve bank to be drawn upon in bad years. This idea is as old as the biblical Joseph's granary, but there was considerable disagreement over whether such a world granary should be under national or international controls. Second, there was almost universal recognition of the need to increase the world's agricultural production. On the techniques and methods of achieving this goal, however, sharp differences continued to persist. The point had not yet been reached where famine, wherever it took place, was seen as the enemy of mankind as a whole. When asked when a man should eat, the Cynic Diogenes said 2,500 years ago: "A rich man when he will, a poor man when he can." In general, this melancholy answer is still valid in today's world.

The 1980s did not bring much improvement. The Western nations, plagued by recession, became more penurious in their foreign aid policies. When a horrendous famine struck Ethiopia and tens of thousands of children died there like flies, the industrial world was slow to respond. Finally, a rock concert organized in London in 1985 raised 70 million dollars for the starving Africans. Yet, by and large, the world's rich were still getting richer and the poor were still getting poorer.

The disruption of the international money markets was a third source of global economic crisis. The collapse of several large banking institutions in 1974 sent shudders of fear through the financial community. A report published by the International Monetary Fund in 1974 showed that the OPEC countries were unable to spend more than a fraction of their earnings and were accumulating unspendable claims on the consumer countries. These claims were increasing at the incredible rate of $60 billion a year. Debts of this size—like World War I reparations—can never be paid, or even serviced, across the exchanges. Debtor nations might have no choice but to repudiate their debts. Moreover, the OPEC countries tended to invest their "petrodollars" in the strongest industrialized countries, which needed these investments least, rather than in the poor though less credit-worthy developing nations. Finally, the gradual decline in the value of the American dollar and the inflation that was raging in most Western countries in the seventies deepened the international monetary disorder even further. The Western nations were, in effect, issuing claim checks on their countries for a product that burnt up in the atmosphere.

The rich-poor global economic confrontation became even more acute by a dramatic rise in world population. The tragedy has been that the resource-poor developing nations have been precisely those with the sharpest rises in their birth rates. The birth rate itself has become a fairly dependable way of distinguishing developing from developed countries. There are few exceptions to the rule of thumb that developing countries have birth rates above thirty per thousand while developed countries have birth rates well below thirty per thousand. It is estimated that the planet's population of 4.5 billion in 1980 will grow to more than 8 billion by the year 2000. The largest growths will take place in those countries least able to afford them.

In the light of the above projections, few responsible statesmen would argue for unlimited population growth. Most agree that in the long run, the necessity for "zero population growth" will be seen as a truism rather than a slogan since the alternative of unending population growth in a world of scarce and finite resources is patently absurd. Obviously, the combination of dwindling resources and rising populations presents a mortal danger to the planet.

There are sharp differences, however, over the process by which population growth will decline and eventually cease and the need for efforts directed specifically toward this end. The debate is essentially one of international politics, crosscut by ethical principles, and religious and ideological doctrines. The main differences, however, fall fairly neatly across the great divide between the rich and the poor countries of the world.

In general, the rich industrialized countries incline toward the need for special population programs and policies. They maintain that unrestrained population growth is the principal cause of poverty, malnutrition, and environmental disruption. They also tend to believe that it is a fundamental human right for each person to determine the size of his or her family, including the right to contraception and abortion. Finally, the developed countries are inclined to believe that too rapid population growth seriously intensifies other social and economic problems and thus tends to disrupt society.

On the other hand, many of the poor countries regard the motives of rich countries, which are pushing them to adopt aggressive population programs, with suspicion. These rich countries went through a period of rapid population growth as a component of their own development processes, and their current efforts to restrain population growth in the developing countries are perceived as an attempt to maintain the status quo by retarding the development of these countries—in short, a form a racial imperialism. Many of the poorer countries also adopt a religious doctrinal position that population is not a serious problem. Be faithful and multiply, they say. God will provide. Moreover, the world has already shown that Malthus' predictions were incorrect; the same is true of the neo-Malthusian predictions and solutions.

Not all nations fit neatly into these two general categories, of course. China, for example, practices population control at home but, in her bid to support the nations of the Third World, opposed such measures at the Bucharest Population Conference of 1974. And India, though poor, has embarked on a systematic population control program. On the whole, however, the general pattern that emerges is a melancholy one: The world's rich nations are approaching zero population growth while the poor are still multiplying with headlong speed.

A survey of oil, food, money, and people in our time thus shows us a world torn between rich and poor, producers and consumers, a world of rising costs and dwindling supplies, of growing populations and declining production. The economic struggle for power may degenerate into global chaos unless a balance is struck among the three major types of states in today's world: the oil-producing states, which seek a high return for their diminishing resources; the developed nations, which find the industrial civilization they have built up over centuries in jeopardy; and the developing nations, which face the disintegration of their striving for development as a result of price policies over which they have no control.[5]

Perhaps the most widely publicized plan for bridging the gap between the world's rich and poor has been the project known as the New International Economic Order. In 1974 Algeria convened a special session of the United Nations General Assembly in order to explore various ways of transferring wealth from the rich to the poor. At first, the industrialized countries complained bitterly, but gradually, over the years, a North-South confrontation gave way to a North-South dialogue. Innumerable proposals were advanced by the Third World majority in the United Nations. Their essence was always the same: the world's poor wanted one-quarter of the world's goods and resources by the year 2000. By 1980 the poor had turned the United Nations into a kind of collective bargaining agent through which they demanded their seat at the world's table. The New International Economic Order had become their vehicle.

By the 1980s the poor demanded three concessions from the rich: doubling the rate of foreign aid; legalizing cartels to push up the prices of raw materials produced by developing countries; and lowering trade barriers against finished products sold by the poorer nations. The rich, in turn, resisted the demand that the UN General Assembly—dominated by Third World countries—be authorized to deal with these critical matters. They insisted that Western-controlled bodies such as the International Monetary Fund (IMF) and the General Agreement on Tariffs and Trade (GATT) be entrusted with crucial decisions. The rich, in short, were fearful of being soaked by the poor. And the poor became bitter as they contemplated a world that was two-thirds hungry and one-third on reducing diets.

It is also important to remember that the poor are not entirely without economic power. Southern Africa, for example, by the 1980s, had become the "Persian Gulf of minerals." The region contained 52 percent of the world's reserves of manganese, 52 percent of cobalt, and 95 percent of chromium. Manganese is indispensable to steel production. A single mine in Zaire provides the bulk of America's and Western Europe's cobalt, a necessary element in jet aircraft production. And without chromium, available in Zimbabwe, Western industries could not make cars, computer components, airplanes, stainless steel, and hospital equipment. Some African states even have petroleum. Nigeria, for example, declared its readiness in 1980 to use oil as a political weapon, if necessary, to persuade the United States to withdraw its corporate investments from the Republic of South Africa. Hence, the Third World's grip on certain vital resources can only be ignored by the West at its own peril.

Solutions for these economic confrontations will not be easy to find. Logic and reason may founder on the rocks of selfishness and fear. It is both logical and reasonable that the "old rich" of the developed world should join hands with the "new rich" of the OPEC countries in order to grant concessional food and oil supplies to the poor nations of the Fourth World. It is quite another thing for "have" nations to act in such a manner toward "have-not" nations. It is one thing to talk about the need for a general restructuring of rich-poor economic relations for the purpose of creating a more just and workable global economic order. It is quite another to translate the rhetoric into a concrete act of policy through a "survival pact" between the world's rich and poor. Both producers and consumers have legitimate claims and will have to seek to reconcile them for the common good. But for real progress to be made, economic breakthroughs will not be enough. The poor will need patience and fortitude and the rich will have to make spiritual and moral breakthroughs in order to develop the compassion and the empathy that will move us closer to the brotherhood of man.

THE DEBT BOMB

The confrontation between the world's rich and poor has reached its most explosive form in the so-called "debt bomb." Never have so many nations owed so much money with so little promise of repayment. By the mid-1980s, about thirty developing countries all over the Third World owed the colossal sum of $700 billion to a group of Western banks, governments, and international institutions. Half of this sum was owed by Latin American countries. Of these, Brazil and Mexico were in debt for $100 billion each, and Argentina owed $50 billion. A major default by one of the debtors could trigger a financial crisis of catastrophic proportions. The risks, according to United States Federal Reserve Chairman Paul Volcker, were "without precedent in the post-war world." The global economy was sitting on a debt bomb. How did this situation come about?

The origins of the debt crisis date back to the first OPEC "oil shock" in 1973. Suddenly, the oil-rich nations began to earn billions of dollars. On the other hand, poor nations who had no oil found themselves hard pressed to pay for much higher energy costs. The answer to the problem for both rich and poor lay in a magic new concept: recycling. The oil-rich nations deposited most of their excess wealth in the world's major banks; these, in turn, lent the "petrodollars" to the developing countries that needed to buy oil or were eager to modernize their economies. This new business became a bonanza for many banks. A bank arranging a loan deal normally received a service fee of one-eighth of one percent. On a $1 billion loan, this produced an instant profit of $1.25 million. Not surprisingly, the competition was keen, and between 1973 and 1982 more than sixty banks entered the international lending business each year. There was not much concern about repayment terms. The fact that Mexico sat on oceans of oil or Zaire on mountains of copper was thought to be collateral enough. And if one bank did not compete for the business, another would. Finally, life was glamorous. Meetings were held in beautiful resorts in exotic locations. It was an easier and far more exciting way to make money than to negotiate a loan with some coal concern in Pittsburgh.

Borrowing countries snapped up the petrodollar loans with enthusiasm. Most were assured that their economies would grow faster than oil prices. Besides, since international loans were mainly in dollars, and inflation in the United States was rising during the 1970s, borrowers believed that they could repay loans taken today with cheaper dollars tomorrow. Thus, going into debt seemed a painless alternative to prudence and belt-tightening. Yet, the day of reckoning was on the horizon.

During the first years of the Reagan administration, inflation declined and the dollar strengthened vis-à-vis other currencies. No longer could loans be paid off with less expensive dollars. Now, the contrary was true. Even more important, rising oil prices had triggered a global recession that depressed commodity prices on which the borrowing countries depended. Sugar, cotton, coffee, and copper fell to new lows. Tanzania's President Julius Nyerere put it plainly: to buy a seven-ton truck in 1981, his country had to produce four times as much cotton, or three times as much coffee, or ten times as much tobacco as it took to purchase the same vehicle five years earlier.[6] Thus, the developing countries found themselves in a classic squeeze: rising debt costs were eating up ever larger chunks of declining export earnings. In most borrowing countries, interest payments that did not even reduce the principal devoured more than half of export earnings. In some cases, particularly in Latin America, debt service payments exceeded all export revenues. Obviously, a crunch was in the making.

The first SOS was sent out by Mexico in 1982. With oil prices declining, that nation requested a postponement of interest payments. Since banks regarded the payment of interest as the main criterion of a "performing loan," this request, in the words of J. P. Morgan Guaranty's chairman, was "like an atom bomb dropped on the world financial system."[7] Thirteen leading American, Japanese, British, and West German bankers worked around the clock for two weeks in a kind of money-raising telethon to put together a rescue package. Why did the bankers work so desperately to help out Mexico? Because if

Mexico defaulted, some of the lending banks might have gone broke. Thus, for the first time in history, international bankers had to face a cruel paradox: if they made a small loan to a borrower, they owned a piece of him, but if they made a huge loan and the borrower threatened to default, it was the borrower who owned the bank. Hence, the banks, in desperation, had to violate Gresham's Law and throw good money after bad in order to prevent borrowers' defaults and, ultimately, their own.

Mexico's fate was soon shared by Brazil, Argentina, and a dozen other developing countries. The International Monetary Fund (IMF) soon had to participate in almost monthly rescue operations. The IMF was a currency pool supported by over 140 countries. Its purpose was to provide loans to countries in trouble. It was never, however, designed for the kind of crises which it was now called upon to resolve. Besides, it followed fairly conservative fiscal practices and usually exacted strict austerity measures as a condition for its help. Among these were import restrictions and wage controls that did not endear it to the borrowing countries. IMF help usually presented the debtor country with a stark dilemma: if it chose to default, it would be ostracized by the world capital markets; if it accepted IMF terms and practiced austerity, the result might be depression and riots in the streets. As one observer put it: "if the IMF route might leave a Latin American dictator swinging from a tree branch, he may decide to go the default route."[8]

By the mid-1980s, no easy solutions were in sight. What seemed certain was that in the not too distant future the lending institutions would have to take a beating by either writing off some of the loans or sharply reducing interest rates or both. Many bankers looked to the U.S. Federal Reserve for help in case of a default. Few bankers, however, understood that this "debt bomb" was much more than just another financial crisis. What was at stake was the fate of millions of poor people in the Third World who, unless the rich practiced unprecedented wisdom and generosity, were faced with disaster or revolution.

THE EAST-WEST ECONOMIC CONFRONTATION

There is hope that a major military conflict between East and West may be avoided. Power confronts counterpower and the condition of mutual deterrence has decreased the diplomatic influence of military force. Even in the political arena the contest has narrowed to a jockeying for limited advantage. In addition, centrifugal tendencies in both camps have infused the political distribution of power with new elements of flexibility. But a *decisive* victory is still possible in the *economic* theater of the East-West struggle. Both superpowers are aware of this fact. The Soviet leadership has repeatedly asserted that its capacity to outproduce the West will usher in the victory of communism without the necessity of military conflict. Its major weapon in this arena of the power struggle is economic and industrial competition. A succession of "plans," ranging from five-year plans to twenty-year plans, testifies to this continuing effort. The Western nations, especially the United States, have responded to this challenge by reasserting the continued necessity to outproduce the Soviet Union and to retain healthy and prosperous economies. Indeed, East and West have been engaged in a fierce industrial race. A brief review of this relationship is quite revealing.

In 1958 Premier Khrushchev proclaimed a bold Seven-Year Plan which was to give the Communist bloc greater industrial production by 1965 than the rest of the world put together. Indeed, the Soviet premier added that by 1970 the Soviet Union would have the highest standard of living in the world and would be outproducing the United States both in absolute terms and on a per capita basis. Under the Seven-Year Plan, heavy industrial output was to increase by almost 100 percent and light industry by 50 percent. Capital investment and foreign trade were scheduled for a 70 percent increase as were food, industry, and agriculture. In addition, the plan promised an increase of at least 40 percent in real income and the realization of a gigantic housing program.

In 1961 the Seven-Year Plan was superseded by an even more ambitious Twenty-Year Plan, which was to bring the Soviet Union to the threshold of true communism. The new plan, announced at the Twenty-second Congress of the Communist Party of the Soviet Union, envisaged the creation of "the material and technical basis of Communism" during the first decade and the introduction of "the principle of distribution according to need" by the end of the second. Specifically, the Soviet leadership pledged itself to "surpass the strongest and richest capitalist country, the U.S.A., in production per head by 1970," and to "leave the overall volume of United States industrial output far behind by 1980." Huge increases were planned for all sectors of heavy industry as well as for agricultural production. The plan also included sharp rises in the standard of living and blueprints for the solution of the housing problem. The overall goal of the Twenty-Year Plan was clearly to make the Soviet Union the richest and most powerful nation in the world.

By the time of Khrushchev's fall, it had become clear that the ambitious goals of the Twenty-Year Plan could not be realized. Neither industrial nor agricultural production measured up to expectations. In 1976 the Brezhnev regime announced a new Five-Year Plan with more realistic objectives. National income was to increase by 7 percent a year, industrial production by 8 percent, and agricultural production by 25 percent. The new Soviet regime also increased profit incentives for factory managers and collective farm chairmen. By the late 1970s the Soviet economy showed marked improvements in both the industrial and agricultural sectors. Thus, central economic planning seems to remain a permanent feature of the Soviet system. Only the targets change. The challenge to the West remains. Hence, a rough projection of present Soviet economic plans into the 1980s may be useful.

There are several factors that operate in favor of the Soviet Plan. First, the mineral wealth of the Soviet Union far exceeds that of the United States. While American leadership is much concerned with the conservation of natural resources, the Soviet Union is just beginning to exploit the vast energy resources of Siberia and the Soviet Far East. With respect to most raw materials, the Soviet Union has the base to support larger industrial production than the United States. Second, the high degree of technological advance is an important factor in the raising of production and labor efficiency. Third, the Soviet labor force may be manipulated relatively freely. Manpower may be transferred from factories to farms and back again without serious repercussions to the economy. Moreover, strikes and similar labor crises restricting production do not exist in the USSR. Finally, and most important, the planned Soviet economy does not seem to be threatened by recessions or depressions. Indeed, as one American student of the Soviet economy has noted, in every year since 1946 Soviet industry has produced more than the previous year, and there is no reason to suppose that this steady upward movement will not continue.

On the other hand, there are also formidable obstacles in the path of Soviet economic planning. First, while it is true that the natural resources of the Soviet Union are almost inexhaustible, they are located for the most part in the thinly populated regions of the country. A large-scale migration of workers to Siberia would therefore be necessary to exploit these resources for production. Second, enormous capital investments are needed for the realization of production targets. But the Soviet government at the same time also promised a housing construction program, an increased living standard, and shorter work hours. It is questionable whether these production and consumption goals can be attained simultaneously. Soviet economic growth in 1980, for example, was less than one percent. Third, Soviet agriculture often was in serious trouble. Poor harvests frequently forced the Soviet government to purchase large quantities of wheat in Western markets in order to feed its people. The huge Soviet grain purchases from the United States in the 1970s are cases in point. In the light of these events it is most doubtful whether the highly ambitious agricultural targets can be attained. Fourth, Soviet planning is based on the premise of relative internal stability within the Soviet bloc, an unlikely assumption as events in Poland in 1980 indicated. The economies of the Eastern European countries are expected to contribute their share toward the targets. The recurrence of an event like the Czechoslovak crisis of 1968 would seriously jeopardize the fulfillment of the plan. Moreover, the increasing efforts made by Eastern European countries to establish closer economic ties with the West make their contributions to the Soviet plan less and less predictable. Finally, the Soviet leadership takes for granted a very slow rate of economic growth in the United States.

Of all the "imponderables" in the equation, this last is perhaps the most important. On the one hand, the Soviet hope seems by no means unreasonable. Since 1950 the Soviet economy had been growing at a rate roughly twice that of the United States, and in 1958 the Soviet bloc for the first time surpassed the United States in steel production. On the other hand, a sense of urgency has been growing in the United States. American leadership of both parties has become increasingly convinced that the Soviet plan represents a strategy with which the USSR counts on winning the East-West struggle without war. The United States has realized that if indeed communism should succeed in "burying" the capitalist system—to use former Premier Khrushchev's phrase—it is more likely to do so through higher production statistics than through nuclear bombardment. Hence the leadership of both major parties in the United States has shown itself deeply concerned about staying ahead of the Soviet Union in industrial capacity. Yet it seems questionable whether this sense of urgency can be sustained over a long period of time. The energy crisis of the 1970s and the recession of the 1980s have made the American economy very vulnerable. It is true that in times of crisis the United States has always been able to out-produce its adversaries. The reaction to Pearl Harbor is a case in point. But the Communist challenge is unprecedented in that it is not an immediate but a long-range challenge that demands relentless, all-out effort. Americans may not have that kind of discipline. The Soviet hope, of course, is that the West-ern economies will disintegrate from maladies resulting from their own "inner contradictions."

Yet, when one contemplates the tensions that presently exist within the Communist camp one is apt to conclude that communism is at least as vulner-able to inner contradictions as are the Western nations.

Perhaps the greatest paradox of the economic struggle between East and West lies in the fact that, as they have developed, the economies of the Soviet Union and of the United States have become increasingly similar. In both so-cieties, good performance is rewarded with "capitalist" incentives. The suc-cessful Soviet factory manager or collective farm chairman is the recipient of bonuses, special funds, and numerous fringe benefits. While his standard of living is still far lower than that of an American executive—as, of course, the Soviet standard of living in general is much lower—the motives that spur him on are very similar. There remain, of course, great differences between the two systems. First, in the United States waste and inefficiency are not penalized by the government. In Communist countries, in contrast, failure to fulfill the quota may result in disciplinary action or dismissal. A serious discrepancy be-tween target and actual accomplishment may be interpreted as sabotage and lead to internment in a labor camp. Second, the prevailing role of the United States government in relation to transactions with the rest of the world is that anything is permitted unless it has been restricted by the state. The Soviet rule is just the reverse: nothing is permitted unless it is initiated by the state. Fi-nally, when the nation's economic interest is at stake, the Soviet government commands while the United States will tend to exhort or cajole. The two na-tions' approaches to the energy crisis highlighted this difference: the Soviet government simply ordered its managers and technicians to develop the re-sources of Siberia; but the shale deposits of Colorado will be developed only when entrepreneurs decide that the combination of threats and promises by the government is enough to move them to action.

It is very likely that over the years the economic similarities between the two societies will increase. The great emphasis on production may even lead to a degree of ideological erosion. The typical Communist party member is no longer a fiery orator or an idealist visionary, but a calculating administrator and technocrat. The common dictates of industrial production may divest the

East-West struggle of its messianic ideological character. Once universalist ideology atrophies, the fierceness of the struggle may abate. Hence, it is possible that the East-West industrial competition may in the end prove an indirect path to international order. The two great antagonists may settle for coexistence without victory or defeat. The nuclear age no longer permits a decisive military victory over one of the superpowers. The only possible victory can occur in the economic realm.

Even China has given up ideology for pragmatism. The real crime of the "Gang of Four," who went on trial for their lives in 1980, was that they had brought China to the brink of economic chaos in the 1960s. Chiang Ching, Mao Tse-tung's widow, the fiery ideologue of bygone days, had now become Public Enemy Number One. China had embarked upon a mixed economy with distinct "capitalist" overtones. Trade with the United States and with Japan was booming; China had joined the World Bank and the International Monetary Fund; Chinese enterprises were encouraged to make profits; banks were giving loans to Chinese "entrepreneurs" seeking to export goods; farmers were allowed to sell their produce in the open market; taxation was introduced; China even developed a modest rate of inflation and for the first time, in 1980, its national budget showed a deficit. It almost seemed as if communism had become an embarrassment to China's leaders. Single-minded in their goal to modernize their nation and to catch up with the Soviet Union, the new pragmatists paid lip service to Mao's heritage, but in practice emulated the United States. It was more than likely that in the East-West economic competition of the 1980s, China would be counted with the West. In the space of two short decades, one billion people had apparently switched sides.

THE "WAGING" OF ECONOMIC AID

The massive transfers of wealth and the dislocations that have taken place as a result of the oil, food, and debt crises of the 1970s and 1980s have tended to occupy the center of the stage of the international economy. The sheer amounts that have changed hands stagger the imagination and have made regular economic "foreign aid" figures appear minuscule by comparison. This has not meant, however, that economic aid has ceased to be a weapon in the international struggle for power. The struggle has merely become more complex and multifaceted. Hence, the subject deserves careful analysis.

Both the United States and the Soviet Union have become increasingly convinced that to win ultimate victory they must gain the allegiance of the world's uncommitted nations. As a result, the competition between East and West for the favor of these nonaligned nations continues to be intense. As one scholar has pointed out, "global politics have come to resemble more and more the domestic politics of a two-party system."[9] The uncommitted countries play the role of the often crucial independent vote. In order to win this floating vote, both parties promise prosperity and economic welfare. Both parties encourage industrialization. Both parties attempt to appeal to the vital center.

The United States de-emphasizes its traditional associations with paternalistic colonialism, while the Soviet Union disclaims its revolutionary militancy. In short, both superpowers attempt to appeal to the new nationalism on whatever grounds seem most likely to elicit a favorable response. At the same time, the new nations themselves, having become fully aware of their strategic position, have increasingly used the East-West struggle to advance their own causes. In the process, economic aid has developed into a major instrument in the international power struggle and one that again clearly illustrates how extensively and intimately the two chief phases of that struggle—the East-West and the rich-poor—are linked.

Ever since the launching of President Truman's Point Four Program in 1949, Western, and especially American, aid to "underdeveloped areas" has been a permanent and expensive fact of life. And though it has been continuously attacked on many grounds, and often sharply curtailed, few have gone so far as to suggest that it be ended altogether. Annual debates on the budget for economic aid programs have no longer challenged their basic purposes but have been confined to questions as to what sums should be allocated to them and how they ought to be administered. Examination of the growing literature on the subject shows that there are several telling motives that in fact underlie Western foreign aid policies. First, there is the economic argument—advanced in the United States as early as 1952—that the developing countries possess many of the ingredients of economic and strategic strength. The nature of the United States' economy has made it dependent on these areas for critical raw materials, and so the United States must participate in the continued development of these resources, a vital basis of its power. A second line of reasoning maintains that foreign aid is a tool in the East-West struggle, an important weapon in the competition with the Soviet Union for the support of the nonaligned countries. This argument, a favorite of members of Congress "selling" foreign aid to their constituencies, assumes that economic aid buys grateful allies and is therefore a highly effective defense against Communist infiltration. Since communism feeds on poverty, this argument holds, raising the standard of living should prove the best way to combat and prevent it.

A third ground on which foreign aid is justified is the hope that it will contribute to the establishment and strengthening of democracy, or at least prevent a state from turning to communism. This hope is rooted not only in considerations of power. Rather, as is true of the Soviet Union as well, the United States feels flattered and reassured when it sees its own type of institutions apparently vindicated by being adopted and made to work elsewhere. For that reason alone, it would prefer the world to be covered with as many democratic and as few Communist societies as possible.

Fourth, American foreign aid is intended to help provide a sound economic and social basis for the political stability and military strength of the United States' allies. In some areas, such as Taiwan, South Korea, and South Vietnam, the aid given went well beyond these economic and social considerations and was frankly designed first and foremost to build up the military effectiveness of the countries concerned. Results were mixed: quite effective in

Taiwan, uncertain in South Korea, and totally ineffective in South Vietnam. A similar logic has underlain the economic aid the United States has given to the two Communist states that to date have defied Soviet domination—Yugoslavia and Poland. The American assumption in undertaking this step was that whatever weakened Moscow's control strengthened the United States. It appears that these Western efforts to attract Communist countries were not unsuccessful. In the case of Yugoslavia, it is very likely that the prompt American offer to shore up Tito's government against Stalin after the former's expulsion from the Cominform in 1948 strengthened the position of the Yugoslav leader and made it possible for him to pursue a fairly independent course. Poland, too, developed a measure of independence, as the workers' demands for free trade unions in the 1980s demonstrated.

An impressive synthesis of most of the above arguments in favor of foreign aid was advanced by Professors Millikan and Rostow in a Report to the Senate Special Committee to Study the Foreign Aid Program.[10] As their main thesis the authors recommended that the United States employ its resources to create and encourage conditions for self-sustaining economic growth in the developing countries. Such growth, they held, would lead to the evolution of politically stable and viable democratic societies that could not easily be victimized by Communist promises or intimidation. The authors' premise in this argument was, of course, that there is a necessary causal connection between growing economic strength and the development of democratic values and institutions. Yet can this premise really be accepted as axiomatic? If it could— since economic development has in fact been steadily advancing in most of the uncommitted countries—would not democracy throughout the world have shown more victories, or even promises, than it actually has? It would seem, indeed, that the relationship between economic conditions and political institutions is considerably more complex than Millikan and Rostow have maintained.

The administration of American foreign aid has been highly complex. Almost 85 percent of the annual budget approved for foreign aid has been earmarked for military equipment and defense. The other 15 percent is designated as economic aid for development or defense support. Such support is in part military aid disguised as economic aid. In countries where American assistance pays for the development of a national power arsenal, defense support is economic aid disguised as military assistance. Hence, in practice, the distinction between "military" and "economic" aid is often not apparent. Ninety-nine percent of the entire foreign aid budget is handled bilaterally between the United States and the recipient countries. Less than one percent is channeled through the United Nations and its specialized agencies. The Congress has been very hesitant to allocate more generous funds to the UN's economic aid and technical assistance programs. The reasons for this have been several: unwillingness to yield financial control over American dollars to the General Assembly, reluctance to make the United Nations financially dependent upon any *one* power, suspicion that the United Nations was too responsive to Communist machinations, and a continuing preoccupation with immediate rather than long-range defense and security problems. This reluctance has been an important factor in causing the chronic shortage of funds that has afflicted the work of the United Nations in economic aid and technical assistance to developing areas.

The Soviet Union for a long period showed little interest in economic competition for the uncommitted nations. Under the iron dictatorship of the aging Stalin, its main concern continued to be with the consolidation of "socialism in one country" and Soviet hegemony in Eastern Europe. After Stalin's death, however, the new leaders were quick to see significant "built-in" advantages that the Soviet Union enjoyed vis-à-vis the West in its relations with the nations of Asia, Africa, and the Middle East. It could come to the nations that had just emerged from colonialism as the main protagonist of national self-determination; to the nonwhite peoples of the world it could come as a partly Asian nation; in countries where the merchant had long been an object of contempt, it could emphasize its hostility to capitalism; to fledgling agricultural states yearning for modern industrial economies it could present itself as the nation that had launched the interplanetary age; and lastly, it could exploit its theory of the "inevitability" of a Communist victory by persuading the peoples of the new nations that by following the precepts of Marxism-Leninism they would have history on their side and could make the leap to progress almost through an act of faith.

The new Soviet leadership lost no time in utilizing these advantages and taking up the instrument of economic aid with a vengeance. Suddenly, Nehru was no longer an imperialist lackey, but a glorious leader of a free people. Nasser, who had been attacked as a Fascist usurper when he first rose to power, became the hero of a nation exploited by Western colonialism. Actual economic aid began to be offered by the Soviet Union in 1954, five years later than the United States. The formal occasion of this action was the extensive tour of Asia that Khrushchev and Bulganin undertook in that year. As the two Soviet leaders visited country after country, they accompanied their own offers of aid with vehement denunciations of Western aid as camouflaged imperialism in which "the flag would follow the dollar." They particularly hammered at the American policy of attaching "strings" to its aid programs and sought to convince their listeners that American aid was never motivated by a disinterested humanitarianism but was solely intended to prevent the forward march of communism. Khrushchev and Bulganin pointed to the Soviet Union as the classic example of a nation that had attained industrialization without "imperialist aid." Hence, industrialization Soviet style—and with the aid of "good red rubles" with no strings attached—was recommended as infinitely preferable to American "gilded missiles."

The Soviet theme of anti-imperialism fell on ready ears in Asia and soon made necessary a reevaluation of American aid policy. For it was indeed true that until the mid-1950s the United States had customarily attached political conditions to its foreign economic assistance. In exchange for extensive aid to South Vietnam, for example, the United States had exerted a degree of pressure on the government of that country to install a pro-American premier,

Ngo Dinh Diem. In addition, a Vietnamese army was equipped with American weapons and training facilities, but was expected in return to resist any possible Communist aggression from the North. The Soviets branded this as an example of "Yankee Imperialism" working hand in glove with French colonialism. The result of this maneuver was that Ho Chi Minh, the Communist and anti-French leader of North Vietnam, gained a great deal of popularity, while Premier Diem was regarded in many Vietnamese circles as *"l'homme d'Amerique."*

In this altered situation following the appearance of the Soviets on the scene, the task of the United States became increasingly difficult. Most importantly, it now became possible for an opportunistic neutralist to "play both sides of the street" and to hold out his political friendship to the highest bidder. If the United States demanded unacceptable political conditions, the recipient was now in a position to say: "If you do not give me aid without strings, I know someone who will." One striking example of this is the history of the Aswan High Dam. In 1956, President Nasser conceived this ambitious project in order to control floods, add irrigation, and provide power for his growing economy. The United States offered to finance the construction of the dam. Shortly thereafter, however, Nasser bought some armaments from Czechoslovakia and decided to recognize Communist China, whereupon Secretary of State John Foster Dulles withdrew the American offer. Contingent offers by the United Kingdom and the World Bank collapsed as well. At this juncture the Soviet Union stepped into the breach and offered to build the dam. The Egyptian president accepted the Soviet offer without hesitation and subsequently the Aswan High Dam was built with Soviet funds and Soviet engineers. Eight years later, Nikita Khrushchev visited Aswan to accept the tribute of a grateful Nasser.

The United States aid programs to nonaligned nations now made every effort to avoid strings of any kind. In general, American aid—and the implied political support that inevitably went with it—was therefore placed in the hands of the ruling elites that were in fact in control. Unfortunately, however, the members of these traditional elites were often the people in the countries concerned who were most closely associated with large-scale land ownership and with the former colonial powers. Though still in control, they were actually being opposed as "reactionaries" by more and more of the people. Hence, by supporting these traditional groups, the United States tended to be popularly identified with them and to become maligned as an intruding force helping to impede social and political progress. Moreover, as a result of their support by the United States, the members of the traditional elites in question felt free in a number of instances to be less than scrupulously honest and public-spirited in their administration of American aid funds. Indirectly, this contributed even further to the unfavorable popular image of the United States. As a result, although the introduction of American money and influence aided in preparing the way for industrialization and higher popular economic expectations, the Communists frequently found themselves in the better position to mobilize the population as a whole in the pursuit of these objectives. By assuming leadership against the "conservatives" backed by the United States, Communist parties were able steadily to strengthen their positions and even, in Indonesia, for example, managed for a time to participate in government in such key roles as regular cabinet positions.

The above analysis should not convey the impression that American aid without strings has had no beneficial results. Indeed, most nonaligned countries have responded very favorably to the scrupulous observance of the recipient nations' sovereign rights. But just as often it has unwittingly played into the hands of Communist interests. And as this has been perceived in the United States, the entire subject of economic aid as an instrument of policy in the East-West struggle has come under extensive reexamination. Yet almost no one has gone so far as to recommend that foreign economic aid to the new nations be stopped altogether. For though such a policy might have pleased a few economy-minded congressmen, it would obviously have alienated the new nations whose neutrality, if not support, the United States badly needed. At best, it might align the United States with static and conservative regimes, perhaps pro-Western but growing progressively more alien to the heartbeat of their countries. Such regimes would almost certainly be unstable and probably would in the long run prove unable to resist the factions championing the example of Soviet-style industrialization.

These, then, were the horns of the American dilemma in regard to economic aid. On the one hand, continued emphasis on aid with or without strings; on the other, a policy of withdrawal; with either alternative possibly having equally disastrous consequences. The dilemma seemed even more acute because many Americans looked at Soviet aid to the uncommitted nations in largely one-dimensional terms. They wondered at the "blindness" of the nonaligned leaders and their failure to see that Soviet aid missions had all the earmarks of Trojan horses. This attitude failed to take into account the Afro-Asian view of the Soviet Union. To be sure, it is difficult enough for a nation to see itself as others see it. It is far more difficult to see a second nation as a third sees it.[11] Yet this is precisely the root of the competition. The Soviet Union has been able to project itself into the thinking of the uncommitted nations somewhat more successfully than the United States. The truth is that Soviet aid has been much more attractive to many of the new nations than many Americans would care to admit. To most of the Asian and African leaders communism is merely an alternative to democracy—an alternative, in fact, which many believe may be able to produce the desired effects more quickly. In brief, the choice from the point of view of the recipient country is not one between good and evil. It is not even primarily a question of Soviet or Western aid. Rather, it is the much more practical question of how much can be sought and "safely" accepted from either or both.

Fortunately for the United States, the built-in advantages enjoyed by the Soviet Union in its appeal to the Afro-Asian nations are at least partly offset in many of the countries concerned by considerable and ever-growing suspicion of Communist leadership. The Soviet Union's representation of itself as a partly Asian country, for example, has by no means entirely obscured the fact that the country is governed by white men and has frequently adopted a repressive policy toward its minority groups. The antireligious overtones of communism are repulsive to the Hindu, Buddhist, and Moslem elements that are widely scattered throughout the neutralist countries. The totalitarian features of the Soviet Union are deeply suspect in countries like India, with a spiritual tradition of nonviolence. Finally, there are profound misgivings about Communist expansionary goals and the tactics of subversion and political domination. The Soviet invasion of neutral Afghanistan in 1980 alerted the nonaligned countries to this danger. These handicaps frequently neutralize communism's built-in advantages and have compelled the Soviet Union to administer its aid program with the utmost circumspection and the most scrupulous respect for the sovereignty of the recipient countries.

In purely quantitative terms, the Soviet aid program has spent approximately one tenth of the amount expended by the West. It should be pointed out, however, that most Communist nations share in the program. An indication of the range of these activities may be gathered from the following selective summary:

Czechoslovakia provided technical aid in the construction of a meat-processing plant and sugar refinery in Afghanistan. Sixteen Soviet experts conducted a survey of possible industrial and agricultural investment projects in Cambodia. Soviet technical experts have made studies in India of possibilities for a pharmaceutical industry, glass and electric-power plants, and heavy machinery manufacturing. Hungarian experts advised on the construction of hydro-electric and diesel stations in Indonesia. The U.S.S.R. assisted in modernization of spinning looms and mills in Lebanon. Czechoslovakia provided technical aid in the establishment of a flour mill in Paraguay. Polish engineers assisted in construction of an enamelware factory in Egypt. East German experts conducted a survey of water resources, and assisted in the construction of waterworks and water systems in the Sudan. Czechoslovakian technicians assisted in the construction of an international airport in Damascus and in the construction of an oil refinery in Syria. Czechoslovakia provided technical assistance in the construction of a cement factory in Yemen.[12]

In 1959, for example, missions from the entire Soviet bloc entered Guinea, the only African country to have seceded from the French Community. Virtually the entire economy of that new nation was affected by Communist economic aid, and only several years later did the United States enter the competition effectively.

Before we embark on a more detailed comparison of the economic aid administered by East and West, it should be mentioned that several Western nations besides the United States made sizable contributions. The United States has, of course, been the single most important purveyor of aid. Britain made substantial grants—largely through the instrumentality of the Colombo Plan—to develop the economies and raise the living standards of several Asian nations. This effort was not limited to members of the Commonwealth, but extended to Burma, Thailand, Nepal, and Indonesia. In addition, Britain extended large-scale assistance to its former colonies in Africa. The same was true of France and African members of the French Community. Most recently, West Germany has made some notable contributions to the Western program. Indeed, Germany's role is becoming increasingly important.

The effectiveness of economic aid, however, cannot be judged primarily in quantitative terms. If that were so, the economic struggle would have been won by the West long ago. In order to analyze the dynamics of the struggle correctly, we must proceed to a qualitative assessment of the several specific types of aid used by both East and West in the Third World.

Both East and West made long-term aid commitments. While the West poured great quantities of foodstuffs and consumer goods into the uncommitted countries, the Soviet Union preferred to build monuments to itself. For example, the United States shipped vast quantities of wheat to India and provided vital technical assistance in Indian irrigation projects. While American technicians and engineers were widely scattered throughout the subcontinent, the Soviets concentrated their effort in Central India. In Bhilai, the Soviets erected a giant steel mill with a capacity of a million tons of ingots. The plans for the mill were drawn up by Soviet engineers but its construction was a joint Indian-Soviet effort. A great deal of machinery and equipment was brought from the Soviet Union and the project was financed by a Soviet credit to the Indian government. The total cost of the plant exceeded $200 million. Most important, when construction was completed, the Soviet engineers went home and the plant belonged to the Indian government to be used for the benefit of the Indian economy. A similar example of Soviet "impact" aid was the construction of asphalt roads in Afghanistan. The roads were financed by Soviet credit and built with Soviet machinery under the supervision of Soviet engineers. In 1980, Soviet tanks used these roads in their invasion of the country. Western aid to Afghanistan, on the other hand, had consisted largely of consumer goods.

In any objective evaluation, Western aid to the Indian and Afghanistan economies was vital. It was applied throughout the entire economies of the two nations, kept them from foundering, and greatly facilitated national planning. Yet once wheat has been consumed, it is easily forgotten. The Bhilai steel mill and the modern roads of Kabul, in contrast, have a decidedly more permanent "glamour value." To the casual observer, they furnish proof of Soviet generosity. More important, perhaps, they point up the Soviet ability to make long-range commitments for the construction of specific major industrial projects. Until the establishment of the International Development Association (IDA) in 1960, the United States was severely handicapped in its long-range planning by the requirement for annual congressional approval of most foreign aid expenditures. Since then, IDA has made "soft loans" to numerous Third World nations. The United States began to realize in 1960 that it was precisely this type of long-range capital assistance that was required to guide most of the new nations over their initial planning period toward the goal of industrialization. Many Western projects of this kind had to grow out of private initiative. But this meant higher interest rates, a search for profit, and the continued presence of Western personnel. Western capital construction aid looked askance at waste because it was motivated at least in part by private economic considerations. The persistence of the American fixation on "private enterprise" tended to inhibit the use of economic aid as an instrument of governmental policy. The Soviet leadership, on the other hand, considered the question of economic returns completely irrelevant. Its motives were to win the psychological and political allegiance of the new nations.

Both East and West have wooed the uncommitted with lavish gifts. Once again the Western, especially the American, practice has been to give "grants" in the form of commodities and technical assistance. The Soviet bloc does not give grants. Instead, it brings "gifts." The Soviets have been very conscious of the psychological truth that a grant is something a richer nation gives a poorer, whereas a gift is a matter between friends. Gifts from the Soviet bloc again follow the "monument" pattern. For instance, the Soviet government constructed a technological institute in Rangoon as a gift to the people of Burma. In return, Burma presented the Soviet people with "a gift of rice." This type of ceremonial gift exchange was so successful that it was frequently repeated elsewhere. The Soviets have given hospitals, sports centers, hotels, and exhibition halls to the uncommitted nations. In most instances, the recipients were permitted to demonstrate their appreciation by a gift of surplus commodities. The monetary value of the gifts from the Communist bloc countries has usually been relatively small, but their significance has far transcended their cash value. A Soviet glamour gift frequently receives more publicity than a multimillion dollar United States grant of cash, commodities, equipment, or technical assistance. An amusing by-product of East-West economic competition was the fact that some of the nonaligned countries refused any form of economic aid at all unless it was an outright gift. Cambodia, for example, laid down this condition in 1960: "It refused categorically to accept loans of any kind. Even a generous Soviet offer of a very long-term, interest-free credit was rejected on the grounds that an obligation to repay would in some way constitute an abridgment of Cambodia's sovereignty."[13] This strange pattern reached its logical extreme in the case of Indonesia. Former President Sukarno announced repeatedly that he had *rewarded* the United States by *accepting* its gifts. This curious psychological inversion became one of the most astounding phenomena of the East-West struggle.

It is not always true that Third World leaders prefer outright grants. Most of the larger uncommitted countries are the recipients of loans from both East and West. Loans do less violence to the sense of dignity and independence of the recipients and a borrowing country feels not like an object of charity but like an equal. It is simply engaging in a normal economic exchange in which it is paying fairly for what it receives.[14] Burma even insisted on paying for its Soviet gift with a symbolic gift of rice of its own. Similarly, the Burmese premier preferred an American loan to a grant, stating that: "We prefer to pay for it, as this forms a more solid basis of friendship than acceptance of gifts."[15]

There are, indeed, several further considerations in the debate concerning gifts versus loans. For one thing, as an American expert on the subject pointed out, "Credits are twice-blessed; they bless by maintaining the sense of dignity of the recipient when first extended, and they bless by securing the gratitude of the recipient if payments are reduced or forgiven. Grants would serve neither of these ends."[16] On the other hand, there is the important matter of the interest rate. Soviet loans typically carry an interest charge of 2 to 2.5 percent. Thus the Indian government is paying the Soviet Union 2.5 percent interest on the Bhilai steel mill. In contrast, the interest rate charged by the United States government, the World Bank, and private Western firms usually ranges between 4 and 5 percent. For a project comparable to the Bhilai steel mill that was financed by the World Bank and by a United States loan, the Tata Iron and Steel Company Ltd. and the Indian Iron and Steel Company are paying the World Bank 4.75 percent. The Soviets have emphasized their low interest rate, especially in those areas of Asia, Africa, and the Middle East where the money-lender is an object of scorn. Their purpose has been to try to portray the West as an exploiter of the poverty of the underdeveloped countries and to present their own program as one of mutual benefit. While the political elites in the nonaligned nations know, of course, that a large proportion of Western aid consists of grants that need not be repaid, when loans are compared with loans the comparison is favorable to the Soviet Union. For in fact the 2 percent interest rate strikes a delicate balance. It is high enough to safeguard the national pride and sensitivity of the new nations, yet it is low enough to seem to lend plausibility to the denunciation of the West as a rapacious Shylock. Soviet capacity to manipulate its interest rate is one of the advantages of a state-controlled economy. It would be idle to expect an American firm to abandon traditional investment practices and pour money into unstable developing countries without the expectation of a reasonable economic return. When funds placed in an American savings bank or government bonds yield 10 percent or more, it is difficult to persuade Western business to extend loans abroad for 2 percent or less.

A final matter of crucial importance concerns the method of repayment of aid credits. At first, "gold clauses" were inserted into all agreements for Western loans. In order to protect the lender from inflation, the borrower had to pledge himself to repay the credit in hard currency—American dollars or British pounds sterling. But usually hard currency was in short supply in the new nations. When Soviet credit appeared on the scene, the Russians announced their willingness to accept repayment in local currency or in the form of commodity exports from the recipient countries. This gave the Soviet Union a great advantage in the economic struggle. Burma, for example, would have liked to repay a United States loan by exporting parts of its rice surplus. But the United States was burdened with a rice surplus of its own. Moreover, the Soviet negotiators made it a policy not to require a detailed economic justification before granting a loan for a particular development project. Whereas the Soviets emphasized speed, Americans often became bogged down in endless surveys and preparatory missions. As one scholar has put it: "After battling with the hardheaded bankers, skeptical lawyers and insistent economists who run Western and international aid programs, it is a welcome relief for the negotiators of the underdeveloped countries to deal with the openhanded and eager Russians."[17]

The publicity that accompanies the economic aid program of East and West has an important bearing on the overall picture. A Soviet decision to extend a loan or give a gift is invariably announced as a "unanimous desire of the Soviet people" to bring economic and social welfare to the developing countries. Conversely, the annual foreign aid appropriation by the American Congress is usually preceded by an acrimonious debate over the merits of the recipient. Invariably, a small but articulate minority inveighs against "the great giveaway" and the pouring of American funds "down rat holes and bottomless pits." Frequently, Third World leadership is not sufficiently sophisticated to perceive that Soviet unanimity is a fabrication or, on the other hand, that violent opponents of foreign aid are in a minority in the United States. The net result is that small Soviet gifts or loans often receive more favorable notices than do much larger quantities of Western aid.

Perhaps the crucial advantage of the Communist aid program is its claim never to have attached any strings, economic or political, to its assistance. It was, indeed, this Soviet self-restraint that compelled the West to adopt similar policies. In the meantime, however, the fact that the West *did* attach political conditions to its early programs gave the Communist bloc a great propaganda advantage. By widely proclaiming a "no strings attached" policy, the Soviet Union capitalized on the intense emotions of anticolonialism in the new sovereign countries. All industrial establishments constructed by members of the Soviet bloc became the property of the recipient country. By contrast, private Western companies often constructed plants and continued to operate them for profit. While it cannot be denied that private investment made great contributions to economic growth in many developing countries, the high interest rate was often seen as an "economic string" leading to ultimate political dependence. The Russians, on the other hand, built their monuments and went back home. Quite obviously it would be puerile to regard the Soviet refusal to attach political strings as a manifestation of disinterested humanitarianism. But it would be equally naive to assume that Communist economic aid missions always and necessarily serve as a camouflage for espionage and conspiratorial activities.

It is very likely that economic aid without strings is seen by the Soviet Union as the best way to achieve ultimate control. For there may well be Communist strings of a more hidden nature. First, a tradition of correct behavior, once established, may cause a lowering of the guard in the recipient nation. As Communist aid grows, the day may come when the economy of the uncommitted country will have become dependent on the continued flow of Soviet aid. At that point political pressure may be applied: first as a gentle reminder to the recipient state that its behavior is not sufficiently "friendly"; then, perhaps, as a warning that behavior should become "friendlier." In short, once economic dependence is established, political dependence may shortly follow. A pro-Soviet coup, as in Afghanistan in 1979, may then precede an actual takeover.

On balance, Soviet policy seems to subordinate immediate subversion to the more ambitious and longer-range goal of economic and political dependence. During the "infiltration" stage, the Soviet program increases the appeal of nonalignment in Asia, Africa, and the Middle East since it strengthens the bargaining power of the new nations vis-à-vis the West. The likelihood that immediate conspiracy is not a factor would seem to be borne out by the fact that there is no direct correlation between Soviet foreign aid policy and the role of the Communist party in the recipient countries. The five largest recipients of Soviet aid in the 1970s were India, Egypt, Afghanistan, Indonesia, and Cuba, each of which received more than $300 million in credits. In these five recipient countries, the Communist party was legal in India, outlawed in Egypt, nonexistent in Afghanistan where there was no political party system under the king, virtually purged in Indonesia, and ruling in Cuba. Only Afghanistan was physically absorbed after many years of patient infiltration. Communist objectives are thus clearly attuned to the long run. They have been planned well and have demonstrated great sensitivity to the peculiar psychology of the new nationalism. It is here that the difference between East and West has been at its most striking. While the West has often attempted to impose conditions *before* aid was to be given, thus frequently antagonizing the recipients, the Soviet bloc has posed as a benefactor seeking no payment at all. In truth, the ultimate price may be high indeed, but will not be exacted until long *after* economic aid has been absorbed.

Before leaving the subject of "strings" attached to foreign aid, a word must be said about the human rights initiatives of President Jimmy Carter. The President insisted that American representatives in multilateral lending institutions vote to block funds from going to seven countries which the House of Representatives had defined as human rights violators: Angola, Cambodia, Cuba, Laos, Mozambique, Uganda, and Vietnam. While moralists approved the measure, critics noted that the list of violators omitted American allies such as South Korea, Chile, and Brazil. There was anxiety that the new measure would politicize major lending institutions such as the World Bank and thus invite retaliation. The Soviet Union and China were quick to accuse the United States of hypocrisy and the application of a double standard to its policy of human rights. The dilemmas which American foreign policy had introduced into the détente process were thus extended to the field of foreign aid.

Under the Reagan administration, Central America was singled out for special attention. The $8 billion in aid recommended for the five countries of the region by the Kissinger Commission was supposed to be divided about equally between military and economic aid. On the question of "strings," the Commission was divided. While all twelve members were deeply concerned about right-wing "death squad" activities in El Salvador, for example, they differed on the wisdom of imposing conditions. Some of the members held the view that, while the right-wing vigilantes were most undesirable, they were at least anti-Communist and therefore "our SOBs." Other members argued that minimal conditions guaranteeing basic human rights and freedoms should be imposed. If these were not observed, the United States should severely curtail or even terminate its aid to El Salvador. The Congress, too, recommended that the Salvadoran military make some improvements in the area of human rights. Yet, in President Reagan's view those military officers could hardly be given a failing grade on human rights without forfeiting the game to Moscow. Hence, "human rights" certifications of foreign aid recipients tended to be rather token under the Reagan administration.

No analysis of Communist economic aid would be complete without a consideration of the policies of the People's Republic of China. Peking's first aid and project to a non-Communist country was launched in 1956 with a grant to Cambodia. Later that year, Nepal became the beneficiary of Chinese economic aid. That small nation, fearful of political intervention, went so far as to insist that no Chinese technical personnel accompany the shipments. In September 1957 Ceylon received a grant for the improvement of rubber plantations. In addition to outright gifts, the Chinese also experimented with long-term loans to Third World countries. Following the pattern set by the Soviet Union, Peking attached no conditions whatever to its aid agreements.

In the 1960s, the Chinese stepped up their aid program considerably. A large loan was granted to Burma, and trade and aid missions were established in Africa. The largest single Chinese project in Africa became the Tanzam railway, for which large credits were extended to Tanzania and Zambia. Several Latin American countries became recipients of Chinese aid, in particular Peru, Chile, and Guyana. In the Middle East, Iraq, Syria, and Southern Yemen became beneficiaries during the 1960s.

During the turbulence of the Cultural Revolution, Chinese aid was sharply curtailed, but by the 1970s, once again it had assumed major proportions. In 1970, for example, the Chinese extended credits for $700 million to seven recipient countries, including a $200 million loan to Pakistan, while Soviet aid during that year, including aid to Cuba, amounted to a total of only $600 million, which was shared by ten countries. By the 1980s, Chinese foreign aid had grown substantially while both Soviet and American aid had declined. Peking generally extended its aid on soft terms, with low or no interest rates and long-deferred repayments. In most instances, trade agreements and an exchange of missions accompanied the aid pacts, and advisors were sent to the countries where Chinese projects were underway. The construction of a major railway in Tanzania was a case in point.

A word should be said about purely military aid. Here the United States and the Soviet Union are still the main protagonists and the linkage pattern between them and the new nations is striking indeed. In 1965 and again in 1971, for example, India and Pakistan fought wars in which both used American weapons that had been given to them for defense against communism. In 1967, almost $3 billion worth of Soviet military equipment that had been given by the USSR to the Arab states was destroyed or captured by Israel. The Soviet Union replaced most of the destroyed equipment, which made possible the Egyptian-Syrian attack on Israel in October 1973. Both the United States and the Soviet Union extended military aid to their respective clients during that war, and when in 1974 the Soviet Union once again embarked on a massive rearmament program for Syria, the United States felt compelled to do the same for Israel. Thus, military assistance plays a large role in the economic struggle for power. It may make the new nations more dependent on a superpower, but the superpower, in turn, may become embroiled in the wars of its client and thus run the risk of confrontation with its superpower adversary.

In the field of arms *sales,* the United States clearly dominates the market. In the mid-1980s the annual arms traffic throughout the world was worth well in excess of $20 billion. Half of these arms were sold by the United States, with the Soviet Union a close second. Britain, France, and West Germany were responsible for the remainder. Nations in the Middle East were the main purchasers. In 1978, for example, the United States sold jet aircraft to Israel, Saudi Arabia, and Egypt. In the war between Iran and Iraq in the 1980s, the latter fought with French arms. The net result of these arms infusions has been destabilization. Wars among Middle Eastern countries comparable to the conflict between Iran and Iraq have become more likely. Nor is such arms traffic likely to diminish so long as the struggle between the superpowers continues unabated.

One final observation is in order: it pertains to Soviet and American educational aid to foreign students. Before 1980 the preponderance of students from Third World countries studied in the United States rather than in the Soviet Union. Under the Reagan administration, however, Fulbright fellowships were severely curtailed. Hence, far fewer foreign students could afford to attend American universities. The Soviet Union, on the other hand, increased the number of scholarships available to students willing to attend a Soviet university or a school in a country friendly to the Soviet Union. The net result was that, by the mid-1980s, a young bureaucrat about to enter government service in a Third World country was more likely to have attended Moscow or Lumumba University than American University or Harvard. Given the fact that scholarships constituted a totally insignificant amount when compared to the defense budget, for example, it appears that the United States may have acted in a penny-wise and pound-foolish manner. Be that as it may, the economic struggle for Third World allegiance is bound to continue at every level of human experience.

THE FUTURE OF THE ECONOMIC POWER STRUGGLE

As we complete the final two decades of the twentieth century, the nature of the economic power struggle will no doubt become more and more global in nature. Interdependence is no longer an abstraction or a slogan, but has become an economic reality. The crucial distinction will no longer be between capitalists or Communists, blacks or whites, rich or poor, but between those who perceive the world as an arena for competition among self-contained economic entities, and those who perceive it as a "global village"—as Planet Earth, which will survive as one or not at all.

In that sense, much of the material in this chapter does not augur well for the future because it still reflects a provincial mentality. But that is still largely the state of today's world. We are still quite far from a "new international economic order."

One thoughtful student of the international economy conjured up a vision which he described as "The Ghost of the World Future." The vision is nightmarish, but could become the reality of the coming generations unless our growing global interdependence will lift up the nations of the world instead of dragging them down together:

I awoke at about 2 A.M. this morning and saw a thin, emaciated-looking man standing in front of my bed.

"Who are you?" I asked.

"I am the ghost of the world future," he answered.

And with that he grabbed me with a bony hand and took me on a voyage through time and space. We came somehow to a dwelling where two old people, a man and a woman, were sitting at a table.

"Who are these people?" I asked.

"They are your children," said the spirit.

"But they are old and bent and their hair is gray," I said.

"Of course. This is the year 2030," said the spirit.

"But why are they living underground, in a joyless house with no windows?"

"It is too dangerous above ground," the spirit explained, "too much radioactivity, for one thing. You see, around 1990, a missile with one hundred independently-targeted nuclear warheads was launched by accident from a submarine—no one is sure whether it was American, Russian, or Chinese, or one of the submarines operated by the Mafia—and since then atomic bombs have been exploded almost every year by nations or terrorist organizations."

"Why is this house so bare?" I asked. "It looks like a prison."

"The world economy collapsed around 1984," answered the spirit. "Surely you are not surprised. The economies of the poor nations collapsed first—particularly those who were exploding nuclear devices or buying jet aircraft when they couldn't feed their people—and then even the advanced industrial nations began to disintegrate under the arms burden. But probably the richest countries could have survived if the Arabs hadn't decided to withdraw 500 billion of their petrodollars from the Eurodollar market one weekend in the summer of 1984."

"Why are my children all alone?" I asked. "Didn't they marry, don't they have children?"

"I'm sorry to tell you that your daughter's husband and your son's wife died in a terrorist raid on the city many years ago. There is no effective government anymore, you know."

"But surely *their* children had children—surely there must be grandchildren to comfort them in their old age?"

"There are no grandchildren. When world population passed 12 billion in the year 2020, all but a relatively few privileged couples were sterilized."

"Why are they nibbling those strange pills at the table?" I asked.

"That's their dinner. You can't expect them to eat bread, now that it's selling for $300 a loaf."

At that point an entire wall of the room suddenly lit up and the image of a man appeared about ten-feet high in living color.

"What's that?" I asked.

"It's time for the evening television news," the spirit answered. "You see, the one thing that people still have is television. It's bigger and better than ever, and it takes their minds off their problems."

"Spirit," I said, "I can stand no more. You must tell me something: Is this a vision of what *must* be, or is it only a vision of what *might* be if mankind doesn't change its ways?"[18]

This future must *not* be. In the second half of this book we shall examine humanity's efforts to avert it in its struggle toward international order.

REFERENCES

1. Walter J. Levy, "World Oil Cooperation or International Chaos," *Foreign Affairs*, July 1974, p. 696.
2. Conversation with the author at the United Nations, December 1980.
3. *The New York Times*, January 8, 1981.
4. The Trilateral Commission, *A Turning Point in North-South Economic Relations*. New York, 1974, p. 9.
5. Address delivered by Secretary of State Henry A. Kissinger before the 29th United Nations General Assembly, September 23, 1974. Press Release USUN-118(74), September 23, 1974, pp. 8–9.
6. "The Debt Bomb," *Time*, January 10, 1983, p. 46.
7. *Ibid.*, p. 48.
8. Stuart Greenbaum, Professor of Banking and Finance, Northwestern University, quoted in *Time, Ibid.*, p. 50.
9. George Liska, *The New Statecraft: Foreign Aid in American Foreign Policy*. Chicago: University of Chicago Press, 1960, p. 5.
10. Max F. Millikan and Walt W. Rostow, *A Proposal*. New York: Harper, 1957, *passim*.
11. Joseph S. Berliner, *Soviet Economic Aid*. New York: Praeger, 1958, p. 137.
12. *Ibid.*, p. 44.
13. Hans Heymann, Jr., "Soviet Foreign Aid as a Problem for U.S. Policy," *World Politics*, July 1960, p. 533.
14. Berliner, *op. cit.*, p. 147.
15. *The New York Times*, March 13, 1957.
16. Berliner, *op. cit.*, p. 150.
17. *Ibid.*, p. 154.
18. Richard N. Gardner, "The Ghost of the World Future," *The Inter Dependent*, October 1974, p. 6. Reprinted by permission of *The Inter Dependent*, © 1974, United Nations Association of the U.S.A.

BIBLIOGRAPHY

Adelman, M. A. *The World Petroleum Market*. Baltimore: Johns Hopkins Press, 1972.
Allen, Loring. *OPEC Oil*. Cambridge: Oelgeschlager, Gunn and Hain, 1979.
Bairoch, Paul. *The Economic Development of the Third World Since 1900*. Berkeley: University of California Press, 1975.
Barbera, Henry. *Rich Nations and Poor in Peace and War*. Lexington, Mass.: Lexington Books, 1973.
Bartie, Wolfgang. *China's Economic Aid*. New York: Holmes and Meier, 1975.
Bauer, P. T. *Equality, the Third World, and Economic Delusion*. Cambridge, Mass.: Harvard University Press, 1981.

Berelson, Bernard, ed. *Population Policy in Developed Countries.* New York: McGraw-Hill, 1974.

Brown, Lester R. *In the Human Interest: A Strategy to Stabilize World Population.* New York: Norton, 1974.

Brunner, Karl, ed. *The First World and the Third World.* Rochester, N.Y.: University of Rochester, 1978.

Brzezinski, Zbigniew K., and Huntington, Samuel P. *Political Power: U.S.A.–U.S.S.R.* New York: Viking, 1964.

Bundy, William P., ed. *The World Economic Crisis.* New York: Norton, 1975.

Cheng, Chu-yuan. *China's Economic Development.* Boulder, Colo.: Westview Press, 1982.

Clark, Paul G. *American Aid for Development.* New York: Praeger, 1972.

Commoner, Barry. *The Poverty of Power: Energy and the Economic Crisis.* New York: Knopf, 1976.

Connelly, Philip, and Perlman, Robert. *The Politics of Scarcity: Resource Conflicts in International Relations.* New York: Oxford University Press, 1975.

Copper, John F. *China's Foreign Aid: An Instrument of Peking's Foreign Policy.* Lexington, Mass.: Lexington Books, 1976.

Destler, I. M. *Making Foreign Economic Policy.* Washington, D.C.: Brookings Institution, 1980.

Eckes, Alfred E., Jr. *The United States and the Global Struggle for Minerals.* Austin: University of Texas Press, 1979.

Freeman, David S. *Energy: The New Era.* New York: Walker, 1974.

George, Susan. *How the Other Half Dies: The Real Reasons for World Hunger.* Montclair, N.J.: Allanheld, Osmun, 1977.

Goldman, Marshall I. *Soviet Economic Aid.* New York: Praeger, 1967.

Goulet, Denis. *The Cruel Choice: A New Concept in the Theory of Development.* New York: Atheneum, 1971.

Harkavy, Robert E. *The Arms Trade and International Systems.* Cambridge: Ballinger, 1975.

Hartland-Thunberg, Penelope. *Trading Blocs, U.S. Exports, and World Trade.* Boulder, Colo.: Westview Press, 1980.

Heilbroner, Robert L. *An Inquiry into the Human Prospect.* New York: Norton, 1974.

Higonnet, Rene P.; Jorge, Antonio; and Salazar-Carillo, Jorge. *Foreign Debt and Latin American Economic Development.* Elmsford, N.Y.: Pergamon Press, 1983.

Hunter, Robert E., et al. *The United States and the Developing World: Agenda for Action.* Washington, D.C.: Overseas Development Council, 1973.

Johnson, Gale D. *World Agriculture in Disarray.* New York: St. Martin's Press, 1973.

Kamarck, Andrew M. *The Economics of African Development.* New York: Praeger, 1971.

Kenen, Peter B., ed. *International Trade and Finance: Frontiers for Research.* New York: Cambridge University Press, 1976.

Kissinger, Henry A. *The Report of the President's National Bipartisan Commission on Central America.* New York: Macmillan, 1984.

Klinghoffer, Arthur Jay. *The Soviet Union and International Oil Politics.* New York: Columbia University Press, 1977.

Kolko, Joyce. *America and the Crisis of World Capitalism.* Boston: Beacon Press, 1974.

Kuznets, Simon. *Population, Capital, and Growth.* New York: Norton, 1973.

Lefever, Ernest W. *Nuclear Arms in the Third World: U.S. Policy Dilemma.* Washington, D.C.: Brookings Institution, 1979.

Levinson, Jerome, and De Onis, Juan. *The Alliance That Lost Its Way: A Critical Report on the Alliance for Progress.* Chicago: Quadrangle Books, 1970.

Levy, Walter J., and Conant, Melvin A., ed. *Oil Strategy and Politics, 1941–1981.* Boulder, Colo.: Westview Press, 1982.

Liska, George. *The New Statecraft: Foreign Aid in American Foreign Policy.* Chicago: University of Chicago Press, 1960.

Little, Jane Sneddon. *Euro-Dollars: The Money Market Gypsies.* New York: Harper & Row, 1975.

Maddox, John. *Beyond the Energy Crisis.* New York: McGraw-Hill, 1975.

Marer, Paul, and Montias, John Michael. *East European Integration and East-West Trade.* Bloomington: Indiana University Press, 1980.

Maurer, Harry, and Mirow, Kurt Rudolf. *Webs of Power: International Cartels and the World Economy.* Boston: Houghton Mifflin, 1982.

Mesarovich, Mihajlo, and Pestel, Eduard. *Mankind at the Turning Point: The Second Report to the Club of Rome.* New York: Dutton, 1974.

Monroe, Wilbur F. *International Monetary Reconstruction: Problems and Issues.* Lexington, Mass.: Lexington Books, 1974.

Moran, Theodore H. *Multinational Corporations and the Politics of Dependence: Copper in Chile.* Princeton, N.J.: Princeton University Press, 1974.

Mosley, Leonard. *Power Play: Oil in the Middle East.* New York: Random House, 1973.

Murdoch, William W. *The Poverty of Nations: The Political Economy of Hunger and Population.* Baltimore: Johns Hopkins Press, 1981.

Myrdal, Gunnar. *The Challenge of World Poverty: A World Anti-Poverty Program in Outline.* New York: Pantheon, 1970.

Nagorski, Zygmunt, Jr. *The Psychology of East-West Trade: Illusions and Opportunities.* New York: Mason and Lipscomb, 1974.

Neuberger, Egon, and Tyson, Laura D'Andrea, eds. *The Impact of International Economic Disturbances on the Soviet Union and Eastern Europe.* Elmsford, N.Y.: Pergamon Press, 1980.

O., Bohdan, and Szuprowicz, Maria R. *Doing Business with the People's Republic of China.* New York: Wiley, 1978.

Odell, John S. *U.S. International Monetary Policy.* Princeton, N.J.: Princeton University Press, 1982.

Olson, Mancur. *The Rise and Decline of Nations: Economic Growth, Stagflation, and Social Rigidities.* New Haven, Conn.: Yale University Press, 1982.

Olvey, Lee D., Jr. *The Economics of National Security.* Wayne, N.J.: Avery, 1984.

Peterson, J. E. *The Politics of Middle Eastern Oil.* Washington: Middle East Institute, 1983.

Pfaltzgraff, Robert L., Jr. *Energy Issues and Alliance Relationships: The United States, Western Europe and Japan.* Cambridge: Institute for Foreign Policy Analysis, 1980.

Philip, George. *Oil and Politics in Latin America.* New York: Cambridge University Press, 1982.

Pierre, Andrew J. *The Global Politics of Arms Sales.* Princeton, N.J.: Princeton University Press, 1982.

Pigou, Arthur C. *The Political Economy of War.* London: Macmillan and Company, Ltd., 1940.

Pisar, Samuel. *Coexistence and Commerce.* New York: McGraw-Hill, 1970.

Poneman, Daniel. *Nuclear Power in the Developing World.* Winchester, Mass.: Allen & Unwin, 1982.

Report of the European Security Study. *Strengthening Conventional Deterrence in Europe: Proposals for the 1980's.* New York: St. Martin's, 1983.

Robbins, Lionel C. *The Economic Causes of War.* London: Jonathan Cape, 1939.

Rustow, Dankwart A., and Mugno, John F. *OPEC: Success and Prospects.* New York: New York University Press, 1976.

————. *Oil and Turmoil: America Faces OPEC and the Middle East.* New York: Norton, 1982.

Sampson, Anthony. *The Money Lenders.* New York: Viking, 1982.

————. *The Seven Sisters: The Great Oil Companies and the World They Made.* New York: Viking, 1975.

Schumpeter, Joseph A. *Capitalism, Socialism and Democracy.* New York: Harper, 1950.

Servan-Schreiber, Jean-Jaques. *The World Challenge: OPEC and the New Global Order.* New York: Simon & Schuster, 1981.

Smith, Adam. *Paper Money.* New York: Summit Books, 1981.

Spengler, Joseph. *Population Change, Modernization, and Welfare.* Englewood Cliffs, N.J.: Prentice-Hall, 1974.

Spero, Joan Edelman. *The Politics of International Economic Relations.* New York: St. Martin's Press, 1977.

Tendler, Judith. *Inside Foreign Aid.* Baltimore: Johns Hopkins Press, 1975.

Thompson, Kenneth S. *Foreign Assistance: A View from the Private Sector.* Notre Dame, Ind.: University of Notre Dame Press, 1972.

Thorp, Willard L. *The Reality of Foreign Aid.* New York: Praeger, 1971.

Thurow, Lester C. *The Zero-Sum Society.* New York: Basic Books, 1980.

Tironi, Ernesto, and French-Davis, Ricardo, eds. *Latin America and the New International Economic Order.* New York: St. Martin's, 1982.

Turner, Louis. *Oil Companies in the International System.* London and Boston: Allen and Unwin, 1978.

Tussie, Diana. *Latin America in the World Economy.* New York: St. Martin's Press, 1983.

Vakhrushev, Vasily. *Neocolonialism: Methods and Maneuvers.* Moscow: Progress Publishers, 1973.

Wallerstein, Mitchel B. *Food for War—Food for Peace.* Cambridge: Massachusetts Institute of Technology Press, 1980.

Walters, Robert S. *American and Soviet Aid: A Comparative Analysis.* Pittsburgh: University of Pittsburgh Press, 1970.

Ward, Barbara, et al. *The Widening Gap: Development in the 1970s.* New York: Columbia University Press, 1971.

Wattenberg, Ben J., and Whalen, Richard J. *The Wealth Weapon: U.S. Foreign Policy and Multinational Corporations.* New Brunswick, N.J.: Transaction Books, 1980.

Weissman, Steve, et al. *The Trojan Horse: A Radical Look at Foreign Aid.* San Francisco: Ramparts Press, 1974.

White, John. *The Politics of Foreign Aid.* New York: St. Martin's Press, 1974.

Widstrand, Carl, ed. *Multinational Firms in Africa.* New York: Africana, 1976.

Williamson, John, ed. *IMF Conditionality.* Washington: Institute for International Economics, 1983.

Willrich, Mason. *Energy and World Politics.* New York: Free Press, 1975.

Wionczek, Miguel S., ed. *LCD External Debt and the World Economy.* Mexico: El Colegio de Mexico, 1978.

Wriggins, W. Howard, and Guyot, James F. *Population, Politics, and the Future of Southern Asia.* New York: Columbia University Press, 1973.

Yu, George T. *China's African Policy: A Study of Tanzania.* New York: Praeger, 1975.

Zwass, Adam. *Monetary Cooperation Between East and West.* White Plains, N.Y.: International Arts and Sciences Press, 1975.

Part Three

THE INTERNATIONAL STRUGGLE FOR ORDER

Chapter 8

Diplomacy and Political Order

Diplomacy is the art of avoiding the appearance of victory.

METTERNICH

THE NATURE OF DIPLOMACY

Diplomacy may be defined as the conduct of international relations by negotiation. It is a process through which nations attempt to realize their national interests. It is, of course, not always an instrument of political order. Its object at times may be the intensification of a struggle between nations, or it may be a neutral tool that regards order as irrelevant to the pursuit of the national interest. But more often than not, diplomacy is an important instrument of political order, for the very process of negotiation implies that nations settle their differences through peaceful change within the framework of a given system rather than by resorting to the overthrow of the system through violence. When a nation has decided in favor of war, the instrument of diplomacy becomes superfluous. But so long as the national interest dictates the avoidance of war, diplomacy works on behalf of peace. And since most nations feel most of the time that their policies may be realized by means short of war, diplomacy has been, and remains, a major highway to political order.

Diplomacy antedates the nation-state system by almost two thousand years. The city-states of ancient Greece had developed diplomatic intercourse to a high level. On reading Thucydides' *Peloponnesian War*, one is struck by the profound insights that the ancients had gained into the subtle arts of negotiation. If the Greeks made a major contribution to the essence of diplomacy—the accommodation of conflicting interests—the Romans' contribution was the equally important one of investing the practice of diplomacy with legal authority. The reemergence of the city-state system in Italy during the Renaissance was once more accompanied by a great burgeoning in the arts of diplomacy. Machiavelli's *The Prince* was the most famous of many contemporary discourses on the subject. The coming of the nation-state system in the seventeenth century ushered in an age of even greater diplomatic activity. This era of the so-called old diplomacy dominated the scene until World War

I. When we contemplate the quaint practices that prevailed during these three hundred years—boudoir intrigues, powdered wigs, and "waltzing congresses"—we are tempted to smile indulgently. But before we decide that this period is of only historical and archaeological interest, we would do well to remember that the "waltzing Congress of Vienna" of 1815 ushered in a century in which there occurred not a single major world war. The diplomatic dramas in which Metternich, Castlereagh, and Talleyrand were the major actors are well worth rereading.[1] Hence, before we turn to an analysis of the more modern techniques of negotiation, we shall evaluate the traditional methods of diplomacy.

Hans Morgenthau has defined the task of diplomacy as a fourfold one:

> Diplomacy must determine its objectives in the light of the power actually and potentially available for the pursuit of these objectives. Diplomacy must assess the objectives of other nations and the power actually and potentially available for the pursuit of these objectives. Diplomacy must determine to what extent these different objectives are compatible with each other. Diplomacy must employ the means suited to the pursuit of its objectives. Failure in any one of these tasks may jeopardize the success of foreign policy and with it the peace of the world.[2]

Eighteenth- and nineteenth-century diplomacy seems to have fulfilled these conditions rather well. Few nations set themselves goals that were not commensurate with their power. Only rarely did nations make gross errors in assessing the power or the objectives of others. Underrating or overrating the power of the antagonist was the exception, not the rule. Nations constantly compared their own goals with those of others and weighed their compatibility. Since the national substance of a nation was rarely if ever threatened, it was generally possible to compromise on most outstanding issues. Sometimes nations resorted to a threat of force. But most of the time, traditional diplomacy was characterized by a spirit of compromise. The hallmark of the old diplomacy was the rule of *quid pro quo*.

The greatest success of traditional diplomacy was, as we have mentioned, the Congress of Vienna of 1815. At Vienna, the diplomats of Austria, Prussia, Britain, Russia, and France managed to negotiate their differences and as a result ushered in one of the longest periods of peace in Western history. How was this feat accomplished? In the first place, the fundamental structure of the international system was accepted by the negotiating powers as "legitimate." No nation at Vienna threatened the existence of the others with aspirations to world conquest. Nor did the congress have to cope with the presence of any revolutionary power whose ideology dictated the absorption of the others. Each of the participants advanced limited objectives and expressed them in terms of limited territorial claims and counterclaims. This happy state of affairs provided the second condition of success, namely, that each nation found itself in a relationship of reasonable satisfaction and security vis-à-vis the others. This point has been well stated by Henry A. Kissinger in his analysis of the Vienna Congress:

Since absolute security for one power means absolute insecurity for all others, it is obtainable only through conquest, never as part of a legitimate settlement. An international settlement which is accepted and not imposed will therefore always appear *somewhat* unjust to any one of its components. Paradoxically, the generality of this dissatisfaction is a condition of stability, because were any one power *totally* satisfied, all others would have to be *totally* dissatisfied and a revolutionary situation would ensue. The foundation of a stable order is a *relative* security—and therefore the *relative* insecurity—of its members. Its stability reflects, not the absence of unsatisfied claims, but the absence of a grievance of such magnitude that redress will be sought in overturning the settlement rather than through an adjustment within its framework.[3]

The conditions that contributed to the success of the Congress of Vienna do not prevail in the modern world. Yet if we study the Vienna Congress we find that there are important insights to be gained nevertheless. These do not, of course, derive from the *conditions* of the international order in 1815. They apply, rather, to the diplomatic *conduct* by which the diplomats at Vienna pursued their objectives.

All important negotiations at the Congress of Vienna took place in private. Only the ministers and their most trusted subordinates participated in the crucial discussions. Camouflaged by the glitter of nineteenth-century Vienna and the pomp of the Habsburg court, the diplomatic interchanges proceeded strictly behind closed doors. In our own time "secret diplomacy" has become a term of disapprobation. And to be sure, secrecy often led to extreme suspicion even among the diplomats of the earlier period. Thus, when Prince Metternich, the Austrian plenipotentiary, was told that the Russian ambassador in Vienna had died during the negotiations, he was reported to have asked: "Ah, is that true? What may have been his motive?" Yet despite its inevitable drawbacks, this method gave the statesmen of the time a priceless advantage that contemporary diplomats have largely been denied: it enabled them to conduct their negotiations in private, free from the pressures and inhibitions of constant publicity.

The old diplomacy fell into disrepute with the coming of the twentieth century. Liberal optimists who believed that power politics could be banished from the earth through the establishment of a universal League of Nations took a dim view of the old-fashioned secret diplomacy and considered it the symptom of a corrupt and bygone era. The new spirit was expressed most eloquently by Woodrow Wilson in his Fourteen Points: "Open covenants of peace, openly arrived at, after which there will be no private understanding of any kind, but diplomacy shall proceed frankly and in the public view." The advocates of the "new diplomacy" urged that not only the results of diplomacy should be made public, but that even the process of negotiation itself ought to be subject to the scrutiny of the people. The implication was that the business of diplomacy was too important to be entrusted to diplomats alone. The principles of democratic government demanded that in matters affecting the vital interests of the nation the public be kept informed and allowed to express itself at every stage of the proceedings. The reason for this, as Wilson and the proponents of open diplomacy saw it, was that the national interest was safer in the hands of the public than it would be if left in the hands of some elite group, no matter how well versed in the arts of negotiation the latter might be.

It is a curious irony that Wilson, the great advocate of open diplomacy, seldom practiced it. His efforts to realize his dream—the creation of the League of Nations—were conducted with considerable secrecy. When he returned from Versailles, he confronted the American people with a *fait accompli*. The Senate's refusal to ratify the treaty incorporating the League of Nations was in some measure attributable to the fact that the senators had not been taken into the President's confidence during the formulation of policy. Wilson wanted the "consent," but not the "advice" of the Senate and the people. In other words, the major architect of "open convenants openly arrived at" was one of the great practitioners of secret diplomacy. Nevertheless, the impact of the new Wilsonian conception was enormous. To a world grown deeply weary of war and the struggle for power, the prospect of a new system of international conduct that, in the words of one caustic observer, would no longer be governed by "men who were sent abroad to lie for their country,"[4] looked desirable indeed.

Yet it soon became evident that if the new diplomatic techniques dispelled some long-standing fears, they also raised some serious problems. There was little disagreement that the *results* of diplomatic negotiations should be disclosed to the people, but many observers began to question the wisdom of exposing the *negotiations* themselves to the searchlight of publicity. It was soon discovered that under such conditions an atmosphere was created that precluded genuine bargaining. It became increasingly difficult, if not impossible, for a diplomat to yield on a point, to give up a claim, or to admit that there was at least a modicum of justice on the other side when he knew that each such action would be condemned by his compatriots as an act of cowardice and as a retreat in the face of the enemy. Thus, more and more frequently, diplomacy fell victim to publicity. Diplomats came to the bargaining table with maximum demands which they defended "on principle." Positions grew brittle, compromise became the exception rather than the rule, and the negotiators tended to address the audience rather than each other. This transformation of diplomacy into an instrument of propaganda was accelerated by the rapid development of the media of communication. A diplomat who was not only exposed to the physical presence of an attentive public but had to cope with a network of television cameras as well was not likely to run the risk of looking like a fool or a knave before millions of people.

Secret diplomacy seldom involved more than a small number of negotiators. The new diplomacy, in contrast, has through the coming of the United Nations and the various regional organizations acquired an even further complicating dimension in that most negotiations must be conducted multilaterally. Once a dispute is brought before the United Nations, for example, it becomes the business of the entire General Assembly. Representatives from more than one hundred fifty nations express themselves on the matter while the entire world watches. Such a state of affairs is hardly conducive to effective bargaining. The issue generally is not resolved through negotiations but through attempts by the leading forces in the General Assembly to obtain a majority vote with which to defeat a recalcitrant minority. It need not be emphasized that this method frequently exacerbates differences among nations instead of composing them.

All these developments have radically changed the nature of both diplomacy and the diplomat. While a plenipotentiary attending the Congress of Vienna had large powers of discretion, the modern diplomat is frequently little more than a messenger who communicates the instructions of his government. Frequently heads of state even short-circuit their emissaries altogether by dealing with each other directly. During World War II, for example, Roosevelt, Churchill, and Stalin by no means relied solely on the talents of their diplomats. In fact, many of their most vital policy decisions were hammered out in telegrams and long transatlantic telephone conversations among themselves. In the 1970s and 1980s, this kind of "back channeling" was even more extensive. Key negotiations with the Soviet Union in the Nixon, Ford, and Carter administrations were usually carried out by secretaries of state directly with long-time Soviet ambassador Anatoly Dobrynin. This procedure did not please Malcolm Toon, the United States ambassador to Moscow. And Joseph Sisco, who was twice offered the Moscow embassy by Richard Nixon, turned down the post. "So long as Nixon and Kissinger were around," Sisco said, "they were going to be the Soviet desk officers. And if I decided to go to Moscow, Nixon would have a personnel problem within six weeks." Clearly, a talented diplomat desires to be more than a messenger, travel agent, or innkeeper.

The modern phenomenon that may combine all the weaknesses of the new diplomacy most dramatically is the "summit conference." Geneva in 1955, Paris in 1960, and Glassboro, New Jersey, in 1967, became the capitals of the world while heads of state met there to air their differences. The participants found themselves cast in the role of gladiators, with the rest of humanity as their audience. While most of the onlookers desperately hoped for peace, few were willing to tolerate the kind of compromise that the attainment of real peace would have required. The unprecedented publicity led to an equally unprecedented inflexibility; the inflexibility found expression in little more than repetitive propagandistic flourishes; and in the end, the heads of state parted company: in 1955, in an "improved atmosphere" but without any concrete results; in 1960, in animosity and disillusionment; and in 1967, once again, without tangible results. There are times, of course, when a summit may break the ice after many years of nonrelations and frozen hostility. President Nixon's visit to China in 1972 was a case in point. Sadat's mission to Jerusalem in 1977 was another. While none of the stubborn problems besetting Sino-American or Arab-Israeli relations was actually resolved at those historic meetings, the atmosphere between the hostile countries was certainly improved. Similarly, the Moscow Summit of May 1972 improved Soviet-American relations and marked the occasion of the first superpower arms control agreement since World War II. And when, in 1978, President Carter invited Prime Minister Menachem Begin of Israel and President Anwar Sadat of

Egypt to Camp David, the negotiations among the three heads of state leading
to the Egyptian-Israeli peace treaty were kept essentially secret. Even "sum-
mitry" was more successful when conducted privately. On balance, "sum-
mitry" may be helpful under certain very specific conditions but rarely
manages to dissolve substantive policy differences.

It is clear from the above that the high hopes that were originally entertained for open diplomacy have not been warranted. Public control of the negotiating process has not necessarily yielded superior results. Sometimes, open
covenants stridently proclaimed may even set back the process of accommodation. A brief vignette about Jewish emigration from the Soviet Union will serve
to illustrate this point.

Fewer than a thousand exit visas were issued to Soviet Jews in 1970, but in
1971, according to both Soviet and American sources, the figure jumped to
around fifteen thousand. It rose again in 1972 to around thirty thousand and
reached a peak of thirty-five thousand in 1973. This sharp rise was a bonus of
détente, specifically of a comprehensive trade agreement that Nixon and Kissinger had signed with the Soviet Union in October 1972. Then, suddenly, entered open diplomacy.

Senator Henry M. Jackson led the forces that were skeptical about
détente in general and were reluctant to grant most-favored-nation trading
status to the Soviet Union without getting something in return. What Jackson
sought, however, was not a concession in the economic field but a commitment
from the Soviet government on free Jewish emigration from the Soviet Union.
To this end, he proposed an amendment to the trade bill. This demand
touched off a bitter and protracted conflict between Kissinger and Jackson
over the merits of détente, a conflict that was exacerbated greatly by the outbreak of war in the Middle East in October 1973.

Jackson and his followers attacked Kissinger's concept of détente, claiming that it was a kind of one-way street in favor of the Soviet Union. The Russians, he argued, were always getting the better bargain. "We sell the Soviets
cars," exclaimed a critic of détente in a Detroit plant, "and they sell us parking
places in Siberia." In addition, the critics maintained, the Soviet Union had
violated the spirit of détente by encouraging the Arab assault on Israel in October 1973. Instead of consulting with the United States and looking for ways
to stave off the conflict, the Soviet leadership had aided and abetted Egypt and
Syria in mounting their surprise attack. It was plain that the Russians were
reaping the benefits of détente but not living up to their obligations. Hence,
the United States should insist on a major concession: the lifting of restrictions
on Jewish emigration from Russia to Israel.

Kissinger strenuously opposed the Jackson amendment to the Soviet trade
bill, not because he approved of Soviet domestic policies, but because he
thought that the stipulation was inappropriate and counterproductive. Its use
denied the possibility, in his opinion, of normal commercial contacts so long as
certain basic ideological conflicts remained unresolved. In short, if the United
States loudly rattled the skeletons in the Soviets' political closet, the Russians
would probably respond in kind. Once the skeletons emerged from both clos-

ets, détente would be endangered. And as Kissinger never tired of pointing out, the overriding goal of détente was the avoidance of nuclear war. Besides, the Soviet attitude toward the leading capitalist nation had changed. Khrushchev had come to the United States in 1959, saying "We shall bury you." Yet when Brezhnev visited the United States in 1973, not a word was said about the burial of capitalism. Instead, Brezhnev's approach was more along the lines of "We want to borrow from you." Trade, in Kissinger's opinion, could serve to promote political détente only if trade was in fact kept politically neutral. The result of the Jackson initiative was an angry Soviet rejection, in January 1975, of the entire trade agreement on the grounds that such interference in Soviet internal affairs could not be tolerated. By then, the annual rate of Jewish emigration had declined to around twenty thousand and by 1976 it had fallen to less than fifteen thousand.

During the 1980s, with a new cold war chilling relations between the superpowers, Jewish emigration diminished to a trickle. A highly visible Jewish dissident, Anatoly Shcharansky, on whose behalf thousands of petitions had been submitted from the United States and Western Europe, was languishing in a Soviet prison.

Hence, quiet diplomacy was clearly more effective in this case. Obviously, the Soviet Union was unprepared to let itself be influenced in its domestic policies by public pronouncements emanating from the United States. Open diplomacy had had a boomerang effect. Today, trade and Jewish emigration remain enmeshed in a complicated stalemate. A significant increase in emigration would speak more eloquently than public moral rhetoric. The lesson may be validly applied in the opposite direction, too. How would America respond if the Soviet Union proclaimed that it would sign another SALT agreement only if the United States agreed to remove all racial discrimination? The point clearly seems to be that most public, official attempts to lecture a sovereign power are generally self-defeating.

In other types of situations, on the other hand, the methods of open diplomacy may be exactly what are needed. Several such examples were the United Nations conferences held in 1974 on the deepening crises of food shortages and the population explosion. The very acuteness of these crises made open discussion of their global implications a necessity. Since what happens to the world's food supply and the world's people is everybody's business, multilateral conferences on these matters were the proper forum for seeking agreement.

To generalize, we may say that secret negotiations seem more helpful when their function is a sensitive one, such as mediation between two adversaries. The Middle East diplomacy of Henry Kissinger, for example, has shown that in an age of "open covenants openly arrived at," the older type of diplomatic strategy may make a most important contribution. Jimmy Carter also realized this truth during the negotiations at Camp David. Indeed, this modern version of secret diplomacy has been a direct outcome of the failures of the new multilateralism. On the other hand, the more positive aspects of order-building, like the passage of new international legislation, lend themselves more readily to the new diplomacy. In most cases, however, effective order-building requires a discriminating and sensitive application of both principles. Hence the diplomat is clearly far from obsolete. It is only that the demands upon him have become more rigorous and that he must operate under immensely more difficult conditions. We must therefore turn from our consideration of diplomacy in general to an examination of the nature of the diplomat himself.

The best portrait of the modern diplomat is probably that painted by Sir Harold Nicolson in his classic treatise, *Diplomacy*. First among the diplomat's virtues, according to Nicolson, must be truthfulness. By this he means "not merely abstention from conscious misstatements but a scrupulous care to avoid the suggestion of the false or the suppression of the true."[5] The modern diplomat must also possess the quality of intellectual integrity. Ideally, too, he should be good-tempered or, at least, able to keep his temper under complete control at all times. A display of anger, for example, is regarded as a betrayal of weakness. When Napoleon flung his hat upon the carpet in front of Prince Metternich in June 1813, the latter knew that the emperor's strength was ebbing. Next on the list is patience, which Nicolson considers an indispensable quality for the successful negotiator. Modesty is considered important since vanity may tempt the diplomat into imprudence. The negotiator should also bear a special loyalty to his country, a loyalty that will prompt him to tell his government what it ought to know rather than what it wants to hear. And finally, the author reminds us that he has not forgotten the qualities of intelligence, knowledge, discernment, prudence, hospitality, charm, industry, courage, and tact. He has simply taken them for granted.[6]

It is clear from the above that the combination of characteristics required of the diplomat is unusual indeed. Yet even if people who measure up to this high standard can be recruited, the measure of success they may achieve in the job of international order-building remains to the largest degree dependent upon the complex and trying conditions under which they must work.

For example, so long as even one of the negotiators dogmatically adheres to universal aspirations, diplomacy's perennial quest for compromise is bound to continue to be frustrated. When two combatants, each claiming to represent the one true secular religion, meet in the arena, there remains almost no room for accommodation at all. Both tend to invoke the authority of God or the historical process and forget that "they meet under an empty sky from which the gods have departed."[7] Proselytizing should have little room at the bargaining table. Only to the extent that the negotiator can free himself from the onesidedness and biases of his own particular ideology is he able to think and feel himself into the position of other diplomats. Such empathy can contribute a great deal to successful negotiation. For though it in no way implies a yielding of one's own position, it makes possible the placing of questions at issue in as broadly conceived and mutually respecting a framework as possible.

The modern statesman-diplomat in a democracy faces a unique dilemma of responsibility to his nation. From this he cannot escape, whether he engages in secret or in open negotiations. Should his goals simply reflect the will of the people whose servant he is supposed to be? Or does his greater knowledge of the international scene entitle him to lead the people in some new direction if he believes that the common man's judgment is in error? Moreover, how important is domestic support, politically speaking? The experience of Woodrow Wilson and the League of Nations demonstrated that the statesman-diplomat ignores his people at his own peril. But the generation that ratified the United Nations Charter hailed this same man, repudiated only a quarter century before, as a great visionary. The fate of Wilson therefore seems to indicate that the diplomat who would also be a statesman must lead more than follow. Yet since he cannot but act on incomplete knowledge, and so can never "prove" that his vision is correct, this task may be a trying and cruel one. As Henry A. Kissinger has pointed out in his analysis of the Congress of Vienna,

> The statesman is therefore like one of the heroes in classical drama who has had a vision of the future but who cannot transmit it directly to his fellowmen and who cannot validate its "truth." Nations learn only by experience; they "know" only when it is too late to act. But statesmen must act *as if* their intuition were already experience, as if their aspiration were truth. It is for this reason that statesmen often share the fate of prophets, that they are without honour in their own country, that they always have a difficult task in legitimizing their programmes domestically, and that their greatness is usually apparent only in retrospect when their intuition has become experience. The statesman must therefore be an educator; he must bridge the gap between a people's experience and his vision, between a nation's tradition and its future. In this task his possibilities are limited. A statesman who too far outruns the experience of his people will fail in achieving a domestic consensus, however wise his policies; witness Castlereagh. A statesman who limits his policy to the experience of his people will doom himself to sterility; witness Metternich.[8]

Two decades after he wrote *A World Restored*, Henry Kissinger became Secretary of State. In many ways, his unique form of diplomacy was rooted in the intellectual insights of his academic career and represented a remarkable fusion between scholarship and statesmanship. The impact of his diplomacy was so profound that it merits special attention.

Henry Kissinger differs from most American statesmen in the sense that his policies were based on doctrine and deliberate design rather than on the more pragmatic day-to-day approach that has been typical of American diplomacy. This doctrine, which rested on three main pillars, emerged very clearly in *A World Restored*. The reason Kissinger undertook this study was that he was interested in the manner in which the European statesmen of the early nineteenth century secured the peace of Europe for a hundred years. He found three answers to this question. First, to be secure, a peace must be based on a negotiated settlement, with all sides in equilibrium, rather than on a victor's peace. Everybody is a little bit unhappy, but no one is completely unhappy. Thus, no one will try to overthrow the settlement through yet another war, and the relative insecurity of each guarantees the relative security of all. Second, a victorious power, in order to have peace, will not attempt to annihilate the vanquished but will coopt it into the established order by giving it something of its own substance. Thus, the victor decontaminates the defeated of his revolutionary ardor and transforms him subtly from a "have not" into a "have" nation. Third, in the absence of a globally controlled system, the best guarantor of peace is balance and, hence, a balancer is essential. This balancer will seldom ask the question, "Who is right and who is wrong?" but rather, "Who is weak and who is strong?" He will throw his weight on the weaker side whenever an imbalance occurs and by so doing restore the equilibrium and maintain the peace. Hence, peace, to Henry Kissinger, is a bonus of a successful balance policy.

Kissinger's policy, in fact, was a transplantation process of these three concepts into the modern world. The first principle was adopted in the Middle East, where Kissinger's policy supported neither Israel nor the Arabs but was committed to the principles of balance and equilibrium that made possible the disengagement treaties separating Israel from Syria and Egypt. He hoped to achieve a modern peace of Westphalia without victory or defeat. The second principle was applied to the Soviet Union, which received gigantic credits from the United States, and unlike Mr. Khrushchev who in 1959 talked about "burying" capitalism, Mr. Brezhnev began to be engaged in "borrowing" from capitalism. Kissinger's hope was that, subtly and over time, a community of economic interests would be established between the capitalist and communist worlds. The third principle was illustrated by President Nixon's trip to China, which created a triangle between the Soviet Union, China, and America in which Kissinger attempted to place the United States into the role of balancer, where it would be wooed by both China and the Soviet Union.

The weaknesses of the Kissinger diplomacy flowed from the fact that the transplantation had perhaps been too literal. This was, after all, not the early nineteenth century, but the late twentieth, and the world's center of gravity no longer rested in Europe. Kissinger was often accused of paying more attention to the adversaries of the United States than to her friends, and of not being sufficiently sensitive to the aspirations of the small and poor nations of the Third World. More fundamentally, perhaps, he followed the famous dictum of the classical German poet Johann Wolfgang von Goethe, in his essay *Poetry and Truth:* "If I had to choose between justice and disorder, on the one hand, and injustice and order, on the other, I would always choose the latter." In short, he tended to make stability a goal in itself. This, at times, compelled him to sacrifice humanitarian considerations on the altar of a larger strategic vision. During the war between India and Pakistan in 1971, for example, Kissinger "tilted" toward Pakistan and China because these two allies were weaker than the alliance on the other side, India and the Soviet Union. But by choosing Pakistan, he gave that government the green light to persecute and chase into exile ten million Bengalis without arousing any criticism from the United States. Kissinger responded to this critique by stating that the alternative might have been a major Soviet incursion into the Indian subcontinent, which would have been a greater evil. Of the two evils, he thus chose the lesser in an inherently tragic world.

Unlike John Foster Dulles, who divided the world into "good" and "evil" states and tended to judge those in the middle as "immoral," Henry Kissinger perceived the international arena as infinitely more complex. In his view, the statesman could only seldom choose between right and wrong. Most of the time, he had to choose between one right and another right or one wrong and a greater wrong. And there was no escape from choice itself for, as Camus reminded us, "not to choose is also a choice." Nor could one wait until all the facts were in, because, by then, foreign policy had become history.

Most basically, perhaps, the balancing approach may be becoming obsolete in a world in which some of the greatest challenges are global in nature, requiring global responses. The four modern Horsemen of the Apocalypse are called energy crisis, famine, population explosion, and environmental disruption. As Kissinger himself had realized, these problems could only be tackled through a comprehensive approach which fully accepted the interdependence of the world as a fact of modern life in the last quarter of the twentieth century. One may agree or disagree with Kissinger's approach to diplomacy. But it is impossible to ignore the fact that his approach was based on a consistent philosophic doctrine that evolved over a quarter of a century of reflection and experience, a doctrine, moreover, that displayed a remarkable fusion between scholarship and statesmanship.

ETHICS, POWER, AND THE STATESMAN

If the task of the diplomat is difficult, that of the statesman who instructs him is indeed formidable. For the latter, the greatest challenge of all concerns the role of ethics in a world of power. What is the relationship between "personal" and "political" morality? Does diplomacy leave room for morality at all? How should we judge a statesman—by his intentions or by the consequences of his actions? What should be the criterion of success for the statesman-diplomat? In short, what must concern us now is the problem of statesmanship and moral choice.

Diplomacy in the era of Woodrow Wilson looked confidently to the possibility of continuous progress in the relations among nations toward the goal of justice and brotherhood. Most contemporary observers of the new diplomacy were convinced that the inherent rationality and morality of man could not fail to assert themselves in diplomatic intercourse. The growth of democratic institutions would help immeasurably in this process. It was assumed, also, that statesmen would conduct diplomatic relations exclusively on a basis of goodwill and cooperation. In other words, this group of thinkers, whom we shall call the "idealists," deeply believed that it was only a question of time until a congruence would be achieved between personal and political morality. The cataclysm of World War II, however, cast serious doubts on these assumptions. It was no longer at all clear that historical progress toward cooperation among nations was inevitable. Nor was there sufficient evidence for the assertion that human nature was infinitely improvable. As a result, a second group of thinkers emerged who were no less concerned about peace and justice than were the idealists, but who felt that the very nature of the international struggle set unavoidable limits to the moral aspirations of man. These "realists" were convinced that international behavior was governed by its own objective laws, the most important of which was an immutable struggle for power. The idealist who attempted to deal with international relations in terms of morality did so at his own peril. Thus, at one end of the diplomatic spectrum, the Wilsonian idealists hoped to infuse international behavior with high moral standards. At the other end, the realists contended that international relations were neither moral nor immoral. The latter, indeed, defining the relations among nations as predominantly a matter of power, saw considerations of morality as irrelevant.

A careful analysis of the dilemmas of statesmanship indicates that the dichotomy between idealists and realists is too simple. The purely idealist statesman would be a saint, while a purely Machiavellian one would be a beast.[9] Few statesmen, however lofty their purposes, dare to ignore the reality of power, but equally few statesmen, however Machiavellian, venture to ignore the existence of morality. The crucial difference between interpersonal and international relations is not that the former permit moral behavior, whereas the latter do not. It resides, rather, in the fact that personal behavior is usually judged by an ethic of *intention* while that of the statesman is essentially one of *consequence.* Morgenthau cites an interesting example that illustrates this point:

> Neville Chamberlain's policies of appeasement were, as far as we can judge, inspired by good motives; he was probably less motivated by considerations of personal power than were many other British prime ministers, and he sought to preserve peace and to assure the happiness of all concerned. Yet his policies helped to make the Second World War inevitable, and to bring untold miseries to millions of men. Sir Winston Churchill's motives, on the other hand, have been much less universal in scope and much more narrowly directed toward personal and national power, yet the foreign policies that sprang from these inferior motives were certainly superior in moral and political quality to those pursued by his predecessor.[10]

The Suez crisis of 1956 excellently illustrates the multiple facets of this problem. President Eisenhower's decision to support Egypt and the Soviet Union against Britain and France was justified in terms of "a single standard of international morality which must be applied to friend and foe alike." This was clearly an ethic of intention. The British and French, on the other hand, justified their military expedition in terms of its ultimate consequence—the reassertion of their legal rights in the Suez Canal. This difference in interpretation of what constituted "morality" led to a great deal of bitterness and confusion. If we dig further, the problem becomes even more complex. Is not the logical extension of an ethic of consequence the dreadful formula that the end may justify the means? This was a question that the British and French found difficult to answer after the Suez affair. Conversely, cannot "moral" intentions at times lead to "immoral" consequences? To be specific, the moral act of President Eisenhower might have destroyed NATO and resulted in a far more immoral consequence—Soviet domination of Western Europe.

It should be obvious from the above discussion that power and morality are inseparable and must be so considered by the statesman. Perhaps it is helpful to think of the two as two concentric circles, of which power is the larger. Morgenthau, for example, asserted repeatedly that what he regarded as a morally dubious policy of the United States in Vietnam had hurt America's power position in other parts of the world. Or to take a hypothetical example, let us suppose that the United States promises Portugal a large loan. It then decides to withdraw the offer, breaking its promise. As a result, Portugal leaves NATO and becomes nonaligned. If this actually occurred, it might be said that the United States lost some of its power because it acted unethically. In some cases, therefore, power may be said to *include* morality. Of course, Portugal would base its decision on a multiplicity of factors, only one of which would be the American breach of promise. Hence, this generalization, like all others on ethics and power, is subject to exceptions. At times, indeed, morality may be the larger of the two concentric circles. Thus, America's moral stand in the Suez crisis won the admiration of many uncommitted nations in the East-West struggle. This friendship, although it was not expressed in terms of new military allies, no doubt added power to the international position of the United States in some parts of the world.

More generally, so far as the role of ethics in foreign policy is concerned, there is a dual tradition in American diplomacy. On one side of the spectrum was the *Realpolitik* of a Henry Kissinger who conceived of peace as the result of equilibrium rather than of justice and who never tired of pointing out that diplomacy, to be successful, had to be based on power and had to risk resort to war. On the other side were the globalism of a Woodrow Wilson who wanted to make the world "safe for democracy," the moral crusade of a John Foster Dulles or a Ronald Reagan who divided the world into free and unfree states, and the missionary zeal of a Jimmy Carter who declared that the abuse of human rights was no longer any single nation's exclusively domestic business. But as we have seen, these two principles have never been applied mutually exclusively in practice. Just as Kissinger could not remain indifferent to problems of morality, Wilson and Carter were forced to recognize the reality of power. Neither a beast nor a saint would make an effective architect of a modern foreign policy.

The subtle interdependence between ethics and power compels the statesman to engage in a process of continual balancing. He is forever having to weigh alternatives. And in this enterprise it is very rare for the merits in favor of one course of action to be clearly greater than the arguments for another. As one careful student of diplomacy has pointed out:

> The merits in argument for and against an acceptable line of action never occur in ratios of 100 to 0 or even of 80 to 20. They tend rather to occur in the order of 55 to 45 or even 51 to 49. Even at best, the arguments against a line of action in foreign policy tend to be almost as weighty as the considerations in favor. Yet these small margins of difference constitute the distinction between success and failure and are all-important.[11]

Almost never is the statesman called upon to decide between a clear-cut right and a clear-cut wrong. Here international relations resemble interpersonal behavior; most decisions must be taken along a continuum of varying shades of gray. But there does remain one crucial difference: the fact that the statesman's decision may affect the lives of millions of his fellow men.

Lest all this seem a study in confusion, let us, for illustrative purposes, examine the alternatives of a decision that reversed American policy of a quarter of a century: President Nixon's trip to China in 1972.

On the positive side, there were several arguments to be made. First, the decision made it possible once again to establish relations with China on the basis of reality rather than fiction. As a result, exchange programs were planned, and journalists, intellectuals, and athletes were able to visit each other's countries. Second, a modest trade relationship was begun. Third, the American move placed the Soviet Union on the defensive. Finally, the American policy reversal was decisive in seating China in the United Nations.

On the negative side, the United States paid a heavy price. In the first place, since the American President chose not to forewarn Japan of his imminent move, that nation went into "Nixon shock" and began to perceive the United States as a rather capricious ally. Second, Chiang Kai-shek on Formosa felt betrayed by the United States, and, similarly, a number of America's military allies in Asia, notably South Korea and the Philippines, developed serious reservations about the value of the American commitment. In short, critics of the move thought that the President might have confused motion with progress.

Thus, the China decision, like most major foreign policy decisions, had its benefits and its costs. Arguments for and against were balanced fairly evenly. Nor did any one side of the argument have a monopoly on ethical considerations. Each side could, and did, adduce persuasive moral arguments for its respective position.

The case of China shows that the statesman must act with the tragic knowledge that he cannot choose between good and evil but only among varying stages of evil. Indeed, whatever decision he makes, *some* evil consequences are bound to result from it. In such a situation, is it not easier to abstain from *any* decision? Yet such "abstention from evil does not at all affect the existence of evil in the world but only destroys the faculty of discriminating between different evils. The perfectionist thus becomes finally a source of greater evil."[12] This tragic condition has been painted in all its starkness by Morgenthau:

> We have no choice between power and the common good. To act successfully, that is according to the rules of the political art, is political wisdom. To know with despair that the political act is inevitably evil, and to act nevertheless, is moral courage. To choose among several expedient actions the least evil one is moral judgment. In the combination of political wisdom, moral courage and moral judgment, man reconciles his political nature with his moral destiny. That this conciliation is nothing more than a *modus vivendi*, uneasy, precarious, and even paradoxical, can disappoint only those who prefer to gloss over and to distort the tragic contradictions of human existence with the soothing logic of a specious concord.[13]

The Chinese case also demonstrates that the statesman must come to grips with at least three different modes of thinking. First, he must ask the question of power: Could the United States afford to ignore the increasing strength of the regime in power in Communist China? Second, the question of morality: Should the United States deal with a nation which it had condemned repeatedly as an aggressor? And third, the question of law: Could the United States expect China to obey the legal norms established by the international community? Morgenthau maintains that the statesman, if he is a political realist, should maintain the autonomy of the political sphere and merely ask himself the question of power.[14] This would seem too one-dimensional a view, for as we have seen, most of the time power *includes* considerations of morality and law.

Perhaps these dilemmas appear even more starkly in another example: President Nixon's decision to mine the North Vietnamese ports and to order all-out bombing attacks on Hanoi and Haiphong in 1972. These actions tested the determination of the Soviet Union and China to stand by their North Vietnamese ally. When no action was forthcoming either from Moscow or from Peking, President Nixon realized that he had won his gamble and that he had effectively isolated North Vietnam. Thus the war was brought to an end for American combat soldiers, but at a price that aroused the moral indignation of many nations and that of many Americans. Was this brutal means justified to attain the end of the war? Or could another, less dreadful, way have been found? Once again reasonable men may differ, but what remains beyond question is that power and morality are inextricably intertwined, and that the statesman may be confronted by choices that are awesome and terrible.

We are left, finally, with the ultimate question which formed the central point of the famous controversy between Socrates and the Sophists over two thousand years ago: Whose standard of morality should the statesman apply? Should he seek universal principles of justice, as did Socrates? Or should he readily admit that morality and justice are bound by time and space, as did the Sophists? If he pursues the former goal too far, he becomes a dogmatist; if he yields to the latter view too easily, he will be emasculated by a sloppy relativism. Indeed, the unending question for meaningful choices in a tragic world is the most difficult task confronting the modern statesman-diplomat as political order-builder.

TERRORISM AND THE TWILIGHT OF DIPLOMACY

By the mid-1980s, the world's diplomats were very much concerned. Since 1971, there had been hundreds of terrorist assaults on embassies and diplomatic missions. More than half of these had taken place in the 1980s. Twenty-five countries had been victimized, with the American embassy personnel held captive by Iran only the most widely publicized example. A diplomat's job, formerly held sacrosanct, had become as dangerous as that of a policeman in an angry crowd. Seldom before in modern history had diplomacy been so dangerous a calling. Some career diplomats expressed the fear that terrorism had struck at the very heart of diplomacy itself. A survey of the most significant of these terrorist attacks makes melancholy reading.

On December 28, 1972, four Palestinian "Black September" terrorists seized the Israeli embassy in Bangkok, Thailand. After negotiations with the Thai government, they surrendered the hostages and fled to Egypt. On March 1, 1973, "Black September" terrorists seized the Saudi embassy in Khartoum, Sudan, and killed several American and Belgian diplomats. After three days, they surrendered to Sudanese authorities. On September 13, 1974, three Japanese Red Army terrorists seized the French embassy in The Hague, Netherlands. They demanded—and got—a ransom of $1 million, flew to Damascus on a French plane, and surrendered to the Palestine Liberation Organization. On April 24, 1975, terrorists seized the West German embassy in Stockholm, Sweden, and demanded the release of twenty-six Baader-Meinhof gang members being held in German prisons. Two diplomats were killed before the terrorists surrendered. On December 4, 1975, gunmen demanding independence for Molucca seized the Indonesian consulate in Amsterdam, Netherlands, and took thirty hostages, including sixteen children. The terrorists only gave up after a sixteen-day siege during which one hostage died and three were injured. On December 21, 1975, three people were killed and seven wounded when six pro-Palestinian terrorists seized eighty-one persons attending an OPEC conference in Vienna, Austria. The terrorists fled to Tripoli, Libya. On June 15, 1977, three members of a Croatian separatist movement shot their way into the Yugoslav mission to the United Nations in New York, seeking to take the ambassador hostage. After wounding a chauffeur, they surrendered to the police. On March 26, 1979, Palestinians stormed the Egyptian embassy in Kuwait to protest the conclusion of a peace treaty between Egypt and Israel. On May 4, 1979, guerrillas in San Salvador seized several ambassadors as hostages in the French and Costa Rican embassies. Some of the hostages were held for a month before they were released. Two months later, Colombian guerrillas seized twenty diplomats from eighteen countries, including the papal nuncio, the American envoy, and thirteen other ambassadors. Only after protracted negotiations lasting several months were the diplomats released. On July 13, 1979, Palestinian terrorists attacked the Egyptian embassy in Ankara, Turkey, killed two security guards, and took nineteen hostages. On January 13, 1980, peasants and students seized the Spanish embassy in Guatemala City to protest army repression. Two embassy staff members and two Guatemalan officials were killed. On March 2, 1981, Pakistani terrorists hijacked a Pakistani airliner and flew it to Damascus, demanding the freeing of fifty-five Pakistani political prisoners in exchange for more than one hundred passenger hostages. After twelve days of negotiations, the government of Pakistan bowed to the hijackers' demands. Terrorism had chalked up another victory in its assault on civilization. In May 1981 a Moslem terrorist shot and severely wounded Pope John Paul II in St. Peter's Square in Rome, and in 1983 terrorists destroyed the American Embassy in Beirut. In June 1985, forty American passengers on a TWA airliner were hijacked by Shi'ite terrorists and held as hostages in Beruit for two weeks.

The United States, as a major target of left-wing discontent, has been disproportionately victimized over the years, even aside from Teheran. From 1971 to 1984, the State Department listed more than five hundred significant terrorist actions against American diplomatic installations or individuals. Five top officials were killed, including the ambassador to Afghanistan and the president of the American University in Beirut. The terror on embassy row everywhere took its toll on the morale of career diplomats. Diplomacy had suddenly become a very dangerous profession.

Perhaps most frightening is the fact that some of the most devastating acts of terrorism in the 1980s were apparently initiated not by crazed individuals but by coldly calculating leaders of sovereign states. By the mid-1980s, for example, the would-be assassin of Pope John Paul II confessed that he had been in the pay of the Bulgarian KGB. Since the Bulgarian KGB was clearly a puppet of its Soviet master, strong circumstantial evidence pointed to Yuri Andropov, the deceased Soviet leader and ex-KGB boss, as the prime mover to eliminate the troublesome Polish Pope. The destruction of the Korean airliner in 1983 and the murder of 269 innocent people may also be cited as an example of state-initiated terrorism. And the three suicide missions that led to the death of hundreds of American and French soldiers in Beirut was apparently of Iranian or Libyan origin. A case could in fact be made that a car bomb triggered the American withdrawal from Lebanon.

It is clear from the above examples that, apart from state-initiated terrorism, most of this kind of violence has emanated from postcolonial Third World countries. Not only have most terrorists perceived themselves as "freedom fighters," but the new nations of the Third World have been less inclined than Western states to abide by the old rules of discourse among nations. Modern diplomacy was, after all, a Western invention developed by European diplomats. The "inviolability" of embassy grounds and diplomats, too, was a Western concept. In the aftermath of the Hungarian revolution in 1956, for example, Cardinal Jozsef Mindszenty sought asylum in the American embassy in Budapest. In 1984 in London, on the other hand, the Libyan embassy became a source of terrorism when gunmen sprayed the streets below with machine-gun fire, killing a policewoman. The British had to let the killers go since the Libyans threatened to take reprisals against the British embassy in Tripoli. It appeared that Libyan leader Muammar Qadaffi was in personal charge of the operation.

Thus, traditional principles of diplomacy are no longer accepted by many of the new nations, such as Khomeini's Iran or Qadaffi's Libya. In short, the West wanted to export its diplomatic way of life, and this simply did not work. A custom that had evolved over five hundred years of time had virtually broken down in a single decade. And, as a consequence, as we move toward the year 2000, diplomacy itself is now on trial.

REFERENCES

1. For a perceptive analysis of the Congress of Vienna, see Harold Nicolson, *The Congress of Vienna.* New York: Harcourt, Brace, 1946; or Henry A. Kissinger, *A World Restored.* Boston: Houghton Mifflin, 1957.
2. Hans Morgenthau, *Politics Among Nations.* 3d ed. New York: Knopf, 1960, pp. 539–540.
3. Henry A. Kissinger, "The Congress of Vienna," *World Politics,* January 1956, pp. 264–265.
4. This is a statement attributed to a British ambassador, Sir Henry Wotton, cited by Sir Harold Nicolson in *Diplomacy.* New York: Oxford University Press, 1955, p. 44.
5. Nicolson, *op. cit.,* p. 110.
6. *Ibid.,* p. 126.
7. Morgenthau, *op. cit.,* p. 259.
8. Kissinger, *op. cit.,* p. 329.
9. Morgenthau, *op. cit.,* p. 14.
10. *Ibid.,* p. 6.
11. Charles Burton Marshall, *The Limits of Foreign Policy.* New York: Henry Holt, 1954, p. 33.
12. Hans J. Morgenthau, *Scientific Man versus Power Politics.* Chicago: University of Chicago Press, 1952, p. 202.
13. *Ibid.,* p. 203.
14. Morgenthau, *Politics Among Nations,* pp. 11–12.

BIBLIOGRAPHY

Ball, George W. *Diplomacy for a Crowded World: An American Foreign Policy.* Boston: Atlantic-Little, Brown, 1976.
Bell, Coral. *The Conventions of Crisis.* New York: Oxford University Press, 1971.
Berman, Maureen R., and Zartman, I. William. *The Practical Negotiator.* New Haven, Conn.: Yale University Press, 1982.
Carlton, David, and Schaerf, Carlo, eds. *Contemporary Terror: Studies in Sub-State Violence.* New York: St. Martin's, 1981.
Carter, Jimmy. *Keeping Faith: Memoirs of a President.* New York: Bantam Books, 1982.
Cecil, A. *Metternich, 1773–1859: A Study of His Period and Personality.* New York: Macmillan, 1933.
Cooper, Sir Alfred D. *Talleyrand.* New York: Harper, 1932.
Craig, Gordon A., and George, Alexander L. *Force and Statecraft: Diplomatic Problems of Our Time.* New York: Oxford University Press, 1982.
Craig, Gordon S. *From Bismarck to Adenauer: Aspects of German Statecraft.* Baltimore: Johns Hopkins Press, 1958.
———, and Gilbert, Felix. *The Diplomats: 1919–1939.* Princeton, N.J.: Princeton University Press, 1953.
Crenshaw, Martha, ed. *Terrorism, Legitimacy, and Power.* Middletown, Conn.: Wesleyan University Press, 1983.
Dickson, Peter W. *Kissinger and the Meaning of History.* New York: Cambridge University Press, 1978.
Eban, Abba. *The New Diplomacy: International Affairs in the Modern Age.* New York: Random House, 1983.

Evans, Ernest. *Calling a Truce to Terror: The American Response to International Terrorism.* Westport, Conn.: Greenwood Press, 1979.

Foster, J. W. *The Practice of Diplomacy.* Boston: Houghton Mifflin, 1906.

Goodwin, Geoffrey, ed. *Ethics and Nuclear Deterrence.* New York: St. Martin's, 1982.

Graubard, Stephen R. *Kissinger: Portrait of a Mind.* New York: Norton, 1973.

Hankey, Maurice P. A. *Diplomacy by Conference.* New York: Putnam, 1946.

Hoffmann, Stanley. *Duties Beyond Borders: On the Limits and Possibilities of Ethical International Politics.* Syracuse, N.Y.: Syracuse University Press, 1981.

Hoopes, Townsend. *The Devil and John Foster Dulles.* Boston: Little Brown, 1973.

Iklé, Fred Charles. *How Nations Negotiate.* New York: Praeger, 1964.

Kennan, George F. *American Diplomacy, 1900–1950.* Chicago: University of Chicago Press, 1953.

———. *Memoirs: 1925–1950.* Boston: Atlantic-Little, Brown, 1967.

———. *Memoirs: 1950–1963.* Boston: Atlantic-Little, Brown, 1972.

Kissinger, Henry A. *White House Years.* Boston: Little, Brown, 1979.

———. *Years of Upheaval.* Boston: Little, Brown, 1982.

———. *A World Restored: Metternich, Castlereagh, and the Problems of Peace 1812–1822.* Boston: Houghton Mifflin, 1957.

Macomber, William. *The Angels' Game: A Handbook of Modern Diplomacy.* Briarcliff Manor, N.Y.: Stein and Day, 1975.

Mayer, Arno J. *Politics and Diplomacy of Peacemaking: Containment and Counterrevolution at Versailles, 1918–1919.* New York: Knopf, 1967.

Mayer, Martin. *The Diplomats.* New York: Doubleday, 1983.

McCamy, James L. *Conduct of the New Diplomacy.* New York: Harper & Row, 1964.

McDermott, Geoffrey. *The New Diplomacy and Its Apparatus.* London: Plume Press, 1973.

Nicolson, Harold. *The Congress of Vienna, a Study in Allied Unity: 1812–1822.* New York: Harcourt, Brace, 1946.

———. *Diplomacy.* New York: Oxford University Press, 1950.

———. *The Evolution of Diplomatic Method.* New York: Macmillan, 1955.

———. *Peacemaking, 1919.* Boston: Houghton Mifflin, 1933.

Pillar, Paul R. *Negotiating Peace: War Termination as a Bargaining Process.* Princeton, N.J.: Princeton University Press, 1983.

Randle, Robert F. *The Origins of Peace: A Study of Peacemaking and the Structure of Peace Settlements.* New York: Free Press, 1973.

Sherwood, Robert E. *Roosevelt and Hopkins.* New York: Harper, 1948.

Spender, Sir Percy. *Exercises in Diplomacy.* New York: New York University Press, 1970.

Sterling, Claire. *The Terror Network.* New York: Holt, Rinehart, and Winston/Reader's Digest Press, 1981.

———. *The Time of Assassins.* New York: Holt, Rinehart, and Winston, 1984.

Stoessinger, John G. *Henry Kissinger: The Anguish of Power.* New York: Norton, 1976.

Thayer, Charles W. *Diplomat.* New York: Harper, 1959.

Watson, Adam. *Diplomacy.* New York: McGraw-Hill New Press, 1982.

Yost, Charles. *The Conduct and Misconduct of Foreign Affairs.* New York: Random House, 1972.

Chapter 9

International Law and Political Order

Inter armis silent leges. In the clash of arms the laws are silent. We may add that in the truce of arms the laws are heard.

WALTER LIPPMANN *The Public Philosophy*

INTERNATIONAL RELATIONS AND THE RULE OF LAW

Between the evolution of political order among nations and the development of world law—a body of rules and principles of action that are legally binding upon states in their relations with one another—there is undoubtedly a vital connection, yet there remains wide disagreement on the nature of this connection. Many observers of the international scene feel that political order-building has to precede the establishment of a rule of law; that, in fact, a legal consensus can only grow in the soil of a community based on social and political harmony. Others are equally convinced that the establishment of a rule of law can help knit the bonds of social and political order, that the promulgation of legal documents such as convenants and treaties can weave the fabric of community. The former tend to favor a "political" approach to order-building and prefer to work through the processes of political accommodation and diplomacy; the latter are inclined toward a "legal" approach and look with greater hope to the role of international law. In the present chapter we shall be concerned with this legal approach to political order.

The modern law of nations has its origins in antiquity and in medieval times. It has four chief roots. A first important source is the work of classical writers. The most famous of these is Hugo Grotius, frequently described as the "father of international law." His fame rests mainly on a monumental work, *The Law of War and Peace*, published in 1625 as an impassioned protest against the carnage of the Thirty Years' War. It was this treatise that laid the groundwork for the modern laws of war. A key passage in its preface sounds amazingly modern:

Throughout the Christian world I observed a lack of restraint in relation to war, such as even barbarous races should be ashamed of; I observed that men rush to arms for slight causes, or no cause at all, and that when arms have once been taken up there is no longer any respect for law, divine or human; it is as if, in accordance with a general decree, frenzy had openly been let loose, for the committing of all crimes.[1]

A second significant source of international law is custom. If certain customary practices among nations persist for a long period of time, and if no state expressly rejects them, they eventually may be absorbed into the body of international law. For example, it had long been the custom to exempt unarmed fishing vessels from war booty. Finally, in 1900, this custom came to be recognized as law.[2] This role of custom, however, illustrates a major problem of international law. Since only those practices become law that are not strongly opposed by any state, the rules that nations observe represent only a lowest common denominator. It is for this reason that international law is not only threatened by the ever-present danger of not being abided by, but it is also permanently plagued by low moral standards. The reason for this is, of course, that while international law is intended to control states, it is in effect controlled by them.

A third major source of international law derives from treaties. These have played an important role since the days of Greek antiquity. Thucydides' *History of the Peloponnesian War*, for example, speaks extensively about treaties among the city-states of the ancient Mediterranean world. The Congress of Vienna, the Versailles Settlement, the United Nations Charter, and NATO have all rested on treaties that have contributed importantly to international law. Yet, though more specific than custom and requiring the deliberate commitment of states through ratification, treaties also are often ambiguous and do not necessarily ensure just relationships among nations, for the treaty makers' first responsibility is attempting to strike a delicate balance between justice and peace. If they overemphasize the former, the peace may be lost—witness Versailles. The same is true if they lean too much toward the latter—witness Munich. The revision of a treaty is often an arduous and painful process. It took fourteen years of negotiations between Panama and the United States, for example, to renegotiate a 1903 treaty governing the Canal Zone, which had granted the United States control "in perpetuity" and to transfer sovereignty over the Zone to Panama by the year 2000.

The fourth important source of international law is the decisions of courts. The contribution of international tribunals in the establishment of international law is a recent development, largely a product of the twentieth century. The most important of the judicial bodies have been the Permanent Court of International Justice under the League of Nations and the International Court of Justice under the United Nations system.

Traditionally, only states have been subjects of international law. In the absence of a higher secular arbiter, each state has tended to recognize or refuse to recognize its fellow members of the world community. The practice of recognition has followed fairly arbitrary rules of co-option which each state has developed on its own. Since the advent of the United Nations, the practice of "collective recognition" has gained currency. In the case of the birth of new states, such as Israel and Ghana, admission to the United Nations has become a kind of imprimatur by the world community. This rise of "collective recognition" may be a hopeful sign for the development of more uniform legal standards. Our generation has also seen the extension of international law to subjects other than states: semigovernmental organizations such as the Jewish Agency; nongovernmental organizations like the International Red Cross; international organizations such as the United Nations and its specialized agencies; and, perhaps most important, individuals, who also now have rights and duties before international law. Even stateless people have come to enjoy at least a minimum of international protection. And for the first time in history the attempt was made at Nuremberg in 1945 to bring individuals before the bar of international law.°

The question of jurisdiction over individuals demonstrates that the problem of "progress" in international law is a highly complex one. It would be too one-dimensional to state that international law advances simply by the expansion of jurisdiction. The ambiguity of the problem was demonstrated during the Nuremberg War Crimes Trials in 1945.

The Nuremberg Tribunal was set up by the victorious powers—the United States, the Soviet Union, Britain, and France—to try the major leaders of the Nazi government. The indictment against them was threefold: (a) crimes against peace (i.e., planning, preparing, initiating, or waging aggressive war or taking part in a common plan to do so); (b) war crimes (i.e., violations of the rules of war); (c) crimes against humanity (crimes against civilians before or during the war). On the basis of one or more of these counts, a number of the leading Nazis were either executed or given prison sentences, while others were acquitted. However, several questions have been raised as to the legality of the Nuremberg trials. For example, since international law had never before applied to individuals, was not the Nuremberg judgment ex post facto? Some observers felt that the Nuremberg trials set a dangerous precedent. In a future war, would it not be possible—on the basis of the Nuremberg judgment—for the victor nation to bring to trial the statesmen of the defeated country? To take the point ad absurdum, if in a war between the United States and the Soviet Union the latter should be victorious, might not the victor try an American President as a "warmonger and imperialist aggressor"? Hence, it is difficult to assert with finality that the subjecthood of individuals under international law has necessarily served the cause of world order. And even if this were so beyond a doubt, it must be remembered that, before international law was able to hold individuals criminally liable, it first had to destroy the sovereignty of the nation of which they were members.

The dubiousness of the Nuremberg precedent prompted the General Assembly of the United Nations to direct its International Law Commission to formulate the principles of international law established at Nuremberg. The commission in its findings approved the principle of individual responsibility and denied the immunity of high government officials who committed crimes

---

° While an attempt was made by the victorious powers after World War I to bring to trial certain German "war criminals," including Kaiser Wilhelm, these so-called Leipzig Trials were a failure.

in the name of obedience to orders. But the commission was also convinced that the ad hoc character of the Nuremberg trials pointed up the necessity for a Criminal Chamber of the International Court of Justice. However, owing to disagreement among the major powers, an international criminal code does not yet exist. From the above example one may draw the possible conclusion that "progress" in international law is perhaps better served through the development of its "facilitative" rather than its "punitive" aspects.

If international law still applies largely to states, it is also primarily interpreted by states. Self-judgment as the logical adjunct of sovereignty still dominates the scene. Only minor incursions have been made into the principle of "domestic jurisdiction." The only international body with military enforcement power is the United Nations Security Council, and its power is severely curtailed through the veto of the Big Five. The rule of self-judgment also applies in questions of revision and repeal of international law. For example, the Western powers took the position that the Potsdam Agreement could only be revised with the unanimous consent of the signatories. They invoked the principle of *pacta sunt servanda*—"pacts must be observed." The Soviet Union, on the other hand, desirous of evicting the Western powers from Berlin, invoked the opposing principle of *rebus sic stantibus*—"matters have changed." Quite clearly, such an explosive political issue cannot be settled by judicial means, but can only yield to the processes of diplomacy.

In view of the tremendous obstacles in the path of international law, it is remarkable that in certain limited areas a respectable body of substantive law has in fact crystallized. International law has come to serve a useful function in the demarcation of boundaries among states; the acquisition of a "no man's land" and the regulation of minor territorial disputes fall in this category. Even in this area, however, great difficulties may arise. It has been impossible, for example, to agree upon a uniform definition of territorial waters. The law of the sea, too, has been the subject of numerous inconclusive global conferences. Similarly, each state still claims sovereignty over its airspace. International law also defines the privileges and immunities of ambassadors, of heads of state, and of their immediate entourage. Certain rules have developed on the basis of reciprocity under customary international law. Ambassadors, for example, may not be taxed and may be sued only with their own consent. High-ranking United Nations officials also enjoy "diplomatic immunity." Finally, the right of political asylum for refugees has long been sanctioned by customary international law.

The law of nations also facilitates normal and peaceful relations among nations. Numerous claims by one state against another have been settled through "good offices," mediation and arbitration tribunals, and judicial decisions. A useful body of law also exists for the purpose of regulating strained and hostile international relations. For example, under the Drago Doctrine of 1902, international law holds that the forcible collection of debts through blockade is illegal. An attempt has also been made to determine the rights and duties of neutrals in times of war. Of course, the fiercer and more "total" war has become, the more difficult it has been to define these rights and duties.

International law has also attempted to come to grips with war itself. Two approaches have dominated international legal thinking. The first has been a modern version of the assumption that first guided Hugo Grotius: that war cannot be eliminated by legal means, but that its worst horrors may be somewhat mitigated through the development of laws governing its conduct. An impressive body of laws aimed at this end today exists. To name but a few: the Geneva Protocol of 1925 on the Prohibition of Chemical and Bacteriological Warfare and Poison Gas; the Geneva Convention of 1929 on the Treatment of Sick and Wounded; the Washington Pact of 1935 for the Protection of Museums and Historic Sites; the London Protocol of 1936 regulating submarine warfare; the Hague Convention of 1938 outlawing inhuman weapons; and the Geneva Convention of 1949 governing the protection of civilian populations. The observance of these laws of war has varied. International laws proved almost completely impotent during World War II, though even Hitler decided against the use of poison gas for fear of retaliation in kind. The laws of war have been observed far more scrupulously in the nuclear age. For example, owing to the fear of an atomic holocaust both sides decided to keep the Korean conflict limited and demonstrated a considerable respect for the laws of war.

The second attempt by international law to deal with war has been its legal prohibition. In 1928, in the Kellogg-Briand pact, most states of the world "renounced war as an instrument of national policy." But no sanctions were included in the pact against a possible aggressor. During the entire lifetime of the League of Nations, international lawyers grappled with the intricate problems of defining "aggression" and of deciding what constituted a "just," that is "defensive," war. It was impossible to reach agreement and in the end the League of Nations Covenant in fact left certain loopholes for legal resort to war. Similarly, the United Nations Charter, while expressly outlawing war, permits the creation of regional arrangements for the purpose of collective self-defense. The United Nations, however, after more than two decades of legal controversy, in 1974 finally emerged with a definition of aggression. Needless to say, the definition was so ambiguous that its application in a concrete case of war remains very dubious indeed.

The record demonstrates that of the two approaches to dealing with war, the more realistic is through the development of laws governing its conduct. The elimination of war is clearly not a legal problem, but the most brutal effects of modern warfare may perhaps be somewhat softened through the development of such a body of laws. Perhaps not surprisingly, as the horrors of war in our time have increased there has also occurred a revival of concern and respect for laws concerning the waging of war.

On the whole, we must admit that the contribution of international law to the building of political order has been modest. In the first place, most international disputes simply do not lend themselves to a judicial approach since they are much too deeply involved in questions of power and prestige. Hence international law, unlike domestic law, suffers from a paucity of cases and cannot easily grow into a codified system. A second obstacle is the stubborn fact that the very states that are to be governed by international law are the sovereign masters of that law, rather than its servants. In other words, international law suffers from the lack of a centralized enforcement agency. These truths have raised the question of whether there is such a thing as international law at all. The record shows that the answer is definitely in the affirmative, yet it also shows that the main usefulness of international law is in technical and fairly noncontroversial matters. In these areas, it has crystallized into a respectable body of international rules and regulations which are invaluable aids in the normal day-to-day conduct of international relations.

As a general rule, the "legal approach" to political order-building has been most effective among those nations that are held together by a sense of political community. But law has not been able to produce this community. Rather, its existence has seemed to depend on the prior existence of a cultural and political community. Where there is no such community—as in the relations between the two superpowers—the "political approach" of diplomacy is likely to yield more fruitful results than the judicial. Indeed, the true relation between diplomacy and international law has not been one in which the latter has displaced the former, but one in which more successful diplomacy has resulted in more ungrudging consent to better laws.

The most ambitious example of the legal approach to political order in our time is the International Court of Justice. We shall now explore the question of whether this institution accurately reflects the role of international law in general.

THE INTERNATIONAL COURT OF JUSTICE

The International Court of Justice, better known as the World Court, came into existence in 1945 as part of the United Nations system. Actually, the Court was a reincarnation rather than a birth. It was the successor to the Permanent Court of International Justice of the League of Nations. The old World Court had been one of the more successful institutions of the League. In the eighteen years of its activity, it had rendered thirty-two judgments and had handed down twenty-seven advisory opinions. The new World Court broke the continuity as little as possible. It established itself at the Hague and the statute governing its activities became virtually a carbon copy of its predecessor.

The fifteen justices of the Court are elected for nine-year terms by a majority of votes in the General Assembly and the Security Council. The veto power of the Big Five does not apply. The statute of the Court provides that the justices be chosen "from among persons of high moral character who possess . . . recognized competence in international law." They should also represent "the main forms of civilization and the principal legal systems of the world." Hence, individuals rather than states are to be elected to the Court. This proviso, it was hoped, would increase the Court's impartiality. It was also assumed that the fifteen justices would represent a wide geographic distribution and that no two members of the Court would be of the same nationality.

These clauses were inserted owing to the conviction of the founders that the impartiality of the Court would have to be safeguarded as much as possible. They realized that the judicial value of the Court as an international tribunal might be totally defeated if the justices were to be swayed by national loyalties or the political interests of particular states. On the other hand, the founders had to make their peace with the fact that judges, like other human beings, were nationals of a particular country, and that the Court might have to deal with explosive political issues on which national sentiment would run high and on which Olympian dispassionateness would be hard to achieve. One important concession was made in this direction in the statute. If a case were to come before the Court and there was no judge of the nationality of one of the parties among the permanent justices, that party would have the right to choose an additional ad hoc judge of its own or any other nationality. This right has been exercised invariably. The Court was thus an expression not only of the hope that the justices would rise above all national allegiance and serve only the law, but also of the realization that this high level of detachment might not always actually prove possible.

The record of the World Court, while modest, indicates the nature of the relationship between political order-building and the rule of law. The Court has been involved in four different types of cases: it has dealt with both the East-West and the colonial-anticolonial conflicts; it has passed on disputes within the Western Hemisphere; and it has been called upon to interpret the legal competence of the United Nations. A closer look at some significant cases from each of these four areas will shed further light on the role of the Court.

The World Court's *cause célèbre* was the Corfu Channel case, involving two countries separated by the Iron Curtain—Albania and Great Britain. This was the only contentious East-West case ever to come before the Court. In October 1946 two British warships were sunk by mines as they passed through the Corfu Channel in the territorial waters of Albania. Forty-four British sailors were killed and the British government brought the matter before the Security Council, where a resolution that held Albania responsible for the tragedy was vetoed by the Soviet Union. Subsequently, the question of responsibility was referred by both parties to the International Court of Justice. Since there was no Albanian judge on the Court, a Czechoslovak justice—Judge Ecer—was appointed to the Court, which now comprised sixteen members. The British contention was that the Albanian government had laid the mines or must have known about them, that it was therefore guilty of criminal negligence, and that it should therefore be held responsible. Albania claimed that the British ships had violated its sovereignty and that its action was a justifiable act of self-defense. The Court, in an eleven to five opinion, held in favor of the British contention. As a result of this opinion, the British government requested that the Court also fix the amount of damages to be paid by Albania. Although the Albanians claimed that the Court had no jurisdiction over this part of the case, the Court held that the decision of the two parties to submit the dispute gave it the right to fix the damages as well. In a ten to six opinion, the Court held that the Albanian government must have known of the existence of the mines and should therefore pay compensation to Great Britain. The amount of the damages was fixed at $2.4 million. The six dissenting justices contended that it had not been proved that the Albanian government knew of the mines and that Albania could therefore not be held liable. The dissenting justices represented Egypt, Brazil, the Soviet Union, Poland, Yugoslavia, and Czechoslovakia. Albania refused to honor the decision of the Court, despite the fact that the majority opinion had been based on numerous reports by experts who had visited the localities adjacent to the scene of the incident. In thus declining to pay the amount awarded, Albania has become the first state in history to "refuse in principle to comply with the decision of the Court in a contentious proceeding to which it was a party."[3] Neither the Court nor the British government has been able to enforce the decision.

A second problem involving the East-West struggle reached the Court in November 1947 when the General Assembly requested an advisory opinion on the controversial question of the admission of new members to the United Nations. The Court was asked to pass on the question of whether a member state could make its consenting vote subject "to the additional condition that other states be admitted." The General Assembly's request for an advisory opinion on this matter grew out of the Soviet Union's proposal of a membership "package deal." This was rejected by the United States, which held that each application should be considered on its individual merits. The Court, in a nine to six opinion, upheld the American view and declared that Article IV of the Charter, stating that admission was to be open to all "peace-loving" states, was to govern admissions procedure rather than extraneous political considerations. The minority, which included not only the Soviet, Polish, and Yugoslav justices, but also the French, British, and Canadian members of the Court, contended that the question of membership was essentially a political one and that political considerations were therefore admissible. Though the decision itself was superseded through a membership "package deal" in 1955, the fact that it witnessed three Western justices voting with the anti-Western minority has made it of more than passing interest. What was significant was not the "rightness" or "wrongness" of the opinion of these three Western justices but the simple fact that what they considered to be an objective appraisal of the case led them to an opinion that contravened that of their national governments at the time.

The only colonial issue to reach the Court to date has concerned the disposition of Southwest Africa, which had been a mandate under the League of Nations. The Court has been concerned with various aspects of this problem intermittently since 1950. In that year the General Assembly requested an advisory opinion on whether or not the former mandate could be administered as an integral part of South Africa. The issue aroused much interest because of South Africa's adamant refusal to place the territory under any form of international supervision. The Court, in a unanimous opinion, declared that "the United Nations [was] entitled to exercise supervisory functions over the administration of the mandate, and [that] the Union acting alone [was] not competent to modify the international status of the territory."[4] Specifically, the

court stated that the Union government was under the obligation to submit periodic reports on the status of Southwest Africa to the United Nations. In a
later case, in 1956, the Court upheld the legality of oral reports to the UN from
the contested territory.

In the third round, in 1962, the Court took yet another step when, by a
vote of eight to seven, it rejected South Africa's objections to its jurisdiction.
On the basis of this opinion, the two plaintiffs, Ethiopia and Liberia, submitted
lengthy substantive briefs. The Union of South Africa, too, submitted its defense. In July 1966, by the narrowest possible majority—a seven to seven tie
being broken in favor of South Africa by the "casting vote" of the president,
Sir Percy Spender of Australia—the Court dismissed the complaint against
South Africa on the grounds of insufficiency of legal interest on the part of the
complaining states. The Court, in short, decided not to decide. The reaction of
the Afro-Asian group was violent. It expressed its disinclination to resort to the
Court in the future and secured the passage of a resolution in the General Assembly withdrawing the right to administer Southwest Africa from South
Africa and conferring this right upon the General Assembly. Defenders of the
decision, on the other hand, asserted that it was better for the Court to dismiss
the case than to make a decision against South Africa that would have been
unenforceable. Thus, sixteen years of litigation came to an end. The Court's
ultimate role in the colonial struggle, as in the East-West struggle, had been
negligible.

In 1972, in a dramatic move, the UN Security Council decided to meet in
Addis Ababa, Ethiopia, in order to underline the importance of the problems
besetting Africa. In one of its resolutions it strongly urged a United Nations
role in "Namibia"—the new African term now used for the territory of Southwest Africa—and requested the Secretary-General to travel there in order to
see to it that the resolution was implemented. Secretary-General Kurt Waldheim duly went to South Africa and tried his best to persuade the South African government but to no avail. For all practical purposes, South African
control over Namibia remained intact, despite an African initiative in 1974 to
expel South Africa from the United Nations that was blocked by American,
British, and French vetoes in the Security Council, and despite a General Assembly decision, taken a few weeks later, to suspend South Africa's participation. Four major UN organs—the World Court, the General Assembly, the
Security Council, and the Secretary-General—had come to grief on the unyielding rock of South African sovereignty. Only the diplomatic initiative of
Secretary of State Henry Kissinger in 1976 finally managed to move Namibia
closer to black majority rule and independence. And by the early 1980s, with
Zimbabwe's emergence as a sovereign state, Namibia's freedom was only a
matter of time.

While the Court's role in the settlement of disputes involving the two
great political struggles has been minimal, it has played a significant part in
intraregional controversies, especially within the Western Hemisphere. Here
the Court has made an important contribution to political order-building.
Some of these cases have been fairly technical, as for example the question of

fishing rights by Britain off the Icelandic coast, or a claim to the ruins of the ancient temple at Angkor which strained relations between Cambodia and Thailand. Others have had greater political import. One of the most typical of these cases to reach the Court was a boundary dispute between Honduras and Nicaragua. In November 1960 the Court ruled that Nicaragua was obligated to give effect to a 1906 arbitration award settling its boundary with Honduras. This award had been made by King Alfonso XIII of Spain, who had established a boundary line that would cause the transfer to Honduras of frontier regions claimed by Nicaragua. In 1912 Nicaragua had challenged the award, and repeated attempts to settle the issue had failed. Finally, in 1957, the Organization of American States brought about an agreement between the two countries to submit the case to the World Court. The Court supported the 1906 award by a vote of fourteen to one. The dissenting vote was cast by a Colombian justice who had been designated by Nicaragua as ad hoc judge for the case. The dissenting opinion held that the 1906 arbitration award was invalid because of errors made by the arbitrator. The permanent judges, however, ruled in favor of Honduras and declared that the king of Spain had been a proper arbitrator under the terms of an 1894 treaty between Nicaragua and Honduras and that Nicaragua had accepted the king's decision at the time. Nicaragua complied with the decision.

The broader significance of this case was the fact that justices from both sides of the Iron Curtain ruled in effect that once a valid arbitration award is made in an international dispute, it becomes effective and remains so despite any lapse of time in its implementation. The judgment displayed a broad support for the principle of arbitration and laid the groundwork for the future settlement of similar international disputes. When, on the other hand, Australia complained about France's atomic testing activities in the Pacific, the latter paid no attention and even refused to appear in Court.

Perhaps the most important contribution of the World Court to international order-building has been the strengthening of the United Nations as a juridical and political entity. When Count Folke Bernadotte, the United Nations mediator in Palestine, was assassinated by a Jewish terrorist group, the United Nations requested an advisory opinion on the question of whether the world organization was entitled to bring a claim against a state for damages caused to the United Nations by injuries suffered by one of its representatives while acting on its behalf. The Court, in an eleven to four opinion, held that the United Nations was entitled to claim such reparation. The majority, in a far-reaching opinion, stated that

> Fifty states, representing the vast majority of the members of the international community, had the power, in conformity with international law to bring into being an entity possessing objective international personality, not merely personality recognized by them alone, together with capacity to bring international claims.[5]

Thus, the United Nations was granted a "personality" by the Court, a kind of sovereignty all its own which the majority saw implied in the Charter:

Under international law, the Organization must be deemed to have those powers which, though not expressly provided in the Charter, are conferred upon it by necessary implication as being essential to the performance of its duties.[6]

The four dissenting justices—Egyptian, Polish, Russian, and American—held that this "implied powers clause" was not inherent in the Charter. On the strength of this advisory opinion, the United Nations claimed reparations from Israel for the death of Count Bernadotte and injuries to other United Nations personnel in the pursuit of their duties. The government of Israel has honored these claims. Thus, the Court helped to endow the United Nations with an international legal personality entitled to protect its officials by bestowing upon them the legal status of world civil servants.

In July 1962 the Court once again interpreted the United Nations Charter in a very important advisory opinion. In response to a request by the General Assembly, the Court declared, by a vote of nine to five, that the expenses of the United Nations Emergency Force (UNEF) and the United Nations Congo Force (ONUC) constituted expenses of the United Nations within the meaning of Article 17, paragraph 2 of the Charter, which declares that "the expenses of the Organization shall be borne by the members as apportioned by the General Assembly."[7]

By this opinion, the Court confirmed the General Assembly's authority to impose legally binding assessments on the member states. In effect, a two-thirds majority could now bind the entire membership, including those states that voted in the negative. In that sense, the opinion signified a tentative step toward the principle of international taxation by the world community and lent support to the principle of majority rule in international relations. It also gave the Assembly and the Security Council free rein to establish peace forces of the UNEF or ONUC type and to provide for their financing, thus underwriting the late Secretary-General Dag Hammarskjöld's conception of the UN as a "dynamic instrument" capable of executive action, in contrast to the notion of the UN as a mere "static conference machinery."

Despite the far-reaching implications of the opinion, its practical effects on the UN treasury were not too significant. The two great powers that had refused for reasons of political opposition to pay for UNEF or ONUC—the Soviet Union and France—continued to withhold payment. But thirty-one smaller states that had been in arrears for reasons of alleged financial hardship decided to clear their accounts.[8]

Any analysis of the World Court must be tempered with caution, for the number of cases that have been brought before it have thus far been few—fewer, indeed, than the number earlier submitted to the League of Nations Court. Moreover, it is difficult to determine the Court's role as an impartial arbiter in political disputes. It is true that in both East-West cases, the justices from the Soviet bloc voted with the minority, but this fact alone is inconclusive evidence. It may be explained by political considerations but it may also be attributable to the fact that the justices have been trained in different legal systems and rooted in different political beliefs. On the other hand, the vote of the three Western justices in the membership case indicated a high degree of objectivity.

An obvious and irritating problem consistently plaguing the Court has been that of enforcement. The World Court has no police power by which it can actually implement its decisions against recalcitrant parties to a dispute. When Albania refused to abide by its decision and the Union of South Africa paid no attention to its advisory opinion, the Court was helpless. The Albanian fiasco even raised the question of whether it might not have been better for the Court to stay out of a dispute in which it would be unable to enforce a decision. Some observers have argued that in this instance the Court had "frozen" a quarrel rather than resolved it and that it might have been wiser to leave the matter to the political processes of diplomatic negotiations. Iran was another case in point. In September 1980, the World Court, in a unanimous ruling, ordered Iran to release the American hostages who had been held captive for almost a year. The United States' legal advisor to the Department of State called the ruling "splendid." Nonetheless, Iran not only ignored the opinion entirely but failed to appear before the Court. Nothing could be done to enforce the Court's decision.

In 1984 the Court suffered another setback, this time at the hands of the United States. In April of that year Nicaragua lodged a complaint against the United States, charging that the mining of its ports was an illegal intrusion in its domestic affairs. The United States announced that it was suspending its acceptance of World Court judgments on matters concerning Central America for a period of two years. Moreover, it asserted that Nicaragua had never filed its instruments of ratification and thus had no right to plead before the Court in the first place. The Nicaraguans declared that the United States was guilty of aggression and should be compelled to pay damages. "If the United States does not accept the Court's decision," the Nicaraguan representative announced, "it becomes an outlaw government."

On May 10, 1984, the World Court ruled unanimously that the United States should cease to blockade or mine the ports of Nicaragua. It also asserted by a vote of 14 to 1, with the American judge dissenting, that Nicaragua's political independence "should be fully respected and should not be jeopardized by any military action." In effect, the Court dismissed American procedural objections and found in favor of Nicaragua.

The United States, while rejecting the Court's jurisdiction, nonetheless ceased the mining activities in Nicaragua's harbors. The blockade, however, had been quite ineffectual anyway, and most of America's allies had voiced strong objections. France had even undertaken to remove some of the mines. Thus, the American decision had little to do with the World Court ruling. In the light of the United States' appearance before the Court as plaintiff four years earlier in the Iranian case, its disrespect when it was a defendant was, to say the least, inconsistent. The American judge on the Court apparently realized this inconsistency when he voted with the majority to order the United States to halt the mining. Had the United States not chosen to do so voluntarily and for reasons unrelated to the ruling, the Court could have done nothing to enforce its decision.

Next to enforcement, the Court's most serious problem has been how to encourage nations to avail themselves of its services. In Article 36 of the statute (the so-called optional clause) the Court has given states the opportunity to recognize "as compulsory, *ipso facto* and without special agreement, in relation to any other state accepting the same obligation, the jurisdiction of the Court in all legal disputes." Thirty-eight states have signed this optional clause, and it therefore seems that any legal disputes concerning any one of them would automatically fall under the Court's jurisdiction. This, however, has not been the case, because most states have found it necessary to qualify their adherence to the optional clause through numerous reservations. These reservations have done much to choke off the Court's jurisdiction, since in most cases states have tended to define almost everything as remaining "within their own domestic jurisdiction." To make matters worse, some states have reserved the right to decide unilaterally which matters were to be within their domestic jurisdiction. This was the legal basis on which Iran denied jurisdiction to the Court during the hostage crisis and the United States did the same in its dispute with Nicaragua. Many observers interested in strengthening the Court have pointed out that a beginning could be made if nations withdrew their reservations of unilateral competence to determine which matters were to fall within their domestic jurisdiction. As early as 1959, the Commission to Study the Organization of Peace made a sensible recommendation that still awaits adoption by the United States:

> There is a widespread recognition, reflected in President Eisenhower's 1959 State of the Union message, that the United States has set a bad example for other states in qualifying its ratification of the optional clause so severely as to make that ratification virtually meaningless. No amount of exhortation by American leaders in favor of promoting the rule of law in international affairs would be so effective as the simple act of transforming United States ratification of the optional clause into a genuine acceptance of the Court's compulsory jurisdiction in legal disputes. Such an act might stimulate widespread alteration of attitudes toward the International Court of Justice and pave the way for the full realization of the Court's potential as an instrument for the settlement of disputes and the clarification and development of international law. The Court has a limited but vitally important role to play in the evolution of world order, and it is essential that its opportunities for service through both decisions and advisory opinions be expanded.[9]

The plight of the International Court of Justice is a fairly accurate reflection of the plight of international law in general. The great issues of international relations—the East-West and the colonial-anticolonial struggles—have remained largely outside its purview. The reason for this is that matters of national prestige and power status have been so much involved that nations have been unwilling to submit such disputes to judicial settlement. Even if states were more inclined to submit disputes to the Court, the problem of enforcement in an anarchic world would still remain. Hitler could not be stopped by a court decision. On the other hand, the World Court has made a vital contribution to order-building in technical and fairly noncontroversial matters, and—in intraregional disputes—even in some important political questions. Perhaps most important, it has become the constitutional arbiter of the United Nations Charter.

REFERENCES

1. *De jure belli ac pacis libri tres,* in *Classics of International Law,* Francis Kelsey, trans., *Prolegomena,* p. 20.
2. U.S. Supreme Court, 1900, *Paquete Habana and the Lola,* 175 U.S. 677.
3. Oliver J. Lissitzyn, *The International Court of Justice.* Carnegie Endowment for International Peace. New York: St. Martin's Press, 1951, p. 80.
4. *Ibid.,* p. 94.
5. *Ibid.,* p. 59.
6. Advisory Opinion Concerning Reparation for Injuries Suffered in the Service of the United Nations, *International Organization,* August 1949, p. 575.
7. International Court of Justice, *Certain Expenses of the United Nations (Article 17, paragraph 2 of the Charter), Advisory Opinion of 20 July 1962:* I.C.J. Reports, 1962.
8. John G. Stoessinger, et al., *Financing the United Nations System.* Washington, D.C.: Brookings Institution, 1964.
9. Report of the Commission to Study the Organization of Peace, *Organizing Peace in the Nuclear Age.* New York: New York University Press, 1959, p. 14.

BIBLIOGRAPHY

Alexander, Lewis M., ed. *The Law of the Sea.* Columbus: Ohio State University Press, 1967.

Andrassy, Juraj. *International Law and the Resources of the Sea.* New York: Columbia University Press, 1970.

Baldwin, Malcolm F., and Page, James K., eds. *Law and the Environment.* New York: Walker, 1970.

Bassiovni, Cherif M., ed. *International Terrorism and Political Crimes.* Springfield, Ill.: Charles C. Thomas, 1975.

Bowie, Robert R. *Suez 1956: International Crises and the Role of the Law.* New York: Oxford University Press, 1975.

Bozeman, Adda B. *The Future of Law in a Multicultural World.* Princeton, N.J.: Princeton University Press, 1971.

Brown-John, C. Lloyd. *Multilateral Sanctions in International Law: A Comparative Analysis.* New York: Praeger, 1975.

Buderi, Charles L. O., and Caron, David D. *Law of the Sea: U.S. Policy Dilemma.* San Francisco: Institute for Contemporary Studies, 1983.

Cattan, Henry. *Palestine and International Law: The Legal Aspects of the Arab-Israeli Conflict.* New York: Longman, 1973.

Chayes, Abraham. *The Cuban Missile Crisis: International Crises and the Rule of Law.* New York: Oxford University Press, 1974.

Cohen, Jerome Alan, ed. *China's Practice of International Law: Some Case Studies.* Cambridge, Mass.: Harvard University Press, 1972.

D'Amato, Anthony. *The Concept of Custom in International Law.* Ithaca, N.Y.: Cornell University Press, 1971.

Davidson, Eugene. *The Nuremberg Fallacy: Wars and War Crimes Since World War II.* New York: Macmillan, 1973.

Deutsch, Karl W., and Hoffmann, Stanley, eds. *The Relevance of International Law.* Cambridge, Mass.: Schenkman, 1968.

DeVisscher, Charles. *Theory and Reality in Public International Law.* Princeton, N.J.: Princeton University Press, 1968.

Ellias, T. O. *Africa and the Development of International Law.* Leiden: Sijthoff, 1972.

Evans, Alona E., and Murphy, John F. *Legal Aspects of International Terrorism.* Lexington, Mass.: Lexington Books, 1978.

Falk, Richard A. *Legal Order in a Violent World.* Princeton, N.J.: Princeton University Press, 1968.

――――. "The Southwest Africa Cases: An Appraisal," *International Organization,* Vol. XXVI, No. 1, Winter 1967.

Fawcett, James. *Law and Power in International Relations.* Boston: Faber and Faber, 1982.

Fisher, Roger. *Improving Compliance with International Law.* Charlottesville: University Press of Virginia, 1983.

Galloway, L. Thomas. *Recognizing Foreign Governments: The Practice of the United States.* Washington, D.C.: American Enterprise Institute, 1978.

Gong, Gerrit W. *The Standard of 'Civilization' in International Society.* New York: Oxford/Clarendon Press, 1984.

Goodwin-Gill, Guy S. *International Law and the Movement of Persons Between States.* New York: Oxford University Press, 1978.

Gross, Leo, ed. *The Future of the International Court of Justice.* Dobbs Ferry, N.Y.: Oceana, 1976.

Henkin, Louis. *How Nations Behave: Law and Foreign Policy.* New York: Praeger, 1968.

Hollick, Ann L. *U.S. Foreign Policy and the Law of the Sea.* Princeton, N.J.: Princeton University Press, 1981.

Jessup, Phillip C. *A Modern Law of Nations.* New York: Macmillan, 1948.

――――. *The Price of International Justice.* New York: Columbia University Press, 1971.

Kelsen, Hans. *The Law of the United Nations.* New York: Praeger, 1950.

Kissinger, Henry A. *White House Years.* Boston: Little, Brown, 1979.

Kuper, Leo. *Genocide: Its Political Use in the Twentieth Century.* New Haven, Conn.: Yale University Press, 1982.

Lauterpacht, H. *International Law and Human Rights.* New York: Praeger, 1950.

Luard, Evan, ed. *The Control of the Sea-Bed. A New International Issue.* New York: Taplinger, 1974.

――――. *The International Regulation of Wars.* New York: New York University Press, 1972.

Matte, Nicolas M. *Aerospace Law.* Toronto: Carswell, 1969.

McDougal, Myres S.; Lasswell, Harold D.; and Chen, Lung-chu. *Human Rights and World Public Order.* New Haven: Conn.: Yale University Press, 1980.

Okolie, Charles Chukwuma. *International Law Perspectives of the Developing Countries.* New York: Nok, 1978.

Pomerance, Michla. *The Advisory Function of the International Court in the League and U.N. Eras.* Baltimore: Johns Hopkins Press, 1973.

Rosenne, S. *The World Court.* New York: Oceana, 1962.

Schwarzenberger, Georg. *International Law and Order.* New York: Praeger, 1971.

Seidman, Robert B. *The State, Law and Development.* New York: St. Martin's Press, 1978.

Stone, Julius. *Israel and Palestine: Assault on the Law of Nations.* Baltimore: Johns Hopkins Press, 1981.

Teclaff, Ludwick A., and Utton, Albert E., eds. *International Environmental Law.* New York: Praeger, 1974.

Thompson, Kenneth W. *The Moral Imperatives of Human Rights: A World Survey.* Washington, D.C.: University Press of America, 1980.

Trooboff, Peter D., ed. *Law and Responsibility in Warfare: The Vietnam Experience.* Chapel Hill: University of North Carolina Press, 1975.

Turkin, G. I. *Theory of International Law.* Cambridge, Mass.: Harvard University Press, 1974.

Vincent, R. J. *Nonintervention and International Order*. Princeton: Princeton University Press, 1974.

Vyshinsky, Andrei. *Law of the Soviet State*. New York: Macmillan, 1948.

Wright, Quincy. *Contemporary International Law: A Balance Sheet*. New York: Doubleday, 1955.

Chapter 10

The United Nations System and Political Order

Out of this nettle, danger, we pluck this flower, safety.

SHAKESPEARE *Henry IV*, I, 3

THE IDEA OF THE UNITED NATIONS

The United Nations is the most ambitious order-building experiment in history. In one very fundamental sense, its conception is rooted in the past. Its edifice was erected in times of war, during a period of concerted effort to defeat the Axis powers. The Organization was to be called into existence "to kill another Hitler in the shell ere he become too great." The nations were to be "united" against a criminal outlaw. In that sense, the United Nations was to prevent another World War II, just as the League of Nations before it had been created to prevent another World War I. Few of the United Nations' founders at San Francisco were aware of the titanic proportions of the coming East-West struggle. The rock on which the United Nations was to stand was to be the unity of the Great Powers, which would assume among them the major responsibility for peace and order. The United Nations was ill-equipped to deal with a world in which this unity would no longer exist and ill-prepared to answer the vital question: "Who will control the controllers if they should fight among each other?" In that sense, the thinking of the founders was oriented backward in time rather than forward. The future was mobilized once more to slay the dragons of the past.

But in another, equally fundamental sense, the conception of the United Nations was broad and forward-looking. The new world organization was to be created "to save succeeding generations from the scourge of war." But how to accomplish this end when so little was known about the causes of war and the roads to peace? The answer, which found its expression in the structure of the United Nations, was at once simple and sophisticated. It was simple in its failure to anticipate some of the major causes of subsequent international conflict.

But it was sophisticated in the various new trails it blazed in the pursuit of peace.

To enable it to work toward its goal, the United Nations was equipped with six major organs. The ambitious task of achieving collective security was assigned to the Security Council. Based on the assumption that peace was indivisible and that the Big Five—the United States, the Soviet Union, Britain, France, and China—could reach unanimity, the Security Council was to be the great international guardian of peace. If challenged by an aggressor, it would confront him with an incontrovertible law based on the irresistible force of the world community.

If the Security Council was thus to find the road to peace through military security, a second major United Nations organ, the General Assembly, was to utilize the time-honored technique of talking things out. It was to function as the world's forum, a Parliament of Man in embryo, a meeting-place in which all member nations were to confer on the basis of sovereign equality. The General Assembly's underlying assumption was that the rational, and sometimes irrational, airing of disputes among nations could contribute importantly to the pacific settlement of those disputes as well as to peaceful changes in the system of international relations itself.

A third principal organ, the Economic and Social Council, was created in the belief that a great deal of international strife was rooted in poverty and misery and that, therefore, the United Nations should do its utmost to help raise standards of living and improve economic conditions throughout the world. Since the founders of the United Nations saw colonialism as another frequent source of war, they felt it necessary also to employ the new world organization to mitigate the anger of dependent peoples against their colonial masters. Hence, to devise a technique whereby independence could be gained with as little bloodshed as possible, they provided a fourth major organ, the Trusteeship Council. The theory behind this latter institution was that if the colonies could be viewed as responsibilities to be shouldered, rather than real estate to be owned and exploited, the colonial nations might prove more amenable to the liquidation of their empires, with the result that violent eruptions of the struggle over colonialism might be avoided. Yet another cause of war was believed by the founders of the United Nations to lie in the absence of common legal standards among nations. For this reason, they included within the United Nations framework the World Court, which we have analyzed earlier (see Chapter 9). The purpose of the World Court was to pass on justiciable disputes and, by building on precedent, to lead in the creation of a uniform international legal system. Finally, the founders of the United Nations were convinced that the maintenance of peace required a nucleus of men and women whose loyalty was first and foremost not to any particular nation but to the entire international community. To head such an international civil service, they established a sixth major organ of the United Nations, the Office of the Secretary-General.

The United Nations was thus designed to attack the problem of war on six principal fronts, each the responsibility of one of its major organs. In addition, the struggle for international peace and stability was also to be waged in a number of more peripheral ways. These became the province of the so-called specialized agencies. Like the United Nations' main organs, these specialized agencies were designed to serve their own particular tasks, and all of them shared the same theoretical assumption. They were based on the premise that sovereignty—the behavior of nations as though they were a law unto themselves—vastly increased the danger of war. Whereas the major organs, however, were to attempt to persuade the nations to give up portions of their sovereignty, the specialized agencies were intended to proceed more indirectly. Their purpose was to engage the nations in enterprises of common interest and thus to bring them actively together in spite of their sovereignty. The reasoning behind this method was that if the United Nations could induce nations to cooperate in economic, social, and cultural activities, giving up some of their sovereignty in these relatively noncontroversial areas, habits of collaboration and a fabric of cohesion would develop that gradually might be transferred to matters of more vital political significance. It was hoped that the nations would then yield some of their sovereignty because it had become superfluous. This indirect approach to peace of the specialized agencies, working toward international cooperation and compromise in regard to specific matters of common interest, was the technique of functionalism.[1]

The specialized agencies that were absorbed into the United Nations system can be divided roughly into two groups. The first group, whose major purpose was to broaden and facilitate communication among nations, included the Universal Postal Union (UPU), the International Telecommunication Union (ITU), the International Civil Aviation Organization (ICAO), the World Meteorological Organization (WMO), and the Inter-Governmental Maritime Consultative Organization (IMCO). Some of these, like UPU and ITU, antedated the creation of the United Nations by several decades. Others, like IMCO, did not come into existence until years after the ratification of the Charter. But all were made part of the United Nations system and all were based on the premise that good "housekeeping" and good communications among nations might decrease the dangers of war.

It is less easy to generalize about the specialized agencies in the second group. For lack of a better term they may be called the "welfare" agencies, in the sense that each was intended to improve world economic, social, and cultural conditions and thus build defenses for the peace. The oldest of these, the International Labor Organization (ILO), was to better conditions of labor throughout the world on the assumption that the equalization of labor standards was a necessary condition of peace. The Food and Agriculture Organization (FAO) hoped to raise nutritional levels and improve agricultural technology. The International Refugee Organization (IRO), conceived as a temporary agency, was to find resettlement opportunities for the uprooted and homeless of the world. It was based on the assumption that nations could make a common effort to salvage refugees from intolerance and thus learn to yield part of their sovereignty in this common enterprise. The World Health Organization (WHO) was based on the premise that ill health and epidemics might be precursors of war. Hence, the objective of this agency was to be the attainment by all peoples of the highest possible level of health. The United Nations Educational, Scientific and Cultural Organization (UNESCO) was established by the framers of the United Nations because they believed that nations' ignorance of one another's ways and lives was a common cause of distrust leading to war. Hence UNESCO was to advance understanding among nations through research and the exchange of scholars and scientists. The International Bank for Reconstruction and Development (IBRD), or World Bank, was to bind up the wounds of war through loans for the reconstruction of devastated areas and to better the chances of peace by granting loans for the development of resources in lesser-developed countries. The International Development Association (IDA), an affiliate of the World Bank, was formed to provide long-term loans at low interest rates to underdeveloped countries that could not obtain World Bank loans. The International Finance Corporation (IFC), another affiliate of the bank, was to promote the growth of productive private enterprise in the developing countries. The International Monetary Fund (IMF) was to aid peace through the promotion of exchange stability and the use of a fund to support weak currencies. Finally, and more recently, the International Atomic Energy Agency (IAEA) was to consecrate the energy of the atom to the cause of peace, and the United Nations Industrial Development Organization (UNIDO) was to encourage the industrial growth of developing countries.

The idea of the United Nations was thus a multidimensional one. But though it was much more ambitious in its conception than the comparable post–World War I project of the League of Nations, it did not attempt the impossible. The UN founders were quite aware that the members of the world organization about to be born were not ready for anything like a world government. They knew that as yet, at least, the only world government that could hold together the heterogeneous population of the earth would have to be one based on force. And this would hardly be an improvement over what already was.

In not attempting the impossible, the founders of the UN were realists. But in seeking to go to the very limits of the possible, they were also visionaries. And necessarily so, for the idea of the United Nations had to take into account the full import of the cruel paradox that, in the nuclear age, the national sovereignty of nations would have to be controlled by an international order, but that this international order would have to be created and even controlled by sovereign nations. The plan therefore had to combine the dictates of national power with those of international order. We shall now see how the United Nations as a working reality has measured up to the original conception.

THE UNITED NATIONS: A BALANCE SHEET

The Security Council and Collective Security

The complexity of the United Nations system makes analysis a formidable task. It makes little sense to evaluate the world organization as a whole. Each organ has its distinctive goals and tools and has established its own unique record. In order to do justice to the United Nations family, each of its members must be considered separately. We shall begin with the organ that the framers of the Charter conceived as the hub of the organization—the Security Council.

The Security Council was given extensive powers to keep the peace. It was to consist of eleven members, of which five—the United States, the Soviet Union, Great Britain, France, and China—were to be permanent. Six nonpermanent members were to be elected by the General Assembly for two-year terms. The Charter empowered the Security Council to recommend means of peaceful settlement of disputes; if a nation committed an act of aggression, the Council would have the power to apply sanctions against the aggressor. These might range from the severance of diplomatic relations to the taking of collective military measures. With a view to the latter, there was also contemplated a Military Staff which would be permanently available to the Security Council.

It thus seemed that the principle of collective security, embodied in the Security Council, had at last acquired teeth. Since the Big Five were to dominate the Council, no aggressor would be able to challenge such an overwhelming agglomeration of power. Yet the Big Five, fully conscious of their preponderant power and their primary responsibility in keeping the peace, demanded proportionate privileges. They not only insisted on their permanent status on the Council, but also demanded that if a Council decision concerned a matter of substance and not a mere question of procedure, the majority would have to include all five of the permanent members. This was the origin of the much discussed "veto power," by which each of the five Great Powers could prevent the Security Council from taking action. This veto power deserves careful analysis.

The exact original wording of Article 27 of the Charter, which gives the right of veto, is as follows:

1. Each member of the Security Council shall have one vote.
2. Decisions of the Security Council on procedural matters shall be made by an affirmative vote of seven members.
3. Decisions of the Security Council on all other matters shall be made by an affirmative vote of seven members including the concurring votes of the permanent members; provided that in decisions under Chapter VI, and under paragraph 3 of Article 52, a party to a dispute shall abstain from voting.

The principal questions to which the veto power was to apply were the admission of new members to the United Nations, enforcement actions to meet a threat to the peace, proposals for the peaceful settlement of disputes, amendments to the Charter, and the election of a Secretary-General.

Three of the Great Powers at San Francisco—the United States, the Soviet Union, and Great Britain—insisted on the right of veto. None of them would have acceded to the United Nations without that right. China and France at first took a more flexible position, but the rigid stand of the Big Three soon resulted in their equally firm insistence on the veto rule. As a further safeguard of their sovereignty, moreover, the Great Powers insisted that the decision as to whether a vote was to be substantive or procedural was itself a substantive question and hence subject to the veto. This meant that in theory at least, anything was vetoable that a Great Power might choose to veto. Needless to say, this possibility of the use of the veto being expanded to apply to any matter at all did not augur well for the effective functioning of the Security Council. It thus seemed that from the very beginning the Great Powers' uncompromising insistence on their sovereignty, combined with the intensification of the East-West struggle, might well turn the Security Council into a moribund agency.

It has almost become a cliché to assert that the Security Council has been paralyzed through the Soviet Union's abuse of the veto power. While there is some validity to this charge, the truth is far more complex. It is true that the Soviet Union has been responsible for more than 80 percent of the total number of vetoes cast. By the mid-1980s it had cast well over one hundred vetoes. But the figures themselves do not sufficiently explain the picture. In the first place, the Soviet Union has not had a monopoly of negative votes. The negative votes of the other Great Powers were usually not classed as vetoes because others of the Big Five—as well as some nonpermanent members—voted the same way. As Norman J. Padelford has pointed out:

> It is clear from the record that when the Soviet Union finds its vital interests at stake there are now no other great powers generally inclined to stand with it. Therefore the negative vote of the Soviet delegate usually becomes a sole veto, accompanied ordinarily only by the vote of whatever satellite holds a non-permanent seat on the Council. When other great powers, particularly the United States and Great Britain, find their national interests at issue they can usually persuade other permanent members to go along with them either in casting a multiple negative vote sufficient to stop a proposal without the stigma of exercising a sole veto (or near-sole veto), or to join in introducing and passing a resolution more suitable to their desires.[2]

Second, the Western powers on the Security Council have been able to make the Soviet Union appear even more obstructionist by forcing votes on issues that they knew would elicit a Soviet veto. Thus over half of the Soviet vetoes were cast against the admission of Western and Western-oriented nations to the United Nations. Italy's application, for example, was vetoed six times before that nation was finally admitted as part of a "package deal" in December 1955, as a result of which sixteen new members were permitted to join the United Nations. Finally, the Soviet Union has declared that it has been forced to use the veto extensively because of the composition of the Security Council. In the words of Premier Khrushchev in 1958:

> It is common knowledge that the majority in the Security Council is composed of the votes of countries dependent, in one way or another, primarily economically, on the U.S.A. Thus, the Security Council in its present composition cannot be regarded as an impartial arbiter, and that is why it has of late ceased to play the important role in the maintenance of international peace and security which devolved upon it by virtue of the United Nations Charter.[3]

It is true that when Khrushchev made the above statement, there was no member of the Security Council upon whose support the Soviet Union could count. The Soviet Union was the only Communist state with a vote in the Security Council. Eight votes were controlled by military allies of the United States in NATO and SEATO. Two members—Iraq and Sweden—were neutralists in the East-West struggle. In the following year, Sweden was replaced by Italy, a member of NATO, and Iraq by Tunisia. Thus, in 1959, the composition of the Security Council began to resemble that of a Western military alliance. A good illustration of a typical case is provided by the U-2 plane episode in 1960. In May of that year, the Soviet Union brought the case before the Security Council and introduced a resolution branding the flights by American planes over Soviet territory as "acts of aggression." Two states—the USSR and Poland—voted in favor of the Soviet motion; seven states—Argentina, China, Ecuador, France, Italy, the United Kingdom, and the United States—voted against. The latter were all members of the Western alliance system. Two nonaligned states—Ceylon and Tunisia—abstained.

This pattern began to change somewhat in 1966, when four nonpermanent members were added to the Security Council. The passage of a resolution now required nine affirmative votes instead of seven. Since the enlargement of the Council was undertaken primarily for the benefit of the new nations, most of which were nonaligned on East-West issues, it now became more difficult for the United States to control the Council. In 1966, for example, when the United States attempted to have the Vietnam question inscribed on the Council's agenda, it found itself dependent upon the vote of Jordan. The move succeeded, but just barely. The days of an automatic American majority or of a "hidden veto" achieved by mobilizing this majority against a Soviet-sponsored resolution were over. United States influence was still very great, but now had to depend on bargaining and persuasion rather than reliance on an absolute majority.

On the whole, the Security Council has tended to narrow rather than expand the scope of the veto power. It established that the abstention of a Great Power was not tantamount to veto, and, in the Korean police action decision of 1950, went even further by declaring that the absence of a Great Power should merely be regarded as abstention but not as a veto *in absentia.* Perhaps most important, the potential threat inherent in the "double-veto" has not materialized. It has been used relatively sparingly.

The tendency to blame the veto power—especially its excessive use by the Soviet Union—for the decline of the Security Council is to confuse the symptoms with the causes. The membership of the Security Council reflects the two great political struggles of our time. The Great Power veto has simply been a constant reminder that, in an international system of sovereign nation-states, no important action may be taken against a major power without its consent. In fact, it may be argued that abolition of the veto might increase the danger of war, since the majority might then be tempted into precipitous action against the recalcitrant superpower. The unanimity principle has also taught the lesson that, in the nuclear age, the technique of arriving at decisions by counting votes has not been the most fortunate one for the solution of international problems. The principle of voting by majority does make sense in a homogeneous political context, but in a world of profound schisms, negotiating with the opponent rather than out-voting him may be a wiser method of intercourse. All this is not to say that the veto has been a blessing. But certainly, it has not been the unmitigated evil that some observers have made it seem to be. Indeed, many Soviet vetoes have been circumvented through action in the General Assembly or through other means.

The significance of the Security Council in the overall context of the United Nations family has gone through an interesting cycle. Briefly, what has occurred has been a threefold progression. First, beginning in the early 1950s, the Security Council began to go into eclipse as the Uniting for Peace procedure brought an increasing number of matters concerning international peace and security before the General Assembly. Second, the Assembly in turn, beginning in the middle 1950s, began to pass increasingly vaguely worded resolutions and thus invested the Secretary-General with greater policy-making authority. And finally, in the early 1960s, the Security Council experienced a significant revitalization. The veto power provides a very important clue to this threefold constitutional development. A closer look at the three periods is revealing.

The decline of the Security Council and the concomitant rise of the General Assembly during the first ten years of the UN's existence are well-known facts, which may be documented by several data. First, the frequency of Security Council sessions declined sharply during the first decade, and the scope of the political issues it considered narrowed considerably. In 1948, for example, the council held 168 meetings, whereas in 1955 only twenty-three were held. Eighty-one of the vetoes cast by the Soviet Union were tallied up from 1946 to 1955. The Uniting for Peace Resolution passed in 1950 was a direct response of the Assembly—under strong American pressure and over vehement Soviet opposition—to the creeping paralysis of the Council.

Its own mandate thus broadened, the Assembly, beginning in 1955, in turn widened that of the Secretary-General. The missions of Dag Hammarskjöld to Peking in 1955, to Suez in 1956, to Lebanon in 1958, and again to the Congo in 1961 were all based on Assembly resolutions that gave the Secretary-General increasing policy-making powers. Indeed, the abortive Soviet attempt to replace the Office of the Secretary-General with a veto-bound triumvirate was in essence an effort to extend the principle of the veto into the UN Secretariat.

Beginning in 1960, one could observe a definite resuscitation of the Council. The growing membership of the Assembly made the Soviet Union somewhat more hesitant in its use of the veto. The USSR knew that if it wielded the veto on a vital matter, the Assembly would immediately step into the breach. Hence, it began to prefer to keep control over even undesirable operations rather than to relinquish the reins to an unpredictable Assembly, and now tended to abstain where it might have vetoed before. The paradoxical conclusion of this development is that the Council was revived by—of all things—the Assembly.

A cross-section of actual disputes brought before the Security Council shows a mixed record. In 1946 the Security Council urged Iran and the Soviet Union to settle a dispute through direct negotiations. The prodding was successful. In 1947 the Security Council successfully acted as midwife in the birth of Indonesia. The Security Council's role in a protracted dispute between Greece and the Soviet Union from 1946 to 1950 was inconclusive. In the struggle between India and Pakistan over Kashmir, the Security Council used the technique of mediation but was unable to reach a permanent settlement. In the Palestine dispute, Security Council mediation helped produce a cease-fire and an armistice but no final settlement. On the question of Berlin, the Security Council proved impotent. The Korean case was the Council's only authorization of collective military sanctions. The results were inconclusive. (For a full discussion of the United Nations action in Korea, see Chapter 12.) In 1960 the Security Council was confronted with the complex problems encountered by the newly independent Congo. In the early 1960s, while still concerned with the Congo, the Council again turned its attention to the problems raised by the apartheid policy of the government of the Union of South Africa. While it brought a solution for the Congo's ills within reach by 1964 (see Chapter 12 for an analysis of UN peace-keeping operations in the Congo and the Middle East), it was unable fundamentally to affect the attitudes of the South African government. In 1967 the Council managed to produce a cease-fire in the wake of the six-day Arab-Israeli war, and in 1968 a Western-led initiative to condemn the Soviet Union for its invasion of Czechoslovakia was blocked by a Soviet veto.

The 1970s witnessed significant changes in the power balance of the Security Council. As the United States lost its automatic majority, it too resorted to the use of the veto power. American virginity was lost in March 1970 when the United States cast its first veto to prevent the use of force against the regime of Southern Rhodesia. Subsequently, the United States used its veto to defeat hostile majorities on issues primarily concerning Middle Eastern and African affairs. By the mid-1980s, thirty American vetoes had been cast. Most of these were cast against Middle Eastern resolutions that the United States considered unbalanced and against the use of force to bring down the two white minority regimes in Southern Africa. In 1977, for example, the United States approved an arms embargo against South Africa but joined Britain and France in vetoing a resolution that would have imposed full economic sanctions against the Pretoria government. Another typical American veto was one cast in 1983 against a resolution that would have condemned Israel for settling the West Bank. Yet another was cast in 1985, once again to prevent mandatory economic sanctions against the government of South Africa, which had just proclaimed a state of national emergency.

The composition of the Council changed dramatically with the seating of the People's Republic of China in 1971. The old bipolar tug of war between the Soviet Union and the United States gave way to a new and different constellation. This became clear during the Indo-Pakistan war of 1971 when the Soviet Union backed India and China supported Pakistan. The Security Council was paralyzed not by the familiar United States–Soviet deadlock, but by a Chinese-Soviet confrontation during which the latter cast three consecutive vetoes. In 1972 China cast its first veto in order to block the admission of Bangladesh to the United Nations. It now seemed as if effective Council action would be possible only through consensus of the Big Three, no longer just the Big Two. Despite this new and complicating element, the Security Council did not break down. Every six months it managed to extend the mandate of the peace force in Cyprus (UNFICYP), which it had established in 1964. The mandate continued even during the hostilities that erupted on the island in 1974. In 1973 and 1974, in the wake of the October War in the Middle East, the Security Council even managed to create two new peace forces: a United Nations Emergency Force (UNEF II), which was to supervise the disengagement agreement between Israel and Egypt, and a United Nations Disengagement Observer Force (UNDOF), which had similar responsibilities in the wake of the Syria-Israeli agreement. (See Chapter 12.) The Chinese, who could have vetoed all these efforts, chose not to participate in the voting. Thus, the worst expectations of the pessimists did not materialize.

When one considers the structure and political limitations under which the Security Council must function, what is impressive is not that it has accomplished so little, but that it has achieved so much. True, it has not been able to compel a Great Power to do anything against its will or to take action against a small power that has the backing of a great one. In 1980, for example, the Security Council called upon Iran to release the American hostages, but the Soviet Union vetoed a resolution that would have punished Iran with economic sanctions. Iran thus got away with its kidnapping of embassy personnel. And in 1983 the Soviet Union vetoed a resolution that would have censured it for shooting down a Korean airliner, resulting in the death of 269 innocent people. Yet, the Council has at times interposed the authority of the United Nations between the superpowers and has thus managed to nip possible military clashes between them in the bud. The peace-keeping operations dispatched by the Council to the Congo, to Cyprus, and to the Middle East were cases in point. Finally, the recent tendency to adopt decisions by consensus rather than by majority voting may be seen as an encouraging trend.

The General Assembly

The General Assembly was conceived as a world forum, a talking-shop in which the world's nations were to be given the broad mandate "to discuss any questions or any matters within the scope of the Charter." It was to be the largest although not the most important organ of the United Nations. Each nation, large or small, was to have one vote. The Assembly was to have no enforcement powers but merely the authority to recommend courses of action. Like a national legislature, it was organized into committees. A survey of its seven standing committees gives a bird's eye view of the Assembly's responsibilities: two Committees on Political and Security Questions; an Economic and Financial Committee; a Social, Humanitarian, and Cultural Committee; a Trusteeship Committee; an Administrative and Budgetary Committee; and a Legal Committee. Thus the Assembly was given the power to discuss almost

anything within the purview of the Charter: the maintenance of peace and security; the financial contributions of member states, the raising of economic,
social, education, and health standards; the disposition of former colonies; the
promotion of human rights; and the development of international law. Much
United Nations activity was to be initiated in the Assembly and also was to be
approved by it. The Assembly was to be the world's town meeting, but its
bailiwick was to be a highly heterogeneous society of nation-states. It was to
have no power of compulsion; enforcement was to be the exclusive domain of
the Security Council.

When, quite early in the life of the UN, it became apparent that the Security Council—paralyzed by the unanimity rule—was falling victim to the
East-West struggle, the Assembly was given certain "implied powers" through
a liberal interpretation of the Charter. In 1947 the Assembly voted to create
an Interim Committee, or Little Assembly, which was to meet whenever circumstances might require during intervals between sessions of the Assembly.
More important was the so-called Uniting for Peace Resolution adopted by the
Assembly in November 1950. This resolution grew out of the American conviction that the Security Council action to meet aggression in Korea had been
made possible only through a fortuitous circumstance—the absence of the Soviet delegation. Hence, the United States proposed that the Assembly exercise
a residual responsibility in any threat to the peace in case the Security Council
was hamstrung by the veto. The resolution contained five major provisions of
far-reaching import:

1. It authorized the General Assembly to meet on short notice in an emergency in
   which the Security Council was prevented from acting, and to recommend appropriate collective measures, including the use of armed force when necessary.
2. It established a fourteen-nation Peace Observation Commission to observe and
   report on dangerous situations in any part of the world.
3. It asked all members to maintain in their armed forces special elements which
   could be made available for United Nations service on call of the Security
   Council or the General Assembly.
4. It established a fourteen-nation Collective Measures Committee to study and
   report on these and other methods for maintaining and strengthening international peace and security.
5. It urged all United Nations members to renew their fidelity to the United Nations, honor its decisions, and promote respect for human rights and achievement of economic stability and social progress.

The resolution became the subject of heated controversy. The Soviet Union,
holding to a narrow interpretation of the Charter, declared that most of its
provisions were illegal. The United States, on the other hand, construing the
Charter more broadly, declared that the provisions were in accordance with
its spirit and that they clearly served the need of strengthening international
peace and security. The resolution was adopted by a vote of 52 to 5, with 2
abstentions. It greatly broadened the scope of the General Assembly which, as
a result of its new mandate, was able to deal with several matters of security:
the Chinese military intervention in Korea, the Suez crisis of 1956, Soviet in-

tervention in Hungary, the Lebanese crisis of 1958, and the Congo crisis of 1960. Thus, the Assembly became a backstop of the Security Council. The Charter, like a constitution, had shown itself to be amenable to interpretation in order to keep pace with changing events.

Since its inception, the United Nations has rapidly been approaching the ideal of universal membership. It started out with fifty-one original members, and for years the East-West struggle resulted in a policy of competitive exclusion of new applicants. "Package deals" in the mid-1950s resulted in the admission of over a score of new members, and by the 1980s—following the birth of many newly sovereign states in the Third World—membership in the Assembly was approaching the 160 mark.

The most significant consequence of the Assembly's growing comprehensiveness has been the emergence of blocs and the development of bloc voting. The Assembly has thus tended to become one of the arenas in which the two major political struggles of our time are being waged. In fact, the Assembly has begun to take on the complexion of a multiparty system. The uneven degree of discipline within each bloc or party has made the picture somewhat analogous to the French Parliament under the Fourth Republic. Roughly speaking, six blocs have emerged in the Assembly: the Afro-Asian bloc (the largest but least cohesive) has at times commanded over seventy votes; the Latin American bloc has been able to muster twenty votes, the Atlantic Community eighteen, the British Commonwealth twenty, and the Arab bloc ten. The most highly disciplined group has been the Communist bloc which, not including Yugoslavia, has controlled nine votes.

The vast majority of votes taken in the General Assembly have involved one or both of the two great political struggles. According to the voting rules of the General Assembly, important questions are to be decided by a two-thirds vote, and "other matters" by simple majority. In view of this fact it is clear that, under certain conditions, some blocs—singly or in combination with others—may exercise what amounts to a collective veto over decisions of the General Assembly. Theoretically, for instance, the Afro-Asian bloc, if united, could effectively block any important decision. In practice, however, this has not tended to occur. The Afro-Asian bloc has often been deeply divided. Also, party discipline has been loose and, in many instances, "crossing the floor" has become a frequent phenomenon. In this connection, it is useful to point out that in the General Assembly—unlike a national legislature—there are not two but three sides to a controversial question. Abstentions are freely recorded and frequently their high number has demonstrated that many nations have refused to stand up and be counted in the East-West or the colonial-anticolonial struggle.

The question of who controls the General Assembly may best be answered by looking at some important votes. Votes on East-West issues may be grouped into three rough categories. First, there are those in which the United States is clearly in control and only the Soviet bloc is in opposition. A resolution passed in 1962 to continue the efforts of the UN Commission for Unification and Rehabilitation of Korea (UNCURK) was a case in point. The vote was

63 in favor, 11 opposed, with 26 abstentions. On others, the United States manages to control a sizable majority, but has to lobby intensively to attain it. Thus, in 1960 it managed to persuade most Latin American, Western European, and French-speaking African states to vote for Kasavubu rather than Lumumba to represent the government of the Congo. The vote was 53 in favor, 24 opposed, and 19 abstentions. Finally, on some crucial issues, the United States was defeated. The case *par excellence* is the issue of Chinese representation, which has come before every General Assembly since 1951. Because of its special interest, the voting pattern on this question will be analyzed in depth.

During the decade from 1951 to 1960, the issue of Chinese representation came before every Assembly under the so-called moratorium device. Using this technique, the United States proposed each year that consideration of the question be deferred. This position was adopted by the Assembly at every session until 1960.

Three conclusions suggest themselves from this voting record. First, the absolute number of votes in favor of moratorium remained fairly constant during the ten years. But since the membership of the UN increased by 65 percent during this same period, the relative number of states supporting the American position significantly declined. Second, up until 1959, the total number of votes in favor was always an absolute majority and exceeded the combined votes of those opposed, abstaining, or absent. Finally, in 1960, for the first time, the American position was in serious jeopardy when the supporters of the moratorium won by only a plurality and were in turn exceeded by the combined votes of the opposition, abstainers, and absentees.

Thus in 1961 the United States had to fight the issue on its merits when the Assembly decided to consider it as an "important question." But, at the very same time, China's attack on India alienated nonaligned sentiment in the United Nations. Hence during the next three years the United States was actually able to improve its position. The votes in 1961, 1962, and 1963 were 48:37:19, 56:42:12, and 57:41:12, respectively. No vote was taken in 1964. In 1965, the United States just held the line in a tie vote of 47:47:20. By 1966, the excesses of the Cultural Revolution on the Chinese mainland had alienated some of the Afro-Asian nations and the United States position gained again to 57:46:17. In 1967, the vote was 58:45:17, and in 1968 it was 58:44:23.

As China began to normalize its foreign relations, UN sentiment in its favor began to rise once again. The vote in 1969 was 56:48:21, and in 1970 a majority of 51 members actually voted to seat the People's Republic and to oust the Chiang Kai-shek regime, with 49 opposed and 25 abstaining. Only a previously adopted resolution that a two-thirds majority would be necessary to seat the mainland government prevented its victory that year.

The moment of truth came in 1971. The China question was being debated at the very time presidential aide Henry Kissinger was in Peking to prepare for President Nixon's forthcoming visit to the Chinese capital. The American position at the UN reflected this shift in policy. George Bush, the United States representative, now favored the seating of the People's Republic on the Security Council but wanted to retain representation for the Chiang Kai-shek regime in the General Assembly. A majority of UN members felt otherwise. After considerable procedural wrangling, the General Assembly, in a dramatic vote taken on October 25, 1971, defeated the "important question" resolution by a majority of 59:55:17. This cleared the way to seat the representatives of the People's Republic by a simple, rather than a two-thirds, majority. Such a resolution, which had in fact been sponsored by Albania for over a decade, was now passed by a large Assembly majority of 76 votes in favor, 35 against, and 17 abstentions. As of October 25, 1971, China was to be represented in all principal UN organs exclusively by the mainland government. The American honeymoon with the United Nations had definitely come to an end.

On issues of colonialism there have also been changes in voting patterns. First, the Afro-Asian members, supported by the Soviet bloc and many Latin American countries, consistently urged strong resolutions against Portugal and South Africa. At first, the United States tended to vote against such resolutions. Thus, in 1962, the Assembly, by a vote of 57 in favor, 14 opposed, and 18 abstentions, declared that Portugal's policy in Angola constituted a threat to world peace and recommended an arms embargo against the colonial power. During the same year, by a vote of 67 in favor, 16 opposed, and 23 abstentions, it condemned South Africa's racial policies and called for sanctions against the Union government. The United States opposed both these resolutions on the grounds that the call for sanctions was ill-advised. In 1966, however, the United States supported a resolution passed by a vote of 114:2, terminating South Africa's mandate to govern Southwest Africa and declaring that the territory would henceforth be the direct responsibility of the world organization. The United States, though, was not prepared to support a resolution passed by the Assembly later establishing a special UN council for the administration of Southwest Africa. Here it expressed its ambivalence in the form of abstention. And when the General Assembly, in November 1974, by a vote of 91 in favor, 22 against, and 9 abstentions, decided to suspend the South African delegation from its deliberations without prior authorization by the Security Council, the United States joined those who voted against. Thus, by the 1970s, the forces of anticolonialism were clearly in command of the General Assembly. Only in 1977, after Henry Kissinger had placed the United States on record as favoring black majority rule in Southern Africa, did Andrew Young, President Jimmy Carter's new ambassador to the UN, begin to cast clear-cut votes against the white minority regimes though he, too, opposed the use of force against them.

A good case can be made, in fact, that by the mid-1970s the radical wing of the new Afro-Arab-Asian nationalism had captured increasing control of the General Assembly. Various "national liberation" groups demanded and received legitimacy. The most prominent case in point was the decision of the General Assembly in 1974 by overwhelming vote to invite Yasir Arafat, the leader of the Palestinian Liberation Organization, to address the world body. When Arafat appeared, he was accorded all the ceremonial honors usually reserved for heads of state. Only 4 states out of the 138 that then made up the Assembly's membership had opposed the invitation, the United States among them. When during the Palestine debate Assembly president Abdelaziz Bouteflika in effect curbed Israel's right to speak by limiting the debate to one speech from each country, this ruling was vainly opposed by the United States. And when the Assembly, in late November 1974, by a vote of 89 to 8, with 37 abstentions, affirmed the right of the Palestinian people to be free and sovereign and, in a companion vote of 95 to 17, with 19 abstentions, awarded permanent observer status to the Palestine Liberation Organization, the United States again was on the side of the opposition. The trend spilled over from the General Assembly into one of the UN's "nonpolitical" specialized agencies. The General Conference of UNESCO adopted several highly controversial resolutions unfavorable to Israel including one that rejected Israel's request to participate in UNESCO's European regional grouping. On December 6, 1974, the United States delegate, John A. Scali, warned the General Assembly that when the majority rule becomes "the tyranny of the majority, the minority will cease to respect or obey it."

These Third World victories in 1974 took place as a result of an informal "deal." The Arabs and Communists joined the Africans in suspending South Africa, and the Africans and the Communists joined the Arabs in recognizing the Palestine Liberation Organization. As a result, many Western observers felt that the world organization, which had been formed to help small nations keep the great powers from making war, had now made it difficult for the great powers to keep small nations from starting wars.

An analysis of the above voting patterns demonstrates that on issues involving the East-West struggle, the United States so far has generally been able to muster majorities on matters vital to its national interest. Owing to the rise of the Afro-Asian-Arab bloc this American power is no longer automatic but has demanded increasing diplomatic and persuasive efforts. In the China vote of 1971, the United States actually found itself in the minority. But even in 1974, when the Afro-Asia-Arab bloc controlled a commanding majority in the Assembly, the United States lobbied successfully to maintain American forces in Korea under the United Nations flag, and to keep the American-backed Lon Nol government of Cambodia in the United Nations, against a determined Chinese-sponsored effort to give the seat to the government-in-exile of Prince Norodom Sihanouk. The United States barely held the line, however, on the latter decision, with a vote of 56 in favor to 54 against, with 24 abstentions. Besides, the Lon Nol government collapsed a few months later, as the Communist insurgents took over Cambodia. In the colonial struggle, however, the United States has abdicated leadership in the General Assembly. The Afro-Asians are in control here, demanding rapid action. The closer they come to their goal of eliminating colonialism, the more insistent they become on erasing its last vestiges from Africa. Toward this end they are eager to push the UN's powers to their limit—and even beyond. In terms of the overall distribution of power in the General Assembly, the UN's progress toward universality has resulted in some reduction of the influence of both of the two superpowers and a corresponding net gain for the more radical forces of the new nationalism.

Turning to the accomplishments of the General Assembly, a cross section reveals a mixed record. It has provided opportunity for the exploration of a whole galaxy of political disputes. The forum of the Assembly has had the beneficent effect of subjecting explosive disputes to the scrutiny of world public opinion, although it has also lent itself to endless and often repetitive oratory which has frequently debased the process of deliberation. But on the whole, the Assembly has shown inventiveness and flexibility in its approach. It was able to restore the *status quo ante bellum* after the Suez crisis of 1956 and, in the process, to improvise a new instrument for policing the peace—the United Nations Emergency Force (UNEF). (For a full discussion of UNEF and other UN peace forces, see Chapter 12.)

At the same time, it found itself tragically unable to take effective action to stop the Soviet Union in Hungary in 1956 or in Czechoslovakia in 1968. Similarly, it was unable to inject itself into the conflict in Vietnam. In the Middle East, its pro-Arab posture did not encourage an atmosphere that was conducive to negotiations between the warring parties. Since 1978, for example, the PLO has urged the Assembly to call on the Security Council to cut off trade with Israel. Even though more than 100 members voted for such resolutions in 1978 and 1979 and 98 members approved another in 1980, there was no visible impact. And even though, in 1980, 143 members censured Israel for the annexation of the Arab sector of Jerusalem, this resolution only hardened Israel's determination to retain the entire city as its capital. Voting simply proved to be no substitute for meaningful negotiations.

The work of the Assembly has not been limited to the handling of disputes. Great inventiveness has been demonstrated in the area of international law-making. It was under the aegis of the General Assembly, for example, that the International Atomic Energy Agency was born. The Universal Declaration of Human Rights and the Convention on Genocide were similarly notable achievements of the General Assembly's initiative. Though the former did not become a legally binding instrument, the latter succeeded in attaining that status, albeit subject to ratification by member states. The General Assembly also approved three vitally important instruments of arms control: the Outer Space Treaty of 1967; the Nuclear Non-Proliferation Treaty of 1968; and the Sea-Bed Treaty of 1971. And in 1974 it authorized the establishment of a United Nations University with headquarters in Tokyo and regional centers throughout the world.

In addition, the General Assembly has exercised a number of important housekeeping responsibilities. In this capacity it has supervised the activities of the Economic and Social Council, the Trusteeship Council, and the specialized agencies. Furthermore, it has had key electoral duties. In conjunction with the Security Council, it elects the Secretary-General and the justices of the World Court, and passes on the admission of new members. It also elects the ten nonpermanent members of the Security Council. On this last matter, feelings have often run high and gentleman's agreements among the competing blocs have tended to develop. The Assembly has also had the responsibility of fixing the contribution of each member state to the United Nations' budget.

The rise of the Afro-Asian-Arab bloc has brought the one nation–one vote rule under heavy fire. It has become increasingly difficult for the Great Powers, especially the United States, to accept the fact that Chad's or Iraq's vote should have the same weight as that of a major power. The question has been raised whether it was reasonable to expect the United States or the Soviet Union to accept decisions reached by a body in which a nation with a small and largely illiterate population and an underdeveloped economy should have the same voice as a superpower, or whether the United States, which has contributed one fourth of the budget, should have the same voting power as a nation with an assessment of less than 0.1 percent. These considerations have led to many informal "weighted voting" proposals designed to bring voting power into line with the realities of political power and influence in the Assembly. These proposals have all foundered on the question of what would constitute an objective criterion for weighting. Should it be population, military strength, literacy, wealth, or other more intangible factors? Moreover, since the distribution of power among nations is in constant flux, whatever weighting was decided upon would require constant revision. For these reasons, the Assembly's system of equality has been retained despite its obvious inequities. This may, however, lead to a growing preference by the superpowers for conducting important business outside the framework of the United Nations, where they would not have to worry about the votes of uncommitted countries. In any case, it seems increasingly likely that all concerned—small powers as well as large—will have to face the fact that, in the nuclear age, voting is a poor substitute for genuine deliberation and compromise.

Another ambitious plan of the Assembly has been the projection of its influence into territories that are quite literally uncharted. Aware that the Antarctic continent and outer space could easily become objects of the power struggle, the Assembly has moved with dispatch to provide a forum for the advancement of a novel and most important principle: that neither *terra incognita* on this planet nor in outer space should be subject to ownership or control by individual states but, instead, should be considered the domain of the international community as represented by the United Nations. The Assembly has shown wisdom by having risen to this new challenge before, rather than after, actual crises have developed. And many member states have looked with considerable favor upon the principle of United Nations jurisdiction over the fruits of man's new discoveries.

If we look at the overall record of the General Assembly, it becomes clear that the major political controversies have shifted, during the past decade, from an East-West to a North-South axis. The New International Economic Order, which we discussed in Chapter 7, is a case in point. The division between the developed and the developing countries has been exacerbated by two special problems: first, racial discrimination in South Africa and Rhodesia and second, the conflict between Israel and its Arab neighbors. Since 1980, for example, more than half of the resolutions passed by the Assembly have dealt with either Israel or South Africa. Yet neither of these two nations has paid much attention to the General Assembly.

During the years of cold-war political confrontation between East and West, the United States had a relatively easy time in the General Assembly. Of the original fifty-one members of the United Nations in 1945, at least thirty-five were closely associated with the United States, only five with the Soviet Union, and only ten were nonaligned. In those early years, the United States delegation could easily muster majority votes and even two-thirds votes when required.

The United States did not hesitate in those years to use its "automatic majority" in its own national interest. Former Ambassador Scali would have done well to concede, in his comments on the "tyranny of the majority," that the United States was once able to keep Communist China out of the United Nations, to persuade the United Nations to intervene in Korea, and to shift peace-keeping from the Security Council, in case of veto, to the General Assembly under the Uniting for Peace Resolution of 1950.

Today, the shoe is on the other foot. Because of the liquidation of the colonial empires, the more than one hundred developing countries, usually backed by the Communist countries, can easily muster a two-thirds vote in the General Assembly. Perhaps the most dramatic and controversial event that shook the General Assembly during the 1970s was a vote taken on November 10, 1975, defining Zionism as "a form of racism and racial discrimination." The vote was 72 in favor, 35 against, with 32 abstentions and 3 delegations absent.

The majority, consisting of all the Communist states save Rumania and most Third World countries, charged Israel with white settler and military expansion policies reminiscent of the imperialist powers of a bygone era. Those states in opposition, led by the United States and the Western European powers, deplored the resolution as infamous and harmful to the United Nations cause.

It was indeed ironic that, thirty years after the death of Hitler, the victims of the worst excesses of racism in modern history should now be accused of a similar transgression. There was little doubt that the anti-Zionist resolution was a triumph for the forces of radicalism among the Third World, and that these forces, armed with centuries of anticolonial fury and modern petrodollars, had now come close to making the UN General Assembly into their vehicle. But a closer scrutiny of the vote does not suggest that the General Assembly had succumbed to a wave of anti-Semitism of the Hitler variety. The reasons for the anti-Zionist vote were much more complex.

In the first place, a number of Third World votes were simply bought with petrodollars. Second, several African states supported the resolution for reasons of Third World solidarity without much substantive knowledge about either Israel or Zionism. As the delegate of Mauritius put it, "Many people voted without knowing what Zionism is. I am confused." Third, many delegates supported the anti-Zionism drive because they were against what the Palestinians told them Israel was: a white imperialist military state reminiscent of the Western colonial regimes. Fourth, Israel was perceived by many of the nations of the Third World as the protégé of the United States, which in turn was perceived by them as the military leader of all the former colonial powers in NATO. Fifth, Israel, it was pointed out, was settled largely by whites, and its early leaders were Europeans from Russia. Finally, many states voted for the resolution because of fear of Arab oil retaliation or abstained for similar reasons, as in the case of Japan.

Thus, the anti-Zionism vote of 1975 signified the confluence of a number of factors. The most prominent were the petrodollar, opportunism, and ignorance, as well as pride and prejudice. One final observation about the resolution is worthy of mention: those nations that voted in favor were largely dictatorships, both of the left and of the right, while those in opposition were largely, though by no means exclusively, the Western democracies. In the General Assembly of the 1970s, the democracies numbered less than two dozen states and appeared almost like an endangered species.

Similar resolutions were passed in other UN bodies, and even some specialized agencies, such as UNESCO and ILO, became arenas of political contention. The American response was one of anger. In 1976, Secretary Kissinger announced that the United States would reduce economic assistance to countries that had voted against the United States in the United Nations. He also declared his intention to take the United States out of the International Labor Organization, which had passed a number of Third World–sponsored anti-Western resolutions. He was supported in this move by George Meany, head of the American Federation of Labor and Congress of Industrial Organizations (AFL-CIO), which represented American workers in the ILO. Meany also objected to the presence of Soviet officials in the governing body of the ILO. In 1977, the United States made good on its threat and withdrew from ILO membership, thus depriving that specialized agency of 25 percent of its budget. The move was symptomatic of the American dissatisfaction with having become a minority party in the United Nations. Money was used as a tangible weapon to express that growing discontent. The United States chose to return to the ILO under the Carter administration in 1980.

Under the Reagan administration, the United States became increasingly disillusioned with the General Assembly. Its preoccupation with East-West issues made the United States impatient with the Assembly's North-South perception of most of the world's conflicts. On one occasion in 1984, a member of the United States delegation declared in a moment of pique that, if the United Nations should choose to leave New York, the Americans would gladly wave goodbye as the delegates sailed into the sunset. The President, while not endorsing this comment, did suggest that it might make sense for the United Nations to divide its working year between New York and Moscow. In addition, the State Department announced that the United States would withdraw from UNESCO within two years unless that specialized agency's anti-Western bias and wasteful financial practices were promptly corrected. Clearly, the United States had put much distance between itself and the world body since the days of John F. Kennedy, who had described the United Nations as "the cornerstone of American foreign policy."

It will take patience and understanding for the United States to adjust it-self to a United Nations shaped and dominated by Third World nations, most of which were born since the end of the Second World War. It must be re-membered, however, that the General Assembly reflects the interests and ob-jectives of politically motivated governments and thus reflects the politics of a world that itself has changed profoundly since the years of the cold war. In every debate, there are grounds for differences on the merits of both sides of every argument. It is the essence of statesmanship to reconcile these compet-ing interests and differing points of view for the common good, through nego-tiation and compromise. Just as very few decisions of the American Congress satisfy all its members, very few decisions of the United Nations will satisfy all its members. Because the Congress may make mistakes in the eyes of some citi-zens, these mistakes do not justify scrapping the Constitution. Similarly, be-cause the General Assembly makes mistakes in the eyes of the United States, these mistakes do not justify scrapping the Charter. In the long run, the success of the United Nations system will not depend upon the votes on some specific issues in a particular session of the General Assembly, but rather, in the words of the Charter, upon "harmonizing the actions of nations in the attainment of these common ends."

The Economic and Social Council

The framers of the United Nations Charter were profoundly impressed by the functional theory of international order-building. This conviction found its most ambitious institutional expression in the Economic and Social Council (ECOSOC). This organ was to be an instrument for coordinating an entire gal-axy of functional activities, ranging from aid to needy children to technical as-sistance to lesser-developed areas. The common denominator of all these activities was the functional premise that the bonds of international political order could be forged more readily by first concentrating on specific common problems in the politically less formidable spheres of economic, social, and cultural affairs. It was hoped that such activities could be kept out of the arena of political controversy and that the habits of collaboration thus developed might little by little reach over into the strife-torn areas of political and even military security. In order to emphasize and facilitate this work, the Economic and Social Council became one of the principal United Nations organs.

ECOSOC was made up originally of eighteen members, elected for three years by the General Assembly. In 1966, the membership was enlarged to twenty-seven, and in 1980 it stood at fifty-four. Although the Charter contains no specific membership provisions, in practice the permanent members of the Security Council have had permanent seats on ECOSOC as well. The rest of the membership has tended to reflect the power alignments of the General Assembly, although there has been a slight imbalance in favor of the more ad-vanced industrial states. ECOSOC is responsible to the Assembly and, in ef-fect, has frequently served as a committee of the Assembly on functional matters. Since ECOSOC itself is not an operational organ, most of its energies have been absorbed in coordinating the numerous commissions which are

under its control. There are eight such functional commissions in all. They
deal with a wide variety of subject matter: transport, statistics, population, social matters, human rights and protection of minorities, status of women, commodity trade, and narcotic drugs. In addition, ECOSOC has set up a number
of regional commissions: the Economic Commission for Europe (ECE) and
parallel bodies for Asia and the Far East, Latin America, and Africa. There are
also four special voluntary programs which depend for their support exclusively upon donations from governments and private sources: the United Nations Children's Fund (UNICEF); the United Nations Development Program
(UNDP), consisting before the merger of 1966 of two separate bodies known as
the Expanded Program for Technical Assistance (EPTA) and the Special Fund;
the United Nations High Commissioner for Refugees (UNHCR); and the
United Nations Relief and Works Agency for Palestine Refugees in the Near
East (UNRWA). Finally, ECOSOC receives reports from all the specialized
agencies. The difficulties in coordinating this vast array of functional bodies
have therefore been enormous. In general, the job has been somewhat easier in
economic than in social fields, and less trying in regional than in global matters. But ECOSOC's role as a clearing-house for the UN's functional activities
has been complicated even further through the participation in its affairs of
various citizens' organizations. Among these, and enjoying consultative status
in ECOSOC, have been such nongovernmental organizations as the YMCA,
the YWCA, and the U.S. Chamber of Commerce.

So great has been the proliferation of functional activities under UN auspices that they virtually defy systematic analysis. Ironically, among the organs
coordinated by ECOSOC there have even developed certain empire-building
tendencies. In areas of overlapping activity, some agencies have claimed "sovereignty" over responsibilities to which other agencies have at the same time
stoutly laid claim. And inevitably, the problem of deciding priorities is a difficult one at best. Given the inescapable realities of a limited budget, who, for
example, is to determine which will be more conducive to the building of international order: the exchange of scientists or advancement in the status of
women?

During the cold-war years, economic development sometimes became a
casualty of the struggle between the superpowers. The full fury of the cold war
hit UN economic development programs for the first time in 1960, when Premier Fidel Castro of Cuba applied to the Special Fund for aid. Up to that time,
the eighteen-member Governing Council of the Special Fund had made it a
rule to keep politics out of their deliberations. Annual programs were always
voted on as a package. The Soviet Union had acquiesced in projects for Formosa, South Korea, and South Vietnam, while the United States had regularly
voted for projects in Communist countries like Poland and Yugoslavia. But in
1961, when the Cuban project came up for consideration before the Governing Council the United States undertook a major diplomatic effort to stop
it. In this effort it was unsuccessful. When the United States tried to round up
the seven votes necessary to block the project in the eighteen-member council,
it discovered that the other members were unwilling to aid in the precedent-

breaking consideration of a single project. They were afraid that this might lead the Soviet Union to force separate votes on aid to Formosa, South Korea, and South Vietnam, or Egypt on aid to Israel. There was a general concern that approval of individual projects would reintroduce political considerations and turn the Special Fund into an East-West battleground. Hence, the United States decided not to press for a vote that it could not win. In Feburary 1963 the UN decided to go ahead with the project, a step that elicited a violent re- action in the United States Congress. Yet if the United States had pressed the issue to a showdown, it would have jeopardized a considerable number of de- velopment projects that it liked for the sake of one small one that it did not like.

Despite these disturbing incursions of the cold war into UN development activities, there has been an overall sense of remarkable progress. The General Assembly, at its sixteenth session in 1961, proclaimed a Development Decade to mobilize support for the poorer nations of the earth. A second Development Decade was announced in 1971 and a third in 1981. The UN Development Program and the specialized agencies were seen as the chief instruments of this bold plan. What is perhaps most encouraging about the Development Program is the fact that a broad consensus exists in the United Nations on the matter of future support. No nation seriously questions its existence. The de- bate is over how much and how quickly it should grow. And in this debate, the vast majority of the UN membership will probably continue to support a policy of gradual expansion, especially in view of the commanding position of the developing countries. In 1972, for example, the UN Development Program announced a grant of $250 million over a five-year period to assist sixteen countries in their plans for economic growth. The grants were decided by UNDP's forty-eight-nation Governing Council and ranged from $50 million for India to $5 million each for Honduras and Costa Rica.

In December 1964, the General Assembly, prodded by the developing nations in ECOSOC, passed a resolution creating a new United Nations organ, the UN Conference on Trade and Development (UNCTAD). The main pur- pose of the Conference, as seen by the "Group of 77" developing nations, is to help the poor nations of the world rectify the imbalances in their international trade and thus to achieve industrialization and economic self-sufficiency. To- ward that end, the conference, which includes the entire UN membership, meets at least once every four years and its permanent organ, the Trade and Development Board, once every six months. An UNCTAD secretariat, headed by a secretary-general, has its headquarters in Geneva, where the first confer- ence convened in 1964.

UNCTAD is now a regular United Nations body in which the poor regu- larly confront the rich and demand better terms for their economies. It has become the principal forum for negotiating commodity agreements, for exam- ple. The conference has not remained insulated from political controversy, however. At first, the Soviet Union and the United States engaged in a kind of "aid race" for the allegiance of the poor nations, but by the 1970s the richer nations developed a tougher attitude and the aid race was gradually replaced

by a silent United States–Soviet agreement not to accede to unreasonable demands. Thus, UNCTAD has highlighted the political patterns that link the
East-West struggle with that of the world's poor for their place in the sun.

There is a measure of competition between ECOSOC and the General
Assembly. The former is constituted on a regional basis and consists of only
fifty-four members, while the latter comprises the entire UN membership.
Hence, the rich industrialized nations have more influence in ECOSOC than
in the General Assembly, where the developed countries are outnumbered.
When the World Food Conference in 1974 decided to establish a World Food
Council, for example, the United States and the Soviet Union wanted to make
the new organ responsible to ECOSOC, while the Third World nations preferred that the General Assembly serve as the coordinating umbrella. A compromise solution was finally worked out with the Food Council reporting to
the Assembly through the Economic and Social Council. In 1978, the General
Assembly, in an effort to coordinate all these activities, empowered the Secretary-General to appoint a Director-General for Economic and Social Operations.

ECOSOC continues to be one of the six principal organs of the United
Nations and continues to serve as an important clearing house for functional
programs. But recently it has become more of a technical organ than a political decision-making body. As the divisions between rich and poor, consumers
and producers, have assumed increasing importance in the United Nations,
ECOSOC's political role has been eclipsed to a considerable extent by the
General Assembly. During the Twenty-ninth session in 1974, for example, the
General Assembly adopted a Charter of Economic Rights and Duties of States
which was highly favorable to the developing countries. The vote was 120 in
favor, 6 against, including the United States, with 10 abstentions. The adoption of this new document was one of the events that brought about former
Ambassador Scali's warning about the "tyranny of the majority." Since then,
the Assembly, rather than ECOSOC, has been the leading forum for resolutions related to the advancement of the New International Economic Order.

The Trusteeship Council

The concept of trusteeship was devised by the United Nations' founders primarily as a weapon against the struggle they anticipated over the liquidation
of colonialism. If only the United Nations could turn the colonies from lucrative benefits into "sacred trusts," the quest for dependencies might die from
lack of incentive. Colonial powers might develop greater inhibitions in their
quest for colonies, and anticolonial powers greater patience in their struggle
for independence. If, indeed, colonialism was a cause of war, then the United
Nations should make as international as possible the administration of dependent areas and the process by which their colonial status finally came to be
terminated. This, in general terms, was the thinking that underlay the concept
of trusteeship.

In setting up the Trusteeship Council, the UN founders were able to build on the precedent of the mandate system of the League of Nations. While the League's mandate system had in essence been a thinly disguised technique of annexation, with its Permanent Mandates Commission controlled exclusively by colonial powers, it nevertheless represented a first tentative attempt at internationalization. The United Nations' framers were determined to expand this experiment considerably. Their first step was to dispose of the mandates that had been held by the now-defunct League system. For the most part, these were immediately turned into trusteeships of the United Nations. Exempted from this transfer, however, were the former Middle Eastern mandates—Syria, Lebanon, Jordan, and Israel—which were soon to achieve national independence; Southwest Africa, which was lost to the United Nations because of the stubborn refusal of the Union of South Africa to permit it to be placed under trusteeship; Japan's Pacific holdings, which were taken over as a so-called Strategic Trust Territory by the United States; and Somaliland, which had not been a League mandate and which was entrusted to Italy. Beyond these changes, the trusteeship system continued very much in the footsteps of the League. Britain was to administer Tanganyika and parts of Togoland and the Cameroons; the remainder of Togoland and the Cameroons remained under France; Ruanda-Urundi continued as a Belgian trust; to Australia were entrusted Nauru and New Guinea; and New Zealand was to administer Western Samoa. In all, the Trusteeship Council was thus to supervise eleven trust territories, seven of them in Africa, and a total population of fifteen million people.

The most radical departure from the League precedent was the widespread conviction among UN members that administration not only of trust territories but of *all* colonial possessions should be internationalized. This principle became the subject of heated controversy. The colonial powers insisted that the colonial possessions were to be under their jurisdiction exclusively, whereas the anticolonial bloc saw no further justification for the continuation of colonialism at all. The outcome of this struggle was Chapter XI of the Charter, The Declaration Regarding Non-Self-Governing Territories, which represented a modest triumph for the forces of anticolonialism. For one thing, the United Nations was no longer to use the term "colony." In its place was to be substituted the more innocuous phrase "Non-Self-Governing Territory." In addition, the colonial powers committed themselves to transmit information on economic, educational, and social conditions in their respective dependencies. The new nations pressed for the submission of political information as well, but the colonial powers insisted that this matter be left to their own discretion. Thus, when the new trusteeship system was launched, it was not only responsible for the administration of eleven trust territories but also, for the first time in history, possessed the power of imposing a minimum of international control over all colonies.

In composition, the Trusteeship Council was originally a fourteen-nation body, with its membership divided equally between colonial and anticolonial powers, or in United Nations terminology, "administering" and "nonadministering" powers. Australia, Belgium, France, Italy, Great Britain, New Zealand,

and the United States represented the first group. The Soviet Union and China
plus five other nonadministering powers made up the anticolonial bloc. As a
result of the liquidation of two thirds of the trust territories, the size of the
Trusteeship Council has diminished considerably. By 1980 it consisted of only
five states: the permanent members of the Security Council. The transition
from trusteeship status to independence has, on the whole, been orderly. The
exodus began in 1960 with the granting of independence to Cameroon, Togo,
and Somalia. Tanganyika was next, receiving independence in 1961. On January 1, 1962, Western Samoa became the first independent Polynesian state
and on the same day the Belgian trust, Ruanda-Urundi, was transformed into
two independent countries, Rwanda and Burundi. By 1980 only the Pacific Islands remained under the authority of the Trusteeship Council.

Each of the trust territories was administered under a Trusteeship Agreement. These agreements were concluded between the administering powers
and the United Nations, but in most cases the former were able to determine
the nature of the agreement. The United States, for example, insisted that the
Pacific Islands be made into a Strategic Trust Territory under the Security
Council, and therefore subject to American veto. The terms of the agreements
were approved by the General Assembly, to which the Trusteeship Council
has been responsible on all important matters. Like ECOSOC, the council has,
in effect, become a committeee of the Assembly. Owing to the stronger representation of the colonial powers on the Trusteeship Council, its recommendations—especially those dealing with advancement toward self-government in
the trust territories—have at times been criticized by the General Assembly as
lacking in vigor. Responsibility for the supervision of Non-Self-Governing
Territories, under Chapter XI of the Charter, has not been exercised by the
Trusteeship Council itself but by a separate body, the Committee on Information from Non-Self-Governing Territories. The membership of that committee
has been patterned after that of the council.

Where the Trusteeship Council was directly involved in its dealings with
the trust territories, its responsibilities were threefold: preparation of annual
reports, examinations of petitions, and dispatch of visiting missions. Annual
reports were based on lengthy written questionnaires, to be completed by the
administering powers. If the replies seemed incomplete or unsatisfactory, the
Trusteeship Council had the right to proceed to written and oral cross-exami-
nation. On the basis of these reports, the council then formulated its own recommendations for the General Assembly. These recommendations were
far-reaching and related to economic development, health services, educational facilities, labor conditions, and the participation of the indigenous population in the affairs of government. The Trusteeship Council also permitted
the inhabitants of trust territories to submit petitions on specific grievances.
This procedure was a radical departure from the League precedent, since it
by-passed the colonial power and established direct contact between the trust
and the United Nations. At first this opportunity was utilized infrequently, but
during and since the 1950s the number of petitions grew considerably. A typical petition brought before the Trusteeship Council concerned the fate of the

Ewe tribe in West Africa, which claimed that the boundary line between French and British Togoland divided its people. The following excerpt will convey its flavor:

> About 2 years ago both french and british government promised to have constituted a conventional zone for the amendment of the frontiers regulations, amidst the Ewe people. This problem is very hard to be solved, because it is impossible for two persons to wear one trousers. Only their guilty conscience forced them to make this promise, but in reality they are unfit to complete this task just like two persons suggesting of wearing one trousers.
>
> Therefore we beg to have explained the things to the general assembly of the UNO properly; in order to have considered or rescue from this cruelty in due time.[4]

On the whole, the Trusteeship Council took such petitions very seriously. The council's most effective device was the visiting mission. Every three years the council dispatched missions to each of its territories. These ventures were not only of great symbolic value but had the great advantage of actual contact with the populations of the territories. At times there was friction between the visiting missions and the administering powers over the tempo of advancement toward self-government. This was not surprising, since the visiting missions were generally most interested in how quickly the administering powers were eliminating themselves, whereas the latter tended to regard the trusts as quasi-colonies. But most of these tensions were fruitful and yielded worthwhile results.

While the Trusteeship Council has been a notable success, as its overall record indicates, it has not always been able to remove the trust territories from the colonial power struggle. Libya, for example, became the subject of a heated political controversy among the several powers eager to administer it as a trust. Since no solution satisfactory to all seemed possible, Libya was granted its independence. This was a case in which the necessity for trusteeship was clearly apparent but in which, owing to the disagreement of the powers concerned, it could not be worked out in practice. Of the consequences of this fact for Libya itself, Inis L. Claude, Jr., has written that ". . . in terms of the objective of the rational and orderly liquidation of colonialism, the excessive prolongation of dependence [was] hardly more unfortunate than the premature conferment of independence."[5]

In a general analysis of the United Nations trusteeship systems, several factors emerge. For one thing, while the system has had little effect on the rate at which colonies have been liquidated, it has contributed considerably to making their liquidation more *responsible*. Moreover, in view of the fact that most of the trust territories have already received independence, the Trusteeship Council may soon find itself without a function. Of course, a liberal interpretation of the Charter would open the possibility of bringing new trusts under the council's responsibility. There are still a few colonies that might be possible candidates, although the political atmosphere in the General Assembly strongly favors immediate independence without an intermediate stage.

Perhaps the most significant feature of the trusteeship system has been its

prophylactic quality. It has belied the facile assumption that the United Nations has been ineffective because of its inability to enforce decisions. Trusteeship has proved that effectiveness without sanctions is possible. As Claude has
pointed out, it has attempted to deal with a situation *before* rather than *after* it
reached the crisis stage.[6] In the Congo the United Nations was compelled to
create a kind of trusteeship after the crisis had become acute.

In the general struggle over the liquidation of colonialism, the trusteeship
system has played a significant, but not decisive, role. More recently, with the
influx of new African and Asian members into the United Nations, the Trusteeship Council has dealt more with the problems of Southern Africa than with
the problem of the single remaining trust territory. The original concept of
the trusteeship system—to prepare the territories for independence with all
deliberate speed—has been expanded by the General Assembly to apply to *all*
colonial possesssions via the Declaration Regarding Non-Self-Governing Ter-
ritori :s. On the whole, the United Nations institutions set up to deal with
problems of colonialism have been successfully used by the anticolonial majority of the General Assembly in its relentless drive toward full self-determination for all dependent peoples.

The Secretary-General and the Secretariat

One of the greatest fears of the founders of the United Nations was that the
new world organization would be no more than the sum of its parts—a group
of delegates each loyal to his own nation and perceiving the world through the
particular lenses of his own nationality. The men and women at San Francisco
were deeply convinced that one important road to international order could
be constructed by providing the United Nations with a nucleus of people who,
for the duration of their tenure as world civil servants, would place loyalty to
the world community on an equal level with their other, more parochial commitments. It was this notion of international loyalty-building that provided the
basis for the Office of the Secretary-General and of his staff, the United Nations
Secretariat.

The Office of the Secretary-General of the United Nations is not without
precedent. The League of Nations had also made provision for such a post. Its
first incumbent, Sir Eric Drummond, a British civil servant, was primarily an
administrator who made it his policy to remain aloof from the political disputes that were sapping the life-blood of the League. Albert Thomas, on the
other hand, the Director-General of the League's International Labor Organization, set quite another precedent. Not content with anonymous administrative responsibilities, he ventured into the uncharted land of international
statesmanship and did not shrink from taking a stand on controversial policy
issues. Weighing these two precedents and tending to prefer the latter, the UN
architects endowed the Office of the United Nations Secretary-General with
political as well as administrative powers. The Secretary-General was not only
to be the chief administrative officer of the United Nations, but, in the words
of the Preparatory Commission in 1945, his Office was to represent

A quite special right which goes beyond any power previously accorded to the head of an international organization. The Secretary-General more than anyone else will stand for the United Nations as a whole. In the eyes of the world, no less than in the eyes of his own staff, he must embody the ideals and principles of the Charter.[7]

This conception of the Office led to the inclusion in the Charter of Article 99, which set forth the Secretary-General's significant political powers: "The Secretary-General may bring to the attention of the Security Council any matter which in his opinion may threaten the maintenance of international peace and security." The founders of the UN thus clearly intended the Secretary-General to be an international statesman, a kind of conscience of the world. In order to equip him adequately for this role, they gave him what, in some respects at least, amounted almost to the power of acting as a twelfth member of the Security Council.

The first imcumbent of the Office was Trygve Lie of Norway. Lie used his political powers abundantly and frequently took positions in the conflicts among the major powers. In the early years he tended to stay aloof from the most inflammable issues of the East-West struggle but defended the interest of the world community as he conceived it by taking stands on minor political disputes. He supported the European Recovery Program and opted in favor of the partition of Palestine. Soon thereafter, however, he became embroiled in political controversies of the first magnitude. Early in 1950 Mr. Lie advocated the seating of the Chinese Communist delegation in the United Nations and provoked the extreme displeasure of the United States. Several weeks later he strongly supported the American initiative in the "police action" to repel aggression by North Korea, and went so far as to label the North Koreans as the aggressors. While this action reconciled the United States, it provoked the implacable hostility of the Soviet Union. When, in late 1950, the question of Lie's reappointment came up, the United States threatened to veto the appointment of any other candidate, while the Soviet Union declared with equal conviction that it would not tolerate him. The United States prevailed upon the General Assembly to extend his term, but the value of Trygve Lie as a peacemaker between East and West was irretrievably impaired. In November 1952, after two years of fruitless bickering, Lie resigned from the post of Secretary-General.

The experience of Trygve Lie pointed up the great dilemma, if not the inherent contradiction, of international statesmanship. The Secretary-General, to be an effective spokesman for the interests of the world community, must at times take a stand on major current political issues. But he also has to retain the confidence of all the actors in the drama. The utmost diplomatic skill and political sensitivity are needed for this task. Lie, for example, never violated the Charter. He took positions on both sides of the East-West struggle and became the object of severe criticism by both antagonists. But whereas one was willing to forgive, the other thought he had gone too far. Hence his effectiveness as a possible bridge-builder was ended.

These lessons were not lost on Trygve Lie's successor, Dag Hammarskjöld of Sweden. Hammarskjöld had been an economist and chairman of the Swedish National Bank as well as Deputy Minister for Foreign Affairs. He had never been a member of a political party and was known to have a "passion for anonymity." By background he was a civil servant, not a politician. Not surprisingly, therefore, the new Secretary-General approached his Office with somewhat greater restraint than had his predecessor. Unlike Lie, Hammarskjöld at first chose not to take overt political initiative. Public diplomacy was replaced by quiet diplomacy. This is not to say that the increasing ferocity of the two great international political struggles left the new Secretary-General untouched. But Mr. Hammarskjöld's approach to political disputes differed in two important respects from that of his predecessor. First, he always attempted to gain authority for his actions from the Security Council or the General Assembly. Second, most of his diplomatic maneuvers were carried on behind the scenes, away from the searchlight of publicity. The former habit gained him the confidence of the major powers, while the latter made possible agreements without serious loss of face for any nation. A survey of Mr. Hammarskjöld's major activities in this respect is quite revealing.

In 1954 the Secretary-General flew to Peking to negotiate the release of eleven American airmen who were interned there as United Nations personnel. Virtually no publicity was released about the trip, but a year later the airmen were released. In 1956, during the Suez crisis, the Secretary-General was confronted with an international problem of the first magnitude. Two permanent members of the Security Council were accused of military aggression and a third, the Soviet Union, threatened them with rocket bombardment. In addition, the Arab states and Israel seemed locked in mortal combat. Mr. Hammarskjöld, under the authority of the General Assembly, equipped the United Nations with an unprecedented military instrument, the United Nations Emergency Force (UNEF), which helped to restore order to the troubled area. (For a more detailed analysis of UNEF, see Chapter 12.) By taking this action, the Secretary-General became deeply involved in the political drama being acted out in the Middle East. But as always, his decisiveness was tempered with circumspection. Mr. Hammarskjöld's declaration before the Security Council, when that body met to consider the Middle Eastern crisis, is worth quoting:

> The Principles of the Charter are, by far, greater than the Organization in which they are embodied, and the aims which they are to safeguard are holier than the policies of any single nation or people. As a servant of the Organization, the Secretary-General has the duty to maintain his usefulness by avoiding public stands on conflicts between Member Nations unless and until such an action might help to resolve the conflict. However, the discretion and impartiality thus imposed on the Secretary-General by the character of his immediate task may not degenerate into a policy of expediency. He must also be a servant of the principles of the Charter, and its aims must ultimately determine what for him is right and wrong. For that he must stand. A Secretary-General cannot serve on any other assumption than that—all Member Nations honour their pledge to observe all Articles of the Charter. He should also be able to assume that those organs which are

charged with the task of upholding the Charter will be in the position to fulfill their task.

The bearing of what I have just said must be obvious to all without any elaboration from my side. Were the Members to consider that another view of the duties of the Secretary-General than the one here stated would better serve the interests of the Organization it is their obvious right to act accordingly.[8]

This declaration, expressing Mr. Hammarskjöld's conception of his office, not only won him the Council's confidence during the Suez crisis but also resulted in his unanimous election to a second five-year term of office. This second term, moreover, was marked by a growing tendency in both the General Assembly and the Security Council to grant the Secretary-General broad powers for the exercise of his quiet diplomacy. The Assembly requested Mr. Hammarskjöld to facilitate the withdrawal of foreign troops during the Lebanese crisis in 1958. In 1960, when racial violence in the Union of South Africa convened the Security Council in an emergency session, a strong resolution against the Union government would have produced a British or French veto whereas a weak resolution might have provoked a Soviet veto. But East and West and colonial and anticolonial governments alike were able to agree on a mild resolution requesting the Secretary-General to use his good offices with the Union government in order to ameliorate racial tensions.

In mid-1960, when the Belgian withdrawal from the Congo left the new republic strife-torn and threatened by Great Power intervention on the model of the Spanish Civil War, the talents of the Secretary-General were called upon once more. Acting under the authority of the Security Council, he organized a United Nations Force, excluding the Great Powers, which was to restore peace and order in the Congo until responsible self-government could be established. When the Congo was threatened by civil war through the secession of the province of Katanga, Mr. Hammarskjöld—again after securing Security Council authorization—entered Katanga at the head of the United Nations Force to prevent a major conflagration. By this time, the Secretary-General had won the respect of most observers and had established the unique political value and significance of his Office. As James Reston put it in August 1960:

In the present state of diplomatic relations between East and West, it is unlikely that agreement could have been reached between Washington and Moscow on what should be done [in the Congo]. But in the all-night debate both the United States and the Soviet Union were able to agree, as they have had to do in several crises in the past, to trust in the intervention of the U.N. Secretary-General, Dag Hammarskjöld.

This remarkable man is proving to be one of the great natural resources in the world today, and it is difficult to think of another in the field of world diplomacy who could do the job as well.

He is tireless. He is infinitely patient. He is sensitive to the slightest troublesome breeze in the world. He knows exactly what his job will let him do and forbid him from doing. And he knows when to be ambiguous; he also knows when to be precise.

When he said that the Congo was "a question of peace or war," the Security

Council paid attention, because he does not use three-letter words often or care-
lessly.

That he has exercised these powers with such skill as to win the respect, if
not the affection, of the contending states is one reason why the U.N.is now a refuge for common sense in a satanic world.[9]

As the Congo crisis developed further, however, Hammarskjöld began to
run into major difficulties. Though ordered to do so by Patrice Lumumba, the
deposed premier of the fledgling republic, he refused to withdraw the United
Nations Peace Force. He maintained that Lumumba did not speak for the
Congo and that it was necessary for the force to remain until peace and order
were restored. This action resulted in a vehement attack on the Secretary-
General by the Soviet Union, which had supported Lumumba in the Congolese power struggle. Disappointed by its setback in the Congo, the Soviet
Union now accused the Secretary-General of having exceeded his authority. At
the Fifteenth General Assembly, Premier Khrushchev violently attacked Mr.
Hammarskjöld, demanded that his Office be abolished, and proposed that in
his place there ought to be a three-man committee representing the Communist bloc, the Western bloc, and the uncommitted countries. The Secretary-
General refused to resign and stated that he was no longer deferring primarily
to the Great Powers—a radical shift from his position during the Suez crisis.
His position was firm and clear: "I would rather see that Office [the Secretary-
Generalship] break on strict adherence to the principle of independence, impartiality and objectivity than drift on the basis of compromise."[10]

The Assembly affirmed his stand by a resounding vote of confidence of 70
to 0 with the nine Soviet bloc countries, the Union of South Africa, and France
abstaining. While it thus seemed clear that the Soviet triumvirate proposal
would not be adopted, two other suggestions were made, both with a view to
curtailing the Secretary-General's powers. Premier Nkrumah of Ghana offered
a plan to equip the Secretary-General with three deputies, chosen from the
East, West, and Third World blocs, each with "clearly defined authority" in
United Nations affairs. And Prime Minister Nehru of India proposed an advisory committee from different geographical areas, a sort of inner cabinet
whose views and perhaps even approval would have to be sought on any important matters.

The tragic death of Dag Hammarskjöld on the eve of the opening of the
Sixteenth General Assembly caused great anxiety, since the Soviet Union had a
veto over the election of a successor. Actually, the Soviet leadership was quite
aware that it could not get the "troika" plan through the Assembly, but hopeful that it would be able to effect a drastic cutback in the power of the Office.
The United States attempted to rally the General Assembly behind its view
that the Secretary-General's authority must not be compromised and that a
single person be named in an acting capacity until a new Secretary-General
could be elected. President Kennedy expressed this view forcefully before the
Assembly:

However difficult it may be to fill Mr. Hammarskjöld's place, it can better be
filled by one man rather than by three. Even the three horses of the troika did not

have three drivers, all going in different directions. They had only one, and so must the United Nations executive. To install a triumvirate, or any rotating authority, in the United Nations administrative offices would replace order with anarchy, action with paralysis, and confidence with confusion.[11]

A number of Soviet attempts to get support for a troika at the undersecretary level were unsuccessful and, on November 3, 1961, the General Assembly upon recommendation of the Security Council unanimously named U Thant of Burma Acting Secretary-General for the remainder of Dag Hammarskjöld's term.

This decision postponed the troika issue until April 10, 1963, when Hammarskjöld's term of office was to expire. But Soviet reservations about U Thant were apparently dispelled by his conciliatory mediation during the Cuban crisis of 1962, and he was elected to a full term, retroactive, according to his own wish, to his designation as Acting Secretary-General. The Office itself had now moved eastward from Trygve Lie of Norway, a NATO country, and Hammarskjöld of neutral Sweden, to a citizen of a neutralist country in Asia.

U Thant, though very different in background and training from his predecessor, nevertheless introduced no sharp changes in policy. Most of his energies at first were taken up with the continuing crisis in the Congo and the looming threat of bankruptcy which the United Nations faced as a result of having mounted two major peace-keeping operations. Still as Acting Secretary-General he played a major role in the establishment of the UN Temporary Executive Authority (UNTEA), which supervised the transfer of West New Guinea from the Netherlands to Indonesia. And in 1964 he met a major challenge when called upon to put together a UN peace force to keep apart the warring factions on Cyprus and to prepare the way for a more fundamental solution for the problems of that tormented island.

In 1966, U Thant was elected unanimously to another five-year term. He accepted reluctantly, and only after great pressure had been put on him by many member states, both large and small. The continuing escalation of the war in Vietnam and his own inability to bring the combatants to the negotiating table gnawed at him. Moreover, he had been unable to improve substantially the finances of the Organization. In 1967, acceding to the demand of Egypt's President Nasser, he decided to withdraw the UN Emergency Force from the Middle East, where it had been stationed for more than a decade. Though political controversies continued to surround him, he nevertheless continued to enjoy the support of most of the membership. Whatever opposition there was remained fairly passive and never reached the vehemence of the attacks that had been made upon his two predecessors. In 1971, after two full terms in office, U Thant retired from his post, the first Secretary-General to do so with the blessing of most members, whether large or small. His successor was an Austrian, Kurt Waldheim.

The election of the fourth Secretary-General was particularly significant because it coincided almost exactly with the seating of the People's Republic of China in the United Nations. Despite Cassandra-like predictions emanating from many quarters that the Chinese would make difficulties, none occurred.

Mr. Waldheim received the support of the five permanent members, which made his election unanimous. During his first term in office, the new Secretary-General already displayed considerable initiative. He offered the UN's good offices in the settlement of the Vietnam conflict, traveled to numerous countries on a variety of missions, and worked tirelessly to put the UN's financial house in order. In 1972, after Palestinian guerrillas murdered eleven Israeli athletes at the Munich Olympics, he took the initiative in asking the General Assembly to discuss the problem of terrorism on an international scale. In 1974, he visited fourteen famine-stricken countries in the Sahelian region of Africa in order to draw the world's attention to their plight. In the wake of the October War in the Middle East, he set up two new peace forces in the area, separating the Israelis from Egypt and from Syria. And when hostilities erupted on Cyprus, he maneuvered adroitly in order to maximize the effectiveness of the small United Nations peace force on that troubled island. On the whole, he tried his best to be an activist Secretary-General, but to do so without antagonizing any of the major powers. This was not an easy task since Mr. Waldheim's constituency was both larger and more complicated than that of each of his three predecessors. In 1976, the membership rewarded Mr. Waldheim by electing him for a second five-year term.

The fifth Secretary-General, Javier Perez de Cuellar, was a professional diplomat from Peru. His tenure, which began in 1982, was one of considerable frustration. Though an extremely tactful and even self-effacing man, de Cuellar was not able to involve the United Nations in the Great Power conflicts in a truly meaningful sense. The Lebanese tragedy ran its melancholy course without the United Nations and not even Britain and Argentina permitted a role for the world body during the Falklands crisis. Perhaps de Cuellar's most significant achievement was his decision, in 1983, in an unusually blunt and straightforward report, to draw the world's attention to the rapidly declining role of the United Nations. In none of the major world conflicts, the Secretary-General asserted, had the United Nations been allowed to inject itself into the peace-making process. Even multinational peace-keeping forces in the Middle East, which in earlier years used to be provided by United Nations, were now being carried on by NATO powers. Unless this negative trend was reversed, the Secretary-General warned, the UN's future looked bleak indeed.

In a general evaluation of the Secretary-Generalship, it is probably fair to say, as did Trygve Lie upon looking backward on his experience, that the office is "in many ways . . . far ahead of our times."[12] And always, it remains beset by an unavoidable dilemma. If, in the fulfillment of his duties, the Secretary-General speaks out too loudly, he will incur the wrath of one or more of the Great Powers and thus doom himself to inefficacy. Yet if he refuses to speak out at all, he dooms himself to sterility. To live under the strains of this dilemma and play the most forceful possible part in the work of the United Nations in spite of it requires a most gifted and unusual man.

If the Secretary-General is the world's chief civil servant, the United Nations Secretariat is its international civil service. This international staff has not limited its activities solely to United Nations Headquarters in New York City. Each of the autonomous specialized agencies in the United Nations family has its own director-general and secretariat. The functions of the various levels of the Secretariat have been largely of a "housekeeping" nature. The Secretariat's responsibilities have been legion and have included the planning of conferences, the gathering of information, interpreting, and the publication of a yearbook. In all these activities the international civil servant must demonstrate scrupulous objectivity in order not to antagonize any member government. Employment policy for members of the Secretariat was laid down in Article 101 of the Charter:

> The paramount consideration in the employment of the staff and in the determination of the conditions of service shall be the necessity of securing the highest standards of efficiency, competence, and integrity. Due regard shall be paid to the importance of recruiting the staff on as wide a geographical basis as possible.

It was hoped to combine the principles of merit and geography. While competence should be the main criterion, a truly international service could not be indifferent to considerations of nationality. But once a national of a member state had joined the Secretariat he was expected to take an oath of allegiance to the United Nations and not to accept instructions from any government. In other words, during the time of his tenure the world civil servant—like his chief, the Secretary-General—was expected to contribute to international order-building by developing a loyalty to the world community.

The potential and at times actual conflict between the demands of a national and a world outlook have frequently placed a great strain on members of the Secretariat and on the Secretary-General. A principal source of that strain was the United States government which, in the early 1950s, subjected American members of the Secretariat to intensive loyalty investigations. Although not a single member was convicted, large sections of the American public began to regard the Secretariat as a sanctuary for American Communists and saboteurs. The United States government exerted great pressure on Trygve Lie to dismiss those American members of his staff who had been accused of disloyalty to the United States. The Secretary-General faced a formidable dilemma: if he acceded to the American demands, he would impugn the integrity of the international civil service; if he refused, he ran the risk of alienating a government without whose support the United Nations could hardly continue to exist. In his plight, he asked the opinion of a special committee of legal advisers. This group suggested that membership in the Secretariat in no way abrogated the loyalty a person owed to the state of which he was a citizen, and that, therefore, Lie was justified in dismissing "disloyal" Americans. Accordingly, nine American members of the Secretariat with permanent contracts who had refused to answer questions of investigating committees or had invoked the Constitutional privilege of silence were dismissed from active service. One year later, however, an Administrative Tribunal of the United Nations ruled that the dismissed employees were entitled to compensation. The General Assembly—over American opposition—voted to make

amends after having requested an advisory opinion of the World Court, which
supported the view of the Administrative Tribunal. Nevertheless, the U.S.
Congress, in a concurrent resolution, declared that no American funds paid to
the UN could be used to pay compensation to the dismissed UN officials.[13]

This episode demonstrated that in a conflict between national and world
loyalty in the Secretariat, the national probably remains paramount. This is
further borne out by the fact that in early 1961, the Soviet Union extended its
critique of the Secretary-General to the Secretariat and demanded that the
entire staff be reorganized on the basis of equal representation for "the three
main groups of states—socialist, neutralist, and Western." Thus, until the international civil service can ask for and find in its members unreserved world
loyalty, the Secretariat member must continue to reconcile his national and
international allegiances as best he can. That a fruitful synthesis between national and world loyalty is indeed possible has been demonstrated in a classic
statement by C. Wilfred Jenks, one of the early pioneers of a global civil service:

> A lack of attachment to any one country does not constitute an international
> outlook. A superior indifference to the emotions and prejudices of those whose
> world is bounded by the frontiers of a single state does not constitute an interna-
> tional outlook. A blurred indistinctness of attitude toward all questions, pro-
> ceeding from a freedom of prejudice born of lack of vitality, does not constitute
> an international outlook. The international outlook required of the international
> civil servant is an awareness made instinctive by habit of the needs, emotions,
> and prejudices of the peoples of differently-circumstanced countries, as they are
> felt and expressed by the peoples concerned, accompanied by a capacity for
> weighing these frequently imponderable elements in a judicial manner before
> reaching any decision to which they are relevant.[14]

It could justly be said of the United Nations civil service that seldom has
so much been done for so many by so few. In New York, Rome, Paris, Geneva,
and Vienna, there have emerged small but compact nuclei of a nascent world
loyalty. They have often been threatened with disintegration but have always
managed somehow to survive. By 1980, the number of international civil servants dispersed throughout the world approached the 15,000 mark.[15]

"It may be true," said Dag Hammarskjöld shortly before he died, "that in
a very deep human sense there is no neutral individual, because everyone, if he
is worth anything, has to have his ideas and ideals. . . . But what I do claim is
that even a man who is in that sense not neutral can very well undertake and
carry through neutral actions because that is an act of integrity."[16] This statement, which was made in response to Premier Khrushchev's blunt assertion
that no man could be neutral, probably best expresses the philosophical conception of the international civil service.

Case Study: The United Nations Conference on the Human Environment

In June 1972, about 1,200 delegates from 114 nations met for two weeks in
Stockholm, Sweden, in order to produce a framework for international action

to halt the deterioration of the environment and to conserve the earth's dwindling resources. The UN Conference had been four years in the making and was initiated by a 1968 resolution of the General Assembly, originally proposed by the government of Sweden. It was to be man's first global attack on the deepening environmental crisis, and it was mounted under the aegis of the United Nations.

Man has always lived in two worlds: the "biosphere," which is the world of natural things from which he draws his physical existence, and the "technosphere," the world of tools and artifacts, of social and political institutions that he forged for himself. For centuries, the planet's fields and forests, its reserves of fertile soil and minerals, its oceans and rivers could carry without strain the entire freight of man's technological inventions and desires. In the last few decades, however, and with explosively increasing force in the last few years, the balance between the planet's biosphere and the technosphere has been critically affected. Man no longer lives almost overwhelmed by the scale of his environment. It is the environment that is beginning to be overwhelmed by man. At stake is nothing less than the quality of life on this planet.

From its inception the United Nations has been concerned about the quality of life for the peoples of the world, and its involvement with environmental issues dates back to the 1949 International Technical Conference on Conservation. The Stockholm Conference of 1972 was convened under UN auspices because the UN alone had the worldwide system through which an essentially cooperative and international response to the global challenge could be launched. It also provided a forum in which industrialized and developing countries could most easily meet to discuss and devise joint policies for development which would enhance, rather than injure, the shared biosphere. And finally the UN, as a continuing body, could set in motion a whole range of actions without which fragmentation and disunity would continue to mark man's approach to his global environment.

Under the leadership of Maurice F. Strong, the secretary-general of the conference, the delegates debated multiple aspects of a single theme: How should man control his growth to save the planet earth?

At one end of the spectrum were the advocates of a "zero-growth" world, one in which the current progressive deterioration of the environment, degrading the quality of the world's air, land, and water, would be virtually brought to a halt. It would be a world in which population would be stabilized and the consumption of raw materials held to a level not substantially greater than the production of such materials. Energy use would be compatible with the planet's long-term reserves of nuclear and fossil fuels. Those supporting this view believed that social chaos and major wars would erupt over access to the world's depleting resources unless the industrialized countries decided to arrest their heedless growth.

At the other extreme were those—largely the developing countries—who saw no need in the foreseeable future to alter the emphasis on growth. They contended that a zero-growth world would lead to the destruction of the world's economies, which must expand in order to prosper.

In this tug-of-war between "environmentalists" and "developmentalists"

Secretary-General Strong took a middle course. "No growth is not a viable policy for any society today," he said. "Indeed, people must have access to more, not fewer, opportunities to express their creative drives. But these can only be provided within a total system in which man's activities are in dynamic harmony with the natural order." "To achieve this," he added, "we must rethink our concepts of the basic purposes of growth. Surely we must see it in terms of enriching the lives and enlarging the opportunities of all mankind. And if this is so, it follows that it is the more wealthy societies—the privileged minority of mankind—which will have to make the most profound, even revolutionary, changes in attitudes and values."[17]

Mr. Strong's carefully charted middle course between the advocates of development and the defenders of the environment avoided a confrontation between the have and the have-not nations at the conference. The latter feared that if the advanced countries set high environmental standards for their imports, this would seriously damage the export capabilities of poorer nations. Brazil, for example, asked to be compensated for building environmental protection devices into its new automobile plants. Lurking in the background was the suspicion of Third World nations that the industrial countries might set limits on international pollution that would inhibit the poor nations' uphill fight toward industrialization.

The tension between the rich and the poor overshadowed the usual manifestations of the East-West struggle. The Soviet Union boycotted the conference because East Germany was denied full participation. China, however, was in attendance and cast its lot squarely with the have-not nations. In addition, China mounted an attack on the United States for "wanton bombing" in Vietnam. The Chinese delegate also demanded "reparation payments" from the United States and other industrialized nations. He insisted that, since the advanced countries were responsible for the largest amounts of environmental pollution to date, they owed the developing countries both reparations and assistance in development. The Chinese delegate made a major bid for the leadership of the have-not nations when he exclaimed: "We must not give up eating for fear of choking." Since the poor outnumbered the rich by a ratio of about two to one at the conference, this statement received wide support and acclaim. When a vote was taken, however, to halt all atomic testing, China was one of the three states voting against the resolution, with the other negative votes being cast by France and Gabon.

The deliberations at the conference were divided into six subject areas: problems of human settlements, national resources, pollution, national development, environmental organization, and environmental education. Three committees, each made up of members of all the participating delegations, dealt with two of these subjects each. All committee decisions had to be reviewed by the conference as a whole, which in turn submitted its own report to the General Assembly.

In the end, the conference was able to point to some very notable accomplishments. In the first place, it ratified a Declaration on the Human Environment. The first draft of this document was a delicately balanced compromise between the rich and the poor that had been hammered out in dozens of diplomatic sessions before the Stockholm meeting. In the middle of the conference itself, however, the Chinese, claiming that they had had no part in the drafting of the declaration, demanded that the entire document be reopened for debate. The motion was successful, and after lengthy debate a revised document was approved. The new declaration was tilted somewhat more in the direction of those who perceived poverty as a more important problem than pollution. Like its predecessor, the Universal Declaration of Human Rights, the Declaration on the Human Environment was binding on no one. But it was hoped that it would set a standard of environmental behavior that would be observed voluntarily by most of the membership of the United Nations.

The second concrete achievement of the conference was a set of "action plans." At the core of these was to be "Earthwatch"—the systematic monitoring and assessment of global conditions as a basis for national measures to curb environmental abuses. Typical examples of such action plans included an appeal to all nations to minimize the release of toxic metals and chemicals into the environment; a global early-warning system designed to monitor changes in the world's climate and levels of air pollution; and action to save certain species, such as the whale, from complete extinction.

Finally, the conference established a new environmental coordinating unit in the United Nations. This permanent new organ, consisting of a fifty-four-member governing council, a small secretariat, and an executive director—set up under the aegis of the Economic and Social Council—was to follow up on the world community's continuing concern with the environmental crisis beyond the immediate confines of the Stockholm Conference. The financing of UN environmental activities was to be arranged through the creation of a voluntarily supported Environment Fund. Only the immediate administrative costs of the coordinating unit were to be borne by the UN's assessed regular budget.

The most dramatic decision taken by the General Assembly in the wake of the Stockholm Conference had to do with the geographical location of the new secretariat that was to coordinate the UN Environmental Program. Most Western diplomats, who expected the secretariat to be placed in Geneva or in New York after a routine debate, were startled by the unified and forceful efforts made by Asian, African, and Latin American countries to establish the secretariat in a developing nation, namely in Nairobi, the capital of Kenya.

Most of the Western states, particularly the United States, the United Kingdom, and Sweden, defended the view that the establishment of the environment secretariat should be determined primarily by factors of efficiency, effectiveness, and cost. When judged by these standards, Geneva or New York seemed to be logical choices.

The developing countries, in an intense and emotional debate, held that the site of the environmental headquarters was essentially a political decision. One of the most remarkable features of the debate was the extraordinary display of bloc solidarity and discipline in evidence among the developing states. Even when a UN Secretariat estimate revealed that the annual cost of the environment secretariat in Nairobi would be $2.3 million, whereas the cost in Geneva would come to only $1.4 million, this did not change a single vote. The delegate of Kenya stated that if, in fact, it cost a little more to build a UN agency in a developing state, the United Nations would "in effect pay a little rent for the omissions of the past."[18] China supported the pro-Nairobi group, but the Soviet Union, torn between its superpower status and its efforts to woo the poor nations, found itself among the abstainers.

Thus, the developing nations, in their drive for status and prestige as well as funds, established a new principle: the observance of geographical representation in the establishment of new UN bodies. In a more fundamental sense, the Nairobi decision symbolized the growing rift between rich and poor and underlined with growing force the emergence of a new power constellation at the United Nations.

Environmental breakdown does not respect national or ideological boundaries. It threatens Capitalists and Communists, the rich and the poor alike. The environmental challenge may yet prove to be the great leveler of international relations. It might even become a catalyst toward a saner world order since it may compel nations to cooperate on basic problems common to all. Perhaps the greatest achievement at Stockholm lay in the fact that more than one hundred nations found it possible to face a crisis before it had reached the point of no return and to take action on a global basis to arrest it. Most delegates sensed that the planet would survive the ecological crisis as a whole or not at all. Hence they turned to the United Nations as a logical means of action. This decision also infused new life and hope into the world organization itself. Having languished for years with the realization that it could not free the planet of most of its wars and political crises, the United Nations could now draw new strength from the hope that it might make a major contribution toward making life on this planet worth living at all.

The Global Conference Approach: Planetary Management

The 1970s and 1980s witnessed an integrated approach by the United Nations to some of the world's most critical problems. A series of global conferences was organized under UN auspices to address the main challenges to an endangered Planet Earth. The first of these was the World Conference on the Human Environment held in Stockholm in 1972, which was the subject of the special case study above. The year 1974 saw a whole bevy of global conferences: the Sixth Special Session of the General Assembly on raw materials and development; a Conference on the Law of the Sea, held in Caracas; a World Population Conference, held in Bucharest; and a World Food Conference, held in Rome. All these conferences emphasized the need to respond to planetary challenges with planetary initiatives. What became painfully clear during the debates in Stockholm, New York, Caracas, Bucharest, and Rome was that interdependence was no longer a slogan or an abstraction but had become a gut reality. Planetary crisis demanded planetary management.

The Sixth Special Session of the General Assembly on raw materials and development met in New York in April 1974 in order to search for a more just and viable basis for international economic cooperation. A package of proposals was adopted including a Declaration and Program of Action on the Establishment of a New International Economic Order. The poor countries demanded the establishment of a special emergency fund and rejected as insufficient an American proposal for a $4 billion assistance program for the most seriously affected. The oil-rich Arab nations pressed the point that the industrialized countries should shoulder the main burden of aiding the world's poor. The Western nations rejected this point of view and the session ended with few concrete achievements. The plight of the poor was clear to all but no consensus was reached as yet on how to share the responsibility of helping them.

The United Nations Conference on the Law of the Sea was held in Caracas in the summer of 1974 after six years of preparation. It continued into the 1980s with numerous conferences held in other world capitals. The major problem areas before the conference were the establishment of the limits of national jurisdiction over territorial waters presently ranging from three to two hundred miles; fisheries questions; preservation of the marine environment; the establishment of international machinery to regulate activities on the high seas such as the dumping of waste into the oceans; passage through international straits; the exploitation of the mineral resources of the seabed; and the conduct of scientific research. Negotiations were arduous, but the conferences represented tentative first steps in the direction of a new international regime governing the world's oceans. The participating nations all agreed that the need for new laws was urgent and that the process of forging them should be continuous.

The World Population Conference that was held in Bucharest in August 1974 placed the problem of population squarely onto the front pages of the world's agenda. Since population was related to the issues of economic development, diplomacy, human rights, and institutional change, it was analytically impossible to insulate it from the crosscurrents of international politics. Despite wide divergencies among the participating countries, a consensus was reached on a World Population Plan of Action which looked toward a target of reducing world fertility from 38 per 1,000 to 30 per 1,000 by 1985. In addition, there was general agreement on certain key principles of population planning and individual human rights. For example, all countries agreed to respect and ensure the right of persons to determine, in a free, informed, and responsible manner, the number and spacing of their children, and to encourage the participation of women in educational, social, economic, and political life on an equal basis with men. On the whole, the Bucharest Conference symbolized the evolution of the international population movement from a preoccupation of scholars and students to a global need and a major political force. As in the Conference on the Law of the Sea, the delegates realized that only a beginning had been made, and that the problem required the continuous and vigilant attention of the United Nations and its member states.

In November 1974, most of the world's nations gathered in Rome on the occasion of the first World Food Conference in history, sponsored by one of the United Nations' specialized agencies, the Food and Agriculture Organization. The delegates met under the specter of famine in Africa and on the Indian subcontinent and amid reports that the world's food reserves had reached levels that were dangerously low. Flood, drought, and fertilizer shortages had created grain shortages that were estimated at 20 million tons. The United States, Canada, and Australia agreed to make emergency food supplies available on a short-term basis. The most concrete long-term achievement of the Rome Conference was the establishment of a World Food Council, which was to serve as an umbrella organization to funnel food and money to needy nations. Donor nations consisting of the "old rich" of the industrialized West and the "new rich" of the oil-producing areas agreed to provide both food and money to ensure that 10 million tons of food would be shipped annually to the needy nations. The conference also accepted a proposal by Secretary of State Kissinger for a system of nationally held but internationally coordinated grain banks for emergency needs in natural disasters. The conference also adopted a declaration accepting the removal of the scourge of hunger and malnutrition as the objective of the international community as a whole. All things considered, the Rome meeting signified the beginning of a global survival pact between the rich and the poor nations of the world.

The global conferences held under the UN's aegis in 1974 were an impressive beginning. They were primarily diagnostic in nature and tried to focus attention on the most dangerous illnesses of Planet Earth. In some cases, as in Bucharest and in Rome, there were attempts to prescribe a cure even though the sovereign states gathered there insisted on the right of final decision. What emerged with clarity and force, however, was the new insight that the real divisions in the world of the 1970s and 1980s were no longer between capitalists and Communists, or white and nonwhite, young and old, or even rich and poor, but between those who could see only the interests of a limited group and those who could see the interests of mankind as a whole. The 1970s saw the beginnings, through the United Nations, of a world environment policy, a world energy policy, a world food policy, and a world population policy, to bring man and nature into balance.

The "planetary management" movement continued to gather momentum throughout the 1970s. In 1975, a global conference was held in Mexico City to raise the status of women throughout the world. At a "Habitat" Conference, held in Vancouver, Canada, in 1976, delegates pondered the question why, all over the world, people tended to migrate from rural areas to urban centers. And in 1977, a conference took place in Nairobi, Kenya, to mobilize the world in a battle against the creation and spread of deserts.

While skeptics have tended to dismiss these conferences as little more than global debating sessions, this seems too bleak an assessment. Whatever the achievements or failures of this form of "planetary management" in the first decade of its existence, the global "town meetings" represent the first evolutionary pooling of the world of its intellectual and financial resources in the battle against dangers that are common to all of humanity. They are the first gropings by the passengers of Spaceship Earth toward a common survival policy. The disruptions of the 1980s will no doubt underline with even greater force the need for "planetary management."

Financing the United Nations System

Before attempting a general evaluation of the United Nations system a word must be said about financing, especially in view of the fact that this issue threw the Organization into a major crisis in the early 1960s, and again in the early 1970s. While the United Nations was engaged in major peace-keeping responsibilities, there was never a shortage of Cassandras predicting that the Organization would end with a bang. However, during the height of the UN Operation in the Congo there existed a real possibility that it might end with a whimper. A fiscal crisis developed in the early 1960s that became a threat to the very life of the Organization. The heart of the crisis lay squarely in two operations that the United Nations had mounted to keep the peace: the United Nations Emergency Force in the Middle East (UNEF) in 1956 and the United Nations Congo Force (ONUC) in 1960.

Altogether, the UN system spends a little over $2 billion annually—or a fraction of what it takes to run the New York City government for a year. First, there is the regular assessed budget for the normal day-to-day expenses of the Organization, amounting to about $500 million a year. Second, there are the assessed budgets of the specialized agencies, which come to roughly twice that sum. Third, there are the special voluntary programs such as the Children's Fund, which subsist solely on the generosity of governments' and private citizens' voluntary contributions, amounting to approximately another $500 million a year for four programs.

Finally there are the expenses for peace-keeping operations. The UN Operation in the Congo (ONUC) cost the United Nations roughly $120 million a year and the expenses of the UN Emergency Force (UNEF) which patrolled parts of the Arab-Israeli border between 1956 and 1967 came to approximately $20 million a year. Since these two major UN peace forces had been responsible for the Organization's fiscal crisis, their financing deserves special analysis.

Never have so many people argued so much about so little money, the reason being that the financial problem of the peace-keeping operations was, in reality, a political problem. The financial crisis was first and foremost a political crisis over the proper role that the UN was to play in the national policies of its member states. And only secondarily was it a crisis over the financial burdens of UN membership.

When the General Assembly authorized the establishment of UNEF in 1956, Dag Hammarskjöld urged that a special account be set up to finance the force as a collective responsibility of the entire membership. Most of the Western members supported the Secretary-General in this view, but the Soviet bloc asserted that the "aggressors" should pay, namely Britain, France, and Israel. Between these two opposing views, yet a third emerged: most of the new nations claimed that everyone should pay something, but that the Great Powers, which had special privileges under the Charter, should also shoulder special responsibilities and pick up the major portion of the bill. This "rebate formula" won the day: the costs of UNEF were assessed upon the membership, but the underdeveloped nations were given rebates of 50 percent and the wealthier nations were invited to make up the deficits through voluntary contributions.

During the next few years, however, deficits gradually developed. The Soviet Union, for example, opposed the force on political grounds and hence was unwilling to pay. And many of the smaller nations, though approving of the force, claimed that they were unable to pay even their reduced assessments. By 1960, when the Congo Force was created, the problem of arrears had all the earmarks of a major crisis.

The problem of paying for the $120 million ONUC budget brought the United Nations to the brink of bankruptcy. The Secretary-General once again supported the principle of collective responsibility. This time the Western nations broke ranks. France was unwilling to pay and joined the Soviet Union in its political opposition. The majority of the membership agreed to another rebate formula, but this time the reductions granted the poorer states reached 80 percent.

The deficits now began to mount sharply. Two permanent members were unwilling to pay, and over half the membership claimed incapacity to pay. By late 1961 the UN debt approached the $100 million mark, and the General Assembly was forced to take emergency action. First, it authorized a $200 million bond issue and invited governments to subscribe, hoping to tide the peace forces over until a more permanent solution could be found. And second, it requested an Advisory Opinion of the World Court as to the legal status of the peace force assessments. (For a full discussion of this opinion, see Chapter 9.) The response to the bond issue was fairly generous. By 1963 sixty governments had purchased approximately three fourths of the total subscription, with the United States buying half of the total amount. This made it possible to meet the costs of the two forces until early 1963 without having to assess the membership during that period. The Court Opinion, as we have seen in the preceding chapter, did not persuade the Soviet Union and France to clear their accounts, but did elicit payments from numerous smaller nations, totaling over $6 million.

With the bond money exhausted, the General Assembly had to meet in emergency session in May 1963. It appropriated an amount of $42,500,000 for the two peace forces for the last six months of 1963 and granted a 55 percent reduction to the developing countries. In December it appropriated $17,750,-000 for UNEF for 1964, but decided to allot only $15 million to carry ONUC until the end of June 1964. The majority of the members were in no mood to continue massive peace-keeping operations indefinitely. The combined cash appropriations for UNEF and ONUC for 1964 amounted to less than one fourth of those appropriated for 1963.

In keeping with its increasingly conservative mood, the General Assembly gradually retreated from the principle of collective responsibility for the funding of peace-keeping operations. Thus, in 1962 the costs of the UN Temporary Executive Authority in West New Guinea (UNTEA) were divided evenly between the two direct beneficiaries, the Netherlands and Indonesia, and in 1963 the costs of a UN Observer Group sent to Yemen were split between Egypt and Saudi Arabia. And in 1964, the costs of the UN Peace Force dispatched to Cyprus had to be raised through voluntary contributions.

Finally, in 1964, the United States and the Soviet Union had a major showdown over the payments for UNEF and ONUC. The United States insisted that every member state that was in arrears for more than two years would have no vote in the General Assembly under Article 19 of the Charter. The Soviet Union rejected this view and was supported by France in the case of ONUC. The United States, despite strenuous efforts, was unable to muster enough support in the General Assembly for its strict interpretation of Article 19. An impasse resulted that produced the famous "voteless" Nineteenth Session. Finally, in August 1965, Ambassador Arthur J. Goldberg abandoned this position, but declared that the United States, too, would henceforth reserve its right not to pay for peace-keeping operations of which it disapproved. Thus, the assessment principle, the financial bedrock of collective responsibility in peace-keeping, was, temporarily at least, defeated.

At the heart of the financial crisis was, of course, the fact that no power, least of all a great power, would adopt or easily pay for a policy that it considered inimical to its national interest. Thus, the United States supported the peace forces essentially because it found them compatible with its own national goals. Yet the question might well be raised as to what United States policy toward ONUC might have been if Kasavubu instead of Lumumba had been killed. And the Soviet Union opposed the peace forces because UNEF challenged the formation of a Soviet bridgehead in the Middle East and ONUC forced the liquidation of a Soviet bridgehead in the Congo. To sum up, the positions of the major powers had relatively little to do with finances per se. In the case of the middle and smaller powers, money per se played a far larger and, in some instances, a decisive role. Hence, while the financial crisis of UNEF and ONUC was caused primarily by the political attitude of the few, it was deepened considerably by the real or alleged financial limitations of the many.

After the seating of the People's Republic of China in the United Nations, it was the turn of the United States to regard UN finances with a more penurious eye. In the wake of a popular wave of anti-UN feeling in 1972, the House Appropriations Committee, without consulting any of the organs of the United Nations, moved to reduce the American contribution to the regular budget from 31 percent to 25 percent. In view of the fact that under the UN Charter only the General Assembly had the right to determine the assessments for the regular budget, this unilateral action was widely interpreted as illegal. On sober second thought, the United States brought the question of its contribution before the General Assembly in the fall of 1972. Reluctantly, the world body approved the reduction of the American contribution to 25 percent. The impact of the American move on the UN treasury was serious but not catastrophic since the admission of the two Germanys to the United Nations in 1973 more than made up the difference. China, too, in an unprecedented move, offered to raise its contribution to the regular budget from 3 to 7 percent over a period of several years.

By the late 1970s, the financing of the three peace-keeping operations was determined exclusively by the Security Council. The Cyprus Force continued to subsist solely on the basis of voluntary contributions, but the assessment principle was applied once again to the two new peace forces in the Middle East. The Soviet Union made a contribution for the first time to UNEF II and to UNDOF in 1973 and 1974 respectively. China expressed its ambivalence toward the United Nations' role in the Middle East by refusing to pay for the two forces. In 1979, UNEF II was terminated because the peace treaty between Israel and Egypt had rendered it unnecessary. Thus, in the 1980s, the finances of the United Nations were not in the desperate straits in which they found themselves during the 1960s. A shortage of funds continued to plague the Organization as virtually a chronic affliction.

In the last analysis, the difficulties that continue to plague the financial structure of the United Nations are largely symptoms of the great political rifts that characterize the contemporary international scene. The United States and British threats, in 1984, to withdraw from UNESCO within two years, ostensibly in protest against wasteful financial practices, was a case in point. The underlying reason was the Anglo-American objection to UNESCO's anti-Western philosophical bias. The quest for technical formulas and legal or fiscal remedies will probably not succeed unless it is preceded by more fundamental political accommodation. Such accommodation must await a greater degree of harmony among the differing conceptions of what member states want the United Nations to be: a conference forum with no executive or legislative powers—which is the goal of those wishing to "walk backwards into the future"; an organization with very limited and carefully circumscribed executive powers—which, with variations, is the view of most member states; or an organization of increasing independence and authority—more than the mere sum total of its parts—which was the aim of Secretary-General Hammarskjöld when he first defended the financing of peace forces as a collective responsibility of the entire membership.[19]

THE UNITED NATIONS IN PERSPECTIVE

We are now ready to attempt a somewhat more general analysis of the United Nations family. A look at the record of each of the principal organs shows clearly that in no case have the hopes of the United Nations' founders been realized completely. Each organ has developed a life of its own, often quite different from the original conception, and has made its own unique contribution.

The record of the Security Council is uneven. It has not attained the goal of collective security, but the Great Powers have often been able to agree on investing the Secretary-General with significant responsibilities for keeping the peace. The General Assembly has certainly not become the world's parliament, but has shown a capacity for improvisation far greater than any of the UN's founders would have dared to predict. It has also shown a remarkable talent for international law-making, and it continues to be the last remaining global forum in which the two great political struggles are waged in an atmosphere of parliamentarianism. By the early 1980s, however, the Third World majority had become so commanding that the Western nations felt outnumbered. While a generation earlier small nations had found it difficult to prevent great powers from making wars, by the 1980s the great powers had discovered the need to restrain small powers from starting wars that might engulf the superpowers. The war between Iraq and Iran was a case in point. Neither ECOSOC nor the specialized agencies have realized the original functionalist hope, since most economic, social, and cultural work has been too permeated with political significance. But the proliferation of functional activities under the aegis of ECOSOC has yielded a multitude of global "good works" of unprecedented magnitude and unquestioned value. While colonial dependencies never became "sacred trusts of civilization," the trusteeship system has doubtless contributed to the peaceful liquidation of Western colonialism. But unless new trusts are added, the Trusteeship Council may disappear from the United Nations family. The World Court's role has been modest. It has not been able to contribute much to global order-building but has managed to consolidate the gains of international law in the Western world. Of all the United Nations organs, the Office of the Secretary-General has come closest to approximating the conception of the framers of the Charter. It has, indeed, become the repository of an invaluable new treasure—international statesmanship.

In 1956, the United Nations invented the concept of a peace force. Since then more than 300,000 men have seen service as "soldiers without enemies" in five UN peace forces: three in the Middle East, one in Cyprus, and one in Africa. While none of these small peace forces could ever stop a war, they have nonetheless served as valuable buffers between contending armies.

Lately, the United Nations has been the object of a great deal of criticism in many quarters. Especially after the General Assembly passed the anti-Zionist resolution, the UN's popularity in the West declined precipitously. Its alleged impotence in dealing with political crises is also often blamed for its declining reputation. This criticism overlooks the fact that many disputes are brought to the UN only when the crisis has become acute and violence has already erupted. Nations all too frequently "dump" quarrels into the lap of the UN when they literally no longer know what else to do. Thus, they make of the UN a kind of "receiver in bankruptcy" and then proceed to blame the Organization for that sad state of affairs. In that sense, there is nothing wrong with the United Nations except its membership.

Given such adverse conditions, the UN has actually done rather well. But its task as crisis manager would be a great deal easier if nations submitted disputes *before* they went critical. It is wiser to deal with crises when they are still manageable than to engage in brilliant rescue operations at the brink of disaster. In that sense, the planetary conferences on population, food, resources and development, environment, and the laws of the sea held under the UN's aegis during the 1970s and 1980s were responses made in time by the world community to crises that endangered mankind as a whole.

In the final analysis, the most striking characteristics of the United Nations have been its *elasticity* and *adaptability*. The League of Nations, which did not subscribe to as eclectic an approach to peace as the United Nations, crumbled after the first onslaughts. The United Nations, on the other hand, has developed multiple lines of defense against war. In its short life span it has been tested at least as severely as was the League of Nations. It has managed to respond to a multitude of challenges with amazing resiliency, an unmatched gift for innovation and improvisation, and a realistic sense of the politically possible.

The fact that the United Nations has survived four turbulent strife-torn decades is in itself a political miracle.

REFERENCES

1. For a full development of the functional approach to peace, see David Mitrany, *A Working Peace System.* London: Royal Institute of International Affairs, 1946.
2. Norman J. Padelford, "The Use of the Veto," *International Organization*, June 1948, pp. 231–232.
3. Quoted by Arthur N. Holcombe, "The Role of Politics in the Organization of Peace," *Organizing Peace in the Nuclear Age.* New York: New York University Press, 1959, p. 97.
4. Petition by E. M. Attiogbe, spokesman for the Ewe tribe, cited by John MacLaurin, *The United Nations and Power Politics.* London: Allen and Unwin, 1951, pp. 354–355.
5. Inis L. Claude, Jr., *Swords into Plowshares.* 2nd ed. New York: Random House, 1959, p. 369.
6. *Ibid.*, pp. 370–372.
7. Cited by H. G. Nicholas, *The United Nations as a Political Institution.* New York: Oxford University Press, 1959, p. 153.
8. United Nations Security Council, *Official Records*, Eleventh Year, 751st Meeting, October 31, 1956, pp. 1–2.
9. *The New York Times*, August 10, 1960.
10. *New York Herald Tribune*, September 27, 1960.
11. Address by President Kennedy to the General Assembly, September 25, 1961, in *Documents on American Foreign Relations 1961*, pp. 473–484.
12. Trygve Lie, *In the Cause of Peace.* New York: Macmillan, 1954, p. 80.
13. House Congressional Resolution 262, 83rd Congress, August 20, 1954.
14. Cited by Claude, *op. cit.*, p. 204.
15. Bernard D. Nossiler, "Parkinson's Law at the UN," *New York Times Magazine*, November 23, 1980, p. 60.
16. Cited in Wilder Foote, ed., *Dag Hammarskjold: Servant of Peace, A Selection of His Speeches and Statements.* New York: Harper & Row, 1962, p. 351.
17. *The New York Times*, June 11, 1972.

18. *Ibid.*, November 11, 1972.
19. For a full analysis of the UN's financial problems, see John G. Stoessinger et al., *Financing the United Nations System.* Washington, D.C.: Brookings Institution, 1964.

BIBLIOGRAPHY

Akrasanee, Narongchai, et al. *Asean and the Pacific Community.* Jakarta: Centre for Strategic and International Studies, 1984.

Alcock, Anthony. *History of the International Labor Organization.* New York: Octagon Books, 1971.

Bailey, Sydney D. *The Procedure of the UN Security Council.* New York: Oxford University Press, 1975.

Barkenbus, Jack N. *Deep Seabed Resources.* New York: Free Press, 1979.

Beichman, Arnold. *The "Other" State Department.* New York: Basic Books, 1968.

Boyd, Andrew. *Fifteen Men on a Powder Keg.* Briarcliff Manor, N.Y.: Stein and Day, 1971.

Brook, David. *Preface to Peace.* Washington, D.C.: Public Affairs Press, 1964.

Brown, Lester R. *World Without Borders.* New York: Random House, 1972.

Brown, Seyom, et al. *Regimes for the Ocean, Outer Space, and Weather.* Washington, D.C.: Brookings Institution, 1977.

Burns, Arthur Lee, and Heathcote, Nina. *Peace-Keeping by UN Forces: From Suez to the Congo.* New York: Praeger, 1963.

Buzan, Barry. *Seabed Politics.* New York: Praeger, 1976.

Claude, Inis L., Jr. *Swords into Plowshares.* 4th ed. New York: Random House, 1971.

Cox, Arthur M. *Prospects for Peacekeeping.* Washington, D.C.: Brookings Institution, 1967.

Cox, Robert W., and Jacobson, Harold K. *The Anatomy of Influence: Decision-Making in International Organization.* New Haven, Conn.: Yale University Press, 1973.

Dayal, Rajeshwar. *Mission for Hammarskjöld: The Congo Crisis.* Princeton, N.J.: Princeton University Press, 1976.

Denoon, David B. H., ed. *The New International Economic Order. A U.S. Response.* New York: New York University Press, 1979.

Eichelberger, Clark M. *Organizing for Peace.* New York: Harper, 1977.

El-Ayouty, Yassin. *The United Nations and Decolonization.* The Hague: Nijhoff, 1971.

Falk, Richard A. *This Endangered Planet.* New York: Random House, 1971.

Finchman, Charles, and Van Rensburg, William. *Bread upon the Waters: The Developing Law of the Sea.* Jerusalem: Turtledove, 1980.

Finger, Seymour Maxwell. *Your Man at the U.N.* New York: Rawson, Wade, 1980.

Foote, Wilder T., ed. *Dag Hammarskjold: Servant of Peace.* New York: Harper & Row, 1962.

Galenson, Walter. *The International Labor Organization: An American View.* Madison: University of Wisconsin Press, 1981.

Gati, Toby Trister, ed. *The U.S., The U.N., and the Management of Global Change.* New York: New York University Press, 1983.

Goodrich, Leland. *Korea: A Study of United States Policy in the United Nations.* New York: Harper, 1956.

———. *The United Nations in a Changing World.* New York: Columbia University Press, 1974.

Gordenker, Leon, ed. *The United Nations in International Politics.* Princeton, N.J.: Princeton University Press, 1971.

————. *The UN Secretary-General and the Maintenance of Peace.* New York: Columbia University Press, 1967.

Gordon, King. *UN in the Congo.* New York: Carnegie Endowment for International Peace, 1962.

Haas, Ernst, ed. *Scientist and World Order: The Uses of Technological Knowledge in International Organizations.* Berkeley: University of California Press, 1978.

Hazzard, Shirley. *Defeat of an Ideal: A Study of the Self-Destruction of the United Nations.* Boston: Atlantic-Little, Brown, 1973.

Hiscocks, Richard. *The Security Council: A Study in Adolescence.* New York: Free Press, 1974.

Hoggart, Richard. *An Ideal and Its Servants: UNESCO from Within.* New York: Oxford University Press, 1978.

Jackson, Richard L. *The Non-Aligned, the U.N. and the Superpowers.* New York: Praeger, 1983.

James, Alan. *The Politics of Peace Keeping.* New York: Praeger, 1969.

Jessup, Philip C., and Taubenfeld, Howard J. *Controls for Outer Space.* New York: Columbia University Press, 1959.

Kay, David A. *The New Nations in the United Nations, 1960–1967.* New York: Columbia University Press, 1970.

Kim, Samuel S. *China, the United Nations, and World Order.* Princeton, N.J.: Princeton University Press, 1979.

Lall, Arthur. *The UN and the Middle East Crisis, 1967.* New York: Columbia University Press, 1968.

Lefever, Ernest. *Crisis in the Congo.* Washington, D.C.: Brookings Institution, 1965.

Leontieff, Wassilly, ed. *The Future of the World Economy: A United Nations Study.* New York: Oxford University Press, 1977.

Lie, Trygve. *In the Cause of Peace.* New York: Macmillan, 1954.

Lipgens, Walter. *A History of European Integration, 1945–1947.* New York: Clarendon Press/Oxford University Press, 1982.

Meron, Theodor. *The United Nations Secretariat.* Lexington, Mass.: Lexington Books, 1977.

Mitrany, David. *A Working Peace System.* Chicago: Quadrangle Press, 1966.

Murphy, John F. *The United Nations and the Control of International Violence.* Totowa, N.J.: Allanheld, Osmun, 1983.

O'Brien, Conor Cruise. *To Katanga and Back.* New York: Simon and Schuster, 1963.

Olson, Robert K. *U.S. Foreign Policy and the New International Economic Order: Negotiating Global Problems, 1974–1981.* Boulder, Colo.: Westview Press, 1981.

Orbach, William W. *To Keep the Peace: The United Nations Condemnatory Resolution.* Lexington: University Press of Kentucky, 1977.

Rikhye, Indar, et al. *The Thin Blue Line: International Peacekeeping and Its Future.* New Haven, Conn.: Yale University Press, 1974.

Rosner, Gabriella. *The United Nations Emergency Force.* New York: Columbia University Press, 1963.

Rothstein, Robert L. *Global Bargaining: Unctad and the Quest for a New International Economic Order.* Princeton, N.J.: Princeton University Press, 1979.

Rovine, Arthur W. *The First Fifty Years.* Leiden: Sijthoff, 1970.

Rubenstein, Alvin Z., and Ginsburgs, George, eds. *Soviet and American Policies in the United Nations: A Twenty-five Year Perspective.* New York: New York University Press, 1971.

Saurant, Karl P., and Hasenpflug, Hajo, eds. *The New International Economic Order: Confrontation or Cooperation Between North and South?* Boulder, Colo.: Westview Press, 1977.

Schachter, Oscar. *Sharing the World's Resources.* New York: Columbia University Press, 1976.

Scott, George. *The Rise and Fall of the League of Nations.* New York: Macmillan, 1974.

Sewell, James Patrick. *Functionalism in World Politics.* Princeton, N.J.: Princeton University Press, 1966.
———. *UNESCO and World Politics: Engaging in International Relations.* Princeton, N.J.: Princeton University Press, 1975.
Stoessinger, John G. "Atoms for Peace: The International Atomic Energy Agency," in Arthur N. Holcombe, ed., *Organizing Peace in the Nuclear Age.* New York: New York University Press, 1959, pp. 117–233.
———, et al. *Financing the United Nations System.* Washington, D.C.: Brookings Institution, 1964.
———. *The Refugee and the World Community.* Minneapolis: University of Minnesota Press, 1956.
———. *The United Nations and the Superpowers.* 4th ed. New York: Random House, 1977.
Stone, Julius. *Conflict Through Consensus: United Nations Approaches to Aggression.* Baltimore: Johns Hopkins Press, 1966.
U.N. Security Council. *U.N. Security Council Resolution 242: A Case Study in Diplomatic Ambiguity.* Washington: Institute for the Study of Diplomacy, School of Foreign Service, Georgetown, 1981.
Urquhart, Brian. *Hammarskjöld.* New York: Knopf, 1972.
U Thant. *View from the U.N.* New York: Doubleday, 1978.
Wainhouse, David W., ed. *International Peace Observation.* Baltimore: Johns Hopkins Press, 1966.
Waldheim, Kurt. *Building the Future Order.* New York: Free Press, 1980.
———. *The Challenge of Peace.* New York: Rawson, Wade, 1980.
Ward, Barbara. *Progress for a Small Planet.* New York: Norton, 1979.
Wilson, Thomas W., Jr. *International Environmental Action: A Global Survey.* New York: Dunellen, 1971.
Zacher, Marc W. *Dag Hammarskjöld's United Nations.* New York: Columbia University Press, 1970.
Zuijdwijk, Ton. *Petitioning the United Nations: A Study in Human Rights.* New York: St. Martin's, 1982.

Chapter 11

Regionalism and Political Order

Ours is essentially a tragic age, so we refuse to take it tragically. The cataclysm has happened, we are among the ruins, we start to build up new little habitats, to have new little hopes. It is rather hard work: there is now no smooth road into the future: but we go round, or scramble over the obstacles. We've got to live, no matter how many skies have fallen.

D. H. LAWRENCE *Lady Chatterley's Lover*

THE IDEA OF REGIONALISM

Regionalism may be defined as a grouping of three or more states whose goal is the formation of a distinct political entity. A regional arrangement is a voluntary association of sovereign states that have developed fairly elaborate organizational tools to forge among them such bonds of unity. A purely military alliance among nations that do not pursue the goal of political order-building is not a regional arrangement. The Triple Entente was a purely military pact, but NATO, though primarily devised for defensive purposes, may be considered a regional arrangement since it has developed purposes other than military.

We have seen the role of regional arrangements as instruments of the international struggle for power. We shall now analyze their role as contributors to international order. Before we proceed to representative case studies, however, we must examine the concept of regionalism as a form of order-building.

Regionalism is based on the assumption that universalism is today still premature and too ambitious. Those who feel that the time is not yet ripe for order-building on a global scale want to use regionalism as an essential stepping-stone. They envisage the development of political unity within delimited geographic areas, which could then be used as building blocks in the construction of a future, world-wide political order. The classic statement of this idea was that of Clarence K. Streit, who, in his *Union Now*, proposed the unification of democratic countries in order to form the nucleus for a future world government. Streit conceived of regionalism as a vital intermediate stage in an organic evolution toward the more ambitious goal of globalism. Other propo-

328

nents of regionalism, however, have felt that in view of the continuing heterogeneity of the world, it as yet makes little sense to speak of a world-wide political order at all. First, they insist, a universal framework of values and a global sense of community must be developed.

Regionalist thinkers have differed not only on goals but also on methods. Some have preferred the federal approach to order-building. This approach has emphasized the necessity for participating states to yield parts of their sovereignty to a "supranational" body. The latter would then, in effect, have some of the powers of a new state and its decisions would be binding on the member governments. The federal approach has tended to concentrate especially on the legal instruments of order-building, such as constitutions. Still other regionalists have advocated the functional method, and have pointed out the necessity for economic, social, and cultural cooperation as a prerequisite to political integration. The functionalists have tended to shy away from the formation of "supranational" organs and, instead, have encouraged the development of as many forms of intergovernmental collaboration as possible.

We have seen earlier how little we know about the nature and the causes of war. This is, of course, simply another way of admitting how little we know about the process of political order-building. Little empirical work has been done to examine the claims of the regionalists in relation to world order, or the approach of the federalists as opposed to that of the functionalists. Most of the arguments advanced have been based on the dubious foundations of historical analogy, popular belief, and dogmatic preference. There is ample descriptive and analytical literature about the regional and global arrangements that already exist, but relatively little material on the *process* whereby regional orders are actually built. One of the most illuminating studies of this kind was prepared by a group of scholars at Princeton University.[1] This study made a careful analysis of ten cases in which regional order-building had attained the level of "security-communities," a condition in which warfare among the members had become so highly improbable as to be practically out of the question. The authors distinguished between two types of security-community: one that had resulted from a formal merger of previously independent units into a single larger unit—like the United States; and a second, of a more pluralistic nature, which retained the legal independence of separate governments. This pioneering study in the formation of security-communities affords some penetrating insights into the dynamics of regionalism.

The Princeton study cast serious doubt on the validity of several popular beliefs that have long served as premises for regionalist thinking. The study exploded the notion of an organic, almost automatic evolution of the world into larger units; in fact, the authors pointed out that the closer they got historically to modern conditions and to our own time, the more difficult it was to find the successful formation of security-communities. Nor did the widely held belief that the establishment of one successful "security-community" would have a bandwagon effect stand up under scrutiny. Even more important, the authors placed in question the popular notion that a principal motive for the regional integration of states had been the fear of anarchy or of warfare among themselves. These important negative findings were matched by equally significant positive insights into the nature of the integrative process.

The authors isolated several conditions that they considered essential for the establishment of regional security-communities. In all successful cases they found a compatibility of values and expectations among the participating units. These common values were most helpful when they were incorporated in similar types of political institutions, thus creating a common political way of life. The authors further discovered that the competition between the federalist and the functionalist approaches to political order-building was largely irrelevant to the dynamics of regional integration. While they did find that the establishment of pluralistic security-communities through functionalism was somewhat easier than the creation of amalgamated security-communities through federalism, the difference was not considered crucial. What did seem decisive for the outcome was whether the integrative process was accompanied by widespread expectations and experiences of joint rewards for the participating states. In this regard, the functional technique seemed somewhat more successful, since it usually implied strong economic ties that, in the cases where regionalism proved successful, in turn led to economic rewards for the member states. Another essential condition was seen in a marked increase in political and administrative capabilities of the participating states, as well as in the presence of superior economic growth within the region. Other preconditions for the establishment of security-communities appeared to be the presence of a multiplicity of unbroken links of social communication and considerable mobility of people among the states concerned. Finally, a degree of mutual predictability of behavior was considered an essential prerequisite.

In addition to these general conditions, the authors developed the concept of "take-off," which they used to describe the conditions most favorable to the *beginning* of regional integration. The study pointed out that nations have been more likely to begin the process when they have felt strong rather than when they have seen themselves as weak. The authors also discovered that a military alliance usually turned out to be a relatively poor pathway toward building a security-community, since "the presence of excessive military commitments—excessive in the sense that they were felt at the time to bring considerably more burdens than rewards—had a disintegrative effect."[2] Finally, the study pointed out that not all security-communities were "final," but that, indeed, it was possible to cross, recross, or even stand poised upon a broad threshold of integration.

A great deal of research has taken place in the fields of international organization and regional integration since the Princeton study appeared. One particularly fine study was *Power and Interdependence* by Robert O. Keohane and Joseph S. Nye.[3] In it the authors explored the costs and benefits of mutual dependence in international relationships. They wisely pointed out that rising interdependence was not creating a brave new world of cooperation to replace the bad old world of international conflict. "As every parent of small children knows," the authors noted, "baking a larger pie does not stop disputes over the size of the slices."[4] Interdependence has conferred some benefits upon states, but it has also made them more vulnerable. The energy dependency of oil-consuming states on OPEC is only one example of such new vulnerability. Interdependence is, therefore, not an unmixed blessing.

These pioneering studies have forced us to reexamine a number of widely held beliefs about both the relationship of regionalism to world order and the dynamics of the regional order-building process in general. None of the ten cases selected for the Princeton study went beyond World War II. We shall therefore attempt to apply a similar empirical analysis to some of the representative regional political groupings of our current period. We must remember, of course, that the process of regional integration does not proceed only on a political level. Most of the existing regional entities have followed a whole range of pathways to unity. But each has tended to emphasize one approach more than others. NATO, for example, has stressed military bonds of unity; the European Coal and Steel Community and the Common Market have operated largely in the realm of economics; and the Council of Europe has stressed the principles of political association. The regional arrangements that are based primarily upon economic and military premises are discussed elsewhere in this volume. (For an analysis of military arrangements, see Chapters 6 and 12; economic arrangements are discussed in Chapters 7 and 13.) The present analysis will concern itself with those regional instruments of order-building that are *primarily* political in character.

POLITICAL ORDER-BUILDING IN EUROPE

The Council of Europe

The ideal of a politically united Europe has its roots in antiquity. It makes its appearance in the political and philosophical literature of each major epoch in European civilization. But at no time prior to our own era had the movement for European unity been a popular one, capturing strong and widespread support. Indeed, the European idea had remained largely an abstraction, the preserve of philosophers and visionaries. Only after World War I did it enter into the thinking of statesmen and diplomats as a concrete possibility and, perhaps, even as a necessity. The Balkanization of Europe in the wake of World War I made many thoughtful observers fearful of the danger of a new struggle and so led them to look and work toward the gradual acceptance by the sovereign states of Europe of a common political mechanism. Foremost among the advocates of a united Europe was a count of the Holy Roman Empire, Richard Coudenhove-Kalergi.[5] He first expressed his thoughts in a book, *Pan Europa*, published in 1923, and he organized the first Pan-European congress, in Vienna, which mobilized public opinion for his ideas. The promotional efforts of the count and his followers succeeded, in the inter-war period, in winning over several prominent European statesmen. Aristide Briand of France, one of the great European figures in the League of Nations, and Gustav Stresemann of Germany made European unity a cornerstone of their national policies. But these early efforts were doomed to failure. The death of Stresemann, the

lengthening shadow of Hitler over Europe, and the incapacity of the League of
Nations drove the ideal of European union into temporary eclipse. Yet even
during the darkest days of World War II, statements by the most prominent
European leader of the Allied powers gave indication that the ideal would
emerge with increased vitality once Europe was again at peace. As early as
October 1942, Winston Churchill expressed the hope that

> Hard as it is to say now, I trust that the European family may act unitedly as one
> under a Council of Europe. I look forward to a United States of Europe in which
> the barriers between the nations will be greatly minimized and unrestricted
> travel will be possible. We must try to make this Council of Europe into a really
> effective League, with all the strongest forces woven into its texture, with a High
> Court to adjust disputes, and with armed forces, national or international or
> both, held ready to enforce these decisions and to prevent renewed aggression
> and the preparation of future wars. This Council when created, must eventually
> embrace the whole of Europe, and all the main branches of the European family
> must someday be partners in it.[6]

It had taken a Hitler to compel Europe to take union really seriously. At
war's end, Sir Winston and Count Coudenhove found massive support among
the statesmen of Europe. In May 1948 an attempt was made to organize the
first truly continental demonstration of unity—the Congress of Europe. This
congress, held at The Hague, was the birthplace of the Council of Europe.

It is noteworthy that each of the major European countries produced
statesmen deeply committed to the European Movement. All of them came
from the border lands of their respective countries and all of them shared a
cosmopolitan world view. The list of these European-minded political leaders
is impressive indeed: Konrad Adenauer of Germany, staunch fighter against
the tyranny of Hitler and devoted disciple of Stresemann's European policy;
Leon Blum and Robert Schuman of France, who carried on the tradition of
Briand; Alcide de Gasperi of Italy, who saw in unity the fulfillment of a Christian ideal; Paul-Henri Spaak of Belgium; Sir Winston Churchill, one of the
grand architects of the idea but one who remained ambivalent about the role
of Britain in such a venture; and finally, Count Coudenhove, the pioneer who
had indefatigably prepared the way.

In January 1949 the foreign ministers of the major European powers convened and drafted the Statute of the Council of Europe. The council's primary
goal, as set forth in Article I, was to be the achievement of "a greater unity
between its Members for the purpose of safeguarding and realizing the ideals
and principles which are their common heritage." Progress toward unity was
to proceed on several fronts. The statute listed an extensive range of subjects
that were to be within the competence of the council. Among them were legal
matters, human rights, and cultural and social questions. While no specific reference was made to political questions in the statute, it was clearly implied
that the council was to function as essentially a political body. It was to consist
of a Committee of Ministers whose members were to be the foreign ministers
of the member states and of a Consultative Assembly whose membership was
to be drawn from the legislatures of the participating countries. The original

membership of the council comprised ten states: Belgium, Denmark, France, Ireland, Italy, Luxembourg, Holland, Norway, Sweden, and Great Britain. Since then, seven more have been added: Austria, West Germany, Greece, Iceland, Cyprus, Turkey, and Switzerland. The council's membership policy was conceived as open-ended and it was hoped that it might serve as a first step toward a United States of Europe.

It is an ancient truth that organizational realities tend to be far more modest than the ideas that underlie them. In view of its broad membership base, it is not surprising that both of the council's main organs have witnessed a continuing struggle between two quite differing conceptions of what European unity should be and how it might best be achieved. On the one hand have been the "federalists," favoring a "supranational" organ with real powers; on the other have been the "functionalists," who have advocated the more traditional "transnational" path to unification. The former have consistently urged that the member states yield more of their sovereignty to the council, whereas the latter have jealously sought to preserve their sovereign rights. The preferability of the supranational approach has been defended by France, West Germany, Italy, and the Benelux countries, which together have come to be known as The Six. More conservative, the transnationalists have been led by Great Britain, which has continued to see itself not only as a European power but, at the same time, as the leader of the Commonwealth. This British ambivalence toward Europe has been aptly expressed in a classic statement of Sir Winston Churchill: "We have our own dreams and our own tasks. We are linked but not comprised. We are with Europe, but not of it. We are interested and associated but not absorbed."[7]

The council's organizational structure reflects a clear-cut victory for the more conservative approach. Neither the Committee of Ministers nor the Consultative Assembly has supranational powers. Both are intergovernmental arrangements in which sovereignty has been entirely preserved. Any resolutions are merely recommendations and must be ratified by the participating member states before they become binding. The Committee of Ministers is the executive organ, consisting of one representative from each member state. In principle, these should be the respective foreign ministers; in practice, they have frequently been alternates. All important decisions are made unanimously, "in the belief that this procedure serves the interests of European unity better than the imposition of the will of the majority on a reluctant minority."[8] Once decisions are reached, the ministers are to take the initiative for their adoption in their respective national governments.

The council's deliberative organ has been the Consultative Assembly. Its membership has comprised 132 delegates, with representation ranging from three in the case of Iceland and Luxembourg to eighteen for France, Great Britain, and West Germany. The assembly has borne only a superficial resemblance to a national parliament. Although there have developed various party groupings, the assembly has, in effect, been an assembly of individuals rather than a body of legislators representing constituencies.

One is tempted, in the light of the above, to conclude that the council has

been little more than a debating society of European parliamentarians on va-
cation in Strasbourg and speaking for no one but themselves. Indeed, such a
judgment could be supported by some of the facts. For one thing, the mandate
of the council has been so broad that it has frequently led to vagueness. The
tendency to make unity a goal in itself has led to an absence of specific pro-
gramming. Moreover, while the delegates have frequently been enthusiastic
about proposals in Strasbourg, they have suffered from inertia when it came to
taking up the same matters in their own parliaments. The main weakness of
the Council of Europe has thus not been its lack of supranational authority but
its lack of a clearly defined program. The capacity to deal with everything in
breadth has led to few accomplishments in depth. Nevertheless, the organization's record is not without its significant positive achievements. For example,
there has developed in the council an interesting tendency toward transnational party caucusing. The leaders of the Italian Center Party, for instance,
have gotten along better with their political counterparts in the German and
French delegations than with their respective opposition parties at home.
Though the contribution of this phenomenon to regional order-building cannot yet be accurately assessed, other achievements of the council have been
more concrete. Its most significant accomplishment has been in the field of
human rights. Intensive debates in both organs of the council led to a deep
concern with this subject in the parliaments of the member staffs. In effect, the
Council of Europe thus provided a springboard for the adoption of the European Convention of Human Rights. This became a legally binding document
signed and ratified by all members of the council. The following Human Rights
were to be guaranteed:

> Security of persons; exemption from slavery and servitude; freedom from arbi-
> trary arrest, detention or exile; freedom from arbitrary interference in private
> and family life, home and correspondence; freedom of thought, conscience and
> religion; freedom of opinion and expression; freedom of assembly; freedom of as-
> sociation; freedom to unite in trade unions; the right to marry and found a fam-
> ily.[9]

Implementing the provisions of the convention, a European Commission on
Human Rights was created, the first international body established by governments and competent to receive and act on individual petitions concerning
violations of the rights set forth in the convention. Moreover, there was set up
a European Court on Human Rights, whose function was to be the adjudica-
tion of infringements of the convention. These institutions have gone far beyond the purely hortatory Universal Declaration of Human Rights passed by
the United Nations General Assembly. This is due mainly to the regional character of the experiment but also, in some degree, to the impetus provided by
the Council of Europe. The recognition of obligations in the matter of these
rights and freedoms has become the principal condition of membership in the
council.

    As a working reality, the Council of Europe has fallen far short of the am-
bitious conception of the founders of the European Movement. But for all its

vagueness and lack of authority, it has served one vital function: it has remained the only European forum that has included countries neutral in the East-West struggle and in which, therefore, it has been possible to discuss the problems of Europe as a whole. By contrast, the European Parliament, which was constituted for the first time in 1979, only served the ten member states of the European Economic Community. The tension arising from the differences among the council's members have led to fruitful and sometimes tangible results. It has, of course, remained true that the council has been able to do no more than propose policies, leaving to its individual members the choice of adopting policies in question. Yet even this act of proposing has constituted an important encouragement to the member states to pursue their common quest of European political order-building.

NATO

NATO is not only the West's major military instrument in the East-West struggle. It has been, at the same time, intended as a major means for the advancement of European unity. In fact, it was quite clear to the founders of NATO that without strong political bonds the Treaty's effectiveness as a military alliance would be minimal. This was the reason for the inclusion in the NATO Charter of its Article II:

> The Parties will contribute toward the further development of peaceful and friendly international relations by strengthening their free institutions, by bringing about a better understanding of the principles upon which these institutions are founded, and by promoting conditions of stability and well-being.

NATO includes two organs that are to contribute to political integration in the North Atlantic Community. One is the North Atlantic Council, composed of the foreign ministers of the member countries and concerned chiefly with military matters. Yet since the exchange of military intelligence necessary for joint planning has made it almost impossible for members of NATO to go to war against one another, the council's work has profound political implications as well. The other politically significant NATO organ is its unofficial Parliamentarians' Conference. This conference draws its membeship from all fifteen NATO countries and acts as a consultation forum for the coordination of national policies among member states.

The main weakness of NATO's nonmilitary work has been that statesmen have tended to "inform other member countries about decisions of national policy that have already been taken unilaterally, instead of consulting them fully before making decisions."[10] (For an analysis of NATO as a military alliance, see Chapter 6). Clearance in NATO has at times been noticeably absent during the formulation stage of policy. This became tragically clear during the Suez crisis of 1956, when Britain and France failed to consult with the United States. The divergence between American and Anglo-French policies seriously weakened the bonds of NATO and resulted in the adoption by the North Atlantic Council in 1956 of a proposal to establish a Committee of Three to study possibilities for the improvement of consultation procedures among the NATO powers. This committee, consisting of the foreign ministers of Norway, Italy, and Canada, expressed the opinion that NATO had been concerned too much with problems of military strategy and too little with progress toward political unity. The withdrawal of French forces from the NATO integrated command in 1966 further weakened the alliance. As NATO Headquarters were moved from Paris to Brussels, the prospects for strengthening political bonds in the Atlantic Community seemed to recede further into the distance. And when, in 1974, hostilities erupted on Cyprus and strained relations between Greece and Turkey to the breaking point, virtually severing Greece's ties with NATO, political integration in the alliance suffered yet another setback.

In overall perspective, however, the political cohesion of NATO has nevertheless been quite remarkable. It is frequently forgotten that under the NATO Charter, member states are merely obligated to do what they "deem necessary" in case of an outside attack. Moreover, all policy decisions must be reached by unanimous vote. In purely structural terms, national sovereignty looms larger in NATO than in the United Nations Charter, where majority decisions are possible. Hence, as Claude has pointed out, "the flight of security-minded statesmen from the veto-bound Security Council of the United Nations to NATO was not an escape from a primitive to a more advanced form of international organization so far as voting procedures are concerned, for the North Atlantic Treaty permits a much more thoroughgoing application of the veto principle than the Charter provisions concerning the Security Council."[11] The explanation may be found in the fact that political cohesion in NATO, despite all the tensions and all the setbacks, is relatively high. For this reason, NATO as a political reality means more than the structural provisions safeguarding the sovereignty of its member states would seem to indicate.

During the 1970s and 1980s, NATO as a military alliance has come under increasing scrutiny. In the view of many Western analysts, NATO is becoming an alliance in search of a new cause. If it is to survive as a viable entity, its members will have to build unity less on the basis of deterrence and more on the integrative cement of a common political community.

Western European Union

A third major European regional arrangement that has promoted political order-building is the Western European Union (WEU). The European statesmen resuscitated a treaty that had been superseded by NATO. This was the Brussels Treaty of 1948, which had created a joint command for British, French, and Benelux forces. The Brussels Powers agreed that this structure might be expanded to admit Germany and Italy. The latter proposal proved generally acceptable and quickly crystallized into the Western European Union, which came into force in May 1955 after parliamentary ratification by the seven member states.

In terms of supranationality, WEU falls short of military union. There is no fusion of armies nor is there a central organ with decision-making powers in matters of common defense. Each member state continues to have a national army and exercises a veto power over its disposition. WEU's central policy-making organ is its council, composed of the foreign ministers of the seven member states. The more important defense questions, such as the size of the armed forces to be contributed by each member state, must be approved unanimously. But decisions on types of conventional weapons to be used are taken by majority vote in the council. In addition to the council, a deliberative body, the assembly, coordinates the military policies of the seven states. This assembly has a purely advisory status and its members have usually been the same parliamentarians who also attend the meetings of the Consultative Assembly of the Council of Europe.

In sum, WEU has been a useful order-building device. It is a "little NATO" within NATO. Yet, by having succeeded in attracting Britain to its purposes and activities WEU, several years before Britain joined the Common Market in 1971, made a major contribution to the European political order-building process.

If we apply to the Council of Europe, NATO, and WEU the criteria formulated in the Princeton study of the building of security-communities, we see that all three rate rather high. For one thing, all three of these European regional arrangements involve nations with a fairly high compatibility of values, expectations, and political forms. In NATO and WEU, which are held together by the need for common security, the expectation of joint rewards is great. In the Council of Europe, which is concerned more with the goal of unity than with the achievement of tangible returns, it is almost entirely absent. Save for Portugal, moreover, all the nations concerned enjoy relatively high levels of economic development. Mobility of persons is also very considerable, being highest among the nations of WEU and lowest in NATO—owing to the rather restrictive immigration policies of the United States and Canada. On the whole, political integration is fairly high in WEU and NATO, but quite low in the Council of Europe. The crucial factor seems to be the expectation of joint rewards from the integrative process. This is present in the two military alliances but not in the Council of Europe. Yet the authors of the Princeton study have warned that though an outside military threat may provide the original impetus toward political order-building, more permanent unions derive their main support from other factors.[12] This would seem to indicate that the high degree of political integration in NATO and WEU may be transitory unless it is buttressed through specific programs that hold out to the member nations the promise of substantial and sustained rewards of a nonmilitary kind as well. NATO officials seem to have recognized this fact. On the occasion of the thirtieth birthday of the alliance in 1979, all member states stressed the need to forge political, economic, and social bonds in addition to those imposed by the dictates of collective self-defense.

OTHER EXPERIMENTS IN REGIONAL ORDER-BUILDING

The Organization of American States

One of the earliest post–World War II regional arrangements to be established was the Organization of American States (OAS). The treaty, which formalized the solidarity of the Western Hemisphere against both external and internal threats to the peace, was the culmination of a long and arduous road to inter-American political order. The highlights of this history of hemispheric relations are well worth reviewing.

The famous Monroe Doctrine of 1823 declared that the United States reserved to itself the right to act as the protector of Latin America in case of outside aggression:

> We owe it, therefore, to candor, and to the amicable relations existing between the United States and those [European] powers, to declare that we should consider any attempt on their part to extend their system to any portion of this hemisphere as dangerous to our peace and safety.

In 1904 President Theodore Roosevelt interpreted the doctrine to mean that in cases of intra-hemispheric disputes the United States could also exercise the right of "an international police power." This controversial Roosevelt Corollary gave rise to several instances of United States intervention in the Caribbean. In all of these interventions—in Cuba, Haiti, the Dominican Republic, Nicaragua, and Panama—the United States attempted to restore political and economic stability. However, the novel interpretation that the Monroe Doctrine not only forbade intervention from Europe but permitted United States intervention in order to forestall any *possible* European incursion, led to widespread resentment in Latin America. At the turn of the century, the Latin American nations began to exert pressure upon the United States to renounce its claims to intervene. Gradually, these efforts met with success. The Roosevelt Corollary was officially discarded in 1926, and the Good Neighbor Policy initiated by Franklin D. Roosevelt in 1933 put an end to the practice of unilateral intervention. The Axis threat to the Western Hemisphere during World War II consolidated inter-American solidarity even further. And when the Americas emerged victorious, the time was ripe for the conclusion of a regional arrangement dedicated both to the maintenance of reciprocal security and to a common effort toward political order-building.

Accordingly, delegates from the twenty Latin American nations and from the United States met in Rio De Janeiro and drafted the famous Rio Treaty—an Inter-American Treaty of Reciprocal Assistance. Article III, the heart of the treaty, provided that "an armed attack by any state against an American state shall be considered as an attack against all American states." This provision was in essence a recognition of the fact that the Monroe Doctrine had become multilateralized. It also furnished a pattern for the NATO Charter that would be concluded two years later. The drafters of the Rio Pact, unlike the framers of NATO, were not solely concerned with protection against external aggression. Most of the members were equally eager to guard against the possibility of internal schism. The immediate reason for their apprehension was the government of Argentina, which had sided with the Axis during World War II. Argentina was the only member state which wanted a treaty only against aggression by non-American states, but its position was voted down. The Rio Treaty as first constituted in 1947 was primarily an instrument of military security against internal and external attack. A year later, at a conference in Bogotá, Colombia, the pact was further elaborated by the inclusion of provisions for political order-building. This new and sophisticated system, in the words of the then American Secretary of State, George C. Marshall, was to be "the very heart of hemispheric organization." It was named the Organization of American States (OAS).

The structure of the OAS provides for an eclectic approach to political order-building. An annual Assembly of Foreign Ministers constitutes the organization's main organ. The foreign ministers consider all urgent problems of internal and external security. Conference procedure for the settlement of intra-hemispheric disputes differs from that which governs cases of outside attack. The procedure adopted for the former is as follows: first, the foreign ministers may issue a call to the parties to cease hostilities; next, they may recommend various techniques of conciliation and mediation; they may then impose diplomatic and economic sanctions; and finally, if all the foregoing measures fail, they may recommend the use of armed force to restore order. It is significant that the first three of these provisions may be initiated by a two-thirds vote, which thereby becomes binding on all members. There is no veto. However, in the case of military enforcement measures, no state may be compelled to contribute armed forces without its consent. In the eventuality of an external threat, the arrangement is somewhat looser. The member states are obligated merely to consult with one another in order to arrive at a common policy, but each state may do what it "deems necessary" to help the victim—or not to help it.

In addition to its central organ, the OAS also works through several subsidiary bodies. There is, first, the OAS Council, which is the organization's central administration and coordinating organ. Second, there is an Inter-American Economic and Social Council, but, unlike its United Nations counterpart, this is not a major organ and does not have a very extensive program. Third, an Inter-American Cultural Council, designed for the promotion of friendly relations and cultural understanding among the American peoples, is patterned after UNESCO. The OAS also enjoys the services of a very active Inter-American Council of Jurists, which roughly parallels the International Law Commission of the United Nations. Finally, OAS, like the United Nations, has its international secretariat, the Pan-American Union. This is headed by a secretary-general who is chosen by the Inter-American Conference for a ten-year term, not subject to reelection.

A survey of the OAS structure indicates that the attention of the organization is about equally divided between the negative function of resolving disputes and the positive task of political integration. The achievements of OAS in the former category have been considerable. In December 1948 Costa Rica complained to the council that Nicaragua was trying to overthrow its government through revolution. The council blamed Costa Rica for negligence and Nicaragua for not preventing the revolutionary activity. A Committee of Five was appointed to mediate between the disputants. The effort was successful and the two parties signed a Treaty of Friendship in 1949. In 1950 Haiti accused the Dominican Republic of fostering subversion aimed at the overthrow of the Haitian government. The OAS Council found the Dominican Republic responsible and called upon it to desist from further subversive activities in the Western Hemisphere. In June 1954 a more complicated issue arose. The pro-Communist government of Guatemala charged Honduras and Nicaragua with U.S.-inspired aggression. The matter was discussed first in the United Nations Security Council, but it was decided that that body would not pursue the matter further until OAS had completed its investigation. This investigation never took place because the Guatemalan government was overthrown and replaced by a new, anti-Communist government. As a result, the matter was dropped by all concerned. In 1955 Costa Rica charged Nicaragua with fomenting a revolt. The OAS Council was successful in settling the matter through an investigating committee which made a series of recommendations accepted by both parties.

Four serious intra-hemispheric crises occupied the OAS in the 1960s. The first concerned the policy of subversion that had been pursued by the Dominican Republic in 1960 against Venezuela, including a plot to assassinate the Venezuelan president. The organization decided to take a strong stand against the Dominican Republic not only in the light of this specific provocation but because it was determined to end the thirty-year dictatorship of Generalissimo Trujillo. For the first time, the OAS decided to apply sanctions against one of its members for actions against another. The punishment consisted of a collective break in diplomatic relations and of "partial sanctions," including the suspension of arms shipments. The assassination of Trujillo in 1961 radically changed the Dominican picture and in 1962 the OAS voted to end the sanctions.

The second crisis grew out of the Cuban revolution and the apparent desire of Premier Fidel Castro to turn his revolution into an export commodity. The fact that the Soviet Union had gained a firm foothold in Cuba was especially distasteful to the United States and introduced further complications. The United States wanted desperately to prevent the spread of communism in the Western Hemisphere but was now forced to pursue this aim within the context of a multilateral conference, rather than by a unilateral wielding of the Monroe Doctrine. The other delegates were not as openly fearful of the Cuban revolution, but expressed varying degrees of ambivalence. Nevertheless in 1962, by a two-thirds vote, the foreign ministers at Punta del Este declared the Marxist-Leninist foundations of Castro's Cuba incompatible with membership in the Organization of American States. Cuba was also explicitly excluded from the Inter-American Defense Board and had an arms embargo imposed upon it. In October 1962, during the missile crisis, the OAS unanimously endorsed the American naval quarantine and Argentina and Venezuela actually sent ships to help United States naval forces. The response of the OAS to the missile crisis marked the first time that any military action was taken by the organization against a country in the Western Hemisphere. It took a dozen years for the first signs of a thaw to appear. In 1974 two American senators visited Cuba to explore the possibility of rapprochement; but despite this move, the OAS failed to remove the quarantine against Cuba. In 1975, at a meeting in Costa Rica, the OAS finally lifted the sanctions against Cuba that had been imposed in 1964.

Another precedent was set in January 1964 when the OAS took up a dispute involving the United States. Panama charged the United States with aggression after American troops had fired on Panamanian demonstrators in the Canal Zone. A more basic cause of the dispute, however, was the Panamanian demand to renegotiate the 1903 treaty giving the United States sovereign rights in the Canal Zone "in perpetuity." The OAS found itself in a dilemma. On the one hand, it wanted to help a small sister republic, but on the other, it was loath to place the United States in the role of the accused. Thus, it constituted itself as an "organ of consultation" to look into the charges and to help the two parties in reaching an amicable settlement. The peace-keeping mechanism of the organization was adapted to the situation in a flexible and imaginative manner. Finally, in 1978, Panama and the United States managed to renegotiate the 1903 treaty bilaterally and to transfer sovereignty over the Canal Zone to Panama by the year 2000.

A highly controversial situation arose in April 1965 when the United States decided to intervene in the Dominican Republic and sent in marines in order to stave off an alleged Communist coup. Proponents of the move defended it by pointing out that the United States could not afford another Castro, but critics deplored the unilateral intervention and feared the imminent end of the Good Neighbor Policy. In order to give the intervention a semblance of multilateralism, the United States in May 1965 requested an inter-American military force for the restoration of order in the Dominican Republic. The OAS foreign ministers, in a vote of fourteen to five, which was barely the required two-thirds majority, authorized the force. The five states opposing its creation resented what they felt to be an OAS ratification of American unilateralism. Nevertheless, the first inter-American military force entered Santo Domingo in May 1965, and thus established yet another precedent in the evolution of the OAS as an intra-hemisphere peace-keeping organ. In late 1966, after a little over a year of successful peace-keeping, the force was withdrawn from Santo Domingo.

The order-building task of the OAS has been made rather difficult because the Latin American countries and the United States have had different reasons for supporting the organization. For Latin America, OAS implied the legal sanctification of American nonintervention in the affairs of the hemisphere. It was also seen as a device for countering the supremacy of the "Colossus of the North." And most important, the Latin American countries looked forward to economic and technical assistance from the United States. The motives of the United States were somewhat different. From the American viewpoint, the OAS was to be a vital regional alliance in the East-West struggle. In 1961 the United States, in an effort to reconcile these different perspectives, launched a massive economic development program within the context of the OAS—the Alliance for Progress.

The Alliance for Progress got off to a fairly slow start. Tensions between the United States and the Latin American members of the alliance over American trade and aid policies retarded progress. In particular, the Latin Americans resented the requirement that American goods and services would have to be purchased with American aid funds. The United States, during the early years of the alliance, also continued to give bilateral aid to Latin American countries. This disappointed those who preferred greater emphasis on a multilateral program of hemispheric development. Finally, in 1966, at a major conference at Punta del Este, President Johnson and eighteen other heads of state, in a "Declaration of the Presidents of America," outlined plans for a Latin American common market to be in operation twenty years hence. The foundation for this emerging common market would be laid through multinational projects, the modernization of agriculture, the development of science and technology, and the advancement of education.

The continued presence of dictatorships—notably in Cuba, Haiti, and Paraguay—has had a retarding effect on order-building. Some members have advocated the encouragement of democracy in the Western Hemisphere but others have declared that such a policy would negate the principle of nonintervention. The organization has not been able to pursue both goals simultaneously. In addition, many Latin American countries have lacked internal stability. Coups d'état are not infrequent. In 1961 a coup ended a thirty-year dictatorship in the Dominican Republic and in 1964 another stemmed the drift toward anarchy in Brazil. During the early 1980s unrest was rampant in Nicaragua and El Salvador. Besides, OAS members such as Venezuela and Mexico disagreed profoundly with United States policy in these two Central American countries.

In the light of these divergent patterns and interests, unity and solidarity have been expressed primarily in general statements, with more concrete steps in order-building proving difficult, if not impossible. Despite its many shortcomings, OAS remains one of the most advanced regional arrangements in the world. It alone has provisions for internal security and has acquitted itself well in this respect. On the other hand, its progress toward political integration has been far more hesitant. If we apply the criteria of the Princeton study, we notice that OAS is not blessed with a system of common values—which the authors considered one of the essentials for the building of a security-community. However, OAS meets another key condition admirably. All its members have high expectations of concrete rewards. Although these expectations differ—being primarily military in the eyes of the United States and economic in the view of Latin America—they are nonetheless effective. At present, therefore, OAS may be considered what the Princeton group would call a "pluralistic security-community" at a low level. Further political integration would seem to depend on continuing and expanded expectations of joint rewards and on the improvement and enlargement of communications that will enhance mutual responsiveness among the members.

The Arab League

The most prominent regional arrangement in the Middle East has been the Arab League. It was organized on the eve of the San Francisco Conference in 1945 and comprised seven states: Egypt, Syria, Lebanon, Jordan, Iraq, Saudi Arabia, and Yemen. The purpose of the league as set forth in its Charter was

> ... to strengthen the ties between the participating states, to coordinate their political programs in such a way as to effect real collaboration between them, to preserve their independence and sovereignty, and to consider in general the affairs and interests of the Arab countries.

In practice, "strengthening the ties" between the members of the Arab League was a subordinate goal. There were two overriding causes for the creation of the league: first, to present a united front against the return to the Middle East of French and British colonialism; and second, to prevent the creation of a Jewish state in Palestine.

The most powerful organ of the league has been the Majlis, a council comprising the prime ministers of the member states. All important decisions, including any kind of collective action, have required unanimity. Majority decisions have been binding only on those states that have voted for a particular resolution. On intraleague disputes, the council may act by majority vote, provided the "independence, sovereignty or territorial integrity of a member are not involved." As a result of this reservation, all but very minor questions have in practice required unanimous decision. In 1950 the structure of the Arab League was developed further by the adoption of a Treaty of Joint Defense and Economic Cooperation modeled after the NATO Pact. Like NATO, this treaty stipulated the peaceful settlement of all disputes among the members; stated that an attack upon one was to be regarded as an attack upon all; and included a statement that armed attack from the outside would be met by collective military measures. In addition, for the purpose of coordinating the economies of the Arab countries, it created an Economic Council consisting of the member states' ministers of economic affairs. Finally, the office of a secretary-general was added whose incumbent was to be appointed by a two-thirds vote of the Council.

The formal structure of the Arab League has had relatively little to do with the actual policy-making process. In the opinion of one expert student of the Arab League:

> The real activities of the League are carried on in private and secret talks and through conversations held outside regular meetings. The careful elaboration of agreements, with each stage consigned to writing—so customary in the West—is utterly unfamiliar. When the prestige of man comes into conflict with the prestige of the written word, the former prevails. Furthermore, the activities of the

League are unknown and misunderstood abroad, and even in the Arab world, because the organization has been reluctant to secure publicity for its activities.[13]

The league's official purpose and its formal structure thus provide few clues to its actual goals and operations.

In its first aim, the liberation of Egypt, Lebanon, Syria, and Libya from colonial rule, the Arab League was clearly successful. When France attempted to resume control of Lebanon and Syria in 1945, the league pressed for submission of the dispute to the United Nations Security Council. When in 1946 the Security Council took up the problem, the league presented a united front and succeeded in preventing the French from returning to Lebanon and Syria. Similarly the league supported the complete evacuation of British troops from Egypt. When Egypt emerged as an independent state after seventy-two years of British rule, this victory was attributable in no small measure to the efforts of the Arab League.

Finally, the Arab League played a decisive role in securing the independence of Libya by acting as the spokesman for that new state in the United Nations. Actually, the intervention on behalf of Libya probably owed its success more to the inability of the Big Four to agree on a new status for Libya than to the inherent strength of the league itself. When neither the Big Four nor the United Nations was able to decide what to do with the former Italian territory, the Arab League's insistent pressure for independence weighed heavily in the balance. Libya became independent in 1951 and was admitted as the eighth member of the Arab League in 1953. The Sudan received its independence and joined the league in 1956, and two years later Morocco and Tunisia were admitted. Kuwait became a member in 1961 and in the following year Syria resumed its separate seat, which it had relinquished by joining the United Arab Republic. Finally, in 1962 Algeria became the thirteenth member of the Arab League. By the early 1960s it was clear that the first major political goal of the league—the emancipation of the Arab states from Western colonialism—had been achieved.

In its second major objective, the prevention of the Jewish state in Palestine, the Arab League has failed. In 1946 the league developed a common policy toward Palestine: Jewish immigration and land purchases were to be stopped; Jewish products were to be boycotted; and Palestine was to be admitted to the league as an independent Arab nation. An attempt was made to create a common front against the creation of the state of Israel by threatening a general war for the liberation of the area if the new state were to come into being. When on May 15, 1948, Israel achieved its independence, the secretary-general of the Arab League informed the United Nations Security Council that the league was forced to intervene "to achieve peace and order and to restore the territory to the Arabs of Palestine."[14] In its war against Israel, however, the latent internecine schisms within the league quickly came to the surface. It found itself unable to coordinate the armies of its members. Since each state claimed the honor for itself, the League Council was not even able to agree on a commander-in-chief. "Iraq refused to accept an Egyptian commander. Egypt rejected an Iraqi general. And the commander-in-chief of the Jordan army was of British origin and therefore out of the question. The result was that each Arab army that entered Palestine fought on its own."[15] When in May 1949 Israel was admitted to the United Nations, the league faced complete defeat. The state that the league had vowed to destroy was not only in existence but was now recognized as an official member of the world community. The league defeat was made even more bitter when one of its members, Jordan, declared itself ready to accept the establishment of Israel and seemed intent on annexing the remaining portions of Palestine. Under the impact of total defeat the league began to disintegrate completely. Iraq and Jordan developed an increasing suspicion of Egyptian domination in the league and accused the secretary-general, Azzam Pasha, of pro-Egyptian leanings. As a result, an innocuous former civil servant, Abdel Khalek Hassouna, was appointed to the post. Nevertheless, Iraq refused to pay its membership contribution to the league and began to look around for new allies. To the consternation of the entire league, Iraq became the keystone of the Baghdad Pact, linking it to Britain, Turkey, Iran, and Pakistan. Only a revolution in 1958 brought it back into the fold. Jordan narrowly escaped expulsion because of its flirtation with Israel. The Arab League as a regional arrangement seemed to have turned into a complete debacle.

The pattern of internal conflict among the Arab states continued. In 1961 the United Arab Republic disintegrated and Syria seceded. Later that year, a bitter feud erupted between Egypt and Saudi Arabia over Yemen. In 1962 Syria lodged a formal complaint with the Arab League, charging that President Nasser was trying to effect a reunion of Syria with Egypt by forcible means. In 1963 Iraq's Premier Kassem was assassinated by pro-Nasser revolutionaries. In Syria the nationalistic Baath party took control. During the same year actual warfare broke out between Algeria and Morocco over the ill-defined Sahara border. After a league call for a cease-fire, a shaky truce was established.

In 1967 almost all of the above conflicts were temporarily obscured when war erupted between Israel and three members of the Arab League, Egypt, Syria, and Jordan. Again, however, there was little effective coordination among the Arab armies, although King Hussein of Jordan placed his armed forces under Egyptian command. Shortly after the war, the members of the league met at Khartoum, in the Sudan, to discuss future policies toward Israel but, once again, many of the stubborn intra-Arab rivalries came to the surface and made any concerted policy difficult.

In late 1973, in the wake of the October War, the Arab League experienced a dramatic resurgence. The key to its new-found power, of course, was oil, or rather the ability to agree for the first time on a common oil price policy vis-à-vis the consuming countries. While only a few of the Arab League states—Saudi Arabia, Kuwait, Algeria, and the United Arab Emirates—were major oil producers, all league members benefited from the new policy. The ability to affect the Middle East postures of powerful industrialized states such as the United States and Japan gave the Arab League a new sense of heady confidence and power. Traditional rivalries were submerged and at a summit meeting in Rabat, Morocco, in 1974, the Palestine Liberation Organization was given the status of a government in exile. The league's anti-Israel policy, doomed to failure for over a quarter of a century, was suddenly infused with fresh hope in the mid-1970s. The league's new-found ability to act in unison led to significant policy successes that, in turn, endowed it with an internal cohesion and vigor that it had not exhibited since its inception. But then again, President Sadat's dramatic visit to Jerusalem in 1977 divided the league into a moderate group led by Egypt and a more radical alignment led by Syria.

By 1980 the Arab League was virtually a shambles. It was difficult to find two Arab countries that enjoyed friendly relations with one another. The immediate cause of this disarray was the Iraqi-Iranian war. Libya and Syria leaned toward Iran while Jordan and Saudi Arabia supported Iraq. Syria and Jordan had come close to war and Iraq was trying to replace Egypt as the "gendarme" of the Persian Gulf. The PLO, locked in a power struggle with Israel, was still trying to establish a Palestinian state. When the Arab League met in Amman, Jordan, in November 1980, Syria, Libya, Algeria, Southern Yemen, Lebanon, and the PLO refused to attend. Clearly, the unity of the Arab League had reached a new nadir.

The Arab League as a regional arrangement has not invested much energy in forging concrete political instruments of internal political order. One such peace-keeping operation was a joint Egyptian–Saudi Arabian military force dispatched to Kuwait in 1961 to replace British troops which had entered the newly independent country to protect it against the irredentist claims of Premier Kassem of Iraq. In addition, beginning in 1972, the league, under the leadership of its new secretary-general, Mahmoud Riad, took on the responsibility of mediating between Palestinian guerrillas and several Arab governments, such as Lebanon, that had large numbers of guerrillas on their soil. In 1979 a Syrian "peace-keeping" force entered war-torn Lebanon. Other nonpolitical order-building efforts have included the passage by the League Council of legislation for inter-Arab private international law, the dissemination throughout the Arab world of the language of the Koran, and the organization of several cultural, scientific, and educational conferences.

If we analyze the Arab League in terms of the criteria of the Princeton study, we encounter the strange paradox of a regional arrangement that fulfills almost none of the essential conditions of a security-community. The absence of common values and mutual responsiveness among the members of the league is all too evident. The hostility between pan-Arabism and pan-Islam, the traditional authoritarianism of the monarchies and the rampant nationalism of the new republics, the fratricidal strife within the camp of the new nationalism—all these have made a mockery of unity in the Arab League. And yet there were times when it has held together. It held together because it was able to offer its members the expectation of two great rewards: the liquidation of Western colonialism and the destruction of Israel. It made a vital contribution to the achievement of the first objective and this success has solidified its bonds. Its total failure in the latter over more than thirty years almost brought about its disintegration, but in the mid-1970s the oil weapon infused it with new hope and strength. Then, by the 1980s, it almost succumbed to fratricidal slaughter. Ironically, however, since opposition to Israel is the one thing that *all* league members save possibly Egypt have in common, the league's very existence appears to depend on the continued existence of the entity that it seeks to destroy. Because of its primarily negative goals, moreover, the league has done little to advance political order in the Middle East. And, as the authors of the Princeton study have pointed out, a unity that is based chiefly on common hostility against an outside force is bound to be transitory, since it imposes too many burdens and realizes too few rewards. Hence, it seems safe to say that unless the Arab League develops more positive methods of integration, it may face complete disintegration.

The Organization of African Unity

The Organization of African Unity (OAU) was created at the Conference of African Nations meeting in Addis Ababa, Ethiopia, in May 1963 with thirty-one independent African nations attending.

There was some disagreement among the delegates over the best method of furthering the cause of African unity. President Nkrumah of Ghana urged the creation of a unitary African state with a strong central government, but the conference was more impressed with the more moderate proposals of Emperor Haile Selassie of Ethiopia, who quickly became the major spokesman of the majority view.

The conference decided upon a basic charter which listed the goals of the new organization: freedom, dignity, and equality for all Africans; continuation of the struggle against colonialism; preservation and consolidation of the territorial integrity of the members; and the establishment of common institutions. These aims were to be pursued in harmony with the United Nations Charter.

The conference was also able to agree on institutions for the OAU. It established, as the supreme authority of the OAU, an Assembly composed of the heads of the member states which would meet at least once every year; a Council of Ministers to meet at least twice a year, with each country having one vote and decisions to be made by simple majority; and a Secretary-General and Secretariat. In addition, a special Commission for Mediation and Arbitration of inter-African disputes was set up. The costs of the new organization were to be met by assessing the members, using the United Nations scale as a model.

Since its inception in 1963, most of the energies of the OAU have gone into the struggle to eliminate the vestiges of Western colonialism in Africa. The heads of the member states have met at least once a year and much of their planning has centered on speeding the decolonization process. In 1964, for example, they decided to deny OAU ports and airfields to ships and planes that served South Africa. In 1965 the delegates unanimously urged Britain to use force against Rhodesia if the latter would seize independence from Britain. In 1966 the members urged the UN Security Council to adopt mandatory sanctions against the Smith regime in Rhodesia. During the late 1960s and the 1970s two-thirds of the OAU's budget was set aside to help guerrilla activity in the "white redoubt" countries of Southern Africa. When, in April 1980, Zimbabwe emerged as the fifty-first sovereign black African state, the OAU had only two targets left for liberation: Namibia and apartheid's last fortress, South Africa.

The OAU, however, has also been increasingly concerned about peace-keeping among its own members. In 1964, for example, it established a permanent commission to arbitrate border disputes. In 1965, it arranged for liaison with the UN General Assembly. In 1966, at the OAU Council of Ministers' meeting in Addis Ababa, the members were sharply divided over the seating of the Ghanaian delegation in the wake of Nkrumah's ouster. In 1967 the OAU sent a six-man mission to Lagos in search of Nigerian-Biafran peace and Zambia agreed to serve as moderator in the border dispute smoldering between Kenya and Somalia. At the same conference, UN Secretary-General U Thant urged the OAU to pay more attention to internal peace-keeping. While in 1968, the war between Nigeria and its breakaway province of Biafra assumed the proportions of a major human tragedy, Somalia ageed to resolve its boundary dispute with Kenya. In 1972 the OAU's prestige was further enhanced when the UN Security Council held a series of meetings in Addis Ababa for the express purpose of underlining the urgency of the problems that were besetting the African continent. And in 1981 an OAU peace-keeping force consisting of troops from Nigeria, Senegal, and Zaire arrived in Chad in an effort to replace Libyan forces.

While much of the momentum of the OAU is still derived from its original anticolonial raison d'être, it is beginning to exhibit some of the earmarks of a pluralistic security-community at a low level in its increasing role as internal peace-keeper. As colonialism recedes more and more into the past, it seems safe to predict that this latter function of the OAU will assume greater prominence in the future.

The British Commonwealth

Another case study in political order-building deals with the British Commonwealth. This is a unique international phenomenon and defies easy definition. As one observer has put it, "If it did not exist you could not invent it."[16] The Commonwealth's uniqueness as a regional arrangement lies in the first instance in the fact that it originated not as a congeries of independent states, but as an empire. The other regional arrangements we have analyzed have attempted to build unity by forging bonds where none have existed before. The Commonwealth, in essence, represents an effort to create political unity through the dissolution of existing political bonds that have become too onerous. For this reason the roots of the Commonwealth are radically different from those of other regional arrangements.

The present membership of the Commonwealth comprises thirty-one states, consisting of almost one billion people. The thirty-one members are: Australia, Barbados, Botswana, Canada, Ceylon, Cyprus, Fiji, Gambia, Ghana,

Guyana, India, Jamaica, Kenya, Lesotho, Malawi, Malaysia, Malta, Mauritius, New Zealand, Nigeria, Pakistan, Sierra Leone, Singapore, Swaziland, United Republic of Tanzania, Tonga, Trinidad and Tobago, Uganda, the United Kingdom of Great Britain and Northern Ireland, Western Samoa, and Zambia. The Union of South Africa withdrew from the Commonwealth in 1961 and became the Republic of South Africa. In addition to the sovereign states listed above, the Commonwealth also includes a number of dependencies that are in the process of transition toward sovereign status.

It is difficult to discern what common purpose holds together this highly diversified group of states known as the Commonwealth. Very generally, however, the Commonwealth can be said to be dedicated to at least two objectives: common defense against external threats and common policies for economic betterment. The organizational structure of the Commonwealth is extremely loose. It has neither charter nor treaty and membership in it confers no legal rights and imposes no legal obligations. In terms of formal machinery, the Commonwealth is the least developed of all regional arrangements. The most important of the Commonwealth institutions is a symbolic one—the Crown. Even India and Pakistan, although republics, have accepted the Crown as a symbol of their free association in the Commonwealth. The wearer of the Crown dedicates herself equally to many different peoples and many different faiths. Yet the Crown is considered indivisible. In L. S. Amery's telling metaphor, "it is a jewel of many facets, not a string of disconnected pearls."[17] The informality of Commonwealth relations is reflected in the main political organ, the Conference of Prime Ministers. This conference is simply an annual or biennial forum with no executive authority. Resolutions that may be passed by the conference merely have the status of recommendations until ratified by the individual members. This procedure is analogous to that in the Committee of Ministers of the Council of Europe. The conference is primarily a means of consultation rather than an organ for reaching decisions. But the techniques of consultation and the exchange of information among the Commonwealth countries have reached a high level of sophistication. Each member sends to each of the others a High Commissioner whose relationship to the host country is far less formal than that of the ordinary ambassador. In addition, massive exchanges of personnel in fields of mutual interest at the administrative level have helped to solidify the bonds of the Commonwealth. Common defense problems are discussed and functional matters like shipping and communications receive close attention. There also exists a Commonwealth Secretariat.

The complete absence in the Commonwealth of any pretensions to supranationality has not prevented large areas of friction among the members. Ireland preferred to leave the Commonwealth rather than discuss its differences with Great Britain. Burma decided to leave it when granted independence. The membership of India introduced serious disputes with other members: the struggles with Pakistan over Kashmir and Bangladesh and the perennial friction with the Union of South Africa over the question of apartheid.

The Commonwealth has not been able to evolve any common parliamentary or executive institutions. All such efforts have come to nought, owing to the stubborn insistence of each member on its complete sovereignty. Among the many paradoxes of the Commonwealth is the fact that whatever unity it has achieved as a regional arrangement has been attained without the development of institutional limitations on the sovereignty of its members.

Measured in terms of its own purposes, the record of the Commonwealth has been a mixed one. One of its most notable achievements has been its ability to attract into what once was an empire countries that only recently and after long and bitter struggles succeeded in emancipating themselves from colonial tutelage. All the former colonial countries that joined the Commonwealth after receiving independence did so by their own free will. In an age of colonial liquidation and widespread anticolonial emotionalism this has been a remarkable accomplishment indeed. In 1979, at Lusaka, the members of the Commonwealth even hastened the emergence of Southern Rhodesia as independent Zimbabwe. The goal of common defense, on the other hand, has been achieved only partially. At the time of Britain's gravest crisis, during World War II, the members of the Commonwealth fought freely on its side—though some, like India, exacted a heavy price. In the post–World War II world, however, the stategic interests of many of the member countries turned elsewhere. Canada solidified its ties with the United States. Because of its racial policies, the Union of South Africa became the *bête noire* of the Commonwealth and incurred the special animosity of such formerly colonial lands as Ghana and India. Australia and New Zealand, joined in the ANZUS Treaty, looked for protection more and more to the United States than to Great Britain. And India, attempting to follow its own independent course between East and West, more and more subordinated its commitment to the Commonwealth to the dictates of its own evolving strategy of "nonalignment."

How far this dissolution of strategic ties within the Commonwealth has progressed may be seen from the voting behavior of the Commonwealth countries in the United Nations. Of all the blocs in the General Assembly, the Commonwealth bloc has been the least cohesive. In fact, owing to wide divergencies on matters of foreign policy, its members have tended to vote almost completely independently. On the crucial matter of the Anglo-French invasion of Suez, only Australia and New Zealand supported the position of the United Kingdom. Ceylon, India, and Pakistan voted against Britain, and Canada and South Africa abstained. This lack of foreign-policy consensus has been fairly typical of the so-called Commonwealth bloc. Indeed, on any matter about which the members of the Commonwealth have strong convictions, each state can usually be expected to act strictly as it sees fit.

In its second purpose, that of improving economic relations, the Commonwealth has been more successful, although the devaluation of the British currency in 1967 sent shock waves throughout the Commonwealth. All parts of the Commonwealth, with the exception of Canada, share a "sterling area" in which trade and investment are greatly facilitated. Economic aid and technical assistance are administered under Commonwealth auspices through the Colombo Plan. This plan has been one of the most concrete incentives for

Commonwealth membership in the lesser developed areas of the world. Its projects are undertaken as a joint enterprise on the basis of local development plans and mutual consultation.

Finally, the mobility of people among the member states has been fairly high. It would be too ambitious to speak of a "Commonwealth citizenship." But in many instances, Commonwealth status facilitates the right to enter or leave member states or to qualify for naturalization. Most of the Commonwealth countries afford privileges to other members not generally accorded to citizens of foreign countries. When, for example, the government of Uganda decided to expel most of its citizens of Asian heritage, Britain made a major effort to offer these refugees new homes.

In terms of the Princeton study, the Commonwealth can hardly be considered a security-community. The unity in political and security matters that once characterized the British Empire has been greatly weakened by powerful new centrifugal tendencies. The common commitment to parliamentarianism is threatened by the political instability of the new members in Africa. It would, moreover, be difficult to speak of the existence of common values throughout the Commonwealth. On the other hand, expectation of joint rewards has been fairly high. Membership in the Commonwealth has brought with it concrete economic benefits through joint projects like the Colombo Plan and the unhampered flow of trade. Informal order-building has been continuous without infringements of the members' sovereignty. Perhaps the most important factor of all in explaining the Commonwealth's continuing resiliency has been the fact that rewards and the expectation of rewards have always greatly exceeded burdens and responsibilities.

The Association of Southeast Asian Nations (ASEAN)

Our final case study will focus on Asia. In 1967, fearful of being drawn into the Indochina conflict, five Southeast Asian countries proclaimed themselves as "a zone of peace and neutrality." Thus was born the Association of Southeast Asian Nations (ASEAN), consisting of Indonesia, Malaysia, Thailand, the Philippines, and Singapore.

During its first ten years ASEAN resembled a debating society rather than a solid organization. But by the early 1980s, largely because of the powerful economies of the five participating states, ASEAN had become a force to be reckoned with. Although it had no supranational powers, ASEAN had become an extremely useful instrument of regional communication. It had enabled the leaders of the region to become better acquainted with one another and to understand each other's perspectives. On numerous occasions ASEAN has spoken with a collective voice to the United States, China, Japan, and the Soviet Union.

Perhaps the major weakness of ASEAN has been that leadership in its five member countries has remained heavily dependent upon a few individuals: Ferdinand Marcos in the Philippines, Kriangsak in Thailand, Lee Kwan Yew in Singapore, Suharto in Indonesia, and Hussein Onn in Malaysia. Thus, the bonds of regionalism had to develop without the benefit of parliamentary democracy. In addition, each member state has had its own particular problems with a neighboring great power.

In the Philippines, the United States has come under crossfire from the government and its critics, with the latter demanding that Washington pressure Marcos to call for free elections, and the government insisting that no interference in internal affairs be tolerated. Thailand has been desperately concerned about the conflicts that have been raging on its borders. Not only have refugees from the Indochina conflict flooded into Thailand but there has been great anxiety that the fighting between pro-Soviet Vietnam and pro-Chinese Kampuchea might spill over the borders into Thailand. The question of whether Thailand might become another domino has also worried Malaysia and virtually defenseless Singapore. Indonesia, too, was torn between its continuing concern over the long-range problem of China and the more immediate problem of Vietnam. Thus, despite their differences, the five members of ASEAN were able to agree upon one fundamental goal: to keep the region free from great power intervention.

Aware of the growing economic dynamism of the region, the superpowers have begun to pay attention. Vice President Walter Mondale toured the area in 1978 and President Carter played host to a conference of ASEAN ministers in Washington a few months later. China's Vice Premier Teng Hsiao-ping also visited the five countries and even went to the extraordinary length of genuflecting before the Crown Prince of Thailand. The Soviet Union, too, has wooed ASEAN, but has had a relatively cool reception because of its alliance with Vietnam.

The ASEAN community has attained the level of a low-level pluralistic security community even though its members are far from being parliamentary democracies. They have achieved this status because they all agree on one overriding objective: to maintain the neutrality of the area from outside disputes. So far, they have not only achieved this goal, but their strong economies have made them objects of courtship by big powers aiming to expand their markets. Far from threatening them militarily, the United States, China, and Japan have begun to look to ASEAN as a large potential market. Hence, it is very likely that ASEAN's bonds will tighten further as its members continue to coordinate their economic policies vis-à-vis the outside world. Originally, the five members of ASEAN were fearful of intrusion. By the mid-1980s that danger had decreased significantly. Economic power had begun to shift away from Europe and America. The ASEAN countries have all been beneficiaries of this shift.

REGIONALISM AND THE UNITED NATIONS

The relation between regional arrangements and the United Nations has been a subject of heated controversy. Attitudes on the subject have fallen along a wide spectrum. At one extreme have been those who have defended the necessity of regional arrangements as building blocks toward globalism. Those who have advanced this view have held that regionalism is not only compatible with the United Nations but, in fact, is an essential stepping-stone to the world organization's successful functioning and further development. Winston Churchill expressed this position most forcefully when he stated before the opening of the San Francisco Conference that "there should be several regional councils, august but subordinate, and these should form the massive pillars upon which the world organization would be founded in majesty and calm."[18] At the other extreme in the controversy have been those who have tended to regard regional arrangements as little more than poorly camouflaged power alliances, evil creations of an anarchic world that are wholly incompatible with the principle of collective security.

At the San Francisco Conference, the problem of regional versus global organization was one of the thorniest issues. Many prospective members of the world organization were deeply committed to regional arrangements that antedated the United Nations Charter. The Inter-American system, the Arab League, and the British Commonwealth commanded the loyalty of more than a score of the nations which assembled at San Francisco. The American republics wished to safeguard the hemispheric system, the Arab states were jealous of the rights of the Arab League, Britain had an eye on the Commonwealth, the Soviet Union wished to exempt its mutual assistance pacts from Security Council control, and most of the small states were suspicious of the Security Council because of the veto power. On the other hand, some members of the conference were deeply committed to universalism and tended to regard regional arrangements as a menace to peace and order. The interplay among these forces produced a compromise solution that was reflected in the Charter in a grudging acceptance of the fact that regionalism was here to stay and that its existence had to be reconciled with the principle of world organization. At first, there was an attempt to make regional organizations like the OAS into operating arms of the United Nations. Very soon, however, it had to be admitted that the very raison d'être of the regional organs was the preservation of their autonomous status vis-à-vis the United Nations. This autonomy was expressed as the right of "collective self-defense," recognized in Article 51 of the Charter. Under this provision NATO, OAS, and the Arab League were in practice exempted from external control by the United Nations. Soviet regional arrangements found a similar escape clause in Article 53 of the Charter, permitting "collective self-defense" against "enemy states" in World War II. Thus the Charter was compelled to recognize the coexistence of regionalism and universalism.

The problem for regionalists and universalists alike has, therefore, become the quest for a viable and productive division of labor between the two forms of political organization in order to maximize progress in order-building. If we compare the order-building record of the various regional organizations with that of the United Nations, the "building-block theory" advocated by the regionalists does not hold up. The Commonwealth, which prides itself on its sophisticated consultative machinery, has on several occasions been compelled to request the help of the General Assembly. It did not succeed in solving the stubborn conflicts between India and Pakistan over Kashmir and Bangladesh. Similarly, NATO was impotent in the three-cornered struggle involving three of its members over Cyprus, and the problem was handed over to the United Nations. The vital disagreements between the United States and Britain and France over the Suez question could not be composed within the framework of NATO. Only the OAS, with its highly developed order-building institutions, has made a creditable showing and has effectively dealt with serious disputes among its members. On the whole, NATO, the Commonwealth, and the Arab League have had to ask far more from the order-building capacities of the United Nations than they have been able to contribute to the resolution of international conflicts themselves.

If the record of the regional arrangements as independent instruments of order-building is thus not impressive, the reason would seem to lie chiefly in the fact that many of their energies have been absorbed in the two great struggles of our time. As major strategic instruments in these struggles, they have, in fact, been designed and operated so as to preserve the greatest possible degree of autonomy vis-à-vis the United Nations. This situation has, in turn, been reflected in a tendency to discuss more and more of the great international issues outside the world organization's framework. In the words of one scholar of regionalism, "The United Nations has been placed in a position of inferiority so that now the links between the regional arrangements and the world organization exist at the practical pleasure of the former."[19] This increasing habit of bypassing the United Nations on vital issues of high politics and security also troubled the late Secretary-General, Mr. Hammarskjöld, who urged a reversal of the trend:

> In recent years, the main attention has been concentrated on measures designed to give a measure of security on a regional basis, in the absence of a more universal system of security. If there is now to be a serious and sustained exploration of the possibilities for cooperation on a wider basis, the world organization must necessarily gain a new dimension.[20]

The problem of achieving a balance between regionalism and globalism cannot be solved in the theoretical realm. Each situation must be examined on its own merits and requires its own particular division of labor. In order to demonstrate the complexity of the problem, let us take the example of the peaceful uses of atomic energy. Should atoms-for-peace be given to needy nations through the universal channel of the United Nations International Atomic Energy Agency (IAEA)? Or should such a program be administered through regional organs like the European Atomic Energy Community (Euratom) in Western Europe? This case study shows that each problem requires its own unique solution.

It is generally agreed that the developmental aspects of atomic energy for peaceful purposes can and should be shared among organizations at the regional as well as the global level. It would indeed be difficult to make a case for totally shifting to the International Atomic Energy Agency all of the many atomic development activities that are at present being carried out through the various regional arrangements. Yet in view of the fact that the different atomic powers maintain different safeguard criteria and insist upon different standards of inspection, the entire matter poses a most difficult dilemma: how to share atomic development activities on different levels and, at the same time, work out the responsibility for adequate and generally acceptable control.

To the donor, the regional approach to atomic development may often seem preferable to working through United Nations channels. The donor's freedom to choose the recipient and to define precisely the conditions for cooperation may even result in more extensive assistance. In the case of United Nations assistance, in contrast, the donor's influence on the recipient must proceed through the machinery of the IAEA Board of Governors and the General Conference. For this reason, United Nations assistance cannot be identified with any one country and tends to assume a more apolitical character than its regional counterpart. This explains why United Nations assistance is at times preferred by the underdeveloped countries and why regional arrangements are frequently favored by donors. Finally, as recipients like to point out, an international organization like IAEA may be better suited for atomic development by virtue of the fact that its membership includes both the advanced and the underdeveloped areas—which means that it can fulfill the function of an intermediary more satisfactorily than can a regional organization.

For certain types of atomic development and research, cooperation through regional arrangements may often be more effective than through IAEA. The Western European and the Latin American countries, for example, form regions that are reasonably homogeneous both geographically and technologically. These factors inevitably favor a regional approach to the development of atomic energy. Moreover, regionalism may also in many cases be better suited to furthering atomic research. The European Organization for Nuclear Research (CERN), founded in 1956, is composed of twelve Western European countries at comparable stages of atomic research development. Its Eastern counterpart, the Joint Institute for Nuclear Research, also founded in 1956, consists of eleven countries from the Soviet bloc. Both these organizations are based on the common experiences and goals of the countries comprising their respective regions and, undoubtedly, derive considerable scientific and technological benefits from this fact.

Agencies engaged in nuclear development will probably continue to proliferate. It is not possible to make a case for exclusively regional or exclusively global nuclear development. In the absence of a general principle, the IAEA will have to adapt itself to constantly changing patterns of development.

In the area of control, however, uniform safeguards must be imposed to avert disaster. In 1974, for example, India announced a nuclear explosion and became the sixth member of the "nuclear club" as a direct result of having been party to a bilateral agreement with Canada. The donor nation had assumed that its assistance would be used exclusively for peaceful purposes. The IAEA is in a logical position to play the coordinating role in this task. Yet it is prevented from doing so because some regional and bilateral controls are less stringent than those demanded by the United Nations. Euratom, for example, does not require certain controls that are insisted upon in the IAEA Statute. However, since the member states of Euratom are also signatories to the IAEA Statute, this obstacle is by no means insurmountable. Moreover, periodic reports of the "disappearance" of fissionable materials and the growing threat of "nuclear theft" by terrorist groups makes the need for global inspection and control more urgent than ever before.

There are three possible ways in which regional development and control functions might be brought under the IAEA. First, the nuclear powers might arrange for IAEA to take over regional programs in their entirety. This is the hope of the IAEA's Director-General but is unlikely to materialize. Second, regional arrangements might continue, with the parties requesting the IAEA to assume responsibility for the administration of safeguards. The IAEA Statute permits this, and its realization is possible. The United States has already taken the initiative in bringing some of its bilateral agreements under IAEA control. Third, the regional arrangements might cover the same broad fields of development and control as are covered by IAEA. This is the most likely development. IAEA can therefore be expected to discharge a function of piecemeal coordination, dealing with limited and specific situations as they arise from day to day. The size of reactors, division of labor in isotope research, and concrete inspection provisions are likely to be some of the typical problems of coordination that IAEA will face. The reconciliation of regionalism with globalism in atomic energy will thus become primarily a process to be managed, rather than a problem to be solved.

The case of atomic energy demonstrates the extreme complexity of the relationship between regionalism and globalism. In this particular case, the regional approach seems quite appropriate for the developmental aspects, whereas in the matter of control a world approach seems required. Each problem, however, demands its own careful study and its own particular solution. Excessive theorizing and generalizing are likely to contribute very little.

The record supports neither the building-block theory of regionalism nor the opposite contention that regional arrangements are necessarily antithetical to the principles of the United Nations Charter. Rather, the evidence shows that frequently the United Nations has been a second line of defense for regionalism and that sometimes regional arrangements have served as backstops for the world organization. Certainly there is ample room for both types of political order-building on the international scene.

REFERENCES

1. Karl W. Deutsch et al. *Political Community and the North Atlantic Area.* Princeton, N.J.: Princeton University Press, 1957.
2. *Ibid.,* pp. 190–191.

3. Robert O. Keohane and Joseph S. Nye, *Power and Interdependence.* Boston: Little, Brown, 1977.
4. *Ibid.,* p. 10.
5. Richard Coudenhove-Kalergi, *An Idea Conquers the World.* London: Putnam, 1953, p. ix.
6. Cited by A. H. Robinson, *The Council of Europe.* New York: Praeger, 1956, pp. 1–2.
7. Cited by Arnold J. Zurcher, *The Struggle to Unite Europe.* New York: New York University Press, 1958, p. 6.
8. Political and Economic Planning (PEP), *European Organisations.* London: Allen and Unwin, 1959, p. 132.
9. Oscar Svarlien, *An Introduction to the Law of Nations.* New York: McGraw-Hill, 1955, p. 443.
10. PEP, *op. cit.,* p. 206.
11. Inis L. Claude, Jr., *Swords into Plowshares.* 2nd ed. New York: Random House, 1959, p. 199.
12. Deutsch et al., *op. cit.,* p. 156.
13. B. Y. Boutros-Ghali, "The Arab League," *International Conciliation,* May 1954, p. 394.
14. United Nations Doc. S/745, May 16, 1948.
15. Boutros-Ghali, *op. cit.,* pp. 411–412.
16. K. C. Wheare, "The Nature and Structure of the Commonwealth," *American Political Science Review,* December 1953, p. 1016.
17. L. S. Amery, *Thoughts on the Constitution.* New York: Oxford University Press, 1953, p. 169.
18. Cited by Claude, *op. cit.,* p. 120.
19. Edgar S. Furniss, Jr., "A Re-examination of Regional Arrangements," *Journal of International Affairs,* IX (1955), 84.
20. Cited by Norman D. Palmer and Howard C. Perkins, *International Relations.* Boston: Houghton Mifflin, 1957, p. 641.

BIBLIOGRAPHY

Andemicael, Berhanykum. *The OAU and the UN.* New York: Africana, 1976.
Aron, Raymond, and Lerner, Daniel, eds. *France Defeats the EDC: Studies in an International Controversy.* New York: Praeger, 1956.
Axline, W. Andrew. *Caribbean Integration: The Politics of Regionalism.* New York: Nichols, 1979.
Britain in Western Europe—WEU and the Atlantic Alliance. London: Royal Institute of International Affairs, 1956.
Bromberger, Merry and Serge. *Jean Monnet and the United States of Europe.* New York: Coward-McCann, 1969.
Bull, Vivian A. *The West Bank—Is It Viable?* Lexington, Mass.: Lexington Books, 1975.
Burr, Robert N. *Our Troubled Hemisphere: Perspectives on United States–Latin American Relations.* Washington, D.C.: Brookings Institution, 1967.
Crawford, Oliver. *Done This Day: The European Idea in Action.* New York: Taplinger, 1970.
Deutsch, Karl W., et al. *France, Germany, and the Western Alliance.* New York: Scribner, 1967.
———. *The Nerves of Government.* Glencoe, Ill.: The Free Press, 1963.
———, et al. *Political Community and the North Atlantic Area.* Princeton, N.J.: Princeton University Press, 1957.

El-Ayouty, Yassin, and Brooks, Hugh C. *Africa and International Organization.* The
    Hague: Nijhoff, 1974.
————, ed. *The Organization of African Unity after Ten Years: Comparative Per-*
    spectives. New York: Praeger, 1975.
Feld, Werner J., and Wiedgen, John K. *Domestic Political Realities and European*
    Unification. Boulder, Colo.: Westview Press, 1977.
Fifield, Russell H. *National and Regional Interests in ASEAN.* Singapore: Institute of
    Southeast Asian Studies, 1979.
Geiger, Theodore. *The Fortunes of the West: The Future of the Atlantic Nations.*
    Bloomington: Indiana University Press, 1973.
Goodman, Elliot R. *The Fate of the Atlantic Community.* New York: Praeger, 1975.
Hall, H. Duncan. *Commonwealth: A History of the British Commonwealth of Na-*
    tions. New York: Van Nostrand Reinhold, 1971.
Harrison, Reginald J. *Europe in Question: Theories of Regional International Inte-*
    gration. New York: New York University Press, 1975.
Hudec, Robert E. *The GATT Legal System and World Trade Diplomacy.* New York:
    Praeger, 1975.
Ionescu, G., ed. *The European Alternatives: An Inquiry Into the Policies of the Euro-*
    pean Community. Alphen aan den Rijn, Netherlands: Sijthoff, 1979.
Jordan, Robert S. *The NATO Internatinal Staff Secretariat 1952–1957.* New York:
    Oxford University Press, 1967.
Jose, James R. *An Inter-American Peace Force Within the Framework of the Organi-*
    zation of American States. Metuchen, N.J.: Scarecrow Press, 1970.
Keohane, Robert O., and Nye, Joseph S. *Power and Interdependence.* Boston: Little,
    Brown, 1977.
Krause, Lawrence. *U.S. Economic Policy Toward the Association of Southeast Asian*
    Nations: Meeting the Japanese Challenge. Washington, D.C.: Brookings Institu-
    tion, 1982.
Laqueur, Walter. *The Rebirth of Europe.* New York: Holt, Rinehart, and Winston,
    1970.
Leuthy, Herbert. *France Against Herself.* New York: Praeger, 1955.
Liska, George. *Europe Ascendant.* Baltimore: Johns Hopkins Press, 1964.
Mally, Gerhard. *The European Community in Perspective.* Lexington, Mass.: Lexing-
    ton Books, 1973.
————. *Interdependence: The European-American Connection in the Global Con-*
    text. Lexington, Mass.: Lexington Books, 1976.
Marquand, David. *Parliament for Europe.* London: Jonathan Cape, 1979.
McDonald, Robert W. *The League of Arab States.* Princeton, N.J.: Princeton Univer-
    sity Press, 1965.
Myrdal, Gunnar. *Realities and Illusions in Regard to Inter-Governmental Organiza-*
    tions. New York: Oxford University Press, 1955.
Nye, J. S. *Peace in Parts: Integration and Conflict in Regional Organization.* Boston:
    Little, Brown, 1971.
Pfaltzgraff, Robert L., Jr. *The Atlantic Community: A Complex Imbalance.* New
    York: Van Nostrand Reinhold, 1969.
Pryce, Roy. *The Politics of the European Community.* Totowa, N.J.: Rowman and
    Littlefield, 1978.
Reid, Escott. *Time of Fear and Hope: The Making of the North Atlantic Treaty*
    1947–1949. Toronto: McClelland and Stewart, 1977.
Robertson, A. H. *The Council of Europe—Its Structure, Functions and Achievements.*
    New York: Praeger, 1956.
————. *Human Rights in Europe.* Manchester, England: Manchester University
    Press, 1977.
Sanger, Clyde, and Smith, Arnold. *Stitches in Time: The Commonwealth in World*
    Politics. New York: Beaufort Books, 1983.

Sasse, Christoph, ed. *Decision Making in the European Community*. New York: Praeger, 1977.

Schaetzel, Robert J. *The Unhinged Alliance: America and the European Community*. New York: Harper & Row, 1975.

Slater, Jerome. *The OAS and United States Foreign Policy*. Columbus: Ohio State University Press, 1967.

Von Geusau, Frans A. M. Alting. *Beyond the European Community*. Leiden: Sijthoff, 1969.

Woronoff, Jon. *Organizing African Unity*. Metuchen, N.J.: Scarecrow Press, 1970.

Young, Oran R. *Resource Management at the International Level: The Case of the North Pacific*. New York: Nichols, 1977.

Chapter 12

The Military Struggle for Order

To take arms against a sea of troubles.

SHAKESPEARE *Hamlet*, III, 1

DILEMMAS OF DISARMAMENT

The following is a description of Hiroshima shortly after the city was destroyed by an atomic bomb in August 1945:

> People are still dying, mysteriously and horribly—people who were uninjured in the cataclysm—from an unknown something which I can only describe as the atomic plague.
>
> Hiroshima does not look like a bombed city. . . . I write these facts as dispassionately as I can, in the hope that they will act as a warning to the world. In this first testing ground of the atomic bomb . . . it gives you an empty feeling in the stomach to see such man-made devastation. . . . I could see about three miles of reddish rubble. That is all the atomic bomb left. . . . The Police Chief of Hiroshima . . . took me to hospitals where the victims of the bomb are still being treated. In these hospitals I found people who, when the bomb fell, suffered absolutely no injuries, but now are dying from the uncanny after-effects. For no apparent reason their health began to fail. They lost appetite. Their hair fell out. Bluish spots appeared on their bodies. And then bleeding began from the ears, nose and mouth.
>
> At first, the doctors told me, they thought these were the symptoms of general debility. They gave their patients Vitamin A injections. The results were horrible. The flesh started rotting away from the hole caused by the injection of the needle. And in every case the victim died.
>
> A peculiar odour . . . given off by the poisonous gas still issues from the earth soaked with radioactivity; against this the inhabitants all wear gauze masks over their mouths and noses; many thousands of people have simply vanished—the atomic heat was so great that they burned instantly to ashes—except that there were no ashes—they were vaporised.[1]

The bomb here mentioned, it should be noted, is now considered obsolete. Its capacity for destruction has been dwarfed by an even more total weapon—the hydrogen bomb. That this development has engendered a more intensive quest for disarmament than ever before in history is by no means surprising. Indeed, the price of failure in this quest is not likely to be merely the kind of devastation that was loosed on Hiroshima and Nagasaki. It may well be the extinction of man as the dominant form of life on this planet.

Since 1945 the issue of disarmament has assumed paramount importance and has unceasingly occupied the thinking of statesmen and technical experts everywhere. The United Nations General Assembly has dealt with it during every session and it is safe to predict that this pattern will continue. The two major antagonists in the East-West struggle have both agreed that disarmament is the most important problem facing the world today.[2] Yet, despite a strategic arms limitation treaty agreed upon at the Moscow Summit of 1972, not a single weapon, atomic or conventional, has been scrapped by treaty. Instead, we are still witnessing the fiercest and most relentless arms race in history. Why? In order to answer this question, we must analyze the disarmament dilemma in all its complexity.

If the objective of the political order-builders is a world without major disputes, the hope of those who would build order through disarmament is a world without weapons. In the view of the latter, arms races cause wars. If, as they see it, arms are permitted to accumulate, they will sooner or later be used. An arms race therefore becomes a relentless and self-propelling march to war. Both sides strain furiously to maintain or reclaim the lead. Finally, the tension reaches such a pitch that war is almost welcomed as a liberating explosion. If, on the other hand, nations are deprived of the means to fight, the proponents of disarmament maintain, wars will either cease to exist or, at worst, become relatively harmless. In the telling phrase of Maxim Litvinov: "the way to disarm is to disarm."

Here we encounter the first crucial problem. Is it true, as the advocates of disarmament hold, that arms races cause the political tensions that drive nations to war? Or are the political order-builders correct in asserting that though arms races may precipitate war, the real source of international conflict must be sought in the political tensions between nations that lead to arms races in the first place? The former tend to regard the arms race as a basic cause of war, the latter merely as a symptom of political pathology. Both groups are prepared to admit that the problem is really a circular one: that arms races breed political tensions; that these in turn lead to the development and acquisition of more destructive weapons; and that this situation raises temperatures even further—until the violent climax is reached. But the two groups differ as to the most effective point at which to intervene in the vicious circle. Those who see arms races as a basic cause of war assert the primacy of international order-building through disarmament. They maintain that halting the arms race will lead to a reduction in political tensions, which will likely result in an even further scrapping of weapons. On the other hand, a growing number of observers are defending the view that disarmament efforts are bound to fail unless they are preceded by more fundamental political accommodation. The way to disarm, according to this latter view, is not to begin by disarming but to concentrate instead on the settlement of political differences.

One of the most articulate spokesmen for the primacy of disarmament was the British Nobel Prize winner Philip Noel-Baker. This scholar attacks the thesis that disarmament can only be a consequence, never a cause, of improvement in international relations. In support of this view, Noel-Baker cites the Rush-Bagot Agreement of 1817 between Britain and the United States, which disarmed the Canadian frontier. In his view, this agreement was a great contribution to the establishment of friendly relations between Canada and the United States. He also points to the 1922 Washington Naval Disarmament Convention, which reduced the navies of Britain, the United States, and Japan, as producing a remarkable improvement in international relations. He suggests that the convention nipped in the bud an impending struggle for supremacy of the seas and played a major part in creating cordial relations between Britain and the United States. From these examples, the author concludes that the ending of the East-West nuclear arms race by a disarmament treaty would improve international relations, reduce tensions, and facilitate the settlement of outstanding political disputes.[3]

The opposing view was most eloquently defended by Hans J. Morgenthau. He attacks the view of the military order-builder as unrealistic. "Men do not fight because they have arms, but they have arms because they deem it necessary to fight." If deprived of weapons, nations will employ all their resources for the development of new ones. In fact, Morgenthau continued, the threat of all-out nuclear war may have been the most important single factor that has prevented the outbreak of general war in the nuclear age. The removal of that threat through disarmament might indeed increase the dangers of war. Disarmament might do away with weapons but not with the will and the technical knowledge to produce these weapons. In support of his argument, Morgenthau cited the Treaty of Versailles which, in his view, was a blessing in disguise for German militarism. Disarmament compelled Germany to project its military thinking in the future, to look at problems of strategy and technology *de novo*. Far from removing German ambitions of conquest, disarmament merely equipped it to fight World War II while France was ready merely for a repetition of World War I.[4] Hence, Morgenthau concluded, the first step toward order-building must always be political rather than military. Disarmament *in vacuo* is bound to be a failure.

In view of the sharp disagreement on the nature and significance of disarmament, it is necessary to subject the modern record of disarmament negotiations to careful scrutiny. Why did most of them fail? What was the secret of success of the few that did not? Does the record provide any clues for the crucial disarmament negotiations of our own time?

Before embarking on a survey of the disarmament record, it is useful to bear in mind a definition and three important distinctions. Central to the concept of disarmament is the term *reduction*. An actual reduction of weapons must take place before we can describe an act as *dis*armament. The first of the three distinctions is between *general* disarmament, which refers to efforts involving all nations, and *local* disarmament, which includes only a limited number of countries. The second is between *quantitative* disarmament, which concerns the reduction of all types of weapons, and *qualitative* disarmament, which concentrates upon a specific category of weapons. It is also useful to remember that the reduction of nonatomic weapons is referred to as "conventional disarmament," while "nuclear disarmament" refers to the reduction of atomic stockpiles.

In the entire history of the nation-state system up to World War II, there are on record only two disarmament conferences that proved successful. Both were local and quantitative. The first was the Rush-Bagot Agreement, concluded in 1817, limiting the naval forces of Canada and the United States to three vessels each on the Great Lakes. The agreement resulted in the demilitarization of the United States–Canadian frontier. With certain revisions that were added during World War II, the agreement has remained in force.

The more significant of the two successful ventures in disarmament was the Washington Treaty of 1922 for the Limitation of Naval Armaments. The aim of the treaty was to determine ratios for the allocation of capital ships among the major naval powers. The United States and Britain were to have the largest navies, while Japan, France, and Italy were given smaller allocations. A ratio of 5:5:3:1.67:1.67 was finally established for the capital ships of the United States, Britain, Japan, France, and Italy, in that order. As a result, the three leading countries scrapped approximately two-fifths of their capital ships. In regard to cruisers, destroyers, and submarines, however, the Washington Treaty failed to reach agreement. The London Naval Conference of 1930 attempted to complete the work begun at Washington by limiting the tonnage of naval craft other than capital ships. Parity for cruisers, destroyers, and submarines was agreed upon between the United States and Britain, while Japan was limited to two-thirds of American or British strength. Neither France nor Italy was a signatory to the London Treaty. Italy demanded parity with France, as in the Washington Agreement. This parity France was now unwilling to grant.

The agreements hammered out so painstakingly in Washington and London were not destined to endure. In 1934 Japan demanded parity with Britain and the United States in all naval craft. When this demand was rejected, Japan abrogated the treaty and embarked on an ambitious naval rearmament program. Hence, of the two successes on record, only the Rush-Bagot Agreement may be considered permanent. The Washington Treaty was moribund after a decade.

Unhappily, the list of failures is far longer. The pattern was set at the First Hague Peace Conference in 1899, when twenty-eight nations expressed themselves on the desirability of a reduction in armaments but were unable to agree on a specific formula. The failure was repeated by forty-four nations meeting at the Second Hague Peace Conference in 1907. As the Russian delegate put it at the time: "The question was not ripe in 1899, it is not any more so in 1907. It has not been possible to do anything on these lines, and the Conference today finds itself as little prepared to enter upon them as in 1899."[5] The next effort took place at Versailles in 1919, when disarmament was imposed upon Germany. As that nation became increasingly restive under the terms of the

"Versailles Diktat" during the 1920s, the League of Nations sought desperately to keep German armaments at a minimum. Finally, a World Disarmament Conference was convened at Geneva in 1932. But that conference met under the shadow of Hitler, who was to come to power several months later. When Germany embarked on a relentless arms program in 1933, the World Disarmament Conference had to concede defeat.

Six years of world war, culminating in the ghastly spectacle of atomic destruction, convinced the founders of the United Nations that disarmament should be a permanent item on the agenda of the new world organization. Accordingly, in January 1946 the General Assembly created the Atomic Energy Commission for the specific purpose of eliminating atomic weapons from the nations' military arsenals. In addition, a Commission for Conventional Armaments was established by the Security Council in February 1947. When neither of these two organs made any progress, the General Assembly, in 1952, amalgamated them into one Disarmament Commission. This body originally consisted of the members of the Security Council plus Canada. However, each time the commission failed to achieve a consensus, the General Assembly attempted to remedy the matter by enlarging its membership. Finally, the General Assembly itself became a forum for disarmament proposals that were thinly camouflaged propaganda maneuvers in the East-West struggle rather than serious overtures to negotiation. Premier Khrushchev's proposal for general and complete disarmament, which he made in the General Assembly in 1959, was a case in point. Since 1954, indeed, Geneva, Vienna, and Moscow, rather than the United Nations, have become the meeting places for serious negotiations. The conferences that have been held there have usually included an equal number of representatives from East and West.

Thus, since the end of World War II, disarmament negotiations have been a permanent phenomenon. Yet none of the many conferences that have been held—whether inside or outside of the United Nations—has accomplished the elimination of a single atomic or conventional weapon. Even the Moscow Summit of 1972 was no exception. It achieved a limitation on the building of additional arms, not a reduction of existing arms. The most intensive disarmament efforts in Western history have been a virtual failure. The only successes on record antedate World War II, and one of these was of too brief duration to be termed an unqualified success. We shall now look into the causes of this discouraging record.

One important reason for these many failures is the inherently *static* nature of all disarmament. It is a fact of international life that many nations are constantly engaged in attempts to manipulate the existing distribution of power in their favor. An increase in armaments is an obvious means to accomplish this end. The goal of disarmament, on the other hand, is in essence the freezing of a certain distribution of power which will be acceptable to some, but never to all the powers concerned. Most nations conceive of themselves as dynamic actors on the international scene, hoping to move from strength to strength. Such states will have little patience with policies that would deprive them of an important means whereby they can grow in power and stature. Indeed, one of the greatest obstacles to disarmament is the fact that nations are less concerned with what they are than with what they would like to be.

The technical counterpart of this political truth has been the enormous difficulty of *measurement*. Each disarmament conference has to grapple with this stubborn problem. Once the delegates get down to specifics, they constantly find themselves compelled to "compare apples with oranges." Which is more valuable to a military arsenal—a destroyer or a tank? How does the striking force of the American Strategic Air Command compare to the Soviet land army? How many Polaris missiles should be scrapped for each Soviet intercontinental ballistic missile? How do four million men in reserve compare to one million in active service? Precision is almost impossible to attain. Each side in the East-West struggle has advanced proposals that would leave its superiority intact or reduce that of the other side. Since both the United States and the Soviet Union conceive of themselves as dynamic contestants for supremacy, neither has been willing to accept an arms reduction that would freeze it at a level of inferiority. Salvador de Madariaga has illustrated the point admirably through the analogy of an imaginary conference of animals at which "the lion wanted to eliminate all weapons but claws and jaws, the eagle all but talons and beaks and the bear all but an embracing hug."[6]

The crucial cause of the failure of most disarmament negotiations is, of course, the absence of mutual trust. In technical terms this has meant that each side has attempted to impose rigorous requirements of *inspection* and *control* on the other in order to ensure that an agreement, once reached, would not be violated. Control and inspection are to be the technical substitute for mutual trust. But this condition has invited a circular problem: each side requires control because it does not trust the other; yet, the acceptance of a control system itself demands a high degree of mutual trust. In short, whenever nations have taken the position that there can be no disarmament without security, they have had to realize that foolproof security is equally impossible. A degree of mutual confidence is necessary for both disarmament and security. The major powers have been unable to escape from this predicament.

The control problem proved to be an insurmountable obstacle at the very beginning of the nuclear disarmament negotiations in the United Nations Atomic Energy Commission in 1946. At that time, when the United States still had an atomic monopoly, it proposed a far-reaching control plan known as the Acheson-Lilienthal Report, or Baruch Plan. The purpose of the plan was to ensure that atomic energy would be used exclusively for peaceful purposes. To accomplish this end, the United States proposed the internationalization of all facilities producing atomic power. All atomic plants would be owned and operated by an Atomic Development Authority that would have the powers of inspection, accounting, and licensing. The American hope was to place atomic energy firmly under international control before the Soviet Union would end the American monopoly and engage in an atomic arms race with the United States. The plan was widely heralded as a generous offer which would place the power of the atom under the authority of a limited world government. The Soviet Union's response, however, was negative. It insisted upon the continuance of national ownership and operation of atomic plants and advanced a plan of its own, which proposed the destruction of all existing stocks of nuclear weapons and a legal prohibition of their future manufacture. Only after existing stockpiles had been destroyed and a treaty outlawing nuclear weapons concluded would the Soviet Union be ready to proceed to international inspection. Most immediately, then, the impasse revolved around the problem of priorities. The United States insisted on the priority of international inspection before it was willing to undertake the destruction of its nuclear stockpiles. Control would have to come first and disarmament would follow. The Soviet Union, on the other hand, insisted on the prior destruction of American stockpiles before it was willing to allow international inspection. It reversed the sequence: disarmament must come first and control would follow.

It would seem from the above that the United States' offer was a generous one, whereas the Soviet Union's rejection was an unreasonable act of caprice. After all, the United States made its offer at a time when it had an atomic monopoly. It would therefore appear that the Soviet Union, which had not yet developed its own atomic bomb, could only gain from the internationalization of atomic power. Actually, however, the picture is considerably more complex. It is true that the American offer was an enlightened act of statesmanship. But it is equally true that, given the state of mistrust between the two superpowers, there were valid reasons from the Soviet point of view for rejecting the Baruch Plan. First and most important, the plan would have perpetuated the American monopoly of atomic weapons. And beyond that, the Soviet Union feared that the proposed Atomic Development Authority would be dominated by the Western powers with the Eastern bloc in a permanent minority without the right of veto. In the words of Andrei Gromyko, the Soviet delegate:

> The Soviet Union is aware that there will be a majority in the control organ which may take one-sided decisions, a majority on whose benevolent attitude toward the Soviet Union the Soviet people cannot count. Therefore, the Soviet Union, and probably not only the Soviet Union, cannot allow that the fate of its national economy be handed over to this organ.[7]

Most basically, Soviet suspicions grew out of the realization that only the United States would be in a position to cheat, i.e., withhold weapons from the authority, while the Soviet Union would be compelled to accept a permanent position of inferiority. All this is not to say that the United States' offer was not farsighted. What does seem clear, however, is that its chances of acceptance would have been considerably greater if it had permitted the continuation of national atomic research in the Soviet Union.

The struggle over priorities that began in 1946 continued without letup until the Moscow Summit of 1972. The United States and the Soviet Union both agreed that a viable disarmament treaty would have to include provisions for the prohibition of nuclear weapons as well as acceptable arrangements for control. The Soviet Union consistently defended the priority of prohibition in numerous "ban the bomb" proposals. These proposals were unacceptable to the United States, which feared that the Soviet Union would not accede to control once prohibition was accepted. The United States' insistence on the priority of control, on the other hand, was unacceptable to the Soviet Union because the latter consistently tended to regard all international inspection as a form of espionage. Hence the paradoxical situation that though both powers accepted the principle of simultaneous disarmament and control, they were unable to translate it into practice. Each side continued to postpone what for it would be the greater sacrifice and, instead, encouraged the opponent to take the first step. To try to expedite matters, the French in 1958 introduced the ingenious formula: "Neither control without disarmament, nor disarmament without control but, progressively, all the disarmament that can at present be controlled."[8] Though this proposal met the problem in principle, it, too, could not be applied in practice.

Fundamentally, the impasse stemmed from the fact that American proposals assumed a good deal of Soviet confidence in the United States, while the Soviet counterproposals assumed an equal amount of American faith in Soviet intentions. When the two rivals realized that this premise of mutual trust did not exist, they sought substitutes in various technical requirements for inspection and control. Yet they soon concluded that even such technical devices could never be completely foolproof; cheating would continue to be possible regardless of how intricate the safeguards. Indeed, there clearly seemed no other alternative: good faith was a necessary premise for *all* disarmament negotiations and arrangements.

A further reason for the failure of disarmament negotiations may be found paradoxically enough, in the very interest that the subject has continued to evoke in world public opinion. In the words of India's late Prime Minister Nehru:

> The arms race affects us nations and peoples everywhere, whether we are involved in wars or power blocs or not. . . . There can be little doubt about the deep and widespread concern in the world, particularly among peoples, about these weapons and their dreadful consequences.[9]

The testing of hydrogen weapons on both sides of the Iron Curtain and the resulting problem of atomic radiation intensified public indignation the world over. Disarmament became the most emotional issue before the United Nations General Assembly. Not surprisingly, the rise of this passionate popular interest and involvement led both sides in the conflict to engage in open diplomacy. Vying for the allegiance of the uncommitted countries where disarmament was a burning issue, the two superpowers themselves turned the disarmament negotiations into a weapon in the East-West struggle. Open diplomacy in the sensitive and frequently technical field of disarmament inevitably culminated in propaganda battles in which both East and West felt compelled to appeal to the audiences rather than to each other.

Each side faced a similar dilemma in the conduct of these public negotiations. The demands of security forbade the advancement of proposals that the other side found genuinely acceptable. But the power of publicity demanded

that the proposals appear as reasonable as possible in order to avoid the onus
of sabotaging the negotiations. Hence, a curious pattern developed that one
observer aptly called the "gamesmanship of disarmament."[10] This "game" was
played according to certain tacit but well-defined rules:

> Every plan offered by either side has contained a set of proposals calculated to
> have wide popular appeal. Every such set has included at least one feature that
> the other side could not possibly accept, thus forcing a rejection. Then the pro-
> posing side has been able to claim that the rejector is opposed to the idea of dis-
> armament *in toto*. The objectionable feature may be thought of as the "joker" in
> every series of proposals.[11]

As a result of this game, the illusion was sometimes created that the two sides
had narrowed their differences. Actually, what had happened was that each
side had expanded its range of acceptable proposals to ensure popular appeal,
but had made equally sure that a "joker" would force rejection of the entire
package. The Baruch Plan contained such a joker: the insistence that there be
no veto on the question of sanctions against violators of the control agreement.
Acceptance of this joker would have placed the Soviet Union in a position of
permanent military inferiority. Soviet proposals made similar use of the joker
technique. A typical case was a Soviet proposal, made on May 10, 1955, in
which the USSR agreed to reduce its land armies to a maximum figure desired
by the three Western powers. For five years the Western negotiators had proposed a reduction of Chinese, Soviet, and American forces to one million men
each, with 650,000 each for France and the United Kingdom. But as public
pressure mounted and the July 1955 Summit Conference drew nearer, the
French delegate to the conference, Jules Moch, stated that "The whole thing
look[ed] too good to be true." The spokesman for the United States, on the
other hand, made the following, more optimistic statement:

> We have been gratified to find that the concepts which we have put forward over
> a considerable length of time, and which we have repeated many times during
> these past two months, have been accepted in a large measure by the Soviet
> Union.[12]

As it turned out, Moch's suspicions were fully justified. The proposal was indeed too good to be true. The Soviet concession was made conditional upon
agreement that "states possessing military, naval and air bases in the territories
of other states shall undertake to liquidate such bases."[13] In other words, the
Soviet joker was a demand for the dissolution of the Western alliance system—a condition, of course, that was completely unacceptable without prior
settlement of the major political differences between East and West. It is significant, nevertheless, that despite the obviousness of this joker, the onus for
the collapse of the manpower reduction talks was placed by most observers at
the Summit Conference squarely upon the United States. The public, eager for
results, was hypnotized by what appeared to be a generous proposal and did
not notice the jokers. Even as astute an observer as Philip Noel-Baker failed to
perceive the deceptiveness of the Soviet bid. In his book, *The Arms Race*, he
refers to May 10, 1955, the day of the Soviet manpower reduction proposal, as

"the moment of hope," and attributes its failure directly to what he feels to have been the dogmatic unwillingness of the American State Department to disarm at all.[14]

Perhaps the really classic example of gamesmanship was Premier Khrushchev's dramatic proposal for "general and complete disarmament," made before the General Assembly in September 1959. In his speech, the Soviet premier suggested that "over a period of four years, all states should carry out complete disarmament and should divest themselves of the means of waging war."[15] The premier envisaged the dissolution of all armies, navies, air forces, general staffs, war ministries, and military schools as well as the destruction of all atomic weapons and missiles. Especially in the uncommitted countries, the publicity value of the Russian leader's speech was quite high, even though, by the late 1950s, the effectiveness of disarmament propaganda had begun to reach a point of diminishing returns. Yet as always, there was a joker. And this time it was the vagueness of the new proposal's references to the matter of control provisions. Indeed, the most to which the Soviet premier would commit himself was the establishment of "an international control body in which all states would participate."[16] Yet Mr. Khrushchev presumably knew full well that as far as the West was concerned, no disarmament proposal would be acceptable unless it at the same time provided for a rigorous and full-scale inspection system.

A final reason for the failure of disarmament is undoubtedly the fact that one of the two main negotiators is a totalitarian power and, as such, a closed society. It is true that the unwillingness to accept international inspection has not always been a Soviet monopoly. As Claude points out, the United States expressed similar suspicions of foreign inspection in 1919 and again in 1927.[17] But in the United States and most other Western countries, this attitude appears now to have been largely transcended. In 1958, for example, the American Institute of Public Opinion conducted an extensive poll in six nations—the United States, Britain, France, West Germany, India, and Japan—to determine the climate of opinion in regard to international inspection of disarmament.[18] The following three questions were asked.

1. Would you favor or oppose setting up a world-wide organization which would make sure—by regular inspections—that no nation, including Russia and the United States, makes atom bombs, hydrogen bombs, and missiles?
2. If this inspection organization were set up, would you favor or oppose making it each person's *duty* to report any attempt to secretly make atom bombs, hydrogen bombs, and missiles?
3. If you, yourself, knew that someone in [name of country] was attempting to secretly make forbidden weapons, would you report this to the office of the world-wide inspection organization in this country?

The first question simply referred to a general disarmament proposal; the second, however, raised a potential conflict of values between national and international loyalty; and the third posed the problem of conflicting loyalties in its starkest form. Hence it was expected that favorable responses would be highest to question one and lowest to question three. Actually, the overall results of the six-nation poll were striking: an overwhelmingly positive response to all three questions in all six countries. Japan ranked highest, with West Germany, India, France, the United States, and Britain following, in that order. From these results the authors concluded that "Inspection by the People was not as visionary a proposal as one might have thought."[19] This conclusion is perhaps overly optimistic, since the authors did not take into account the probable differences between people's reactions to a set of hypothetical questions and their possible reactions when confronted with an actual situation. Yet the study did permit the conclusion that a cross section of the citizens of six democratic nations was definitely in favor of some form of international inspection of disarmament. The very fact, on the other hand, that the Soviet Union did not permit such a poll was itself indicative. Like all closed societies, it has been obsessed with the importance of national sovereignty. And, of course, national sovereignty reaches its most absolute form in matters of military security. In view of this difference in the underlying political logic of East and West, differences between the two sides on such technical matters as to whether inspection or prohibition should have priority, or as to the allocation of specific ratios, are, in the last analysis, merely surface manifestations. The really fundamental difference, rather, must be sought in the basically different characters of the two types of societies: the Western system, more "open" than that of the East, has been able to absorb at least a minimum of international authority; the Soviet Union, largely a "closed" society, has regarded all forms of foreign control as a menace and, hence, anathema.

We are now left with the crucial substantive question of whether the record indicates that order-building through disarmament is a valid approach. The evidence suggests that it is not. Disarmament seems to be not so much a means for the attainment of political order as a product of its achievement. We have seen that, as a rule, nations will be concerned with disarmament only when they are engaged in a power struggle; yet it is precisely this condition that makes the attainment of disarmament so difficult. Even the Washington Treaty of 1922 cannot be cited as an argument in favor of the effectiveness of disarmament. Most of the capital ships that were discarded under the terms of the treaty were obsolete and would have been scrapped anyway. The vessels considered most important in a future war were cruisers, destroyers, and submarines. And significantly, it was in these three categories that the five signatory powers failed to reach agreement. In fact, it might be said that all the treaty accomplished was a "naval holiday" in the building of capital ships that freed the energies of the five nations to engage in an arms race in the production of other naval craft that were considered more vital to the needs of modern warfare. Even if one rejects this uncharitable interpretation of the Washington Treaty, it would be difficult to regard it as a significant instrument of international order-building in view of the fact that Japan repudiated it the moment its new policy of imperialism dictated such a course. Disarmament as a direct approach to order seems feasible only when nations are interested in the enhancement rather than in the reduction of one another's strength. It is probably an exaggeration to claim, as does one authority, that because of the many technical obstacles involved, "even such inveterate friends as the United States and Britain probably could not agree on a formula of mutual arms limitation."[20] After all, the Rush-Bagot agreement of 1817 between the United States and Canada was just such a case. Yet the irony of this agreement lies in the fact that it was probably unnecessary since it was concluded between two neighbors, both of whom by then considered war between them most unlikely.

The discouraging record of disarmament in the modern world supports the proposition that order is fundamentally not a military problem. Disarmament negotiations per se will not reduce the tensions between the major powers unless such efforts are preceded by at least a minimum of success in the settlement of outstanding political differences. This is really another way of saying that the problem of disarmament is not disarmament at all, but is in essence the problem of forging the bonds of political community among nations. We have seen earlier that we know little about the causes of war. Similarly, we do not know enough about the process of community-building. Why should a pilot under orders drop a lethal weapon on a defenseless city in "enemy" country, but refuse to drop it on his own? At first glance, this question may seem naive. But when one considers its human implications, it is not. For if we could answer it, the issue of disarmament would have become largely irrelevant. As an order-building strategy, disarmament is chiefly concerned with symptoms. The real causes of the disease must be sought at a deeper level.

The frustrations over disarmament have led some thinkers to approach the problem in a somewhat different way: arms *control* rather than disarmament. Whereas the disarmer is primarily concerned with the actual scrapping of existing weapons, the arms controller is more interested in stabilizing the climate in which these weapons exist and in the prevention of additional arms buildups. The emphasis here is less on hardware and more on psychology. The hope is that progress can be made on issues related to disarmament, which might act as confidence-builders and ultimately lead to actual disarmament agreements. In December 1959, for example, a treaty was signed among twelve nations with claims in Antarctica demilitarizing that continent. The signatories pledged themselves neither to establish military fortifications nor to carry out military maneuvers in the Antarctic. In 1963, in the wake of the Cuban missile crisis, the Soviet Union and the United States established direct communications—a "hot line" between the White House and the Kremlin—and reached agreement on the peaceful uses of outer space. In 1964 the United States offered one of its large nuclear reactors to international inspection by a United Nations agency, and in the same year the two superpowers agreed on cutbacks in their stockpiles of fissionable materials—the raw materials for atomic weapons—thus retarding the growth of "overkill" capacity on both sides.

In 1967 the two superpowers, after lengthy negotiations, agreed to work in earnest on a formula for a treaty banning the proliferation of nuclear weapons. In January 1968 they presented a joint draft treaty on nonproliferation to the seventeen-member Disarmament Conference in Geneva. The draft treaty was designed to freeze the "nuclear club" at its membership of five: the United

States, the Soviet Union, the United Kingdom, France, and Communist China. Several hurdles confronted the negotiators. First, neither France nor China was expected to sign. Second, certain "threshold" countries such as India and Israel were reluctant to sign, the former for fear of China and Pakistan and the latter because of Egypt. Finally, the matter of inspection posed formidable obstacles. Would the treaty be policed through self-inspection, regional bodies such as Euratom, or a United Nations organ, such as the International Atomic Energy Agency? These and other knotty problems defied easy solution and made progress on the treaty slow and arduous. Nevertheless, the very fact of superpower cooperation on such a sensitive issue as nonproliferation provided grounds for optimism. In June 1968 another forward step was taken when the UN General Assembly, in a vote of 95 in favor, 4 against, and 21 abstentions, gave its blessing to the draft treaty. Three nuclear and forty nonnuclear ratifications were now needed to make the document into a binding treaty. In March 1970, the nuclear nonproliferation treaty officially entered into force without the adherence of China and France. It has worked relatively well since then, although in 1974 India became the sixth member of the world's exclusive nuclear club. In 1981, however, Israel took unilateral measures by destroying an Iraqi nuclear installation in a preemptive strike. This event indicated the possibility that, in the future, states would depend more upon themselves than upon treaties to prevent the spread of nuclear weapons.

Several other arms control treaties are deserving of mention: In 1967 the two superpowers agreed on a treaty in which each pledged itself not to militarize outer space. The treaty was approved by the UN General Assembly in 1967 and entered into force that same year. In 1971 a similar treaty was signed in relation to the seabed and the ocean floors. In 1976 the Soviet Union and the United States agreed on a ban against environmental warfare and in 1978 they approved a similar ban against chemical warfare. It is important to note that none of these efforts achieved an actual reduction of existing weapons, but each went a long way in preventing their further dissemination and in preventing the construction of new weapons.

These arms control achievements have not been insignificant. Without them, the world would be an even more dangerous place. Nuclear testing would poison the air and water; the superpowers might try to annex the moon and other planets; nuclear weapons would be emplaced on the bottom of the sea; tidal waves might be loosed and earthquakes triggered; and there might be a dozen nuclear powers instead of six. If, indeed, the nuclear nonproliferation treaty should break down, nuclear terrorism might become the biggest threat facing humanity. There are already some disturbing signs that point in this direction.

In July 1975, the mayor of New York City received the following unsigned note:

> We have successfully designed and built an atomic bomb. It is somewhere on Manhattan Island. We refer you to the accompanying drawing in 1/8 scale. We have plutonium and explosives for the bomb to function. This device will be used at 6 P.M. July 10 unless our demands are met. Do not notify the public. This will result in hysteria and the use of the bomb.[21]

The extortioners demanded $30 million in small unmarked bills. The FBI deposited the money at a designated drop site, but no one claimed it. The extortioners made no further contact.

Suppose that the bomb had gone off, or that some future nuclear terrorist might be more successful. The contemplation of such nightmares makes one realize that arms control, despite its imperfections, is useful nonetheless. It is *not* disarmament. But it is a great deal better than nothing. Unfortunately, since 1980 not a single arms control treaty has been signed between the superpowers.

In view of the current emphasis on arms control rather than on disarmament, two arms control treaties are included as case studies: The first will deal with the partial nuclear test ban signed in Moscow in 1963, which was the first specific symptom of the new United States–Soviet détente; and the second will describe the most significant fruits of that détente reached a decade later: the Strategic Arms Limitation Treaties.

THE CESSATION OF NUCLEAR TESTING IN 1963

The goal of nuclear test cessation was always more modest than that of disarmament since it implied no reduction of stockpiles nor any fundamental change in the arsenals of the negotiating powers. A nuclear test ban would accomplish two things: it would limit the further development of nuclear weapons already stocked in great quantities in the Soviet Union, the United States, Britain, and France; and it would halt further contamination of the world's atmosphere through radioactive fallout.

If disarmament has been the most important general problem before the General Assembly, the cessation of nuclear weapons testing was the most crucial specific issue related to disarmament. The pressures on the nuclear powers, especially by the atomic have-not nations, were enormous. In 1959, for example, the General Assembly passed by overwhelming majorities four resolutions urging a moratorium on nuclear tests. These resolutions were primarily a reflection of a worldwide concern with the damage to human health if tests were to continue.

Scientists have differed widely on the amount of damage that radioactive fallout inflicts on the human system. But all agree that there are at least four areas in which *some* harm is certain to result. For one thing, it has been established that exposure to radiation shortens the human life span. In the opinion of Dr. H. J. Muller, a leading American geneticist, the shortening of the life span is "by far the most serious of the long term effects on the exposed person himself."[22] The second danger derives from strontium 90, a radioactive substance produced by nuclear explosions but unknown in nature. This by-product of atomic tests causes cancer of the bone. Opinions differ on the extent of the damage but there is wide agreement that each test results in bone cancer being incurred by a number of people. Most scientists also agree that children are more susceptible to the poison than adults.[23] Leukemia, a fatal disease of the white blood cells, has also been related to strontium 90.[24] Finally, the most

far-reaching effects of fallout seem to be genetic mutations in future generations. Again, estimates vary but there is wide agreement among geneticists
that nuclear tests will be responsible for a considerable number of stillbirths,
embryonic deaths, and defective mutations.[25]

As a result of constant prodding by the General Assembly, the Soviet
Union, in May 1955, took the initiative in seeking a test ban. During the following year the Soviet Union pressed the United States for the conclusion of a
bilateral agreement. The Soviet position was that the question of a test ban
could be separated from the general problem of disarmament and that controls
to detect violations were unnecessary. As Premier Bulganin wrote to President
Eisenhower in 1956:

> It is a known fact that the discontinuation of such tests does not in itself require
> any international control agreements, for the present state of science and engi-
> neering makes it possible to detect any explosion of an atomic or hydrogen bomb,
> wherever it may be set off. In our opinion this situation makes it possible to sepa-
> rate the problem of ending tests of atomic and hydrogen weapons from the gen-
> eral problem of disarmament and to solve it independently even now, without
> tying an agreement on this subject to agreements on other disarmament prob-
> lems.[26]

The Western powers agreed to discuss a test ban as a separate issue but flatly
rejected the Soviet assertion that controls were unnecessary. In a counterpro-
posal, the United States, Great Britain, and France suggested test cessation
under an international control system. The Soviet Union declared itself willing
to negotiate the vexatious matter of inspection. The next difficulty arose when
the United States insisted on the need to continue testing until a cut-off agreement and a control plan had actually been negotiated. At this point, great
pressure was exerted on the American government by a large majority in the
General Assembly to agree to an informal test ban pending the conclusion of a
formal treaty. Opinion among leading American scientists was deeply divided
on this issue. On the one hand, Dr. Linus Pauling, an American Nobel Prize
winner, represented a considerable body of opinion when he demanded that
test be halted immediately:

> Each added amount of radiation causes damage to the health of human beings all
> over the world and causes damage to the pool of human germ plasm such as to
> lead to an increase in the number of seriously defective children that will be born
> in future generations. An international agreement to stop all testing of nuclear
> weapons now could serve as a first step towards a more general disarmament, and
> the effective abolition of nuclear weapons, averting the possibility of a nuclear
> war that would be a catastrophe to all humanity.[27]

The case for continuing tests was largely defended by scientists in the United
States Atomic Energy Commission. In the opinion of Dr. Edward Teller, a
leading scientist, testing had to continue because

> further tests will put us into a position to fight our opponent's war machine while
> sparing the innocent bystanders. One development of the greatest impor-
> tance is the progressive reduction of radioactive fallout. Clean weapons of this
> kind will reduce unnecessary casualties in a future war.[28]

Dr. Teller's colleague in the AEC, Dr. Willard F. Libby, also justified atomic tests on grounds of national defense:

> It is not contended that there is no risk to human health. Are we willing to take this very small and rigidly controlled risk, or would we prefer to run the risk of annihilation which might result, if we surrendered the weapons which are so essential to our freedom and actual survival?[29]

While the United States was engaged in weighing the alternatives of a provisional test ban, the Soviet Union, in March 1958, announced a unilateral cessation of nuclear tests. Once again on the defensive, the United States proposed a meeting of technical experts to study the feasibility of a control system to detect violations of a test ban. This conference, attended by an equal number of scientists from East and West, took place in July 1958 and submitted a positive report, calling for three steps by which a detection system might be implemented:

1. A network of control posts around the globe. About 170 would be land-based. Of these, 10 would be in the United States, 14 in the USSR, and 8 in Communist China. The remaining land-based posts would be distributed on the continents and on large and small oceanic islands. Ten additional posts would be on ships.
2. Creation of an "international control organ," which would run the global system, pick the staff, select the detection devices, study reports, and generally see to it that no nation violated the test suspension agreement.
3. Use of weather reconnaissance aircraft to sample the air for radioactivity. They would rush to a suspicious area to see if a bomb had been set off or whether the tremor was due to other causes.[30]

The scientists' report, while welcomed by the negotiators, raised important new problems. What would be the composition of the "international control organ"? What would be the voting procedure? Would there be a veto? What would be the authority of the inspectors? Serious bargaining took place on all of these questions at Geneva. The West suggested a veto-free control commission to be headed by a neutral administrator. The Soviet Union, however, insisted on a three-man directorate and the right of veto. The negotiators also disagreed on the number and role of the inspectors in the field. The West demanded international and mobile inspection teams with freedom of access to any area where an illegal atomic test was suspected. The Soviet Union emphasized the primacy of self-inspection but accepted the admission in principle of "foreign specialists" from the West. Another technical problem presented itself when the United States announced that it had underestimated the difficulty of detecting underground nuclear explosions. The United States position was that such explosions would be almost indistinguishable seismographically from natural shocks such as earthquakes. Hence, the American government demanded that the number of control stations be raised from 180 to 600.

More threatening than the technical problems of an atomic test ban was the sword of Damocles of the "nth nation." The main negotiators were three nuclear powers—the United States, the Soviet Union, and Britain. But France, of course, was already developing its own nuclear arsenal, and it was estimated that in the not too distant future several new nations would join the nuclear club: Belgium, Canada, China, Czechoslovakia, East Germany, West Germany, India, Israel, Italy, Japan, Sweden, and Switzerland.[31] Would the new atomic powers agree to be bound by a treaty to which they were not a party? France, for example, insisted on the completion of a series of tests while the Big Three were engaged in negotiations in Geneva. Far more serious, even, was the problem of Communist China. The 1958 Geneva report of the technical experts recommended that 8 of the 180 control stations be placed on mainland China. If the international control organ were placed under United Nations authority, would it be reasonable to expect Communist China to admit United Nations control posts on its territory while it was not a member of the world organization? Even if the control organ were set up outside the United Nations framewowrk, would Communist China consider itself bound by a treaty with nations that continued to refuse to recognize it as a legal government?

Despite the numerous difficulties, a remarkable lessening of differences occurred during 1959 and 1960, but in late 1961 the Soviet Union broke the informal moratorium and tested weapons of unprecedented explosive force. By the time of the Cuban missile crisis a test ban agreement seemed more remote than ever. Yet the resolution of that crisis seemed to convince the Soviet leadership that more could be gained from a détente with the West than from a policy of intransigence. At any rate, in July 1963 Paul-Henri Spaak of Belgium reported that Premier Khrushchev seemed genuinely interested in a test ban. A few days later, American and British negotiators, led by Averell Harriman and Lord Hailsham respectively, arrived in Moscow to explore the seriousness of Soviet intentions. After five days of negotiations, tentative agreement was reached and a copy of the draft treaty was publicized on July 24. All nuclear tests in the atmosphere, under water, and in space were to cease, but underground tests were to be permitted. On August 5, Soviet Foreign Minister Andrei Gromyko, United States Secretary of State Dean Rusk, and British Foreign Secretary Lord Home put their signatures to the document. After a protracted debate, the United States Senate, on September 24, ratified the treaty by a vote of 80 to 19. A large majority of the world's nations quickly followed suit and deposited their instruments of ratification. A decade of arduous negotiations had finally produced concrete results.

On the negative side, France and China made a common front against the treaty. The former was bent on its own independent nuclear force and the latter attacked the treaty as a fraud and saw it as further proof of Soviet duplicity. Also, the test ban was only partial and underground tests continued to take place in many parts of the world. Nevertheless, most observers agreed with President Kennedy's assessment of the treaty as a step toward reason and away from war. In specific and immediate terms, it solved a major problem of public health by halting the further contamination of the atmosphere by radioactive fallout. More broadly, it was the first East-West agreement in the tensely guarded realm of military security.

THE STRATEGIC ARMS LIMITATION TREATIES

On May 26, 1972, President Richard M. Nixon and Soviet Party Chairman Leonid Brezhnev signed in Moscow two historic arms control documents which represented the culmination of almost three years of arduous strategic arms limitation talks (SALT) in Helsinki and in Vienna.

The first document was an Anti-Ballistic Missiles Treaty of unlimited duration which placed limits on the growth of Soviet and American strategic nuclear arsenals. The treaty established a ceiling of two hundred launchers for each side's defensive missile system and committed both sides not to build nationwide anti-missile defenses. Each country was limited to two ABM sites, one for the national capital and the other to protect one field of ICBMs. Each site would consist of one hundred ABMs.

The United States already had a protected ICBM field in North Dakota and thus, under the terms of the treaty, could add an ABM site around Washington. The Soviet Union already had an ABM site for the defense of Moscow and thus was permitted to add an ABM site to protect an ICBM field. At the time of the agreement, the Soviet Union had a total of 2,328 missiles, 1,618 ICBMs and 710 on nuclear submarines, compared with 1,710 for the United States—1,054 ICBMs and 656 on submarines.

The second concrete arms control achievement of the Moscow Summit was an Interim Agreement limiting ICBMs to those under construction or deployed at the time of the signing of the agreement. This meant the retention of 1,618 ICBMs for the Soviet Union, including 300 large SS-98, and 1,054 for the United States, including 1,000 Minutemen and 54 Titans. The agreement also froze the construction of submarine-launched ballistic missiles on all nuclear submarines at existing levels—656 for the United States and 710 for the Soviet Union. However, each side could build additional submarine missiles if an equal number of older land-based ICBMs or older submarine missile launchers were dismantled. The agreement was to be in force for five years and both sides pledged themselves to "follow-up negotiations" in order to achieve a full-fledged treaty.

Neither arms control instrument signed at Moscow placed limitations on the qualitative improvement of offensive or defensive missiles, nor were ceilings imposed on the number of warheads that could be carried by offensive missiles or on strategic bombers permitted each side. Modernization of missiles, including the emplacement of new missiles in new silos, was permitted. Both sides pledged "not to interfere with the national technical means of verification of the other party," and each side retained the right to withdraw from either agreement if it felt that its supreme national interest was in jeopardy.

The two agreements managed to freeze a rough balance into the nuclear arsenals of the two superpowers. There remained "missile-gaps," of course, in specific weapons. The United States, for example, retained the lead in the technology of "multiple independently targeted reentry vehicles" (MIRVs) while the Soviet Union possessed a larger quantity of missile launchers. Nevertheless, the overall effect was one of achieving a rough equilibrium.

The process of achieving this equilibrium went through eight stages lasting almost three years. SALT 1 was held in Helsinki in late 1969 and was exploratory without any formal proposals submitted by either side. SALT 2, held in Vienna from April to August 1970, got down to specific proposals. The two superpowers agreed in principle on the terms of a defensive missile treaty that would have limited each side to one hundred missiles each around Moscow and Washington. But several months later, the American delegation, fearful of Congress, backed away and advanced a new proposal which would have given the United States a four-to-one advantage. This was angrily rejected by the USSR, and it took a few more months before the original two-site 200-missile compromise was reaffirmed. SALT 3, held in late 1970, broke up in disagreement over offensive arms. SALT 4 took place in Vienna from March to May 1971 and during this period President Nixon and Chairman Brezhnev began to engage in top-secret correspondence. The result was a Soviet initiative proposing an ICBM freeze as well as an ABM treaty. SALT 5, held from July to September 1971 in Helsinki, saw further progress on the proposed ICBM freeze. SALT 6, in late 1971 and early 1972, produced the outlines of the ABM treaty, and SALT 7, the last round before the Moscow Summit, led to the inclusion of submarine-based missiles in the accord. The final accords were thus the result of protracted and painstaking bargaining and negotiations.

Several conclusions are worthy of note in connection with the two Moscow agreements. In the first place, the observation made earlier with regard to disarmament, namely that a measure of political accommodation must precede agreement on a technical formula, seems to apply with equal logic to arms control. It must be remembered that Soviet-American relations had improved significantly by the early 1970s, partly due to the common determination to resolve long-standing differences in Europe and partly due to the Soviet fear of China. At any rate, the political climate had thawed considerably since the days of the cold war. Second, the SALT agreements did not depend primarily on verification to be effective. Each side knew that, if it cheated and "surprised" the other with a devastating nuclear attack, the other side, though mortally wounded, could still inflict a retaliatory blow that would be "unacceptable" to the offender. Hence, the agreements were not based primarily on mutual trust, but on the mutual capacity to absorb a first strike. Besides, each side continued to spend gigantic sums on antisubmarine warfare (ASW). Since, in the mid-1970s, the stability of the nuclear deterrent was based mainly on the invulnerability of nuclear submarines and their missiles, a significant breakthrough in ASW by either side could destabilize the balance in a more serious way than an ABM system. Finally, however, there is no doubt that even if the two agreements did not qualify as disarmament, they nevertheless signified a momentous breakthrough in superpower relations and a modest step toward a saner world.

In November 1974 another advance was made. At their first meeting, in Vladivostok, President Ford and Soviet Party Chairman Brezhnev agreed to an overall ceiling of about 2,400 nuclear missiles and bombers on each side, with about half of these being missiles with multiple nuclear warheads (MIRVs).

The advance was modest since these ceilings were high and, furthermore, were only quantitative. No restrictions were set on the development of qualitative improvements such as missile flight tests to increase accuracy or the development of land-mobile and air-mobile intercontinental ballistic missiles (ICBMs). Nor was the development of cruise missiles launched from submarines restricted under the terms of the accord.

Secretary Kissinger expressed the hope that SALT II would "put a cap on the arms race" for ten years "between 1975 and 1985." This "cap," however, did not signify a reduction of existing stockpiles of weapons, but merely a quantitative limitation on the development of further weapons. In that sense, the Vladivostok accord was a modest achievement.

The verification issue began to haunt Kissinger in 1975 and placed in serious question further progress toward SALT II. Admiral Elmo R. Zumwalt, retired chief of naval operations, declared in December 1975 that the Soviet Union had committed "gross violations" of the SALT I accord of 1972 and that Kissinger had not properly informed President Ford. He charged that the Soviets were constructing launch silos for additional missiles and thus were surreptitiously upgrading their ABM defensive potential. He also accused the Soviets of converting "light" ABM missiles into "heavy" ones and thus violating the spirit of SALT I. Kissinger heatedly denied the charges and was supported in his defense by the CIA. By this time, however, the ire of the Soviets was aroused. *Pravda* not only denied any violations of the 1972 accord, but in turn voiced serious doubts about American compliance. It now blamed the United States for the delay in reaching a final SALT II agreement, which, Brezhnev had hoped, would be sealed by the time the Twenty-Fifth Communist Party Congress was to convene, in February 1976.

Progress toward SALT II was also stalled over two new weapons which the United States and the Soviet Union wanted to add to their respective arsenals. The Pentagon had developed a "cruise missile," which was a long-range, jet-propelled, extremely accurate guided nuclear bomb that could be launched from a bomber, a ship, or a submarine. Pentagon spokesmen declared that, since the cruise missile traveled through the atmosphere, it should not be included in the SALT II ceiling of 2,400 ICBMs, which traveled through space. The Soviet Union insisted that the "cruise missile" be included in the ceiling. At the same time, the Soviets had developed a new "Backfire" bomber, which, they declared, should be excluded from SALT II because of its limited range. The Pentagon, insisting that air-to-air refueling could enable it to reach the United States and return, demanded its inclusion in the ceiling. Thus, by early 1976, the future of SALT II was very much in doubt. The allegations of cheating by the Soviet Union, the dispute over the inclusion of newly developed weapons in the overall ceiling, and a deepening suspicion of Soviet behavior in Angola and in the Middle East made Kissinger's position on SALT II extremely vulnerable. It seemed that despite the breakthrough of SALT I, the safety of the superpowers still depended, first and foremost, on their capacity for mutually assured destruction. SALT had made a dent in the balance of terror, but it was little more than a beginning.

President Carter continued to pursue SALT II. During the first year of his presidency, negotiations were stalled because the new American initiatives on human rights and the encouragement Carter extended to Russian dissidents angered the Soviet leadership. By 1978, however, another breakthrough was in sight. Each superpower was prepared to place a ceiling of 2,250 on its total of land- and sea-based missiles and long-range bombers, almost a 10 percent reduction from the Vladivostok limits. In addition, three separate ceilings were placed on weapons armed with multiple warheads: 1,320 for land- and sea-based missiles and for bombers equipped with cruise missiles; 1,200 for land- and sea-based missiles alone; and 800 for land-based missiles alone. Finally, in June 1979, SALT II was signed by President Carter and Soviet Party Chairman Brezhnev. It set an overall ceiling of 2,250 on each side's strategic arsenal of missiles and bombers and provided "subceilings" on weapons such as land-based American missiles equipped with multiple warheads and Soviet "heavy missiles." Congressional approval of the treaty would open the way for final ratification.

But then in early 1980, the Soviet Union invaded Afghanistan. SALT II was the major casualty of that decision. A new militancy rose throughout the United States and President Carter decided not to submit the treaty to the Congress. President Ronald Reagan's top priority was not arms control, but a massive armaments program. Once again, the two superpowers resumed their march toward Armageddon.

By the early 1980s the arms race had once more become a terribly expensive fact of life. Even though arms control negotiations between the superpowers resumed in 1985, the money devoted each year to military expenditures amounted to more than the total income of all the peoples of Africa and South and Southeast Asia. It was nearly three times what all the world's governments spent on health, nearly twice what they spent on education, and nearly thirty times what industrialized countries gave in aid to developing countries. These massive military expenditures have risen over the years despite the modest arms control agreements that are still in effect. Arms control has thus managed to slow down the mad momentum toward nuclear death, but not to arrest it.

AN INTERNATIONAL POLICE FORCE AND COLLECTIVE SECURITY

The framers of the United Nations Charter foresaw that the elimination or even the substantial reduction of armaments would be an extremely difficult task. They had considerably greater faith in the possibility of fashioning a world in which arms would be redistributed and organized in such a way that lawbreakers could be confronted by preponderant military power. As the postwar world developed, however, the growing fury of the East-West struggle made it almost impossible for the UN Security Council really to function as the planned-for instrument of collective security. Consequently, the standing United Nations Armed Force that was envisaged by the UN founders in Article

43 was never permitted to come to life. It seemed, indeed, as though the East-West struggle would permanently prevent the creation of the one international instrument that could be the most valuable of all for military order-building: a permanent and powerful international police force. What had happened, of course, was that the would-be international policemen had fallen out among themselves.

Yet if we survey the record, the East-West struggle has nevertheless not prevented the United Nations from engaging in military action to defend collective security. On six different occasions the United Nations has managed effectively to meet serious threats to the peace. The first military action under the United Nations flag was fought in Korea from 1950 to 1953. In 1956 a United Nations Emergency Force was set up to restore order in the Middle East. In 1960 a United Nations Force was given prime responsibility for insulating the newly independent Congo from the East-West struggle. In 1964 a UN force was dispatched to Cyprus to prevent civil war between the island's Greek and Turkish communities. And in 1973, 1974, and 1978 three UN buffer forces were dispatched to the Middle East to supervise disengagement agreements. Each of these experiences had been unique in its highly improvised character; each has involved the UN in a most explosive situation and so has had a high quality of drama; and while all of them have fallen short of the original concept of collective security, each has made an important contribution to military order.

The Korean "Police Action"

We have seen earlier that in Korea the mobilization of an international police force was made possible only through the absence of the Soviet delegate from the Security Council in June 1950. But once the Council was freed from the paralyzing veto—albeit only temporarily—it was able to organize military action swiftly and effectively. This first modern effort of international policing therefore deserves careful analysis.

On June 27, two days after the North Korean attack, the Security Council called upon all members to "furnish such assistance to the Republic of Korea as may be necessary to repel the armed attack and to restore international peace and security in the area."[32] On July 7 the Council recommended that such forces and other assistance be placed under a Unified Command under United States operational control. It also authorized the Unified Command to use the United Nations flag. The response of the member nations to this first modern experiment in collective security was encouraging. Fifteen members other than the United States and the Republic of Korea offered to contribute troops: Australia, Belgium, Canada, Colombia, Ethiopia, France, Greece, Luxembourg, the Netherlands, New Zealand, the Philippines, Thailand, Turkey, the Union of South Africa, and the United Kingdom. In addition, thirty-seven other members offered to contribute a wide range of supplies and services, including food, clothing, medical supplies, and transportation.

Since almost 90 percent of the non-Korean forces fighting under the United Nations flag were United States forces, and since it had been the United States that had taken the initiative in this UN action, it was only logical that the Unified Command should be primarily an American operation. Accordingly, General Douglas MacArthur was placed in charge of the United Nations Command and, for all practical purposes, the United Nations Police Force became identical with the Far East Command of the United States. South Korean troops were integrated into American companies and joint actions with other United Nations allies were conducted through liaison officers. Moreover, since the United States was bearing by far the largest share of the load, this preponderant American military role was accepted by all concerned as perfectly fair and proper.

While questions of military coordination in Korea were thus largely solved through the commanding position of the United States, the problem of providing the United Nations Force with political guidance presented almost insuperable obstacles. So long as the United Nations Forces were south of the 38th parallel, the problem was not acute. But by August 1, 1950, the day the Soviet delegate returned to the Security Council, the United Nations Forces were fast approaching the 38th parallel. A decision had to be made whether to stop at that point or to carry UN operations beyond it. In view of the Soviet Union's return to the Security Council and the consequent certainty of its veto in the matter, the decision had to be made by the General Assembly. Under American pressure, but with considerable misgivings, the General Assembly voted to authorize the entrance of United Nations Forces into North Korea. Yet in effect, this and subsequent decisions were made by the United States rather than by the General Assembly itself. In November 1950, after the Chinese intervention, there was formed a Committee of Sixteen for interallied consultation, but in practice the United States almost always prevailed. American domination of the international police force became most evident in the controversy involving the commander, General MacArthur. Most of the allies, and many Americans, viewed MacArthur's intentions to bomb military bases in Manchuria as a serious provocation to the Chinese. The removal of the general from the United Nations Command did not, however, take place in deference to the wishes of the allies, but was fundamentally the result of the general's challenge to the authority of his Commander-in-Chief, the President of the United States.

This first experiment in blocking aggression through an international police force was neither an unqualified success nor a complete failure. On the negative side, it owed its activation to a fortuitous circumstance—the Soviet Union's temporary absence from the Security Council; it fell far short of a genuine collective security action; though initiated as a "police action," it developed into a limited war; instead of crushing the aggressor, it resulted in the signing of an armistice with him on the basis of equality; it was in effect chiefly an American enterprise and, aside from the forces of the Republic of Korea, involved the participation of only thirty-six thousand combatants from the other United Nations countries; and its political direction was dominated chiefly by the United States. In fact, if it had not been for American initiative, the international police force in Korea would not have come into existence at all.

On the other hand, the Korean experience broke precedent in several important ways. It saw sixteen nations fighting as a United Nations army, under the United Nations flag, and led by a United Nations commander. Moreover, despite the disproportionate role played by the United States, its image as a United Nations action has remained largely intact. Most important, the United Nations Force succeeded in halting aggression and restoring what was in effect the *status quo ante bellum*. Even when comparing this achievement with the League of Nations' dismal failure in Manchuria in 1931, it would be an exaggeration to characterize it as a complete success. Yet the fact remains that the United Nations Force in Korea took a big step along the road to collective security.

The greatest weakness of the Korean action was the lack of planning for the transition from military enforcement to the tasks of consolidating the peace. Though the aggressor had been thrown back, Korea remained as politically divided as before—and, ironically, along a line only a short distance from the 38th parallel where the fighting had begun. At best, therefore, the United Nations action provided a breathing spell during which political differences could once more be subjected to negotiation. This in itself was a great service. Yet the final lesson of Korea is nonetheless clear: that the pursuit of order through purely military techniques is bound to fail unless it is shored up by equally determined efforts to reach a political settlement.

Historically, the Korean experience has by no means been an unmixed blessing. In the United Nations of the 1980s, the Korean "police action" of the 1950s was widely regarded as an historical anomaly. Moreover, since it had placed the UN at war with China, the People's Republic harbored a great deal of resentment. And perhaps most important, the history of the Korean War had made it difficult, if not impossible, for North Vietnam to regard the United Nations as an impartial mediator in its war with the United States during the 1960s and 1970s.

The Four United Nations Peace Forces in the Middle East

United Nations military action in the Middle East was considerably less dramatic than the Korean campaign. The first UN Emergency Force that was dispatched to the troubled area never exceeded six thousand men. Moreover, UNEF was never meant to be a fighting army. Its purpose, rather, was to serve as a symbol of the UN's involvement which, it was hoped, would succeed in bringing about the neutralization of the disputed areas. Its unique achievement, in which it went importantly beyond the Korean action, was that it constituted for the first time a genuine international police force that was not dominated by any single power. In fact, all of the Great Powers were specifically excluded from it. For this reason the significance of UNEF greatly transcends its modest physical dimensions.

The father of the United Nations Emergency Force was Lester B. Pearson of Canada. When on November 2, 1956, the General Assembly was locked in acrimonious debate over British-French-Israeli action in Suez, Pearson proposed that peace and security be restored through a United Nations Force. United States and Afro-Asian approval encouraged the Canadian diplomat to draft a resolution requesting the Secretary-General to draw up a plan for the creation of an international military force to be submitted to the General Assembly within forty-eight hours. The Canadian resolution passed without a negative vote at a time when Britain and France were still bombing Egyptian territory. Secretary-General Hammarskjöld and Mr. Pearson immediately set about to improvise the force. They decided to appoint Major General E. L. M. Burns, chief of staff of the United Nations Truce Supervison Organization in Palestine, as head of the new United Nations Command. The next vital decision concerned the composition of troops to be sent. The Secretary-General thought it wise to exclude the Great Powers from the force. It would have been ill-advised to deputize Britain and France as United Nations policemen, since Egypt would never have agreed to admit them. If the United States were included, the Soviet Union would demand a role, and hence it was best to keep the two superpowers out altogether.

To the delight of leading United Nations officials, twenty-four members agreed to make troops available for the enterprise, with offers ranging from 1,180 from Canada to 250 from Finland. However, this delight began to give way to embarrassment when, in order not to jeopardize relations with Egypt, it became necessary to reject some of the offers. For example, the Canadian contingent, especially a battalion of the "Queen's Own Rifles," resembled the British too much in appearance. Pearson tactfully decided to use them as maintenance and administrative personnel in roles where they would be least conspicuous. New Zealand troops were politely rejected because New Zealand had voted with Britain and France in the General Assembly on the Suez affair. Pakistan was considered unsuitable because it was a member of the Baghdad Pact and an irritant to India. Troops from the Soviet bloc—Czechoslovakia and Rumania—were not "rejected" but simply not "activated."[33] Finally a contingent of six thousand troops from ten countries—Brazil, Canada, Colombia, Denmark, Finland, India, Indonesia, Norway, Sweden, and Yugoslavia—was ready for action.

The composition of the force was very important since its admission to the contested area depended upon the permission of Egypt. Though this condition was distasteful to many members of the Assembly, it was, according to the Secretary-General, the "very basis and starting point" of the entire operation. In effect, Egypt therefore had a veto over the national makeup of the force and could, as well, determine the length of its stay in the Suez area. On November 12 Egypt granted UNEF permission to enter. Shortly thereafter, Britain, France, and Israel were persuaded to withdraw from Egyptian territory and UNEF proceeded to neutralize the contested boundary zones. Its function became essentially that of a "buffer" between Israel and Egypt.

In May 1967 President Nasser abruptly demanded that UNEF be withdrawn from the borders which it had patrolled for over a decade. Secretary-

General U Thant complied with the Egyptian demand, though with serious misgivings, and the force was promptly removed.

U Thant's decision was a very controversial one. The Secretary-General was widely criticized for giving in too hastily to Egyptian pressure. Critics pointed out that while it was true that UNEF's presence on the Egyptian border depended on the consent of the Egyptian government, the Secretary-General could have stalled by requesting an emergency session of the Security Council or of the General Assembly and thus gained time. The Israeli delegate to the UN, Abba Eban, stated caustically that "the umbrella was removed at the precise moment when it began to rain." The Secretary-General defended his action by pointing out that there would have been no legal basis for maintaining the force on Egyptian soil without that nation's consent. Moreover, the force had never been permitted to patrol on the Israeli side of the border, and when the Israeli government was asked whether it would invite the UNEF troops to its side after leaving Egypt, Israel had refused to do so. Both governments were within their legal rights, the Secretary-General asserted.

A further complication in the picture was the fact that two nations that had given contingents to UNEF—India and Yugoslavia—were removing their forces even before the Secretary-General had given the order to withdraw. Moreover, several UNEF soldiers were killed by Egyptian troops who threatened that unless UNEF were promptly withdrawn, it would be regarded as an "army of occupation." Finally, the Secretary-General reasoned that if he did not comply with the request of a sovereign government, it might be infinitely more difficult to obtain consent for the admission of a peace-keeping force in a future crisis. Given all these conflicting considerations, the Secretary-General made his difficult and fateful choice.

An overall analysis of the UNEF experience points up a striking dilemma for any international peace force. In order to be an effective instrument of collective security and a respectable military force, it must include one or more of the Great Powers. But if it does, it is likely to find itself dominated by a Great Power, as was the case in Korea, and to suffer a proportionate loss of its international character. Hence, since in order to steer clear of the East-West struggle it must exclude the Great Powers, a truly international force can hardly be more than a buffer. The Korean Force, organized and operated as an instrument of enforcement, came closer to the ideal of collective security in terms of its *action*. The Middle East Force, though compelled to limit itself to the task of neutralization, more closely approached the collective security ideal in terms of its *composition*. While its dependence on the sufferance of Egypt made it a fragile instrument of peace-keeping, it nevertheless helped to restore peace in the Middle East in 1956 and to maintain an uneasy truce on the Israeli-Egyptian border for over a decade.

The second UN Emergency Force (UNEF II) was established immediately after the conclusion of the Yom Kippur war, in late October 1973. The force was deployed by the Security Council for an initial six-month period, subject to renewal, along the disengagement line that had been negotiated between Israel and Egypt by Secretary Kissinger. UNEF II differed from its predecessor in three important respects. First, it was placed under the exclusive mandate of the Security Council. This meant that it could not be terminated *during* each six-month period except with the unanimous consent of the permanent members. Every six months, however, each of the Big Five had the power to prevent its prolongation when the Security Council voted on the renewal of the mandate. Thus, UNEF I could be killed at any time by the host country, but UNEF II could be killed only at regular six-month intervals by the veto of a permanent member. Second, while the troop composition of UNEF II consisted primarily of small neutral countries, Poland became a part of the force in addition to Austria, Sweden, Finland, Ireland, Ghana, Senegal, Kenya, Nepal, Panama, Peru, Canada, and Indonesia. Thus, a Warsaw Pact nation for the first time became a member of a UN peace force. And finally, another precedent was set when the Soviet Union agreed to share in the $30 million assessed budget, which was authorized by the Security Council for the first six-month period, as well as in several subsequent appropriations of similar amounts. China, however, decided not to participate in the votes either authorizing or extending the peace force nor did it choose to share in the costs, even though these were defined as regular "expenses" in accordance with Article 17 of the Charter.

UNEF II operated at a level of approximately seven thousand men under the direction of a Finnish commander, Major-General Siilasvuo. The Security Council maintained tight political control, and despite some minor areas of friction, the force operated very effectively. When violence erupted in Ireland, however, the Irish contingent was withdrawn. UNEF II, like its predecessor, still consisted of borrowed troops who could be recalled at will by their national governments. In 1979, in the wake of the peace treaty between Israel and Egypt, UNEF II was terminated. There was a consensus that, during the five years of its existence, it had acquitted itself well.

In May 1974, in the wake of the disengagement arrangement that had been worked out by Secretary Kissinger between Israel and Syria, the Security Council established a small UN Disengagement Observer Force (UNDOF). The new force was to draw its contingents from UNEF. Five hundred Austrians, 350 Peruvians, 100 Canadians, and 100 Poles were transferred for patrol duty to the Golan Heights. Once again, the Security Council authorized an initial six-month period and once again China did not vote. UNDOF's expenses were subsumed under the UNEF budget. A formula was worked out under which those nations that contributed troops to UNEF or UNDOF received reimbursements so that they did not have to shoulder a double burden of both manpower and money. UNDOF performed creditably under the leadership of Brigadier-General Gonzalo Briceño Zevallos of Peru, who exercised his command under the watchful eye of the Security Council. In the mid-1980s UNDOF was still patrolling the Israeli-Syrian border, keeping incidents there to a minimum.

In late November 1974, after a trip by Secretary-General Waldheim to the Middle East, Syria acquiesced to a six-month extension of UNDOF's mandate to patrol the Golan Heights, and the Security Council approved the prolongation. Thereafter, regular six-month renewals were granted by the

Security Council to both UNEF II and UNDOF. Thus, by the early 1980s, UN peace-keeping operations had clearly become the exclusive province of the Security Council.

In 1978 the Security Council authorized a United Nations Interim Force in Lebanon (UNIFIL), which was to supervise the withdrawal of Israeli forces from southern Lebanon. UNIFIL was brought to a strength of about six thousand men, most of whom were drawn from small neutral states. However, the force also included a thousand French paratroopers. The job of UNIFIL was particularly difficult since fighting was still in progress and the numerous warring factions made it almost impossible to define UNIFIL's mandate clearly. The little force was to prevent not only clashes between Israeli forces and PLO guerrillas, but also clashes between Lebanese Christians and Moslems. Ultimately, it was hoped, authority over Lebanon would revert to the Lebanese government. It was a credit to UNIFIL that by the mid-1980s the force was still operating in Lebanon. It had outlasted the multinational peace-keeping force organized by the United States. Perhaps the more neutral composition of the UNIFIL explained its greater longevity. Soldiers from Fiji, Ghana, Ireland, Nepal, the Netherlands, Norway, Senegal, and Sweden probably did not constitute as much of a threat to the Lebanese Moslems as did the troops from four former colonial countries.

The United Nations Congo Force (ONUC)

Perhaps the most complex military challenge to confront the United Nations was the one that occurred in the Congo between 1960 and 1964. Historians may differ with Mr. Hammarskjöld's view that the United Nations' task in the Congo was the most important responsibility that the world organization had to shoulder in the first fifteen years of its lifetime, but most will agree that the Congo problem required every diplomatic and military resource that the United Nations could possibly muster.

We have seen earlier that the United Nations was first called into the infant African republic in order to take the place of Belgian troops whose sudden withdrawal had left the Congo in a state of political unrest verging on anarchy and civil war. The Secretary-General's problems in putting together a United Nations Force for the Congo resembled those that had been faced in the Middle East. Once again, the Great Powers had to be kept out of the conflict. Furthermore, it was deemed advisable to employ mostly African troops for the United Nations Force. The Secretary-General, together with UN Under-Secretary Ralph J. Bunche, appealed to the new African nations for support. The response again was encouraging: almost all the African nations offered contributions. In addition, troops were accepted from Ireland, Sweden, Indonesia, Malaya, the United Arab Republic, and India. At its high point, the Congo Force comprised over 20,000 men from twenty-nine different countries. The task of the force became vastly more complex, however, when tribal warfare broke out between the central government in Leopoldville under Premier Lumumba and secessionist movements in the two provinces of Katanga and

Kasai. The United Nations Force faced an almost insoluble dilemma: how to restore order while avoiding the charge of intervention in a civil war. As in the Middle East, the presence of the force had to be approved by a sovereign government. But whereas in the case of Egypt, President Nasser had retained control, the Congolese government was in a state of disintegration. The premier and the president of the central government were locked in a power struggle. Moreover, the Soviet Union gave material help to the Lumumba government in direct contravention of the wishes of the United Nations Command and refused to pay its share of the cost of the Peace Force. Racial tension entered the picture when ex-Premier Lumumba accused the non-African contingents of the force of being pro-Belgian. Several member states withdrew their contingents from the force in protest against "neocolonialism."

Financial crises constantly threatened the life of the force. Even after the General Assembly recognized President Kasavubu as the legitimate spokesman for the Congo, United Nations personnel were beaten up by Congolese and frequently had to shoot in self-defense. The UN troops were authorized to use force "only in the last resort." Some were killed. All these factors conspired to make the operation a most difficult and delicate one. While the tribal fighting was going on, the United Nations Force could do little more than protect civilians. It served as a sort of fire brigade: though unable to prevent the outbreak of civil war, it managed to keep it within bounds. Most important, the United Nations Force prepared the ground for the more difficult and complex task of restoring political stability in the Congo.

The Congo experience was a repeat performance of UNEF, with all of UNEF's difficulties vastly magnified. Again, the force had to be improvised at a moment's notice. It, too, was dependent on the good will of a sovereign state, this time a fledgling state on the verge of collapse. Once again, the Secretary-General had to race against time in order to forestall Great Power intervention. The force itself, once established, again was little more than a buffer, but this time its task was not limited to patrol duty in the desert. It had to keep brutal tribal warfare in the jungle to a minimum and even to assume some of the administrative functions of government. Finally, like UNEF, the Congo Force accomplished its primary mission before it was disbanded in 1964: it succeeded in preventing the Congo from becoming a seedbed of a general war.

The United Nations Cyprus Force (UNFICYP)

In March 1964 yet another peace-keeping experiment was launched, this time in Cyprus. When the Greek and Turkish communities on that island found themselves unable to resolve their differences and civil war became an increasingly ominous threat, the Security Council met in emergency session and authorized a peace force. Once again, the force was tailored to the situation. Three thousand British troops already on the island were deputized as UN policemen, and in addition Canada, Sweden, Ireland, and Finland contributed troops, bringing the total up to seven thousand men. The new force also differed from previous ones in its financing arrangements. Since the mood was definitely set against another assessment, the $6 million required for six months was raised through voluntary contributions, with $2 million supplied by the United States, $1 million by the United Kingdom, and the remainder by Greece, Turkey, Italy, Australia, and the Netherlands. The Cyprus Force also set a new precedent in that the Secretary-General appointed a high-level diplomat as mediator to help bring about a political settlement between the two hostile communities. By 1968 the Cyprus Force was the only major UN peace-keeping operation still in the field. It was still on active duty in the early 1970s, though its strength had been reduced to three thousand men. China's accession to the Security Council did not lead to the termination of the force. When the Council considered the extension of the force in 1972, fourteen members voted in favor. China, not wishing to disrupt the consensus, chose to abstain rather than to veto. Despite its voluntary financial base, the Cyprus Force had become an important military order-builder in the Mediterranean.

In late 1973, when UNEF II was being organized, its first contingents were drawn from the force on Cyprus which, as a consequence, was reduced to a level of two thousand men. But when hostilities erupted on the island, UN-FICYP had to be brought up to its original strength of over four thousand men. Costs were kept low, because Britain provided the logistical support base for the force, and never exceeded $12 million a year. During the hostilities on Cyprus, the Secretary-General had to maneuver deftly in order to maintain the strictly neutral character of the force and not to incur the wrath of the Security Council. A number of peace soldiers were killed in the crossfire between Greek and Turkish Cypriots. On the whole, UNFICYP acquitted itself remarkably well under heavy pressure. By the mid-1980s, the Security Council had renewed its mandate more than forty times. Given the political struggles that divided the Security Council, this was an extraordinary achievement.

A PERMANENT PEACE FORCE?

The six United Nations experiences in peace-keeping just discussed were all successful in at least one sense: they restored military order and thus bought time. In the past quarter of a century, more than 300,000 "soldiers without enemies" have served in this capacity. It is an open question whether the six peace forces prevented general conflagrations, and it is clear that they were not examples of genuine collective security. But that their limited success provided renewed opportunity for political order-building is indisputable. This is a major accomplishment, especially since the six ventures all operated under the handicap of starting out as complete improvisations.

The fact that peace-keeping seems to have become an integral UN responsibility has convinced an increasing number of observers that an even more effective performance would be possible if a permanent international peace force were established under United Nations authority. Article 43 of the Charter, which contemplated such a force, was never implemented because of the intensity of the East-West struggle. Yet the experiences of the six peace forces leave no doubt that even a modest force with permanent status would prove very valuable.

It is immediately apparent that such a force would have to be a very different one from that contemplated under Article 43. The framers had assumed that concerted military action by the Great Powers would nip any conflict in the bud. Ironically, however, in the six crises the peace depended not on how quickly the Great Powers could be brought to the scene, but on how successfully they could be kept at arm's length. Hence, the Great Powers would probably have to be excluded from a permanent force, at least at the beginning.

In composition, such a force might consist of long-term volunteers recruited individually by the United Nations, with quotas for different nations. The commanding officer and other high-ranking personnel might be chosen from nationals of middle and smaller states. The force would not be furnished with heavy arms or atomic weapons, but might have its own permanent bases and training depots. Its Commander-in-Chief would be the Secretary-General.

Proposals along these lines have been considered in United Nations circles and have received a mixed reaction. There have been several serious reservations. First, it has been pointed out that such a permanent force would have to be very large and expensive to be able to meet different kinds of emergencies. Korea, for example, necessitated a fighting force to repel an armed attack; UNEF I and II as well as UNDOF were patrol forces in the desert; ONUC had to help save a new country from anarchy and civil war; and the Cyprus Force was needed to prevent two hostile communities on an island from sparking off an international crisis. Thus, the argument runs, the unique character of each experience suggests an ad hoc approach. Second, few nations would be willing to commit troops to the United Nations for unspecified future operations and to give the Secretary-General the authority of Commander-in-Chief over these forces. Third, in view of the melancholy financial histories of UNEF and ONUC, it is most doubtful whether the membership would be willing to underwrite the costs of a standing UN Force.

The above difficulties suggest a more modest approach. There is a growing consensus that the next step should not be an existent UN Force, but a flexible call-up system under which members would be asked to earmark contingents for UN duty on a standby basis. By the mid-1980s, Denmark, Norway, Sweden, Finland, Canada, Italy, and the Netherlands had already offered to earmark units for UN use under such an arrangement. Nevertheless, the knotty problem of political control of these units remains to be solved; and, unless the nations earmarking the troops also "pay their own beat," the fiscal obstacles may prove insurmountable.

If such a standby UN Force could be established as a first step toward a permanent force, the results would be most beneficial. Such a force would be a most useful instrument in the struggle for military order. But its function in the general quest for order would still be a *transitional* one. As the record of disarmament and arms control negotiations has clearly demonstrated, military instruments per se cannot create political order. But a standby or permanent

UN Peace Force might at least make a limited contribution by preparing the ground. It might thus embody the best that military order-building has to offer in our time.

REFERENCES

1. Peter Burchett, reporting for the *London Daily Express,* September 5, 1945; cited by Philip Noel-Baker, *The Arms Race.* New York: Oceana, 1958, pp. 119–120.
2. A joint statement by President Eisenhower and Premier Khrushchev made at Camp David in 1959.
3. Noel-Baker, *op. cit.,* p. 86.
4. Hans J. Morgenthau, *Politics Among Nations.* 3rd ed. New York: Knopf, 1960, pp. 410–411.
5. James Brown Scott, *The Proceedings of The Hague Peace Conference of 1907,* Vol. I. New York: Oxford University Press, 1920, pp. 89–90.
6. Cited by Inis L. Claude, Jr., *Swords into Plowshares.* 2nd ed. New York: Random House, 1959, p. 308.
7. Security Council Official Records, March 5, 1947, p. 453.
8. Yves Collart, *Disarmament: A Study Guide and Bibliography on the Efforts of the United Nations.* The Hague: Nijhoff, 1958, p. 55.
9. Cited by Joseph Nogee, "The Diplomacy of Disarmament," *International Conciliation,* January 1960, p. 280.
10. *Ibid.,* p. 282.
11. *Ibid.*
12. Noel-Baker, *op. cit.,* p. 22.
13. Nogee, *op. cit.,* p. 286.
14. Noel-Baker, *op. cit.,* pp. 12–30.
15. General Assembly Official Records, Fourteenth Session, September 18, 1959.
16. *Ibid.*
17. Claude, *op. cit.,* p. 314.
18. William M. Evan, "An International Public Opinion Poll on Disarmament and 'Inspection by the People': A Study of Attitudes Toward Supranationalism," *Inspection for Disarmament,* Seymour Melman, ed. New York: Columbia University Press, 1958, pp. 231–250.
19. *Ibid.,* p. 234.
20. Claude, *op. cit.,* p. 308.
21. Larry Collins, "Combating Nuclear Terrorism," *The New York Times Magazine,* December 14, 1980, p. 37.
22. "Race Poisoning by Radiation," *Saturday Review,* June 9, 1956.
23. "The Biological Effects of Bomb Tests," *New Statesman and Nation,* June 8, 1957.
24. *The New Scientist,* May 16, 1957.
25. Noel-Baker, *op. cit.,* p. 255.
26. Cited by Nogee, *op. cit.,* p. 263.
27. *The New York Times,* January 14, 1958.
28. Cited by Noel-Baker, *op. cit.,* p. 261.
29. *The New York Times,* June 8, 1957.
30. *New York Herald Tribune,* September 1, 1958.
31. Nogee, *op. cit.,* p. 298.
32. United Nations Doc. S/1511, June 27, 1950.
33. William R. Frye, *A United Nations Peace Force.* New York: Oceana, 1957, p. 23.

BIBLIOGRAPHY

Barton, John H. *The Politics of Peace: An Evaluation of Arms Control.* Stanford, Calif.: Stanford University Press, 1981.

————, and Weiler, Lawrence D., eds. *International Arms Control: Issues and Agreements.* Stanford, Calif.: Stanford University Press, 1977.

Bellany, Ian, and Blacker, Coit D., eds. *The Verification of Arms Control Agreements.* London: Cass, 1984.

Caldicott, Helen. *Missile Envy.* New York: Morrow, 1984.

Clark, Duncan L., and Brauch, Hans Guenter, eds. *Decisionmaking for Arms Limitation.* Cambridge, Mass.: Ballinger, 1983.

Clough, Ralph N., ed. *The United States, China, and Arms Control.* Washington, D.C.: Brookings Institution, 1975.

Dyson, Freeman. *Weapons and Hope.* New York: Harper & Row, 1984.

Epstein, William. *The Last Chance: Nuclear Proliferation and Arms Control.* New York: Free Press, 1976.

Fabian, Larry L. *Soldiers Without Enemies: Preparing the United Nations for Peacekeeping.* Washington, D.C.: Brookings Institution, 1971.

Fromm, Erich. *May Man Prevail?* New York: Doubleday, 1961.

Harbottle, Michael. *The Impartial Soldier.* New York: Oxford University Press, 1970.

Harvard Nuclear Study Group. *Living With Nuclear Weapons.* Cambridge, Mass.: Harvard University Press, 1983.

Jensen, Lloyd. *Return from the Nuclear Brink: National Interest and the Nuclear Nonproliferation Treaty.* Lexington, Mass.: Lexington Books, 1974.

Jessup, Philip C., and Taubenfeld, Howard J. *Controls for Outer Space.* New York: Columbia University Press, 1959.

Kemp, Geoffrey, Pfaltzgraff, Robert L., and Ra'anan, Ure, eds. *The Superpowers in a Multinuclear World.* Lexington, Mass.: Lexington Books, 1974.

Kolkowicz, Roman, et al. *The Soviet Union and Arms Control: A Superpower Dilemma.* Baltimore: Johns Hopkins Press, 1970.

Larson, Thomas B. *Disarmament and Soviet Policy.* Englewood Cliffs, N.J.: Prentice-Hall, 1969.

Leachman, Robert S., and Althoff, Philip. *Preventing Nuclear Theft: Guidelines for Industry and Governments.* New York: Praeger, 1972.

Lehman, John F., and Weiss, Seymour. *Beyond the Salt II Failure.* New York: Praeger, 1981.

Levine, Robert A. *The Arms Debate.* Cambridge, Mass.: Harvard University Press, 1963.

Melman, Seymour, ed. *Inspection for Disarmament.* New York: Columbia University Press, 1958.

Moskos, Charles C., Jr. *Peace Soldiers: The Sociology of a United Nations Military Force.* Chicago: University of Chicago Press, 1976.

Myrdal, Alva. *The Game of Disarmament: How the United States and Russia Run the Arms Race.* New York: Pantheon, 1977.

Newhouse, John. *Cold Dawn: The Story of SALT.* New York: Holt, Rinehart and Winston, 1973.

Noel-Baker, Philip. *The Arms Race.* New York: Oceana, 1958.

Payne, Samuel Burton, Jr. *The Soviet Union and SALT.* Cambridge: Massachusetts Institute of Technology Press, 1980.

Potter, William C., ed. *Verification and SALT: The Challenge of Strategic Deception.* Boulder, Colo.: Westview Press, 1980.

Quester, George. *The Politics of Nuclear Proliferation.* Baltimore: Johns Hopkins Press, 1973.

Rosner, Gabriella. *The United Nations Emergency Force.* New York: Columbia University Press, 1963.

Schelling, Thomas C. *The Strategy of Conflict.* Cambridge, Mass.: Harvard University Press, 1960.

———, and Halperin, Morton H. *Strategy and Arms Control.* New York: Twentieth Century Fund, 1961.

Scoville, Herbert, Jr., and Tsipis, Kosta. *Can Space Remain a Peaceful Environment?* Muscatine, Iowa: Stanley Foundation, 1978.

Seaborg, Glenn T. *Kennedy, Khrushchev, and the Test Ban.* Berkeley: University of California Press, 1981.

SIPRI. *Nuclear Proliferation Problems.* Cambridge: Massachusetts Institute of Technology Press, 1974.

———. *Safeguards Against Nuclear Proliferation.* Cambridge: Massachusetts Institute of Technology Press, 1975.

Smith, Gerard. *Doubletalk: The Story of SALT I.* New York: Doubleday, 1980.

Stegenga, James A. *The United Nations Cyprus Force.* Columbus: Ohio State University Press, 1968.

Stoessinger, John G. "Atoms for Peace: The International Atomic Energy Agency," in Arthur Holcombe, ed., *Organizing Peace in the Nuclear Age.* New York: New York University Press, 1959, pp. 117–233.

Wainhouse, David W., et al. *Arms Control Agreements.* Baltimore: Johns Hopkins Press, 1968.

———. *International Peacekeeping at the Crossroads: National Support—Experience and Aspects.* Baltimore: Johns Hopkins Press, 1973.

———, ed. *International Peace Observation.* Baltimore: Johns Hopkins Press, 1966.

Waltz, Kenneth N. *Man, the State, and War: A Theoretical Analysis.* New York: Columbia University Press, 1959.

Willrich, Mason, and Rhinelander, John B., eds. *SALT: The Moscow Agreements and Beyond.* New York: Free Press, 1974.

Wiseman, Henry, ed. *Peacekeeping: Appraisals and Proposals.* Elmsford, N.Y.: Pergamon Press, 1983.

Wolfe, Thomas W. *The SALT Experience.* Cambridge, Mass.: Ballinger, 1979.

Chapter 13

The Economic Struggle for Order

It is not from the benevolence of the butcher, the brewer, or the baker that we expect our dinner, but from their regard to their self-interest. We address ourselves, not to their humanity, but to their self-love, and never talk to them of our necessities, but of their advantages.

ADAM SMITH *The Wealth of Nations*

The world since 1945 has been one gigantic experimental station in economic order-building. But while a generation ago the central problem was to create new institutions where none existed, today it is to get a whole bevy of global and regional economic agencies to work together effectively. The "house of economic order" in today's world looks like a great "booming, buzzing confusion," to use William James' famous description of reality. There is little doubt that it will have to be built from the bottom up rather than from the top down. For the sake of organization and clarity, we have divided the economic order-building institutions into two major categories: global and regional. In the former group there are a number of institutions affiliated with the United Nations, such as the World Bank and the International Monetary Fund, as well as the global conferences on food, population, and environment which have been discussed in Chapter 10. Outside the UN framework, the General Agreement on Tariffs and Trade (GATT) is probably the most significant. In addition, the recent growth of so-called multinational enterprises is deserving of analysis. The most important experiment in regional economic order-building is probably taking place in Western Europe. The second part of this chapter will deal with the evolution of the European Economic Community (EEC), which has managed, in some degree, to transcend the traditional bonds of the nation-state system. Both the global and the regional agencies share the common functionalist premise that the economic path to order may pave the way for the order-builders in the political and military realms. Beyond this, each has been unique, attuned to its own particular objectives and accumulating its own special experiences.

ECONOMIC ORDER-BUILDING AT THE GLOBAL LEVEL

Four horsemen of the Apocalypse are galloping across the world of the 1980s: food shortage, debt crisis, inflation, and population explosion. We have looked at these fearful recent phenomena in the context of the economic struggle for power in Chapter 7. It is essential to remember, however, that the order-building institutions that make up the contents of the present chapter all live in the shadow of these recent apocalyptic developments and have been profoundly affected by them. Their task of building a more stable economic order has, as a result, been made a great deal more difficult, especially on the global level.

The International Bank for Reconstruction and Development (IBRD), or World Bank, and its two affiliates, the International Development Association (IDA) and the International Finance Corporation (IFC), are all members of the United Nations family and are committed to the industrial development of the economically underdeveloped countries. The World Bank is controlled primarily by the rich industrialized countries, but its former president, Robert S. McNamara, underscored the need to bridge the widening gulf between the rich and the poor and used the bank's resources toward that objective. Similarly, the International Monetary Fund (IMF), which also is a nominal member of the UN system, has tended to function primarily as a Western-controlled short-term currency loan operation. Recently, however, pressures have built up to negotiate a reform of the international monetary system, aimed at developing a new system of reserves and settlements to replace the dollar standard and at improving the balance-of-payments adjustment process. The achievement of these objectives would give the fund the power to create international reserves and to influence national decisions on exchange rates and on domestic monetary and fiscal policies. Developments in both the bank and the fund have reflected a steady increase in recent years in the resources of multilateral development and assistance agencies in contrast to static or declining bilateral efforts. The growing economic interdependence of the world has, of course, been the major reason for the faster growth of the multilateral approach. The membership of both the bank and the fund has increased considerably in recent years. Even China joined both institutions in 1980.

The UN conferences on environment, food, and population have been discussed extensively in Chapter 10. Suffice it to say in the present context that perhaps the most impressive feature that these conferences had in common was their truly planetary character. Representatives of all mankind gathered in Stockholm, Rome, and Bucharest in order to forge common action plans against scourges that were common to all. The fact that action plans emerged at all from these town meetings of the world came as a surprise to the skeptics. The UN Environment Program established in Nairobi and the World Food Council established at the Rome Conference were concrete testimonies to the fact that the "New International Economic Order" was not just an empty slogan. A real beginning had been made in the slow and painful evolution toward global consciousness.

The General Agreement on Tariffs and Trade (GATT) today comprises over eighty nations. It was formed originally in 1947 by twenty-three Western nations which were interested in lowering tariff and trade barriers among themselves. A generation later, in the 1980s, the dollar and the British pound sterling had been devalued, Western Europe was struggling on the road to economic unification, and debt crises had begun to plague the world economy. Tariffs, in short, were no longer the most significant hindrance to world trade. Nontariff barriers loomed as far more important. The energy and food crises stimulated a new concern about access to raw materials and a clear need for new ground rules on export controls. It is very likely that GATT will become one of the instruments in such a fundamental revision of the entire world trade system.

Finally, the 1980s have witnessed the rapid growth and proliferation of a unique phenomenon in the global economy: the multilateral enterprise. Observers of these powerful economic entities are sharply divided. Some perceive them as greedy, disruptive colossi, motivated solely by profit; others see them as forces that transcend the iron bonds of the nation-state system and as forerunners of a saner economic order. While both extreme views are exaggerated, it seems that, on balance, the order-building potential of the multinational corporations exceeds their disruptive potential. Hence, they are discussed in the context of the present chapter.

During 1973 a "Group of Eminent Persons" met under the auspices of the UN Economic and Social Council to study the role of multinational corporations in international relations and the process of development.[1] There are currently some two hundred large multinational enterprises which operate simultaneously in twenty or more different nations and are joined together by common ownership and management strategy. The $3 billion of value added annually by each of the top ten multinationals is already greater than the gross national product of some eighty member states of the United Nations, and some observers are predicting that by the end of the century three hundred giant corporations will account for the large majority of world industrial production.[2] Yet, even weak states can and sometimes have nationalized the local affiliate of a multinational corporation. For the foreseeable future, the two kinds of entities will continue to coexist, in uneasy tension.

The relationship of the multinationals to the developing countries is highly complex. At present 95 percent of the world's multinationals are domiciled in highly developed countries, such as the United States, Britain, Germany, France, Japan, Sweden, Holland, and Switzerland. The developing countries need the jobs the multinationals have to offer, but at times political or economic considerations may dictate nationalization. Thus, the multinationals exert massive economic power, but the developing nations retain political power by exercising their prerogatives as sovereign entities.

In rare cases a multinational corporation can influence the foreign policy of a country directly. The impact of the International Telephone and Telegraph Company (ITT) on Chile was a case in point and stimulated the creation of the special UN group. Such examples of private foreign policy are relatively rare. More commonly, the existence of corporations with decision domains crossing several national boundaries has provided an additional instrument that governments may attempt to use in their relations with each other. Manipulation of transnational corporations, however, is an instrument available to the host as well as the home government. The most dramatic example was the 1973 oil embargo. While the companies exerted some independence in diverting non-Arab oil to the Netherlands and the United States, the Arab countries were able to obtain almost total company compliance in regard to Arab oil. Thus, control has worked as a two-way street.

Perhaps the most important order-building function of the multinational corporation is its capacity to tie the global economy together in a more meaningful way. It tends to shift industrial production toward the poorer parts of the globe. It transfers technology and managerial resources from advanced to less-developed countries. It promotes both regional and global economic integration. It may also help to erode the great ideological cleavage between East and West. Already there are more than a thousand agreements between Western corporations and Communist countries.

There is, of course, the danger that the diminution of the role of the nation-state might signal a new feudalism rather than healthy progress. Kings and corporate barons might engage in conflicts and coalitions and the serfs would suffer. If that were to happen, the real global divisions would not be among nations, but between a world city knit together by transnational elites and the diverse but intense parochialisms of the world countryside.

On balance, it seems clear that the role of the multinational corporation in international politics is already very substantial. Its impact is not only economic but political as well. Its challenge is so powerful that it is beginning to elicit concerted responses in the world community. Since these responses are being made manifest at a fairly early stage in the evolution of the multinational corporation, there is hope that its enormous potential will not further exacerbate the struggle for power, but will help pave the way toward a saner international economic order.

ECONOMIC ORDER-BUILDING IN WESTERN EUROPE

It has been at the regional level, and especially in Western Europe, that functional collaboration has been really tested. We shall now examine the various regional arrangements aimed at Western European economic integration. These arrangements include chiefly the Organization for Economic Cooperation and Development (OECD); the European Coal and Steel Community (ECSC); the European Atomic Energy Community (Euratom); and the European Economic Community, or Common Market (EEC). Behind the façade of these prosaic-sounding names, real pioneer work has been accomplished in the forging of economic order.

The nations which signed the Organization for European Economic Cooperation (OEEC) Convention in April 1948 were all members of the Atlantic

Community: Austria, Belgium, Denmark, France, Greece, Iceland, Ireland, Italy, Luxembourg, the Netherlands, Norway, Portugal, Sweden, Switzerland, Turkey, and the United Kingdom. Canada and the United States became associate members while the Federal Republic of Germany and Spain joined soon afterward as full members. Yugoslavia took part as an observer. The machinery of OEEC included a Council composed of all the member governments, an Executive Committee, several Technical Committees, and a Secretariat. Thus equipped, the organization embarked on its two main responsibilities: the apportioning of American aid and the liberalization of trade restrictions in the Western European economy.

The structure of OEEC was the subject of some disagreement. The French wanted a strong executive organ with some supranational characteristics. This was opposed by Britain, which insisted that the new organization remain under the direct control of the participating governments with no abrogation of sovereignty whatsoever. The British view prevailed both in form and in practice and OEEC was constituted as a purely transnational body, a conference of sovereign states in permanent session. The power of decision rested in the council, which was bound by the rule of unanimity. It would be false to assume, however, that the unanimity rule was a hindrance to the work of OEEC. The rule resulted in a practice of careful deliberating at all levels of policy making. In fact, when one or more states threatened to veto a decision, it was not uncommon for them to be "shamed" into agreement. A carefully prescribed procedure, including hearings and cross-examinations, made it almost impossible for a state to claim that it had been left out of the policy-making process. The veto was used only as a last resort. If a state used it too often, it found itself isolated and even ostracized. Diplomatic pressure was usually sufficient to persuade a reluctant member. On the other hand, the veto was a constant reminder to the large states that the smaller ones could not simply be out-voted but had to be persuaded. At times, the strict application of the unanimity rule even enabled the small states to exert a disproportionate amount of influence, as for example, when "a struggle over regulations concerning dried fruit among some of the smaller powers once held up far more important business."[3] But on the whole, the veto rule did not lead to paralysis; rather, it opened new avenues of improvisation and innovation. Of these, perhaps the most important was what OEEC officials came to call the "confrontation technique." The continuous process of intergovernmental consultation that went on at all levels of the organization encouraged a "European way of thinking" and an "OEEC point of view" in the permanent national delegations accredited to OEEC.[4] In making this view known to their national governments and in pressing for its acceptance, these officials imposed a moral obligation upon their governments that could not be lightly ignored. Indeed, the members of OEEC learned always to bear in mind the international consequences of national decisions. To be sure, there existed no legal obligation to do so, but long years of conditioning created a high degree of sensitivity to the interests of Europe as a whole. It may be said of most OEEC officials that this dual loyalty to their own country and to Europe seldom caused any serious difficulties. In most instances it proved possible for them to find a workable balance.

OEEC began as a "crisis organization" primarily concerned with the distribution of American aid. But as European recovery progressed, its second major responsibility, the liberalization of trade, assumed increasing importance. In this respect also, OEEC was very successful. It brought about a great increase in intra-European trade as well as in European production. The OEEC Code of Trade Liberalization resulted in the modification and withdrawal of numerous quota restrictions among the member states. A European Productivity Agency under the aegis of OEEC brought about major improvements in European industrial and agricultural productivity. Yet in the area of tariff reduction, OEEC also suffered a number of failures. Most notable among these were the major rifts that developed on the question of tariff reduction between The Six—France, Italy, West Germany, and the Benelux countries—and the rest of the OEEC membership. The increasing impatience of the Inner Six members of OEEC with the more conservative policies of the Outer Seven placed the organization under strain.

When OEEC went out of existence in 1960, it had demonstrated that a functional organization need not be supranational to be moderately successful. The OEEC had managed to improvise a number of successful techniques of economic cooperation despite its council's unanimity rule. The decisive factor in the organization's success, however, was not structural. It was the fact that OEEC had served two real and tangible purposes—the distribution of Marshall Plan aid and the liberalization of intra-European trade. It was these well-defined purposes that saved it from the fate of the Council of Europe, in whose case cooperation was defined much less concretely and sharply.

In 1961 OEEC was replaced by the Organization for Economic Cooperation and Development (OECD). The new body included the eighteen OEEC members plus the United States and Canada. Its goals were described as close cooperation on economic and business cycle policy, expanded aid to underdeveloped countries, and further progress in trade liberalization. During the 1970s and 1980s, the OECD countries' major challenge was to combat inflation and recession. The OPEC oil cartel had inflicted heavy damage on the industrial oil-importing nations of the OECD. In fact, it may not be incorrect to say that OPEC had become OECD's main preoccupation.

Neither OEEC nor its successor had any supranational features. Quite early in the life of the OEEC, this absence of supranationality gave rise to disagreements and eventually prompted six member nations to launch a far more ambitious project in economic collaboration. In May 1950 French Foreign Minister Robert Schuman made a dramatic announcement. He proposed to pool the resources of the French and German coal and steel industries under a common supranational authority that was to be open to other European countries. The motives underlying this far-reaching proposal were both economic and political. A rational distribution of European coal and steel throughout Western Europe would be highly desirable. But far more important was Schuman's desire to end Franco-German enmity. By the pooling of two raw materials vital for war, military conflict between Germany and France would become next to impossible. The bold conception of the Schuman Plan thus combined both realism and vision.

A month after the initial proposal, negotiations began among six European countries—France, West Germany, Italy, and the Benelux states. The moving spirit behind the negotiations was Jean Monnet, another major architect of the European idea. Monnet's hope was that economic union among the participating states would ultimately lead to political union. He envisaged a supranational authority with well-defined but real powers over coal and steel. Subsequently, other sectors of the economy might be added, leading logically to the goal of political fusion. The treaty negotiations proceeded fairly smoothly, since all participating states saw great advantages in the proposal. The French feared that an uncontrolled revival of the German Ruhr industries might once again herald the start of German aggression. Hence France was willing to give up a degree of control over its own industries in exchange for some control over those in Western Germany. The Germans hoped that the Schuman Plan would greatly improve their coal and steel production, expand markets, and create new outlets for foreign investment. Italy looked forward to new capital and the possibility of relieving its population problem through emigration. The Benelux countries hoped for increased exports and a greater volume of transit trade.

The great disappointment encountered by the negotiators was the attitude of Great Britain. The Six had invited the Labour government to participate but had been turned down. The main objection on the other side of the Channel was to the proposed supranational character of the organization. The British, in consideration of their unique international position and their ties to the Commonwealth, were simply unwilling to allow control of coal and steel to pass to a supranational authority. Prime Minister Attlee rejected the Schuman Plan in the strongest terms:

> We on this side are not prepared to accept the principle that the most vital economic forces of this country should be handed over to an authority that is utterly undemocratic and is responsible to nobody.[5]

Similarly, the Scandinavian countries, Austria, and Switzerland rejected the supranational features of the proposed treaty. Thus, negotiations remained limited to The Six. The entire process took a little over two years. Italy was the last of the members to ratify, in June 1952. In September of that year the new European Coal and Steel Community, creating a single market for coal and steel for the 160 million people of the six participating states, became a reality.

The structure of ECSC before the fusion of its executive with those of the other European communities in 1967 deserves close analysis. At least one of the community's institutions—the High Authority—possessed powers previously exercised only by national governments and some powers that even those governments did not possess. Hence, a real curtailment of national sovereignty by The Six was involved. The core and executive institution of ECSC, the High Authority, made all important decisions. This body consisted of nine members who held office for six-year terms. Eight of these were chosen by agreement among the six member governments and the ninth was co-opted by the other eight. The High Authority never included more than two members of the same nationality. In practice, ECSC's main organ was composed of two members from France, two from Germany, and one each from Belgium, Italy, Luxembourg, and the Netherlands. The ninth member always came from a country providing only one official. The members of the High Authority did not regard themselves as political spokesmen for their respective governments but as international civil servants of an independent European institution. Decisions of the High Authority were made by majority vote but, so far as the outside world was concerned, the principle of collective responsibility was observed.

The main supranational features of the High Authority were threefold: first, its legal right to bypass the six national governments and to deal with the coal and steel industries of the community directly; second, to make binding decisions in its area of competence; and third, to impose sanctions against violators. In carrying out its functions, the High Authority took the following types of action: first, it could direct the industries through decisions which were legally binding in every respect; second, it could act through recommendations; and finally, it could express opinions. Recommendations and opinions usually carried great weight but engendered no legal compulsion. Sanctions against violators of binding decisions took the form of monetary fines. Over twenty industrial enterprises in the community were thus fined, principally for such infractions as exceeding the price ceiling, breaking price equalization schemes, and forming cartels without approval. The fines were usually light but increased in severity if violations continued. The first president of the High Authority was Jean Monnet. During his tenure, Monnet always emphasized that the federal aspects of ECSC were superior in actual power to those of the member governments. "In a sense, Monnet considered the High Authority as the repository of the European General Will, with the evil governments merely the spokesmen for the selfish particular wills."[6] In brief, the High Authority seemed to be the embodiment of "the European point of view."

It would be erroneous, however, to regard the High Authority as a kind of Platonic Nocturnal Council. There were important checks on its power. The most important of these was the Community's Court of Justice, established under the terms of the ECSC Treaty. This court assumed its functions in January 1955. It was composed of seven judges elected for six years and served as an appellate body of redress against the High Authority when that body was accused of exceeding its jurisdiction. Both private firms and member states could appeal to the court, which in fact became the constitutional arbiter of the Schuman Treaty. As such, the court had the power to annul the High Authority's decisions. The record of the court has been marked by a high degree of objectivity and independence. A large number of appeals came before it. On some occasions the court upheld the High Authority against member governments and private enterprises. In 1955, for example, the court rejected an appeal by the government of the Netherlands against the Authority's decision

to maintain ceiling prices for coal and steel. On the other hand, the court upheld appeals by the French and Italian governments and reversed High Authority decisions on the sale of scrap iron.

A second important check on the High Authority's power was exercised
by the Council of Ministers, which was composed of the Ministers for Economic Affairs from the six member countries. The council was introduced as a
result of pressure by the Benelux governments, which were fearful that the
Schuman Community's coercive authority might be too great. The council's
task was to harmonize the actions of the High Authority with those of the participating governments. In practice, the council advised the High Authority
and made sure that the interests and policies of the member countries were
given due weight. It constantly confronted the High Authority with "national"
points of view, thus serving as a vital link between national policy and the
"European policy" of the Authority.

The High Authority also depended for advice upon a Consultative Committee consisting of producers, workmen, distributors, and consumers from the
six member states. Before coming to any important decision, the Authority reviewed any proposed action with the committee. The final institution in the
ECSC structure was the Assembly. Since 1958, the Assembly has also served
Euratom and the Common Market and is now known as the European Parliament. The 142 members of this body were chosen either by the respective
parliaments of the six states or by popular election. The delegates were all parliamentarians and in most cases also attended the sessions of the Assembly of
the Council of Europe. At least once a year the Assembly reviewed the action
of the High Authority, acting very much like a stockholders' meeting. Unlike a
national parliament, it had no legislative power and could not initiate policy.
Its one great power was a negative one: it could remove the High Authority by
a two-thirds vote of censure. This never actually occurred. In practice, the Assembly attempted to influence the shaping of policies. The most interesting
development in this respect was the development of supranational political
parties.[7] It was not uncommon for the Socialist members from the six participating states to form a common front against the Assembly's conservatives, including even their own countrymen.

In sum, the High Authority was a supranational organ with considerable
power over the coal and steel industries of The Six. It must be remembered,
however, that this power applied only to these two sectors of the member
countries' economies and that an effective system of checks and balances was
written into the treaty. If the High Authority was the motor of ECSC, the
Council of Ministers, the Consultative Committee, the Assembly, and the
Court of Justice were its brakes. The total structure of ECSC was thus a
unique phenomenon, falling somewhere along the continuum between a
purely transnational organization and a federal government. Its High Authority certainly had far more power than the central agency of a conventional
international organization, though less than is generally yielded to a federal
government.

We must now assess the accomplishments of this unique functional organization. Some friends of ECSC feared that the community would atrophy and that its supranational features would not long endure. These fears proved unwarranted. The proposed common market for coal, iron ore, steel, and scrap went into effect in 1953. Apparently unconcerned about its isolation, the High Authority launched a massive program. A timetable was laid down by which all tariffs, quotas, currency restrictions, and discriminations among the coal and steel industries were to be eliminated. The High Authority tried its utmost to ensure fair conditions of competition and to eliminate monopolistic buying and selling practices. The Authority's most difficult task was "trust-busting"—implementing the anti-cartel provisions of the treaty. Success on this front was limited because of resistance in all the six member states. French and German industrial interests especially complained that the Authority moved too quickly. Actually, on the cartel question, the High Authority's approach was quite cautious. By and large, the High Authority showed itself to be understanding of special problems and to be dedicated to making the most constructive contribution possible to the industries concerned. Investment in the coal and steel industries of The Six was encouraged. The Authority endeavored to raise loans for the purpose. And it even ventured into the social realm through research into occupational diseases, safety problems, and the harmonization of wage levels and fringe benefits.

There was some friction among the five institutions of ECSC but, on the whole, these tensions were useful rather than damaging. The system of checks and balances built into the treaty worked very well. The four "brakes" attached to the High Authority effectively prevented the latter from assuming the proportions of a Frankenstein monster. Indeed, ECSC became a unique showcase of functional cooperation.

There was, however, one serious weakness from which ECSC suffered: the absence of Great Britain from its membership. Not that the participating powers did not make a determined effort to secure Britain's membership in the organization. They realized from the beginning that the absence of Britain would constitute a very serious obstacle to the building of a European economic order. And they feared that it might eventually even compel The Six to erect protective barriers against Britain and the other nations closely associated with it in economic matters. Yet both Labour and Conservative governments in Britain firmly rejected participation in any supranational body that would entail a formal surrender of sovereignty. In view of their wider commitments to the Commonwealth, the British considered it ill-advised to wed themselves irrevocably to the European continent through ECSC. The net result of this policy, however, was that during the first decade of ECSC's life, Britain and the Scandinavian countries increasingly became economic "outsiders" to the European Six. At first, Britain did not take ECSC seriously, but by 1960 it found itself left out of something of key economic importance. Hence, to try to remedy the situation, in 1960 Great Britain decided to launch a rival economic order-building scheme of its own, the European Free Trade Association. We shall examine this scheme in its proper context below.

On balance, ECSC demonstrated that the delegation of limited sovereign powers to a supranational body could work in practice. When in 1954 the community was left on its own through the demise of the European Defense Community, it was given a short life expectancy. Yet it not only survived, but encouraged The Six to engage in further supranational experimentation among themselves. If it was possible to internationalize coal and steel, could not the same thing be accomplished in other sectors of the economy? Atomic energy, a new source of power with as yet few vested interests, might lend itself to a similar approach. This idea was to provide the seed for the new European Atomic Energy Community (Euratom). By the late 1950s it seemed to many observers that the "sector" approach to economic integration was the most effective road to international order-building that had yet been devised. The basis for this optimism was the impressive record of the European Coal and Steel Community.

The European Atomic Energy Community was born at a meeting of the foreign ministers of "little Europe" in June 1955. What Jean Monnet of France did for ECSC, Paul-Henri Spaak of Belgium accomplished for Euratom. Determined to "relaunch Europe," Spaak guided the draft treaty through a maze of technical committees during the summer of 1955. From this process there emerged the Spaak Report, which became the basis for the Euratom Treaty. After protracted negotiations, the treaty was signed in Rome in March 1957, and after ratification by the six member states went into effect on January 1, 1958. Therewith another sector of the economies of The Six, atomic energy, was absorbed into a supranational community.

The essential purpose of Euratom was the pooling of the atomic energy resources of The Six for peaceful purposes. The treaty steered clear of the military implications of atomic power. This limitation was inserted at the insistence of France, which wanted its defense program to remain outside of Euratom's control. Hence, Euratom's main responsibilities included the development of nuclear research and the dissemination of technical knowledge; the development of uniform health and safety standards; the construction of nuclear reactors for peaceful purposes; and the development of control and inspection measures to prevent the member states from diverting Euratom-supplied nuclear materials to military purposes. The working capital of Euratom was supplied by the United States, which sold 30,000 kilograms of fissionable materials to the community in 1958. Under the terms of the agreement, Euratom was given property rights over these materials. At the insistence of Euratom officials, the community was also given the right of self-inspection by the United States government.

The structure of Euratom was made similar to that of ECSC. "Supranational" authority was vested in a Euratom Commission, which was composed of five members from different nationalities chosen on the basis of their competence. The commission's powers with respect to atomic energy were even greater than those of the ECSC High Authority in matters of coal and steel. This difference may be attributed to three factors: first, the Euratom Treaty was highly technical, which meant that only nuclear specialists could discuss its implications in a meaningful sense; second, the treaty was narrower in scope than ECSC and did not arouse as much resistance; and, most important, atomic energy was a relatively new field in which neither vested interests nor national habits were deeply rooted. Thus it proved relatively easy to endow the new commission with very considerable powers.

Euratom, like ECSC, was a structure with checks and balances. It was decided to make the ECSC Assembly also the parliamentary body of Euratom. Even more significant, the ECSC Court of Justice also became the "conscience" of the Euratom Commission. The court was given the power to remove the members of the commission from office "for cause." In addition, the court became the constitutional arbiter of the Euratom Treaty and was given the right to pass on the legality of commission decisions if these were challenged by the member states.

Euratom has encountered relatively few serious obstacles. Atomic energy was still so new that the benefits to be derived from common action were greater and more apparent than in the conventional industries of coal and steel. Besides, matters of health and safety could be dealt with more efficiently through a community approach. Second, the establishment of Euratom marked the beginning of the injection of order into the confusing array of functional organizations in Western Europe. The Court of Justice and the Assembly began to serve both ECSC and Euratom. By 1958 the "Community" of The Six had come to represent not only form but ever-growing substance. It was quite clear, indeed, that the ultimate objective of The Six was a United States of Europe via the road of economic order.

The second offspring of the ECSC was the European Economic Community (EEC) or Common Market. This is the most ambitious functionalist scheme of our time. The idea for EEC was contained in the Spaak Report of 1956, which forcefully outlined the advantages of further steps toward economic union among The Six. The draft treaty proposed a twelve- to fifteen-year transitional period during which tariffs and quantitative restrictions for all commodities, including agricultural products, were to be eliminated among the six participating states. A single tariff schedule to be applied to outside countries was to be developed; freedom of movement for workers was also envisaged; exchange policies were to be coordinated; a common transportation policy was to be hammered out; and common provisions for social benefits were contemplated. In brief, EEC was to become an arrangement that went much further than the abolition of tariffs and quotas among The Six, and was to be a half-way house toward complete political union.

Once again, Paul-Henri Spaak guided the project through the delicate formative stages. As in the ECSC, each of the prospective member states saw definite advantages. Only France had serious reservations and wanted to bring its overseas territories into the community. France had great bargaining power because the other members feared its volatile parliament. France was especially afraid of competition in the agricultural field and received numerous concessions in that area. France knew well that its participation was indispensable and used its advantage with consummate political skill. West Germany was eager to join since it perceived an opportunity for increasing markets and investment. Moreover, Chancellor Adenauer was deeply committed to supranationality among The Six, even as an ideal. Italy was most impressed by the goal of freedom of movement for workers which, it hoped, would contribute to the solution of its population and unemployment problems. The Benelux countries hoped for increased exports and transit trade. In spite of this favorable climate, negotiations at various times appeared on the point of breaking down. Finally, the EEC Treaty was signed in March 1957 and, together with the Euratom Treaty, went into effect on January 1, 1958.

The institutional structure of the Common Market was again patterned on the example of ECSC. A commission composed of nine members chosen on the basis of "general competence" played the role of the High Authority. It was to perform its duties "in the general interest of the Community with complete independence." Its supranational authority largely flowed from the power to fix and amend the timetables for freeing the various "sectors" from trade restrictions. The Assembly of the ECSC also served the Common Market and was given the power to remove members of the EEC Commission through a vote of censure. The ECSC Court of Justice was also made into a court of appeal in the framework of EEC. Thus the three "Communities" of The Six had a common Assembly and a common Court of Justice. In addition, EEC had a Council of Ministers which served as the link between the community and the national governments. An Economic and Social Committee similar in function to the Consultative Committee of the ECSC completed the institutional picture in the early 1960s.

A dramatic structural step toward union was taken in 1967 when the three executive bodies of ECSC, Euratom, and the EEC were fused into a single fourteen-member European Commission. France, West Germany, and Italy supplied three commissioners each, Belgium and the Netherlands two each, and Luxembourg one. With this event, the pattern of a rudimentary federal structure clearly emerged among The Six.

The policy of Britain has gone through a full circle. As we have seen, Britain was unwilling to join any of the three supranational experiments because of its reluctance to give up any of its sovereign power. In 1950 Britain was courted by The Six. But a decade later the wheel had turned full circle. In 1959, fearful of being left behind and outside, Britain began to woo The Six, but now it was the turn of The Six to be reluctant. France had consolidated relations with West Germany and no longer needed Britain to balance German power in the community. President de Gaulle, eager for French grandeur, saw Britain rather than Germany as his chief rival in the race for nuclear greatness; and it was Britain, not Germany, that had delivered arms to Tunisia—a fact that the new French government, which viewed EEC as as much "Eurafrican" as European, could not easily overlook. Nor did the other members of the Common Market show great eagerness to admit Britain to the community.

In self-defense, Britain therefore assumed the leadership of a rival scheme of her own, the European Free Trade Association. Those European countries that were interested in freer trade but also had reservations about supranationality followed the British lead. In December 1959 Britain, Austria, Denmark, Norway, Portugal, Sweden, and Switzerland signed the Convention setting up the new association. Britain, rejected by the Inner Six, took the initiative in forming the Outer Seven. The seven member states contemplated the abolition of tariffs in annual installments by 1970. This was the main goal. Unlike EEC, the European Free Trade Association did not include planning for agricultural products, transport, and labor movements. It was a far more modest venture to be approached through the traditional transnational channels patterned after the OEEC model.

It soon became apparent, however, that EFTA, with its market of 90 million people, was no match for the 170 million inhabitants of The Six. In August 1961 the British government finally decided to apply for membership in the EEC. Negotiations proved difficult because of Britain's Commonwealth and EFTA commitments, special agricultural problems, and the issue of supranationality. While the British application was pending, EEC in January 1962 moved into its second stage of integration, which involved majority voting on numerous important issues. Even while compromises making it possible for Britain to join were weighed, President de Gaulle, to the dismay of the other EEC members, not to mention Britain itself, vetoed British membership in January 1963. The French president, eager to construct a Western Europe in which France would play a leading role, was intent on excluding what he described as the "Anglo-Saxon presence" from the continent. In 1967 yet another British effort to enter the Common Market came to grief on the rock of French resistance.

The turning point for Britain came in 1969. That year, President de Gaulle was defeated in a referendum on a domestic question and was succeeded by Georges Pompidou. In 1970 Edward Heath led the British Conservatives to a resounding victory over the Labour party. Mr. Heath took Britain's case for entry into the Common Market directly to President Pompidou and found the new French president much more receptive than his predecessor. Protracted negotiations ensued between Britain's Geoffrey Rippon and France's foreign minister, Maurice Schumann. Finally, in early 1972, a new chapter in European history was opened when Britain was formally admitted to the Common Market.

With Britain's accession to EEC, EFTA went into eclipse. Ireland, Denmark, and Norway were invited together with Britain, but Norway refused to join. The welcome extended to Britain was generally warm since the French especially perceived Britain as a counterweight to West Germany, whose economic power was of some concern to France and to the Benelux countries. In June 1975, in a national referendum on membership in the Common Market, the British people by a solid majority vote gave their approval to continued membership. Thus, by the mid-1970s the Common Market was a power to be reckoned with, a group of nine nations comprising more than a quarter of a billion people well on their way toward economic union. In 1981 a tenth nation—Greece—was admitted to membership in the Common Market.

In 1984 the Common Market faced a serious crisis. Huge agricultural subsidies had brought the Community to the brink of bankruptcy. Moreover, Britain demanded a $1.5 billion rebate on its contribution to the Community's budget, which the continental members were unwilling to grant. Once again, customs officials harassed truckers at borders and petty squabbles over relatively insignificant amounts obscured the larger vision of European unity. Nonetheless, in 1985, Spain and Portugal were admitted to the EEC, raising the Community's membership to twelve. Pessimists still complained about "squalid squabbles over money," but optimists continued to adhere to the ultimate vision of a United States of Europe.

Despite the serious pains described above, the Western European economic integration movement has already had profound effects upon the rest of the world. The reaction in the United States has been ambivalent. On the one hand, the United States welcomes a strong and united Europe as a more dependable ally in the struggle against communism; but on the other, the United States confronts real economic power on the other side of the Atlantic, which can no longer be dealt with lightly and which may force major reevaluations of economic policy. The Soviet Union has not been able to ignore the Common Market either. Its answer to the Common Market has been COMECON, an effort to forge a common economic policy for the Eastern bloc countries. COMECON, however, has proved to be no match for the Common Market's economic power. Most Eastern European countries, as well as the Soviet Union itself, are already trading with the EEC. China, perceiving the Common Market as an irritant to the Soviet Union, has expressed its approval. And even the more remote countries in the developing parts of the world have had to pay attention to this bold new experiment now taking place in Western Europe.

We are now ready for a more general evaluation of functionalism as a technique for the building of economic order. On a global scale, as we have seen, the functional approach is still in its infancy. But the efforts undertaken by the World Bank and its affiliates to bridge the gulf between the world's rich and poor have been commendable. Similarly, the UN's global approach to food, resources, environment, and population has demonstrated a nascent consciousness of the world's economic interdependence. And the evidence suggests that the order-building potential of most of the world's proliferating multinational enterprises may outweigh their potential for conflict and disruption.

Our Western European case study in functional order-building on a regional basis affords some interesting insights. For one thing, supranationality per se is not necessarily a precondition for an organization's success. The Organization for European Economic Cooperation was a singularly successful venture although it did not embody any supranational features. What seems to determine an organization's operational effectiveness is whether it has a concrete and tangible job to do. If it does, institutional gadgetry becomes more or less irrelevant. A vague desire for cooperation without clearly defined goals will lead to atrophy; the Council of Europe is a case in point. What distinguishes all the regional economic organizations of Europe, whether supranational or not, is the fact that they have clearly defined operational programs. This was true especially of the three "Communities" of The Six and certainly continues to be true of the Common Market since the accession of Britain. The integration process is also furthered by the fact that all participants have expectations of concrete economic rewards. The nature of these expectations differs from state to state, but all members hope to derive great benefits in one form or another.

The increasing complexity of the European organizational picture cries out for a measure of coordination. It is unlikely that an overall scheme or Grand Design will be acceptable to all the states of Western Europe in the immediate future. The ultimate objective of some Western European states is nothing less than a United States of Europe. This aim is not yet shared by others, especially Britain and France. Coordination will probably have to proceed within each of the two camps. Some progress has been made. Already, the three "Communities" share a common Assembly, a common Court of Justice, and a common Executive. These may be the forerunners of a European federal system.

Perhaps the most encouraging by-product of functional experimentation in Western Europe has been the development of a "European outlook." The constant process of consultation and the complexity of international machinery have persuaded most Western European statesmen to consider national policy decisions in the broadest possible context. In 1979, for example, the members of the Common Market permitted the creation of a European Parliament through direct elections. By the 1980s they pursued coordinated agricultural policies and common external economic relations. Despite occasional setbacks such as Prime Minister Margaret Thatcher's demand in 1984 that Britain's contribution to the funding of EEC should be reduced, the Common Market has become an established fact of European economic life.

In the 1960s the Common Market had six members. In the 1970s it had nine; in 1981 the admission of Greece brought the membership to ten; and the admission of Spain and Portugal in 1985 doubled the Community's original membership.

The entry of Greece will cost the Common Market $2 billion in economic aid over the next five years. That cost will triple before Portugal and Spain are also integrated. There are other problems ahead. Free movement of labor, capital, and goods means that additional millions of southern workers will migrate and compete with northern labor. Cheap agricultural products will irritate French and Italian farmers. True, the more developed European partners will gain a larger market for industrial products, plus investment opportunities in low-wage areas. But those will not compensate for the costs.

The compensating factor should be political consolidation. A stronger democratic bloc should emerge, with a stronger voice in world affairs. A Common Market of twelve nations will begin to assume continental, if not world, importance. It will stretch from near the polar icecap in Greenland to sunny Crete in the eastern Mediterranean. The Common Market population will increase 20 percent to over 300 million. Its area will expand by 50 percent. Its gross domestic product will edge ahead of that of the United States. It will have half the votes in the OECD, the economic coordinating center for the industrial democracies. And Greece's 4,600 ships will make the EEC the world's most powerful maritime bloc, with a third of the world's merchant shipping tonnage. The Common Market's trade already exceeds that of the United States.

Size, of course, will bring new tensions. The Nine had a harder time agreeing than The Six. Twelve nations will make consensus even harder to achieve. But the Common Market has, over a bumpy road, overcome far more serious strains. And its history shows that the poorer countries, such as Italy and Ireland, benefit more than the rich. The odds are that Greece, Spain, and Portugal will, too.

Yet, there is a danger in the evolution of economic groupings such as the Common Market. If these regional bodies should claim a new kind of "sovereignty" for themselves and develop into a form of regional nationalism, their purpose would be defeated. Even more important, recession has threatened the very fabric of some of the democracies upon whose political and economic strength the survival of the European integration movement depends. Nations do not integrate when they are weak, but only when they are strong. On the whole, however, the functional organizations have shown an amazing talent for improvisation and muddling through innumerable difficulties. Functionalism on a regional basis has become one of the most powerful instruments in the international struggle for order. The European Communities may well be the forerunners of the first political system transcending the sovereign nation-state since Machiavelli wrote *The Prince* almost five hundred years ago.

THE WORLD ENERGY CRISIS

The entire world today stands at the edge of an awesome watershed: the coming energy transition. For decades the rich industrial countries depended on cheap oil as their major energy resource. Most poor developing countries, until recently, eagerly looked forward to their own entry into the petroleum era. But the Arab oil embargo of 1973–1974, the Iranian revolution, and the war between Iraq and Iran rudely reminded the industrial countries of their dependency and the poor countries of their poverty. The price of oil had risen from $2 a barrel in 1960 to $40 in 1980. Even though oil prices had declined substantially by the mid-1980s, the long-term outlook was still disturbing. A CIA report, released by the White House in April 1977, had predicted that "in the absence of greatly increased energy conservation, projected world demand for oil [would] approach productive capacity by the early 1980s and substantially exceed capacity by 1985."[8] In short, the world will probably run out of oil before the end of the century. Ours may be the last generation of the petroleum era. What will our children and grandchildren use as *their* major energy resource? Will we prepare them for the inevitable transition? Or will we say, with the last of the French monarchs, "Après nous, le déluge"? That is the real challenge of the energy crisis.

"Each new inventory of world oil reserves has been more disturbing than the last," President Carter declared in his address to the American people on April 18, 1977. A dramatic shift has occurred in the global supply-and-demand situation. While consumers were in control in the 1960s, the picture changed in the 1970s, and according to most projections, will continue to change in the same direction during the 1980s and 1990s. For the world to maintain its current rate of consumption and yet keep its reserves intact, we would have to discover another Kuwait roughly every three years, or another Texas or Alaska roughly every six months.[9] Clearly, this seems a most unlikely prospect.

Let us look at the inventory a bit more closely. The United States produces approximately 10 percent of the world's petroleum. Regrettably, America's oil is now almost certainly half gone. Most experts agree that the rate of extraction will decline sharply after 1985, with total depletion a real prospect by the end of the century. The Middle East has roughly 30 percent of the world's oil, of which one-tenth has been consumed. The Soviet Union has 25 percent, of which one-tenth has been used up. Africa has about 10 percent, most of which is still in the ground. Latin America is believed to have 10 percent, of which one-fifth has been consumed, and Western Europe produces less than 5 percent. The remaining 10 percent is distributed throughout other parts of the world. The trilateral nations—the United States, Western Europe, and Japan—face an immediate oil squeeze. Most other areas still have ample oil to meet their immediate requirements. But the oil-short nations encompass most of the world's industrial base and all import huge amounts of oil from the oil-rich regions. Even if one assumes a relatively peaceful Middle East—a dubious assumption at best in the light of events in Iran and Iraq—the prospects are bleak. It is highly probable that the world will have reached the end of its oil supplies sometime before the year 2000. What, then, are the alternatives as we enter the twlight of an era?

Coal has been the world's most plentiful fossil fuel and has been used for at least two thousand years. There is no shortage of coal, yet it is not likely that coal will ever replace petroleum. At best, it will be a transitional source of energy. There are several compelling reasons for this. In the first place, coal is very unevenly distributed geographically. The Soviet Union, the United States, and China—in that order—have 90 percent of the world's coal resources, with the Soviet Union having nearly twice those of the United States and the United States having about three times those of China. This uneven distribution may be politically significant. The Soviet Union, for example, has a much higher percentage of the world's coal than the Middle East has of the world's oil. Second, even though world coal resources seem adequate for at least two hundred years, only a portion of these resources is "recoverable." In an average mine, only about half of the coal is actually mined, with the rest being left standing as "pillars." Third, as everyone knows, coal mining is an unpleasant, unhealthy, and often dangerous occupation. And finally, a conversion to coal as a major energy resource would create formidable environmental problems. Specifically, it would release huge amounts of carbon dioxide into the atmosphere, which might raise the earth's temperature to a dangerous level. Conversely, some scientists have warned that soot might blanket the Northern Hemisphere, shield the sun, and thus usher in a new ice age. Either way, the climatic consequences of a new coal era might prove catastrophic. Coal will never replace petroleum.

Many countries have long nurtured the hope that nuclear power would reduce their dependence on oil and perhaps even replace it altogether. As early as 1960, for example, the U.S. Air Force invested over $1 billion in an attempt to build a nuclear-powered airplane. Some critics pointed out that the plane would be too heavy and cumbersome to be militarily useful. Others feared that radioactive debris would be scattered all over the countryside if the plane should crash. In 1962 President Kennedy finally ordered the project scrapped. This episode foreshadowed some of the dilemmas posed by nuclear power.

The dream of replacing oil with atomic energy seems to be fading fast. In the first place, nuclear power is not cheap. Research and development as well as capital construction costs are formidable. The hope for "electricity too cheap to meter" has proved to be unfounded. Second, the dangers of converting to a nuclear-powered world are legion. Problems of radiation, radioactive waste, and reactor safety loom large. Even worse, it is very difficult to divorce the peaceful from the warlike atom, as the history of the International Atomic Energy Agency has amply shown. India's explosion of a "peaceful bomb" in 1974 is another compelling example of this danger. The nuclear nonproliferation treaty does not cope adequately with these perils. Moreover, in a nuclear world, terrorists and criminals would have far more ready access to nuclear bombs, with potentially disastrous consequences for society. Perhaps the only way to deal with these dangers would be to centralize far more authority in the hands of governments. Such a course of action, obviously, would not be very desirable. Optimists have always regarded a nuclear world as a forward step. But if humanity today stands at the edge of an abyss, a step forward is not necessarily progress.

More recently, some energy experts have turned to the sun for new hope. One scholar, for example, maintains that, by the year 2000, the sun's inexhaustible energy could provide 40 percent of the global energy budget, by furnishing heat and electricity.[10] Wind and water could also be tapped more efficiently. Solar energy, this advocate declares, would be clean, cheap, safe, and self-sustaining.

While the prospect of a solar-powered world is seductively attractive, it is not likely to be translated into reality in the near future. The sun, despite its enormous heat, is not very efficient as an energy provider. Solar power involves using a source which has a temperature of 6,000 degrees centigrade to heat water to less than 100 degrees. The almost boundless potential of the sun, while theoretically available to us, simply still eludes us in practical commercial terms. Solar energy is indeed a hope, but it is a rather distant hope.

A more hopeful prospect may be natural gas. Huge supplies of natural gas are available for industrial use in the United States and Canada. Some of the excess could be stored as a reserve in nonproductive wells. There are industries that now burn oil that could convert to gas without much difficulty. The search for new synthetic fuels, while expensive, must also not be abandoned. It may take an imaginative combination of the old and of the new.

Perhaps our best chance to get through the transition period without major turbulence may lie in conservation. A barrel of oil saved may be as useful as a barrel produced—perhaps even better in some respects. In view of the fact that the waste of energy throughout the industrialized world is enormous, conservation has vast possibilities. More than half of the current U.S. energy budget is waste. For the next quarter of a century, the United States could meet all its new energy needs simply by improving the efficiency of existing uses. One must bear in mind here a crucial distinction between curtailment and conservation. Curtailment means a cold, dark house; conservation means a well-insulated house with an efficient heating system. Gas-guzzling cars might have to give way to less conspicuous, more energy-efficient models. Small may truly have to become beautiful. A vigorous conservation program might see the world through the energy transition without becoming hooked on hazardous technologies or unreliable sources of supply.

The search for new sources of energy will be painful and competitive. But there is a strangely positive side to it as well. We shall have to struggle for our survival. Hence, there is bound to be a great deal of international cooperation. The long-term demands for energy are so gigantic and the economic and political linkages among nations are so strong that, as a practical matter, competition may very well give way to cooperation in conservation, research, development, and discovery. The energy transition will not respect national boundaries or sovereignties. Any contribution to the global energy supply is bound to be of general benefit. For essentially selfish reasons, nation-states will be obliged to wish each other well.

In 1492 Imperial Spain financed the explorations of Christopher Columbus in the New World. During the next one hundred years, the flow of precious metals from the New World made Spain one of the dominant states of Europe. When Philip III assumed the throne in 1598, he was convinced that the glory of Spain would last forever. What he did not know, however, was that the flow of gold and silver had already peaked. During the next century, it declined precipitously. This unanticipated decline brought the Spanish Empire to its knees. Spain had had its golden moment in the sun.

The Spanish experience may hold a special meaning for our modern world. The industrial nations were shaped by the availability of cheap oil at least as much as Spain was by the flow of gold and silver.[11] But unlike Spain, we can see the end ahead, and can choose to begin a meaningful transition. Unless we do so, we may share the fate of Spain. Once again, as so often in the past, the challenge is plain: we shall have to learn to change *before* we are shaken and shattered into doing so. Hopefully, we shall not have to learn again through trauma and catastrophe.

REFERENCES

1. United Nations Economic and Social Council, *The Impact of Multinational Corporations on Development and on International Relations*, E/5500/Rev. 1, 1974.
2. Joseph S. Nye, Jr., "Multinational Corporations in World Politics," *Foreign Affairs*, October 1974, p. 153.
3. *Ibid.*, p. 58.
4. *Ibid.*, p. 53.
5. *Hansard*, June 27, 1950.
6. Ernst B. Haas, *The Uniting of Europe.* Stanford, Calif.: Stanford University Press, 1959, p. 456.
7. *Ibid.*, Chap. 11.
8. Central Intelligence Agency, *The International Energy Situation: Outlook to 1985*, April 1977, p. 1.
9. *The National Energy Plan*, White House Press Release, April 29, 1977, p. VIII.
10. Denis Hayes, *Rays of Hope.* New York: Norton, 1977, p. 155.
11. *Ibid.*, p. 47.

BIBLIOGRAPHY

Baranson, Jack. *Technology and the Multinationals.* Lexington, Mass.: Lexington Books, 1978.

Barnet, Richard J., and Müller, Ronald E. *Global Reach: The Power of Multinational Corporations.* New York: Simon and Schuster, 1975.

Benoit, Emile. *Europe at Sixes and Sevens.* New York: Columbia University Press, 1961.

Bergsten, Fred, C. *Toward a New World Trade Policy.* Lexington, Mass.: Lexington Books, 1975.

————, et al. *The Future of the International Economic Order: An Agenda for Research.* Lexington, Mass.: Lexington Books, 1973

————; Horst, Thomas; and Moran, Theodore H. *American Multinationals and American Interests.* Washington, D.C.: Brookings Institution, 1978.

Buckenell, Howard III. *Energy and the National Defense.* Lexington: University Press of Kentucky, 1981.

Butler, David, and Kitzinger, Uwe. *The 1975 Referendum.* New York: St. Martin's Press, 1976.

Cairncross, Sir Alec, et al. *Economic Policy for the European Community: The Way Forward.* New York: Holmes and Meier, 1975.

Campbell, Duncan C., and Rowan, Richard L. *Multinational Enterprises and the OECD Industrial Relations Guidelines.* Philadelphia: Industrial Research Unit, Wharton School, University of Pennsylvania, 1983.

Caves, R. E. *Multinational Enterprise and Economic Analysis.* New York: Cambridge University Press, 1983.

Cline, William R., ed. *Trade Policy in the 1980's.* Washington: Institute for International Economics, 1983.

Cohen, Benjamin J. *Organizing the World's Money.* New York: Basic Books, 1977.

Curzon, Victoria. *The Essentials of Economic Integration: Lessons of EFTA Experience.* New York: St. Martin's Press, 1970.

Dam, Kenneth W. *The GATT: Law and International Economic Organization.* Chicago: University of Chicago Press, 1970.

De Vries, Margaret G., ed. *The International Monetary Fund 1966–1971.* Washington, D.C.: International Monetary Fund, 1976.

Dosser, Douglas; Gowland, David; and Hartley Keith. *The Collaboration of Nations: A Study of European Economic Policy.* New York: St. Martin's Press, 1982.

Douglass, Gordon K. *The New Interdependence: The European Community and the United States.* Lexington, Mass.: Lexington Books, 1979.

Evans, John W. *The Kennedy Round in American Trade Policy: The Twilight of the GATT?* Cambridge, Mass.: Harvard University Press, 1971.

Feld, Werner J. *Multinational Corporations and U.N. Politics: The Quest for Codes of Conduct.* Elmsford, N.Y.: Pergamon Press, 1980.

———. *Transnational Business Collaboration Among Common Market Countries.* New York: Praeger, 1970.

Gilbert, Milton. *Quest for World Monetary Order.* New York: Wiley, 1980.

Grunwald, Joseph, et al. *Latin American Economic Integration and U.S. Policy.* Washington, D.C.: Brookings Institution, 1972.

Haas, Ernst B. *Beyond the Nation-State.* Stanford, Calif.: Stanford University Press, 1965.

———. *The Uniting of Europe.* Rev. ed. Stanford, Calif.: Stanford University Press, 1968.

Holland, Stuart. *Uncommon Market.* New York: St. Martin's Press, 1980.

Holzman, Franklyn D. *Foreign Trade Under Central Planning.* Cambridge, Mass.: Harvard University Press, 1974.

———. *International Trade Under Communism.* New York: Basic Books, 1976.

Hossain, Kamal, ed. *Legal Aspects of the New International Economic Order.* New York: Nichols, 1980.

Hürni, Bettina S. *The Lending Policy of the World Bank in the 1970s.* Boulder, Colo.: Westview Press, 1980.

John, Ievan G., ed. *EEC Policy Towards Eastern Europe.* Lexington, Mass.: Lexington Books, 1976.

Johnson, Harry G. *Technology and Economic Interdependence.* New York: St. Martin's Press, 1976.

Kaser, Michael. *Comecon: Integration Problems of the Planned Economies.* New York: Oxford University Press, 1967.

Kennet, Wayland, ed. *The Futures of Europe.* New York: Cambridge University Press, 1976.

Kindleberger, Charles P., ed. *The International Corporation.* Cambridge: Massachusetts Institute of Technology Press, 1970.

Kitzinger, U. W. *The Challenge of the Common Market.* Oxford: Basil Blackwell, 1961.

———. *Diplomacy and Persuasion. How Britain Joined the Common Market.* London: Thames and Hudson, 1973.

Kozma, Ferenc. *Economic Integration and Economic Strategy.* Boston: Nijhoff, 1982.

Lawrence, Robert M., and Heisler, Martin O. *International Energy Policy.* Lexington, Mass.: Lexington Books, 1980.

Machlup, Fritz. *Remaking the International Monetary System: The Rio Agreement and Beyond.* Baltimore: Johns Hopkins Press, 1968.

Madsen, Axel. *Private Power: Multinational Corporations for the Survival of Our Planet.* New York: Morrow, 1980.

Mason, Edward S., and Asher, Robert E. *The World Bank Since Bretton Woods.* Washington, D.C.: Brookings Institution, 1973.

Mason, Henry L. *The European Coal and Steel Community: Experiment in Supranationalism.* The Hague: Nijhoff, 1955.

Maull, Hanns. *Europe and World Energy.* London and Boston: Butterworths (with the University of Sussex European Research Centre), 1980.

Meyer, F. V. *The European Free Trade Association.* New York: Praeger, 1960.

Mitrany, David. *A Working Peace System.* Chicago: Quadrangle Press, 1966.

Myrdal, Gunnar. *An International Economy.* New York: Harper, 1956.

Nyilas, Jozsef, ed. *Integration in the World Economy: East-West and Interstate Relations.* Leiden: Sijthoff, 1976.

Okigbo, P. N. C. *Africa and the Common Market.* Evanston, Ill.: Northwestern University Press, 1967.

Phatak, Arvind V. *Managing Multinational Corporations.* New York: Praeger, 1974.

Preeg, Ernest H. *Traders and Diplomats.* Washington, D.C.: Brookings Institution, 1970.

Rahl, James A., ed. *Common Market and American Antitrust.* New York: McGraw-Hill, 1970.

Reid, Escott, W. *Strengthening the World Bank.* Chicago: Adlai Stevenson Institute, 1973.

Rostow, Walter W. *Stages of Economic Growth.* Cambridge: Cambridge University Press, 1959.

Seers, Dudley, and Vaitsos, Constantine, eds. *Integration and Unequal Development: The Experience of the EEC.* New York: St. Martin's Press, 1981.

————, ————, eds. *The Second Enlargement of the EEC: The Integration of Unequal Partners.* New York: St. Martin's Press, 1982.

Stobaugh, Robert, and Yergin, Daniel, eds. *Energy Future: Report of the Harvard Business School Energy Project.* New York: Random House, 1979.

Taylor, Paul. *The Limits of European Integration.* New York: Columbia University Press, 1983.

Turner, Louis. *Multinational Companies and the Third World.* New York: Hill and Wang, 1973.

Twichett, Kenneth J., ed. *Europe and the World: The External Relations of the Common Market.* New York: St. Martin's Press, 1976.

Van Brabant, Jozef M. *East European Cooperation: The Role of Money and Finance.* New York: Praeger, 1976.

van de Laar, Aart. *The World Bank and the Poor.* Boston: Nijhoff, 1980.

Vernon, Raymond. *Sovereignty at Bay: The Multinational Spread of U.S. Enterprises.* New York: Basic Books, 1971.

————. *Storm Over the Multinationals: The Real Issues.* Cambridge, Mass.: Harvard University Press, 1977.

Wells, Louis T., Jr. *Third World Multinationals: The Rise of Foreign Investment From Developing Countries.* Cambridge: Massachusetts Institute of Technology Press, 1983.

Whitman, Marina v. N. *Reflections of Interdependence.* Pittsburgh: University of Pittsburgh Press, 1979.

Wightman, David. *Economic Cooperation in Europe—A Study of the United Nations Commission for Europe.* London: Stevens and Heinemann, 1956.

Wiles, P. J. D. *Communist International Economics.* New York: Praeger, 1969.

Wilkins, Mira. *The Maturing of Multinational Enterprise: American Business Abroad from 1914 to 1970.* Cambridge, Mass.: Harvard University Press, 1974.

Zartman, William I. *The Politics of Trade Negotiations Between Africa and the European Economic Community.* Princeton, N.J.: Princeton University Press, 1971.

Part Four

TOWARD A THEORY OF INTERNATIONAL RELATIONS

Chapter 14

Perception and Reality in World Politics

Behold! human beings living in a sort of underground den, which has a mouth open toward the light and reaching all across the den; they have been here from their childhood, and have their legs and necks chained so that they cannot move, and can only see before them; for the chains are arranged in such a manner as to prevent them from turning round their heads. At a distance above and behind them the light of a fire is blazing, and between the fire and the prisoners there is a raised way; and you will see, if you look, a low wall built along the way, like the screen which marionette players have before them, over which they show the puppets. I see, he said.

And do you see, I said, men passing along the wall carrying vessels, which appear over the wall; also figures of men and animals, made of wood and stone and various materials; and some of the prisoners, as you would expect, are talking, and some of them are silent?

This is a strange image, he said, and they are strange prisoners. Like ourselves, I replied; and they only see their shadows, or the shadows of one another, which the fire throws on the opposite wall of the cave?

True, he said: how could they see anything but the shadows if they were never allowed to move their heads?

And of the objects which are being carried in like manner they would see only the shadows?

Yes, he said.

And if they were able to talk with one another, would they not suppose that they were naming what was actually before them?

Very true.

And suppose further that the prison had an echo which came from the other side, would they not be sure to fancy when one of the passers-by spoke that the voice which they heard came from the passing shadow? No question, he replied.

To them, I said, the truth would be literally nothing but the shadows of the images. That is certain.

Plato "Allegory of the Cave" Republic, VII

This book has attempted to present an analysis of international relations in our time. In so doing, we have dealt with a wide range of phenomena. For the purpose of ordering this body of material, we have employed two key concepts. First, and very broadly, we have analyzed world politics in terms of the ever-present tension between the struggle for power and the struggle for order among nations. We have seen that these two struggles are at many points closely interwoven. Indeed, the very soil which produces struggles for power also provides the nourishment for new institutions of order. Thus, World War I brought forth the League of Nations and World War II the United Nations. The Suez crisis of 1956 and the Congo crisis of 1960 led to the creation of unprecedented UN peace forces. The Cuban missile crisis of 1962 ushered in a bevy of arms control agreements. And the excesses of nationalism in Germany and Italy led to the dawn of European unity. Similarly, every struggle for order among nations also involves some kind of power struggle. Witness the United Nations, the most imaginative instrument for order-building thus far devised, yet at the same time the arena for some of the most stubborn vying for power in history. The evidence suggests that self-styled realists and idealists are both wrong: power alone is no reliable guide through the landscape of international politics, nor is the quest for order. The relationship between power and order in world politics is inherently dialectical in nature. Fundamentally, therefore, these two pervasive struggles must be recognized as two sides of a single coin.

Within this broad and general conceptual framework, we have introduced a specific substantive theme as our second key concept: the linkage between the triangular East-West struggle involving China, Russia, and the United States, and the struggle between North and South, the rich and the poor. The pattern of interdependence between these two great conflicts of our time is woven into the entire fabric of contemporary international relations. The struggle for power and order may be seen as the essence of international relations everywhere and always. The East-West struggle and the struggle between the rich and the poor provide their particular form of expression here and now.

To these two organizing concepts which deal with the substance of world politics we may now add a third, which concerns a further vital dimension of international relations: *the frequent and highly significant differences between the way nations perceive one another and the way they really are.* For the titanic struggles among the nations of our time are not only waged on the basis of objective realities. They are also fought out in the realm of imagery and illusion. It is the thesis of this concluding chapter that there are often great gaps between *perception* and *reality* in world politics and that these integrally affect all aspects of international relations, deeply exacerbating the international struggle for power and seriously slowing down the international struggle for order.

The assumption underlying this thesis is that to some degree, at least, international relations are what people think they are; or, to put it in other words, that, under certain conditions, men respond not to realities but to fictions that they have themselves created. To say that there are no objective problems in world politics would be gross exaggeration. But the stage of world politics lends itself all too easily to the development of wide gaps between what that reality is and the way it is perceived. And because of this fact, perception probably plays as important a role in international relations as does objective reality itself.

Before we can analyze the significance of perception in international relations, we must define it and search out its origins. Perception in international relations may be defined as the total cognitive view a nation holds of itself and of others in the world. As such, it is a most complex phenomenon and includes both reality and distortion. There is little doubt that many nations much of the time see themselves and others the way they really are; but it is equally certain that many nations much of the time see themselves and others in stereotyped one-dimensional ways. Nationalism and ideology contribute much to seeing other nations as "bad" and one's own as spotless. Stereotyped images on one side elicit similar ones on another, often compounding the distortion. Even worse, if one believes a stereotype long enough it may become reality by setting in motion the mechanism of the self-fulfilling prophecy. Thus, if a nation believes that another is its implacable enemy and reiterates this often enough, making it the guideline of its national policy, it will eventually be right.

Our first task, then, is to isolate those factors in a nation's overall perception that are distorted; to extrapolate from the composite picture of reality and illusion the elements of illusion. Here we encounter a major difficulty. Throughout this book, we have referred to nations as if they were cohesive entities speaking with a single voice on the world scene: "The United States agreed," "the Soviet Union feared," "India proposed." Such statements, while unavoidable in an analysis of international relations, tell only part of the story. The next crucial question we must ask ourselves is *who* in the United States agreed, *who* in the Soviet Union feared, and *who* in India proposed. Put differently, *who* is it that speaks for nations in world politics? To answer this question, we must analyze the nature of public opinion and its impact on a nation's decision-making process in international relations. Then, we must attempt to differentiate between those decision makers and "influencers" who tend to perceive the outside world in terms of preconceived images and stereotypes and those who evaluate their environment more in accordance with objective reality.

It would, of course, be folly to attempt a generalized answer that would be true for all nations. Fortunately, excellent studies have been made of the impact of public opinion and of stereotypes on the foreign policy-making process of three different types of nations. Walter Lippmann's study, *Public Opinion*, and Gabriel Almond's *The American People and Foreign Policy* are both classics dealing with the American scene.[1] Alex Inkeles' *Public Opinion in Soviet Russia* gives us a revealing picture of that aspect of the Soviet Union.[2] And Gabriel Almond and James S. Coleman have edited and contributed to a study on *Politics of the Developing Areas* which provides many valuable insights into the public opinion and decision-making process of the emergent nations.[3] A comparative analysis of these studies yields much valuable information on the role of distorted perception in world politics.

It was Walter Lippmann who first subjected perception in American politics to a scrupulous analysis. In his trailblazing study, he pointed out that, for most people, "the world they have to deal with politically is out of reach, out of sight, out of mind."[4] Hence, the only reaction they can have to an event that they can neither reach, see, nor care about is one conditioned by their mental predisposition toward that event. Almond further refined this theme and applied it more specifically to Americans' reactions to matters of foreign policy. He discovered that only a small segment of the American public—the elite—is able to grasp the complex realities of international relations. This group consists largely of interest groups, professional organizations, and government officials. A second layer of American public opinion he identified as the "attentive public," those people who, while not themselves experts, continuously expose themselves to information on matters of world politics. The vast majority of Americans, however, Almond discovered, respond to matters of foreign policy largely on the basis of mood. They tend to exhaust their emotional and intellectual energies in private pursuits and thus approach problems of world politics with a perfunctory attitude. Moreover, they feel that "they cannot affect foreign policy anyway," and that, therefore, a serious investment of time and energy is not worthwhile. As a result, this "mass public" tends to respond to the complex reality of world politics with simplified and frequently distorted images. It has replaced the real environment with a "pseudo-environment" largely compounded of prejudices and stereotypes.

As a result of these observations, it follows that the mass public is to some extent responsible for distorted American perceptions of world politics. Most scholars feel that this mass public exerts a great deal of influence through its electoral powers. Lippmann argues, however, that such control, to be beneficial, must emanate from a broadly educated public. If the mass public continues to perceive public policy in terms of "pictures in their heads," Lippmann sees the coming of a functional derangement between the mass of the people and the government in which "the people will have acquired power which they are incapable of exercising, and the governments they elect will have lost power which they must recover if they are to govern."[5] Carl J. Friedrich, on the other hand, has greater faith than Lippmann in the good political sense of the common man.[6] Be that as it may, it is clear that as a result of mass public influence, *some* degree of distortion enters the American perception of world politics, and that when "the United States speaks" in world affairs, its position is therefore to *some* degree colored by images which depart from reality.

It is subject to serious doubt, however, whether Lippmann and Almond are justified in locating the source of distortion primarily in the mass public. The record of American foreign policy suggests the possibility that distortions may also originate in the elite. The relationship between the mass public and the elite seems to be a highly complex one. At times the interaction between the two may further compound distortions. At other times, the elite may serve as a corrective and educate the mass public. But on some occasions, and this is not less important, the mass public may have a sounder perception than the elite. It was the policy elite surrounding the American President in 1961, for example, not the mass public, that misperceived the situation in Cuba that in turn led to the fiasco of the Bay of Pigs. Nor did the "best and the brightest" in the American foreign policy establishment of the 1960s and 1970s have a monopoly of wisdom in Vietnam. Many students with far less formal education perceived the situation much more clearly and fought hard to avert a national disaster. At any rate, the gaps between perception and reality that exist in the American view of world politics are not readily attributable to any one segment of the American people.

Studies of public opinion in Soviet Russia also suggest great distortions in the Soviet perception of world politics. But while in the United States it is difficult to locate the source of these distortions, in the Soviet Union, the main locus may be identified as the elite—the Communist party. As we have seen in an earlier chapter, Communist ideology to some degree colors the lenses through which the Soviet regime perceives the world. These lenses are distributed to the mass public in the Soviet Union through cadres of professional agitators who do their best to ensure that the "new Soviet man" will perceive world politics through the reddish prism of Communist ideology. Ideology thus provides a kind of built-in distortion. As Inkeles points out in a striking analogy, this effort is only partially successful:

> The figure most apt for describing the state of Soviet public opinion is that of a forest fire. On the broad peripheral front the blaze rages in full intensity. Here is found a thin line of convinced and confirmed Communists. But behind this line comes a much larger area, which has already been swept by the flames and which now boasts only glowing embers. This is the line of the half-believers, which includes some party members as well as the nonparty supporters of the regime. And beyond that there lies a still broader sweep of the burned-over timber, in which here and there a spark still glows but which is predominantly cold, ashen, and gray. The work of mass persuasion is the wind which fans this blaze. But like the wind in the forest fire, it not only spreads the flames but hastens the burning, and behind the line of flames and embers it can only stir up little swirls and eddies of ash.[7]

Thus the Soviet Union, too, is bound to perceive world politics to some extent in terms of distorted images and stereotypes. Since these are rooted primarily in Communist ideology, the width of the gap between perception and reality in Soviet foreign policy is determined by the degree to which the Soviet leaders themselves uncritically accept the doctrine with which they so relentlessly proselytize the rest of the world. Yet here, too, a caveat is necessary. There may be times at which commitment to Communist ideology may clarify rather than distort reality. For example, a convinced Communist was probably better able to predict the coming decline of Western colonialism than many non-Communists, though he would not have expected the colonial powers to be as acquiescent as they have been with respect to decolonization. The overall record suggests, however, that the elements of distortion in the Communist world view are far greater than the elements of clarification.

It is an open question to what extent personal contact between national leaders and peoples reduces the power of distorted imagery. It is difficult to say whether Nikita Khrushchev's visit to America in 1959 confirmed or reduced whatever false perceptions he might have had of the United States. The visit was probably too brief to make a deep impression either way. Similarly, one cannot say with certitude whether President Nixon's visits to China and to the Soviet Union in 1972 displaced clichés about communism that he might have believed with more realistic perceptions of Chinese and Soviet life. Probably the visits helped to decontaminate the minds of American, Soviet, and Chinese leaders of shopworn slogans at least to some extent since they were all vitally interested in establishing new relationships with one another, and thus were more responsive to reality. It seems clear, however, that President Sadat's dramatic visit to Jerusalem in 1977 after almost thirty years of conflict between Israel and Egypt moved these two nations closer to reality. Sadat himself declared that the largest part of the Arab-Israeli problem was psychological and that this block had to be removed before progress on substantive issues could be made at all. China's Vice Premier Teng Hsiao-ping's visit to the United States in 1979 and President Reagan's return visit to China in 1984 no doubt had beneficial effects on the relations between the two nations.

The Third World nations present yet a third pattern of the impact of public opinion on the foreign policy-making process. As several expert students of the developing nations have pointed out, there is a minimum of contact between the government elite and the mass public in most of the new nations:

> There exists a wide gap between the traditional mass and the essentially modern subsociety of the Westernized elite. The latter controls the central structures of government and essays to speak and act for the society as a whole. This elite subsociety is the main locus of political activity and of change in the society at large.[8]

There are exceptions to this pattern, of course. India, for example, is a democracy in which there exists an intimate connection between public opinion and the government elite. But in most cases, the new nations have evolved authoritarian forms of government in which a high degree of alienation between the mass public and the government is typical. Hence, the pattern differs from that of the United States, since, in the developing nations, the mass public is, politically speaking, relatively powerless. It also differs from the Soviet and Chinese models since the leadership, as a general rule, does not make a concerted attempt to indoctrinate the population with an ideology. Iran under the Ayatollah Khomeini was a striking exception to this rule.

The attitudes of most Third World leaders are deeply colored by their colonial past. In their case, the memory of colonialism persists much longer than the fact. Once again, therefore, some distortion does result. To put it as precisely as possible, the degree of divergence between perception and reality in the new nations' view of world politics is determined by the degree to which the memory of colonialism outlives the reality. In Iran, for example, the bitter memories of the late pro-American Shah prevented an accurate perception of the United States.

Now that we have at least a tentative insight into the nature of public opinion and its effect on a nation's perception of world politics, we may attempt to propose a tentative answer to the following important question: Which element in a nation's population is most responsible for the degree of distorted imagery that affects its government's perception of the international scene?

In our analysis of three different examples, we have seen that the governments of the United States, of the Soviet Union, and of most of the Third World nations are all subject to some degree of distorted perception. In the United States, it is difficult to identify the precise source of distortion. It may be found in a subtle interplay between the mass public and the elite in which each may act on the other as either a reinforcing or a corrective agent, depending upon the specific circumstances. In the Soviet Union and in China, the locus of distortion is more easily identifiable as the Communist party elite, which, to some degree, at least, perceives the world through the lenses of what it defines as Marxism-Leninism. The Soviet or Chinese mass public has little chance to act as a corrective, but tends to absorb at least some of the party ideology, thus compounding the distortion. In the emergent nations of the authoritarian type, where there is relatively little contact between the elite and the mass public, the source of distorted imagery is usually the leadership itself.

Of the three cases studied, the United States is probably least susceptible to distorted imagery. There is no built-in distortion through a prescribed ideology. Moreover, the very complexity of the American foreign policy-making process provides a kind of check-and-balance system which prevents extreme distortions from being translated into policy. The built-in quality of Communist ideology, on the other hand, no doubt injects considerable distortion into Soviet and Chinese perceptions of world politics. But it would be misleading to assume that this ideological factor always and under any circumstances produces a distorted image of the outside world. After all, it is not demonstrable that the Soviet or the Chinese leadership uncritically accepts the Marxist-Leninist conception of international relations. Certainly, the Chinese leaders today are far too pragmatic to do so. While it is difficult to generalize about the emergent nations, it seems fairly safe to say that those with authoritarian forms of government also experience a good deal of distortion, falling somewhere along the spectrum between the Soviet Union, China, and the United States.

Now that we have examined the nature of the perception factor in the anatomy of a nation, we may proceed to an analysis of some of the major gaps between perception and reality in present-day world politics.

The two main political power struggles of our time are being fought on the dual plane of perception and reality. First, if we consider the East-West struggle, it is obvious, as we have seen earlier, that a great number of objective differences exist which defy easy solution. But to a considerable degree, the conflict also takes place in the realm of distorted imagery. On the Soviet side, the main cause of this distortion is Communist ideology. Quite early in the Soviet Union's life, the ideological factor generated a distorted self-image of historically ordained invincibility. It was also responsible for a perception of other nations that did not tally with reality. Thus, the Soviet Union tended to view the West through Marxist-Leninist lenses as being engaged in an effort to impose "capitalist encirclement" on the Soviet Union. Indeed, the Soviet leadership began to believe that it understood the West better than the West understood itself and as a result struggled not so much with the West as with its image of the West.

The West, in turn, became seriously affected by Soviet imagery and, despite a number of striking blunders committed by the Comintern during its first thirty years of operation, tended to perceive the Soviet Union as a kind of chess master on the world scene. The West's self-image, in turn, approached a collective inferiority complex. This "superman" view of communism and the inferiority complex that followed made the West more fearful of the image of the Soviet Union than of the Soviet Union itself. Indeed, the hypnotic spell that the Soviet Union was able to cast over the West became one of that nation's greatest assets in the struggle. It resulted in a "psychological lag," in the sense that the West remained hypnotized by the Soviet Union at a time when most of the inroads into the Western orbit were being made by China. In sum, the net result has been a twofold distortion. The two superpowers have struggled not only with each other, but also with their perceptions of each other. This divergence between perception and reality exacerbated the conflict enormously.

Only when the cold war abated during the 1960s, and the desire for détente grew on both sides of the Iron Curtain, did the old stereotypes give way to more realistic perceptions. By the 1970s, the Soviet Union and the United States had entered a relationship that included elements of *both* conflict and cooperation. As cooperation grew, so did the willingness and the capacity on both sides to perceive complex realities rather than to remain wedded to simple-minded and one-dimensional clichés. Policies began to be shaped less on shadows and fears and more on facts. By the early 1980s, however, an American President once again perceived the Soviet Union as "the focus of evil in the world." And since that President was a masterful "communicator," that perception no doubt came to be shared by a large segment of the American population. Thus, by 1983, the atmosphere prevailing between the two superpowers was a great deal more conducive to distortion than that which had prevailed a decade earlier. Only by 1985, with the resumption of arms control negotiations and the ascendancy to power in Russia of Mikhail Gorbachev, a younger and more pragmatic leader, did the reality principle once again begin to assert itself.

The struggle between North and South also bears the stamp of distortion. Although the record demonstrates that Western colonialism is largely a phenomenon of the past, the new nationalism acts as if it were very much alive.

Indeed, as we have seen, in the life of the new nations the past often lives on with a fierce intensity. Khomeini's hatred for the late Shah of Iran is a case in point. And his perception of the United States as "the great Satan" because of its previous friendship with the Iranian monarch no doubt helped precipitate the hostage crisis and the agony that followed. Although our case studies of interaction between nationalism and colonialism (Chapter 4) demonstrated that the colonial experiment was a very diversified experience, ranging from outright exploitation to the bestowal of generous benefits, the new nationalism always regarded, and still regards, the entire colonial record as an unmitigated evil and fails to differentiate among the many varying shades of the spectrum. Our case studies also failed to support the conception held by most leaders of the Third World that their movement was antithetical to imperialism. Indeed, we have seen that the new nationalism may readily become a seedbed for new conflicts. This is what happened in the relations between Jewish and Arab nationalism in the Middle East. To hear Arabs and Israelis describe each other at times seemed like listening to two sets of fantasies with little relation to the realities in the countries concerned, and even less to the images each country had of itself. Similarly, the devil images held by Iran and Iraq about each other during their war in the 1980s bore only a small resemblance to reality. These vast gulfs between perception and reality were at the heart of the conflicts in the Middle East and the Persian Gulf. Hence, not only the struggle over colonialism but also the struggle between divergent forms of nationalism is intensified by gaps between perception and reality.

No less affected by this type of distortion has been the relationship between the two political struggles for power. Engagement in one of the two major conflicts has tended to obscure an accurate perception of the other. The United States has perceived the world primarily in terms of East and West; Zimbabwe, on the other hand, has seen the great divide between black and white. The United States has often been uncommitted in the struggle between nationalism and colonialism and has frequently been accused of nonalignment by the new nationalist powers. But the new nations have been equally uncommitted in the East-West struggle in which the two superpowers have perceived *them* as nonaligned. In short, the perceptions of the major protagonists have largely remained limited to only one of the two great political struggles. However, each protagonist has been sufficiently aware of the struggle in which he has not seen himself directly involved to exploit it for his more conscious purposes. Thus both the Soviet Union and the United States, though primarily concerned with the East-West struggle, have consistently striven to gain support for themselves by seeking to play the most advantageous possible role in the North-South struggle.

The divergencies between perception and reality in the political power struggle of our time thus boil down to this: though both titanic conflicts are inseparably connected and are being waged simultaneously, those involved in the East-West struggle see the world chiefly in terms of this dichotomy, and those engaged in the North-South struggle see that conflict as all-important. Moreover, similar distortions characterize the views of each other held by the protagonists in each of the two struggles separately. And in every case, the imagery tends to depict the "enemy" as a more deadly threat than the objective record would seem to justify. As a result, the political struggle is greatly intensified in all its aspects.

The gap between fact and fiction has been even more dangerous in the military realm. Until the Cuban missile crisis of 1962, the United States and the Soviet Union had held the most extreme images of one another. The United States was convinced that "conquering the world for communism" was the sole motivation of the Soviet alliance system. On the basis of this view, it sought to arm itself with an irresistible destructive capacity through the policy of massive retaliation. When this posture was criticized as too exclusively nuclear-minded, the United States began to experiment with an image of Benthamite rationality through the more flexible policy of graduated deterrence. The Soviet Union, for its part, developed an image of the West of "imperialist aggression and encirclement" bent upon the destruction of communism. Logically enough, the view each side held of its own camp was one of defense against the other.

The great danger in the military struggle between the United States and the Soviet Union during the 1950s and 1960s lay in the possibility that the extreme image that each side held of the other might have become reality, and that the circle of suspicion and countersuspicion might have precipitated a "preventive" war. If each side had continued to believe that the other was its mortal enemy, this view might have influenced behavior to such a point of rigidity and compulsiveness that the "inevitable conflict" could have been a self-fulfilling prophecy. The missile crisis cleared the air between the superpowers, at least to some extent, and introduced a larger measure of reality into their relations. After the invasion of Afghanistan in 1980, however, with a massive arms build-up gathering momentum on both sides, these dangerous cold war images began to dominate superpower relations once again.

Distortion was massive in the early relations between the China of Mao Tse-tung and the United States. The Korean War and the conflict in Vietnam accelerated this process, and by the late 1960s a vicious spiral had been set in motion. Both China and America began with the a priori assumption of the other's implacable hostility; the power of this conviction caused all the adversary's actions to be interpreted as confirming the validity of the original assumption; hence, the adversary was found hostile a posteriori as well, since his actions had "proved" that the original assumption was correct. The very actions that the Chinese perceived as an American plot to encircle them were perceived by the Americans as necessary measures to forestall Chinese aggression. Confronted by a series of American policies that appeared to them to prove American enmity toward them, the Chinese embarked upon an increasingly virulent "Hate America" campaign that the United States in turn took as proof of their implacable hostility toward America. What seemed patently provocative to one appeared obviously defensive to the other. In this tragic spiral of reciprocally negative reinforcement, the borderline between real and imagined threats tended to blur and finally disappear altogether.

It is easy to see why political accommodation would be well nigh impossible under such conditions. On a deeper psychological level, such devil mirror images are the stuff that holy wars are made of. For to each side in the conflict, the enemy is not quite human and it becomes difficult, if not impossible, to identify with any part of him. Hence, each adversary is left with his fears and terrors which are in no way allayed by their failure to materialize. Such fears, however, can call forth a reality as terrible as the most anguished nightmare. This was the peril of the encounter between China and America. With the visit of President Nixon to China in 1972 and the extrication of the United States from the Vietnam war in 1975, the danger began to diminish. And by the 1980s, when Vice Premier Teng Hsiao-ping embarked on rapprochement with the United States, the old devil images had almost disappeared. Within a single generation, the Soviet Union had replaced the United States as China's major adversary.

One cannot help but wonder, when one contemplates the spectacle of American businesspeople and tourists streaming into China in the mid-1980s, how transient was the cause that had sent American soldiers to die in Korea and Vietnam. In those not-so-distant days, the Chinese were perceived as monstrous architects of evil; today, they are seen as friendly business partners in a common enterprise. Is it not frightening to see how quickly perceptions can change about the same people? And that these perceptions may sway men toward life or toward death?

The United States and the Soviet Union are still engaged in a relentless economic struggle with each other. Each covets the distinction of being the world's leading industrial power. This economic competition has led to a curious paradox: in the imagery of each superpower, the economic system of the antagonist is alien, pernicious, and to be eradicated. In reality, the exigencies of competition have led to a high degree of mutual emulation which, in turn, has made the economies of the Soviet Union and the United States increasingly alike. The hostile images dictate further competition but this competition will probably increase the objective similarities between the two economies still further. It is therefore possible that the common dictates of industrial production may divest the East-West struggle of some of its messianic ideological character. Once global ideology atrophies, the fierceness of the struggle may abate. Hence the gap between perception and reality in the economic realm is a danger chiefly in the short run. In the long run—assuming that the two great antagonists settle for coexistence without victory or defeat—it may actually prove a force making for order.

Yet both superpowers are aware that at least in the economic realm a decisive victory is still possible in the East-West struggle. They have become convinced that such a victory can be won by gaining the allegiance of the world's uncommitted countries. Both sides have therefore waged the economic struggle with the weapon of foreign aid. In this competition, too, images have greatly diverged from realities. Both superpowers, aware of the sensitivities of the new nations, have attempted to project an image of selflessness and generosity. The secret of success in the economic struggle seems indeed to lie in the realm of imagery. Not only must each of the superpowers learn to see itself as the new nations see it, but it must learn how the new nations perceive the other "enemy" superpower. It is difficult enough for a nation to see itself as others see it; it is far more difficult to see a second nation as a third sees it. Yet this ability is turning out to be of the utmost importance in the economic competition for the new nations. The Soviet Union has been able to project itself into the thinking of the uncommitted nations somewhat more successfully than the United States. It has frequently been able to exploit the anticolonial images of the new nationalism to its own advantage. In its reaction to the "blindness" of the nonaligned leaders in accepting Communist aid, the United States has failed to comprehend a most basic fact: that to most of the new nations, communism is not an unmitigated evil, but merely an alternative to democracy—an alternative, in fact, that, as they see it, may quite possibly produce the desired results faster. Moreover, the West has tended to define democracy primarily in terms of political liberty. In countries without a tradition of democracy, this has often seemed like a luxury commodity. The Soviet Union, on the other hand, has tended to emphasize economic security, a more meaningful concept in countries where this is the overriding concern.

Aware of their strategic position in the East-West struggle, most of the new nations have developed an often rather inflated self-image. This has led to curious psychological inversions—almost an upside-down world. At times, the new nations have "rewarded" one of the superpowers by accepting its gifts or loans. Because of the peculiar constellation of world politics, and the linkage of the two great political struggles, the power of the new nations has vastly increased. So long as the two superpowers continue to believe that the uncommitted countries may vitally affect the distribution of power, this strange divergence between perception and reality is likely to persist.

In addition, the debt crisis, food shortages, financial dislocations, and the population explosion have widened the gulfs between the world's rich and poor. The severity and suddenness of these developments have led to serious perceptual distortions that have exacerbated the objective conflicts even further. There is little if any empathy for another point of view. The poor nations of the Third World see only their own misery, and in their anger and desperation perceive the rich nations as greedy Shylocks. The oil-producing countries cannot understand complaints about high oil prices in light of the expensive technology and other resources that they must import. And the industrialized nations of the West, fearing for their standard of living and their technological achievements, have little patience with the oil producers and little sympathy for the world's poor who outnumber and therefore threaten them.

In sum, then, an analysis of the political, military, and economic aspects of the international struggle for power reveals that on the whole great divergencies exist between perception and reality. In the political realm, these divergencies exacerbate the fierceness of both the East-West struggle and the struggle between rich and poor. This is also largely true in the military arena. In the economic struggle, the picture is more mixed. In the conflict of the East-West relationship, the gap between perception and reality seems to work in the direction of cooperation as well as conflict; but in North-South relations, the negative elements are clearly dominant.

The relationship between perception and reality has also affected the international struggle for order. In the political realm, the United Nations is a case in point. Public opinion studies show that, in the United States, for example, the mass public and even the attentive public tend to evaluate the United Nations fairly indiscriminately. There is little awareness of differences among the major organs of the world organization. It is either praised or condemned as a whole. Images swing all the way from cynical disillusionment through apathy to an exaggerated "panacea" view. Yet the record of the United Nations demonstrates that it is quite impossible to generalize about the world organization in its entirety. The performance of each of its major organs and specialized agencies has been different. In other words, in the imagery of the United States there is little or no awareness of the United Nations' most important characteristics: its elasticity, and the fact that it is working on many fronts and with varying degrees of effectiveness at one time. The unfortunate result of this one-dimensional image is to encourage all-too-quick disillusionment. The failure of a single UN organ, such as the Security Council, or the adoption of the anti-Zionist resolution by the General Assembly, seem like failures of the organization as a whole. Hence, American support of the United Nations has tended to be based on the very unstable factor of popular oversimplification. This gap between perception and reality has thus slowed the development of a firm and dependable basis of support for the United Nations.

Such distortion also extends to specific institutions of the United Nations. The veto power of the Big Five in the Security Council affords an interesting example. In the Soviet view, this power saves the USSR from being continuously outvoted in an organization consisting largely of non-Communist nations. The United States, while equally adamant on maintaining the veto power, holds the view that the Soviet Union has used it excessively and thus crippled the organization. Neither of these views tallies with the record. The truth is that only a few of the many Soviet vetoes cast in the Security Council have been final. Many of them have been circumvented through action taken in the General Assembly under the Uniting for Peace Resolution or otherwise.[9] Besides, during the 1970s and 1980s, the United States cast far more vetoes than the Soviet Union. Thus, the view that the veto can paralyze the world organization as a whole—a view held by the Soviet Union, the United States, and most of the new nations—does not square with the facts.

The tug-of-war between regionalists and globalists also has relevance to our thesis. Typically, regionalist thinkers conceive of globalism as either premature or altogether unworkable. Internationalists, on the other hand, have developed an image of regional arrangements as harmful roadblocks on the path to world order. Neither perception leaves room for what the record demonstrates: that frequently globalism has served as a second line of defense for regionalism and that regional arrangements have served as backstops for the world organization. Certainly, there is ample room for both types of political order-building on the world scene. In this case, the gap between perception and reality has sometimes led to unnecessary friction between the two approaches and thus slowed down the advance toward political order.

A serious divergence exists in the military realm of political order-building. The widespread view that arms races cause wars has led to a passionate popular demand for disarmament everywhere. This, in turn, has led to a propagandistic corruption of diplomacy in disarmament negotiations because diplomats have been compelled to address a world audience instead of engaging in the exacting business of searching for a technical disarmament formula. As we have seen earlier, the popular assumption that arms races cause wars is very oversimplified. The record shows that an arms race is merely the symptom of a deeper pathological condition. It is very likely that the search for a technical disarmament formula is bound to fail unless it is preceded by a more fundamental political accommodation. The same observation may validly be made of arms control, as the arduous road to the SALT agreements amply demonstrates. Indeed, the history of disarmament and arms control negotiations supports the proposition that order is fundamentally a political, not a military, problem. This gap between the simple popular image of disarmament and the complex reality has caused a great deal of cynicism, disillusionment, and waste of energy.

The economic field alone has escaped serious distortions. The functionalist hope has largely been vindicated by the record on the regional level, and even on the global level promising beginnings have been made. Within the framework of Western Europe, two basic conceptions of economic order-building have developed, both of which have enjoyed a measure of success. Supranational and more traditional intergovernmental organizations alike have mushroomed. Wherever a concrete task had to be accomplished, the record has been good, regardless of the formal structure of the organization. Since a well-defined task has existed in most instances, serious gaps between perception and reality have been avoided. One interesting development is worthy of mention: the widely prevalent conception that a clear line of demarcation may be drawn between national governments and international organizations no longer seems to be valid. Recent developments, chiefly in Western Europe, indicate that the two are beginning to blend into one another. Indeed, some regional organizations, like the European Communities, may some day exercise powers previously enjoyed only by national governments. Whether these groupings will justify the fear of the globalists and develop into a kind of regional nationalism remains to be seen. For the present, accomplishments have not fallen too far short of expectations. Hence, an unusual congruence exists between perception and reality in economic order-building in Western Europe.

In conclusion, then, the gaps between perception and reality have exacerbated the fierceness of the international struggle for power and also have done much to slow down the advance toward international order. In view of this fact, it seems vital for students of international relations to expose themselves to the work of scholars in the area of human perception—sociologists, social psychologists, and even depth psychologists. This is not to say that the objective realities of world affairs should be neglected. Yet since these are as vast and difficult to contend with as they are, the least we can hope for is that they not be rendered even more complex and inaccessible to reason by our unsubstantiated preconceptions. The perils of our age demand our every effort to see and deal with the world as it really is. Once again man must escape from Plato's Cave, in which he perceives only shadows instead of realities. Only when our reason thus acquires passion will we remove the Sword of Damocles which has been suspended for far too long over our tormented world.

REFERENCES

1. Walter Lippmann, *Public Opinion*. New York: Macmillan, 1922; Gabriel Almond, *The American People and Foreign Policy*. New York: Harcourt, Brace, 1950.
2. Alex Inkeles, *Public Opinion in Soviet Russia*. Cambridge, Mass.: Harvard University Press, 1950.
3. Gabriel Almond and James S. Coleman, *The Politics of the Developing Areas*. Princeton, N.J.: Princeton University Press, 1960.
4. Lippmann, *op. cit.*, p. 29.
5. Walter Lippmann, *The Public Philosophy*. Boston: Little, Brown, 1955, p. 14.
6. Carl J. Friedrich, *The New Image of the Common Man*. Boston: Beacon Press, 1950, *passim*.
7. Inkeles, *op. cit.*, p. 323.
8. Almond and Coleman, *op. cit.*, p. 535.
9. For a complete analysis of this point, see John G. Stoessinger, *The United Nations and the Superpowers*. 4th ed. New York: Random House, 1977, pp. 3–25.

BIBLIOGRAPHY

Aron, Raymond. *Politics and History: Selected Essays*. New York: Free Press, 1978.

Boulding, Kenneth E. *Stable Peace*. Austin: University of Texas Press, 1978.

Brams, Steven J. *Game Theory and Politics*. New York: Free Press, 1975.

Brecher, Michael. *Studies in Crisis Behavior*. New Brunswick, N.J.: Transaction, 1979.

Brown, Seyom. *New Forces in World Politics*. Washington, D.C.: Brookings Institution, 1974.

Cantril, Hadley. *The Human Dimension: Experiences in Policy Research*. New Brunswick, N.J.: Rutgers University Press, 1967.

Carr, Edward H. *The Twenty Years' Crisis, 1919–1939: An Introduction to the Study of International Relations*. London: Macmillan and Company, Ltd., 1946.

Cohen, Raymond. *Threat Perception in International Crisis*. Madison: University of Wisconsin Press, 1979.

Cottam, Richard W. *Foreign Policy Motivation*. Pittsburgh: University of Pittsburgh Press, 1977.

Falk, Richard A. *A Study of Future Worlds*. New York: Free Press, 1975.

Fox, William T. R., ed. *Theoretical Aspects of International Relations*. South Bend, Ind.: University of Notre Dame Press, 1959.

Fromkin, David. *The Independence of Nations*. New York: Praeger, 1981.

Fromm, Erich. *The Anatomy of Human Destructiveness.* New York: Holt, Rinehart and Winston, 1973.
Gilpin, Robert. *War and Change in World Politics.* New York: Cambridge University Press, 1981.
Handel, Michael I. *The Diplomacy of Surprise: Hitler, Nixon, Sadat.* Cambridge, Mass.: Center for International Affairs, Harvard University, 1981.
Harrison, Horace V., ed. *The Role of Theory in International Relations.* Princeton, N.J.: Van Nostrand, 1964.
Heilbroner, Robert L. *Marxism: For and Against.* New York: Norton, 1980.
Hoffmann, Stanley, ed. *Contemporary Theory in International Relations.* Englewood Cliffs, N.J.: Prentice-Hall, 1960.
————. *Primacy or World Order: American Foreign Policy Since the Cold War.* New York: McGraw-Hill, 1978.
Holsti, Ole R.; Hopmann, Terrence P.; and Sullivan, John D. *Unity and Disintegration in International Alliances: Comparative Studies.* New York: Wiley, 1973.
Jaguaribe, Helio. *Political Development: A General Theory and a Latin American Case Study.* New York: Harper & Row, 1973.
Keohane, Robert O., and Nye, Joseph S. *Power and Interdependence: World Politics in Transition.* Boston: Little, Brown, 1977.
Kothari, Rajni. *Footsteps into the Future: Diagnosis of the Present World and a Design for an Alternative.* New York: Free Press, 1975.
Kratochwil, Friedrich V. *International Order and Foreign Policy.* Boulder, Colo.: Westview Press, 1978.
Lenin, Vladimir I. *Imperialism, the Highest Stage of Capitalism.* New York: International Publishers, 1939.
Lieber, Robert J. *Theory and World Politics.* Cambridge, Mass.: Winthrop, 1972.
Liska, George. *International Equilibrium: a Theoretical Essay on the Politics and Organization of Security.* Cambridge, Mass.: Harvard University Press, 1957.
————. *Russia and the Road to Appeasement: Cycles of East-West Conflict.* Baltimore: Johns Hopkins Press, 1982.
Machiavelli, Niccolo. *The Prince and the Discourses.* New York: Modern Library, 1950.
Machlup, Fritz. *A History of Thought on Economic Integration.* New York: Columbia University Press, 1977.
Mahan, Alfred T. *The Influence of Sea Power Upon History, 1660–1783.* Boston: Little, Brown, 1898.
Mendlovitz, Saul H., ed. *On the Creation of a Just World Order: Preferred Worlds for the 1990's.* New York: Free Press, 1975.
Mitrany, David. *A Working Peace System.* Chicago: Quadrangle Press, 1966.
Morgan, Patrick M. *Theories and Approaches to International Politics.* 2nd ed. Palo Alto, Calif.: Page Ficklin, 1975.
Morgenthau, Hans J. *Dilemma of Politics.* Chicago: University of Chicago Press, 1958.
————. *Politics Among Nations: The Struggle for Power and Peace.* 5th ed. rev. New York: Knopf, 1978.
————. *Scientific Man vs. Power Politics.* Chicago: University of Chicago Press, 1946.
————. *Truth and Power.* New York: Praeger, 1970.
————, and Fox, William T. R. "National Interest and Moral Principles in Foreign Policy," *American Scholar,* Spring 1949.
Niebuhr, Reinhold. *Christianity and Power Politics.* New York: Scribner's, 1952.
————. *The Irony of American History.* New York: Scribner's, 1952.
————. *Moral Man and Immoral Society: A Study in Ethics and Politics.* New York: Scribner's, 1932.
Osgood, Robert E., and Tucker, Robert W. *Peace, Order and Justice.* Baltimore: Johns Hopkins Press, 1967.

Pentland, Charles. *International Theory and European Integration.* New York: Free Press, 1973.

Pettman, Ralph. *Human Behavior and World Politics.* New York: St. Martin's Press, 1976.

Pfaltzgraff, Robert L., Jr. *Contending Theories of International Relations.* New York: Lippincott, 1971.

Reynolds, Charles V. *Theory and Explanation in International Politics.* New York: Barnes and Noble, 1974.

Rosecrance, Richard N. *Action and Reaction in World Politics.* Boston: Little, Brown, 1963.

Rosenau, James N. *International Politics and Foreign Policy: A Reader in Research and Theory.* Glencoe, Ill.: Free Press, 1961.

————, ed. *Linkage Politics: Essays on the Convergence of National and International Systems.* New York: Free Press, 1969.

Seton-Watson, Hugh. *Nations and States.* Boulder, Colo.: Westview Press, 1977.

Singer, Marshall R. *Weak States in a World of Powers: The Dynamics of International Relationships.* New York: Free Press, 1972.

Smith, A. D. *Nationalism in the Twentieth Century.* New York: New York University Press, 1979.

Snyder, Glenn, and Diesing, Paul. *Conflict Among Nations.* Princeton, N.J.: Princeton University Press, 1978.

Snyder, Richard C., et al. *Decision-Making as an Approach to the Study of International Politics.* Princeton, N.J.: Princeton University Press, 1954.

Sterling, Richard W. *Ethics in a World of Power, the Political Ideas of Friedrich Meinecke.* Princeton, N.J.: Princeton University Press, 1958.

————. *Macropolitics.* New York: Knopf, 1974.

Stoessinger, John G. *Nations in Darkness: China, Russia, and America.* 4th ed. rev. New York: Random House, 1985.

————. *Why Nations Go to War.* 4th ed. New York: St. Martin's Press, 1985.

Thompson, Kenneth W. *Understanding World Politics.* South Bend, Ind.: University of Notre Dame Press, 1975.

————, and Myers, Robert J., eds. *Truth and Tragedy: A Tribute to Hans J. Morgenthau.* Washington, D.C.: New Republic, 1977.

Tuchman, Barbara W. *The March of Folly: From Troy to Vietnam.* New York: Knopf, 1984.

Waltz, Kenneth N. *Man, the State, and War: A Theoretical Analysis.* New York: Columbia University Press, 1959.

Walzer, Michael. *Just and Unjust Wars.* New York: Basic Books, 1977.

Wolfers, Arnold, and Martin, Lawrence W., eds. *The Anglo-American Tradition in Foreign Affairs.* New Haven, Conn.: Yale University Press, 1956.

Wright, Quincy. *A Study of War.* Rev. ed. Chicago: University of Chicago Press, 1968.

————. *The Study of International Relations.* New York: Appleton-Century-Crofts, 1955.

Index

About the Author

On the eve of World War II, John G. Stoessinger fled from Nazi-occupied Austria to Czechoslovakia. Three years later, he fled again, via Siberia, to China, where he lived for seven years. In Shanghai, he served with the International Refugee Organization.

Dr. Stoessinger came to the United States in 1947, received his B.A. degree from Grinnell College in 1950, and then went to Harvard, where he earned his Ph.D. degree in 1954. He entered the teaching field immediately and has taught at Harvard, M.I.T., Columbia, Princeton, and the City University of New York. In 1969, he led the International Seminar on International Relations at Harvard University. He has received Honorary Degrees of Doctor of Laws from Grinnell College, Iowa, and from the American College of Switzerland. He is now Distinguished Professor of International Affairs at Trinity University in San Antonio, Texas.

Dr. Stoessinger is the author of ten leading books in international relations: *The Might of Nations: World Politics in Our Time*, which was awarded the Bancroft Prize by Columbia University in 1963 as the best book in international relations published in 1962. The book has gone through eight editions (1962, 1965, 1969, 1973, 1975, 1979, 1982, 1986). He also has authored *The Refugee and the World Community* (1956); *Financing the United Nations System* (1964); *Power and Order* (1964); *The United Nations and the Superpowers* (1965, 1970, 1973, 1977); *Nations in Darkness: China, Russia, and America* (1971, 1975, 1978, 1986); *Why Nations Go to War* (1974, 1978, 1982); and *Henry Kissinger: The Anguish of Power* (1976). Dr. Stoessinger also served as Chief Book Review Editor of *Foreign Affairs* for five years and is a member of the Council on Foreign Relations.

From 1967 to 1974, Dr. Stoessinger served as Acting Director of the Political Affairs Division at the United Nations. During the academic year 1978–1979, he served as Presidential Professor at the Colorado School of Mines.

Dr. Stoessinger's autobiography, *Night Journey*, was published in 1978. His latest book, *Crusaders and Pragmatists: Movers of Modern American Foreign Policy*, was published by W. W. Norton in 1979, 1985.